5e

Procedures & Theory
for Administrative Professionals

Patsy Fulton-Calkins, Ph.D.
Adjunct Professor, Educational Consultant, Dallas, TX

Karin M. Stulz, M.A. ED.
Northern Michigan University, Marquette, MI

THOMSON
SOUTH-WESTERN

Australia · Canada · Mexico · Singapore · Spain · United Kingdom · United States

THOMSON

SOUTH-WESTERN

Procedures & Theory for Administrative Professionals
By Dr. Patsy Fulton-Calkins and Karin M. Stulz

VP/Editorial Director:
Jack W. Calhoun

VP/Editor-in-Chief:
Dave Shaut

Senior Publisher:
Karen Schmohe

Acquisitions Editor:
Joseph Vocca

Project Manager:
Dr. Inell Bolls

Production Editor:
Carol Spencer

Production Manager:
Tricia Boies

Director Educational Marketing:
Carol Volz

Marketing Manager:
Lori Pegg

Channel Manager:
Brian Joyner

Marketing Coordinator:
Cira Brown

Manufacturing Coordinator:
Charlene Taylor

Media Technology Editor:
Liz Prigge

Media Developmental Editor:
Matthew McKinney

Media Production Editor:
Ed Stubenrauch

Design Project Manager:
Rik Moore

Cover and Internal Design:
Lou Ann Thesing

Photo Research:
Darren Wright

Copyeditor:
Marianne Miller

Production House:
GGS Information Services, Inc.,
Litten Editing and Production, Inc.

Rights and Permissions Manager:
Linda Ellis

Printer:
World Color/Taunton, MA

Cover and Part Opener Images:
© PhotoDisc, Inc.

For permission to use material from this
text or product, contact us by
Tel (800) 730-2214
Fax (800) 730-2215
http://www.thomsonrights.com

For more information
contact South-Western,
5191 Natorp Boulevard,
Mason, Ohio, 45040.
Or you can visit our Internet site at:
http://www.swlearning.com

The names of all companies or products mentioned herein are used for identification purposes only and may be trademarks or
registered trademarks of their respective owners. South-Western disclaims any affiliation, association, connection with, sponsorship,
or endorsement by such owners.

Your Course Planning Just Got Easier!

Preface

Message to Student

Procedures & Theory for Administrative Professionals is more than a textbook; it is a complete learning package designed to add to your administrative professional skills. You, no doubt, have taken a number of courses in preparation for your career as an administrative professional, including keyboarding, word processing, computer technology, information management, communication, and English among others. This course is a capstone course—one that pulls together the skills you learned previously and adds to your knowledge and understanding of the technical and human relations skills necessary to succeed in your chosen profession.

Your role as an administrative professional in the workplace of today is a challenging one where constant changes in the world frequently impact your job. Some of the major changes include:

- Constant advances in technology
- An increasingly diverse workforce
- A global economy

These changes demand that you learn continually—not necessarily through formal education (although you may seek this venue), but by daily learning on the job, continual reading/research in your field, and taking advantage of opportunities offered through professional organizations. Since your ongoing success demands that you commit to continual learning, this course stresses the importance of that learning and that you adopt the philosophy of learning as a lifelong goal.

Text Organization

Procedures & Theory for Administrative Professionals is comprised of six parts, with a total of twenty chapters.

Key Features

- Learning Goals

  Reveals expected outcomes from studying each chapter

- Summary

  Provides a quick review of major points in each chapter

- Find the Problem

  Provides a short real-life case situation

- Professional Pointers

  Gives several professional growth pointers

- Reinforcement Items

  Provides review questions

- Critical-Thinking Activity

  Provides a case (based on a real-life situation) that demands the use of critical-thinking skills

- Vocabulary Review

  Offers a review of the technological and vocabulary-building terms for each chapter

- English and Word Usage Drill

  Provides a review of the rules given in the Reference Guide of the textbook

- Workplace Applications

  Provides applications tied to the learning goals of the chapter, with the goal(s) identified for each Workplace Application

- Assessment of Chapter Goals

  Provides an opportunity to evaluate completion of the chapter goals

- Team-Building Icon on *Workplace Applications*

  Indicates a collaborative activity involving a group of class members

- Online Icon on *Workplace Applications*

  Indicates use of the Web in conducting research

Learning Styles— Recognizing Differences

Individuals learn in a variety of ways. These learning differences are addressed throughout the textbook by recognizing the tenets of learning theory and utilizing a variety of techniques to address these tenets, including the following:

- Providing *Learning Goals* at the beginning of each chapter

- Coordinating end-of-chapter *Workplace Applications* with the *Learning Goals*

- Utilizing a writing style that reinforces concepts presented with current real-life cases and illustrations

- Presenting case studies based on real-life situations in *Find the Problem* and *Critical-Thinking Activities*

- Providing *Workplace Applications* involving teamwork, individual work, written presentations, and oral presentations

- Utilizing the Web to enhance research skills

- Providing a summary in each chapter to reinforce the important points

- Providing an *Applications Workbook* with activities that support the concepts presented in the textbook

- Providing self-assessment of goal achievement through completion of *Assessment of Chapter Goals*

- Providing PowerPoint slides as an overview of each chapter

New in this Edition

- Chapter 16, Financial Analyses—Organizational and Personal

  As educated wage earners and contributing members of society, students must acquire an understanding of the financial picture of organizations, as well as an understanding of how individuals prepare themselves to achieve their financial goals. This chapter helps to satisfy these needs.

- Find the Problem
  Real-life case situations are presented at the end of each chapter.
- Two additional cases per chapter focus on developing critical thinking.
- A *Vocabulary Review* appears at the end of each chapter.
- An *English and Word Usage Drill* appears at the end of each chapter.
- An *Assessment of Chapter Goals* is included at the end of each chapter.
- New *Workplace Applications*, with at least 50 percent of the applications in each chapter new.
- PowerPoint slides are expanded to include an outline of the major points of each chapter and selected concepts.

Learning Aids

- Key technology and vocabulary-building terms highlighted in each chapter, with definitions for terms given in the chapters and in a glossary
- Numerous illustrations and figures
- Professional pointers at the end of each chapter
- Critical thinking addressed through real-life case situations
- Online research applications designed to reinforce use of the Web
- Chapter summary
- Student CD that contains additional activities and forms for use in *Workplace Applications*
- *Reference Guide* that serves as a review of grammar and punctuation rules, basic formats for letters, and guidelines for business introductions
- Six part tests, with one for each part of the textbook
- Final exam

Instructor Resources

- Comprehensive Instructor's CD that includes learning theory principles, the Learning Goals for each chapter, chapter outlines, teaching suggestions, additional resource suggestions, *Find the Problem*, *Critical-Thinking Activity*, and *Workplace Applications*
- Testing software that offers the instructor the opportunity to create printed tests and choose questions in rank order
- PowerPoint slides for each chapter, including an outline for each chapter and selected concepts within chapters

WebTutor on WebCT and **WebTutor on Blackboard** are also available for use as an online course for distance learning.

The Authors

Dr. Patsy J. Fulton-Calkins' experience in the field is extensive. Her experience in the workplace includes working as an administrative professional for large corporations for six years. Early in her career she completed the CPS certification. Her teaching experience includes more than 17 years at the university, community college, and high school levels.

Courses taught at the community college and high school level include office procedures, keyboarding, business communication, bookkeeping, business law, general business, and vocational office education. At the university level, she taught courses in business and society, senior level management capstone courses, and a general education course covering diversity in the United States. Short courses taught for business and industry include CPS review and communication courses.

In addition to her teaching experience, she has extensive management experience in the following positions:

- Chancellor of Oakland Community College (the CEO), Oakland County, Michigan
- President of Brookhaven College, Dallas, Texas

- Vice President of Instruction, El Centro College, Dallas, Texas
- Vice President of Instruction, Cedar Valley College, Dallas, Texas
- Division Chairperson of Business and Social Science, Cedar Valley College, Dallas, Texas

She also engages in consulting work with community colleges across the nation.

She has traveled extensively within the United States and abroad. Her international travels include China on a Fulbright program for community college presidents, Korea (where she established a sister college with JuSeong College), Hong Kong, England, France, Italy, Germany, Belgium, Switzerland, the Netherlands, Mexico (where she helped establish a language program for community college students), and Canada.

Her educational credentials include a B.B.A., an M.B.Ed., and a Ph.D. Honors include Outstanding Alumnus, University of North Texas; Transformational Leader in Community Colleges; Who's Who in America, Outstanding Woman in Management; listee in *Michigan Women: Firsts and Founders*; Paul Harris Fellow of Rotary International; Beta Gamma Sigma, National Honorary Business Fraternity; and Piper Professor.

Karin Stulz has held a faculty position in the Walker L. Cisler College of Business at Northern Michigan University for the past 14 years. She has extensive experience in the administrative professional field. Her career at Northern Michigan University began with a variety of full-time administrative professional positions. While teaching primarily community college courses, her teaching responsibilities have included courses in office procedures, keyboarding, formatting, machine transcription, and business math, as well as a capstone evaluation course and internship program. In addition, she had taught a wide variety of software application courses, including beginning, intermediate, and advanced word processing, spreadsheets, database, presentation software, and software integration. Karin is active in the College, the University, and the local community. She serves on a wide variety of academic and community committees.

Her educational credentials include a B.S., secondary teaching certification, and an M.A.E. degree. She has also earned specialized certifications through the Microsoft Office Specialist Certification program. Specialized certifications include core certification in Access, Excel, PowerPoint, Word, and expert certification in Microsoft Word 2000. Honors include the *Outstanding Teaching Award* in the Walker L. Cisler College of Business as well as the *Postsecondary Business Teacher of the Year Award* from the Michigan Business Education Association.

Reviewers for This Edition

Special thanks to the following reviewers for their helpful comments during the development of this new edition:

Cheryl Carr
Educational Consultant
Madison, MS

Helen T. Hebert
EA-Remington College
Cleveland, OH

Sharon Massen
Educational Consultant
Westerville, OH

Contents

1

Today and Tomorrow's Workplace

chapter 1

The Workplace— Constantly Changing

LEARNING GOALS

1. Identify forces that are changing the workplace environment.
2. Identify workplace strategies for coping with change.
3. Describe career opportunities available for the administrative professional.
4. Define twenty-first-century workplace requirements.
5. Develop a career plan utilizing effective decision making.

The constantly changing workplace is a reality today. The consistency of the change is evident by the technological innovations that confront you as you work and go about your daily life. Consider the following four examples:

- Today cars have navigation systems that provide graphic directions of how to get from one point to another and a human voice to give verbal directions.
- The workplace is no longer confined to the traditional office; you are able to operate via technology from home offices, from cars, from international cities, or from tropical beaches. JetBlue Airways℠, an airline based at New York's John F. Kennedy International Airport, has its entire force of reservation agents working from their homes.
- In the world after 9/11, technology allows individuals to be scanned using patterns of the iris or fingertip or the shape of the hand or face. Thousands of such systems are being tested or are already up and running. At a handful of airports, face scanners scrutinize passengers. The systems can then compare passing faces against a database of images from FBI lists of suspected terrorists and wanted felons.
- According to some projections, people may be living on Mars by 2017.

In addition to technology, the composition of the workforce is changing constantly. Whether you are preparing to enter the workplace after finishing your studies or you are presently employed either full- or part-time, the increased cultural diversity of the environment is most likely apparent to you. The population of the United States is more diverse today than it has ever been. According to projections, this diversity will continue to increase due to the following:

- Increases in the Asian and Hispanic populations as a percent of the total population of the United States
- Continued immigration to the United States from other countries

© GETTY IMAGES/EYEWIRE

We live in a world of constant technological innovation.

- Increased longevity of the population

As an administrative professional employed in the technological and diverse workplace, your goals must be as follows:

- Proficiency in the field
- Commitment to lifelong learning
- Development of strong human relations, critical-thinking, and decision-making skills

This chapter will help you understand more about the direction of the workplace and the skills you must acquire to be successful as an administrative professional.

Forces of Change in the Workplace

You live in a time when knowledge is exploding dramatically. Terms such as **Information Age** and **Knowledge Age** describe the age in which you live and work. Continual advances in technology drive the changes that occur constantly.

Technological Changes

Technology has spawned the **digital era**—a world fueled by numbers. In this world, everyone wallows in numbers—credit card numbers, **PINs** (personal identification numbers), Social Security numbers, checking account numbers, account numbers for utilities, telephone numbers (with many people using cell phones in addition to regular home and workplace phones), fax numbers, and email addresses (which may include numbers).

If you are employed presently or will begin working soon, you will learn about other technological innovations that have changed the way the administrative professional works. You will discover that computer technology influences the following:

- Procedures used to produce work

- Techniques used to communicate from within and outside the office
- Information available (both amount and type) for making decisions

A Diverse Environment

You will also discover dramatic changes in the work environment, including the ones listed here.

- Greater ethnic diversity
- Increased number of immigrants
- Growth in the number of older workers
- Larger numbers of women in the workforce

Greater Ethnic Diversity

The United States is becoming more ethnically diverse; and based on the statistics of the country's young people, ethnic diversity will continue to increase in the future. For example, demographers identify the group of young people born between 1977 and 1995 as **Generation Y**. Projections are that this population will increase at twice the rate of the total population until 2010. By 2020, this percentage is projected to reach 32 percent. Generation Y is the most ethnically diverse generation to date. While minorities make up 24 percent of **baby boomers** (individuals born between 1946 and 1964), minorities make up 34 percent of Generation Y.[1]

Another comparison that helps to explain how ethnic diversity is increasing is the ethnic diversity of children in 1980 compared to the projected diversity in 2020. In 1980, nearly three-quarters (74 percent) of all children in this country were non-Hispanic whites. Projections are that by 2020, non-Hispanic whites will constitute just over one-half (55 percent) of all U.S. children. By the year 2010, Hispanics are projected to be 19 percent of the child population, replacing blacks as the largest minority group in the child population. The Asian American population is also ex-

Projections are that by 2020, non-Hispanic whites will constitute just over one-half (55 percent) of all U.S. children.

© GETTY IMAGES/PHOTODISC

pected to continue to grow—increasing to 6 percent by the year 2020.[2]

According to the 2002–2003 *Occupational Outlook Handbook*, the ethnic origin of the U.S. workforce by 2010 will grow as follows:

- The white workforce population will grow by 0.9 percent.
- The black workforce population will grow by 1.9 percent.
- The population of Asian and other Pacific Islanders will grow by 3.7 percent.
- The Hispanic population will grow by 3.1 percent.[3]

Increased Number of Immigrants

According to projections, the United States will continue to become home to an increasing number of immigrants. The 2000 census, the latest census (census figures are gathered every 10 years), shows that the percentage of

---

[1] "Faces of the New Millennium," accessed May 5, 2001; available from **www.pubweb.acns.nwu.edu**.

[2] "Racial and Ethnic Composition of U.S. Children," accessed May 5, 2002; available from **www.aspe.hhs.gov/hsp**.
[3] "2002-03 Editions of The Occupational Outlook Handbook and The Career Guide to Industries Available on the Internet," accessed May 5, 2002; available from **www.ftp://146.142.4.23/pub/news.release/ooh.txt**.

U.S. residents born in another country is the highest in 70 years. For example, the 1990 census showed that in Texas, 9 percent of the total population was foreign-born. By comparison, the 2000 census revealed that 13.9 percent of the Texas population was foreign-born. According to the 2000 census, 11.1 percent of the total population of the United States was foreign-born. The overall U.S. population is projected to grow to more than 300 million by 2010 and to 355 million by 2040. Immigrants are projected to become a larger share of the population, increasing steadily until about 2030, when they will level off at approximately 14 percent of the population. The number of children born to immigrants is projected to grow to 45 million by 2040—from roughly 18 percent presently to 27 percent by 2040.[4] Thus, in addition to the growth of Hispanics, Asians, and African Americans in the workforce, this country can expect an increasingly diverse group of workers from numerous countries outside the United States whose native language is not English.

An Aging Workforce

Baby boomers will begin to reach age 65 by 2010; projections are that by 2020, almost 20 percent of the U.S. population will be 65 or older. There will be as many Americans of retirement age as there are 20- to 35-year-olds. According to the Hudson Institute's *Workforce 2020*, retirement patterns are likely to change, with some people who reach age 65 continuing to work due to needing to work or not wanting to retire.[5] Since life expectancies will continue to rise, many financially comfortable Americans may decide that too much leisure time is not the lifestyle they want.

Women in the Workforce

Women, both single and married, continue to enter the workforce in greater numbers than in the past. Women who have children are returning to the workforce while their children are still preschool age. This is particularly true for families raised by single women, a group that is growing significantly.

According to projections, the number of women in the workforce will continue to grow. In the next few years, women will make up 62 percent of new entrants to the workforce. Women also show an entrepreneurial spirit and are launching more businesses than men. This trend will continue in the future. In the next few years, women will own half of small businesses and 50 percent of all American companies. The number of women executives and board members will continue to rise.[6]

A Global Economy

The global nature of the economy is obvious. You merely need to listen to the stock market news each day to understand the interrelatedness of the U.S. economy with economies in Europe, Asia, and other countries around the world. Observe the makes of cars driven in the United States, and you become aware of the number of cars made by companies based in countries abroad. However, many of these companies have plants within the United States and manufacture at least part of their automobile products or even the entire car in this country. Conversely, many car manufacturers in the United States have plants abroad.

Thus, the economy is not only global, but also multinational. The term **multinational** means that a business operates from both within and outside the United States. As businesses look for efficient ways to deliver their products or services, they are considering the

---

[4]Jeffrey S. Passel and Michael Fix, "U.S. Immigration in a Global Context: Past, Present, and Future," accessed May 5, 2002; available from **www.ijgls.indiana.edu/ archive/02/01/passel.shtml**.

[5]Elizabeth Joyce, "*Worforce 2020 Predicts More Older Workers*," accessed May 5, 2002; available from **www.ncoa .org/news/archives/workforce_2020.htm**.

[6]Dr. Terry J. van der Werff, CMC, "Trends for 1999 and Beyond," accessed May 5, 2002; available from **www .globalfuture.com/9901.htm**.

Today women are launching more businesses than men, and the trend is expected to continue.

resources available in other countries. These resources include people and natural resources. U.S. companies can be more profitable when they consider the world as their marketplace.

Workplace Strategies for Coping with Change

In order to produce services and products economically and efficiently, organizations must analyze the way they perform. This focus produces a number of changes that are common in most organizations. Some of these changes are presented in the following sections.

Quality Focus

In a competitive society, businesses must focus on quality. Competitors surpass organizations that fail to provide quality products and services at reasonable costs. An American statistician, the late Dr. W. Edwards Deming, began the quality movement. Deming first introduced his concepts to businesses in the United States but failed to receive their support. In the 1950s, he took his concepts to Japan, where industrialists received him and his ideas enthusiastically. Significant positive productivity results began to emerge in the Japanese industries. Japan today is a major industrial force, producing quality products distributed worldwide. In recent years, American organizations have become aware of the need to focus on the quality of goods and services produced. As a result, organizations now apply Deming's quality principles across a spectrum of production and service industries. This approach to organizational improvement is referred to as **TQM** (total quality management) or **CQI** (continuous quality improvement).

How does TQM affect administrative professionals? How does it change work?

- Administrative professionals are involved in decisions that affect the direction of the business.
- Administrative professionals may have major roles as members of teams that are responsible for turning out products or services.
- Administrative professionals are more involved in meeting the needs of clients and customers.
- Administrative professionals have the opportunity to be creative in helping to solve the problems of the organization.

Changing Organizational Structures

Traditionally, organizational structures used some form of **departmentalization** (subdividing work and workers into organizational units responsible for a task) as a method of organizing work. For example, traditional departments were accounting, sales, information systems, and so on. These departments were set up in a **hierarchical organization** (organized by rank or authority) where vice presidents or the **CEO** (chief executive officer) made final decisions on most matters. Organizations today may use this type of structure when they are small. However, as organizations grow, such a structure can lead to slower decision making and increased competition between departments. Additionally, the world is too complex and change is occurring too rapidly for a few people to be able to make all decisions. Organizational structures are **dynamic** (changing rapidly) rather than **static** (staying the same). Employees within an organization have specialized skills and knowledge that may be far different from those of the CEO. Teams—due to their combined knowledge, strength, and expertise—are often used.

When Cisco's™ president and CEO was asked why Cisco was changing its organizational structure to encompass 11 technology groups, his reply was as follows:

Changing customer requirements and the inherent market opportunity are at the heart of the change. When Cisco created its line of business structure in April 1997, our enterprise, commercial, and service provider customers were building separate networks with predominantly unique product requirements. Today, our customers want our products to move across all customer segments. They want a network of networks that is seamless and has transparent integration across extranets, intranets, and the Internet. As our customers and the industry evolve, Cisco continues to evolve its organization.[7]

The CEO of QUALCOMM™ made a similar statement when asked about organizational structure.

Since its founding in 1985, QUALCOMM has achieved significant growth based on combining technical innovation with rapid product development, marketing, and customer support. This corporate realignment provides our businesses with strong leadership in a responsive organization to encourage and accommodate change and support the global expansion of the market.[8]

Notice that both CEOs mention growth and response to a constantly changing world as reasons for organizational structure changes.

Flexible Workweek

Although a number of organizations still adhere to the traditional five-day workweek and 8 a.m. or 9 a.m. to 5 p.m. hours, the tradition is changing. Companies have begun to establish flexible hours to accommodate changing family structures and needs. Several alternatives to the traditional workweek are gaining in popularity. These alternatives include the **compressed workweek, flextime,** and **job sharing**.

---

[7]"News @ Cisco," accessed November 21, 2002; available from **www.cisco.com**.

[8]"QUALCOMM Announces New Corporate Structure to Focus on Growth Opportunities," accessed November 21, 2002; available from **www.qualcomm.com**.

With a compressed workweek, employees work the usual number of hours (35 to 40) but work fewer than five days. For example, a 40-hour week may consist of four 10-hour days; a 36-hour week may be made up of three 12-hour days.

Flextime is another departure from the eight-to-five workday. With flextime, working hours are staggered. Each employee must work the full quota of time but at periods convenient for the individual and the organization. Under this plan, all employees do not report to or leave work at the same time. For example, with a 40-hour week, one employee may come to work at 7:30 a.m. and work until 4 p.m. (with 30 minutes for lunch). **Core hours** (hours when everyone is in the office) may be from 9:30 a.m. until 2:30 p.m. Flextime helps reduce traffic congestion at the traditional peak hours and allows employees flexibility in their schedules.

Still another departure from the traditional work schedule is job sharing. Under this arrangement, two part-time employees perform a job that one full-time employee would hold. For example, job sharing might be two people working five half days or one person working two full days and another person working three full days. Such a plan can be suitable for parents with small children where one or both spouses want to work on a part-time basis. In addition, job sharing can be suitable for workers who want to ease into retirement by reducing the length of their workday or workweek. Both the employees and the organization can profit from job sharing. Since full-time benefits are generally not paid to part-time employees, the company saves on benefit costs.

Downsizing

Downsizing, reducing the number of full-time employees in an organization, has become a large corporate movement. All you have to do is pick up a newspaper, such as *The Wall Street Journal*™, or a periodical, such as *Fortune*™, to realize the number of organizations that are downsizing. Two major reasons exist for downsizing—streamlining an organization so it is more manageable and cutting **overhead costs** (salary and benefit costs).

Outsourcing

Outsourcing, utilizing an outside company or a consultant to take over the performance of a particular part of an organization's business or to complete a project, is a cost-cutting measure used extensively today. This approach can save the organization money in salary dollars and benefits often granted to employees, such as health insurance and retirement options.

With practices such as downsizing and outsourcing, employees can no longer assume they will work for one organization their entire career. Your grandparents and even your parents may have worked for one employer; however, you cannot expect to do so. Changing jobs is commonplace today and will continue to be a common occurrence in the future.

Tomorrow's Workplace

The workplace of the future, whether it is located in one physical place or in several places involving teleworkers and multinational corporations, promises to be very different in physical appearance. An April 2002 issue of *Newsweek* suggests these physical characteristics for the workplace of the future:

- Remote-access tools, with the worker connecting to the Internet wirelessly over a broadband link, and images and sounds projected to distant locations where the worker is located
- Desks on wheels that can be rearranged for impromptu meetings
- ID badges that open doors and cloak sensitive on-screen information when unauthorized eyes are in range, using a tiny transmitter
- Music pumped through a downward channel of sound, letting employees enjoy tunes privately

Employees can no longer assume they will work for one organization their entire career.

- Lighting that is adjusted to suit every person's individual needs
- Temperature and humidity tailored to each individual's needs
- Microphones at workstations to record speech transmission, thus replacing much of the manual keying done today
- Scenery projected on the wall and changed to meet an individual's needs

The workplace of the future is projected to have desks on wheels that can be rearranged for meetings.

- Gel embedded in chair armrests, allowing conformity to the shape of an individual's arms and elbows[9]

Telework

Many workers have traded in the traditional work environment for **telework**, work that is performed any place and any time using technology. The telecommuting-to-work lifestyle is here to stay. In a few years, according to projections, there will be 30 million teleworkers in the United States. You will learn more about telework in Chapter 13.

Career Opportunities

Numerous career opportunities exist in the administrative professional field. To make wise choices, you need to understand these opportunities, the skills needed for the various specialty areas, and some of the professional growth opportunities available.

One specialty area within the administrative assistant field that will have a large increase in employment through 2010 is

[9]"The Office of Tomorrow," *Newsweek*, April 29, 2002.

medical records and health information technicians.[10]

Additionally, employment growth in the health and legal services industries will lead to average growth for medical and legal assistants and executive administrative assistants. Fast-growing industries (such as personnel supply, computer and data processing services, health and legal services education, engineering, and management) will continue to generate new job opportunities.[11]

Becoming an administrative support supervisor or manager is an advancement possibility for administrative professionals who have demonstrated the necessary competence.

---

[10]"Fastest Growing Occupations and Occupations Projected to Have the Largest Numerical Increases in Employment between 2000 and 2010 by Level of Education or Training," *Occupational Outlook Handbook, 2002-2003,* accessed May 6, 2002; available from **www.bls.gov/oco/ocotjl.htm**.

[11]Ibid.

Medical Records and Health Information Technicians

Job duties for medical records and health information technicians include assembling patients' health information, ensuring that all forms are completed, and inputting necessary information in the computer. Technicians entering the field often have an associate degree from a community college. In addition to general education, course work includes medical terminology, legal aspects of health information, database management, and computer training.

Medical Assistants

The health occupations industry not only is experiencing considerable growth, but also is changing dramatically due to technology and increased costs of health services. In addition to the traditional jobs of working in the office of a medical doctor and working in a hospital,

The medical records and health information field is expected to show an increase in employment through 2010.

positions are also available in health-related organizations such as insurance companies and medical departments of large corporations that provide health-care services.

The American Association for Medical Transcription (AAMT) sponsors a certification program, Certified Medical Transcriptionist (CMT), and publishes a magazine entitled the *Journal of the American Association for Medical Transcription.* The Web address for AAMT is **www.aamt.org**.

Legal Assistants

Growth in the legal service industry will offer employment growth for legal support personnel. The legal field is very specialized, with specialties including criminal, matrimonial, probate, negligence, environment, patent, corporate, malpractice, public interest, and computer law.

Job responsibilities in the legal office include preparing legal documents such as complaints, motions, subpoenas, affidavits, and briefs. Typical duties include the following:

- Processing documents; performing administrative support functions, such as handling records and telephone calls
- Assisting with legal research, such as verifying quotes and citations in legal briefs
- Filing court papers
- Taking notes on proceedings

An avenue of continual growth and learning in the legal field is obtaining certification. Certification information is available from the following organizations: National Association of Legal Secretaries℠ (NALS) and Legal Secretaries International℠. NALS sponsors an Accredited Legal Secretary (ALS) examination and certification program administered by the Certifying Board of the National Association of Legal Secretaries. This organization also administers an examination to certify a legal secretary with three years of experience as a Professional Legal Secretary (PLS). Legal Secretaries International confers the designation of Board Certified Civil Trial Legal Secretary in specialized areas such as litigation, real estate, probate, and corporation law to individuals who have five years of law-related experience and pass the exam. The Web address for NALS is **www.nals.org**; the Web address for Legal Secretaries International is **www.legalsecretaries.org**.

Administrative Support Supervisors and Managers

Administrative support supervisors and managers are employed in virtually every sector of the economy, working in positions as varied as customer service managers and shipping-and-receiving supervisors. The largest numbers are found in banks, government agencies, retail establishments, health-care facilities, insurance companies, and business service firms. Although specific duties vary considerably depending on the organization, common duties include the following:

- Performing administrative tasks to ensure that staff can work efficiently
- Maintaining equipment
- Ordering new equipment and supplies
- Planning the work of the staff
- Supervising the staff
- Overseeing the work of the staff
- Evaluating the individual worker's performance
- Recruiting new employees
- Interviewing prospective employees
- Providing orientation for new employees
- Training new employees in organization and workplace procedures
- Assisting in the resolution of interpersonal conflicts among staff
- Knowing the provisions of labor-management agreements in organizations covered by union contracts[12]

---

[12]"Office and Administrative Support Worker Supervisors and Managers," *Occupational Outlook Handbook, 2002-2003,* accessed May 6, 2002; available from **www.bls.gov/oco/ocos**.

If supervisors and managers are to be successful in their jobs, they must continue to learn and grow. A few organizations that offer educational assistance and support to people employed in management occupations include the ones listed here.

- American Management Association, **www.amanet.org**
- National Management Association, **www.nma1.org**
- Association for Information Management Professionals, **www.arma.org**

Twenty-First-Century Workplace Requirements

Postsecondary education and various professional skills and qualities are essential for success in administrative professional positions. This section identifies some of the major workplace requirements needed to be a successful and productive administrative professional.

Education

According to the authors of *Workforce 2020*, "Upward mobility in the labor force depends, quite simply, on education."[13] Due to our ever-increasing technological world, the level of education for jobs is increasing. Many employers require an associate degree for administrative assistants, and some administrative assistants have a bachelor's degree. In addition to education being essential for obtaining a job, ongoing education is important in keeping a job. Lifelong learning is essential for all individuals who expect to remain productive and promotable workers. In addition to formal education, informal education through reading, attending seminars and conferences, and being active in professional or-

ganizations is essential for maintaining and improving the knowledge and skills needed as work responsibilities change.

You have already learned about several organizations that provide lifelong learning possibilities. Another important association is the International Association of Administrative Professionals℠ (IAAP). This organization is the world's largest association for administrative support staff, with nearly 700 chapters and 40,000 members and affiliates worldwide. IAAP administers certification programs for entry-level and advanced skills. The entry-level skills program is available through the Office Proficiency Assessment and Certification program. The advanced-level certification program awards the Certified Professional Secretary℠ (CPS) designation upon the successful passage of the exam plus the required work experience. The letters *CPS* after an administrative professional's name are indicative of the achievement of the highest professional standard within the field. Figure 1-1 gives more details about this certification. IAAP publishes a magazine called *OfficePro*™; the Web address for IAAP is **www.iaap-hq.org**.

Skills

Certain skills are needed in all administrative professional positions. These skills include the following:

- Communication (listening, verbal presentation, and writing)
- Human relations
- Time management
- Critical-thinking
- Decision-making
- Creative-thinking
- Teamwork
- Technology
- Leadership
- Anger, stress, and time management

Communication Skills

Administrative professionals spend a large part of their workday communicating with

---

[13]"Education Must Improve for 2020 Workforce Success," accessed May 6, 2002; available from **www.heartland.org/education**.

THE CERTIFIED PROFESSIONAL SECRETARY

WHY CERTIFICATION?

Job Advancement—The CPS rating gives you a competitive edge for being promoted and hired.

Professional Skills—You will learn more about workplace operations and build your skills by studying for and taking the CPS exam.

Salary—An IAAP Membership Profile study shows that CPS holders earn an average of $2,228 more per year than those who do not have certification.

Esteem—Attaining the CPS certification demonstrates to your employer that you are committed as a professional.

College Credit—Many colleges and universities offer course credit for passing the CPS exam.

WHO IS ELIGIBLE?

You may take the CPS exam if you are employed as an administrative professional or have at least two years of work experience as an administrative professional, varying according to your level of college education. Students or teachers in a college business education program also may qualify.

WHEN AND WHERE IS THE EXAM GIVEN?

The CPS exam is a one-day exam administered each May and November at over 250 locations across the United States, Canada, and other countries.

WHAT ARE THE PARTS OF THE EXAM?

The exam has three parts:
- Finance and Business Law
- Office Systems and Administration
- Management

Excerpted from **www.iaap-hq.org/cps**

FIGURE 1~1 CPS Certification

---

others. Communication takes the form of emails, letters, faxes, voice mail, telephone calls, written presentations, verbal presentations, and one-on-one conversations. Regardless of the form communication takes, you must be proficient in this area. You must express yourself accurately and concisely in written correspondence, and you must be clear, tactful, and straightforward in verbal communications. Part 2 of this textbook, Effective Communication, will help you improve your communication skills.

Human Relations Skills

As an administrative professional, you interact with many people. Within the company, you work with coworkers, supervisors, and other executives. Contacts outside the com-

pany include customers and visitors to the workplace. The people you encounter are of different cultures, races, ethnicities, and ages. If you are to be successful in working with these diverse individuals, you need to attempt to understand and accept their needs. Throughout your life, you must continue to work on improving your human relations skills. This area is one in which you never completely master the skill but should always attempt to improve. Chapters 2, 3, and 4 will help you improve these skills.

Time Management Skills

Another important skill is the ability to organize your time and work. As an efficient administrative professional, you need to organize your time, paper, electronic files, and calendar so work flows smoothly and tasks are finished on time. Chapter 2 will help you improve your time management skills.

Critical-Thinking Skills

Critical thinking is a unique kind of purposeful thinking in which the thinker systematically chooses conscious and deliberate inquiry. *Critical* comes from the Greek word **krinein**, which means "to separate or to choose." To think critically about an issue means to try to see it from all sides before coming to a conclusion.

As an administrative professional working in a highly technical and rapidly changing workplace, you must think critically about the issues facing you. Doing so can save you time and make your life easier as an individual in the workplace. These skills can also make you a valuable employee for your organization—one who is recognized and promoted. As you are learning and practicing critical-thinking skills, a systematic process of asking appropriate questions will help you. Figure 1-2 lists several questions. Take a few moments to read them; then begin to practice and improve your critical-thinking skills.

CREATIVE-THINKING QUESTIONS

- What is the purpose of my thinking?
- What problem or question am I trying to answer?
- What facts do I need to address this problem or this question?
- How do I interpret the facts or information I receive?
- What conclusions can I make from the information I receive?
- Are my conclusions defensible?
- Have I dealt with the complexity of the situation?
- Have I avoided thinking in simple stereotypes?
- What will be the consequences if I put my conclusions into practice?

FIGURE 1~2 Creative-Thinking Questions

Decision-Making Skills

In your role as an administrative professional, you make decisions daily. If you are to be effective in that process, you must understand and implement proper decision-making steps. The next section of this chapter presents these steps. Study these skills, practicing them throughout this course so you become an effective decision maker in the workplace.

Creative-Thinking Skills

Creativity means "having the ability or the power to cause to exist." Creativity is a process. It is a way of thinking and doing. A creative person understands that multiple options exist in most situations and that he or she is free to choose from a wide variety of options. Creative individuals use more than one set of rules or one method for getting a job done.

Consider this situation. You have decided to take advantage of your company's offer to become a teleworker five days a week. One expectation of you includes being productive as you work from your home; you will have no support from your colleagues. You have two young children who are in the first and third grades. You will be the primary caregiver when they return home from school each afternoon.

How do you think creatively in this situation in order to accomplish your job at the highest level of productivity while meeting your family obligations? How do you set up your home work space to provide for maximum efficiency? How do you provide for your children's needs after school and still get your work done? Take a few minutes to read and think about the tips given in Figure 1-3. Throughout this course, use these tips as you make decisions. Then practice the tips on the job—at the one you have now or will have in the future.

Teamwork Skills

The word **team** can be traced back to the Indo-European word *deuk*, meaning "to pull." Successful teams in the work environment

CREATIVE-THINKING TIPS

- Have faith in your own creativity.
- Attack barriers to creativity. Self-judgment and judging others are barriers to creativity.
- Pay attention to everything around you.
- Ask questions constantly.
- Tackle tasks that are not easy and that require effort.
- Break tasks into small pieces.
- Do one thing at a time.
- Make a game of tasks.
- Know when to stop.
- Stop worrying.
- Block irrelevant thoughts.
- Pay attention to your intuition.
- Concentrate intently on the activity at hand.

FIGURE 1~3 Creative-Thinking Tips

include groups of people who need each other to accomplish a given task. Teamwork skills are similar to interpersonal skills in that they demand that you understand, accept, and respect the differences among your team members. Teamwork also demands that you engage in the following behaviors:

- Treat all team members courteously.
- Build strong relationships with individual members of the team and the team as a whole.
- Learn collectively with the team. Start by developing self-knowledge and self-mastery; then look outward in developing knowledge and alignment with team members.
- Take responsibility for producing high-quality work as an individual team member and encouraging a high-quality team project.

© GETTY IMAGES/PHOTODISC

Teamwork demands that you build strong relationships with team members.

Technology Skills

If you are to succeed in the workplace, you must be competent and current in your knowledge and skills of technology as it applies to your job. You must develop the following:

- Proficiency with computers and current software
- Proficiency in telecommunications
- Capability in researching on the Web
- Competency in using printers/copiers/scanners
- Willingness to research new workforce technology and utilize this technology in the workplace

Later chapters of this book will help you develop these important skills.

Leadership Skills

You will develop leadership skills over time. You begin to develop these skills by seeking out and accepting leadership opportunities. Accepting a leadership position in one of your school's organizations can help you develop leadership skills. As you accept leadership opportunities, learn from each of them. Evaluate yourself or ask a close friend to evaluate you. What did you do well with your leadership opportunity? What did you not do well? How can you correct your mistakes? In Chapter 20, you will learn more about leadership and the application of leadership skills to your job.

Anger, Stress, and Time Management Skills

You live in such a fast-paced world that you may find yourself complaining about how stressed you are. Chronic stress can cause serious health problems and affect your work—not only in the way you perform when you are under stress, but also in the work you miss due to illness. Anger, stress, and time management are all closely related. If you carry around deep-seated anger, you become stressed. In order to be effective in your work life and personal life, you need to understand how to manage your anger and time so you do not become chronically stressed.

Chapter 2 will help you understand how to manage your time and lead a less stressful and angry life.

Success Qualities

In addition to the skills just identified, certain qualities are essential for the success of the administrative professional. These qualities include flexibility, adaptability, integrity, honesty, initiative, and motivation.

Flexibility/Adaptability

Flexible means "capable of being bent or pliable." **Adapt** means "to make suitable to a specific use or situation." The two terms are closely related. You learned earlier in this chapter that the workforce is diverse and constantly changing. You must be able to adapt to new technology, to be pliable when new situations occur, to be willing to think in new ways, and to accommodate the many changes that occur in your work life.

Integrity/Honesty

In the workplace environment, **integrity** and **honesty** mean that you engage in the following behaviors:

- Adherence to a strict ethical code
- Truthfulness
- Sincerity

You do not engage in activities that allow others to question your morals or values.

Initiative/Motivation

The definition of **initiative** is "the ability to begin and follow through on a plan or task." Initiative is taking the tasks you are given and completing them in an appropriative manner. Initiative also means seeking out tasks beyond those assigned by your supervisor. The most highly valued administrative professional has the ability to analyze a task, establish priorities, and see work through to completion. **Motivation** and initiative are closely related. Motivation provides an incentive for someone to act. In taking the initiative to begin a task, you may be motivated **extrinsically** (from outside) or **intrinsically** (from within). For example, you may be motivated to perform a task because it provides a monetary reward for you or because it provides external recognition from your supervisor. Additionally, you may be motivated to perform a task because you are committed to learning and growing. You understand that each task you perform provides you with an opportunity to learn something new.

Your Career Plan

Now that you understand selected opportunities available in the workplace and skills and qualities necessary for the administrative professional, consider your career plan. What are your goals? Where do you want to be in three years? In five years? What steps do you need to take to get there? In order to get to your destination, you must set goals and make effective decisions about reaching your goals. Over time, you should continue to evaluate whether you were able to reach your goals.

Set Appropriate Goals

Personal goal setting involves setting both short- and long-range goals. In order to set goals, you need to take a good look at yourself. Determine what is important to you. Take an inventory of your needs, wants, interests, and abilities. Assume that in developing your master plan, you decide you want your life to consist of career success, good health, financial security, and happiness. You must set some long-range goals that will help you realize these desires. Your goals, for example, may include becoming an administrative manager, having a family, and staying physically and mentally healthy. However, becoming a manager, having a family, and being healthy requires hard work and the accomplishment of many short-range goals.

How do you set short-range goals? You begin by considering the following areas:

- Your strengths and weaknesses
- Your motivation

- Your energy level
- Your ultimate desire to succeed in what you have planned for yourself

Consider the long-range goal of becoming an administrative manager. To do so will require experience, commitment, hard work, and time. Thus, a logical short-range goal may include getting a job that will allow you to use the skills and knowledge you have gained, in addition to providing you with work experience for future opportunities. Salary in your first job may not be your highest priority since you are seeking experience. Money may become a higher priority as you work toward your long-range goal.

Begin setting short- and long-range goals by asking yourself these questions:

- What are my strong points?
- What are my weak points?
- What are my achievements?
- What is my motivation?
- What do I enjoy doing?
- Where do I want to be in three years? In five years?

Keep in mind that your goals will change over time and that you may not reach all of your short- and long-range goals. However, if you go through life never setting goals, you will not reach your maximum potential.

Make Effective Decisions

In your role as an administrative professional, you make decisions daily. It is important that you make good decisions. These decisions may range from recommending new technology to deciding how to handle a difficult client or customer. To make these decisions more effectively, you need an understanding of the decision-making process.

A **decision** is the outcome or product of a problem, a concern, or an issue that must be addressed and solved. Reaching a decision includes the five steps shown in Figure 1-4 and presented in the following section. You should follow these steps systematically when making a decision.

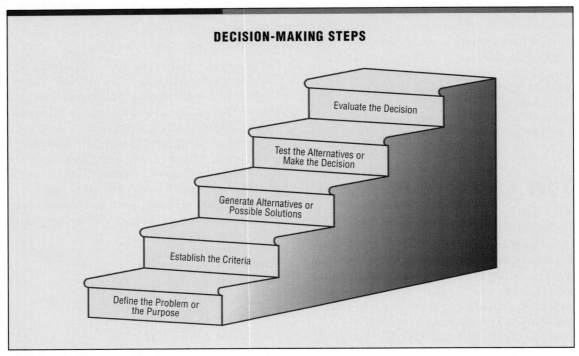

DECISION-MAKING STEPS

Evaluate the Decision

Test the Alternatives or
Make the Decision

Generate Alternatives or
Possible Solutions

Establish the Criteria

Define the Problem or
the Purpose

FIGURE 1~4   Decision-Making Steps

Define the Problem or the Purpose

This statement may sound simple, but it is usually the most difficult step. When attempting to define the problem or purpose, ask yourself a series of questions:

- What problem am I trying to solve, or what purpose am I trying to achieve?
- Why is this decision necessary?
- What will be the outcome of this decision?

Assume you are completing your education and are ready to look for a position as an administrative professional. You know you want to enter the medical field. You have two job offers—one in a small medical office in the suburbs, approximately a 15-minute drive from your home, and one in a large city hospital, approximately a 40-minute drive from your home.

The medical office is small, and the advancement opportunities are limited. However, you understand you may have an opportunity to become an administrative manager, over-

seeing the operations. The office environment is informal, yet professional. People seem to care for one another. The workload of the position is heavy; however, the tasks are varied. The benefits are fair.

The people in the hospital seem very nice, but the pace appears hectic. The workload of the position is heavy, but not varied. The personnel seem too busy to talk with one another. The promotional opportunities appear excellent and include a number of areas from which to choose. The benefits are excellent also. The salary for the hospital position is $200 more per month than the medical office.

Your answers to the three questions might be as follows:

- I am trying to solve the problem of finding a suitable position in the medical field. I want a job that provides good promotional opportunities and challenging work. Since I have a small child who will be staying with a baby-sitter, I do not want to drive long distances to work. I want to be able to spend as much time as possible with my child.

- The decision is necessary because (a) I am finishing my education, (b) I need money to help support my family, and (c) I want to be employed where the work is meaningful.
- The outcome of the decision is my employment in an administrative professional role where the position provides challenges and opportunities and an appropriate starting salary and benefits.

When you finish answering the questions, you should frame the problem in statement form. Your statement may be similar to the following:

My purpose is to find an administration professional position in the medical field within reasonable proximity of my home. This position should be one that provides challenges and opportunities in addition to satisfying my financial needs.

Establish the Criteria

The next step in the decision-making process is to determine criteria needed to make a sound decision. In setting criteria, here are three questions you may ask.

- What do I want to achieve?
- What do I want to preserve?
- What do I want to avoid?

Your answers to these questions in the situation given might be as follows:

- I want employment as an administrative professional in a medical office where promotions are possible.
- I want to use the skills that I have.
- I want to avoid traveling more than 30 minutes to and from work each day.

By asking and answering these questions, you can determine several criteria important to you as you look for a position.

Generate Alternatives or Possible Solutions

The next step in the decision-making process is to begin generating alternatives or possible solutions. For example, you might list the job duties of each position, the promotional opportunities available, and the starting salaries and benefits.

Test the Alternatives and Make the Decision

The effective decision maker tests each alternative using this system:

- Eliminate alternatives that are unrealistic or incompatible with your needs or situation.
- Give additional thought to alternatives appropriate to the situation.
- Select the alternative that appears most realistic, creative, challenging, or satisfying.

For example, one position might have only one promotional opportunity offering a very small salary increase. The work environment in one position might be better than the other position. If neither position meets your needs, you may decide to decline both positions and continue your job search.

Evaluate the Decision

The last step in the decision-making process is evaluating the decision. Evaluation serves two purposes:

- It helps you decide if you have made the right decision for the immediate situation.
- It helps you improve your decision-making skills for the future.

In evaluating your decision, here are some questions you can ask yourself.

- What was right about this decision? What was wrong?
- How did the decision-making process work?
- What improvements are necessary?
- What did I learn from the decision?
- What changes should I make for the future?

Setting appropriate goals and making effective decisions allow you to move in the direction you wish in your career. The decision-making model also helps you deal realistically with your strengths and weaknesses and to minimize the latter as you strive to reach your career goals. ■

SUMMARY

To reinforce what you have learned in this chapter, study this summary.

- The workplace is constantly changing and includes technological changes, a diverse environment, an aging workforce, additional women in the workforce, and a global economy.
- Workplace strategies for coping with change include a quality focus, changing organizational structures, flexible workweeks, downsizing, outsourcing, use of technological equipment, and telework.
- Career opportunities for the administrative professional are expected to be good in medical records and health information, legal services, and medical assistant fields.
- Promotional opportunities for administrative professionals include supervisors and managers.
- Twenty-first-century workplace requirements include greater levels of education and skills such as communication; human relations; time management; critical-thinking; decision-making; creative-thinking; teamwork; technology; leadership; and anger, stress, and time management.
- Success qualities include flexibility/adaptability, integrity/honesty, and initiative/motivation.
- When determining a career plan, set appropriate goals and make effective decisions.

FIND THE PROBLEM

Throughout this course, you will be working for People Pharmaceuticals International. To learn more about this company, read the material on page 1 of your *Applications Workbook*. As a part-time employee, you have had an opportunity to observe some of the human dynamics that occur in the organization. What is the problem in the following situation?

John accepted his first job as an administrative assistant to Pamela Evian, manager of the Human Resources Department for People Pharmaceuticals International. When they were introduced, John shook Pamela's hand vigorously and said, "Hi, Pamela. I am so happy to meet you." Although she responded with a smile and a welcome, the look on her face told John he had done something wrong. Now when he comes to work each morning, he makes a point of going by Pamela's office and greeting her. Her response is always a hurried "Good morning." John wants to make a good impression on his employer, but he has a feeling Pamela dislikes him. What suggestions would you make to John?

PROFESSIONAL POINTERS

Here are some tips to help you take advantage of the possibilities available to you.

- Practice creative dreaming of where you wish to be in your professional life 10 and 20 years from now.
- Know your own beliefs and personal goals; pay attention to what you value.
- Focus on your achievements and your strengths.
- Learn from your failures.
- Create a vision for your future.

REINFORCEMENT ITEMS

1. Identify forces changing the workplace environment.
2. Describe two career opportunities available for the administrative professional.
3. List six necessary twenty-first-century skills.
4. Explain why flexibility and adaptability are essential for success in the twenty-first century.
5. Explain the decision-making model.

CRITICAL-THINKING ACTIVITY

Roberta McPherson has completed her first year at Lincoln Hills Community College in Fort Worth, Texas. Roberta was a C student in high school. However, when she started to college, she decided to concentrate on her studies; as a result, she had a 3.6 grade point average (on a 4-point scale) at the end of the first year. In her first year of college, she had not determined her career course, so she took general education classes. She enjoyed all of her classes, particularly her psychology and computer classes. She talked with one of the school counselors at the end of the year and completed the Myers-Briggs instrument suggested. According to the instrument, Roberta is an extrovert (likes working with people) and a thinker (makes decisions by logical reasoning). Roberta worked part-time in the president's office during the second semester. In this position, she answered the phone, made appointments, keyed reports on the computer, and handled complaints. She enjoyed every aspect of the job—especially dealing with people issues. The president's assistant complimented her several times on her decision-making ability. She urged Roberta to take office systems courses in the fall; she told Roberta she thought the field could be rewarding.

   How should Roberta go about deciding what to do? Roberta has never engaged in personal goal setting. In fact, she has no idea how to begin. However, Roberta is proud of her achievements this past year and is ready to make plans for her future. What advice would you give Roberta about how to set her personal goals? What should she consider? Using the decision-making model presented on pages 20-21 of your textbook, develop a plan you believe Roberta should follow.

VOCABULARY REVIEW

Complete the Vocabulary Review for Chapter 1 given on page 3 of the *Applications Workbook*.

ENGLISH AND WORD USAGE DRILL

Complete the English and Word Usage Drill for Chapter 1 listed on page 5 of the *Applications Workbook*.

WORKPLACE APPLICATIONS

A1-1 (Goals 1 and 3)

Interview one administrative professional who is currently working in the field. You may choose to do the interview by email. Ask the administrative professional these questions:

- How long have you worked as an administrative professional?
- What changes in the workplace environment have you seen since you began working?
- How have you handled these changes?
- What skills do you need to be effective at your job?
- How do you stay current in your field?
- What are the advantages/disadvantages of your current position?
- What advice would you give a student preparing for the same career?

Write a summary of your findings, giving the name of the administrative professional you interviewed and the company affiliation. Present the report to your instructor. Write a thank-you letter to the interviewee.

 ### A1-2 (Goal 1)

Using the Web, research one business merger that has happened in the last year. Attempt to answer this question: What impact will this merger have on the business world and the public? Report your findings to the class. For tips on Websites and Web research, refer to the Preface in your *Applications Workbook*.

A1-3 (Goal 2)

Interview one manager. You may interview the person by telephone. Ask these questions:

- What changes has your organization faced in the last three to five years?
- What steps have you taken to cope with these changes?
- Have you helped your employees understand how to cope with change? If so, how?
- What changes does your organization anticipate within the next year? How do you anticipate the organization will address these changes?

Report your findings to the class.

A1-4 (Goals 3 and 4)

Review the five job openings in your *Applications Workbook*, page 7. Make a list of the types of opportunities available to the administrative professional and the job requirements. Present your report to your instructor in writing, using the memorandum form on the Student CD, SCDA1-4.

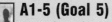 ### A1-5 (Goal 5)

Complete the self-evaluation chart on page 9 of the *Applications Workbook* to help you understand your strengths and weaknesses. Follow the directions given in the *Applications Workbook* for completing the self-evaluation. Working with two classmates or on your own, develop a career plan. If you are working with classmates, discuss with each other your individual strengths and weaknesses. Each person should voice where he or she wants to be in three years and in five years. Question each other as to how you make decisions. What type of information do you need before you make a decision? How do you evaluate a decision? Individually write down where you plan to be in your career in three years and in five years. Explain how you expect to accomplish your goals. Explain how you will evaluate the decisions you make. Write a memorandum to your instructor (using the memorandum form provided on the Student CD, SCDA1-5) explaining how you expect to accomplish your goals and how you will evaluate the decisions you make. Submit the career plan and the memorandum to your instructor. Keep one copy of your career plan for review in Chapter 19.

ASSESSMENT OF CHAPTER GOALS

Did you successfully complete the chapter goals? Evaluate yourself by filling out the form on page 13 of the *Applications Workbook*.

Anger, Stress, and Time Management

1. Determine the effects of stress in the workplace.
2. Identify factors that contribute to workplace stress.
3. Determine the purpose of anger and its resolution.
4. Determine how time may be wasted.
5. Describe the relationship among stress, anger, and time.
6. Apply appropriate techniques for managing stress, anger, and time.

Do you ever have any of these feelings?

- Anger
- Depression
- Anxiety
- Exhaustion
- Stress

Have you ever experienced any of these health problems?

- Headaches
- Backaches
- Muscular problems
- Sleeping problems
- Heartburn

If you answered yes to several of these questions, you are not alone. In the fast-paced, changing world in which you live, many people experience these feelings and health issues all too often. In fact, studies show that between 70 and 80 percent of Americans believe their jobs are stressful.

In addition to adding stress to your job, these factors can cause **negative stress** (factors that cause emotional and mental upset) in your personal life as well as your professional life. You may have one or more of the following responsibilities:

- Attending college and working 40 hours each week

- Assuming responsibility for elderly parents who live with you or who are in rest homes and demand your attention
- Assuming, as a single parent, total responsibility for small children

All of these situations can lead to negative stress. Additionally, you may be the sole wage earner in your household. If so, providing enough money to meet your family's needs is often stressful. Add these personal stressors to the stress of a job, and you may find yourself having difficulty performing successfully on the job and at home. For example, administrative professionals must accomplish a myriad of tasks quickly and accurately in the daily performance of their duties, while at the same time dealing with numerous interruptions. This is no easy task for anyone and can lead to negative stress. No matter how competent and capable you are, you will encounter workdays when nothing seems to go right. Everything you touch seems to fall apart in your hands. You make one error after another. Days like this can produce stress. When you add the demands of a family plus money worries, stress can become a negative factor that affects your health and relationships, causing increased work problems and issues.

Stress, however, is not always negative. In fact, stress can be a positive factor in your life and work. Part of lessening stress involves engaging in the following behaviors:

- Recognizing the difference between good stress and bad stress
- Understanding what bad stress can do to your body if it continues over a prolonged period of time

Stress and Its Effects in the Workplace

Stress is the response of the body to a demand made upon it. Wants, needs, and desires come from stress of some kind. Many positive accomplishments in life relate to feelings of stress.

- If you did not feel a need to achieve, you would not take a challenging job.
- If you did not feel a need to learn, you would not study.
- If you did not feel a need for friends, you would not join social groups.

All of these situations are examples of stress that can make a positive impact on your life. You feel pressure to satisfy needs, wants, or desires that you have; you respond in a positive way to obtain satisfaction. This type of stress is referred to as **eustress**, a beneficial stress that enables individuals to strive to meet challenges.

Now consider negative stress, often referred to as **distress** due to the negative impact it has on your life. For example, if someone you love is sick, you feel distress. If you are unable to keep up with new technology in your office, you feel distress. If you receive a negative performance review at your job, you feel distress. Even the stresses of driving to work in heavy traffic or getting you and your family ready for work each morning can cause negative stress.

If you are unable to cope with stresses, you can become physically, mentally, and/or emotionally ill. Therefore, you must achieve an appropriate balance between the distress in your life and the ability to cope with it. Figure 2-1 graphically illustrates appropriate and inappropriate balances.

Types of Negative Stress

There are two types of negative stress.

- **Acute stress**
- **Chronic stress**

Acute Stress

Acute stress occurs when an individual must respond instantaneously to a crisis situation. For example, if your car goes into a skid on an icy road, you must react quickly. When you experience acute stress, two chemicals are produced in your body—adrenaline and noradrenaline. These chemicals have stimulated people to perform incredible acts in a

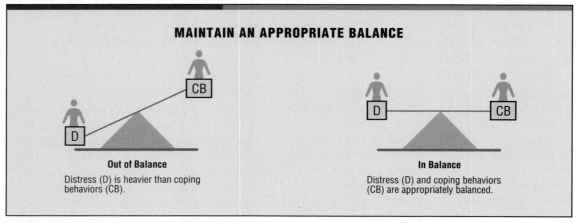

FIGURE 2~1 Maintain an Appropriate Balance

crisis—from lifting extremely heavy objects off injured people (objects they would not be able to lift in an ordinary situation) to fighting off ferocious animals. Immediately after the crisis, however, these heroic people may become weak, their hands may shake, and their knees may quiver. They may even collapse. All of these aftereffects are the body's response to the acute stress event.

Chronic Stress

Chronic stress occurs when a distressful situation is prolonged with no rest or recuperation for the body. Chronic stress triggers the production of different biochemicals in the body. While your body can break down adrenaline and noradrenaline, the chemicals produced by chronic stress cannot be broken down, and they remain in your system where they are capable of damaging your body. Chemicals produced by chronic stress can cause physical problems such as the ones listed here.

- High blood pressure
- Cardiovascular disease
- Migraine headaches
- Ulcers
- Elevated cholesterol
- Weakening of the immune system
- Shortness of breath

- Dizziness
- Chest pains
- Back pains

Chronic stress can also cause emotional problems such as the following:

- Depression
- Withdrawal
- Deep-seated anger
- Self-rejection
- Anxiety
- Loss of self-esteem

Cost of Stress

The cost of stress is high for both the organization and the individual. For the organization, the price can be absenteeism, loss of productivity, and poor work performance. For the individual, the price can be illness and temporary loss of work.

To the Organization

Numerous surveys have shown that employee stress is a major expense for businesses. Here are some of the statistics reported.

- Stress-related claims cost the nation's companies nearly 10 percent of their annual earnings.
- Annually, organizations pay out $26 billion in disability claims related to stress.

- Mental illnesses such as depression, which can result from workplace stress, cost the U.S. economy about $30 million each year.
- Industrial accidents caused by on-the-job stress cost an estimated $32 billion annually.[1]
- Forty percent of job turnover is due to stress.
- Sixty to eighty percent of accidents on the job are stress related.[2]

In an attempt to reduce employee stress, many organizations offer stress-reduction programs in the workplace. These programs include exercise; diet; and stress-reduction techniques such as meditation, relaxation training (including biofeedback techniques), and a change in lifestyle management. Some organizations even offer programs designed to increase fun in the workplace.

To the Individual

The vast majority of workers in the United States say they experience stress on the job. A recent Gallup Poll survey revealed the following:

- Sixty-five percent of workers believe workplace stress causes difficulties.
- Twenty-nine percent of workers have admitted to yelling at coworkers because of workplace stress.
- Fourteen percent said they work where damage to machinery or equipment occurred because of workplace rage.
- Two percent admitted they had actually struck someone.

[1]Toni Knott, "Stress in the Workplace," accessed May 13, 2002; available from **www.cspp.edu/news/stress/htm**.
[2]"Job Stress," accessed May 13, 2002; available from **www.stress.org/job.htm**.

Many organizations offer stress-reduction programs at the workplace.

- Sixty-two percent found that they routinely ended the day with work-related neck pain, 44 percent reported tired eyes, 38 percent complained of hurting hands, and 34 percent reported difficulty in sleeping due to stress.

- Over half said they often spend 12-hour days on work-related duties, and an equal number frequently skip lunch because of the stress of job demands.[3] U.S. workers put in more hours on the job than the labor force of any other industrialized nation. The trend for the number of hours worked has been decreasing in other nations, while the trend in the United States has been increasing.

- According to an International Labor Organization study, Americans put in the equivalent of an extra 40-hour workweek in 2000 compared to 10 years previously.[4]

- In a recent survey, nearly 40 percent of workers described their work environment to be "like a real-life survivor program."[5]

Factors Contributing to Workplace Stress

Some of the factors that contribute to stress on the job are these:

- Role ambiguity
- Job insecurity
- Working conditions and relationships

[3]Ibid.

[4]Ibid.
[5]Ibid.

Americans are working more today than they did 10 years ago.

© GETTY IMAGES/PHOTODISC

- Dual-career families, single parenthood, and extended families
- Anger
- Time
- Money

Role Ambiguity

Role ambiguity exists when individuals have inadequate information about their work roles—when there is lack of clarity about work objectives and expectations. As an administrative professional, you may experience role ambiguity. You may not understand exactly what is expected of you. When this situation occurs, you have the responsibility to find out what your job is. Many companies write **job descriptions** detailing the duties to be performed on the job. If a job description exists for your position, read it carefully. If there is no job description, ask your employer what he or she expects of you.

Job Insecurity

Another factor that contributes to stress on the job is job insecurity. In a volatile economy, organizations are often in the process of downsizing. If your organization is doing so, it is normal to wonder, *Will I be the next to go?* If you have these thoughts, you probably are not able to give your best efforts to the job. Your productivity may suffer.

Working Conditions and Relationships

A number of studies have shown a relationship between working conditions and an employee's physical and mental health. The following conditions impair health:

- A dehumanizing environment—one in which people are treated as objects rather than individuals
- A poor working relationship with a supervisor
- An unsatisfactory working relationship with colleagues

- Lack of trust among people who must work together
- Lack of support from coworkers
- Work overload

Dual-Career Families, Single Parenthood, and Extended Families

In the majority of two-parent families, both parents work. This means that the day-to-day pressures of the job must be balanced against spending time with children and juggling the demands of housework, grocery shopping, meal preparation, yard work, and so on.

In society, divorce is commonplace, which means numerous single parents must also juggle responsibilities of the job, home, and children. The pressures on these single parents can be tremendous.

© GETTY IMAGES/PHOTODISC

Workload pressure can cause stress for dual-career families.

Another factor that can cause negative stress is the need to take care of aging parents. People are living longer today than ever before, and due to advances in medical science, longevity is expected to increase. This phenomenon often means that both children and aging parents need care. Aging parents often live in their children's household, which can result in constant demands on the caregiver.

Anger

You live in a society in which the terms *road rage*, *desk rage*, and *phone rage* have become common terms. According to two studies, the United States has the dubious distinction of having the highest violent crime rate of any industrialized nation. The horror of 9/11 was followed by the spread of the anthrax virus through the mail, resulting in postal workers and others becoming very sick, with some people dying. There has been violence in schools, with teenagers killing other teenagers and themselves. Many people find themselves yelling at someone over the phone for a perceived injustice or misunderstanding. The United States is an angry nation in many ways.

Time

People never seem to have enough time to satisfy the following needs and demands:

- Job demands of an employer
- Children's needs
- Spouse's needs
- Social needs
- Extended family's needs

People are stressed because *they think* they do not have enough time. They often make these or similar statements.

- *Stop the clock; I need more time.*
- *Stop the world; I need to get off for awhile.*
- *There is never enough time in the day.*
- *If only I had more time, I could. . . .*
- *Please slow down.* (to anyone who is in voice range)

Money

There is a very real relationship between time and money. The more money you spend, the more you need to work. The average person is in debt several thousand dollars, as reflected by national credit card statistics. Many people live from one paycheck to the next. Thus, individuals work more to have more money to pay their debts. They have less time to spend with family or on activities outside work. Their stress mounts higher, just as their debts do. It is a vicious cycle that millions in America have trouble breaking.

Anger—Its Purpose and Its Resolution

You have already learned that anger is prevalent in society. Administrative professionals may encounter anger or become angry on the job. Your role as an administrative professional is a complex one. You must have command of the very latest technology, be able to deal with all types of people (even the ones who are angry), and be able to satisfy your employer's needs for efficiency and effectiveness in turning out paperwork. You are expected to keep a stoic face and perform well when your employer is upset or angry—not an easy task, one that requires you to grow and learn continually. You must learn how to deal with your anger and how to help diffuse the anger of coworkers, customers, and clients with whom you come in contact.

Its Purpose

To understand the purpose of anger, consider the following situation:

Margaret and Jose have been married for three years. Margaret has a teenage brother, Rob, who is living with them. Rob has had a rough home

There is a relationship between time and money. Individuals often need to work more in order to have enough money to pay their debts, frequently resulting in not having enough time for family or relaxation.

life. Margaret and Rob's mother and father are divorced. The mother has remarried, but Rob does not get along with his stepfather. Margaret loves her brother and is trying to help him by offering him a place to live, but the third person in the household is interfering with Margaret and Jose's relationship. Jose is a very controlling person and insists on telling Rob how to think, act, and behave. As a teenager, Rob resents being told what to do. Margaret finds she is often angry with Jose because she does not like the way he treats Rob. In fact, she gets so angry that she yells and screams at him. In her anger, she threatens to divorce him. Margaret loves Jose and she knows he loves her. Neither of them wants a divorce, but she is afraid that her anger, which she cannot seem to get under control, is going to drive Jose away, resulting in a divorce.

What purpose is Margaret's anger playing? Anger is a messenger and a shield. Anger as

a messenger tells Margaret something is wrong. Anger as a shield helps Margaret hide her true feelings. In other words, people respond with anger because it is easier than trying to understand the real problem and dealing with it. However, whenever people use anger to mask a problem, they take a step closer to becoming angry individuals who see the world through a lens of anger that blinds them from being able to live a peaceful and happy life.

Its Resolution

How can Margaret deal with the problem? She can use an intervention model coupled with the problem-solving model introduced in Chapter 1. Figure 2-2 shows this model graphically. Controlling anger is actually a problem-solving process. It allows you to take a time-out to focus on what the real message

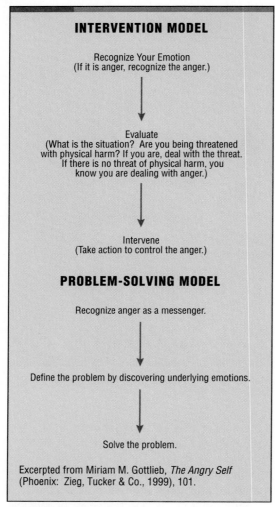

INTERVENTION MODEL

Recognize Your Emotion
(If it is anger, recognize the anger.)

Evaluate
(What is the situation? Are you being threatened with physical harm? If you are, deal with the threat. If there is no threat of physical harm, you know you are dealing with anger.)

Intervene
(Take action to control the anger.)

PROBLEM-SOLVING MODEL

Recognize anger as a messenger.

Define the problem by discovering underlying emotions.

Solve the problem.

Excerpted from Miriam M. Gottlieb, *The Angry Self* (Phoenix: Zieg, Tucker & Co., 1999), 101.

FIGURE 2~2 Intervention and Problem-Solving Models

is underneath the anger. It allows you to question what situation the anger is shielding. Such an approach is not easy. It is much easier to get angry and yell about something than it is to understand anger as a message and strip the anger away to find and deal with the real problem. However, the results of such an approach are well worth it for you as an individual. Such an approach contributes to your long-term health and growth. Not dealing with a problem merely takes you one step closer to becoming an angry person.

Administrative Professionals and Time Wasters

Time is a precious commodity for most people. They never have enough time to get everything done they want or need to do. Administrative professionals are no exception. You, as a busy person in a world of change, will find yourself often lamenting the fact that you do not have enough time—not enough time to do all the tasks at your job, not enough time to handle all the stressors of your professional life and your personal life, and not enough time to relax and enjoy life.

Time—A Resource

In order to control time more effectively, you must understand something about time. You never seem to have the time you need; yet you have all the time there is. **Time** is a resource you cannot buy, sell, rent, borrow, save, or manufacture. You cannot change it, convert it, or control it. It can only be spent. Everyone receives an equal amount of time every day. You spend it even if you accomplish nothing. The term *managing time* is a misnomer. In actuality, managing time means managing yourself in relation to your time.

Time Wasters

Every day you waste time in a variety of ways. If you understand your own time wasters, you can become more effective in managing yourself in relation to your time. Listed here are several common time wasters.

Chatter

If you presently have a job, do you go to work and get busy accomplishing the tasks of the day? Or do you report to work promptly and then spend the first 30 minutes of your workday talking to coworkers about what happened the night before? Certainly, it is important to have some time to talk about topics other than business, but socializing is more appropriate on breaks or at lunch. In most organizations, too much time is wasted in excessive socializing, when employees should be accomplishing the work of the organization.

Disorganization

I had that letter just a few minutes ago, but now I can't find it. It couldn't have disappeared into thin air. Have you ever made such a statement and then proceeded to rummage through the clutter on your desk for 30 minutes in an attempt to find the paper you never should have misplaced? A disorganized and cluttered desk can be a major time waster for administrative professionals. You should know what goes into your desk, what stays on top of your desk, and what goes into your file. Do not clutter your desk with papers that should be filed electronically or manually.

Part of organization is also organizing your day appropriately. For example, if you try to prepare a report, plan a meeting, and do a month's filing all at the most hectic part of the day (when the telephone is ringing constantly and callers are coming and going), the result will be wasted time, nothing accomplished, frayed nerves, and a stressed out or angry feeling. When you have a detailed task to accomplish, plan to do it during a time when interruptions are minimal.

Ineffective Communication

As an administrative professional, you will communicate orally and in writing with people within and outside the workplace—your employer, coworkers, and customers or clients. It is important that the lines of communication between you and others be open and easily understood. Communication in today's workplace is complex, in part due to the various modes of communication that are available. The different modes of communication include email; fax; telephones (with cell phones

A cluttered desk can be a major time waster.

being a constant companion for many people); voice mail; the Web; hard copy (paper) such as letters, reports, and organizational newsletters; in addition to face-to-face communication. Studies have shown that employees communicate with an average of 24 people each day.

Lack of communication or misunderstood communication can cause confusion and loss of productivity. For example, think of the time you waste when you key and format a report incorrectly because you misunderstood instructions from your employer. Or think of the profits a company loses when customers become so unhappy due to ineffective communication that they take their business elsewhere.

Procrastination

Procrastination means trying to avoid a task by putting it aside with the intention of doing it later. Procrastination can be a big time waster. Procrastination takes many forms, but people who habitually procrastinate actually invite interruptions. They prolong telephone conversations, talk with coworkers, take long coffee breaks, or seek excuses to avoid doing their tasks.

Stress, Anger, and Time—The Relationship

Stress, anger, and time are closely related. For example, you get stressed out because you do not have enough time to do your job; you become angry with your husband or children because they are demanding your attention when you are already running as fast as you can in an attempt to keep up with all the demands made on you. In the next sections of this book, you will examine how you spend your time, what your stressors are, and what triggers your anger. You will learn techniques to help manage your stress, anger, and time. Notice that the word *manage* was used since it is impossible to eliminate all stressors or all anger and equally impossible to add more time to the day. Your task is to learn how to

manage these factors so you can live your life as productively and happily as possible.

Techniques for Managing Stress, Anger, and Time

The stress, anger, and time management cycle can become a vicious one. Figure 2-3 illustrates the cycle. Being aware of the relationship between stress, anger, and time and using the techniques listed here can help you lead a less stressful life. These techniques are geared to your professional life; however, they can be used successfully in your personal life as well. Practice them daily and you will reap the rewards.

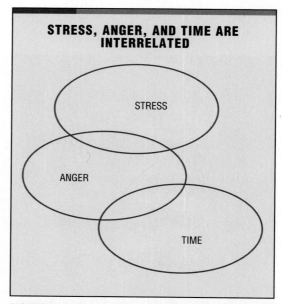

FIGURE 2~3 The Interrelationship of Stress, Anger, and Time

Conduct Audits

To help manage stress, anger, and time, you need to know as much as you can about how you spend your time, what your major stressors are, and what makes you angry. An effective way to discover these factors is to take the time to do an audit. "What?" you may ask. "I don't have time to do these audits. I'm already too busy." Sometimes you need to get off the treadmill of life and take time to analyze what you are doing. In "Workplace Applications" at the end of this chapter, you will complete stress, anger, and time audits. To learn from these audits, you must do the following:

- Determine how often you are stressed and/or angry.
- Determine how much time you are spending in various activities each day.
- Determine positive steps you can take to decrease your stress and anger and to use your time more productively.
- Practice effective stress, anger, and time management techniques.

By looking closely at how often you are stressed, angry, and short of time, you can determine what is and what is not working for you. You will then be able to develop plans periodically to help you control the out-of-control factors.

Clarify Values

Even though you might not give it much thought, you live by a set of values. Generally, you developed these values at an early age. You acquired your values through the teachings of significant others in your life (parents, other relatives, and close friends) and through observing their behaviors. **Values** are principles that guide your life, such as honesty, fairness, love, security, and belief in a higher being. If you have not given much thought to your values recently, try answering these questions:

- What are the highest priorities in my life?
- Of these priorities, which are the most important?

Your thoughtful answers to these questions will help you identify your values. In people's hectic everyday lives, they often lose track of what is most important to them. They may find that their reality has little to do with their core values. However, psychologists say that when people bring together what they do or how they live with what they really value, they experience an inner peace and happiness that impacts every area of their life.

Set Priorities

Many times you will not be able to do everything you are asked to do in one day. You must be able to distinguish the most important items, tasks that should be done first, from less important items, tasks that can wait until a later date. If you are new to a job, you may need help from your employer to determine what items are most important. But once you learn more about the job and your employer, you should be able to establish priorities on your own.

Prepare Daily To-Do Lists

Each afternoon before you leave work, you should prepare a to-do list for the next day. List all tasks, activities, and projects you need to accomplish the next day. Then review your list. Mark the items in this manner:

- Most important matters—A
- Less important items—B
- Remaining items—C

Projects that have a deadline of the following day will be in Category A. In addition, you may have a very large project due next week. In order to get the project done on time, you must break it into parts. One part might be given a Category A priority to be completed tomorrow. On the following day, another part might be given a Category A priority to be completed. By breaking the project into parts and assigning priorities to those parts, the project becomes manageable. What once seemed overwhelming has been accomplished in an orderly and timely fashion.

Category B consists of those items that may be completed the next day, but no serious consequences will result if they are not. Category C consists of items that are fairly unimportant or that may be delegated. If you are going to delegate the items, be clear with the individual who will be doing the task exactly what is expected of him or her. If the project is a complex one, you may want to give the person written instructions.

If you have trouble setting priorities, try the procedure given in Figure 2-4.

Distinguish between Achievement and Perfection

Perfectionism is defined as "a propensity for setting extremely high standards and being displeased with anything else." Some people believe they must do everything perfectly. Certainly, they must achieve and perform well; however, no human being can be perfect. If you blame yourself continually for not doing everything perfectly, you are engaging in energy-draining behavior. Ruiz, in his book *The Four Agreements*, gives this advice:

Under any circumstance, always do your best, no more and no less. But keep in mind that your best is never going to be the same from one moment to the next. . . . your best will sometimes be high quality, and other times it will not be as

---

SETTING PRIORITIES

This tool can be useful if you are having difficulty setting priorities. It is not intended to be used daily. However, if you are new to the process of setting priorities or are having difficulty, the steps help you break down the process into small increments. (*Note:* When keying your list, triple-space so you will have enough space to circle the numbers.)

Step 1
Make a list of 10 things for which you must set priorities. Order is not important at this point. However, do give each item a number 1 through 10.

Step 2
Compare Number 1 with Number 2, and circle the number you believe is most important.

Step 3
Compare Number 2 with Number 3, and circle the number you believe is most important. (*Note:* You probably will be circling a number several times. When you circle a number a second time, make the circle bigger; this will help later when you must count the number of times you circled each item.)

Step 4
Compare Number 3 with Number 4. Circle the most important number of this pair. Compare Number 2 with Number 4; circle the number that is most important. Compare Number 1 with Number 4; circle the number that is most important.

Steps 5-10
Continue to go through the items on your list, comparing each item with every other item and circling the most important number of each set of two.

Last Step
Count the number of ones, number of twos, number of threes, and so on. Your priority list will begin with the number you circled the most. The last item on your list (least important item) will be the number on the list that you circled the least number of times.

FIGURE 2-4 Setting Priorities

good. When you wake up refreshed and energized in the morning, your best will be better than when you are tired at night. Your best will be different when you are healthy as opposed to sick. . . .[6]

Sometimes mistakes can be beneficial. Thomas Edison was asked how he came to hold so many patents. He answered that he dared to make more mistakes than 10 other people and that he learned from each mistake. Thomas Edison understood that the creative process involves trial and error—failure and success.

Use Down Time

If you have down time, you should use it productively. Accomplish those tasks you have been unable to do during your peak workload periods. These tasks may be cleaning out your desk, rearranging files, organizing supplies, or reading articles related to your business or to the technology you use on your job.

Handle Paperwork as Few Times as Possible

Handling paper over and over—putting it in piles on your desk, reshuffling, rehandling, rereading—can be the biggest paperwork time waster. The basic rule is this: *Handle paper once.* Read it, route it, file it, or answer it—but get it off your desk as quickly as possible without handling it repeatedly.

Complete Work Correctly the First Time

At times, as an administrative professional, you may need to redo work you should have done correctly the first time. How do you prevent the need to redo work? Here are several suggestions:

- Get appropriate instructions or procedures before beginning the work.
- Read the file on similar correspondence.

- Understand the scope of the task. What is the final product to be? What expectations does your supervisor have?
- If it is a new task for you, talk with the person (if possible) who did the task before you. Listen carefully to any pointers or suggestions that person gives you.

Organize Your Workstation

Organizing your workstation may not be an easy task, but it must be done if you are to make the most efficient use of your time. When you are working on a project, clear your desk of materials that relate to other projects. Put these materials in a file folder, label the folder with the name of the project, and place the folder in a drawer. Label in/out trays so you know what is incoming material and what is outgoing material. Keep the drawers of your desk organized so you have frequently used supplies in the top drawers.

Practice Speed-Reading

Numerous items that you must read will pass your desk. Before reading correspondence and other materials, organize the material in order of importance. Prepare folders, noting the dates when the materials must be read.

Practice speed-reading. Read for the main thought or idea. If you are reading periodicals or company literature, scan the table of contents first. Then selectively read the articles. Read carefully only the sections that will enhance your knowledge of your job and your organization.

Use Electronic Time Management Systems

A number of time management systems and equipment allow you to organize your work quickly and efficiently.

PIM (Personal Information Management) software allows you to manage a wide variety of information. For example, with PIM software, you can access the following:

- Calendar software, which manages your schedule, address book, and to-do list

---

[6]Don Miguel Ruiz, *The Four Agreements* (California: Amber-Allen Publishing, Inc., 1997), 76.

- Information database software, which handles documents you have downloaded from the Internet or from another source

A number of software packages are available. The three listed below are popular packages.

- Microsoft® Outlook®
- Lotus® Organizer™
- Above & Beyond® 2000

In addition, **PDAs** (personal digital assistants) help you manage time. The PDA, at its most basic, serves as an appointment book, an address book, a to-do list, and a calculator. The functions a PDA performs continue to increase as technology advances. The following list includes several capabilities of PDAs:

- Check email.
- Retrieve telephone calls.
- Transfer data from PIM software.
- Check financial markets.
- Key short letters or reports.
- Access the Web.

Additionally, PDA and cell phone combination units are now available.

Use Good Communication Techniques

Chapters 5 through 9 in this textbook are devoted to a discussion of effective communication techniques, including verbal, written, telecommunications, and presentation skills. You should study these chapters carefully and practice the techniques given to help you become a better communicator. Here are a few suggestions.

- Transmit ideas in simple, clear terms.
- Define terms if necessary.
- Listen carefully.
- Repeat what you think you heard, and ask for clarification if necessary.

You can organize your work effectively and efficiently by using a PDA.

When communicating with others, remain open to new ideas.

- Be sensitive to the communicator's body language as well as to the words being spoken.
- Keep your mind open to new ideas.

Maintain a Proper Diet

What you eat or do not eat affects your overall health. Excessive intake of fat, sugar, salt, and caffeine contributes to poor health and to certain diseases such as hypertension and heart disease. The average cup of regular coffee contains 100 to 150 milligrams of caffeine. As little as 250 milligrams of caffeine can cause nervousness, insomnia, and headaches.

The average American consumes more than 126 pounds of sugar a year. Excessive sugar consumption can result in an increase in triglyceride levels in the blood, which can lead to cardiovascular disease. Too much salt can lead to an increase in blood pressure and the development of hypertension. The wisest course of action is to lower the intake of fat, sugar, salt, and caffeine in your diet.

Maintaining a diet rich in fruits and vegetables is also important. Eating fiber-rich vegetables, fruits, cereals, and legumes helps you maintain a high level of fiber in your diet. A number of these foods are listed in Figure 2-5.

Set Up an Exercise Program

Cardiovascular specialists have found that regular exercise can do the following:
- Lower blood pressure
- Decrease fats in the blood
- Reduce joint stiffness
- Lessen appetite
- Decrease fatigue

HIGH-FIBER FOODS

Vegetables	Fruits	Cereals	Legumes
Artichokes	Strawberries	Oat bran	Lima beans
Sweet potatoes	Figs	Oatmeal	Butter beans
Turnips	Oranges		Black beans
Acorn squash	Pears		Navy beans
Brussel sprouts	Blackberries		Lentils
Broccoli	Mangos		
Carrots	Plums		

FIGURE 2~5 High-Fiber Foods

A few of the many exercises good for your body are swimming, bicycling, jogging, and walking. Participate in an exercise you enjoy. Determine a regular time of day to exercise and do it. When you begin exercising, go slowly. Train your body; do not strain it. If you have any medical problems, consult your doctor about the type of exercise that is best for you.

Get the Proper Amount of Sleep

In India, there is a saying that sleep "nurses all living beings."[7] The proper amount of sleep is essential to mental and physical health. Although the amount of sleep needed varies by individual, studies have shown that people who sleep seven to eight hours a night tend to live longer than people whose sleep is longer or shorter.[8] Yet a number of people have problems getting the proper amount of sleep due to busy schedules and stressful lives.

Even if you do go to bed at the proper hour, you may have difficulty falling asleep. You often have trouble turning off your mind. You rethink what went wrong in your day or begin to plan for the next day. Practicing the following techniques will help you fall asleep:

- Set aside the hour before bed for quiet activities such as reading.
- Take a hot bath.
- Turn off the TV in the bedroom and/or turn down the TV in an adjoining room.
- Practice deep-breathing exercises.
- Create a relaxing scene in your head—waves rolling up on a beach or a mountain stream.
- Be certain your mattress and pillow are right for you—the proper firmness or softness.
- Pay attention to the amount of coffee, tea, cola, and chocolate you are consuming. These drinks can lead to sleep deprivation.

Use Visualization

Visualization is using your imagination to help you relax. Through visualization, you block out unwanted thoughts. In order to achieve the maximum benefits from visualization, get into a comfortable position, relax any muscles that feel tense, and begin to visualize a pleasant scene. For example, you might imagine a sky of white fluffy clouds, ocean waves licking a golden beach, the sun glistening on a snow-covered mountain, or a beautiful sunset over your favorite lake. Focus on the scene for several minutes to block out the tensions of the day. As you visualize, practice some of the deep-breathing techniques listed in Figure 2-6.

[7]Edward Claflin, ed., *Age Protectors* (Pennsylvania: Rodale Press, Inc., 1998), 143.
[8]Ibid.

DEEP-BREATHING TECHNIQUES

- Sit in a comfortable position with your back straight and your eyes lightly closed.
- Focus your attention on your breathing, and follow the contours of the cycle through inhalation and exhalation, noting, if you can, the points at which one phase changes into the other.
- Do the breathing exercise for five minutes once a day.

Excerpted from Andrew Weil, *8 Weeks to Optimum Health* (New York: Alfred A. Knopf, Inc., 1997).

FIGURE 2~6 Deep-Breathing Techniques

Reduce Organizational Dependency

Do not depend totally on the organization for which you work for long-term employment. Educate and train yourself to be employable by a number of organizations. Engage in continuing education to keep yourself up to date on technology and other skills needed in the workplace. This education may be formal (from a college or university) or informal (from professional books and periodicals and attendance at workshops and seminars).

Understand Role Relationships

Be sensitive to the needs of your employer and your coworkers. Know what they expect of you. Know how you fit into the organizational structure. Be familiar with the organizational chart; know who reports to whom. Accept people; be tolerant. Strive to communicate openly and honestly.

Balance Work and Play

Many people comment with a sense of pride that they work a 50- or 60-hour week. Are these people producing a large amount of work? Maybe not. Do they have demanding and challenging jobs? Perhaps. Are they appreciated and respected for their work contri-

butions? Not necessarily. A relationship does exist between hours worked and productivity. Of course, individuals differ in the number of productive hours they can work. However, studies show that productivity decreases after extended periods. Most people realize immediately when they are not being productive. When they become fatigued, the amount of work they produce goes down and their error rate goes up.

You actually can gain new energy by taking time to play. As an adult, you may have forgotten how to relax and, with complete abandon, enjoy the world around you. Some experts writing in the field of creative energy recommend *joy breaks*—stopping for a few minutes to play when feeling overtired or nonproductive. Another way to gain new energy is to take a short exercise break. You might keep athletic shoes at your desk for a short five- or ten-minute break to climb stairs or to take a brisk walk. Such physical activity allows you to release built-up tension, to open blocked thinking, and to trigger creative ideas.

Relax

Deep-breathing exercises are one of the quickest ways to relax your body. Begin by finding a comfortable position, sitting in a comfortable chair or lying down. You may close your eyes if that makes you feel more at ease. Then slowly inhale air through your nose until you feel your lungs fill with air. Next, exhale the air slowly, breathing out through your nose or mouth. Repeat the process until you begin to feel a sense of relaxation.

Use Positive Self-Talk

When you are angry or upset, negative self-talk can escalate your feelings; positive self-talk, on the other hand, can produce positive results. For example, assume you are playing a game of tennis with a skilled opponent. You want to play your best. You miss a ball and say to yourself, *That was terrible; I can't even get a ball over the net.* You are engaging in negative self-talk, and negative self-talk on the tennis court can cause you to miss even more shots. In other words, your negative self-talk is a self-fulfilling prophecy. You decide you are terrible, and you prove yourself right.

Now consider a positive self-talk response. When you miss a ball, you say to yourself, *No big deal; I'll get the next one.* And you do! You make a terrific shot that your opponent is unable to return. When you find yourself engaging in negative self-talk, turn it around by engaging in the following behaviors:

- Recognizing the negative self-talk
- Stopping it immediately
- Beginning positive self-talk

Walk Away

If you can, walk away physically from a situation that makes you angry. If you cannot walk away physically, walk away emotionally. Consider the following example, a common situation that often makes people angry.

You are waiting in line to pay for your groceries. The checker is slow. In addition, no sackers are available, so the checker must sack the items. The person in front of you has forgotten two items and asks the checker if he can go get them; the checker agrees. You have an important appointment, and you must be on time. You find yourself getting angry. You are ready to yell at the person in front of you and at the checker.

What are your choices? You can walk away mentally—count to 10, envision yourself at one of your favorite places having a wonderful time, or hum a song. Or if you really are going to be late for the appointment, you can walk away physically. You can come back to the grocery store at another time.

Do not berate yourself for making a poor shot; negative self-talk can be a self-fulfilling prophecy.

© GETTY IMAGES/PHOTODISC

Talk to a Friend

If a situation at work makes you angry, talk to a trusted friend about what is bothering you. That person may be able to help you understand what is causing your anger and help you decide what you can do about the situation.

Solve the Problem

Chapter 1 presented several problem-solving steps. These steps are valuable in helping you manage your anger, stress, and time. When a situation is causing you to become angry, stressed, and overwhelmed because of the time you are wasting on it, stop! Ask yourself these questions:

- What is the problem?
- What are my alternatives?
- From the alternatives I have generated, what is the best alternative in this situation?

Once you have identified the problem and determined the best alternative in dealing with it, act and evaluate!

- Act on the best alternative—implement it.
- Evaluate the situation: Did the action I implemented solve the problem? If not, why not? Did I choose the wrong alternative? If so, what other alternative can I try?

Success in managing your anger, stress, and time hinges on these behaviors:

- Constant evaluation of the situations that are causing you problems
- Thoughtful decisions that will lessen your stress and anger and help you use your time more effectively

A tough task? Certainly! However, the energy you spend in positive activities is well worth the effort for your mental and emotional health. ■

SUMMARY

To reinforce what you have learned in this chapter, study this summary.

- Stress is the response of the body to a demand made upon it. Stress can be either positive or negative. Eustress is a synonym for positive stress. Distress is negative stress; the two types of negative stress are acute stress and chronic stress.
- The cost of stress is high for both the organization and the individual.
- Factors contributing to workplace stress are role ambiguity; job insecurity; working conditions and relationships; dual-career families, single parenthood, and extended families; anger; time; and money.
- Incidences of anger resulting in violence are prevalent in society and are becoming more common in the workplace.
- Anger can be turned into a positive force by using it as a message and dealing with the problem causing the anger.
- Time is a resource that cannot be bought, sold, rented, borrowed, saved, or manufactured. It can only be spent.
- Time wasters in the workplace include chatter, disorganization, ineffective communication, and procrastination.
- It is important to conduct stress, anger, and time audits periodically.
- Techniques for managing stress, anger, and time include these: clarify values, set priorities, prepare daily to-do lists, distinguish between achievement and perfection, use down time, handle paperwork as few times as possible, complete work correctly the first time, organize your

workstation, practice speed-reading, use electronic time management systems, use good communication techniques, maintain a proper diet, set up an exercise program, get the proper amount of sleep, use visualization, reduce organizational dependency, understand role relationships, balance work and play, relax, use positive self-talk, walk away, talk to a friend, and solve the problem.

FIND THE PROBLEM

Tomoko became very angry on her job this past week due to this situation:

On Monday, Mr. Wilkin, Tomoko's supervisor, reprimanded her for not doing her job well; and in the process, he called her stupid. Two other people in Tomoko's work group overheard Mr. Wilkin's comments. Tomoko was so angry she could think of nothing to say. She merely glared at Mr. Wilkin. Since Monday, Mr. Wilkin has not spoken to Tomoko, and she has not said anything to him—not even a "good morning." Mr. Wilkin had not reprimanded Tomoko before this incident, and she has been working for him for six months. In fact, he often told her she was doing a good job. She is puzzled and ready to quit. Before this situation, she was enjoying her job. How should Tomoko handle the problem? What advice would you give her?

PROFESSIONAL POINTERS

Try these anger, stress, and time management techniques to help you work more productively.

- Keep a journal of situations that make you feel angry or stressed. Writing in a journal and reviewing your thoughts periodically can be like talking to a trusted friend.
- Balance your professional life with a fulfilling personal life. Make time to pursue personal interests and to relax apart from your career.
- Do not allow yourself to lose sight of your vision and purpose in life. Take time to sit quietly and analyze whether you are living your values and being true to your purpose.
- Identify the time of day when you are at your peak. Plan to tackle your most difficult jobs during your peak periods.
- Do not overschedule yourself. Allow an hour or two of uncommitted time each day.

REINFORCEMENT ITEMS

1. Define negative stress and explain its cost to the workplace.
2. List seven factors that can contribute to stress.
3. Describe the purpose of anger.
4. List and explain four time wasters.
5. List eight techniques for managing stress, anger, and time.

CRITICAL-THINKING ACTIVITY

Beverly Tijerina began her career as an administrative professional after obtaining a degree in business with a major in office systems. She served as an administrative assistant for a car dealership for three years. In this position, Beverly was required to greet customers, process sales records for the 30 salespeople, and handle the clerical work required by the service technicians. The job was stressful, but Beverly was happy, felt in control of her work, and was productive on the job.

Due to her outstanding performance, Beverly was offered the position of assistant to the president of the dealership. Beverly knew the job would be challenging and she would have a lot to learn. The job required supervising two employees who had clerical responsibilities, as well as preparing numerous sales reports on spreadsheet software and keeping track of the myriad activities her employer, Mr. Evans, handled. Beverly was not adept at spreadsheet software, so before beginning the position, she took a short course and received certification in Excel®. She had not supervised employees in the past. During the six months Beverly was the assistant to Mr. Evans, she worked hard and logged at least five hours each week in overtime. She now finds she is tired, depressed, and generally unhappy. Some days she feels like telling Mr. Evans she is quitting immediately. Compounding the stressful workload is her manager. Mr. Evans is a nice man, but he is very demanding and is a workaholic and a perfectionist. Beverly believes he has no life outside the company.

- Describe the factors contributing to the stress Beverly is feeling.
- What steps can Beverly take to help her cope with the stress?
- If you were Beverly, how would you attempt to get control of the job?

VOCABULARY REVIEW

Complete the Vocabulary Review for Chapter 2 given on page 15 of the *Applications Workbook*.

ENGLISH AND WORD USAGE DRILL

Complete the English and Word Usage Drill for Chapter 2 listed on page 17 of the *Applications Workbook*.

WORKPLACE APPLICATIONS

A2-1 (Goal 1)

If you are working presently, interview your supervisor concerning stress in the workplace. Ask your supervisor these questions:

- Do you consider the work environment stressful? If so, how?
- What is the cost of negative stress to the organization?

- Does the company offer workshops or seminars for employees on how to handle stress appropriately?
- What suggestions do you have for helping employees deal with stress?

Write a short report of this interview. Submit the report to your instructor, giving the name of the person interviewed and the company.

If you are not working at the present time, use the Web to research two recent articles (within the last year) about the cost of stress in the workplace. Write a short summary of these articles, noting your sources. Submit the report to your instructor.

A2-2 (Goals 2 and 3)

Your *Applications Workbook*, page 19, contains a Stress Audit. Respond to the items given, and score your Stress Audit by using the points listed at the end of the audit. Page 23 of your *Applications Workbook* includes an Anger Audit. Respond to the items given. Save the Stress Audit and the Anger Audit for use in A2-5.

A2-3 (Goals 2 and 3)

You recently joined People Pharmaceuticals International as a part-time clerical assistant to Kurt Rupprecht. You are attending college for the first time, taking five classes. Your classes require much more of your time than you anticipated. You are averaging 25 hours per week on class work and 20 hours per week on your job. Additionally, travel time to and from college and work is taking 10 hours per week. You have an apartment, which you share with two roommates; the three of you share the cooking and cleaning responsibilities. You have little time for fun and relaxation. You feel as if your life is spinning out of control. The job is demanding; your classes are time-consuming; and you feel overwhelmed. You find yourself becoming irritable with your roommates. How can you get the situation under control? Using the techniques suggested in this chapter, determine what steps to take. Submit your answers to your instructor.

A2-4 (Goal 4)

Refer to the Daily Time Logs provided on pages 25-27 of your *Applications Workbook*. For the next five days, use the form to log the time you spend in various activities. Record each day's activities on a different form. If you are employed, log the time you spend in activities at work. If you are not employed, log how you use your personal time. At the end of five days, analyze how you spent your time by answering the questions on the Time Management Analysis on pages 29-30 of your *Applications Workbook*.

A2-5 (Goal 5)

Using the Stress and Anger Audits you prepared in A2-2 and the Daily Time Logs you prepared in A2-4, observe how stress, anger, and time are apparent in your life. Ask yourself these questions:

- How does stress impact my anger?
- How does anger impact my stress?
- How does lack of time impact my anger and my stress?

Write a short paragraph about how the three (stress, anger, and time) are interrelated in your life.

A2-6 (Goal 6)

Use the following items to help you prepare an action plan for managing stress, anger, and time.

- Stress Audit and Anger Audit prepared in A2-2
- Daily Time Log prepared in A2-4
- Paragraph on the interrelatedness of stress, anger, and time in your life prepared in A2-5

State how you will seek to manage your stress, anger, and time during this semester. Team up with two classmates. Each person should review the action plan prepared by another team member. As a team, offer suggestions as to how each of you can improve your plan. Then make necessary changes to your own plan. Submit one copy of your action plan to your instructor, identifying the team members with whom you worked. File another copy of your plan for your records. At the end of the semester, you will assess whether you have met your objectives of managing stress, anger, and time.

ASSESSMENT OF CHAPTER GOALS

Did you successfully complete the chapter goals? Evaluate yourself by filling out the form on pages 35-36 of the *Applications Workbook*.

chapter 3

Ethical Theories and Behaviors

1. Explain the importance of ethical behavior in the workplace.
2. Identify characteristics of an ethical organization.
3. Determine how to achieve ethical change.
4. Determine implications of discrimination in an organization.
5. Identify characteristics of an ethical employee.
6. Determine your commitment to ethical behavior.

Ethics (the systematic study of moral conduct, duty, and judgment) plays an important role in the effectiveness and the long-term viability of an organization. If you wonder about the efficacy of such a statement, pause for a few minutes to think about the ethics (or lack thereof) of two major organizations.

Ethical mismanagement of Enron®, a major energy trading company with headquarters in Houston, Texas, caused an organization to go from a firm that was listed in 2000 by *Fortune* as one of the most admired companies to a bankrupt corporation. Enron's debacle was of such significance to the U.S. economy that Congress led a major investigation through a series of hearings with employees and leaders of Enron. Enron's mismanagement impacted thousands of employees and shareholders who lost significant dollars, with some people losing their life savings. Another major corporation involved in the scandal was Arthur Andersen, employed by Enron as an accounting consultant. The government filed a suit against Arthur Andersen™, charging the company with destruction of tons of paper and thousands of computer files in an attempt to thwart federal regulators investigating Enron. A jury found Arthur Andersen guilty of the charges. A federal judge gave the defunct Arthur Andersen the maximum sentence for its part in the Enron scandal, calling it a warning to the auditing profession.

Unfortunately, these are only two of any number of examples of organizations whose ethics are in question. A writer from *The New York Times*™ expressed these sentiments:

The term **business ethics** *[the study of just and unjust behavior in business] does not have to be an* **oxymoron** *[the combining of incongruous or contradictory terms]. But in today's scandal-*

a-minute atmosphere, it has surely become one. Public trust in corporate America has been undeniably shattered.[1]

However, in contrast are those many organizations that hold ethics sacred in their day-to-day operations. For example, contrast the lack of ethical behavior with some of the ethical statements and policies of three companies listed on *Fortune* magazine's 2002 100 Best Companies to Work For—The Container Store℠, SAS®, and TDIndustries℠.

- The Container Store provides these value-driven benefits for its employees:
  - An environment that ensures open communication
  - Extensive training programs
  - Individual and team-based incentive programs

The cofounders, Kip Tindell and Garrett Boone, state that their goal is not growth for growth's sake. Rather, it is to adhere to a fundamental set of business values, centered around deliberate merchandising, superior customer service, and constant employee input.[2]

- The mission of SAS includes this statement: Our mission is to deliver superior software and services that give people the power to make the right decisions.[3]
- TDIndustries' Culture, Vision & Values statement reads as follows:

TDIndustries strives to model the management style defined by Robert Greenleaf as "Servant Leadership." We firmly believe our shift to this culture over 25 years ago has made us one of the most unique companies in the country—it is to this practice that we attribute our many years of success.[4]

Ethical and unethical behaviors by organizations make a difference in society. People managing organizations and employees of organizations must adhere to some standard of ethics. Business is a cooperative activity, with its existence hinging on ethical behavior. For example, organizations will collapse if their managers, employers, and customers believe it is morally permissible to steal from the organization.

Conversely, ethical behavior by organizations, in addition to being the right thing to do, pays off on the financial bottom line. This is the conclusion of research based on Business Ethics' 100 Best Corporate Citizens list, which shows that the financial performance of socially responsible companies was significantly better than other companies in the S&P 500.[5]

As you study this chapter, take the tenets presented seriously. If you are working presently or will be working when you finish your schooling, you want to be associated with an organization that upholds ethical standards. Ethical behaviors contribute to making the world a better place in which to live and work. Unethical behaviors impact people who are working for the organization as well as the economy.

In this chapter, ethics is a **pragmatic** topic—one to be understood conceptually and practiced in the day-to-day operations of organizations and in the lives of employees within organizations. This chapter provides you with a framework for understanding the importance of ethics and the characteristics of ethical organizations. Additionally, it provides suggestions for practical ethical behavior for administrative professionals.

The Importance of Ethics

As you learned earlier in this chapter, ethics is the systematic study of **moral conduct** (a set

[1]Gretchen Morgenson, "The Big Board Is Standing Up for Independence," *The New York Times*, June 2, 2002.

[2]The Container Store, accessed June 2, 2002; available from **www.containerstore.com**.

[3]Our Company, accessed June 1, 2002; available from **www.sas.com**.

[4]Our Culture—TDIndustries, accessed June 1, 2002; available from **www.tdindustries.com**.

[5]*Good Guys Are Prospering: "100 Best Corporate Citizens Outperform S&P 500 Peers,"* accessed June 1, 2002; available from **www.business-ethics.com**.

of ideas of right and wrong), duty, and judgment. Practically, business ethics is the study of just and unjust behaviors in business. Business ethics requires that judgment be exercised about a proposed act and the anticipated consequences of the act. Business ethics means that individuals within an organization, collectively and singularly, are socially responsible for their conduct.

Ethics—The Roots

So you can understand what religion and some of the great philosophers of history have contributed to ethical thinking, look briefly at both. The major roots of today's ethical principles stem from religion and philosophy. For example, many of the major religions of the world are in basic agreement on the fundamental principles of ethical doctrine. Buddhism, Christianity, Confucianism, Hinduism, Islam, and Judaism teach the importance of acting responsibly toward all people and contributing to the general welfare of the world. In fact, the work ethic still practiced by many in the United States came from what was called the **Protestant ethic**. The Protestant ethic began as a religious teaching in Europe in the fourteenth century and was carried to the American colonies. It encouraged hard work, thrift, and dedication to the task. This philosophy still holds true for millions of Americans.

The great philosophers in history added to the body of knowledge concerning ethics. Here are a few examples of their influence:

- Socrates taught that virtue and ethical behavior are associated with wisdom.
- Plato taught that justice might be discovered through intellectual effort.
- Jeremy Bentham and John Mills taught that morality resides in its consequences and one must maximize the greatest benefit for the greatest number of people.
- Immanuel Kant taught that one must behave in such a way that one's actions can become a universal law.

- Saint Thomas Aquinas taught that ethical behavior in business is necessary to achieve salvation.

In addition to the religious and philosophical roots of ethical behavior, cultures and systems of government teach ethical behavior. For example, the Golden Rule—*Do unto others as you would have them do unto you*—came from many ancient cultures. The Declaration of Independence emphasizes that there are certain *inalienable rights: life, liberty, and the pursuit of happiness.*

The study of ethics began in the classroom in the 1970s. In the 1980s, ethics became a part of the business curriculum, where it progressed from religious and philosophical theory into the pragmatic study of ethical

The Golden Rule—*Do unto others as you would have them do unto you*—continues to be an important concept to uphold in the day-to-day actions of an organization.

behavior and decision making within organizations.

The Why

Why be ethical? This question is debated in academic materials and classrooms. However, it is more than an academic question. At some point, individuals and organizations must answer it. There are numerous ways to do so. You might answer it from a religious or philosophical point of view. You might also answer it from your own value perspective. However, from whatever view you take, the questions and possible answers around ethical dilemmas are not easy. Consider the issue of stem cell research that burst on the scientific scene in November 1998, when researchers first reported the isolation of human embryonic stem cells. This discovery offers great promise for new ways of treating disease, but the ethical questions surrounding stem cell research are being widely debated today, with tentative policies being established.

Opponents of stem cell research believe that human life begins as soon as an egg is fertilized, and they consider a human embryo to be a human being. Therefore, any research that necessitates the destruction of a human embryo is morally abhorrent. Proponents of stem cell research point out that in the natural reproductive process, the fertilization of human eggs can occur, but the eggs sometimes fail to implant in the uterus. They argue that a fertilized egg, while it may have the potential for human life, is not the equivalent of a human being until it has at least achieved successful implementation in a woman's uterus.

In 2001, President Bush decided to allow federal funding of stem cell research, but only on cells already in existence. He decided that for a **cell line** (isolated stem cells from a human embryo that often replicate themselves) already in existence, research is permissible because destruction of an embryo has already taken place. To prevent the federal government from acting in a way that encourages the destruction of human embryos, he refused to allow federal funding for research on any cell line created in the future. However, the debate is far from over, and more issues regarding stem cell research will likely surface.[6]

Overcoming the ethical dilemmas you face now and will face in the future requires great wisdom. An understanding of your own principles of **morality** (a set of ideas of right and wrong) is vitally important. You must do whatever you can to strengthen your ethical understandings and **moral integrity** (consistent adherence to a set of ideas of right and wrong), within and outside the workplace.

---

[6]Stem Cell Research, accessed June 1, 2001; available from **www.aaas.org**.

© GETTY IMAGES/EYEWIRE

Stem cell research has raised a number of issues that demand ethical answers.

The How

How can you, as an administrative professional, make a difference on important ethical issues? As a professional employed in the workplace and as a contributing member of society, you must grapple with answers to this question. However, here are partial answers:

- You can recognize the importance of behaving ethically and how ethical and unethical behavior impact the nation.
- You can constantly seek to understand the corporate culture in which you work and the philosophies of the leaders within the organization.
- You can understand how to achieve ethical change from within.
- You can behave ethically when dealing with your supervisor; your peers; and the customers, clients, and vendors of your organization.
- You can regularly examine your own ethical standards to determine whether you are behaving in ethical ways.

Margaret Mead, a preeminent anthropologist of the twentieth century, stated:

Never doubt that a small group of thoughtful, committed citizens can change the world; indeed, it's the only thing that ever has.

Characteristics of Ethical Organizations

The characteristics of ethical organizations are many. Here are a few important ones.

Environmentally Responsible

An environmentally responsible organization is aware of the possible dangers in business and takes necessary precautions to keep the environment free from pollution. The organization pays attention to **OSHA** (Occupational Safety & Health Administration) regulations regarding careful disposal of waste products. The organization makes it a top priority when

A small group of committed citizens can change the world.

constructing new buildings to cut down as few trees as possible and to protect wetland areas, as well as other areas that are important ecologically.

Internationally Aware

The ethical organization is aware that ethical behavior has different meanings in different countries. Different countries interpret human rights in different ways. In some countries, there is no consideration of gender equity. Even harassment and discrimination are not ethically wrong. Such awareness on the part of U.S. businesses operating in other countries does not mean they adopt the ethical standards of that country. It does mean that U.S. businesses must be knowledgeable about the practices that occur and carefully formulate their own practices and behaviors. Ethical organizations understand the importance of learning the cultures and business customs of the countries in which they operate.

Culturally Committed to Ethical Behavior

Organizational culture is defined as "the ideas, customs, values, and skills of a particular organization." All organizations have a culture. The organizational culture may be one of the following:

- Commitment to behaving ethically
- Verbal commitment with little follow-through
- No commitment to ethics

Employees in ethical organizations are aware of the ethical stance of the organization and realize they are accountable for upholding the ethics espoused by the organization. Preparation and dissemination of mission/value statements are communication vehicles that organizations use to inform employees and customers of their ethics. Consider the following statements made by two companies on *Fortune* magazine's 2002 100 Best Companies to Work For.

- Goldman Sachs[SM]. The business principles of Goldman Sachs include these:

   Our clients' interests always come first. Our experience shows that if we serve our clients well, our own success will follow.

   Our assets are our people, capital and reputation. We are dedicated to complying fully with the letter and spirit of the laws, rules and ethical principles that govern us. Our continued success depends upon unswerving adherence to this standard.

   We stress teamwork in everything we do. While individual creativity is always encouraged, we have found that team effort often produces the best results. We have no room for those who put their personal interests ahead of the interest of the firm and its clients.

   Integrity and honesty are at the heart of our business. We expect our people to maintain high ethical standards in everything they do, both in their work for the firm and in their personal lives.[7]

- Beck Group[SM]. Mission: Revolutionize our industry. . . create the future! Vision: An environment where extraordinary demand for Beck's superior products, services and innovative solutions will result in unique and rewarding experiences for our customers and our people.[8]

Notice Figure 3-1, which outlines several key principles of managing by values.

KEY PRINCIPLES OF MANAGING BY VALUES

- In an organization that truly manages by its values, there is only one boss—the company's values.
- Managing by values is not just another program; it's a way of life.
- Genuine success does not come from proclaiming our values, but from consistently putting them into daily action.
- Real change doesn't happen until it happens inside people.
- Being values-aligned does not occur without changes in our habits, practices, and attitudes. It's easy to spot commitment when you see it— and even easier when you don't.
- Organizations don't make managing by values work—people do.

Excerpted from *Managing by Values* by Ken Blanchard and Michael O'Connor.

FIGURE 3~1 Key Principles of Managing by Values

Honest

An ethical organization is honest when dealing with employees and other organizations and individuals. For example, the company makes its personnel policies clear to all employees. Employees understand salary and promotion policies. In a sales organization, product specifications and pricing structures are clear to external organizations and individuals. An ethical organization holds employees accountable for honesty. Honest employees do not falsify expense reports, time reports, or personnel records.

---

[7]Goldman Sachs Business Principles, accessed June 5, 2002; available from **www.goldmansachs.com**.

[8]The BECK Group—About Beck, accessed June 1, 2002; available from **www.beckgroup.com**.

Committed to Diversity

The ethical organization believes in providing equal treatment to all individuals, regardless of race, ethnicity, age, gender, sexual orientation, or physical challenge. For example, women sometimes face obstacles in the workplace that occur not because of their performance, but because of their gender and how others perceive them. Gays and lesbians often face discrimination based not on who they are or how they perform on the job, but on their sexual orientation. Often minority group members encounter problems based on the **biases** (views based on background or experiences) of others. Such biases can cause **stereotyping** (holding perceptions or images of people or things that are derived from selective perception). Although you may think of stereotyping as negative, it can be positive. For example, stereotyping can help you learn the general characteristics of certain groups, people, or animals. As a small child, you learned that dogs are four-legged animals and are generally friendly to people. As you grew older, you could begin to distinguish among types of dogs and their natures and special characteristics.

Negative stereotyping can cause a premature end to communication and prejudicial behavior that leads to acts of rejection. For example, if an individual has a negative experience with an individual from another country and then decides that all individuals from that country have the same negative characteristics, **prejudice** (a system of negative beliefs and feelings) occurs. Other examples of prejudice are evident when **physically challenged** individuals (persons with a physical handicap) are judged and treated unfairly due to their physical handicaps.

An ethical organization affords equal treatment to all individuals, regardless of race or ethnicity.

© GETTY IMAGES/PHOTODISC

None of this discussion is to imply that the ethical organization advocates a policy that ignores performance issues due to gender, physical challenge, race, ethnicity, or sexual orientation. All individuals must perform their jobs satisfactorily. What is important is giving all individuals the opportunity to do their job regardless of their minority status.

Here is a statement concerning diversity from one of *Fortune* magazine's 2002 100 Best Companies to Work For, QUALCOMM.

You can clearly see, as you walk the halls of QUALCOMM, that diversity is more than a buzz word here—it's an integral part of our company's operation. It's what we call Global Inclusion. It's not a set of rules that gets filed and forgotten, it's not the program of the month; it's a viable philosophy at QUALCOMM that reflects the global nature of business and communications today.[9]

------

[9]QUALCOMM, accessed June 1, 2002; available from **www.qualcomm.com**.

Figure 3-2 explains in greater detail QUALCOMM's stance on diversity.

In dealing with diversity issues, ethical organizations should engage in the following behaviors:

- Ensure that initial employment practices support diversity
- Ensure that promotional opportunities provide for equal treatment of all individuals
- Hold managers accountable for supporting and implementing nondiscriminatory policies
- Assist individuals who have English language deficiencies by allowing them to enroll in on-site or off-site courses at a college or university
- Provide access for the physically challenged to all facilities and provide proper equipment and work space
- Ensure that age differences are not used as an evaluation measure
- Raise the diversity awareness of other managers and individuals by providing seminars on diversity

------

QUALCOMM'S DIVERSITY COMMITMENT

At QUALCOMM, **Global Inclusion** is the catalyst for raising the consciousness about how diversity can positively impact all aspects of our business—employees, customers and communities.

At the heart of **Global Inclusion** is QUALCOMM's commitment to provide all employees, regardless of their backgrounds and perspectives on the world, the opportunity to achieve their personal and professional goals.

Like our customer base, our employees are from many backgrounds. They're free-thinkers who use their unique perspectives to get a new slant on the broad spectrum of technologies we're exploring.

So we like to be different. We want our people to be different. We want our teams charged with the energy that comes from different backgrounds and cultures. And because we're a global company, we want people from around the world helping us build the right products, products that meet the needs of their families and friends, whoever and wherever they are.

Global Inclusion is providing an environment in which individuals from diverse backgrounds can work together to enhance their own lives and contribute to the success of QUALCOMM.

Excerpted from **www.qualcomm.com**.

FIGURE 3~2 QUALCOMM'S Diversity Commitment

Committed to the Community

Ethical organizations understand that they have a social responsibility to contribute to the community. In fulfilling this responsibility, the organizations may engage in any of the following activities:

- Contributing to charities
- Participating in the local Chamber of Commerce and other service organizations
- Working with youth groups
- Supporting the inner city in its crime reduction programs
- Assisting schools and colleges with internship programs
- Encouraging employees to participate in their local communities by recognizing and rewarding employees' endeavors

Notice Figure 3-3, which spells out QUALCOMM's commitment to the communities it serves.

Committed to Employees

Promoting employee productivity is important to ethical organizations. Although fear about job performance and security exists at some level in most organizations, the ethical organization takes steps to reduce such fears.

Here are some ways companies can reduce employee fear:

- Establish realistic job descriptions
- Help employees set achievable goals
- Administer performance evaluations fairly
- Support employees in learning new skills
- Encourage employees to cooperate with each other
- Reward employee creativity
- Provide personnel policies in writing to all employees
- Establish teams to work on significant company issues

Committed to Standards

When carrying out ethical behavior, organizations establish standards that support ethical decision making and quality delivery of products and services. In addition to individual organizational standards, standards are set for entire industries. For example, the **FDA** (Food and Drug Administration) establishes standards for food and drug products manufactured in the United States. OSHA establishes standards for workforce safety. Figure 3-4 shows a portion of the standards established by OSHA.

QUALCOMM'S VOLUNTEER PROGRAM

QUALCOMM's corporate volunteerism program, QUALCOMM Cares, was developed to encourage employee involvement in the community, and is our way of connecting our diverse employee base to local volunteer opportunities. QUALCOMM Cares facilitates employee involvement in rewarding and fun volunteer opportunities, while encouraging the participation of family and friends. QUALCOMM Cares volunteers spend their time at a variety of San Diego non-profit organizations, which serve diverse purposes including: helping people with HIV/AIDS and disabilities, improving the environment, providing food and clothing to the homeless, completing renovation projects, serving and socializing with seniors, helping women in need, creating educational and recreational opportunities for children, and caring for animals. QUALCOMM Cares also offers volunteer team-building projects as special opportunities for internal departments to foster teamwork and celebrate accomplishments, while simultaneously contributing to the improvement of the San Diego Community.

Excerpted from QUALCOMM in The Community, accessed June 5, 2002; available from **www.qualcomm.com**.

FIGURE 3~3 QUALCOMM'S Volunteer Program

PORTION OF OSHA STANDARDS CONCERNING EMPLOYEE EMERGENCY PLANS AND FIRE PREVENTION PLANS

Emergency Action Plan

The emergency action plans shall be in writing and shall cover these designated actions employers and employees must take to ensure employee safety from fire and other emergencies.

- Emergency escape procedures and emergency escape route assignments
- Procedures to be followed by employees who remain to operate critical plant operations before they evacuate
- Procedures to account for all employees after emergency evacuation has been completed
- Rescue and medical duties for those employees who are to perform them
- The preferred means of reporting fires and other emergencies
- Names or regular job titles of persons or departments who can be contacted for further information or explanation of duties under the plan
- The employer shall establish in the emergency action plan the types of evacuation to be used in emergency circumstances.
- Before implementing the emergency action plan, the employer shall designate and train a sufficient number of persons to assist in the safe and orderly emergency evacuation of employees.

"Regulations—Employee Emergency Plans and Fire Prevention Plans," accessed June 4, 2002; available from **www.osha.gov**.

FIGURE 3~4 Portion of OSHA Standards Concerning Employee Emergency Plans and Fire Prevention Plans

Ethical Change

You do not live in a perfect world. Thus, you do not live in a world where all individuals and organizations are ethical. However, many people and organizations strive to make their corner of the world a better place in which to live and work. Assuring that ethical change takes place in an organization is partly the responsibility of management. Management cannot dictate ethical change; they can only provide an environment that encourages ethical change. Although you will not be in a management position when you first begin your career, you may find yourself, at some point, supervising one or more individuals. Figure 3-5 gives several steps management can take to produce ethical change within an organization.

Employees of an organization must take whatever steps are necessary to change their individual behaviors. No one employee can dictate to another how he or she should behave; ethical change for each employee becomes a matter of personal consideration and commitment. In the next section, you will examine factors that can impede ethical change for you as an individual. Additionally, you will consider pragmatic steps you can take to produce ethical change within yourself.

Factors Impeding Ethical Change

A person's background and beliefs often stand in the way of ethical change. As you read the following negative beliefs, ask yourself if you believe any of them.

- Values cannot be changed.
- Organizations are amoral.
- Labels accurately describe individuals.
- Leaders do not behave ethically.

Now examine each of these statements individually.

ETHICAL CHANGE STEPS FOR MANAGEMENT

- Take into consideration the interests of all individuals within the organization. For example, sometimes the welfare of an individual must be preserved (as is the case when unfounded accusations could end a career). Sometimes the welfare of many must be weighed over the good of a few (as in the closing of a plant to sustain the long-term viability of the company).
- Measure the acts of an organization against a variety of ethical yardsticks. For example, the acts of an organization must be balanced against such values as justice, honesty, the good of the stakeholders of the corporation, and the external community.
- Be alert to the pressures and counterpressures of the internal and external environment. Evaluate those pressures in light of the goals of the organization.
- Establish a framework by which to consider the ethical implications of an act and how to achieve the greatest good for the organization and its stakeholders.
- Appoint senior-level management to monitor the actions of the organization as compared to the established organizational ethics.
- Develop an internal mechanism that employees can use to report ethical violations.
- Consistently reinforce ethical standards.
- Establish a training program to allow managers to understand how to bring about ethical change within an organization.

FIGURE 3~5 Ethical Change Steps for Management

Values Cannot Be Changed

Clearly, values can be difficult to change since they are generally adopted at an early age. However, change is possible. Consider this example:

Harold's father (who was divorced from Harold's mother when Harold was two) taught his son that women are inferior to men. Harold's father reared him and sent him to an all-male school from first grade through high school. As a result of his rearing and his lack of exposure to women in significant leadership roles, Harold does not value women in management roles. He believes they are incapable of making good decisions for an organization and of being strong leaders. Harold went to work for a male department manager in a large company. Six months after Harold began his job, his supervisor left for a position in another company. His supervisor was replaced by a woman. Harold decided he should start looking for another job immediately. However, after one month of reporting to his female supervisor, he began to second-guess his long-held assumption that women cannot make good

decisions. He also began to question his lack of valuing women in management roles.

Even though you may have established certain values early in life and held on to them into adulthood, you can change these values if you are open to honestly evaluating situations that suggest a need to change long-held beliefs.

Organizations Are Amoral

Amoral is defined as "lacking moral judgment or sensibility, neither moral nor immoral." History has shown that amoral organizations do not achieve long-term success. If an organization is to achieve long-term success, its values must be clearly defined by management and upheld by everyone in the organization. Employees do not have the authority to establish organizational values even though they, no doubt, are living by their own set of values. The leadership within an organization must be willing to establish the organizational values, live by the established values, make employees aware of the values, and hold employees accountable for living by them.

More women are successfully assuming positions of leadership in organizations.

Labels Accurately Describe Individuals

Generally, when you attach a label to someone, you are not describing that individual accurately. For example, to describe someone by his or her job title clearly leaves out much of who the person is. Or to describe a person as a *team player*, a *bore*, or any other term is restrictive of the whole person's qualities and traits. The point to keep in mind is that labeling hinders, rather than helps, the change process. Labeling individuals affects your view of individuals and often affects the view of significant others in your life. The process of making ethical change within an organization can be harmed by the labeling of individuals.

Leaders Do Not Behave Ethically

Clearly, organizations exist in which individual members of the leadership team do not behave ethically. However, to assume that all management is bad suggests that you are negatively stereotyping management. If you do not want to behave ethically yourself, you can easily shift the blame for your lack of performance to management. The following comments are often made:

- All managers are unethical. Why should I be ethical if my supervisor is not?
- You cannot trust your supervisor.
- Presidents of corporations do not care about the workers; they only care about making huge salaries and pleasing the board to whom they report.

If you find that management within your organization is unethical, you need to leave the organization. When organizational ethics are not adopted by management, the organization is not a good place to work.

Steps Producing Ethical Change

Now that you have looked at factors that hinder ethical change, consider these steps that can help produce ethical change:

- Determine the ethical change required.
- Determine the steps required to achieve the objective.
- Practice the new behaviors.
- Seek feedback.
- Reward yourself and the individuals involved.
- Evaluate the effects of ethical change.

To help you understand how to apply these steps, consider the following situation involving an employee (Theresa), along with examples of the appropriate handling of each step.

Determine the Ethical Change Required

Consider this situation:

You are chairing a task force charged with improving the organization's sexual harassment policy. Theresa is a member of the task force.

When attempting to produce ethical change within an organization, you must follow certain steps.

© GETTY IMAGES/PHOTODISC

She attends the meetings and seems to listen attentively, but she does not say anything during the meetings. Once outside the meetings, Theresa attempts to sabotage the decisions.

When determining the ethical change required, the specific behavior must be considered. What is that behavior?

Not: Theresa is unprofessional in her conduct. Such an analysis is too broad. What does unprofessional behavior mean?

Rather: Theresa does not express her feelings and thoughts in meetings.

Determine the Steps Required to Achieve the Objective

The objective in this situation is to get Theresa to express her thoughts during the meeting—not after the meeting is over. The process you use here is similar to the decision-making process you learned in Chapter 1. You may want to go back and review the process now. After you define the problem, you establish the criteria and generate possible alternatives. In this case, you decide to take the following steps:

- Talk with Theresa in private before the next meeting. Tell her you have noticed she is very quiet in meetings, you value her opinions, and you would like to hear her opinions on issues. Tell her you believe the entire group can benefit from her opinions and suggestions.
- At the next meeting, if Theresa is not forthcoming with comments, ask for her comments. Then thank her when she does express her viewpoints.

Practice the New Behaviors

At each meeting, use the same behavior with Theresa and with any others in the group who are not participating.

Seek Feedback

After a group meeting, talk with a trusted member of the group. Ask that person to evaluate your leadership abilities with the group. Listen openly to the positive and negative comments the person shares. Do not become defensive about negative comments. If you think you are not being successful with the group, you might seek the help of an outside consultant. Invite the consultant to several group meetings to observe you and the group together. Listen to what the consultant has to say, and implement any suggestions made.

Reward Yourself and the Individuals Involved

Once you see a change in Theresa's behavior, reward yourself for bringing about the positive change. Mentally add this success to your list of strengths. Reward Theresa for the change in her behavior by praising her in a one-on-one session. Thank the entire group for its work if the situation warrants it.

Evaluate the Effects of Ethical Change

Is the group more effective in making decisions now that Theresa is voicing her concerns in the meetings? Is the group working together as a cohesive team? Is there a sense of cohesiveness and camaraderie in the group? No doubt, the answer to each of these questions is a resounding yes.

Discrimination—Its Implications for the Organization

You learned earlier in this chapter that the ethical organization does not discriminate due to race, ethnicity, gender, age, sexual orientation, or physical challenge. In fact, in the United States, discrimination is taken so seriously that laws have been enacted to protect citizens against discrimination. These laws are listed in Figure 3-6. Unfortunately, even with laws in place, discrimination continues to occur. In fact, discrimination lawsuits are increasing rather than decreasing. The U.S. **EEOC** (Equal Employment Opportunity Commission) reports that in 1992, 72,302 charges of discrimination were filed by employees against their employers, while in 2001, 90,840 employees filed discrimination lawsuits.[10] Headlines such as the following attest to the

---

[10]"Safeguarding Against Recession Based Discrimination Lawsuits," accessed June 2, 2002; available from **www.bestjobsusa.com**.

FEDERAL LAWS PROHIBITING JOB DISCRIMINATION

- Title VII of the Civil Rights Act of 1964 (Title VII), which prohibits employment discrimination based on race, color, religion, sex, or national origin
- Equal Pay Act of 1963 (EPA), which protects men and women who perform substantially equal work in the same establishment from sex-based wage discrimination
- Age Discrimination in Employment Act of 1967 (ADEA), which protects individuals who are 40 years of age or older
- Title I and Title V of the Americans with Disabilities Act of 1990 (ADA), which prohibits employment discrimination against qualified individuals with disabilities in the private sector and in state and local governments
- Sections 501 and 505 of the Rehabilitation Act of 1973, which prohibits discrimination against qualified individuals with disabilities who work in the federal government
- The Civil Rights Act of 1991, which, among other things, provides monetary damages in cases of intentional employment discrimination

"Federal Laws Prohibiting Job Discrimination," accessed June 4, 2002; available from **www.eeoc.gov**.

FIGURE 3-6 Federal Laws Prohibiting Job Discrimination

fact that discrimination happens and it can be costly to an organization.

$65M Awarded in Sex.Com Case

$1.8 Million Consent Decree Ends EEOC Federal Employment Discrimination Suit in Rockford against Ingersoll

EEOC and Verizon Settle Pregnancy Bias Suit; Thousands of Women to Receive Benefits

Although discrimination may take many forms, only sexual harassment and racial discrimination are considered here.

Sexual Harassment

Studies show that approximately 40 percent of women and 12 percent of men in the workforce are sexually harassed at some point in their careers. What is **sexual harassment**? It is defined by the EEOC as "harassment arising from sexual conduct that is unwelcome by the recipient and that may be either physical or verbal in nature." Three criteria for sexual harassment are set forth:

- Submission to the sexual conduct is made either implicitly or explicitly as a condition of employment.
- Employment decisions affecting the recipient are made on the basis of the recipient's acceptance or rejection of the sexual conduct.
- The conduct has the intent or effect of substantially interfering with an individual's work performance or creates an intimidating, hostile, or offensive work environment.

When sexual harassment is based on the first two criteria, it is referred to as **quid pro quo** (Latin meaning "this for that") sexual harassment. When sexual activity is presented as a prerequisite for getting a job, a promotion, or some type of benefit in the workplace, the behavior is illegal.

The third criterion is referred to as hostile environment sexual harassment. In this situation, the employer, supervisor, or coworker does or says things that make victims feel uncomfortable because of their gender. Hostile environment sexual harassment does not need

to include a demand for sex. It can be the creation of an uncomfortable working environment.

The courts have found that suggestive comments, jokes, leering, unwanted requests for a date, and touching can be sexual harassment. Sexual harassment can occur between people of the same sex; it can also be a woman harassing a man or a man harassing a woman. Victims of sexual harassment can sue and recover for lost wages, future lost wages, emotional distress, punitive damages, and attorneys' fees. EEOC guidelines state that harassment on the basis of sex is a violation of Title VII of the Civil Rights Act and that the organization has a duty to prevent and eliminate sexual harassment. A federal appeals court ruled that an organization is liable for the behavior of its employees even if management is unaware the sexual harassment is taking place. Management is also responsible for the behavior of nonemployees on the company's premises.

For example, if a visiting representative or salesperson harasses a company's receptionist, the receptionist's company is responsible. As a result of these responsibilities, many companies have published policy statements on sexual harassment. A sample policy statement is shown in Figure 3-7.

Once the policy statement is established, it must be communicated to all supervisors and employees, along with a grievance procedure. If you are not made aware of the organization's sexual harassment policy and

---

SEXUAL HARASSMENT POLICY STATEMENT

It is against the policy of the company to discriminate against and/or exclude an employee from participation in any benefits or activities based on national origin, gender, age, sexual orientation, or handicap. Harassment on the basis of sex is a violation of the law and a violation of company policy.

FIGURE 3~7 Sexual Harassment Policy Statement

grievance procedure when you are employed, you should ask for a copy. A sample grievance procedure follows.

Any employee who believes he or she is being sexually harassed on the job shall file a written grievance with the director of Human Resources within 24 hours after the alleged sexual harassment takes place. The grievance is reviewed by the supervisor, and appropriate action is taken. If the employee believes the grievance is not handled satisfactorily, he or she has the right to appeal to the next-level supervisor, with appeal going through the line of authority to the president.

To prevent sexual harassment in the workplace, management has the responsibility of educating its supervisors and employees concerning procedures. If you, as an employee, are faced with sexual harassment, you can seek help or handle the situation yourself, whichever you believe is more appropriate.

Racial Discrimination

In addition to sexual harassment in the workplace, **racial discrimination** also exists. Why? It is based mainly on prejudice, and prejudice is often the result of ignorance, fear, and/or cultural patterns. As past generations viewed groups of people in certain roles and with certain characteristics, those generations learned certain attitudes, passing their beliefs on to the next generation. Changing learned attitudes is a slow process. Strides toward reducing racial prejudice are being made, but even greater strides must be made in the future.

What can be done about racial discrimination? Just as policies must exist to deal with sexual harassment, so must they exist for racial discrimination. Employees who experience discrimination should first seek to correct the problem within the organization by making their concerns known to their supervisor or to the human resources department. If help is not forthcoming, relief can be sought through the EEOC. The local EEOC office should be listed in your area telephone book. Figure 3-8 gives several steps for handling sexual and racial/ethnic discrimination.

Characteristics of Ethical Administrative Professionals

If you are to be an ethical administrative professional, you need to understand the

---

STEPS FOR HANDLING SEXUAL AND RACIAL/ETHNIC DISCRIMINATION

- Know your rights. Know your organization's position on racial discrimination and sexual harassment, what is legal under the EEOC guidelines, and what your employer's responsibility is. Know what redress is provided by Federal Laws.
- Keep a record of all harassment infractions, noting the dates, incidents, and witnesses (if any).
- File a formal grievance with your organization. Check your organization's policy and procedures manual or talk with the director of Human Resources as to the grievance procedure. If no formal grievance procedure exists, file a formal complaint with your employer in the form of a memorandum describing the incidents, identifying the individuals involved in the harassment or discrimination, and requesting disciplinary action.
- If your employer is not responsive to your complaint, file charges of discrimination with the federal and state agencies that enforce civil rights laws, such as the EEOC.
- Talk to friends, coworkers, and relatives. Avoid isolation and self-blame. You are not alone; sexual harassment and racial discrimination do occur in the work sector.
- Consult an attorney to investigate legal alternatives to discriminatory or sexual harassment behavior.

FIGURE 3~8 Steps for Handling Sexual and Racial/Ethnic Discrimination

importance of ethics, ethical leadership, corporate culture, and ethical change. You also need to address your own ethical behavior. Pay careful attention to the following characteristics of ethical administrative professionals.

Make Ethical Decisions

The following people and beliefs influence your personal ethics:

- Your parents
- Significant individuals in your life
- Your peer group
- The culture in which you grew up
- Your religious beliefs

Your personal ethics plus the culture and expectations of the organization for which you work have the potential of making it difficult for you to determine what is right and wrong

Significant others in your life influence your personal ethics.

DIGITAL VISION

in a particular situation. Asking these questions can help you decide what is ethical:

- What are the facts of the situation?
- What are the ethical issues involved?
- Who are the **stakeholders** (people who have an interest in the outcome)?
- Who will be affected by my decision?
- Are there different ways of looking at this issue? If so, what are they?
- What are the practical constraints?
- What actions should I take?
- Are these actions practical?

If you are still unclear about what you should do, ask yourself these questions:

- If my actions appeared in the newspaper, would I feel comfortable knowing everyone was reading about what I did?
- Is what I anticipate doing legal?
- Could I proudly tell my spouse, my parents, or my children about my actions?
- Will I be proud of my actions one day, one week, and one year from now?
- Do my actions fit with the person I think I am?

Support Ethical Behavior

Whenever you, as an administrative professional, encounter someone whose words or deeds indicate that the person is not responding to the ethics of the organization, take a stand. Be sensitive and direct. Let people who are cynical about ethical organizations know that you believe strongly in the concept. Let them know that you believe honesty, concern for society, concern for the future health of the world, and respect for the rights of others are values that belong in the organization.

Refuse to Engage in Negative Workplace Politics

What does the term **workplace politics** mean? It means that the people you know within an organization can be important. It means that networks can exist in which favors

© GETTY IMAGES/PHOTODISC

If your actions concerning an ethical issue appeared in the newspaper, would you feel comfortable knowing everyone was reading the story?

are done for people based on the networks. Workplace politics can be good or bad. Consider this example of positive workplace politics.

Assume that you believe your department records management system is inadequate. You begin to talk with your employer and your coworkers about a more effective system. You also talk with coworkers in other departments, express your concerns, and suggest possible solutions. You are able to garner support, and your employer goes to bat with upper management for the money to get the system. You have used people in the workplace positively to get support for an idea that will benefit the organization.

Workplace politics becomes bad when it is used as a quid pro quo. That is, if you do something for me, I will do something for you, with no consideration of whether that something is good for the organization. It is merely good for you. In other words, you are furthering your own personal interests.

In a perfect world, negative workplace politics do not exist. But the reality is that they do exist. So what do you do about workplace politics? How do you handle them? First of all, you become aware of their existence. When you begin a new job, notice what is happening around you. Become aware of the power bases. Become aware of who knows whom and what the relationships are. Next, hold on to your own value system. Be respectful and polite to everyone. Do not gossip about people in the workplace. Use your awareness of the workplace politics to help yourself do your job. Generally, if you live your values and do your job well, you will be recognized and respected.

Accept Constructive Criticism

If your supervisor recommends that you do something differently, do not take his or her remarks personally. For example, assume you recently set up a meeting for your employer at a hotel where lunch was served. It was the first time you planned such a meeting, and you thought you did a fair job. After the meeting, your employer called you in and told you the room arrangement was not satisfactory and the food choice was poor. How should you respond? First, you deal with the issues at hand. You might ask, "Can we talk about it more? What type of room arrangement would have been better? What type of meal would you suggest?"

Realize that you have much to learn and that everyone makes mistakes. You might also suggest to your supervisor that you would like to review the arrangements with her before the next meeting takes place. With any type of criticism, you want to learn from your mistakes and not make the same mistake twice.

Keep Confidential Information Confidential

Administrative assistants are often privy to information of a confidential nature. For example, they key reports containing confidential information and they are told information by their supervisor that is confidential. The technological age has exacerbated the issues around confidential information in that more and more information is available to all employees in the organization—often with merely a touch of the keyboard. Confidential information, even though it may be divulged innocently to a coworker, can cause irreparable harm to an organization. For example, the divulgence of information concerning a pending lawsuit can cause an organization to lose an important case. As an administrative professional, you must understand the importance of not discussing confidential information with anyone in the organization who does not have the right of access to that information. Even if a longtime friend in the organization asks about a confidential matter, you must not give out the information. A true

friend will respect your ethical stance in not answering the question.

Accept Responsibilities

Ethical administrative professionals understand and accept the responsibilities of their jobs. They perform all tasks to the best of their ability. They do not attempt to pass the blame for incomplete or subpar work on to another individual; they accept responsibility. Also, you may at times be required to assist someone else in doing a task or to work overtime to get your job done. Ethical administrative professionals accept these responsibilities.

Are Honest

Honest administrative professionals avoid hypocrisy. They do not tell white lies to supervisors or coworkers. Even the smallest white lie can cause major damage to one's

Ethical behavior does make a difference in an organization.

DIGITAL VISION

professional reputation. Honest employees do not blame someone else for their errors or break rules and then claim ignorance of the rules. Honest employees do not take organizational supplies or equipment for their own personal use. For example, understanding that workplace copiers are used for the business of the organization, employees do not make personal copies.

Are Loyal

The ethical employee is loyal to the organization, but not in an unquestioning sense. The important issue for the employee and the company is not blind loyalty, but commitment to company directions that support the values. Employees must be allowed to disagree constructively with directions, to speak out on issues, and to be heard by management in the process. However, once a direction is decided, employees must be loyal and productive members of the team. Ethical employees understand and live by this type of loyalty.

Keep the Faith

The ethical employee keeps the faith. The employee understands that changing behaviors is a slow process, but that the commitment to ethics must be upheld even when the organization seems to be mired in behaviors that do not support the stated ethical policies. Certainly, the ethical administrative professional may become discouraged at times. Nevertheless, the ethical employee continues to behave ethically, keeping the faith that others in the organization will eventually adopt appropriate behaviors. A total commitment by all employees to upholding ethical standards makes a company not only a great place to work, but also a success with its clients and customers.

Ethics—Your Call

Although you cannot impact the ethics of an entire organization unless you are in upper management, you can check out an organization's ethics before you accept a position. Here are a few suggestions as to how to evaluate an organization's ethics in the job application process.

- Read the organization's Web page. Are the ethics of the organization mentioned? Is a commitment to diversity mentioned? Is a commitment to the external community mentioned? Is integrity mentioned? Does the organization have professional growth programs for employees?
- Check the history of the organization. Has the company ever made newspaper headlines for behaving unethically?
- Talk with acquaintances who work for the organization. Ask them to describe the ethical environment of the company.

In addition to checking out an organization's stated ethics before accepting a position, you can promise yourself that if for some reason your organization ever begins engaging in grossly unethical behaviors, you will seek employment elsewhere. Senge, in his book, *The Fifth Discipline*, tells this story:

If you put a frog in a cup of tepid water, it will not jump out. The temperature is comfortable. If you continue to turn up the heat gradually over a period of time until the water is boiling hot, the frog will continue to stay in the water and die. The frog adjusts to the increased temperature and does not notice the difference in the environment or the threat to its safety.[11]

The moral of the story is this: Unless you are completely committed ethically, you may stay in an organization that becomes unethical and find yourself supporting the unethical behaviors to the detriment of your own value system and career growth. Commit now to jumping out of unethical waters before you die in them. ■

---

[11]Peter M. Senge, *The Fifth Discipline* (New York: Doubleday/Currency, 1990), 22.

© GETTY IMAGES/PHOTODISC

Commit now to jumping out of unethical waters before you die in them.

SUMMARY

To reinforce what you have learned in this chapter, study this summary.

- Ethics is the systematic study of moral conduct, duty, and judgment—what is right and what is wrong. Business ethics is the study of just and unjust behaviors in business. Business ethics requires that judgment be exercised about a proposed act and the anticipated consequences of the act.

- Ethics has its roots in religion and in the philosophies of some of the great philosophers, such as Socrates, Plato, and Saint Thomas Aquinas.

- The ethical organization is environmentally responsible; is internationally aware; is culturally committed to ethical behavior; is honest; and is committed to diversity, to the community, to employees, and to standards.

- Factors impeding ethical change include the beliefs that values cannot be changed, organizations are amoral, labels accurately describe individuals, and leaders do not behave ethically.

- Steps producing ethical change include determining the ethical change required, determining the steps required to achieve the objective, practicing the new behaviors, seeking feedback, rewarding yourself and the individuals involved, and evaluating the effects of ethical change.

- Two forms of discrimination include sexual harassment and racial discrimination. Sexual harassment is defined as "harassment arising from sexual conduct that is unwelcome by the recipient and that may be either physical or verbal in nature." Racial discrimination is based on prejudice, which is often the result of ignorance, fear, and/or cultural patterns. Laws protect individuals from racial and sexual discrimination, with one of the most important laws being Title VII of the Civil Rights Act.

- Characteristics of ethical administrative professionals include making ethical decisions, supporting ethical behavior, refusing to engage in negative workplace politics, accepting constructive criticism, keeping confidential information confidential, accepting responsibilities, being honest, being loyal, and keeping the faith.

- The decision to act ethically and to seek employment in an ethical organization is a personal one. A person must believe strongly in the concept in order to live his or her beliefs on a daily basis.

FIND THE PROBLEM

Josefina is in her first full-time position as an administrative professional. She has been working for the company for six months. She does not like her supervisor; she believes he is unethical. Josefina talked with Hannah, one of her friends in the company, about her concerns with her employer. Josefina asked Hannah's advice about quitting her job. Yesterday Josefina's supervisor called her in and told her she was being disloyal to him. He explained that he was told she had been spreading vicious rumors about him throughout the company. What is the problem? How should Josefina handle the problem?

PROFESSIONAL POINTERS

Here are some tips for helping you to behave ethically in the workplace.

- Critique ideas, not people.
- Do not publicly criticize your supervisor or your coworkers.
- Do not listen to or pass along gossip about other individuals.
- Check out information you hear from the grapevine. If you know the information is false, say so without becoming emotional. Feed accurate information into the grapevine.
- Communicate in person when appropriate. Even though the majority of communication is through electronic means, face-to-face communication is valuable. It allows you to see a person's reaction to the message and to clarify any misunderstandings quickly.
- Be a good listener, but do not pass on everything you hear. Remember that you must behave professionally; professionalism carries with it lack of pettiness and rumormongering.
- When you have a problem, go directly to the source of the problem in an attempt to correct the situation.
- Appreciate diversity. Understand that people have different values, abilities, and priorities.
- Practice empathy. Putting yourself in the situation of others (figuratively) allows you to relate more closely to the barriers they face or the feelings they have.

REINFORCEMENT ITEMS

1. Why is ethical behavior important in the workplace?
2. List and explain six characteristics of an ethical organization.
3. Explain how ethical change is achieved.
4. Explain how sexual harassment can be reduced in the workplace.
5. Identify six characteristics of an ethical employee.

CRITICAL-THINKING ACTIVITY

Susan has been working as an administrative professional at People Pharmaceuticals for one year. One of her employer's male friends from another company, Timothy Madeley, is a frequent visitor to the workplace. Susan has a pleasant relationship with him, and they usually chat for a few minutes each time he comes to the office, which is three or four times a month. Mr. Madeley is married and he frequently talks about his wife and their three children. On his last visit to see Susan's employer, Mr. Madeley stopped by Susan's office to chat. At the end of the conversation, he said, "Let's have lunch sometime." Susan, thinking she would enjoy a casual meal out, replied, "Sounds good to me." Today as he came into her office after his visit with her supervisor, he said, "I really want to have lunch with you. How about next Tuesday? I have the afternoon free. Maybe you can take the afternoon off so we can enjoy a pleasant outing." Susan was surprised and concerned when he suggested they spend the afternoon together. She did not know how to respond. She merely said, "Let me think about it." How should Susan handle the situation?

VOCABULARY REVIEW

Complete the Vocabulary Review for Chapter 3 given on page 37 of the *Applications Workbook*.

ENGLISH AND WORD USAGE DRILL

Complete the English and Word Usage Drill for Chapter 3 listed on page 38 of the *Applications Workbook*.

WORKPLACE APPLICATIONS

net ## A3-1 (Goals 1 and 2)

Using the Web, access **www.fortune.com** and search for the current year's 100 Best Companies to Work For. Select four companies from the list. Access their Websites using the company name along with the correct Web terminology; e.g., **www.TDIndustries.com**. Search for each company's vision/value/diversity statement. In your opinion, do these statements adequately explain the importance of ethical behavior in the workplace? Why or why not?

Report your findings to the class, or submit a written summary of your findings to your instructor, using the memorandum form provided on the Student CD, SCDA3-1.

A3-2 (Goals 2 and 3)

On page 39 of the *Applications Workbook* is a case study. Read the case and respond to the directions. Submit your responses to your instructor, using the memorandum form provided on the Student CD, SCDA3-2.

A3-3 (Goals 2 and 3)

On pages 41–42 of the *Applications Workbook* are three case studies. Read the cases and respond to the items. Submit your responses to your instructor, using the memorandum form provided on the Student CD, SCDA3-3.

A3-4 (Goals 2, 3, 4, and 5)

As a team of four, interview two managers and two administrative professionals about the ethics of their organizations. Ask these questions:

- Does your organization have a vision/value statement? If so, may I have a copy?
- Does your organization have a grievance procedure for dealing with discrimination? Sexual harassment? If so, what is the policy?
- How does your organization achieve ethical change?
- What characteristics do you believe an ethical employee has?

Present your findings to the class, or prepare a report for your instructor.

A3-5 (Goals 2, 3, 4, and 5)

Using the keywords *ethics*, *discrimination*, and *sexual harassment*, search for articles that address each of these issues:

- The importance of organizations behaving ethically
- Ethical change within an organization
- Response to discrimination in an organization

Submit a summary of the three articles to your instructor, citing your references.

A3-6 (Goal 6)

Using the Web, search for one company's organizational mission/vision statement, as well as other information about the organization's ethical policies. Print a copy of the information you find. Respond to these items about the organization:

- What are the ethics of the organization?
- After reading the organization's ethics, explain whether a match exists between your ethics and the organization's ethics. Be specific in your response.

Finally, complete this statement: To be happy within an organization, I must see evidence that the following ethical behaviors are upheld . . .

Report your findings and your completion of the above statement to the class, or submit your responses to your instructor.

ASSESSMENT OF CHAPTER GOALS

Did you successfully complete the chapter goals? Evaluate yourself by filling out the form on page 44 of the *Applications Workbook*.

chapter 4

Workplace Team and Environment

1. Develop an understanding of effective team behavior and workplace team composition.

2. Demonstrate effectiveness in dealing with diverse environments.

3. Engage in productive team communication.

4. Describe the role of safety and health in the workplace.

I f you are presently working, have you ever had a bad day at work? If so, have you stopped to analyze why that day was a bad one for you? Many bad days are the result of negative relationships with individuals in the workplace. These relationships affect not only your happiness on the job, but also your productivity. If you are unhappy, your work productivity drops significantly.

Another factor that contributes to happiness and productivity in the workplace is the physical environment in which you work. Is it safe? Can you work relatively free from physical harm? Is it a healthy place to work? Is the workplace clean and free from unhealthy factors, such as cigarette smoke? If the answer to any of these questions is no, the productivity of workers suffers. Employees cannot maintain maximum productivity if a threat of physical harm or a threat to long-term health exists. This chapter will help you understand how to work effectively with the workplace team and to contribute positively to a safe and healthy environment.

Teamwork

Teamwork is increasingly important as organizations continue to expand multinationally, adopt new technologies, and look for ways to decrease costs and improve profits. Employers rank teamwork as one of the most important skills for an employee to possess. In fact, studies show that effective teamwork increases worker productivity, decreases absenteeism, produces higher quality products and services, and increases profits for organizations.

What does the word *team* mean? In the workplace, a team is a group of individuals who work together to achieve defined goals. Team effectiveness demands four behaviors from each team member:

• Understanding others

- Accepting different values
- Working together effectively
- Achieving goals

Seek to Understand Others

People who work together must understand and accept the differences that each individual brings to the team. These differences range from ethnicity, race, age, and gender to differences in values and backgrounds. You will encounter a workforce with greater ethnic diversity, an increased number of older workers, and larger numbers of women. As you learned in Chapter 1, diversity in the United States will continue to increase. (To remind yourself of the significance of the projected diversity, you may wish to reread that portion of Chapter 1.) With this great diversity, understanding others can be difficult. Why? A major problem in understanding others is the value differences that are often present. The word *value* comes from the French verb *valoir*, meaning "to be worth." Values are your beliefs. You learn values at an early age from significant people in your environment, such as your parents and other family members. In addition, you learn values from educational, social, and religious structures, such as schools and places of worship.

Values are not inherently good or bad. However, the way in which you live your values may involve behaviors that are either acceptable or unacceptable in society. If you encounter someone who is not behaving appropriately for the values you hold, you may think that person has no values. Such thinking is incorrect; everyone has values. However, the values a person holds may not match your values or may not match the values of society. For example, one might say that Adolph Hitler was value-centered, with one of his values being his desire to build a superior race. However, in his attempt to do so, he engaged in one of the greatest atrocities of history, killing over 8 million Jews.

Practice Acceptance of Different Values

Your job within the diverse workplace is to accept the different values that exist. Certainly you do not have to change your values to correspond to the values of others. However, remember that values are not static. As you grow and change, your values may change also. What is important to remember is that your effectiveness as part of a team depends on your acknowledgment and acceptance of different value structures.

Consider the following situation in which two individuals with different values clash in performing a task.

Benito grew up in Mexico. He is from a large family; he has five brothers and two sisters. As he was growing up, he was taught the value of the family unit. The family worked and played together. Every week a family meeting was held to discuss the activities of family members and the assignment of household chores for the upcoming week. If serious disagreements occurred during the week, a family council was held to settle the differences. Benito approaches his work life the same way. He believes that individuals within an organization should work together closely for the good of the organization.

Sarah grew up in a large city in the United States. Her family is small; she has one sister. Both of her parents worked outside the home while she was growing up. Sarah and her sister were taught to be totally independent. Family unity was not discussed. Her family rarely ate together; each person had his or her own schedule. Sarah's family stressed two main values—respect for the individual and the ability to operate independently.

Recently Sarah served as chair of a team; Benito was a member of the team. Sarah was an efficient chair, assigning each individual team member a task and expecting it to be done. Sarah never encouraged teamwork. Team members came to a meeting, received the assignment from Sarah, and reported to the group at the next meeting. After three team meetings, Benito voiced his concern that the group was not working as a team. Sarah did not seem to understand what he was saying. She suggested that the two of them discuss his concerns after the meeting. Benito became upset and told Sarah she was not listening to him. Sarah then responded angrily that he was not doing his assignments.

Value clashes such as this one are caused by differences in background and experience. Such incidents can cause misunderstandings among workplace team members and make it difficult for individuals to work together. As you work with others in the workplace, you must recognize and understand these differences. You do not need to adopt someone else's values or behaviors, but you cannot judge a person for behaving in ways that are consistent with his or her background, experiences, and values. When clashes occur, you need to find the solution to the problem, rather than lash out at the individual for his or her behavior.

Work Together Effectively

Members of a workplace team are a working unit. The design of almost all workplaces forces individuals into close physical proximity. Even as more and more people are engaged in telework, teams (although very different in composition) exist. When employed in a traditional workplace setting, you usually work on tasks with those people who are physically close to you. You are also generally part of a larger department or division of the organization. Each individual within the department works independently and interdependently to accomplish a variety of tasks. For example, you may be working on a marketing project. As a team, you work to determine the direction and content of the marketing project. As an individual, you prepare one piece of the project. If you are a teleworker, your team may be your clients or customers.

Value clashes can occur because of differences in background and experiences.

Teleworkers' teams often consist of clients.

Achieve Goals

Two sets of goals within an organization are generally important to you—your personal goals and the goals of the organization. For example, you join an organization with certain personal goals. These goals are short-term and long-term. One of your short-term goals may be to learn your job as quickly as possible. One of your long-term goals may be to achieve a promotion to a higher-level position in the organization.

Although your personal goals are important, you must also be committed to the goals of the organization. If your personal goals are inconsistent with the organizational goals, you will not succeed. For example, assume the organization has a short-term goal of developing an employee recruitment plan. The timeline for development is three months. You are asked to be part of the team in charge of developing the first draft of the plan. You have a busy job, but one of your personal goals is to be promoted to a higher-level position. You decide, for career purposes, to be on the team. However, as the team begins

its work, you find you must work overtime several hours each week to complete your regular job duties and finish your tasks on the recruitment plan. You have a small child at home, and one of your values is to be a good parent. You do not believe you can work 10 hours of overtime each week and still be a good parent to your child.

In this situation, your personal values and the organizational values are in conflict. These types of value conflicts often pose real dilemmas for people within the organization as well as the organization itself. Reconciling conflicting goals may require adjustments on your part and the part of the organization. If conflicting goals cannot be worked out, you may need to make personal sacrifices; if the sacrifice is too great, you may need to seek other alternatives. In the example above, you may decide to ask a relative to provide support for your child or you may decide to resign from the committee. If you decide to resign from the committee, you must recognize that you may jeopardize your plan for a promotion; however, you have decided that your child is your most important priority right now.

Workplace Team Composition

The administrative professional is often part of three basic types of teams:
- Project team
- Administrative professional and supervisor team
- Administrative professional and coworker team

Project Team

Project teams are brought together within an organization to accomplish an identified task. The teams are often responsible for a project from start to implementation. For example, the project team may be responsible for developing a diversity recruitment plan. The team must gather statistics on the diversity of the organization in the past and establish the type of diversity picture necessary for the future health of the organization. The next task for the team is to develop a plan to meet the diversity needs. The team may also be involved in evaluating the implementation of the plan after a period of six months or so.

When working in teams, worker **empowerment** is essential. Empowerment implies that individuals have access to the information they need to do the job and the authority and responsibility to do the job without constant checking from the supervisor. Supervisors trust the empowered worker to do the job well and to make decisions consistent with achieving the established goals.

If the project team is to be successful, certain essential criteria are necessary:

- Clarity of purpose
- Technical skills
- Administrative skills
- Interpersonal skills
- Commitment

Clarity of Purpose

The purpose and goals of the project team must be clearly established before the team begins its work. These questions need to be asked and satisfactorily answered:

- What is the team to accomplish?
- When is the team to complete its work?
- What standards will be used to determine whether a project has been completed successfully?
- Who will be evaluating the project?
- What additional resources does the team need outside the organization?
- What is the budget of the team?

As the project team operates, its membership must engage collectively in these behaviors:

- Ensure that team efforts are consistent with corporate-wide objectives.
- Ensure accountability of the team and each team member.

- Make certain that the team conforms to fiscal, legal, and other critical guidelines.

Technical Skills

If technical skills, such as telecommunication and writing skills, are important, careful selection of team members is crucial to ensure that they have the appropriate skills. Training sessions on certain new technologies can be made available to a team. However, there is usually not enough time to bring a **neophyte** (a beginner) in the field up to the level of expertise needed.

Administrative Skills

Administrative skills include the ability to analyze financial data such as budgets, to process paperwork, and to set directions for a project. Since team members generally have various levels of proficiency in administrative tasks, the team should determine at the beginning of a project who is responsible for what particular administrative tasks. If several people need to be proficient in a task, the most proficient individual can provide short training sessions for other team members.

Interpersonal Skills

Interpersonal skills are critical. Team members must be able to work together collaboratively, listen to each other effectively, and resolve conflicts that occur.

Suggestions for working together collaboratively include these:

- Define the purpose of the collaborative project at the first team meeting.
- Choose a chairperson or group leader.
- Determine each group member's skills and expertise.
- Assign tasks to each group member.
- Establish guidelines for completing the task.
- Determine a time for completion.
- Determine product evaluation standards.
- Determine evaluation standards for group members.

Although workers spend a large portion of their time listening to others, they may not

© GETTY IMAGES/EYEWIRE

If a project is to have a successful conclusion, team members must work together collaboratively.

know how to listen effectively. For example, people may spend their time being quietly critical of each other, rather than listening effectively to what others are saying. Listening effectively demands listening for the feelings and the words of the speaker. Listeners may disagree with what the speaker is saying, become angry, and block the speaker's message. Figure 4-1 lists several suggestions for effective listening.

Another important interpersonal skill is conflict resolution. Even the most effective teams have certain areas of conflict. Understanding how to work through conflict is so important that team members may want to engage in a short session on conflict resolution at the beginning stages of a project. Here are several suggestions that can be effective in solving conflicts:

- Identify what is causing the conflict. Is it power, resources, recognition, or acceptance? Many times an individual's needs for these items are at the heart of the conflict.

- Determine what each person in the team needs or wants when a conflict occurs. Be willing to listen to the other person. If you do not understand what the other person is saying, paraphrase what you think you heard and ask for clarification. Be open to what the other person tells you.

- Identify points of agreement. Work from these points first, and then identify the points of disagreement.

- Create a safe environment. Establish a neutral location. Establish a tone that is accepting of the other person's views and feelings. Fear may be behind someone's anger. Let the other person tell you how he or she is feeling. Watch how you position yourself physically in the room. Remember, you have a more difficult time competing

EFFECTIVE LISTENING TECHNIQUES

- Listen for facts.
- Listen for feelings.
- Withhold evaluation.
- Direct your attention to the speaker.
- Maintain eye contact with the speaker.
- Watch for nonverbal communication.
- Remove distractions.
- Ask questions if you do not understand what the speaker said.
- Paraphrase what the speaker said.
- Ask open questions.
- Do not anticipate the speaker.
- Organize what you hear.
- Try to understand the speaker's words.
- Do not get angry.
- Do not criticize.
- Take notes if appropriate.
- Set aside your own preconceptions about the topic being discussed.
- Use listening time productively. People speak at about 150 words per minute and think at about 500 words per minute. Use your thinking time effectively.

FIGURE 4~1 Effective Listening Techniques

with someone who is sitting next to you than with someone who is across the table or room. A circular seating arrangement may be appropriate if you have several individuals involved in a conflict.

- Do not react. Many times individuals act too quickly when a conflict occurs. Step back, collect your thoughts, and try to see the situation as objectively as possible.
- Do not seek to win during a confrontation. Negotiate the issues and translate the negotiation into a lasting agreement.
- Listen actively. Watch the individual's eyes; notice his or her body language.
- Separate people from the issue. When the people and the problem are tangled together, the problem becomes difficult to

solve. Talk in specific, rather than general, terms.

Commitment

Each individual in the team must be committed to the accomplishment of the task and to the individuals within the team. People who are committed to the accomplishment of a task willingly engage in these behaviors:

- Sharing information with one another
- Taking risks
- Expressing their opinions
- Sharing accountability for the results

In demonstrating commitment, team members trust each other. They listen when another team member expresses ideas and opinions. Team members are committed to each other and to the task to be accomplished. By working together in an open and trusting environment, the contribution of each member can be maximized.

Administrative Professional and Supervisor Team

Another type of team in the workplace is the administrative professional and supervisor team. As an employee, you need to be clear about what you owe your immediate supervisor and what your supervisor owes you. Your relationship with your supervisor is of primary importance. Unless that relationship is satisfactory, you will not perform at your highest capacity. At the very least, you owe your supervisor respect, dependability, honesty, and loyalty.

Respect

Respect is showing regard and appreciation for your employer. You owe your employer respect simply because of the responsible position the person holds in the organization. You need to show respect for your employer's decision-making role although you may not always understand or agree with the decisions made. If for some reason you are unable to respect your employer, you need to find another position.

© GETTY IMAGES/EYEWIRE

You owe your supervisor respect, dependability, honesty, and loyalty.

Dependability

Dependability is defined in the dictionary as "trustworthiness." Dependability in practice means you observe the organization's rules regarding work hours, coffee breaks, sick leave, and vacation time. You are at work on time, and you consistently work all hours required. You do not abuse sick leave or vacation policies. You complete work assignments on time; or if on occasion you are not able to do so, you seek help. When you are in the workplace, you give the organizational goals top priority.

Honesty

Honesty means that you are genuine; you are not deceptive or fraudulent. You are truthful, sincere, and fair. You do not play games on your computer or use the Internet for personal matters, such as making travel arrangements or shopping. You do not use email to send personal notes to friends.

Loyalty

The definition of **loyalty** is "the quality of devoted attachment and affection." Loyalty between the administrative professional and the employer is essential. Actions that exhibit loyalty in the workplace include:

- Maintenance of confidentiality when necessary.

- Adherence to the chain of command. If a problem or an issue occurs with your supervisor, talk with him or her first. Your employer does not want to be surprised by concerns about which he or she had no inkling.

- Adherence to organizational values. Be honest with your employer and other employees.

Your employer also has certain obligations to you. Figure 4-2 lists several of these obligations.

SUPERVISOR'S OBLIGATIONS TO THE ADMINISTRATIVE PROFESSIONAL

- Respect. Your employer should be aware of your needs and show respect for you and your abilities.
- Feedback. Your employer should be honest and open with you concerning your work and how it is being evaluated.
- Loyalty. Your employer should present you in a positive light to others. If your employer has a problem with your effectiveness, she or he should talk with you—not others—about the situation.
- Ethical behavior. Your employer is responsible for managing ethically. You should expect your employer to uphold the values and ethics of the organization.

FIGURE 4~2 Supervisor's Obligations to the Administrative Professional

Administrative Professional and Coworker Team

A third important team consists of your coworkers and you. What type of relationship should you have with your coworkers? Consider the following:

- Have you ever been in a situation where one employee who had nothing to do refused to help another employee who was overloaded with work?
- Have you ever been in a situation in which workers spent break times and lunch hours gossiping about other employees?
- Have you ever worked in an environment where small cliques existed?

If you have worked at all, you probably answered yes to one or more of these questions. Uncomfortable situations with coworkers do occur from time to time. Although you cannot avoid these situations entirely, you can reduce such situations by applying effective human relations principles, such as acceptance, cooperation, tact, and fairness.

Acceptance

The dictionary definition of **acceptance** is "favorable reception; approval." You will come in contact with many different people in the workplace. Their backgrounds and interests may be quite different from yours. You may not understand many of these people at first. Because you do not understand them, you may dislike or disapprove of them. As a successful administrative professional, you need to accept other employees without judging them. You should recognize and respect people who are different from you. If you sincerely listen to others, you will learn more about them and avoid conflicts that result from a lack of understanding.

Cooperation

The dictionary definition of **cooperate** is "to work or act together toward a common end or purpose." In the workplace, cooperation means you are willing to work with coworkers for the common good. Since few jobs are performed in total isolation, cooperation is necessary in order to attain organizational goals. You should willingly assist other employees in meeting job deadlines when the situation demands. If one employee has a rush job that cannot be finished without help, you should offer that help, provided you have no top-priority work to complete.

Tact

Tact is defined as "acute sensitivity to what is proper and appropriate in dealing with others, including the ability to speak or act without offending." Tact demands sensitivity to the needs of others. You should consider the impact of what you say and avoid offensive statements. The tactful administrative professional emphasizes others' positive, rather than negative, traits. If you are tactful, you think before you speak. For example, if a fellow employee has just returned to the workplace after a serious illness, let the person know you are pleased that she is back. Avoid asking prying or possibly upsetting questions about her illness.

© GETTY IMAGES/PHOTODISC

Cooperation demands that you work together toward a common purpose.

Fairness

Fair is defined in the dictionary as "having or exhibiting a disposition that is free of favoritism." The fair person does not take advantage of others. You may get an idea from someone else; but if you are fair, you do not take credit for it. Instead, you give credit to the individual who gave you the idea. If you are fair, you also assume your share of responsibility without attempting to get coworkers to do your job.

Administrative Professional and External Team

Although the external team is not as closely constructed as the three previously mentioned teams, it nevertheless has some elements of a team. One or more individuals within an organization who work with individuals outside

the company to achieve specified company goals compose the team.

Outsourcing (using outside firms to perform certain functions of an organization) provides a good example of an external team. For example, assume your organization is outsourcing the implementation of a new telecommunications system. As an administrative professional, you may be on a team that works with this organization. Working with the external team requires the same human relations skills as working with internal teams. Good communication skills and an understanding of the relationship between the outsourcing company and your organization are crucial.

Positive Public Relations

Working with an external team demands good **public relations.** Public relations is the technique of inducing individuals outside the organization to have understanding for and goodwill toward a person, a firm, or an institution. Favorable public relations are crucial to any organization.

The administrative professional must use good public relations when dealing with the external team as well as with visitors, clients, customers, and prospective customers of the organization. Through effective public relations, administrative professionals can increase the likelihood of a prospective customer becoming an established customer and an established customer becoming a repeat customer.

Effective Communication with Workplace Visitors

In many large organizations, a receptionist initially greets all workplace visitors. The receptionist may keep a register in which the name of the visitor, company affiliation, nature of the visit, person the visitor wishes to see, and date of the visit are recorded. After obtaining this information, the receptionist notifies the administrative professional of the caller's arrival. If the visitor is at the company for the first time, the administrative professional's job may include escorting the visitor to the executive's office.

Administrative professionals in small organizations may also serve as receptionists; that is, they have the responsibility of greeting all visitors to the company and directing them to the proper people. Regardless of whether you work in a large or small organization, a number of techniques for receiving visitors are common. These techniques appear in Figure 4-3.

Communication in Diverse Environments

As the diversity of the U.S. workforce continues to grow, you must understand how to communicate with individuals making up this diversity.

Diversity—A Resource

Diversity can and should be a positive force in the workplace. However, understanding and acceptance is necessary. Think back for a minute on the history of the United States. People from different European countries and Africa helped build the United States. In fact, the term **melting pot**, coined by sociologists and meaning "the amalgamation of people of different ethnicities and races into one United States of America," describes the first few hundred years of the integration of people within this country. As the country's diversity continues to grow and people from Mexico, Asia, the Middle East, and other regions of the world seek residency here, the term *melting pot* has limited meaning. New terms, such as **salad bowl** and **quilt**, reflect the diversity more accurately. This country is no longer a group of people who become one big pot of sameness, but is a group of people who retain much of their identity from their homeland and much of their language. If you walk the streets of major U.S. cities, such as New York and Los Angeles, you hear a multitude of languages. In other words, the *salad* has

---

PROPER TECHNIQUES FOR RECEIVING WORKPLACE VISITORS

- When a visitor enters your office, greet the person graciously with a simple *Good Morning* or *Good Afternoon.*
- Learn the visitor's name, and call the person by name.
- Determine the purpose of the visit when it is unscheduled. Avoid blunt questions such as *What do you want?* More appropriate is a question such as *Could you please tell me what company you represent and the purpose of your visit?*
- Make appropriate introductions. See the Reference Guide, page 506, for rules for making introductions.
- Be pleasant to a difficult visitor. Be wary of office visitors who try to avoid your inquiries with evasive answers such as *It's a personal matter.* An appropriate response to such a statement is *My employer sees visitors only by appointment. I will be happy to set one up for you.*
- Handle interruptions well. If you need to interrupt your employer with a message when a visitor is in his or her office, do so as unobtrusively as possible. You may call your employer on the phone or knock on the door and hand him or her a note.
- Let angry or upset visitors talk. Listen and try to understand the visitor's viewpoint. Usually the anger will dissipate after you have listened. Then you can help the person with the concern.
- Do not disclose specific information about the company or your employer to visitors. An appropriate response is *Organizational policy does not permit me to disclose that information. You may want to see Ms. Lu.*

FIGURE 4–3 Proper Techniques for Receiving Workplace Visitors

many ingredients, which remain intact even when mixed. The *quilt* has many different squares, maintaining their beauty even as the quilt is sewn together. In a number of places in the United States today (namely, California, Florida, and Texas), Spanish is the language spoken by many. If the United States is to be a strong country, everyone must practice acceptance and respect for people of diverse backgrounds and experiences.

Ethical and forward-thinking business organizations see diversity as a resource. How? Diverse groups of people bring to the workplace different perspectives, different values, and different ideas. The wise business organization uses these ideas to enrich its products and/or services so they appeal to a broad audience. Thus, the bottom line is that diversity treated with respect is good for the organization. In other words, diversity can make money for businesses. In an article entitled "America's 50 Best Companies for Minorities," *Fortune* related the status of the minority workforce in the top companies committed to diversity. The magazine reported that when companies were asked this question, "Will a multiracial workforce remain a priority for corporate America?" the answer was a resounding yes. According to one manager quoted in a *Fortune* article, diversity must become an integral part of the way a company does business.[1]

Additionally, diversity of ideas within an organization can help individuals grow and learn if they open their minds to hear what others are saying. Thus, diversity becomes a resource for individuals within the organization—a resource that helps each individual grow and be more effective in a highly diverse world.

Cultural Differences

Obviously, people from different countries and cultures bring a variety of thoughts and ideas to the workforce environment. Consider the following differences that exist among people of various countries.

Most people who speak English do not understand that the language and its nuances can be difficult for others to understand. For example:

- We drive on parkways and park on driveways.
- There is neither pine nor apple in pineapple and no grapes in grapefruit.
- Why do we have interstate highways in Hawaii?[2]

How such terminology came into being is confusing. Imagine how puzzling it is for the person attempting to learn English.

Although the British speak English, a number of words have different meanings in Britain than they do in the United States. Consider these examples:

- An elevator is a *lift*.
- The bathroom is a *water closet* or a *loo*.
- The hood of a car is the *bonnet*.
- A cookie is a *biscuit*.
- The subway is the *underground*.

Figure 4-4 lists a few cultural differences that exist between people of different countries. If people are to be effective in dealing with one another, they must continue to learn and grow in their understanding of people from other cultures, races, and ethnicities.

Value and Attitude Clarification

You may not give much thought to how your values are different from other people's values. You may assume that everyone has the same values and then operate from this assumption. Obviously, that assumption is not true, and it can cause communication difficulties if it is not understood.

Also, you may not give much thought to the attitudes you demonstrate. The dictionary

[1]"America's 50 Best Companies for Minorities," *Fortune*, July 8, 2002, 111.

[2]Roger E. Axtell, *Do's and Taboos of Humor Around the World* (New York: John Wiley & Sons, Inc., 1999), 14.

CULTURAL DIFFERENCES

- In Korean culture, smiling can signal shallowness and thoughtfulness.
- Asians avoid eye contact as a sign of respect.
- In France and Mexico, being 30 minutes late to an appointment is perfectly acceptable.
- Latin Americans stand very close to each other when talking; the interaction distance is much less than in the United States.
- Open criticism should be avoided when dealing with Asian employees, as this may lead to loss of face.
- In Japan and China, yes does not always mean "yes." For example, if a person from Japan or China responds to a question in the affirmative, he or she may merely be demonstrating politeness—not acceptance of what you said.
- What is considered humor is not the same in all countries. One should be very cautious when attempting to be humorous; in fact, humor with people of other cultures should be avoided until the individuals know each other better.
- The types of food eaten vary greatly among cultures. For example, corn on the cob, grits, and sweet potatoes are not eaten in countries outside the United States. Muslims and Jews do not eat pork. Dog is considered a delicacy in some Asian cultures.
- Holidays are different; for example, other countries do not celebrate Thanksgiving, as is done in the United States.
- The colors of flowers have different meanings for different cultures. In China, white is the color of mourning; white flowers are sent only to people in mourning.

FIGURE 4~4 Cultural Differences

definition of **attitude** is "position, disposition, or manner with regard to a person or thing." Assume that as a North American, you value punctuality. One of your coworkers is from Mexico. Generally, people from Mexico do not value punctuality as much as North Americans do. One of your coworkers is continually 30 minutes late for work. Although you do not have any supervisory responsibilities, you feel angry because she is consistently late. One day you grumble loudly as your tardy coworker sits down at her desk, "Some people are never on time." Obviously, she hears you and is less than friendly for the remainder of the day. Her interpretation of your remark is that you do not like people from Mexico—in fact, you are hateful toward them. You do value people from other cultures, but your attitude did not reflect your values. Just as you need to understand what you value, you also need to be clear about the attitudes you reflect to others.

Effective Communication Techniques for Diverse Environments

Communication in diverse environments can be improved if all individuals use good techniques. Put into practice these techniques:

Be Respectful

Be respectful of others' culture, background, experiences, and ethnicity. Attempt to remove your own cultural glasses to see the world in the way the person of a different cultural background sees it. Is this difficult? Of course it is. Is it possible? Yes, to a degree. You can never totally understand the world from another person's view, but you can try.

Be Nonjudgmental

Do not be the "ugly American," always comparing others to your own culture and making value judgments when people from other cultures have different values and views. Remove your judging hat. Learn from other cultures, rather than judge them. When you adopt such an approach, you may be surprised to find yourself changing some of your views.

Place Yourself in the Other Person's Position
When someone does something that you do not understand or that makes you angry, try to look beyond the action to the motivations and perspectives of that person. For example, if a person from China fails to make eye contact with you, the behavior is not disrespectful. In fact, just the opposite is true. Not making eye contact is a sign of respect.

Be Flexible
Learn to bend with the situation. If you ask a Japanese coworker his opinion on an issue and he does not respond, do not think he is being rude. Realize that cultures differ. In the Japanese culture, individuals are taught to withhold their personal opinions. An old Japanese proverb says, "Silence is a virtue."

Practice Good Listening Skills
Listen and ask questions. Do not interrupt the speaker. Do not attempt to give your opinion on a particular subject at every opportunity.

Productive Communication

The previous section discussed several techniques to help you in communicating with people of other cultures. Certainly, the techniques are also effective in most communication venues. Additional information in this section discusses workplace communication; these techniques can be effective in many situations.

All organizations have formal and informal communication channels. Your goal as an employee is to be productive in both channels.

Formal Communication
Formal communication channels in an organization may be downward, upward, or horizontal. **Downward communication** consists of messages that flow from management to employees of the company. **Upward communication** includes those messages that travel from employees to management. **Horizontal communication** involves messages flowing from coworker to coworker or from manager to manager.

Informal Communication
In addition to formal communication in an organization, informal channels, often called the **grapevine**, are present. The origin of the term *grapevine* goes back to the time of the Civil War. Messages transmitted by telegraph wires were strung like a grapevine from tree to tree. These messages were often garbled. Today the grapevine has come to mean messages that may or may not be true and that originate from an unknown source.

The grapevine is a natural and normal outgrowth of people working together. The worst feature of the grapevine is untrue communication or rumors. Since rumors and untruths cannot be entirely squelched, the best way to reduce them is with open lines of formal communication. Management needs to give employees the information required to do their jobs. Employees also need to be kept informed about the direction of the organization.

Communication Techniques
This section presents several communication techniques applicable for workplace situations.

Understand the Organizational Structure
When you join an organization, ask for an organizational chart if one is not made available to you. This chart will show you the organizational structure, the relationships between departments, and the levels of administrative authority. Certain portions of the chart may change from time to time, depending on projects of the company. These changes are usually reflected in dotted lines showing new relationships.

Procedures manuals help employees learn more about the structure and the methods of operation of the business.

Understand the Organizational Management Style

Management of an organization has considerable influence on the amount and type of communication within an organization. Management styles include the following:

- Management by coaching and development
- Management by consensus
- Management by information systems
- Management by objectives

Most managers use a variety of styles depending on the situation and needs of the organization. In fact, the word *manager* has come into question by those employed in the management field, as well as by theorists in the field. According to one widely accepted view, traditional management is too restrictive for the needs of today's organizations; the preferred term is *leader*. Here are a few of the differences between a manager and a leader.

- Managers see the world as relatively impersonal and static. Leaders see the world as full of color and constantly blending into new colors and shapes.
- Managers view work as an enabling process, involving a combination of ideas, skills, timing, and people. Leaders view work as developing fresh approaches to old problems or finding options for old issues.
- Managers focus on *how* things need to be done. Leaders focus on *what* needs to be done.

Proponents of the differences between management and leadership make the point that the skills necessary for individuals engaged in moving an organization forward include these:

- Empowering
- Restructuring
- Teaching
- Role modeling
- Questioning

As an administrative professional, you need to try to understand the philosophy of organizational leaders. Their philosophy becomes pervasive in an organization and impacts all decisions of the organization. You will learn more about leadership in Chapter 20.

Write and Speak Clearly

As an administrative professional, you frequently engage in spoken and written communications. Be certain that your communications are as clear as possible. Keep your words simple; refrain from using difficult words to impress others. Express your thoughts, opinions, and ideas concisely. Tell others exactly what you mean. If you do not understand the speaker, repeat what you think the person said in your own words. Ask the speaker to confirm the accuracy or inaccuracy of your statements. If you think the listener has not understood you, tactfully ask the person to repeat what you said.

Be Word Conscious

Words can mean different things to different people. You need to consider how the communicator interprets and uses words. The intended meaning of a supervisor may be misinterpreted by an employee unless both people are using the same point of reference. A good idea is to check your communication with the receiver of the message.

Communicate Ethically

According to the National Communication Association, "ethical communication enhances human worth and dignity by fostering truthfulness, fairness, responsibility, personal integrity, and respect for self and others."[3] Here are several guidelines for helping you to communicate ethically.

- Be clear about your agenda when communicating with others. Do not subscribe to secret agendas; withholding information is dishonest.

- Consider the consequences of being unethical.
- Make a commitment to yourself and others that you will reach resolution when conflict occurs.
- Be responsible and accountable for your words, actions, and judgments. Do not dump your problems and vent your anger on others.
- Use *I* statements and clear language.
- Go directly to the source of your concerns.
- Acknowledge the various levels of power within the organization.
- Let yourself be challenged by new ideas.
- Accept the consequences of your communication.
- Be accurate and truthful about your actions.
- Condemn communication that degrades individuals.
- Advocate sharing information, opinions, and feelings.
- Meet your commitments.

A Safe and Healthy Environment

Everyone prefers to work in a safe and healthy physical environment. If an environment is unsafe and unhealthy, productivity is affected. Employees are often sick and absent. Morale is low. For the employer, an unsafe and unhealthy environment results not only in lost productivity, but also in increased costs in the form of greater medical expenses and disability payments. The impact of the physical environment is great and affects the workplace team either positively or negatively.

As an administrative professional, what would you do if you developed these health problems?

- Your wrists hurt so badly that you could not key material.
- You had so much back pain that you could not sit at the computer for any length of time.

---

[3]"Ethical Communication in Small Groups," accessed June 30, 2002; available from **www.mhhe.com/socscience**.

- You developed vision problems so serious that you could not read small print.

Health problems can result if you do not use proper techniques while working at your computer. This section will help you understand how to take good physical care of yourself.

Ergonomics—A Definition

Ergonomics, according to the dictionary, is "the study of the problems of people in adjusting to their environment; the science that seeks to adapt work or working conditions to fit the worker." Ergonomics comes from the Greek words **ergos** (work) and **nomos** (natural laws). Simply stated, ergonomics is the fit between people, the tools they use, and the physical setting in which they work. The health problems that can occur due to inattention to ergonomic factors demand that you take ergonomics seriously. You should adopt an ergonomic approach to the design of your work site.

Common Injuries

Due to the amount of time people sit at their computers, several common injuries can occur. The generic name given to these injuries is repetitive stress injuries (**RSIs**) or cumulative trauma disorders (**CTDs**). OSHA reports that approximately 2 million workers annually have ergonomic-related injuries, and thousands of these workers miss some work as a result. Thus, RSIs impact workers' health and cost organizations dollars in lost work and insurance claims. The RSIs discussed here include the following:

- Carpal tunnel syndrome (CTS)
- Computer vision syndrome
- Back pain
- Headaches

Carpal Tunnel Syndrome (CTS)

CTS is a condition that occurs due to the compression of a large nerve, the median nerve, as it passes through a tunnel composed of bone and ligaments in the wrist. Symptoms include a gradual onset of numbness, a tingling or burning in the thumb and fingers, pain that travels up the arm and shoulder, and weakness of hands causing difficulty in pinching or grasping objects.

Computer Vision Syndrome

Computer vision syndrome is a term coined by the American Optometric Association for eye complaints related to computer work. The symptoms of computer vision syndrome may include these:

- Inability to focus on distant objects after using the computer for several hours
- Dry or watery eyes
- Blurred vision
- Heaviness of the eyelids or forehead

According to studies, the eyes get extremely dry after people use a computer for a long time. As a comparison, individuals' eyes get dryer from using a computer for an extended time than from reading a book for long periods. Additionally, individuals blink less, from an average of 22 times per minute when not using a computer to only 7 times per minute when using a computer. Glare from a computer screen can also cause eye stress—as can glare from sunlight or from lighting in the workplace.

Back Pain

People who sit for long periods of time are at risk for back disorders. The two greatest problems are sitting upright or forward and not changing position. An upright posture with a 90-degree hip position is unhealthy because the intervertebral discs experience more pressure.

Headaches

Headaches are frequently the body's way of saying something is wrong. Poor head and neck posture, as well as eye strain can be causes of headaches. Stress is another cause.

Prevention—The Key

To avoid common injuries such as repetitive stress injuries, vision problems, back pain, and headaches, you must take certain precautions. Having the right equipment and furniture (keyboards, mouses, chairs, footrests, and so on), as well as maintaining proper posture and taking frequent breaks are preventative measures that help you avoid serious work injuries.

Keyboards

Since the 1980s, numerous new and innovative shapes of keyboards have become available. The basis for the heightened interest in keyboard design centers on the dramatic increase in CTDs in recent years. Ergonomists and designers use a variety of measures to evaluate keyboard designs and keyboard work. These measures include keying comfort, fatigue, user preferences, muscle exertions, physical symptoms, performance, and risk factors.

Four types of keyboards designed to help prevent CTDs include split keyboards, tented keyboards, negative-slope keyboards, and supportive keyboards. Split keyboards attempt to straighten the wrist by changing the orientation of keys. Tented keyboards allow the user to work with the palms angled toward each other. Negative-slope keyboards have extendable legs at the front, rather than the rear, of the keyboard. Supportive keyboards have built-in wrist or palm rests, encouraging straight wrist postures that are more comfortable and nonfatiguing. Additional keyboard designs include scooped keyboards, minimum-motion keyboards, and aligned-row keyboards.

Although the keyboards mentioned have features helpful in reducing CTDs, research does not resoundingly confirm their ergonomic benefits. According to existing research, alternative keyboard features provide greater safety and efficiency for some users, for certain types of discomfort or injuries, and for some tasks than do traditional keyboards. However, research does not support the fact that one keyboard works for everyone. When considering an alternative keyboard design, you should carefully evaluate its features and the appropriateness for you in your particular situation.[4]

Mouse Alternatives

Mouse alternatives include trackballs, mouse pens, mouses that use one finger, and touch tablets, plus a wide variety of mouse shapes and sizes. Additionally, a cordless mouse is now available that allows much greater freedom of movement than the traditional corded mouse. When choosing an alternative to a mouse, evaluate whether the alternative really uses different muscles.

Height-Adjustable Work Surfaces

Desks should be at a height where you can easily key with straight wrists and read or write without slumping forward or without hunching your shoulders. One drawback to height-adjustable work surfaces is that they are more expensive than standard desks.

---

[4]"Ergonomics of Alternative Keyboards," accessed June 30, 2002; available from **www.office-ergo.com**.

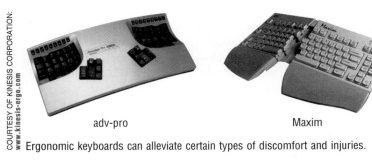

adv-pro   Maxim   Evoltrak

Ergonomic keyboards can alleviate certain types of discomfort and injuries.

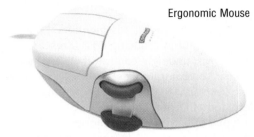

Ergonomic Mouse

Two types of ergonomic mice.

Ergonomic RollerMouse™ Station

CONTOUR DESIGN, INC.

Monitor Arms

Monitor arms allow forward, back, or up-and-down movement of the monitor to accompany posture changes. Arms can be useful for people with neck, shoulder, or upper back discomfort.

Document Stands

Stands reduce distortion of print that occurs when a document is slanted away from the eyes. Stands also reduce neck twisting by bringing the document close to the monitor at a readable angle. Since they allow you to put the paper in front of you, document stands can be useful if most of your work involves looking at paper rather than the screen.

Footrests

Footrests allow different positions for the legs and feet. When using a footrest, you should change foot positions often. Footrests are available that exercise and massage the feet, which can be beneficial.

Task Lights

Task lights are used to reduce eyestrain by illuminating paperwork and reducing the need for bright light. Documents should be illuminated enough to be readable. However, too much light can cause a strong contrast between the brightness of the screen and the document, resulting in eyestrain rather than alleviating it.

Chairs

Adjustable chairs can help you avoid back pain by supporting multiple postures. The usual adjustments on the chairs include backrest, armrest, seat angle, and seat height.

Ergonomic Research

Ergonomic research counters some of the traditional wisdom of what was thought to be correct technique when sitting at the computer. Here are suggestions from the research findings.

- Sit as far away as possible from the monitor. The conventional 18 to 24 inches places you too close to the monitor.
- Conventional practice for mouse placement is to push it away from you. However, research shows that closer is usually better, with the mouse next to the keyboard.
- The chair should be low enough for your feet to be on the floor even when the legs are extended. This research is in opposition to the conventional wisdom of having the legs reach the floor at a 90-degree angle from the knees. Research shows that you should move your legs often; they should not stay in a fixed position.
- Conventional wisdom prescribes an upright posture, with the hips at 90 degrees. However, research supports a hip width of 130 degrees as optimal. This position reduces and evens out pressure on the intevertebral discs.
- Conventional practice recommends rest breaks about 15 minutes long, every 2 hours or so. Research supports very short breaks of 30-seconds every 10 minutes in addition to the normal 15-minute breaks.[5]

---

[5]"Conventional Wisdom" vs. Current Ergonomics, accessed June 30, 2002; available from **www.office-ergo.com**.

Figure 4-5 provides a checklist of ergonomic problems with possible solutions.

ERGONOMIC PROBLEMS—POSSIBLE SOLUTIONS

Problem	Possible Solution
Elbows splayed out from body	Lower work surface Lower chair armrests
Twisting the head from side to side	Bring viewed item closer to centerline of view
Elbow or forearm resting for long periods on hard or sharp work surface	Pad surfaces, corners, and armrests
Rapid, sustained keying	Greater work variety Aggressive break schedule
Significant amounts of hand stapling, punching, lifting, opening mail	Mechanical aids, such as electric stapler or punch; reduce size of lifted load
Prolonged sitting, especially in only one position	Greater work variety Chair that supports posture changes through easy adjustability
Feet dangling, not well supported	Lower chair Lower work surface Footrest
Twisted torso	Rearrange work Provide more knee space Bring mouse and keyboard closer to body
Frequent or prolonged leaning or reaching	Rearrange work Bring mouse and keyboard closer to body
Light sources that can be seen by the worker	Cover or shield light sources Rearrange work area
Reflected glare on computer screen	Shield light sources Glare screen Move monitor so light comes from side angle, not back
Monitor image dim, fuzzy, small, or otherwise difficult to read	Upgrade monitor Use software to enlarge image
Eyestrain complaints	Check all aspects of visual environment Suggest consultation with vision specialist

"A Checklist," accessed July 4, 2002; available from **www.office-ergo.com**.

FIGURE 4~5 Ergonomic Problems—Possible Solutions

Smoking and Substance Abuse

For years, research has made people aware of the health dangers of smoking. Unfortunately, a large number of people continue to smoke. Additionally, substance abuse (alcohol and drugs) is a major problem in society.

Smoking

With the public outcry to smoking, most organizations now have smoke-free environments or designated spaces for smokers. Service industries such as hotels and restaurants still allow smoking in designated areas. However, these areas are generally close to the nonsmoking area, so secondhand smoke can be a problem. Studies have shown that breathing secondhand smoke is unhealthy and that a link exists between secondhand smoke and emphysema and lung disease. Also, eye, nose, and throat irritations can result from secondhand smoke.

Substance Abuse

Substance abuse involves the use of alcohol or drugs to the extent that the habit is debilitating for the individual using the substance. It is a problem of monumental proportions in society. Employees who abuse drugs have high rates of absenteeism and illness. They are absent an average of two to three times more than other employees. Substance abusers also perform at about two-thirds of their actual potential, thus lowering productivity. Shoddy work and material waste can also be the result of individuals who abuse drugs. Substance abusers experience wide mood swings, anxiety, depression, and anger. Even small quantities of drugs in a person's system can cause deterioration of alertness, clear mindedness, and reaction speed.

Security

Employees must believe they are safe in the work environment. Effective organizations establish comprehensive safety plans that are made available to all employees. Elements of an effective safety plan are listed in Figure 4-6.

ELEMENTS OF AN EFFECTIVE SAFETY PLAN

- Management assumes a leadership role in the development and implementation of the plan.
- Responsibility for safety and health activities is clearly assigned to particular people within the organization.
- Possible accident causes are properly identified and eliminated or controlled.
- Appropriate safety and health-related training is instituted.
- An accident record system is maintained.
- A plan for emergencies is developed and distributed to all employees.
- On-the-job awareness and safety and health responsibilities are practiced by every employee.

"Employee Safety," accessed July 4, 2002; available from **www.restaurantville.com**.

FIGURE 4~6 Elements of an Effective Safety Plan

Organizations can use a variety of procedures to protect their employees. Security guards can be stationed at doors to monitor who enters and exists. Doors can have security locks that are opened only by use of a special card. Some organizations place television screens and cameras at various locations. Security personnel monitor these screens for suspicious individuals or behaviors.

Regardless of your organization's policies or procedures to ensure employees' safety, you should establish practices of your own. These are recommended:

- If you work late, notify the security staff. Also tell someone at home that you are working late. Call the person just before you leave to say that you are on your way home.
- If you drive to work, when possible, walk to your car with someone else. Someone from the security staff may be willing to accompany you if you work in a high crime area. Have your car keys ready to unlock your car; then lock it immediately after getting in.

- If possible, situate yourself near others who are working late.
- Work next to a telephone, and have emergency numbers handy.

- Keep all doors to your office locked while you are working.
- If you hear strange noises, call for help. Do not investigate on your own. ■

SUMMARY

To reinforce what you have learned in this chapter, study this summary.

- Team effectiveness demands that team members commit to understanding and accepting one another, to being a productive team member, and to achieving team goals.
- Within the diverse workplace, one must accept differing values.
- The administrative professional works in one of three basic types of internal teams—project team, administrative professional and supervisor team, and administrative professional and coworker team.
- If a project team is to be successful, there must be clarity of purpose, appropriate technical skills, good administrative and interpersonal skills, and commitment to the task.
- For the administrative professional and supervisor team to be successful, the administrative professional must have respect for the supervisor and be dependable, honest, and loyal. The employer's obligations include respecting the administrative assistant, providing appropriate feedback to the assistant, and being a loyal and ethical manager.
- For the administrative professional and coworker team to be successful, there must be acceptance of the individuals within the team and cooperation among the members. Team members also must be tactful and fair with one another.
- The administrative professional may also work with an external team composed of clients, customers, or outside consultants. To ensure success, administrative professionals must demonstrate positive public relations and effective communication when working with these teams of people.
- Diversity of ethnicity, race, gender, and age can be an excellent resource for organizations since diverse groups of people bring different perspectives, values, and ideas to the workplace. Diversity treated with respect is good for business; it can positively impact the profits of the organization.
- Effective communication techniques necessary for understanding people of different backgrounds include being respectful, being nonjudgmental, placing oneself in the other person's position, being flexible, and practicing good listening skills.
- To be effective in formal and informal communication channels, one must understand the organizational structure and management style, write and speak clearly, be word conscious, and communicate ethically.
- Common repetitive stress injuries that can occur in the workplace include carpal tunnel syndrome, computer vision syndrome, back pain, and headaches.
- To avoid repetitive stress injuries, one should have the right equipment and furniture, use proper posture, and take frequent breaks.
- Equipment possibilities that help reduce repetitive stress injuries include ergonomic keyboards, mouse alternatives, height-adjustable work surfaces, monitor arms, document stands, footrests, task lights, and chairs.

- Smoking and substance abuse in the workplace contributes to health problems, absenteeism, poor performance, and depression.
- The organization is responsible for providing a safe place for employees to work. Employees are responsible for observing the safety procedures of the organization and for establishing safe practices for themselves.

FIND THE PROBLEM

People Pharmaceuticals recently employed an individual from Saudi Arabia. You notice that the young man, a part-time employee, is having great difficulty understanding what his job is and how to accomplish it. You rarely see him chatting with anyone in the company and notice he is by himself on breaks and at lunch. You think this is because of the 9/11 tragedy, after which many of your coworkers voiced their fear and distrust of people from the Middle East. You have been with the company on a part-time basis for almost a year and are successful at your job. You wonder whether you should try to help this young man. If you decide to help him, how would you go about doing so?

PROFESSIONAL POINTERS

Here are some tips for working successfully in teams.

- Business is a team sport. No one individual can be successful without the support of his or her fellow employees.
- Every member of a team must be involved; one way to get everyone involved is through appropriate communication.
- No one person has all the answers; all team members' opinions are valuable.
- There is no *I* in the word *team*.
- Teamwork is not about seeking credit for one's individual contributions; it is about the team succeeding.

REINFORCEMENT ITEMS

1. Explain the composition of the workforce team.
2. List and explain criteria that make project teams successful.
3. List and explain five techniques for communicating with diverse groups.
4. List five techniques that enhance team communication.
5. Explain the meaning of ergonomics, and give at least three precautionary measures to prevent RSIs.

CRITICAL-THINKING ACTIVITY

Reynolds & Reynolds is a 15-year-old company providing computer services in the United States and Canada. The company has been very successful over the last 10 years. In this time period, its stock has increased an average of 15 percent each year. The company attributes part of its success to its emphasis on solving problems through a team-based approach. Employees serve on project teams.

Benjamin Toulous was asked by his supervisor to serve on an eight-member team to examine the company's employee evaluation procedures. Benjamin is pleased about serving on this team. He believes he has several good suggestions that will improve the evaluation procedures. After he accepted the invitation to serve, he learned that the team leader was Jennifer Anvil, supervisor in the Accounting Department. Benjamin has little respect for Jennifer; he thinks she is a poor supervisor. He has heard stories from several of her employees about how unfair she is. Although Benjamin has not had direct experience with Jennifer as a supervisor, he believes she is an unacceptable team leader.

What should Benjamin do? Think through the choices he has. As you think about what he should do, use critical-thinking principles, which demand the following:

- Intellectual curiosity
- Willingness to entertain new ideas
- Willingness to acquire new information
- Willingness to evaluate assumptions and inferences

VOCABULARY REVIEW

Complete the Vocabulary Review for Chapter 4 given on page 45 of the *Applications Workbook*.

ENGLISH AND WORD USAGE DRILL

Complete the English and Word Usage Drill for Chapter 4 listed on page 46 of the *Applications Workbook*.

WORKPLACE APPLICATIONS

A4-1 (Goals 1 and 3)
Choose three or four classmates to work with on this project.

The local Chamber of Commerce asks you to write a two-page description of your college/university. The Chamber will be using this description in a publication it is putting together for new companies and individuals moving into the city. You need to include a short history of the college, the number of students enrolled, and the types of programs offered. You also plan to include two or three photos of the college and students. Determine the parts/locations that reflect the "spirit" of the college, and take photographs of these areas.

When you finish the project, discuss how the team process worked. What were the team's strengths? What problems did it have? Did team members lack certain expertise? If so, what? Each member of the team is to fill out the team evaluation form found on the Student CD, SCDA4-1a. Someone from the team should print out enough evaluation forms for the team members, tally the evaluations after they have been completed, and provide the tally results for the team members. Discuss the evaluation as a team. Write a joint memo to your instructor, detailing how the team process worked—the strengths of the team and its deficiencies, if any, and how they were handled. Use the memorandum form on the Student CD, SCDA4-1b. Submit the report that you compiled for the Chamber of Commerce (along with your photographs) and the evaluation memorandum to your instructor.

A4-2 (Goals 2 and 3)

Team up with two of your classmates. Attend a function in your community that attracts a diverse audience—an audience that differs from your own race/ethnicity. The function might be an activity at your college, a church service, a community function, or a musical/cultural event. While attending this function, make a point of talking with individuals who are of different races/ethnicities than you. Pay attention to your style of communication and to the communication of the person with whom you are talking. Write a short report (no more than two pages). Submit your report to your instructor. Include the following information in your report:

- Name and date of the event
- Description of the event
- People with whom you communicated
- Effectiveness (or lack of effectiveness) of your communication
- What you learned from the event

Complete the team evaluation form on the Student CD, SCDA4-2, as individual team members. Discuss your individual evaluations as a team, and compile one team evaluation. Submit your team evaluation to your instructor.

A4-3 (Goal 2)

On page 47 of the *Applications Workbook* is a case study. Read the case and respond to the questions. Submit your responses to your instructor, using the memorandum form provided on the Student CD, SCDA4-3.

A4-4 (Goal 2)

People Pharmaceuticals International is located in Japan, France, and China, as well as in the United States. Using the Web, research the culture and history of one of the company's locations abroad. Choose the one in which you are most interested. Use the keywords *history* and *culture,* along with the name of the country; e.g., *Japanese history* and *Japanese culture.* Use at least three Web sources. Prepare a summary of your findings. Submit your report to your instructor, listing your sources.

A4-5 (Goal 4)

Using the Web, research available ergonomic equipment and furniture. Use at least three Web sources in gathering your information. Use the keywords *ergonomic equipment* and *ergonomic furniture.* Print out pictures of any ergonomic equipment or furniture you find to include in your report. Submit your report to your instructor, listing your sources.

ASSESSMENT OF CHAPTER GOALS

Did you successfully complete the chapter goals? Evaluate yourself by filling out the form on page 48 of the *Applications Workbook*.

2

Effective Communication

chapter 5

Effective Verbal and Nonverbal Communication

1. Define the elements of effective verbal communication.
2. Demonstrate effective verbal communication.
3. Identify nonverbal communication gestures.
4. Demonstrate effective nonverbal communication.

Communication today involves a variety of forms. Much communication is through electronic methods such as email and voice systems. Your first contact when calling a business is often an automated voice system in which you are given multiple directions. For example, if you call the telephone company about a billing question, you may receive this type of message:

Welcome to XYZ Phone Company. For English, press 1. (You also hear directions at this point for someone speaking Spanish.) For all billing questions, press 1. For new service or change of address, press 2. To report a problem with your phone service, press 3. To repeat the menu options, press 9.

If you call an airline company, you may hear a message similar to this one:

Thank you for calling XYZ Airlines. This call may be monitored or recorded to ensure that you receive quality service. For automated arrival or departure information, press 1. For travel using frequent flyer miles, press 2. For travel to and from Canada or in the United States, press 3. For travel anywhere else in the world, press 4.

Although these systems help organizations handle large volumes of calls efficiently, they can be difficult to navigate. By the time you get a live person to help you with your problem, you may be so frustrated that you respond to the person in a negative manner. Additionally, email communication has increased so dramatically that you may communicate for months or even years with individuals you have never seen or spoken with by telephone.

What does this increase in electronic communication mean for your verbal and nonverbal communication skills? Simply stated, by engaging in so much electronic communication, you have fewer opportunities to practice your verbal and nonverbal communication skills. Also, it is much easier to be abusive to a person over the phone or in an email than in person. Yet as an administrative professional, you must develop effective verbal and nonverbal communication skills. You will often deal with a person on the telephone who is frustrated with or angry about an automated voice system and proceeds to take out his or her frustration on you. Additionally, you will use your verbal and nonverbal communication skills daily as you represent your employer, your organization, and yourself to the internal and external public.

Developing verbal and nonverbal communication skills is an ongoing process. No matter how long you have been a student of communication, you can continue to learn more about becoming an effective communicator. As you study this chapter, commit to continually improving and expanding your skills.

Verbal Communication

Verbal communication is the process of exchanging ideas and feelings through the use of words. Initially, the concept of verbal communication seems simple. Everyone understands words and knows what they mean. In actuality, verbal communication is not simple at all. Words, though they may be spelled the same, have different meanings for different people. Add to this situation the complexity of a diverse workforce, and communication can become even more complex. This section offers several techniques to help you become a more effective verbal communicator.

Listen and Understand

Communication is defined in the dictionary as "the *ability to make known; to impart; to transmit information, thought, or feeling so that it is adequately received and understood.*" The first step in effective verbal communication is to *listen*. Have you ever been involved in a situation in which someone did not hear what you said and became angry with you due to what

the person *thought* you said? You can probably answer this question in the affirmative. People do not listen as well as they should; thus, they often do not understand the communicator's verbal message or intent.

Listen Actively

Studies show that most people spend 70 percent of their time communicating. Of that 70 percent, 45 percent is spent listening. However, most authorities agree that listening is the weakest factor in the communication process. Hearing does not constitute listening. A person can hear the words and yet not understand them. **Listening actively** requires that you listen for the meaning as well as the words of the speaker. These techniques will help as you attempt to improve your active listening skills.

- Prepare to listen. Drive distracting thoughts from your mind, and direct your full attention to the speaker.
- Listen for facts. Mentally register the key words the speaker is using, and repeat key ideas or related points. Relate what the speaker is saying to your experiences.
- Do not let your mind wander. Most people speak at approximately 135–175 words a minute, although the brain can process information at about 500 words a minute. Listening allows plenty of time for the mind to wander. Unless you are committed to hearing the speaker, your mind will wander.
- Listen for feelings. Search beneath the surface. Listen to what is and is not being said. Additional suggestions for listening for feelings are included in Figure 5-1.
- Minimize mental blocks and filters by being aware of them. Know your biases and prejudices. Do not let them keep you from hearing what the speaker is saying.
- Question and paraphrase. Ask questions when you do not understand what you have heard. Paraphrase by putting the speaker's communication in your own words and asking the speaker if you have understood correctly.

Studies show that people spend 70 percent of their time communicating.

- Summarize. Clarify the discussion by summarizing it. Effective statements to help clarify a situation include:

  It is my understanding that the major points expressed are . . . .

  The key ideas that have been expressed are . . . .

  In summary, we have agreed to . . . .

By summarizing, you set the framework for examining what has been said. Individuals can then either agree with your summary or point out areas that are incorrect according to their understanding so the group agrees and closure occurs.

Understand the Relationship between Self-Esteem and Communication

Self-esteem is defined as "the way people feel about themselves." Self-esteem and

---

DEAL WITH FEELINGS

- Take time in group situations to talk about how people are communicating.
- Listen at all levels—content, process, and emotion.
- Realize that understanding does not mean agreement.
- Praise in public; reprimand in private.
- Honor the other person's differences before you state your point of view.
- Deal with conflict by getting it out in the open. If conflict is not dealt with, it does not disappear. It may express itself in negative ways.
- If you are working in teams, set ground rules that state how issues will be handled.
- Recognize people when they say or do something you appreciate.

FIGURE 5~1 Deal with Feelings

communication are **intrinsically linked** (being an inevitable part of each other and incapable of being separated). Your self-esteem affects the way you communicate, and your communication is affected by your self-esteem. Everyone begins developing self-esteem or lack of it at a young age. People form opinions of their worth or lack of worth through experiences and feedback they receive from significant others in their lives, such as parents, siblings, friends, and peer groups.

People with low self-esteem are more likely to focus on their failures than their successes. When asked to express their thoughts (and they often have to be asked since they think they have nothing worthwhile to say), they start their answers with statements such as the following:

- *I'm probably wrong, but . . . .*
- *I never was very good at doing this, but . . . .*
- *You don't really want my opinion; I have never done well in that area.*

Examine Your Inference Ladder

You live in a world in which you take action based on your experiences, the data you observe, your assumptions, and the conclusions you draw from your experiences, observations, and assumptions. To help you understand how the inference ladder can cause communication problems, consider this situation:

Tom and Helena work in the marketing department of a large company located in California. Tom is a native of Michigan, and Helena is a native of Texas. They are discussing a marketing project for a client. Helena favors a bold design using several primary colors for the cover of the project; Tom favors an understated monochromatic design. They get into an argument, during which Tom comments in a nasty tone, "I might have known you would suggest such a cover; Texans always have to make a bold statement. When you're in Texas I'll bet you walk around in a ten-gallon hat and cowboy boots." Helena is so furious that she walks away, but her thoughts are, Tom's an idiot. He has never been to Texas. Midwesterners are so boringly conservative.

© GETTY IMAGES/PHOTODISC

I have never been good at golf; I know I am going to slice the ball.

What happened in this communication? Rather than having a positive discussion of what would work best for the client and the audience that receives the brochure, both individuals made assumptions about each other based on where they were born.

Notice Figure 5-2, which illustrates an inference ladder. People's actions and beliefs are influenced by their backgrounds and experiences. From their backgrounds and experiences, they select data and add meaning to the data through their cultural and personal experiences. They then make **assumptions** (something taken for granted or accepted as true without proof) based on the data and the meanings they add. They also draw conclusions, adopt beliefs, and take action. In other words, they draw **inferences** (conclusions

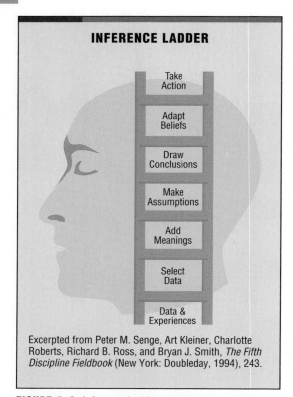

INFERENCE LADDER

Take Action

Adapt Beliefs

Draw Conclusions

Make Assumptions

Add Meanings

Select Data

Data & Experiences

Excerpted from Peter M. Senge, Art Kleiner, Charlotte Roberts, Richard B. Ross, and Bryan J. Smith, *The Fifth Discipline Fieldbook* (New York: Doubleday, 1994), 243.

FIGURE 5~2 Inference Ladder

assuredly. Tom and Helena refuse to work together on the next marketing project. Helena tells her supervisor that Tom is too conservative—that he never has a creative idea—and she will not work with him. Tom tells his supervisor that Helena is not in touch with what California clients want, she only understands Texans. She is so certain she is right that it is impossible to work with her.

Cope with Criticism

It is not easy for anyone to hear criticism. However, no one can escape it. Not only will you be on the receiving end of criticism at times, but you may also find yourself criticizing others. When you are on the receiving end of criticism, engage in these behaviors:

- Listen! Hear the person making the criticism. Give the person time to make his or her critical comments without interrupting.
- Make no excuses for your behavior if you are in the wrong.
- If you do not understand why you are being criticized, ask for specific examples of what you have done wrong.
- Accept the criticism if it is valid. Be positive about your ability to change anything you

derived from premises known or assumed to be true) based on limited data and untested assumptions and take action on their beliefs, which may be fallacious. One of the problems with making assumptions is that people *believe* their assumptions are true. People do not take the time to question their assumptions. Not only do people believe their assumptions are true, but they act on their assumptions. When people make assumptions, those assumptions become their *truth*. People act on their assumptions and often end up creating a stressful situation for no reason.

In Tom and Helena's situation, is it possible to make correct assumptions based on someone's home state? Of course not. Is it possible to assume that all Texans or all Michiganders have similar characteristics? Obviously not. Can acting on these assumptions cause problems with individuals? Most

You always think you are right; unfortunately, you are wrong more than you are right.

have done wrong. Stress the positive—not the negative.

- If the person delivering the criticism is very agitated (perhaps screaming at you), you do not have to listen. Tell the person you will be happy to discuss the problem when he or she is calmer; then leave. You have the right to walk away from an out-of-control situation.

- End the dialogue on a positive note if possible. For example, you might tell the person that you appreciated hearing the comments.

Be Nonjudgmental

The tendency to judge other people often gets in the way of communication. When a person is speaking, you may spend your time judging the person rather than listening to what he or she is saying. That judgment can be as superficial as judging the way the person looks—hair style, dress, pronunciation of words, use of language—or more substantive in nature (but just as dangerous) by judging the person's beliefs and value system. Judgment comes from the listener's frame of reference and experience. If what is said is in agreement with the listener's experience, the listener tends to be positive. If what is said is not in agreement with the listener's experience, the judgment is negative.

In order to prevent or reduce the tendency to judge other people, you need to listen with understanding. You attempt to understand the other person's point of view and try to sense how the other person feels. If you have the courage to listen with understanding, communication improves greatly. You may even find that you have learned and grown in the process.

Willingly Accept Change

In a book entitled *Who Moved My Cheese?*[1] Johnson tells a story about change, with mice and little people as the protagonists, running a maze looking for cheese. Cheese is a metaphor for what you want in life—whether it is a job, a relationship, money, health, recognition, freedom, or spiritual peace. The maze represents where you spend time looking for what you want; for example, your workplace may be the maze. In the story, the mice do better than the little people in dealing with change because they make the problem a simple one. When the cheese moves, the mice move on to other locations where they find more cheese. The little people tend to stay locked in the present situation even though the cheese is gone. The story told in Johnson's book encapsulates how many people handle change. They refuse to accept that change is happening and stay locked in their old, comfortable ways of responding to situations, even to their own physical and financial detriment.

In the fast-paced and changing world, you must accept and grow with change if you want to be a contributing member of an organization. Forward-thinking individuals are not fearful of change; they do not view change as bad. They look for the positives that occur because of change and decide how they can

© GETTY IMAGES/PHOTODISC

When the cheese moves, take advantage of the change and find new cheese.

[1]Spencer Johnson, *Who Moved My Cheese* (New York: G. P. Putnam's Sons, 1998).

contribute to helping change occur. In fact, these people are often called **change agents** (individuals who facilitate change and help others accept change).

Speak and Be Understood

In addition to listening and attempting to understand what others are saying, good verbal communicators seek to speak so they are understood. This statement means that you:

- Concentrate on using language appropriately.
- Resolve conflict when it arises.
- De-escalate noise from the environment.

Use Language Appropriately

The language people use often prevents clear communication. Words in isolation have no meaning. They have meaning only because people have agreed on a particular meaning. You may say, "But what about the dictionary? Doesn't it contain the correct meaning of words?" Yes, it contains the correct meaning as agreed to by **etymologists** (specialists in the study of words). This meaning can be called the objective meaning of a word, and you use the dictionary to determine it. However, cultural differences impact the meaning certain words have for individuals. For example, even though Americans and the British speak the same language, they use words in different ways. In America, waiting in line at a theater for tickets is referred to as *standing in line*; in Britain, it is referred to as *queuing up*.

Meanings of words also change with time. New words come into existence, and other words become obsolete because of lack of use. The computer era has generated different applications for a number of words. For example, a *chat room* in computer terminology is not a room in the standard definition of the word in the dictionary, which is "an area separated by walls or partitions from other similar parts of the structure or building in which it is located." A chat room in computer terminology is a place in computer space where individuals from various locations (even worldwide) come together to talk (share computer messages) through Web connections.

When speaking to be understood, you should engage in the following behaviors:

- Pay attention to the different meanings words can have.
- Clarify your meaning when necessary.
- Be sensitive to whether the individual or group is understanding what you are saying.
- **Paraphrase** (to restate the concept in different terms) when appropriate.

Resolve Conflict

In a perfect world, no conflicts exist. However, there is no such thing as a perfect world. Conflict, no matter how well-meaning individuals may be, can and does occur. What is important for you as an effective verbal communicator is to be able to solve conflicts.

People versus Problems. One of the first steps that needs to be taken when dealing with conflict is to separate the people from the problems. What does this mean? Consider this situation:

Nadia Booluis was appointed team leader of a group working on establishing a mentoring program for new administrative assistants at People Pharmaceuticals. Two team meetings have been held. The first meeting was an introductory session where individuals talked about what directions the project needed to take. For the second session, Nadia had requested that each person come prepared with objectives for the project. Of the eight team members, only two came to the meeting with something written down. A debate about the directions ensued, with two individuals (Jorge and Rebecca) verbally attacking each other. The meeting ended with no resolution about project direction. Several members walked away extremely upset with other team members. As team leader, Nadia must help the team separate the people from the problem.

You may have a difficult time finding your way through the jungle of people problems that often occur in situations and getting to the problem to be addressed and the goals to be accomplished. One way to think about people problems is to separate them into three categories—perception, emotions, and communication.

Perceptions. The dictionary defines **perceive** as "to become aware of directly through any of the senses." Although this definition seems straightforward, understanding someone's perception is not. The way you see the world depends on your beliefs, experiences, and values. For example, one person may see a $75,000 car and think, *How ridiculous! No one should pay that much for a car.* While another person sees the same car and thinks, *One of my goals in life is to be able to drive a car like that.* In attempting to understand another person's perception of a situation, you should withhold judgment while you attempt to think from the person's point of view. Attempting

to understand another person's view is not the same as agreeing with it. You may never agree with the person. Attempting to understand allows you to consider another perspective, which may or may not modify some of your own perceptions. However, you are listening to a different point of view and giving yourself a chance to learn from it.

Emotions. When trying to solve an important problem, people's feelings may be more important than what they are saying. You need to let the emotions surface. What are you feeling? What are other people feeling? At times, you may choose to write down how you are feeling and how you want to feel and ask the members of the group to do the same. As a result, all of you will have a better understanding of your feelings. Do not react to an emotional outburst with an outburst of your own.

© GETTY IMAGES/PHOTODISC

Finding your way through the jungle of people problems that often occur can be difficult.

Communication. In communicating effectively, you can enlist the techniques presented earlier in this chapter, such as the following:

- Listening for facts
- Listening for feelings
- Minimizing mental blocks and filters by being aware of them
- Questioning and paraphrasing

Conflict Definition. Once you separate the people from the problem, your next step is to define the conflict. What is it? Insist that individuals involved in the conflict be specific with their answers. If you are working with a team and a conflict occurs, you may need to define the purpose or mission of the team before you define the conflict. In other words, if the purpose or mission is not clear, people may be confused about what tasks need to be done and what outcomes should be achieved. Conflict can arise from this confusion. In a team situation, the leader must take the time to bring the team together and clarify the purpose or mission.

After the purpose or mission is clear, ask the individuals involved in the conflict to be specific about the disagreement. Use techniques such as asking each person to write down what the conflict is and then having each person verbalize his or her understanding of the conflict in the group.

Collaboration. Once the conflict is defined, your task is to work collaboratively to resolve it. Collaboration relies on creative problem solving to identify solutions. You can use these techniques and activities whether you are working with one individual or a group of people:

- Allow individuals to express risky ideas without correcting them. For example, saying, "Let me play the devil's advocate" is almost certain to cut off creative problem solving.
- Allow people to work through mistakes and discover their own solutions.
- Allow time for the creative process to work.

- Put on your cheerleading hat (praise individuals).
- If necessary, put on your mediator hat and help solve the conflict.

If you are involved in a team, you may need to meet individually with certain members of the team, particularly if individuals are having personal or performance problems. As a team leader in this type of situation, you need to put on your consoling and/or management hats.

Freedom from Blame. As a leader of a team or a person involved in a conflict with one or more people, do not blame others or call people names. Use *I* statements rather than *you* statements. *You* statements can lead to a chain reaction that can go like this.

Person 1: You made a terrible mistake.
Person 2: I didn't make a mistake; you did.
Person 1: You're lying and you know it.
Person 2: I am not. You're the liar.

It is much better to say something similar to the following:

I understand the task is difficult. What do we need to do to fix this problem?

Figure 5-3 lists several additional suggestions for resolving conflicts.

Nonverbal Communication

Although what is said is an important part of communication, another important area is nonverbal communication. If you are suspect of this statement, try walking into a crowded elevator; rather than adopting the normal behavior of turning around and facing the door, stand there and face the other people in the elevator. If you want to create even more tension, smile at everyone. Some may smile in return; others may glare at you; and some may even project fear, thinking you have some evil intent. Why? You have broken the rules of nonverbal elevator behavior in North America.

RESOLVING CONFLICT

- Identify what is causing the conflict. Is it power, resources, recognition, or acceptance? Many times the need for these items is at the heart of the conflict.
- Determine what each person needs or wants. Ask questions to determine what the other person wants. Be willing to listen to the other person. Everyone feels a deep need to be understood. By satisfying that need in the other person, you may be able to lessen the conflict. If you do not understand what the other person is saying, paraphrase what you think you heard and ask for clarification. Be open to what the other person tells you.
- Identify points of agreement. Work from these points first. Then identify points of disagreement.
- Create a safe environment. Establish a neutral location and establish a tone that is accepting of the other person's views and feelings. Acknowledge the other person's feelings. Behind anger may be fear. Let the other person tell you how he or she is feeling.
- Do not react. Many times individuals act too quickly when a conflict occurs. Step back, collect your thoughts, and try to see the situation as objectively as possible.
- Do not seek to win during a confrontation. Negotiate the issues and translate the negotiation into a lasting agreement.
- Listen actively. Watch the individual's eyes; notice body language.

FIGURE 5~3 Resolving Conflict

People use a variety of nonverbal communication methods to convey meaning, including these:

- Body language
- Voice quality
- Time
- Space

As you study this section, know that the statements made here apply only to natives of North America. You have already learned that language has different meanings in different cultures; so do body language, voice quality, time, and space. *You must not assume that nonverbal behavior in other cultures has the same meanings in North America.* Costly and embarrassing mistakes can occur if you make such an assumption. You must study the individual cultures to understand their nonverbal communication. At the end of this section are several paragraphs devoted to nonverbal communication in Asian cultures.

Body Language

Body language is extremely important in face-to-face communication. Assume you are involved in this situation:

As an administrative professional, you have one part-time employee reporting to you. This person generally does a good job; however, today she has made a major error. You call her in to discuss it. When she enters your office, you have a very stern look on your face. You say, "Sit down. I have something very important to discuss with you." When you tell her to sit, you point to the chair on the opposite side of your desk. (This behavior is contrary to your usual behavior of asking employees to sit at a table in your office where chairs are close to each other.) She immediately sits, but does so on the edge of her chair while crossing and uncrossing her arms throughout the conversation. She also alternately bites her lip and stares at the ceiling. At one point, she begins biting her nails.

What does your body language say? First, you let the employee know you have a real problem by the look on your face and the tone of your voice. You do not offer her a chair at the table; you place yourself behind the desk. You place more distance between you and the employee than you usually do. What does the employee's body language say? By sitting on the edge of her chair and biting her nails, the employee lets you know she is concerned. By crossing and then un-crossing her arms, she also lets you know she may not be open to some of what you say. She lets you know she is passively absorbing or ignoring the message by staring at the ceiling. Both of you start the meeting operating at a disadvantage. The conversation may not be a good one unless you modify your behaviors significantly.

People transmit body language through their eyes, face, hands, arms, legs, and posture. *However, you must be careful not to judge a person based on one gesture alone.* You must consider all the gestures a person makes, along with what he or she said. Eye contact is extremely important for North Americans. They tend to believe that people who do not make eye contact with them have low self-esteem, are shy, or are uninterested in what they are saying.

In becoming a student of body language, you should observe the eyes, face, hands, arms, legs, and posture of others.

Eyes

Raising one eyebrow is seen as disbelief; raising both eyebrows shows surprise. Winking may mean that a person agrees with you. When a person looks upward and blinks the eyes, he or she may be considering carefully what you are saying. Wide-open eyes may mean fear. As already noted, avoidance of eye contact in North America is seen as lack of respect, insincerity, or dishonesty. In North America, adults have a tendency to say to a child who is looking down while answering a question, "Are you telling me the truth? Look at me when you talk."

Face

Facial expressions often betray a person's feelings. Common facial expressions include frowns (anger or unhappiness), smiles (happiness), sneers (dislike, disgust), clenched jaws (tension, anger), and pouting lips (sadness).

Hands, Arms, and Legs

Tightly clenched hands or wringing hands usually indicate that a person is under some pressure. Authority and superiority are often indicated when a person stands with his or her hands joined behind the back. Hands that are flat on a table usually indicate a readiness to agree. Hands on hips may indicate aggression, readiness, or even defiance. Boredom or tiredness are indicated by a person resting his or her head in the hands. Tapping or drumming the fingers means impatience.

Crossed arms tend to indicate defensiveness. They seemingly act as a protective guard against an attack by someone, whether that attack is verbal or physical. People who tightly cross their legs seem to be saying they disagree with others. People who have tightly crossed legs and tightly crossed arms usually are feeling negatively about what is being said or what is happening around them. People who cross their legs tightly and kick their feet may be bored. Foot tapping also indicates boredom.

Posture

According to some individuals writing in the field of body language, there are two basic groups of body language postures—open/closed and forward/back.[2] In the open/closed group, people with arms folded, legs crossed, and bodies turned away are signaling they are rejecting people and messages. People with open hands, bodies facing the speaker, and both feet planted on the ground are accepting of people and messages.

The forward/back group indicates whether people are actively or passively reacting to communication. When a person leans forward and points toward the speaker, he or she is actively accepting or rejecting the message. When a person leans back, looks at the ceiling, writes on a pad, and so on, he or she is either passively absorbing or ignoring the message.

Figure 5-4 indicates other meanings for various body positions.

---

[2]"Decoding Body Language," accessed July 12, 2002; available from **www.johnmole.com**.

INTERPRETATION OF BODY LANGUAGE

Listening	Tilts head, makes eye contact, nods
Evaluating	Chews on pencil/glasses, strokes chin, looks up and right
Eager	Leans forward with feet under chair
Bored	Stares into space, doodles
Aggressive	Leans forward with fists clenched
Rejection	Moves back with arms folded and head down, walks with hands in pocket
Defensive	Clenches hands, stands, crosses arms on chest
Lying	Looks down, shifts in seat, glances at you
Anger	Clasps hands behind back
Disbelief, doubt	Rubs eye
Sincerity, openness	Offers open palm
Confidence	Walks briskly with upright posture
Authoritative	Steeples fingers
Indecision	Pulls or tugs at ear

FIGURE 5~4 Interpretation of Body Language

Time

Another important nonverbal communicator is time. Think about the implication time has for North Americans. Being punctual for an interview lets the prospective employer know you care about the position. Being late for an interview sends the reverse message. In a school situation, a late paper or project may result in a penalty for the student.

In other cultures, time may not have the same meaning. For example, in Spain, Greece, Mexico, and Italy, being punctual is not as important as it is in North America. Being 30 minutes late to an appointment is perfectly acceptable. Lingering over a cup of coffee at an outdoor café in Italy is commonplace any time of day; servers do not pressure customers to leave. In contrast, in North America, once their food is served, people eat quickly, expect to have the check by the time they are

Voice Quality

The loudness or softness and the pitch of the voice are nonverbal behaviors that can reveal something about a person. A loud tone of voice usually is associated with anger; a soft tone, with calmness. When two people are talking softly with each other, they are probably at ease. Higher-pitched voices tend to mean that people are tense, anxious, or nervous. People often talk faster when they are angry or tense. In contrast, a low pitch and a slow pace indicate an intimate or relaxed tone. Other forms of nonverbal voice communication include a nervous giggle, a quivering emotional voice, and a breaking stressful voice.

Voice quality is so important that individuals whose voices are important to their job success, such as TV and radio newscasters, spend time and effort to be certain that their voices do not irritate listeners. For example, a nasal or high-pitched voice can be extremely irritating to listeners.

© GETTY IMAGES/PHOTODISC

Being late for an interview can indicate noninterest in the job.

finished eating, pay for their food, and leave immediately. People rarely linger over their meals unless they are enjoying a leisurely meal with friends.

Space

Proxemics (the study of personal and cultural use of space) was coined by E. T. Hall in 1963 when he investigated people's use of personal space in contrast with fixed and semi-fixed feature space, such as partitions within an office and furniture. Hall found that people in different cultures perceive and use space in relationship to fixed and semi-fixed features differently. In addition, North Americans also observe well-established spatial territories when communicating with others.

Behavioral studies show that individuals perceive spatial distances between others differently depending on various relationships with individuals. People use four space differences between themselves and others.

- Intimate distance (6–18 inches) is for embracing or whispering.
- The distance for talking with good friends is 1.5–4 feet.
- Social distance for conversations among acquaintances is 4–12 feet.
- The distance for public speaking is 12 feet or more.

Research supports the fact that violating a person's personal space can have adverse effects on communication. If someone you know gets too close, you back away. If the person knowingly or unknowingly invades *your space*—something you probably take quite seriously, you may avoid other conversations with the individual.

Humans, like animals, establish ownership of certain territories. For example, do you have a certain desk or chair in a classroom that you consider yours? Do you feel displaced when someone else occupies that space? Do you confront the person, saying, "You are in my space?" This act of laying claim to and defending a territory is termed **territoriality**. Territoriality is established so

quickly that by the second class period or by the second series of a lecture, the audience returns to their same seats. If you are working, have you ever arrived at the workplace to find someone else at your desk? If so, what was your reaction? You may have felt violated. You may have wondered or even said, "What are you doing at my desk?"

People also give certain meanings to the types of furniture in an office or the size of the office and the furniture. For example, the offices of vice presidents of an organization are generally of the same size. The president's office is larger, with furnishings that are more lavish. Administrative support personnel often do not have individual offices; instead, they have workstations with modular walls. However, if you are an administrative assistant to the president or even a vice president, you may have your own office.

The proxemics of North American homes also explain how people use space. Some rooms of the home are for public gatherings; for example, the living room. Other rooms are considered off-limits to all individuals, with the exception of the people using the space. For example, the master bedroom and bath are usually off-limits to even close friends.

You have taken my chair. Please move.

Other family members may or may not be welcome in this area. The kitchen or dining room table is usually designed to provide for a cozy, comfortable family atmosphere. The seating arrangement of people gathered around a table provides for direct eye contact and close proximity.

Asian Nonverbal Behavior

As the global village continues to shrink, everyone must become more sensitive, more aware, and more observant of the nonverbal communication of people from other cultures. North Americans must be aware that nonverbal behavior may be quite different in other cultures, and they must respect, learn, and understand the nonverbal nuances of others.

Listed below is information about nonverbal communication common in China, Japan, and Korea. Figure 5-5 lists a number of Asian cultural values.

China
- Generally speaking, China is not a touch-oriented society. Public displays of affection are rare.

ASIAN CULTURAL VALUES

- Respect for elders
- Unquestioning respect for authority
- Loyalty to family
- Concept of shame—one must not bring dishonor or disgrace to family or self
- Control of emotions, self-discipline and self-control
- Education
- Group consensus
- Interdependence
- Perseverance, conformity, loyalty, hard work, and frugality
- Group consensus
- Humbleness

FIGURE 5~5 Asian Cultural Values

- Personal space is much less in China. The Chinese will stand much closer than Westerners.
- Pushing and shoving in stores or when groups board public buses or trains is common. Apologies are neither offered nor expected.
- Silence is perfectly acceptable and customary. Silence is a sign of politeness and of contemplation.
- When walking in public places, direct eye contact is uncommon.

Japan
- Japan is not a touch-oriented society. Public displays of affection are rarely seen.
- Bowing is the traditional greeting.
- No hugging and kissing takes place when greeting someone.
- The Japanese consider it rude to stare. Prolonged direct eye contact is impolite or even intimidating.
- The Japanese consider it insulting to point to someone.
- Smiling in Japan can cover a gamut of emotions—happiness, anger, confusion, regret, or sadness.
- Displaying an open mouth (such as yawning or a wide-open laugh) is considered rude.
- The Japanese like to avoid saying *no*.
- Waving the hand back and forth in front of one's own face means *I do not know* or *I do not understand*.

Korea
- No hugging and kissing takes place when greeting people.
- Public displays of affection are very rare.
- Respect is shown to elderly people.
- Laughter shows many emotions—anger, frustration, and fear.
- Correct posture is important, especially when seated. Koreans do not slouch or put their feet on desks or chairs.
- Entering a room without knocking first is impolite.

- Blowing your nose in public is rude.
- When entering a private home, it is usually customary to remove your shoes.[3]

The Workplace—An Effective Communication Community

The workplace, whether an established location and building or a virtual one in which individuals connect through technology, is a **community**. The workplace is composed of a group of people with certain common interests. Effective communication, both verbal and nonverbal, allows common community interests to flourish. Ineffective verbal and nonverbal communication contributes to the impediment of common community interests.

Throughout this chapter, you examined ways to make your verbal and nonverbal communication more effective. Learning about and practicing effective verbal and nonverbal techniques must continue. Communication is a growth process. As new situations confront you, pay attention to what is and is not being communicated. Consider the people with whom you are communicating. Learn as much as you can about their background and experiences. Attempt to view the world from their point of reference. After a particularly difficult communication situation, evaluate what happened. Determine what went right and what went wrong. For future communication, consider how you might correct what went wrong. Make it your goal to be an effective verbal and nonverbal communicator. ■

[3]Gary Imai, "Gestures: Body Language and Nonverbal Communication," accessed July 12, 2002; available from **www.csupomona.edu**.

The workplace is a community of people with common interests.

© GETTY IMAGES/EYEWIRE

SUMMARY

To reinforce what you have learned in this chapter, study this summary.

- Developing verbal and nonverbal communication skills is an ongoing process. You can always learn more about effective communication with others.

- When listening and understanding, engage in these behaviors—listen actively, understand the relationship between self-esteem and communication, examine your inference ladder, cope with criticism, be nonjudgmental, and willingly accept change.

- Using language appropriately and resolving conflicts enhances effective speech and understanding.

- Conflict resolution involves separating the people from the problems, defining the conflict, collaborating, and not blaming.

- Nonverbal communication can be just as important as verbal communication.

- People use a variety of nonverbal communication methods, including body language, voice quality, time, and space.

- Body language includes gestures made with the eyes, face, hands, arms, and legs, and with posture.

- Body language differs from country to country. North Americans can never assume that the body language of people from another country can be interpreted in the same way as North Americans interpret body language.

- The workplace, whether an established location and building or a virtual one in which individuals connect through technology, is a community in that it is a group of people with common interests. Through effective communication, both verbal and nonverbal, the common community interests are furthered. Often common community interests are ignored due to ineffective verbal and nonverbal communication.

FIND THE PROBLEM

Chan Ying is visiting People Pharmaceuticals from the Gungzhou, China, facility. This is his first visit to Dallas, Texas. You have been asked to pick him up at the airport and bring him to the Dallas office.

You prepare a large sign with his name, Chan Ying, printed in black letters. He does speak English; you do not speak Chinese. When he arrives, you greet him with a low bow and say, "I am happy to meet you Mr. Ying." You hand him your business card, which has your name printed in English. You insist on helping to carry his luggage, although he tells you he can handle it himself. As you drive to the Dallas office, you indicate several historical sites, using your finger to point to the location. Since he has been to the United States previously, you engage him in a conversation about what he likes about the country. You keep up a dialogue throughout your trip. When you get back to the office, you introduce him to Sandra Portales as Mr. Ying. She acknowledges the introduction by shaking his hand and saying, "I am very pleased to meet you, Mr. Chan."

What problems are evident in your communication?

PROFESSIONAL POINTERS

Practice these tips when communicating with others.

- Respect cultures and traditions that are different than your own.
- Avoid stereotyping or generalizing.
- Assume that people can always be trusted until proven otherwise.
- Always seek to understand others and their behaviors.
- Encourage cooperation rather than competition.
- Be willing to compromise.
- Listen to an associate's point of view without interrupting.
- Respond calmly to a loud or angry voice. An angry response only generates anger.
- If you disagree with someone's ideas, deal with the disagreement calmly and rationally—not angrily and emotionally.

REINFORCEMENT ITEMS

1. Define verbal communication and explain why verbal communication is not simple.
2. List six techniques that help you to listen and understand more effectively.
3. Explain four techniques for resolving conflicts.
4. List and explain four nonverbal communicators.
5. Explain what is meant by the statement "The workplace, whether that workplace is an established location and building or a virtual one in which individuals connect through technology, is a community." What relevance does this statement have for communication?

CRITICAL-THINKING ACTIVITY

As a part-time administrative assistant reporting to Kurt Rupprecht, you have been given an excellent opportunity to be part of a workplace team. Kurt will chair the team; he has told you that your role will be more of an observer than a participant. However, he has also told you to feel free to make occasional suggestions. The team is composed of seven administrative professionals (with you being the eighth one); its task is to establish a mentoring program for new administrative professionals joining People Pharmaceuticals. At the first meeting, Kurt delivers the charge to the group—establish a mentoring program for new administrative professionals at People Pharmaceuticals. The mentoring program is to be ready for implementation in six months; the total cost of the mentoring program per new employee is not to exceed $10,000. Kurt asks the group to come to the next meeting with suggestions as to what should be included in the mentoring program and how it should be implemented.

At the second meeting, a major conflict arises. Three individuals in the group suggest that the administrative professionals within People Pharmaceuticals be used as trainers for the new professionals. Two members of the group strongly disagree with this suggestion, stating that the administrative professionals in the company have a biased view and that outside consultants should do the training. Two administrative professionals try to act as mediators in the dispute but have no success. At one point, two people begin screaming at each other, making the following statements:

- You are totally out of touch with reality. Our internal people do not have the skills to conduct the training. Why in the world would you make such a stupid suggestion?

- You are so wrong, but I should have known you would conduct yourself this way. When I discovered you were going to be on the team, I should have declined the invitation to be a part of it. You are always "off the wall" in your suggestions. Do you ever think about what you are going to say before you say it? Your mouth always seems to overload your brain.

Kurt suggests to the group that the meeting be adjourned, stating that tempers need to cool. He asks the team members to come to the next meeting prepared to discuss what happened and how the conflict can be resolved.

After the meeting, Kurt asks you to share with him your impressions of what happened. What do you say to Kurt? What should Kurt do as team leader to help resolve the conflict?

VOCABULARY REVIEW

Complete the Vocabulary Review for Chapter 5 given on page 49 of the *Applications Workbook*.

ENGLISH AND WORD USAGE DRILL

Complete the English and Word Usage Drill for Chapter 5 listed on page 50 of the *Applications Workbook*.

WORKPLACE APPLICATIONS

A5-1 (Goals 1 and 3)

Work in teams of three. Watch two TV variety talk shows (such as *The Oprah Winfrey Show*, *Late Night with David Letterman*, *The Tonight Show with Jay Leno*, or *Larry King Live*) and two news shows in a talk format (such as *Meet the Press* or *Face the Nation*). Answer the following questions about each show your group chooses.

- Is the host an effective verbal communicator? Explain. What elements of effective verbal communication does the host demonstrate?

- How does the host deal with conflict on the show? Explain. Does the host attempt to help resolve conflict? If so, how?

- What nonverbal communication does the host use?

- What nonverbal communication do the guests use?

Present your findings in a written report to your instructor. Identify the shows that you watched, including the names of the hosts and guests.

A5-2 (Goal 2)

Print two copies of the Listening Assessment provided on the Student CD, SCDA5-2. Rate your listening skills and score yourself. Give one copy of the Listening Assessment to a trusted friend or family member. Ask that person to rate you. Compare the ratings and discuss them with the friend or family member.

A5-3 (Goals 2 and 4)

For one week, pay careful attention to your verbal and nonverbal communication. Using the form provided in the *Applications Workbook* on pages 51–54, record the verbal and nonverbal techniques you used and your effectiveness in using them. Evaluate how you could be more effective in the future. If possible, discuss your communication effectiveness with a trusted family member or friend. Ask that person to offer suggestions for improvement. Using the worksheet that you completed, write a memorandum to your instructor, listing the verbal and nonverbal techniques that you used, along with suggestions for improvement. A memorandum form is available on the Student CD, SCDA5-3. Use these headings in your memorandum:

- Verbal communication techniques
- Nonverbal communication techniques
- Improvement of verbal communication
- Improvement of nonverbal communication

A5-4 (Goal 3)

Two locations of People Pharmaceuticals are in France and Japan. Using at least three sources on the Web, research the verbal and nonverbal communication techniques used in these countries. Give an oral report of your findings to the class. Cite the Websites that you used.

A5-5 (Goals 1–4)

Refer to the case study on the Student CD, SCDA5-5a. Read the case and respond to the questions. Write a summary of your responses using the memorandum form on the Student CD, SCDA5-5b. Submit the memorandum to your instructor.

ASSESSMENT OF CHAPTER GOALS

Did you successfully complete the chapter goals? Evaluate yourself by filling out the form on page 55 of the *Applications Workbook*.

chapter 6

Written Communications

1. Demonstrate organizational skills when composing written communication.
2. Apply characteristics of effective correspondence.
3. Apply appropriate planning and writing guidelines.
4. Engage in collaborative writing and research.

Written communications can spell success or failure for a writer and the organization. Consider for a moment the correspondence you receive from organizations. Have these letters ever contained incorrect information? Have any letters ever made you angry? Have you, after reading a letter, decided that you will never do business with the company again?

Have you ever received letters that began with sentences similar to the following?

- Would you like to vacation almost anywhere in the world?
- Would you like to stay in a premier international hotel at a very low cost?

If so, did you continue to read the letter or did you throw it away, realizing it was a sales pitch requiring money from you?

Have you ever received an email from an individual inviting you to a meeting, with the following information missing from the message?

- Purpose of meeting
- Location of meeting
- Time meeting begins
- Projected ending time

Have you picked up an organizational report and read only the first two pages because it was too technical or too poorly organized?

No doubt you answered yes to several of these questions. There is no surer way to make someone upset than to send that person correspondence that is poorly composed, does not contain all necessary information, demeans the reader through its tone, or is so poorly organized that the reader does not understand its purpose.

As an administrative professional, your job often demands that you compose correspondence. When you begin working for an organization, you may compose draft copies of correspondence. As you learn your position and the needs of the organization, you may send out correspondence under your own signature or write final copy for your employer to sign. Being a competent and careful writer is important to your success. This chapter will help you develop techniques for writing effectively.

Written Messages

The administrative professional produces four basic types of written messages—email, memorandums, letters, and reports.

Email

Email is used extensively in the workplace today due to its ease, speed, and relative low cost. Throughout the world, organizations send billions of email messages, and the number is increasing at roughly 138 percent per year. Within a few short years, organizations will use billions of email boxes.[1] In

---

[1]"Email mailboxes to increase 1.2 billion worldwide by 2005," accessed July 27, 2002; available from **www.cnn.com/2001/TECH/internet/09/19/email.usage.idg/**.

Numerous types of written correspondence are generated in the workplace.

© GETTY IMAGES/EYEWIRE

addition to writing email messages in their work lives, many people use email as a source of contact with family and friends. The number of person-to-person emails sent on an average day will probably exceed 36 billion worldwide in a few years.[2] This chapter will help you learn to use an excellent communication tool without abusing it.

Memorandums

Although email is the tool of choice for internal correspondence in most organizations, memorandums continue to have a place in the work world. For example, a memorandum is more appropriate in these situations:

- When the correspondence is relatively lengthy (longer than one-half page)
- When a signed document is needed

As an administrative professional, you may write a number of memorandums. You must pay careful attention to writing a clear, effective memorandum—one in which the reader receives all the necessary information. For example, if you are writing a memorandum to invite coworkers to a meeting, you must let them know the purpose of the meeting, the date and time of the meeting, how long the meeting is expected to last, who will be attending, what participants are expected to do to prepare for the meeting, what participants should bring to the meeting, and so on. Other elements of effective memorandums appear later in this chapter.

Letters

Although organizations communicate extensively with their customers, clients, and employees via telephones, memorandums, and emails, letters remain an important part of organizational communication. Letters are more formal and are the preferred method of communication when writing to current and prospective clients and customers. Letters provide formal documentation that you and

---

[2]Ibid.

your client or customer may want for future reference. This chapter provides the opportunity to improve your letter-writing skills.

Reports

In addition to email, memorandums, and letters, numerous reports are prepared in the workplace. These reports may be informal ones of two or three pages, or they may be formal reports containing a table of contents, body (with footnotes or endnotes), appendices, and references.

Organizational Skills

If you are to be successful in writing, you must develop your organizational skills. A large part of writing effectively is determining the readers' needs, gathering the appropriate information, drafting, editing, and preparing the final product. Additionally, you must be able to organize your time so you can produce the correspondence in a timely manner.

Determine the Goal or Purpose

Many times people start the writing process before they understand clearly what their purpose or goal is. As you begin, ask yourself these questions:

- What is my purpose in writing?
- What do I hope to accomplish?

Before you begin writing the first draft of the correspondence, write a purpose statement. This statement should be short—only a sentence or two. It should state clearly and concisely what you intend to accomplish with the correspondence. If writing the purpose statement is difficult for you, begin by merely putting down what you want to accomplish. For example, you might write these rather rambling thoughts when presented with the task of writing a letter to a colleague.

I must write a letter to Rhea Melrose in our Baton Rouge, Louisiana, office, inviting her to speak to administrative professionals in the Dallas office. We want her to speak sometime in January on a topic that is interesting to administrative professionals. Our group is interested in several areas, including conflict resolution, anger management, and time management. No one knows her, but we have heard she is a good speaker. We have also heard she speaks frequently on anger management and conflict resolution. We do not know if she speaks on time management.

Those thoughts result in this purpose statement:

The purpose of this letter is to persuade Rhea Melrose to speak to administrative professionals in the Dallas office on conflict resolution.

However, before writing the letter, you must be clear about the exact date or suggest two or three possible dates for the presentation. You also need to give Rhea information about who will attend the session.

Analyze the Reader/Audience

An important consideration in the writing process is determining the reader(s). The strongest communications focus on the readers and their needs. You can understand this more clearly if you think about your own personal communications. Do you write the same type of letter to your 80-year-old grandmother as you do to your 10-year-old son? The answer, of course, is no. These two people are quite different in what they need and understand.

Here are some basic questions to ask yourself about the reader/audience.

- What are the values and beliefs of the reader/audience?
- How does the reader typically communicate—with facts or with feelings?
- How old is the reader?
- What is the reader's level of education?
- What attitudes does the reader have? Will the reader be receptive or resistant to the message?
- Does the reader come from a different background? If so, what is that background?

- Is the reader local or international?
- What will the reader do with the document? Will the reader read only a portion of it? Study it carefully? Skim it?
- How much does the reader know about the topic?
- Will the reader resist the message? Will the reader have concerns about the message?
- What will the reader expect from the communication?

Professional Audience

If you are writing to a professional audience (engineers, physicists, lawyers, and so on), you can use technical vocabulary common in the particular field without defining the terms. Additionally, you can deal with the subject immediately, without spending time explaining the background of the material.

General Audience

If you are writing to a general audience, you need to use simple vocabulary and explain any concepts that may be confusing. Additionally, if a concept is complex, you may want to use examples. You should concentrate on what your communication will mean

to the readers and what you expect the readers to do with the information.

International Audience

You learned in the previous chapter that words do not have the same meaning for all audiences. This statement is particularly true for international audiences. Consider these examples of business bloopers.

- In Belgium, General Motors™ used a tag line *Body by Fisher*™. When translated into Flemish, it said *Corpse by Fisher*.
- An American maker of T-shirts in Miami printed shirts for the Spanish market promoting the Pope's visit. Instead of the desired *I saw the Pope*, the shirts proclaimed in Spanish, *I saw the potato*.
- Gerber™ introduced its line of baby food in African markets using the same packaging graphics as were used in the United States (a picture of a baby on the container). Gerber soon learned that African companies routinely put pictures on the label of what is actually inside the container.

When writing for an international audience, make certain that words do not offend or translate into incorrect meanings. Figure 6-1 lists a number of general principles to keep in mind when writing for international audiences.

Gather the Appropriate Information

Once you know the purpose or goal you are trying to achieve with your correspondence, gather the information necessary to begin writing. In gathering the information, you may do the following:

- Peruse the organization's files on the subject if such files exist.
- Talk with you employer (if he or she has any background information).
- Research the topic through the Internet, periodicals, or books.

Organize the Content

Did you ever read a piece of correspondence and, once you finished, realize you did not

© GETTY IMAGES/PHOTODISC

Ask basic questions about your intended audience before you begin writing.

GENERAL PRINCIPLES FOR INTERNATIONAL CORRESPONDENCE

- Use the title of the individual with whom you are corresponding. Do not use first names.
- Use relatively formal language. In the United States, people pride themselves on informality, but people from most other countries do not. Informality often means disrespect.
- Be certain that you understand the order of first and last names. In many Asian countries, the last name appears first.
- Do not use expressions unique to the United States. Do not refer to events that are common only to the United States.
- Use the dictionary meanings of words; do not use slang.
- Be courteous; use thank you and please often.
- Be complimentary when appropriate but do not be excessive in your comments. Such outpourings may be seen as insincere.
- Avoid asking questions that can be answered with yes or no. For a number of other countries, these two words do not have the same meaning as they do in the United States.
- Ask questions tactfully.
- Do not use humor; it may be misunderstood.
- Respect all customs of the country (social, religious, and so on).
- Learn all you can about particular countries; read extensively.
- Translate correspondence into the native language of the country.
- Send business cards that are printed in the native language of the country.

FIGURE 6~1 General Principles for International Correspondence

---

understand what the writer was trying to convey. Why? There could be a number of reasons.

- The writer was verbose.
- The writer failed to clarify the message; the purpose was not discernible.
- The content jumped from one topic to another with no apparent pattern.

Brainstorm (a sudden clever idea; a group problem-solving technique) by yourself or with others if the project is a collaborative one. Brainstorming is a good way to begin to organize content. Write down everything that comes to mind. Then group your ideas. Determine what ideas are related and, thus, should be in the same paragraph. You might label the ideas as Idea 1, Idea 2, Idea 3, and so on. At this point, the ideas do not need to be in order of presentation. Your purpose is to get all similar ideas in the same paragraph. The next step is to determine which idea goes first, which goes second, and so on. For ex-

ample, Idea 3 might be the first paragraph; Idea 1, the second; and Idea 2, the third.

Do not bury the purpose of the document in the middle of the correspondence. The basic organizational structure uses a three-pronged approach. The first part of the document conveys the purpose of the correspondence. The second part supports, informs, and/or convinces the reader. The last part states the desired results, the action, or a summary of the findings.

Draft the Correspondence

Your goal when drafting correspondence is to write down everything you want to say in rough-draft form. Do not spend time agonizing over each word and mark of punctuation. Get your ideas down.

Edit

Your next step is to edit the correspondence. Now that you have completed the draft document, you need to pay careful attention that the document is grammatically correct, the language is clear, the sentence structure is appropriate, the readability level matches the audience, and so on. During the editing process, you are precise—you address the writing mechanics.

Ensure Effective Paragraphs

Effective paragraphs possess unity, coherence, and parallel structure.

- Unity. A paragraph has unity when its sentences clarify or support the main idea. The sentence that contains the main idea of a paragraph is the **topic sentence**. For example, in this paragraph, the topic sentence is at the beginning. However, it may also be at the end of the paragraph. The point to remember is that the topic sentence helps the writer stay focused on the main idea of the paragraph.

- Coherence. A paragraph has coherence when its sentences relate to each other in content, grammatical construction, and choice of words. One method of achieving coherence is to repeat key words in a paragraph or to use certain words for emphasis.

Edit your document for correct grammar, clearness, appropriate sentence structure, and readability level.

© GETTY IMAGES/PHOTODISC

Consider the following use of repetitive words.

The anthropologist described life in a squalid district of New York by telling how much people know about each other—<u>who</u> is to be trusted and <u>who</u> not, <u>who</u> is defiant of the law and <u>who</u> upholds it, <u>who</u> is competent and well informed, and <u>who</u> is inept and ignorant.

- Parallel. Parallel structure also helps you achieve coherence. When grammatically equivalent forms are used, **parallelism** exists. Consider the following illustration of nonparallel and parallel constructions.

  Nonparallel: The position is prestigious, challenging, and *also the money is not bad.*

  Parallel: The position offers prestige, challenge, and money.

Use Appropriate Sentence Structure

Sentences should be simple but varied. Use a combination of sentence structures to keep your reader's attention. There is no formula for determining sentence length, but shorter sentences help keep the reader's attention. Generally, short sentences are also easier to understand. Consider this sentence.

January reports indicate that sales in the pharmaceutical market increased by more than 40 percent, which serves to support the proposed plan presented at last week's board meeting for 20 additional positions.

Did you get lost? The sentence has 32 words. A reader generally loses attention when a sentence is more than 20 words in length. You do not need to count the words in each sentence or limit sentences needlessly. However, you should be aware that readability is generally increased when sentences are short.

Eliminate Passive Voice

Passive voice is present when the subject of the sentence receives the action or is acted upon. It has three characteristics:

- A form of the verb *to be* (*is, am, are, was, were, be, been, being*)
- A past participle (a verb ending in *ed* or *en*)
- A prepositional phrase beginning with *by*

Notice these examples of passive voice.

- The document was written by Mylien.
- The results of the meeting will be sent to you on Monday.

In contrast, **active voice** is present when the subject performs the action. Read the sentences rewritten in active voice.

- Mylien wrote the document.
- You will receive the results of the meeting on Monday.

Do you see the difference? The active voice is clearer and stronger than the passive voice. Is use of the passive voice wrong? No, it does have its uses. For example, the person performing the action may not be known. Additionally, sometimes the writer uses passive voice to obscure who was responsible for the action. For example, in the sentence below, the reader does not know who made the decision.

The decision was made to downsize the organization by 20 percent.

The writer intended to be ambiguous about the decision; the writer did not want the reader to know who made the decision. Although the writer can use passive voice intentionally, if it is overused, it can result in wordy, dull writing. Use passive voice when necessary, but do not overuse it.

Determine Readability Level

Readability is defined as the degree of difficulty of the message. These items contribute to greater reading difficulty:

- Long sentences
- Words with several syllables
- Technical terms

Readability formulas, such as the Gunning Fog Index and the Flesch-Kincaid Index, provide **readability indices**. The higher the readability index, the less readable the message. As a rule, the writer should achieve a readability index of between seventh- and eleventh-grade levels for the average business reader. However, there are exceptions. If you are writing a highly technical report for an expert audience, you may write at the fourteenth or higher grade level. Writers must understand the background and educational level of their audience.

You can check the readability level of your document by activating the software writing aid on your computer. You also can obtain word counts, average words per sentence, sentences per paragraph, characters per word, and passive sentences from this software. Figure 6-2 provides readability statistics.

Prepare the Final Correspondence

Your next step is to prepare the final correspondence. In doing so, you should do the following:

- Check to be certain that the format is appropriate. For example, if it is a letter, did you use an acceptable letter style? If it is a report, is your document formatted correctly? Have you sized your headings appropriately? Have you used boldface and italics to emphasize important points and

Readability Statistics	
Counts	
Words	786
Characters	4251
Paragraphs	106
Sentences	41
Averages	
Sentences per Paragraph	1.4
Words per Sentence	10.3
Characters per Word	4.7
Readability	
Passive Sentences	9%
Flesch Reading Ease	67.2
Flesch-Kincaid Grade Level	8.2
	OK

FIGURE 6~2 Readability Statistics

headings? Do the type sizes and font styles provide for easy readability?

- Run the grammar and spelling package on your computer to help you locate errors.
- Proofread the document on the screen before you print it. Figure 6-3 lists several proofreading tips.
- Print a copy and proofread again.

Evaluate—Process and Time Usage

When you are new at the writing process, take some time at the end of each project to analyze how you spent your time. Were you able to produce the document in a reasonable amount of time? Did you use good organizational skills? Were you able to gather the appropriate information in a

reasonable time period? Did you effectively organize the content before beginning to write? Did you use software aids to assist you in editing your writing? What are your writing weaknesses? How can you correct these weaknesses?

Characteristics of Effective Correspondence

Certain characteristics of effective correspondence are common to letters, emails, memorandums, and reports. As you write, you must pay careful attention to each of the elements given here.

PROOFREADING TIPS

- Proofread your document on the screen before you print it. Scroll to the beginning of the document, and use the top of the screen as a guide for your eyes in reading each line.
- Proofread a document in three steps:
    - General appearance and format
    - Spelling and keyboarding errors
    - Punctuation, word usage, and content
- Read from right to left for spelling and keyboarding errors.
- Use a spell checker.
- If possible, do not proofread a document right after keying it; let the document sit while you perform another task.
- Pay attention to dates. Do not assume they are correct. For example, check to determine that Thursday, November 15, is actually a Thursday. Check the spelling of months; check the correctness of the year.
- Do not overlook proofreading the date, subject, enclosure notation, and names and addresses of the recipients.
- Use the thesaurus if you are not certain a word is appropriate.
- Watch closely for omissions of -ed, -ing, or -s at the ends of words.
- If punctuation causes you problems, check a grammatical source after you have completed all other proofreading.
- Be consistent in the use of commas.
- Be consistent in the use of capital letters.
- Check numerals.
- Be consistent in format.
- Keep a current reference manual at your desk to look up grammar or punctuation rules you question.

FIGURE 6-3 Proofreading Tips

Complete

Correspondence is complete when it gives the reader all the information he or she needs to accomplish the results the writer intended. To help you achieve completeness, ask the *W questions*:

- *Why* is the correspondence being written?
- *What* is the goal of the correspondence? What do I hope to accomplish?
- *What* information is needed before writing the correspondence?
- *Who* needs to receive the correspondence?
- *What* information needs to be included in the correspondence?

Refer to Figure 6-4 for examples of ineffective writing when *W* questions were not asked and corresponding examples of effective writing when *W* questions were asked.

Clear

After reading a message, the reader should be able to determine (without a doubt) the purpose of the correspondence. Clear messages reflect clear thinking. Writing clearly requires good organization and simple expression.

Each sentence should have one thought; each paragraph, one purpose. Business correspondence is not the place to impress a person with your vocabulary. Your aim is to get your purpose across in a simple, concise manner. If a short, easily understood word is available, use it. Your words should *express* rather than *impress*.

Accurate

Get the facts before you start to write. Check your information carefully. If you are quoting prices, be certain you have the correct price list. If you are presenting dates, confirm them.

When you are writing, keep your biases out of the correspondence as much as possible. Your task is to write objectively. Do not slant the information or overstate its significance. Deal with the facts—simply and accurately.

Prompt

A conscientious business correspondent is prompt. Prompt answers to messages say to readers that the writer or organization cares

---

ASKING THE *W* QUESTIONS

Notice the following examples of ineffective writing when the *W* questions were not asked and the corresponding examples of effective writing when the *W* questions were asked.

Ineffective	Effective
Your recent order will be mailed soon. (WHEN?)	Your order of November 15 will be mailed on November 21.
The seminar will be on November 3. (WHERE and WHAT kind of conference?)	The letter-writing seminar will be held in the Green Room at 2 p.m., November 3.
The planning meeting was canceled. (WHAT planning meeting and WHY was it canceled?)	The planning meeting scheduled for November 3 at 2 p.m. has been canceled due to a conflict with the letter-writing seminar scheduled at the same time. The planning meeting has been rescheduled for November 15 at 2 p.m. in the Executive Conference Room.

FIGURE 6~4 Asking the *W* Questions

about them. Conversely, late messages often give the following impressions:

- The writer or organization is indifferent to the needs of the readers.
- The writer is grossly inefficient.

The result in either instance is a negative message. The basic promptness rule is this:

- Reply to email on the same day of receipt.
- Reply to memorandums within one day.
- Reply to letters within three to five days.
- Respond to reports within the timeline established by the cover letter or memorandum.

Concise

Conciseness in writing means expressing the necessary information in as few words as possible. Say what you need to say without cluttering your communication with irrelevant information or needless words. As a checklist for conciseness, ask yourself these questions.

- Are my sentences short?
- Are my paragraphs short?
- Have I used simple, easy-to-understand words?
- Have I used bullets or numbered lists whenever possible?
- Have I avoided unnecessary repetition?
- Have I eliminated excessive information?
- Have I avoided clichés?

Figure 6-5 lists several clichés to avoid.

Courteous

Courteousness in correspondence means using good human relations skills as you write. Treat the reader with respect. Demonstrate that you care about the reader as you write. Keep in mind that writing is similar to talking. When talking with people face-to-face, courtesy and consideration are necessary in order to develop and maintain goodwill. The same or perhaps even greater concern must be evident in written correspondence since only the written word conveys the message; a smile or a friendly gesture cannot be observed.

AVOID CLICHÉS

You have probably read such phrases as *according to our records, at your earliest convenience,* and *under separate cover.* These phrases are clichés; they are overused. Notice the following clichés and the improved wording.

Cliché	According to our files…
Improved	Our files indicate…
Cliché	At the present time…
Improved	Now…
Cliché	In view of the fact that…
Improved	Now…
Cliché	May I take the liberty…
Improved	Omit the phrase and make your statement.
Cliché	Your kind letter…
Improved	Omit kind—people, not correspondence, are kind.
Cliché	May I request a copy.
Improved	Please send me a copy.

FIGURE 6–5 Avoid Clichés

Do not show your anger in a communication. You may be extremely unhappy about a situation, but showing your anger merely compounds the problem. Angry words make angry readers. Both parties may end up yelling at each other through the written word, accomplishing little. Remember, anger and courtesy are not logical partners.

Courtesy also means being considerate. If a person is asking you something, respond. If you are unable to give a positive response, explain why. Explanations let others know you are sincere.

Positive

People hear the word *yes* easier than the word *no.* Certainly, you will not always be able to say yes to someone or something. However, if

Angry words make angry readers.

you use a positive tone when saying no, the reader will respond in a more favorable manner. You set a positive tone by the words you choose and the way you use them. Some words and phrases possess positive qualities, whereas others possess negative qualities. Consider the following negative expressions and their positive equivalents.

Negative
Sorry
Whenever possible
Displeasure
Unsatisfactory
You failed to let us know.
You neglected to send your check.
I hate to inform you that your order has not
    been shipped.
The difficulties are . . .
Do not throw trash on the grounds.

Positive
Glad
Immediately
Pleasure
Satisfactory
Please let us know.
Please send your check.
Your order will be shipped on October 11.
To help you avoid further problems . . .
Please put your trash in the receptacles.

Planning and Writing Guidelines

You must adhere to a number of guidelines when writing email, memorandums, letters, and reports. These guidelines include determining the appropriate format, establishing the basic purpose, conducting research (if necessary), and observing appropriate ethics and etiquette.

Email

Due to its speed and ease of use, email is a major form of communication for organizations and individuals today. Workers spend hours at their place of employment sending and receiving emails. Additionally, people may spend a considerable amount of time at home sending emails to family and friends. In fact, people are so obsessed with email reaching the recipient quickly that they now use an iteration of email called **IM** (instant messaging). If a person's computer is turned on, a message flashes on the screen telling the person that he or she has an IM. In other words, IM lets people know immediately that an email is waiting for them; they do not have to check the email screen to determine whether they have received messages.

Since email is such an important communication tool, you must adhere to certain guidelines, etiquette, and ethics as you use it.

Guidelines

The basic characteristics of effective correspondence presented earlier in this chapter are applicable to email as well:

- Completeness
- Clarity
- Accurateness
- Promptness
- Conciseness
- Courteousness
- Positivism

Several general guidelines, as well as guidelines for etiquette and ethics, apply to email specifically.

- Be appropriately formal when writing email. The rule of thumb is to be almost as formal as you are in standard memorandums. Notice the two messages here. One message is too informal, while the other message is appropriately formal.

  Too Informal

  Ramon, we need to have a meeting soon—can you arrange? I'm free next mon. thks. Tony

  Appropriate

  Ramon,

  We need to meet soon to discuss our division's projected budget for the next six months. Are you available on Tuesday, December 15, from 9 a.m. until 11 a.m.? If so, let me know by this afternoon. We can meet in my office.

  Tony

- Avoid using **emoticons** (faces produced by the Internet counterculture in answer to email being devoid of body language). Here are a few emoticons.

<G>	I'm grinning as I write this sentence.
<LOL>	I'm laughing out loud.
☺	Denotes a smile
;-)	Denotes a wink
:")	Embarrassed
:-!	Foot in mouth
X-(	Mad

- Use the subject line provided on the email form. This line should be concise yet give enough information so the receiver knows the purpose of the message at a glance.
- Think through the purpose of your email before you begin writing.
- Organize the message. Email should not be longer than one screen. If you are writing a memo longer than one screen, send a traditional hard-copy memorandum. People become frustrated when they must scroll from screen to screen and then scroll back to reread something.
- Edit and proofread carefully. Check your spelling. Do not send an email that contains inaccuracies or incorrect grammar. Most email programs allow for checking spelling and grammar. Set the preferences so spelling and grammar are checked.
- Use complete sentences.
- Capitalize and punctuate properly.
- Do not run sentences together.
- Insert a blank line after each paragraph.
- Include your name and title (if appropriate) when replying to an email. Often you can add a signature in your preferences, which will automatically include this information at the end of every email you send.
- Assume that any message you send is permanent.
- Do not double-space your entire message; it takes up too much space and makes the message more difficult to read.
- Be wary of humor or sarcasm. Electronic communication is devoid of body language; thus, the slightest hint of sarcasm could be badly misinterpreted.
- Avoid using all uppercase or all lowercase letters.

Figure 6-6 demonstrates an appropriate format for email.

Etiquette

Use appropriate etiquette when sending email.

- Do not use different types of fonts, colors, clip art, and other graphics in email. Such

SIMULATED EMAIL SCREEN WITH APPROPRIATE FORMAT

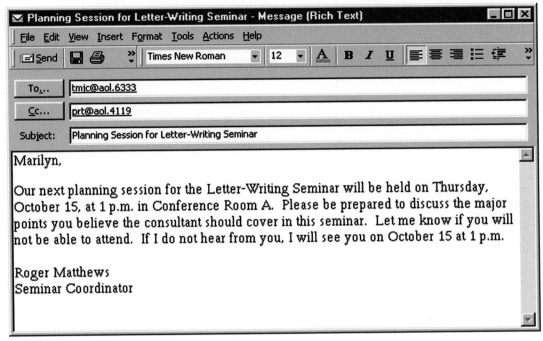

FIGURE 6~6 Email Format

an approach merely clutters your message and takes longer to send and receive, particularly if you include numerous graphics.

- Do not key the message in all uppercase letters. You may emphasize a word or phrase in all capital letters, but use the Caps Lock button sparingly.

- Avoid sending messages when you are angry. Give yourself time to cool down and think about the situation before you send or reply to an email in anger. Take a walk around the office, drink a cup of hot tea to soothe your nerves, or wait 24 hours to respond. In some cases, you may want to make a telephone call or have a personal conversation with the person. You have a more difficult time being angry when you see the person face-to-face or when you hear the person's voice.

- Answer email promptly. The general rule is to read and respond to email once or twice a day (depending on volume).

- Do not send large attached files unless you know the person can receive them. When sending an attachment, ask the receiver to acknowledge receipt.

Ethics

Ethical behavior is important. Ethics in regard to email means you do not misuse the organization's email system.

- Do not send personal email from your office computer.

- When people send you inappropriate email, let them know politely that you cannot receive it. You might say, "I would love to hear from you, but please send any personal email to my home. I cannot receive it at the office."

- Do not use email to berate or reprimand an employee. Do not use email to terminate someone.

- Do not use email to send information that might involve legal action.

- Remember that even if you delete email, it may not actually be deleted. Some organizations make backup tapes of all electronic files. Think carefully before putting something on email.
- Do not respond to unsolicited email.
- Do not forward junk mail or chain letters to a mailing list. This practice is **spamming**, and some organizations have email policies that result in loss of computer privileges for individuals who engage in spamming. Figure 6-7 gives AOL's® policy. Additionally, AOL now allows you to provide them with information about spam by clicking on a button at the bottom of the email screen marked *Report Spam*.
- Do not forward an email unless you know the message is true. For example, you may think you are being helpful forwarding a message about a computer virus. However, when you receive ten email messages concerning misinformation about viruses, you understand the importance of being certain that an email is true before forwarding it.
- Do not include credit card numbers in email messages. It is possible to intercept email in transit; thus, an unscrupulous individual can steal and use someone else's credit card number.

Memorandums

Although email messages have become the preferred vehicle for communicating within the company and short messages sent outside

the company, at times, a memorandum is more appropriate. For example, when the message is longer than one computer screen or a hard copy with a signature is necessary, a memorandum is the better choice.

The characteristics of effective correspondence hold true for memorandums also. Memorandums must be complete, clear, accurate, prompt, concise, courteous, and positive. In style, they are slightly more formal than email, but less formal than letters. The standard memorandum form contains the word *memorandum* and an organizational logo, plus *To, From, Date,* and *Subject* lines. **Pc** (photocopy) or **cc** (courtesy copy) may be in the heading or listed below the body of the memorandum.

General guidelines for writing memorandums include the following:

- Use the first name (or initials) and last name of the individual(s) to whom you are sending the memo.
- Use the job title of the individual if company policy dictates doing so; many organizations do not use titles in memorandums.
- Do not use *Ms.* or *Mr.*
- If you are sending a memorandum to more than one individual, list the names in alphabetical order or by hierarchical order within the company.
- List *pc* or *cc* recipients alphabetically or hierarchically.
- If you are addressing a memo to ten or more people, use a generic classification, such as *Strategic Planning Team*.
- If the memorandum is more than one page, key the additional pages on plain paper. Include an appropriate header on additional pages.

Figure 6-8 presents an appropriate format for a memorandum.

Letters

Letters represent the company to the public—customers, clients, and prospective customers

---

UNSOLICITED BULK EMAIL

America Online, Inc. ("AOL") does not authorize the use of its proprietary computers and computer network (the AOL network) to accept, transmit or distribute unsolicited bulk email sent from the Internet to AOL members.

FIGURE 6~7 AOL's Unsolicited Bulk Email Statement

PEOPLE PHARMACEUTICALS INTERNATIONAL

M E M O R A N D U M

TO: Madelyn Ice
        Liam Nelson
        Rico Osbourne

FROM: Ruth Shank *RS*

DATE: November 15, 2005

SUBJECT: Budget Session

Please be prepared to discuss your budget actuals for the past three months and any changes on your proposed budget (with justification) for the next six months. The budget session will be held in my office on November 23 from 1 to 3 p.m.

cc Darius Hamilton
    Miguel Quinones

FIGURE 6~8 Memorandum Format

and clients. A well-written letter can win friends and customers. Conversely, a poorly written letter can lose customers and make enemies of prospective customers.

Your task as an administrative professional is to assist your employer with writing effective letters. The characteristics of effective correspondence outlined in the sections on email and memorandums hold true for letters as well. Letters must be:

- Complete
- Clear
- Accurate
- Prompt
- Concise
- Courteous
- Positive

Determine the Basic Purpose

Before you begin to write a letter, you must determine the basic purpose for writing. Generally, letters fall into six types:

- Requesting information or seeking a routine action
- Providing information
- Acknowledging information
- Conveying negative information
- Demanding action
- Persuading

The first three types of letters (requesting information, providing information, and acknowledging information) are letters in which the reader's reaction to the message will be favorable or neutral. The next two types of letters (conveying negative information and demanding action) are letters in which the reader's reaction may be unfavorable. Use the **direct approach** in the first three types of letters and the **indirect approach** in the others.

As you write, you want to keep the reader uppermost in your mind and attempt to put yourself in the place of the reader. The approach, called the ***you* approach**, demands **empathy** (identification with and understanding of another's situation, feelings, and motives) on the part of the writer. You must place yourself in the reader's shoes and try to understand the situation from the reader's perspective. If you are trying to sell a product or a service, you must look at the benefits it will offer to the reader. If you are trying to persuade someone to speak at a conference, you must highlight the contributions the proposed speaker can make—his or her unique gifts and skills. When carrying out the *you* approach, adhere to two words of caution: *Be sincere*. Your goal is not to flatter the reader, but to see the situation from the reader's point of view. The *you* approach is important when writing all types of letters; however, it is essential in the persuasive approach, which is discussed on page 139.

Direct Approach. Direct correspondence begins with the reason for the correspondence. If you are making a request or an inquiry, state it. Continue with whatever explanation is necessary so the reader will understand the message. Close the letter with a courteous thank you for action taken or with a request for action by a specific time.

Figure 6-9 is an illustration of a letter requesting information in which the direct approach is used. Notice the format of the letter is block style with open punctuation. If you need additional help in formatting letters, turn to the *Reference Guide* of this textbook on page 508.

Indirect Approach. When writing indirect correspondence, use this format:

- Begin with an opening statement that is pleasant but neutral.
- Review the circumstances and give the negative information.
- Close the correspondence on a pleasant and positive note.

Figure 6-10 is an illustration of a letter using the indirect approach. Notice the format of the letter is modified block style with blocked paragraphs and mixed punctuation.

PEOPLE PHARMACEUTICALS INTERNATIONAL

2405 Main Street
Dallas, TX 75060-9814
214-555-0117

November 20, 2005

Dr. Leonard Montgomery
3418 Melrose Street
Dallas, TX 75201-9702

Dear Dr. Montgomery

Thank you for talking with me last Monday concerning our new cancer drug. At your request, I am enclosing a copy of the research studies.

You will notice that People Pharmaceuticals conducted these studies over a five-year period, using a sample group of 1,500 people. The results were excellent, and we are pleased to offer a drug that has such potential for significantly dropping the cancer mortality rate.

I will call your administrative assistant within the next few days to schedule a follow-up meeting after you have had a chance to review the studies. I look forward to discussing any questions you may have.

Sincerely

Katalina Komanie

Katalina Komanie
Sales Representative

FIGURE 6~9 Letter Using the Direct Approach

PEOPLE PHARMACEUTICALS INTERNATIONAL
2405 Main Street
Dallas, TX 75060-9814
214-555-0117

November 25, 2005

Grace Edwardson
2345 Shady Bend Lane
Dallas, TX 75209-3456

Dear Grace:

Thank you for asking me to speak at your conference in December. I greatly enjoy my association with your group; you truly provide an excellent growth opportunity for managers.

The demands on my time for the next several months are extremely heavy. In addition to a new planning process that I must implement, we have recently employed two new managers who are looking to me for assistance in learning their jobs. As you might expect, I am swamped. I must say no to your request at this time. However, if you need a speaker in the future, please contact me again. I always enjoy talking to your group.

I hope the conference is a huge success. Best wishes in the process.

Sincerely,

Sandra L Portales

Sandra L. Portales
Executive Vice President and
Chief Operating Officer

FIGURE 6~10 Letter Using the Indirect Approach

Persuasive Approach. Use the **persuasive approach** when you want to convince someone to do something or you want to change an indifferent or negative reader's reaction. Your goal is to turn a negative or indifferent attitude into a positive one. When writing a persuasive letter, use the following approach:

- Get the reader's attention quickly; open with the you approach.
- Continue by creating interest and desire.
- Close by asking for the desired action.

Figure 6-11 illustrates the persuasive approach.

Edit, Proofread, and Format

Once you have written a letter, you are responsible for editing and proofreading the document. The grammar and spelling software on your computer can aid you in this job. However, the software will not catch all errors, and certain errors noted by the software may not in fact be errors. Therefore, you must have a good command of grammar and proofread carefully. You also might ask someone else to proofread the document. Remember to follow standard formats when keying a letter.

Reports

The administrative professional's role in preparing reports varies. You may have the responsibility of keying the report, producing the final copies, and distributing the report to the appropriate individuals. Or you may assist with the creation of visuals for the report (charts, graphs, and so on), do research, and draft some or all portions of the report.

Technology has opened up new opportunities for administrative professionals, one possibility being **virtual assistants** (work-at-home professionals who provide numerous business support services, including making appointments, laying out reports, organizing files, and so on). If you are an administrative professional who plans to set up your own business and work independently from a home office, you may find yourself writing a

business plan, a plan that provides the strategic direction for your company's ongoing activities. Such a plan describes what you want to do, how you want to get there, and how you plan to achieve your goals. As a virtual assistant, you also may be responsible for formatting and keying a client's business plan or even assisting the client in writing the plan.

Planning Steps

Whether you are writing a basic report or a business plan, the planning steps should include the following:

- Determine the purpose of the report.
- Analyze the audience who will receive the report.
- Prepare a summary of what should be included in the report.
- Gather information for the report.
- Prepare an outline of the report.
- Draft the report.
- Prepare any necessary graphics, charts, and tables.
- Read and edit the report.
- Prepare the executive summary.
- Print and distribute the report.

A business plan includes these unique elements.

- Strategic directions
- Vision and mission
- Potential investors (if appropriate)
- Target audience
- Opportunities, market strategy, and business strategy
- Proposed organization and operations, management structure, and core competencies
- Financial projections

Most reports involve some type of research. This research may be **primary research**—collecting original data through surveys, observations, or experiments. The research also may be **secondary research**—data or material that other people have discovered and reported via the Internet, books, periodicals, and various other publications. In addition,

PEOPLE PHARMACEUTICALS INTERNATIONAL
2405 Main Street
Dallas, TX 75060-9814
214-555-0117

December 12, 2005

Dr. Consuelo Soto
Soto Management
5121 Valley View
Dallas, TX 75301-7802

Dear Dr. Soto:

Your expertise is needed! Our administrative professionals need your assistance in helping them develop their letter-writing skills. Some of them have several years of writing experience, yet they have not perfected their skills to the level needed. Others are relatively new employees and have had little experience writing letters.

Your work with our employees in the past helped tremendously. They not only learned from your presentation but also enjoyed the experience. We want to offer the workshop during February. Our preferred dates are February 5-6 or February 13-24.

I will call your office next week to talk with you further. I am hopeful that your answer to our request will be an affirmative one. We know you can make a difference in the quality of letters that are sent out by our company. We look forward to working with you.

Sincerely,

Wanda Foster

Wanda Foster
Personnel Manager

FIGURE 6~11 Letter Using the Persuasive Approach

the research may be a combination of both primary and secondary.

Primary Research

If you are conducting primary research, you must decide how you are going to gather the information. You may decide to take these steps:

- Observe situations and individuals.
- Survey or interview groups of individuals.
- Perform an experiment.

Observational research involves collecting data by observing events or actions. Survey research involves collecting data through some type of survey or interview. An interview is usually done in person; however, it may be done over the telephone. Sometimes **focus groups** (people brought together to talk with an interviewer about their opinions of certain events or issues) are used. Acceptable methods of administering surveys include mailing them or giving them in person. For example, you may decide to assemble several people, pass out a survey, and ask them to complete it immediately. Generally, there is a much better **response rate** (the number of people responding to a survey or questionnaire) on surveys administered in person than those done by mail.

Scientific researchers have used experimental research for years; however, business researchers are now using it more and more. Such research may involve selecting two or more sample groups and exposing them to certain treatments. For example, a business may decide to test a marketing strategy before implementing a marketing campaign. Researchers select experimental groups and implement the marketing strategy. Based on the outcome of the research, the business proceeds with the marketing strategy, modifies it, or selects another one.

Secondary Research

Secondary research involves using printed information available from sources such as books, periodicals, and the Web. In the not-too-distant past (1992 or so), research was associated with libraries and librarians helping you find what you needed. You may still go to a brick-and-mortar library to do research. Certainly, these libraries have advantages:

- Libraries carry a huge collection of materials that may offer considerable depth in the subject matter you are interested in researching.
- Libraries have materials that may not be on the Web, including historical, highly specialized, and often quite rare materials.
- Libraries employ librarians to assist you in finding what you need. These people have degrees in Library Science or another equivalent field and can assist you in finding information in their own libraries as well as libraries in other U.S. or world cities.

Visiting Online Libraries. Most libraries have some type of presence on the Web; it may include only their location, hours, and other general information. However, many libraries provide much more information:

- You can search for everything published by a particular author. This type of search is

© GETTY IMAGES/PHOTODISC

Give credit for information you receive from printed sources.

beneficial when you find an article on the Web and want to verify the credentials of the author.

- You can access special collections of the library.
- You can search for documents by subject; libraries offer a more sophisticated subject index than is available on the Web.
- You can verify author names, book titles, publishers, and dates of publication.
- You can borrow books, order photocopies of articles, and make copies from home if the library offers this service.
- You can access a virtual librarian at the **Library of Congress** (U.S. national library that carries more than 17 million books, plus over 100 million other items, such as maps and manuscripts) by using the Web address **www.loc.gov/rr/askalib**.

Clarifying Your Web Search. One of the most difficult parts of searching the Web for information is clarifying your search so you can get information you need. If you do not clarify your search sufficiently, you may find yourself looking at hundreds of articles that do not match what you need. Ask yourself these questions to assist you in clarifying your search:

- Is the Web the best place to look? If you know very little about a topic and believe you are going to need help in narrowing the field to something that fits your needs, you may decide that the library is the best place for you to do your research. There you can get the help of professionals in the field.
- What information do I want? For example, assume you are interested in finding information on ethics. Do you want a history of ethics in the United States? Do you want a history that goes back to early philosophers? Are you interested in business ethics? Are you interested in societal ethics? In other words, you need to narrow your search so you can obtain information that

is helpful for the project in which you are engaged.

- When keying in your search words, enter the most clarifying word first.
- Click *Help* or *Search Tips* on the search engine to learn more about what the search engine can do.

Using Web Search Engines. Although numerous search engines are available, these engines are presently some of the best:

- **www.google.com**
- **www.yahoo.com**
- **www.aol.com**
- **www.askjeeves.com**
- **www.lycos.com**
- **www.msn.com**

Evaluating the Information. Since anyone can place information on the Web, you must determine the credibility of the company or individual hosting the information and the currentness of the data. Ask yourself these questions:

- How do I know if the information is reliable? First, look for current information unless you are interested in the history of a topic. Check the dates given on the Websites. Obsolete information may be worthless to you, even if it does have some historical value.
- What organization or person is hosting the information? Is that person or company credible? If you are looking for company information, the company itself is a good resource. Check the date on the Website. Is it current? If you have information written by a particular individual, try to find out something about that individual. Is the person representing a respected organization? Has the person written in the field previously? What education does the person have? The Website may provide some information about the author. If not, you can do a search of the author's name on the Web or visit the library for credentials on the individual.

Handling Copyrighted Information. Some individuals assume they do not need to credit the source of Web information. This is not true! Just as you must credit the source when quoting information from a textbook or periodical, you also must give credit when you are using a reference you found on the Web. In addition, you cannot print out multiple copies of a copyrighted work on the Web and send it to other people. You can probably print out one copy as long as it is for your own personal, noncommercial use. Some Websites spell out their copyright policies; others do not. Some Websites invite you to distribute freely the information on the site. However, the general rule is to give credit for all information. If no author is listed, which is often the case, list the name of the article or the name of the Website and the date you accessed it. If an author is given, list the author's name first, followed by the title of the article.

"Faces of the New Millennium," accessed May 5, 2002; available from **www.pubweb.acns.nwu .edu**.

Report Parts

An informal report may have only one or two parts—the body and/or an executive summary. Formal reports and business plans contain several parts.

Formal reports usually contain the parts listed below. You can eliminate certain parts, such as the list of tables and illustrations, documentation, bibliography, and appendix, if the report is relatively short and you have done no external research. The following is a list of parts for formal reports:

- Executive Summary
- Title Page
- Table of Contents
- List of Tables and Illustrations
- Body
- Documentation (endnotes/footnotes)
- Bibliography or Reference Section
- Appendix

Executive Summary. The **executive summary** is a one- or two-page summary of the document. It is written for the busy executive who:

- Wishes to preview the report to determine whether he or she wants to read a portion in its entirety.
- Does not need a detailed understanding of all aspects of the report, but does need to know the background, major findings, and recommendations.

The executive summary provides the following information:

- Background—establishes why the report was written; identifies the problem or issues
- Major findings—explains what was discovered
- Recommendations

Title Page. The title page contains the title of the report; the writer's name, title, and department or division; and the date the report is submitted.

Table of Contents. The table of contents lists each major section of the report and the page number of the first page of each section. A table of contents is not required; however, when a report is long, the table of contents helps the reader find particular parts of the report.

List of Tables and Illustrations. If a report contains numerous tables and illustrations, it is appropriate to list each title with the respective page number. This page helps the reader quickly locate and scan the data presented.

Body of Report. You may divide the body into the following major sections:

- Introduction
- Problem statement
- Research methods
- Findings
- Recommendations
- Conclusion

Footnotes/Endnotes/Internal Citations. Place footnotes at the bottom of the page; endnotes, at the conclusion of the document. Internal citations appear within the context of the document.

Bibliography or Reference Section. All references used in a report should be included in a bibliography or reference section. This section includes the complete name of the author(s), the title of the book or periodical, the date of publication, the publishing company, and page numbers.

Appendix. A formal report may contain an appendix that includes supporting information such as tables, statistics, and other pertinent material. Items in an appendix are lettered *Appendix A*, *Appendix B*, and so on. The appendix is the last part of the report.

Business Plans

Although business plans are widely used in the business world, only cursory information on writing them appears in this textbook. If you need to write a business plan, refer to other sources for information about content and format. The parts of a business plan are as follows:

- Title Page
- Table of Contents
- Executive Summary
- Vision and Mission
- Opportunity
- Market Strategy
- Business Strategy
- Organization and Operations
- Management
- Challenges
- Financials
- Appendices and Attachments

Written communications, whether email, memorandums, letters, or reports, should be well-written and follow all elements of good correspondence. If a writer presents a message in an inappropriate format, including numerous grammatical and/or keyboarding errors, the reader's reaction will be negative. Chapter 7 deals with effective report presentation.

Collaborative Writing

Today the workplace uses project teams extensively. These teams gather the appropriate information and write the report. To be an effective member of a writing team, you need to use standard communication skills such as the following:

- Listening actively
- Being nonjudgmental
- Coping with criticism
- Using language appropriately
- Resolving conflict
- Observing body language
- Understanding and accepting cultural differences

You may want to review the suggestions given in Chapter 5 for developing communication skills. In addition to these positive communication skills, your team can produce a better product by following these suggestions.

- Determine the purpose of the writing assignment. What are you to produce? What is the deadline? Are there certain stipulations?
- Determine the audience. Who is to receive the final report? What is their background? How much do they know about the subject matter? In other words, you need to determine at what level you should write the report and how much information you need to give the recipients.
- Select a team leader. The team leader is responsible for the following:
  - Setting the procedures for the team writing meetings
  - Facilitating the meetings
  - Helping the group meet deadlines
  - Solving problems
  - Seeing that the group produces the report in a timely manner

DIGITAL VISION

The team leader must allocate work assignments appropriately if a collaborative product is to be produced in a timely manner.

- Set a work schedule. Decide when and where you are going to meet. Set timelines and stick to them.
- Allocate the work. Define the tasks of each team member. Determine each team member's writing strengths, and use these strengths when assigning tasks.
- Monitor the progress. The group must stay focused and produce the written product by the deadline established.

- Reduce the chance of conflict by:
  - Actively listening to each member of the group.
  - Paying attention to cultural differences that may exist.
  - Acknowledging the worth of the other group members and their points of view. ■

SUMMARY

To reinforce what you have learned in this chapter, study this summary.
- Written communications can spell success or failure for a writer and the organization.
- The administrative professional produces four basic types of written messages—email, memorandums, letters, and reports.

- Email is used extensively in the workplace today due to its ease, speed, and relative low cost.
- When an interoffice communication larger than one-half page needs to be written, a memorandum is the preferred vehicle.
- Letters are the preferred method of communication when writing to current and prospective clients and customers.
- Reports prepared in the workplace may be informal ones of two or three pages, or they may be formal reports containing a table of contents, body, appendices, and references.
- For successful writing, you must develop these organizational skills: Determine the goal or purpose, analyze the reader/audience, gather the appropriate information, organize the content, draft the correspondence, edit, prepare the final correspondence, and evaluate your work.
- The characteristics of effective correspondence include completeness, clarity, accurateness, promptness, conciseness, courteousness, and positivism.
- When writing email, you should use the basic characteristics of effective correspondence in addition to proper formatting, etiquette, and ethics.
- The characteristics of effective correspondence hold true for memorandums. They must be complete, clear, accurate, prompt, concise, courteous, and positive. In style, they are slightly more formal than email, but less formal than letters.
- The six basic types of letters are ones requesting information or seeking a routine action, providing information, acknowledging information, conveying negative information, demanding action, and persuading.
- The *you* approach requires the writer to place the reader at the center of the message.
- Use the direct approach when writing letters requesting information, providing information, and acknowledging information.
- Use the indirect approach when writing letters conveying negative information, demanding action, and persuading.
- The direct approach begins with the reason for the correspondence; the indirect approach begins with a pleasant but neutral statement.
- Use the persuasive approach when attempting to convince someone to do something or change an indifferent or negative reader's reaction.
- The administrative professional may write informal or formal reports. Primary or secondary research is usually required when writing formal reports.
- The parts of a formal report include the executive summary, title page, table of contents, list of tables and illustrations, body, documentation, bibliography, and appendix.
- Collaborative writing has become an important skill for use in team projects.

FIND THE PROBLEM

Kurt Rupprecht, the person to whom you report, asked you to compose a draft memorandum to Maurice P. Templeton, senior vice president and general counsel, asking for his assistance on designing an email ethics policy for People Pharmaceuticals. Sandra Portales will sign the memorandum. Kurt did not give you any other information other than the due date on the memorandum, which is tomorrow. When he gave you the assignment, he said, "You're on your own. Have fun!" You are nervous because you believe he is testing your skills. What should you consider as you begin to draft the memorandum?

PROFESSIONAL POINTERS

Here are some pointers to help you write more effective letters and memos.

- Do not use gender-biased terminology. Avoid such terms since they involve implied or overt stereotyping.

  chairman (use *chairperson*)

  stewardess (use *flight attendant*)

  businessman (use *businessperson*)

  mailman (use *mail carrier*)

- Use plural pronouns when possible to avoid male/female stereotyping.

  Avoid: Each executive has his assigned space.

  Use: All executives have assigned spaces.

REINFORCEMENT ITEMS

1. List and explain the organizational skills necessary in composing written communications.
2. Explain what is meant by effective paragraphs.
3. List and explain the characteristics of effective correspondence.
4. Explain six ethical behaviors you must consider when writing email.
5. List and explain the different types of approaches that may be used in writing letters.

CRITICAL-THINKING ACTIVITY

Janelle VanderWald began her career six years ago as an administrative professional with People Pharmaceuticals. She has an excellent work record and exceptional composition and organizational skills. Two months ago several administrative changes occurred in the company. Some of the managerial positions were eliminated, others were consolidated, and new ones were created. David Khirallah was named senior vice president and chief financial officer. Janelle was promoted, becoming his assistant. Mr. Khirallah is very busy with his new duties; as a result, he doesn't realize how useful Janelle can be to him. Janelle is an efficient assistant, capable of lessening his workload. He composes all of his own correspondence by hand and then gives the documents to Janelle to key. Janelle knows she has the ability to write most of his correspondence. Although Mr. Khirallah is nice, he is very reserved. His conversations with Janelle have been limited. Janelle does not think he dislikes her; she does think he does not know her abilities. She also wonders if he is a "control freak" who does not trust anyone. However, she doubts this is true since he has risen to a high level in the company. Surely, he has been able to delegate work in the past. How should she handle the situation?

VOCABULARY REVIEW

Complete the Vocabulary Review for Chapter 6 given on page 57 of the *Applications Workbook*.

ENGLISH AND WORD USAGE DRILL

Complete the English and Word Usage Drill for Chapter 6 given on page 58 of the *Applications Workbook*.

WORKPLACE APPLICATIONS

A6-1 (Goals 1, 2, and 3)

- A memorandum, a letter, and an email are on the Student CD, SCDA6-1a, SCDA6-1b, and SCDA6-1c. The documents are not well written. Revise them and print copies. Submit the documents to your instructor.
- Write an email to Karen Tomasetti asking her to attend a planning session on November 14. Use the simulated email form on SCDA6-1d.
- Write a memorandum to the individuals listed below, informing them of the monthly managers' meeting on November 21 from 9 a.m. until 11 a.m. Ask them to bring a summary of the division's accomplishments for the last six months and the anticipated direction for the next six months. Use the memorandum form on SCDA6-1e.

  Dennis Schellenger

  Brian Kalpalka

  Sam Weinstock

  Bella Estrada

  Evelyn Claxton

A6-2 (Goal 1)

During your first week on the job, Kurt Rupprecht gave you a letter to write. You had little experience writing letters, and you felt very uncomfortable with his request. However, you were too afraid to ask any questions, so you wrote the letter. When you gave the draft to Kurt, he quickly read it and said you needed to work on your organizational skills. You did not understand what he meant, and you were embarrassed to ask. You merely said, "Certainly, I will do that." Then you returned to your desk frustrated. As you have now learned, organizational skills play a major role in writing effectively. What advice would you give a novice letter writer in how to write letters effectively? Prepare a memorandum to your instructor stating the advice you would give. Use the memorandum form on the Student CD, SCDA6-2.

A6-3 (Goals 1, 2, 3, and 4)

Three situations appear in your *Applications Workbook*, A6-3, page 59. With two of your classmates, compose letters for all three situations. Using the letterhead on the Student CD, SCDA6-3a, print copies on quality bond paper to use for your letters. Print four copies of each form on the Student CD, SCDA6-3b, 6-3c, and 6-3d (one for each of you and one to submit to your instructor). Using the Letter Checklist form on Student CD, SCDA6-3b, determine whether you have included the appropriate information in your letters. Using the evaluation form on the Student CD, SCDA6-3c, evaluate the collaborative writing process. Using the Organizational Skills Form on SCDA6-3d, evaluate your organizational and time management skills. Submit your letters and one copy of each evaluation form to your instructor.

A6-4 (Goals 1, 2, and 3)

Refer to your *Applications Workbook*, A6-4, page 60, for a letter-writing situation. Since this letter pertains to a request outside your work at People Pharmaceuticals, use plain paper. Use an appropriate format.

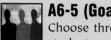

A6-5 (Goals 1, 2, 3, and 4)

Choose three classmates to work with. Conduct primary research by surveying 15 to 20 students on one of these issues: Business Ethics in the United States, Advertising Ethics, Insider Trading and Ethics, or Accounting Firms and Ethics. (If you want to pursue another topic, talk with your instructor about your ideas.) Additionally, as secondary research, use two library sources and two Web sources on the issue you have chosen. As you begin your project, determine the approach you will take. What question(s) will you ask the students? How will you organize your report? What sections will you include in the report? You will not write the report in this activity; your task is to gather all data—both primary and secondary. In Chapter 7, you will produce the report in final form and present your findings to the class in an oral presentation.

ASSESSMENT OF CHAPTER GOALS

Did you successfully complete the chapter goals? Evaluate yourself by filling out the form on page 61 of the *Applications Workbook*.

Presentation Skills

1. Produce a formal report with graphics, using appropriate style and placement.
2. Prepare and deliver a verbal presentation using visuals.

As an administrative professional, you will be responsible for keying and formatting reports frequently. These reports may be informal ones of two- to three-pages or formal ones involving tables, graphics, and reference materials. Informal reports are written in a conversational style, using personal pronouns such as *I*, *you*, and *we*. Major side headings are at the left margin, with a space before and after the heading. Secondary side headings (rare in an informal report) are generally underlined.

Formal reports often require primary and secondary research or both. Tables, charts, and graphics are standard in most formal reports. Gathering information for writing is a time-consuming process. Considerable time and effort is also required during the keying and printing process. An individual or a team may present a formal report verbally, with extensive use of visuals. Since informal reports have few parts, follow a basic format, and require little or no research, your focus in this chapter will be on preparing and presenting a formal report.

Formal Reports

The writer of a formal report often must prepare two or three drafts before formatting the final report. When preparing a draft, you should place the word *draft* at the top of each sheet, followed by the date. You may do so easily by using the *header and footer option* on your software package. Dating each draft is extremely helpful as you work between different drafts in compiling a final copy. Using this approach, you avoid the confusion of determining which copy is the most recent one. Another option is to use your software to revise the date of the draft automatically. Double-spacing your drafts provides space to write in changes by hand.

Outline

Once you have collected and organized the data for a report, whether you gather the data through primary or secondary research or a combination of the two, your next step is to prepare a tentative outline. An outline forces you to think carefully about how you will present the data in the report. Following this step can save you countless hours in the preparation of the report. Through an outline, you organize your thoughts based on the material you gathered. Remember that an outline is a working document; it is not part of the final report. However, the major and minor headings you develop become your major and minor headings in the report. Using an outline format will help keep you organized.

Figure 7-1 illustrates an appropriate format. Notice that the major headings are parallel in structure. For example, all Roman numeral headings are nouns, all second-order headings are nouns, and all third-order headings are **gerunds** (verbal forms that can be used as nouns). The important point for you to remember when outlining is to use parallel structure within each grouping. For example, all Roman numerals must be parallel since they are one grouping. However, all second-order headings do not need to be parallel throughout the outline but must be parallel within their particular section. (All A's, B's, and C's must be parallel under Roman numeral I; all second-order headings must be parallel under Roman numeral II, but they do not have to be the same as those used in Roman numeral I.)

Format

Pay attention to the format you plan to use. The careful writer generally determines format at the beginning of a writing project rather than at the end. Doing so provides the writer the luxury of not having to make numerous changes in the final stages of the report. Here are items you need to consider as you determine the format.

- Print size and font style
- Headings
- Lists
- Margins
- Page numbers
- Title page
- Table of contents

OUTLINE FORMAT

BUSINESS STRATEGY

I. Business Model

  A. Present Revenue Streams

    1. Determining Existing Streams

    2. Establishing Profit Margins

  B. Projected Revenue Streams

    1. Developing Growth Streams

    2. Projecting Profitability

II. Strategic Initiatives

  A. Acquisitions

    1. Establishing Time Frames

    2. Projecting Costs

  B. Timelines

FIGURE 7-1 Outline Format

- Appendixes and attachments
- Executive summary
- Tables

Print Size and Font Style

For the text itself, keep the print size at 12 point. For most people, this size is easy to read, and it looks more professional than a larger size. Also choose a common and easily readable font; for example, Times New Roman. Arial is another acceptable font; in fact, some individuals believe this font style has a more modern look. (The font style used in this textbook is Times New Roman.) Contrast it to the Arial font style used in this sentence. Numerous font styles are available with your software package. You may want to experiment with several different font styles before deciding which one to use. However, remember that you want the report to look professional; you do not want to use a print size and font style that the reader may find distracting or difficult to read. The text of the report is what is important; both the print size and font style should facilitate reading. *Notice how difficult this script style is to read as compared to the other text on this page.*

In the body of the report, you may choose between left-aligned paragraphs and fully justified paragraphs. Although full justification looks clean, with even margins on both sides of the paper, it can leave gaps in the middle of lines, particularly if numerous long words appear in the report. Left alignment is perfectly acceptable.

Headings

So the reader may easily distinguish between sections of the report, use headings throughout your report. When deciding on a font for headings, use the same font style as the body of your document or choose a compatible style. Since Arial and Times New Roman are compatible, you might use Arial for your headings and Times New Roman for the body. Be consistent throughout the report with whatever heading style you choose. However, using the same font style and varying the print size can be effective. Figure 7-2 illustrates how headings can be used with the content of reports.

Level-one headings are usually between 18 and 24 points. You may decide to use boldface print for the first few levels of headings. As you move to second- and third-level headings, the print should be similar in size to the body of the text. You also may use italics or color for various heading levels. First-level headings may be set off with a line below the heading. Other options include the ones listed here.

- Start each first-level heading on a new page.
- Put an additional space between the second- and third-level headings and the following text.
- Use a hanging indent for first-level headings.

Figure 7-3 illustrates different headings.

HEADING FONT STYLES

TITLE PAGE

You should include these elements on the title page:

- Title of the report
- Title of the organization
- Name and title of the writer
- The date (month and year) of the report

Note: Heading is 14-point Arial bold. Content of report is 12-point Arial.

PAGE NUMBERS

Use the header and footer option when preparing draft copies. Include the word *draft* followed by the date; also include page numbers. However, when formatting your final report, include only page numbers.

Note: Heading is 16-point Arial bold. Content of report is 12-point Times New Roman.

FIGURE 7~2 Heading Font Styles

Lists

Lists, used effectively in a report, call attention to important information and contribute positively to the readability level of the report. Software packages contain a variety of bullet styles. Choose an appropriate bullet style, and use it consistently throughout the report. Figure 7-4 illustrates different bullet styles. Be cautious when using extremely large bullet styles within a report. Such styles draw the eye to the bullet rather than to the content. You want to keep the reader focused on the content.

FIGURE 7~3 Different Level Heading Styles

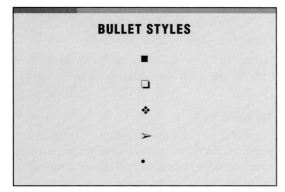

FIGURE 7~4 Bullet Styles

FIGURE 7~5 Justifying Bullets

You can align lists or justify them. However, it is preferable to left-align since justifying can lead to white space in the middle of lines. Figure 7-5 illustrates the white space that can occur when justifying material after bullets.

Margins

If you are not binding a report, one-inch margins around all sides of the report are acceptable. However, if you intend to bind the report (and most reports of more than five pages should be bound), change the left margin to at least 1.5 inches. Before making the final decision on the left margin, determine what type of binding you will use. Refer to "Printing" later in the chapter for more information on binding.

Page Numbers

In the draft stages of a report, you may want to use the header and footer option on the computer to insert the page number, in addition to the title of the report, the word *draft*, and the date. However, when you produce your final report, you will want to use only the page number. You can easily delete the header and footer option and determine where to place the page number. Your software allows you to make this selection—top, bottom, right, left, or center, and if you want the page number on the first page.

The title page does not have a page number. The table of contents has a lower case Roman numeral (ii) as a page number. The executive summary may be the first page of the report or a separate document from the report. If the executive summary is a separate document, the first page does not have a number. However, the remaining few pages do have numbers. (An executive summary is short—only two or three pages.) If the executive summary is included in the report, it follows the table of contents, with no number on the first page. The first page of the actual report is never numbered; the following pages of the report have Arabic numerals. Generally, most page numbers are found at the top right.

If you are going to **duplex** (print on both sides of the page) the final report, you must alternate the position of the page number for every other page. This approach allows the page numbers to be in the same position after final printing is completed.

Title Page
You should include these elements on the title page:

- Title of the report
- Title of the organization
- Name and title of the writer
- Date (month and year) of the report

Figure 7-6 presents a sample title page. Notice that the font style is Times New Roman and includes varying print sizes. The title of the report is the largest print size; the date of the report is the smallest print size.

Table of Contents
The table of contents should list each major section of the report. Figure 7-7 on page 156 shows a sample format for a table of contents.

Appendixes and Attachments
Appendixes and attachments contain information that is important to the readers of the report but not an integral part of the report. For example, if you do primary research, you might include the research questionnaire that you distributed. Additionally, if you have a list of the names of the individuals who completed the questionnaire, you might include this list. You should assign each individual appendix a letter as an official head (Appendix A, Appendix B, and so on.) The appendix is the last part of the report; the page numbers continue in sequential order following the report.

Attachments include any supplementary materials that are **germane** (having a significant bearing) to the report. Attachments will not be in the same format as the report or include page numbers. When attachments are included, the last numbered page has a centered head entitled *Attachments*; the attachments follow that page.

Executive Summary
Use a straightforward format in the executive summary. Since the executive summary is for the busy executive who wishes to preview the report but does not need a detailed explanation, headings and bullets become important formatting tools. Figure 7-8 on page 157 illustrates one format for an executive summary.

Tables
Your software allows you to create tables with ease. You can determine the following:

- Number of columns needed
- Whether columns are the same width or modified to match the length of the text within each column
- Table style
- Color or black and white
- Number of rows and columns

Notice that Figure 7-9 on page 157 uses colors to highlight columns within a table.

Graphics
Graphics, as used in this chapter, include line and bar charts, pie charts, and images created with graphics packages and digital cameras. Graphics provide pictures to help a reader understand and remember the information presented in a report. Graphics also help hold the reader's interest. A report becomes more appealing if well-designed graphics are used. When deciding when and where to place graphics in a report, ask yourself these questions.

- Who is the audience?
- Will graphics help the audience understand the message?
- What purpose will the graphics serve?
- Is the information in the graphics presented in a straightforward manner? Too much information in a graphic can cause confusion for the reader.

BUSINESS ETHICS

PEOPLE PHARMACEUTICALS

Maria Lopez

November 2005

FIGURE 7~6 Report Title Page

TABLE OF CONTENTS

FIGURE 7~7 Table of Contents

EXECUTIVE SUMMARY FORMAT

Background
Why the report is necessary and what the problem or issue is

Major Findings
What was discovered during the research phase

Recommendations
Recommendations made as a result of the discoveries

FIGURE 7~8 Executive Summary Format

- Is the graphic placed appropriately? Does it follow the text to which it refers?
- Has the appropriate type of graphic been selected? If you have selected a bar graph, for example, does it illustrate the concept well? Or would a pie chart or a line graph be more appropriate?

- Will color help get the message of the graphic across to the reader? When using colors, make certain the contrasts are sufficient. For example, two shades of one color, with one slightly darker than the other, generally will not provide adequate contrast.

Charts and Graphs

Software such as Excel allows the user to prepare sophisticated charts and graphs. Figure 7-10 on page 158 illustrates a pie chart using colors. Figure 7-11 on page 159 demonstrates the use of bar charts and line graphs.

Graphics Packages

Graphics packages such as Adobe Photoshop, CorelDRAW, Fo2PIX PhotoArtMaster, Digital Workshop-Illuminatus Opus, and QuarkXPress (image software that pulls unwanted details out of images), along with digital cameras, allow the creative individual to produce top-quality graphics. You can modify colors to get the appropriate depth and hue needed. Figure

AOL (AOL TIME WARNER)
STOCK PRICES FOR SELECTED DATES
DECEMBER 9, 2002 TO MARCH 11, 2003

Date	Open	High	Low	Close	Volume
March 11, 2003	11.25	11.37	11.05	11.11	12,130,000
February 28, 2003	10.85	11.40	10.81	11.32	26,163,300
February 21, 2003	10.66	10.79	10.40	10.60	14,833,700
February 11, 2003	10.45	10.64	10.10	10.20	23,770,900
January 31, 2003	11.80	12.00	11.37	11.66	38,405,000
January 21, 2003	14.70	14.82	14.26	14.35	13,533,000
January 11, 2003	15.25	15.40	15.00	15.03	23,612,300
January 2, 2003	13.15	13.48	12.90	13.31	20,069,900
December 23, 2002	13.20	13.39	13.05	13.24	11,041,600
December 15, 2002	13.29	13.60	13.12	13.40	14,285,700
December 9, 2002	13.65	13.78	12.98	13.80	22,815,000

FIGURE 7~9 Colors Used to Highlight Columns

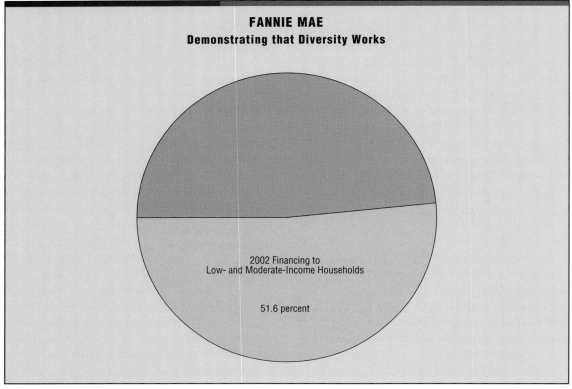

FIGURE 7~10 Pie Chart, Using Colors

7-12 on page 160 illustrates graphics created with digital cameras and graphics packages. Generally, this type of graphic is not necessary in a report; however, organizations often use impressive graphics when creating advertising brochures and annual reports.

Although the administrative professional may not be expected to create complex graphics, the technology today allows it to be done with a minimum of effort. Most organizations employ graphic designers or outsource their materials if they have a need for high-quality graphics.

Quotations

You may quote material from other sources directly or indirectly in a report. If an indirect quotation is used, a footnote reference (explained in "Documentation") is all that is necessary. If the material is a direct quotation, you should handle quotations in this manner:

- Place quoted material in quotation marks.
- Enclose a quotation within a quotation in single quotation marks.
- Show omissions as **ellipses**—three spaced periods (. . .) used to indicate a deletion in text within a sentence; four spaced periods (. . . .) used to indicate a deletion in text at the end of a sentence.

Documentation

Documentation is the process of giving credit to the sources used in a report. If you quote a source directly, use quotation marks around

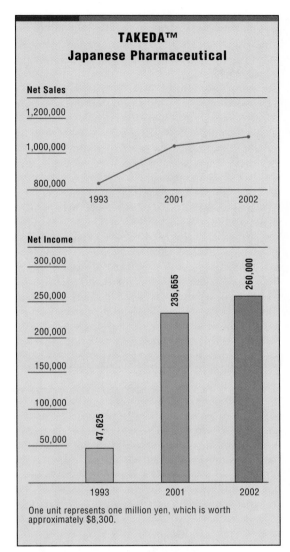

FIGURE 7~11 Bar Chart and Line Graph

note at the bottom of the page that cites the information. Your software allows you to easily add the superscript number within the body of the report and the footnote at the bottom of the page. Footnotes should include the name of the author(s), title of the work, publication city, publishing company, date, and page number of the quote. The following example shows a footnote that references a quote from a book.

Gary McClain and Deborah S. Romaine, *The Everything Managing People Book* (Massachusetts: Adams Media Corporation™, 2002), 85.

The endnote style requires the same superscript number when noting the reference in the text. However, no footnote information appears within the body of the report. Endnote information appears at the end of a paper in a section entitled *References* or *Notes*. The reference notes appear in numerical order according to the superscript; there is a blank space between notes.

1. Gary McClain and Deborah S. Romaine, *The Everything Managing People Book* (Massachusetts: Adams Media Corporation, 2002), 85.

2. Deepak Chopra, *Grow Younger, Live Longer* (New York: Harmony Books™, 2001), 77.

APA and MLA Documentation Styles

Both the **APA** (American Psychological Association℠) and the **MLA** (Modern Language Association) format styles use internal citations. These citations appear in the report itself. The details of the source appear in a section entitled *Works Cited* or *References*. Notice the following ways of handling documentation within a report.

APA Style: According to McClain and Romaine (2002), if you want people to act responsibly, you have to give them responsibility—and hold them accountable for meeting the objective.

MLA Style: McClain and Romaine suggest that if you want people to act responsibly,

the quote within the body of the report. If you paraphrase a source, no quotes are necessary but you credit the source. Documentation may follow several different styles—footnotes, endnotes, and APA and MLA documentation styles. Each style is presented here.

Footnotes and Endnotes

Footnotes are the oldest form of documentation. As the name suggests, you place a foot-

FIGURE 7~12 Graphics Created with Digital Cameras and Graphics Packages

you have to give them responsibility—and hold them accountable for meeting the objective.

Web Citations

With so much information available on the Internet, it is a major resource. When citing Web sources, use a superscript within the body of a report and add the footnote at the end of the page or use the endnote format by adding the appropriate documentation at the end of the report.

One of the issues concerning Internet research is the lack of consistency in documentation. For example, many articles do not give an author, merely a title. Some articles give only a company name, with no title or author name. When documenting your research, use whatever information is available. The example shown does not include an author. If an author's name is provided, place it first, as in a standard footnote notation.

"Email mailboxes to increase 1.2 billion worldwide by 2005," accessed July 27, 2002; available from **www.cnn.com/2001/ TECH/internet/09/19/email.usage.idg/**.

Printing

Reports are generally printed on a workplace printer. However, some reports, such as annual reports, may be sent outside the organization to be printed. You should consider the type of paper to use and, if the report is to be bound, the type of binding.

Paper

When choosing paper, consider the color, finish, and weight. A brighter white looks cleaner than off-white. However, an off-white or light beige color can give your document a unique look. The paper should be a 20- to 24-pound weight with a dull finish, unless you are using numerous graphics and color.

The administrative professional may use workplace copiers to print reports.

In that case, you should choose a glossy paper since color looks better on a glossy finish. As an example, reports sent outside the organization to a number of individuals, such as annual reports, often appear on glossy paper.

Binding

Unless the report is going to only a few people within the organization and is only a few pages in length (3 to 5), you should not staple it. Binding possibilities include the following:

- Three-ring notebook—not the best choice unless the report is an internal one where pages may be added and/or deleted.
- A hard plastic strip that slips over clear plastic front and back covers—an inexpensive binding that works fairly well for internal reports.
- Spiral binding—comes in various colors, with black generally being the most appropriate.

When you choose a binding, consider how the report will be used, the appearance of the entire report, and the cost associated with the binding. You certainly want the report to look professional; however, the cost associated with a high-end print product is not essential if the report is merely an internal document.

Verbal Presentations

Once a report is complete, an individual or a team may present it verbally to a small or large group within the organization. Additionally, with the team approach commonly used in organizations today, administrative professionals sometimes give presentations. These presentations may be informal ones to a small group or formal ones to a large group. You also may have occasion to speak at professional organization meetings. Since presenting can be an important part of your professional life, the remainder of this chapter focuses on proper presentation techniques.

Presenting is not easy for many people. In fact, public speaking is often people's biggest

fear. For most people, becoming an effective presenter is a learned skill. This skill is so important to individuals and organizations that businesses develop training to help people become effective verbal presenters. Like all skill development, you must practice the skill. The next sections will help you develop your presentation skills; the workplace activities will give you the opportunity to practice these skills by presenting to your instructor and classmates.

Release Your Creativity

What do creativity and your learning how to release your creativity have to do with presenting? If you have ever heard dull and boring speakers struggle to present a mundane topic in a routine manner (and most individuals have), you understand the connection between creativity and presentations. Not only is creativity important for producing effective presentations, it is also important when dealing with the constant change that is occurring in the workplace today. In fact, surveys show that one of the skills most wanted by organizations is creative thinking. Employers understand that successful employees can creatively solve problems. You can apply what you learn here about creativity to numerous areas of your work and personal life. Hopefully, a **serendipitous** (desirable but unsought accidental discovery) benefit of increasing your ability to think creatively while preparing and presenting presentations will be your ability to think creatively in numerous workplace situations.

Definition

The dictionary defines **creativity** as "having the ability or the power to cause to exist." Creativity is a process. It is a way of thinking and doing—of making new connections and new linkages. Using creativity often means you are able to solve a problem in new and different ways. Consider this example:

You have a problem convincing one of your coworkers that PowerPoint® slides are important *in an upcoming presentation the two of you are preparing. You keep telling her how important visuals are and how they can help an audience remember more of what they hear. She constantly rejects your ideas. You decide to invite her to a presentation at your local IAAP^{SM} chapter, where you know the presenter will be using visuals. You have heard the speaker on previous occasions, and you know he is an excellent presenter. Your coworker agrees to go. After the presentation, she remarked that the visuals he used helped her remember what he said. Then she laughingly remarked, "I see your point. I'm willing to use visuals in our presentation if you are willing to help prepare them."*

You used your creativity. You presented an important concept to an individual in more than one way. You helped bring about change in her thinking.

Steps in Releasing Creativity

As you commit to getting in touch with your creative self, you must remember that it is a process. You cannot decide one day to become more creative. Becoming creative demands that you do the following:

- Believe in yourself.
- Try new problem-solving techniques.
- Destroy judgment.
- Look and listen.
- Ask questions.

Believe in Yourself. Know that you have creativity. You may not be using it to the fullest, but it is there. Trust yourself. If you have an idea that is different from others, do not assume you are wrong. Try it out. Your idea may be the creative spark to solving a complex problem. Maintain a spirit of inquiry. Experiment with the unknown.

Try New Problem-Solving Techniques. When problems arise, do not lose your creativity. You may need it more than ever. Consider this workplace example:

You planned to present to a small group of coworkers what you believed (due to your research) was a solid idea for making the records manage-

ment system more effective. You talked with your supervisor about your ideas, and she supported the direction you proposed. You prepared your presentation well. You assembled the necessary data. You began your comments by pointing out how cumbersome and ineffective the present records management system was. You continued by pointing out all the flaws of the system and concluded with a new idea for a system that would correct everything that was wrong. You noticed that your coworkers did not seem interested. You wondered why since you heard many of them complain about the system in the past. When you completed your presentation, the group began to tell you why your ideas would not work. You knew your ideas were solid and based on research.

What did you do wrong? You attacked your audience. You knew that several of them had designed the old system, but you did not think it was important to recognize their work. You believed everyone understood the problems with the system.

What should you do next? Try a new way of looking at the problem. Practice the Japanese soft martial art of **Aikido**. Aikido teaches that you should never meet force with force. The person who breaks harmony by attacking or being aggressive in some way fails. By moving in the same direction as the other person, you can effect more change.

Here is an example of how you might use the Aikido concept in this situation. Rather than getting angry and telling the group how wrong they are, you should respond to their concerns with a nonconfrontational statement such as, "You certainly have made some excellent points. Let me continue to work on this project; I'll get back with you." You might even invite one or two members of the group (who have demonstrated some interest in the project) to join you. After doing additional research, you present your ideas to them by first acknowledging their point of view and showing them how their ideas and your ideas can become compatible in producing a better records management system. You find your ideas are accepted; you and the group begin to work together to make the necessary changes. The organization is well on its way to implementing an improved records management system. By using the Aikido concept, you moved with the group rather than struggled against them.

Destroy Judgment. As you are thinking through a problem or an issue, do not be judgmental. Let your thoughts flow freely. Do not discard any of them. Do not let your mind tell you that an idea is no good or ridiculous. To help you destroy judgment (which, by the way, is not easy to do), pay attention to each thought you have. If you begin to become critical of your thoughts, attack the judgmental you. Say to yourself, *Judgment, get out!*

Look and Listen. The story is told of a businessperson who heard that a Zen master (who lived at the top of a mountain) knew the three basic secrets of life. Anyone who knew these secrets would live a happy, fulfilling life. The businessperson climbed for two years to get to the top of the mountain. Once there he approached the old master and asked the master to tell him the secrets. The master said, "Yes, I will tell you. The first secret is pay attention, the second secret is pay attention, and the third secret is pay attention." In other words, you need to pay attention to what you hear, what you think, what others think, and what you see. You need to pay attention to what is happening around you and in the world.

Ask Questions. If you have young brothers or sisters or young children of your own, you have probably laughed about some of the questions they ask. Yet their questions (and the answers they receive) are essential to the

The person who breaks harmony by attacking loses.

DIGITAL VISION

growing and learning process. As people grow older, they do not allow themselves to continue to ask questions. People think they should know all the answers, but obviously they do not. Continuing to ask questions (whatever they may be) helps you get in touch with your creativity. Give yourself permission to ask small, even playful, questions. Let yourself question things you have never questioned in your adult life.

Begin Early

Once you begin to think creatively about the material and about how you will present it, you are ready to do the actual work. Remember, a good presentation is not prepared 30 minutes before it is given. You may get lucky and be able to deliver a presentation with little or no preparation, but that is a rarity. Do

not tempt fate; begin early. You might say, "I don't have time to prepare." If that is the case, do not agree to give the presentation. Beginning preparation three weeks before the presentation is not too soon. Additionally, by beginning early, you can spend a few minutes each day thinking about what you want to say and writing down your thoughts. Then you can come back to your ideas at a later point and revise them or eliminate material that no longer seems relevant. In other words, you have a chance to mull over your thoughts and edit your presentation.

Determine the Purpose

You have probably listened with impatience to speakers who did not make the purpose of their presentation clear. In fact, you may have wondered the following:

- Does the speaker have a point?
- If so, when is the speaker going to get to the point?

To keep you from making that same error, ask yourself these questions as you begin to plan your presentation:

- What do I want the audience to know as a result of my presentation?
- What, if anything, do I want the audience to do as a result of my presentation?

Know the Audience

Who will be in the audience? For example, if your audience is a group of administrative professionals, you know some of their interests. You can use anecdotes or stories that have meaning for them. If you are speaking to a group of colleagues from your workplace, again you know some of their interests. You can tailor your message to meet their needs. If you are speaking to a general audience, keep these questions in mind as you begin to plan your remarks.

- What are the ages of the people who will be in the audience?

© GETTY IMAGES/EYEWIRE

Give yourself permission to ask questions as children do.

- Is the audience **heterogeneous** (completely different) as to gender? Or is the audience **homogeneous** (like in nature)—all male or all female?
- What is the audience's education? Are they high school graduates, college graduates, or a mixture of both?
- What knowledge does the audience have of the subject you will be presenting?
- What will be the size of the audience? Will there be 15 or 50? Numbers make a difference. A small audience allows greater interaction. Questions can be used effectively. With a large audience, there is little chance for interaction other than a question-and-answer period at the end of the presentation.

Consider the Setting

The time and location of your presentation and any other activities that will occur around the same time are important to know. Ask these questions about the setting.

- What time is your presentation? In the morning? Right before lunch? Immediately after lunch? In the evening (before or after a meal)?
- Is there entertainment before or after your presentation, such as a musical group?
- Is there other business occurring before or after your presentation?
- Is the presentation being held in the workplace, a hotel, a conference center, or a school?
- What is the size of the room? What is the configuration of the seating? Is the room a theater-type setting? If the audience is small, are they sitting around a table? Are the chairs to be set up in a circle?

If you have an opportunity to influence the setting, do so. Be certain the size of the room

Know your audience.

DIGITAL VISION

is appropriate. You do not want to be giving a presentation to 12 people in a room designed for 100 people. It will look as though you gave a party and no one came. Nor do you want to give a presentation to 50 people in a room designed for 25. People are not comfortable when they are crowded. Be sure the chairs are comfortable, the temperature is pleasant, the room is clean, the lighting is appropriate, and the acoustics are good.

Research and Select the Material

Research the topic, if necessary, in the library or on the Web. If you are researching on the Web, use several search engines to help you find material. No one search engine has all the material on a particular topic. Comprehensive search engines include **www.google .com**, **www.yahoo.com**, **www.lycos.com**, and **www.askjeeves.com**. Conduct original research if needed. For example, you may be developing a presentation for the local chapter of IAAP on email ethics. Therefore, you decide to do primary research with the IAAP members on ethical and/or unethical email practices they observe in their own organizations.

Individuals usually gather more research than they can use during a presentation. Additionally, audiences absorb only so much information. You do not want to burden your audience by giving them more information than they can comprehend and remember. Your next step is to select the most relevant material appropriate to the subject and audience you are addressing.

Organize the Material

What is the most effective organization? This question has several answers, including the ones listed here. Pick the one that works best for your style.

- Make an outline. Focus on your purpose and identify the material that will help you achieve that purpose.
- Talk out the presentation with a close friend. Some individuals get writer's block when they try to begin by developing an

outline, find themselves staring at a piece of paper, and accomplishing nothing. However, they are very successful at talking through their ideas with a friend. Once they have clarified their ideas in this manner, they are ready to make an outline.

- Make a numerical list of all the points you want to cover. For example, you may have four or five points that you want to cover. You begin by listing these points and then developing each point. Remember that you should not attempt to cover too many points in one presentation. You will lose your audience quickly if you attempt to do so. If you have an audience who is knowledgeable about the topic you are presenting, you may be able to cover as many as ten points; however, that number is too many for most audiences. Generally, with fewer points that are more developed, you will retain the audience's attention to a greater degree.
- Write your ideas on cards; then group your cards into topics.

Develop an Opening

The opening should get the audience's attention immediately. For example, you may do one of the following:

- Tell a story.
- Use a quotation.
- Ask a question.
- Refer to a current event.

It is important to know what *you* do best. If you can never remember the punch line of a joke, do not try to tell a joke. Nothing is worse than beginning with an opening that flops. If you do tell jokes well and decide to do so, make sure the joke is not in poor taste. Humor that is never appropriate includes the following:

- Ethnic and racist jokes—Jokes based on an individual's ethnicity and race are taboo. Even if you are Irish and are presenting to an all-Irish audience, do not tell a joke about the Irish. An ethnic or racist joke is

Organize your presentation materials before you begin writing.

not acceptable, even if the audience is of one race or ethnicity. People may be able to laugh at themselves, but they do not feel good about a speaker calling attention to their weaknesses or inadequacies through humor.

- Gender jokes—Jokes about males or females are not appropriate; nor are jokes about homosexuals. AIDS jokes are also inappropriate. Jokes are not funny when they **denigrate** (belittle) a particular group of people.
- Off-color jokes—Jokes that have sexual connotations should not be told, even if they are told to a male-only or female-only audience. Someone will be offended. Off-color jokes are not appropriate, regardless of the audience makeup.

When you are determining how to open your presentation, ask yourself these questions:

- Is there a link between the story and the presentation?
- Is it a new story or joke? You do not want to relay one that the audience has heard numerous times.
- Am I telling the story as succinctly as possible? You do not want to spend one-third of your time on your opening story.
- If it is a joke, am I timing the punch line well?

Use Language Well

Have you ever been in an audience when two or three people around you were napping or talking among themselves while the speaker was trying to get her or his message across? Or even worse for you, have you ever been delivering a presentation and noticed that several people were nodding off? If your answer was in the affirmative to either of these questions, you understand the importance of speakers getting their message across by using language well and keeping their audience interested. How do you use language well? Here are several techniques that can help you.

- Establish a link with your audience. For example, if your audience is a group of administrative professionals, what concerns does the audience have in common? Make your major points and relate those points to experiences common to both you and the audience.

- Use interesting facts, figures, and quotations. If you are giving a motivational talk on the importance of service, for example, you might remind the audience of the years of service that Mother Teresa gave to the world and use this quote from her: "Love cannot remain by itself—it has no meaning. Love has to be put into action and that action is service."

  When using a quotation, relate the quote to a point in your presentation. A quote dropped in with no relationship to the subject of the presentation seems **contrived** (invented or fabricated). Do not use long quotes; the audience can get lost in the point you are trying to make. Do not overuse quotations—two or three in one presentation are adequate. Do not use often-cited quotations; the audience may have heard the quote so many times that its effectiveness is lost, even if it is a great one.

- Use direct language. Do not use multisyllable words when simpler words would be just as powerful.

- Personalize your talk. Address your audience directly; use *you* frequently.

- Talk in a conversational tone. Use the active rather than the passive voice. For example, do not say "It is believed . . .;" say "I believe . . . ."

- Use **analogies** (comparisons made of two different things by stressing their similarities) to help explain your ideas. For example, stress is like a roller-coaster ride; it has numerous highs and lows.

  Tie the analogy directly to the subject matter of the presentation.

- Speak at an appropriate rate—not too fast and not too slow.

- Speak loud enough that everyone can hear you. Indicate emphasis through variations in tone. Do not speak in a **monotone** (a succession of sounds or words uttered in a single tone of voice).

- Articulate carefully. For example, do not drop the endings of words; say *learning*, not *learnin*.

Develop a Strong Closing

The closing must tie together the opening and the overall purpose of your presentation. The conclusion is your destination. It is the part of your presentation that should take your audience where you want them to be— to what you want them to learn or what you want them to do. A good conclusion gets the audience's attention. It helps them see the relationship between each part of your presentation—between the opening and the body and the body and the conclusion. The closing puts the pieces of your presentation together in a creative and interesting way so the audience leaves thinking you have helped them learn and/or have motivated them. Let the audience know you are ready to conclude by stating simply *In conclusion* or *My final point is . . . .* Make the conclusion short (about 5 to 10 percent of your talk) and powerful. The conclusion can be a moving statement, a story, a call to action, or a challenge. For example, if you are delivering a presentation on human potential, you might end by saying, "I leave you with three challenges—to be the best person you can be, to constantly grow and learn, and to reach the unreachable star." The last few lines of your conclusion should be memorable. Connect with the audience for one final moment—make them laugh and/or make them think.

Prepare Visual Aids

Visual aids, if used properly, can be very effective. According to research studies, on average, people retain the following percentages of what they read, hear, and see.

- 10 percent of what they READ
- 20 percent of what they HEAR
- 30 percent of what they SEE
- 50 percent of what they SEE and HEAR

If you want your audience to remember what you said, show them effective visuals during your presentation.

PowerPoint is a frequently used software package that allows you to display major points to the audience on a projection system. PowerPoint offers these features to help make a visual presentation a powerful one.

- Color—PowerPoint has hundreds of color schemes that can be used to make professional-looking slides.
- Clip art—PowerPoint includes a clip-art collection. If you do not find what you need in the collection, you can purchase clip-art software or download clip art from the Web.
- Through the use of Media Player®, Power-Point accepts movies and sound clips, thus

allowing the audience to see and hear a movie image on the screen.

Although visual aids can be effective, they can also lessen your effectiveness if you do not use them well. Have you ever sat through a presentation where the speaker used ineffective visuals? If so, did they have some of these flaws?

- You could not read the visuals.
- The visuals did not relate to the presentation.
- The visuals were so ineffectively presented that they distracted from the speaker's message.

Have you ever sat through a presentation in which the speaker talked to the visual aids rather than the audience or a presentation where the equipment for presenting the visuals did not work properly?

If you have observed any of these events, you understand that although visuals can add, they can also detract. Figure 7-13 gives several tips for preparing and presenting visuals.

TIPS FOR PREPARING POWERPOINT VISUALS

- Prepare a PowerPoint slide with the title of your presentation.
- Prepare a slide for each of the main points of your presentation.
- Keep the text to a minimum on each slide. Make your points in as few words as possible.
- Have only one graphic for each slide.
- Use the same font styles for all major points on a slide. You may use a different font style for minor points; however, do not use more than two font styles. A slide looks cluttered when you use too many different fonts.
- Make sure the visuals can be seen and read from all parts of the room. If your audience is large, you may need two screens—one on one side of the room and another on the other side of the room.
- Proofread the slides carefully. Check for spelling and content errors. Errors are embarrassing and they detract from a presentation, making the audience wonder about your attention to detail.
- Practice using the PowerPoint slides before the presentation.
- Make sure all equipment is in good working order.
- Make sure you know how to operate all equipment.
- Talk about what is on each slide, but talk to the audience—not to the PowerPoint slide.
- Stand to the side of the projection device when presenting the slides.

FIGURE 7-13 Tips for Preparing PowerPoint Visuals

Rehearse the Presentation

Rehearse the presentation exactly as you plan to give it. If you will be standing at a lectern during the presentation, stand at one during the rehearsal. If you are going to be using a microphone during the presentation, use one during the rehearsal. If you plan to use visuals during the presentation, use them in the rehearsal. Also, you might ask a trusted colleague to listen to and critique your rehearsal presentation. Ask the person to be totally honest with you. You want to be able to correct your errors before you make your presentation. Figure 7-14 lists ten common mistakes people make in presentations. You can avoid these mistakes by planning and rehearsing.

Check the Presentation Room

Be sure to visit the room where you will make your presentation. Know how the room will be set up. Find out where the lectern is going to be if you are using one. Be certain you have the visuals in order. Check your visuals on the actual equipment you will be using. Be certain you know how to use the equipment. If you are at all uncomfortable using the equipment, ask a colleague to assist you by operating the equipment. If you are giving a presentation with PowerPoint, be sure the equipment is working properly and is placed so the audience can see your presentation.

Dress Appropriately

Determine what you will wear several days before the presentation. The usual attire for a woman is a suit or dress; for a man, a suit and tie. Wear something you are comfortable in and that looks good on you. Bright colors are perfectly acceptable. Women should avoid necklaces and earrings that are large and distracting. Rings and bracelets are appropriate, but women should not wear noisy bracelets; they may distract audience members. Men may wear colored shirts and bright ties. The color of the suit should be one that looks good on the man. Men should not wear gold bracelets and a number of rings; they are distracting to the audience. Hair for both men and women should be well groomed and away from the face.

Write Your Introduction

You have already learned that you need to build credibility with the audience. One way to

---

TEN MISTAKES PEOPLE OFTEN MAKE IN PRESENTATIONS

- Failing to prepare with the audience's interests and needs in mind
- Failing to rehearse
- Failing to rehearse with accompanying visuals
- Failing to check the room configuration
- Talking too long; in other words, not knowing when to stop
- Preparing too much material
- Beginning with an inappropriate opening—a story or joke that does not fit the situation or is in poor taste
- Ignoring the body language of the audience and failing to modify the message if the audience is not understanding it
- Trying to appear knowledgeable when you are not
- Failing to prepare a short and powerful conclusion that motivates the audience to action, challenges them, or motivates them to learn more about the subject

FIGURE 7-14 Ten Common Mistakes People Often Make in Presentations

do this is to tell the audience your credentials. How do you do this? First, find out who will be introducing you. Then write a succinct statement (that will take no more than two minutes to deliver) highlighting your major accomplishments, and give it to the introducer. Do not send a packet with pages of information about you and leave it up to the introducer to determine the important points to make. Do not write a long introduction; the audience will become bored, and you lose time that could be used for your message. A good idea is to take a copy of the introduction you wrote with you in case the introducer has misplaced the copy you sent.

Control Nervousness

Understand that nervousness is normal. Even professionals experience it. Barbra Streisand is famous for her stage fright. Remember, one of the greatest fears individuals have (as shown in surveys) is the fear of speaking before an audience. You have already learned how to help control nervousness—prepare and rehearse. A well-prepared and well-rehearsed presentation can eliminate many of your fears. You know who your audience is, what you intend to say, and how you will say it. Here are other suggestions for controlling nervousness.

Day before the Presentation

Remind yourself that you have prepared well. You have followed all of the steps mentioned previously; that is, beginning early, determining the purpose of the presentation, rehearsing, and so on. Burn off some of your nervousness by exercising. Try not to push yourself to the limit with work responsibilities in the few days before a presentation. When you are overly tired, you increase your chances of not doing a good job.

Day of the Presentation

Arrive early enough to check out the microphone, the equipment, and the layout of the room. If changes need to be made, find someone who can assist you in making them.

In the 10 or 15 minutes before your presentation begins, find a private place (maybe a small room away from the gathering audience) and try these relaxation techniques:

- Sit in a straight chair, carry your rib cage high, and breathe deeply. As you exhale, push the air over your lower teeth in a *sss* sound. Focus your efforts entirely on your breathing.
- Walk around. Take a brisk walk for a minute or two. Do some jumping jacks.
- Work off nervous tension by taking deep breaths.
- Realize that some nervousness can help you. You can channel this nervousness into your talk, which will become a positive energy source that adds to your effectiveness.
- Right before you enter the room, swing your arms a few times.
- Remember that the audience is your friend; they want you to succeed.

As You Are Being Introduced

Pay attention to your body language as you are being introduced. Follow these steps:

- Look at the introducer and then look slowly at the audience.
- As you approach the lectern, walk with confidence.
- As you reach the lectern, slow down and collect yourself. Place your notes as high as possible on the lectern so you can refer to them easily.
- Respond to the introduction, but make your response brief. You might say *thank you very much* and exchange a firm handshake with the introducer.

As You Begin Your Presentation

Keep these points in mind:

- Pause for just a moment before beginning your presentation. Let your eyes sweep the room.
- Realize that the audience is much less aware of your nervousness than you are.
- Do not draw attention to your hands, which may be shaking as you begin. For example,

instead of holding a hand microphone, leave the mike on a stand. Do not hold a glass of water. Leave your notes on the lectern; you do not want to call attention to shaking papers.

During the Presentation

Remembering these points will help ensure a successful presentation:

- Maintain eye contact with the audience. As you speak, focus on one side of the room and then (after a period of time) on the other side of the room. Maintain eye contact with as many people as you can.

- Watch for nonverbal feedback from the audience. For example, puzzled looks or blank stares are cues the audience does not understand what you are saying. Modify your presentation as quickly as possible to help your audience understand. Such modification is not easy to do before a large audience, but accomplished speakers learn to read an audience well and to make necessary adjustments.

- Focus on the positive body language (smiles, nodding heads, and so on) coming from the audience. Let yourself feel good about positive reactions.

- Use natural gestures. You may use your arms and hands to emphasize points. However, do not use constant arm and hand motions. Use these motions sparingly and for emphasis only.

- Be natural; do not perform.

- Speak in a normal tone of voice; do not speak too fast.

- Articulate carefully.

Speak with Credibility

According to Malcolm Kushner, an audience gives the speaker credibility or withholds credibility from the speaker. Although you cannot make the audience deem you credible, you can behave in ways that suggest you are a credible individual. How? Here are several suggestions:

- As you speak, demonstrate your competence. Let the audience know you are experienced in your field. Make a few relevant comments about your past experiences.

- Demonstrate your fairness and trustworthiness through what you present.

- Control your nervousness. Speakers who are nervous may be perceived as less credible.

- Do not behave like a high-pressure salesperson. Speakers who are extremely extroverted often come across as less credible than moderately extroverted individuals. You do not want to appear as if you are trying to overpower your audience.

- Have your facts straight; do not make mistakes of fact.

- Do not flip-flop during a presentation. In other words, do not say one thing at one point in your presentation and say the exact opposite at another point in your presentation.[1]

Critique Your Presentation

Within a day after the presentation, critique your performance. Evaluate yourself using these guidelines:

- Be kind to yourself. List the "goods" with the "not so goods."

- Do not try to solve too many problems at once. Pick one or two things to improve each time you give a presentation.

- Realize evaluation is an ongoing process.

- Congratulate yourself by recognizing the improvements you made.

- Make notes to help you the next time you give a presentation.

Additionally, get feedback from other people. You can ask a respected colleague to evaluate you. You or the individuals who asked you to speak may provide evaluation forms for the people in the audience. Ask to see copies of

---

[1]Malcolm Kushner, *Public Speaking for Dummies* (New York: IDG Books Worldwide, 1999), 17-20.

the completed forms and review them carefully. Do not let yourself become upset over a few negative comments. Know that there will always be some negatives.

Present as a Team

You have learned in previous chapters that project teams are used extensively in business today. These project teams often present their report as a team. Such presentations require **collaborative planning** (working together as a team). The techniques presented in the previous section apply to team presentations too. Here are some additional suggestions for team planning.

- Brainstorm what the presentation will include and how to present it. Brainstorming techniques you may find helpful are listed in Figure 7-15.
- Decide who will present each part of the presentation.
- Determine how you will make the transition from one speaker to another. One way is for the speaker who is finishing to mention the next speaker's name.
- Practice your presentation as a group.

BRAINSTORMING TECHNIQUES

- Say each idea aloud as it occurs to you.
- Have a recorder jot down each idea.
- Listen attentively to others' ideas.
- Piggyback on others' ideas.
- Suspend judgment. Do not critique ideas as they are presented.
- Encourage an uninterrupted flow of ideas.
- Expect the outrageous to surface, which is perfectly acceptable in the brainstorming process. Unconventional thinking encourages creativity.

FIGURE 7-15 Brainstorming Techniques

- If graphics are part of the presentation, determine who will prepare them.
- Determine appropriate dress. Speakers should dress in a similar fashion. For example, they may all wear suits.
- Determine how the group will be seated before and after each person's presentation. Will the speakers be on a stage? In what order will they be seated? The first speaker should be closest to the podium. ■

SUMMARY

To reinforce what you have learned in this chapter, study this summary.

- Once you collect and analyze data for a report, the next step is to prepare an outline.
- In determining the format for the report, consider print size and font style, headings, lists, margins, page numbers, title page, table of contents, appendixes and attachments, executive summary, and tables.
- Most formal reports contain some type of graphic, such as line and bar charts, pie charts, and images created with graphics packages and digital cameras.
- All sources used in a report must be acknowledged with appropriate documentation, which may be in the form of footnotes, endnotes, APA and MLA styles, and Web citations.
- Before printing a report, consider the type of paper and the most appropriate binding.
- Once a report is written, it is often presented verbally to a small or large group of people within an organization. In addition, with the team approach commonly used in business today, administrative professionals may give presentations.

- As you begin to prepare presentations, you need to release your creativity. Steps in releasing creativity include believing in yourself, trying new problem-solving techniques, destroying judgment, looking and listening, and asking questions.

- Steps in preparing a verbal presentation include beginning early, determining the purpose, knowing the audience, considering the setting, and researching and selecting the material. Additional steps include organizing the material, developing an opening, using language well, developing a strong closing, preparing visual aids, rehearsing the presentation, and checking the presentation room for proper setup.

- Determine what you will wear several days before a presentation. Be certain that what you select is appropriately conservative and looks good on you.

- Offer to write a brief statement about your credentials for the person who will be introducing you.

- Control your nervousness by preparing well, arriving early enough to check out the room, engaging in relaxation techniques several minutes before you present, and paying attention to your body language as you are being introduced.

- As you speak, you must do so with credibility. You need to demonstrate your competence, demonstrate your fairness and trustworthiness, control your nervousness, have your facts straight, and be consistent in what you say.

- After a presentation, critique your performance.

- When presenting as a team, brainstorm what the presentation will include and how to present it. Carefully think through the details of the presentation, such as who will present each part, how to handle the transition from one speaker to another, and what graphics are appropriate. Also consider who will prepare the graphics, how the team will dress, and how to seat the team before and after each person's presentation.

FIND THE PROBLEM

After you had been at People Pharmaceuticals for three months, Kurt Rupprecht suggests that you join the local chapter of IAAP; he tells you he thinks it will help you professionally. You do join and find that the meetings and activities are helpful. You are active in the chapter. Recently, the IAAP program committee asked you to give a presentation to the members. The committee did not specify a topic. You decide to speak on creativity. A psychology class you took last semester helped you understand the importance of developing your creativity, and Kurt helped you understand the importance of creativity on the job. You believe you can develop a worthwhile presentation on the topic. You select as your title "Let Your Creativity Bloom." You plan to take a dozen daisies and a large vase with you. As you make each point on "Letting Your Creativity Bloom," you will add one daisy to the vase. You also plan to use PowerPoint slides, highlighting one point on each slide. On the day of the presentation, you check out the PowerPoint slides and the equipment, buy the daisies and the vase, load the PowerPoint equipment in the car, and arrange your notes in a folder. You get to the presentation room early, arrange the vase and daisies, and set up the PowerPoint equipment. But the worse-case scenario happens. The equipment malfunctions as you attempt to present your first slide. You apologize to the audience and ask for the audience's indulgence as you attempt to get the equipment working. You are successful; however, it takes you five minutes. The audience is chit chatting with each other during this time. As you begin again, you are distracted because of what happened and you have trouble getting the audience's attention back. The great presentation you prepared does not work. You leave feeling you are a complete failure and vowing you will never again accept a speaking engagement.

What is the problem? How should you have handled the situation? You are embarrassed about the situation, but you think Kurt might be able to help you learn from the experience. He was in the audience, but he has not said a word to you about the presentation. Should you ask for his opinion?

PROFESSIONAL POINTERS

In communication, whether written or oral, the message is affected by the way it is presented. The administrative professional plays an important role in the communication process. As you strive to prepare and assist in the presentation of messages, keep these pointers in mind:

- Be critical of the documents you prepare. Make certain your work is accurate and has a professional appearance.
- Use reference guides for punctuation, grammar, and word usage.
- Continually strive to improve your writing skills. Take writing seminars if possible.
- Develop a manual of preferred document styles and formats for your office if one does not exist.
- Utilize technology to create interesting and professionally prepared documents. Today's readers are accustomed to documents that are visually appealing and that include numerous graphics.
- Seek out opportunities to hone your verbal presentation skills. Realize that your effectiveness in verbal presentations can enhance your marketability.

REINFORCEMENT ITEMS

1. What items should a writer consider when formatting a formal report?
2. What should a writer consider when deciding on types of graphs? List several types of graphics.
3. What steps can you take to help release your creativity?
4. What steps should you take when preparing for a presentation?
5. Explain how you can control nervousness.

CRITICAL-THINKING ACTIVITY

You have a friend who works for the local county tax assessment office as an administrative assistant to the director. The office employs, in addition to the director, two additional administrative assistants and five assessors. Your friend handles most of the correspondence to county residents concerning increased property assessments. She follows a format given to her by the previous person in her position.

Most of the correspondence can follow a standard format by simply changing names, addresses, and assessed property values. Some letters, however, are written to clarify property transactions and inform residents of increased valuations. The director receives numerous complaints from citizens about the letters sent from the assessment office. The citizens complain that the letters are negative in tone, contain incorrect information, and include grammatical errors. Due to the large volume of letters, the director cannot read every word of every letter before he signs them.

Your friend uses her spelling and grammar tools, but she does not check the accuracy of the increased valuations. She keys what the director gives her. A review of the last five letters shows that she missed errors in word usage, misspelled the taxpayer's name, and incorrectly keyed the increased property valuation. A first draft of a letter written by your friend is given on the Student CD, SCDCT7. Your friend asks you to read and evaluate the letter.

- After reading this letter and the situation, what suggestions would you make to your friend?
- Should your friend make any suggestions to the director? If so, what?

VOCABULARY REVIEW

Complete the Vocabulary Review for Chapter 7 given on page 63 of the *Applications Workbook*.

ENGLISH AND WORD USAGE DRILL

Complete the English and Word Usage Drill for Chapter 7 given on page 64 of the *Applications Workbook*.

WORKPLACE APPLICATIONS

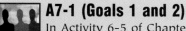
A7-1 (Goals 1 and 2)

In Activity 6-5 of Chapter 6, you and three of your classmates gathered research for a report. Several topics were suggested; however, you also had the option of consulting with your instructor about a topic of your choice. You were to use primary and secondary research. The primary research was to consist of surveying 15 to 20 students on the issue you chose. Your secondary research was to include two library sources and two Web sources.

Your task in this activity is to write a report on the information you collected and present this report orally to your classmates. Additionally, you are to submit the written report to your instructor.

Your written report is to be in proper format and must include appropriate reference information (footnotes or endnotes) and graphics—tables, charts, and so on. The parts of the report are to include the following:

- Title page
- Table of contents
- Executive summary
- Report body
- Appendixes and attachments (including the survey you administered to students)

Excerpts from reports are in the *Applications Workbook*, A7-1, pages 65–69. Review these sample excerpts for proper format.

As a group, verbally present the report to your class (in a presentation of approximately 20 minutes) using visual aids (either PowerPoint slides or overhead transparencies). A sample Power-Point slide is shown on the Student CD, SCDA7-1. Your classmates and your instructor will evaluate your presentation. On the Student CD, SCDA7-2, is an evaluation form. Print one copy for each member of the class and distribute the forms before you present your report.

Tally the results of your classmates' evaluations, and give a summary to your instructor. Write a memorandum to your instructor, using the form on Student CD, SCDA7-3, explaining what you have learned from the class evaluation. Also explain how you would improve the presentation if you gave it again. Submit one copy of your written report to your instructor.

ASSESSMENT OF CHAPTER GOALS

Did you successfully complete the chapter goals? Evaluate yourself by filling out the form on page 71 of the *Applications Workbook*.

chapter 8

Telecommunications— Technology and Etiquette

1. Describe how telecommunications affects individuals' lives today and in the future.

2. Describe the major telecommunication pipelines.

3. Identify messaging services.

4. Use proper cell phone and standard telephone etiquette.

This chapter will help you understand the importance of telecommunications in the world. Additionally, the chapter will help you be conversant about certain telecommunications technology and selected telecommunications equipment and services that are used daily. Although individuals communicate frequently through cell phones, email, and standard telephone service, they do not always use proper telecommunications etiquette. In fact, you may have experienced incidences of rude telephone and email behavior. Due to the prevalence of such behavior, this chapter also focuses on proper telecommunications etiquette for using standard telephone service, cell phones, and instant messaging.

Telecommunications—Its Impact

If you ever doubted the impact that **telecommunications** (the transmission of text, data, voice, video, and images—graphics and pictures—from one location to another) has on individuals, you are probably well aware of its significance since 9/11. As you utilize air travel and pick up friends or relatives from airports, you are aware of the changes telecommunications has brought about in the way airports do business. These changes are merely the beginning of major telecommunication usage in making airplanes and airport terminals safer. According to an article published in *Popular Science*™, the following changes will likely occur by 2007 in airport security procedures.

- Scanners at toll booth-like structures along access roads that aim lasers at vehicles to determine whether they are carrying explosives.

- An ID kiosk (as the first stop for passengers) with a camera and computer linked to facial recognition software that generates a tamperproof, easily trackable photo-ID smart card with a chip containing flight and gate number, check-in time, and a digital version of the facial scan.

- Scans cross-checked against a database of terrorist suspects.
- Checked and tagged luggage examined by a laser scanner that excites the molecules of items inside the bag, then compares the light those molecules emit against a database of chemical components, looking for suspicious combinations of materials.
- Security experts at an airport's command center receiving data from monitors linked to the airport's computer network that process all ID cards, tags, and security devices.
- ID smart cards controlling passenger entry to jetways.
- Cameras monitoring the airport's perimeter, using algorithms that distinguish between, for example, a dog harmlessly brushing against a fence and a human attempting to climb over the fence.
- Jets loaded with hidden cameras in the cockpit, galleys, and cabins, recording activity during flights and sending live feed to security personnel on the ground.
- Passengers, considered dangerous due to biometrics on a smart card that match those on a database of suspects, being sent to a secure area where they commit to an iris scan to confirm their identity.[1]

Star Wars, you say. Not at all. Much of the technology is available today, and the remainder will be available very soon. The gut of the system includes these technological innovations, along with others not mentioned.

- Biometrics—the science of measuring characteristics unique to each individual.
- Iris recognition—a biometric that measures the unique furrows, wrinkles, and cracks in the iris and the muscular part of the eye that surrounds the pupil. (Since no two irises are identical, this biometric is nearly 100 percent accurate.)
- Facial recognition—a biometric that identifies an individual based on a digitized image

Telecommunications is a major part of people's daily existence, affecting much of how they work and live.

of that person's face. (Facial recognition is generally 80 to 90 percent accurate.)

- LIBS (laser-induced breakdown spectroscopy)—A process that shoots a beam of light at an object, exciting its molecules. (As the molecules relax, they emit a pattern of light that is unique for every material.)[2]

Clearly, telecommunications invades every area of people's lives, both personally and professionally.

Pipelines

The telecommunication pipelines discussed here are pipelines that carry video as well as voice. Over the past several years, these

---

[1]Dan Tynan, "Blueprint for a Sterile Airport," *Popular Science*, September 2002, 49-54.

[2]Ibid., 56.

pipelines have changed considerably. In the not-too-distant past, one pipeline carried voice and another pipeline carried video. Telephone companies such as AT&T® and Southwestern Bell™ (one of the Bell family of companies) were giant firms that dealt solely with the delivery and service of telephones and telephone lines. Today traditional telephone companies do not exist. Companies have transformed themselves from delivering a service that connects people via traditional telephone lines to connecting people to people and people to machines through traditional telephone lines and through cable, digital subscriber lines, satellite, fixed wireless, and wireless pipelines. Gone are the days when one or two extremely large companies owned the entire network support infrastructure.

Now there are numerous large communication companies with very diverse missions. To understand this statement better, consider the mission statement of SBC Communications, Inc.™, which includes Ameritech℠, Nevada Bell℠, Pacific Bell℠, Southwestern Bell, and SNET℠. The mission statement is available in its entirety on the Web at **www.sbc.com**.

SBC's mission is to meet our customers where they are—and help them get to where they need to be. That mission starts with the critical local connections SBC provides through its subsidiaries' brands—SBC Southwestern Bell, SBC Ameritech, SBC Pacific Bell, SBC Nevada Bell and SBC SNET, and builds from there with a full range of voice, data and ebusiness services and solutions to meet a wide range of business and consumer needs.

At the same time, SBC is working to be the provider of choice for consumers by enabling access to an integrated package of broadband access, premium data and Internet services and telephony.

As technology and business needs evolve, SBC is continually expanding its data and ebusiness services and capabilities. For our business customers, that means providing services ranging from wide-area networks and IP telephony to applications hosting and emarketplace tools. For residential customers, it means providing instant, *high-speed Internet access that paves the way for home videoconferencing and for online education and entertainment.*[3]

Notice how broad in scope the mission statement is, encompassing various pipelines, ebusiness, and global connectivity—a long way from connecting telephones together through lines strung from one location to another.

Analog Dial-Up

Modem technology that uses **analog dial-up** (connecting devices to a network via a modem and a public telephone network) has been around for many years. The modem allows computers to communicate with each other by converting their digital communications into an analog format to travel through the public phone network. The information then reverts back to a digital format the computer can understand. The word **modem** is an acronym that stands for modulate/demodulate. A computer modem *modulates* data so it can be transmitted over telephone lines in analog form, and a modem *demodulates* incoming signals so the computer's digital processor can understand them. Modems exist in the computer, and a regular telephone line connects the modem from the computer to the external telephone lines. Of the pipelines available for transmitting data and voice today, the modem is the slowest.

The Internet used modem technology from its infancy. However, with the large number of people using the Internet and the continued growth of users (expected to increase to 2 billion in the next few years), modems are considered too slow by many users. Other pipelines, such as cable, digital subscriber line, and satellite (all explained in this section) are much faster.

Cable

Before discussing cable, digital subscriber line, satellite, and wireless, you need a general

---

[3]"SBC-Data Capabilities," accessed November 14, 2002; available from **www.sbc.com**.

understanding of **broadband**, which is short for broad bandwidth. Broadband is a form of digital data transmission that uses a wide range of frequencies to achieve added bandwidth. Broadband is not a pipeline, but is used in DSL, cable, satellite, and wireless pipelines to carry a wide range of frequencies. Inherent in broadband technology, as opposed to modem technology, is greater speed and capacity. By definition, broadband designates a transmission speed of at least 2 million bits per second.

Cable is a pipeline that connects to computers and to a coaxial cable line to provide voice and data transmission. Although cable has been available for years, its original design was as a pipeline for TV only—not for high-speed data traffic. Cable was also designed for one-way television programming. In order to go from one-way service to two-way service, cable pipelines required extensive upgrading. Only in the past few years has this two-way service become available for most of the United States. In certain rural areas, cable pipelines are still not available.

DSL

DSL (digital subscriber line) is similar to cable. It is fast and it uses wires that run to an organization or a home. For example, traditional telephone companies provide DSL service through broadband. Broadband can carry voice, video, images, and data. Cable and DSL pipelines provide extremely fast access to the Web.

Satellite

Television service through a **satellite** (an orbiting vehicle that relays signals between terrestrial communication stations and the earth) has been available for many years. Now satellite service as a high-speed Internet solution is available to everyone in the United States.

Cable was initially designed as a pipeline for TV.

© GETTY IMAGES/PHOTODISC

One of the disadvantages of DSL and cable is that broadband pipelines are not run to certain areas of the country, particularly rural ones; thus, DSL and cable are not accessible to businesses and individuals in these areas. Satellite service makes high-speed Internet access available through an outside antenna and transmit-and-receive electronics integrated into a small indoor unit. The outdoor equipment connects by coaxial cable to an indoor receiver. Broadband by satellite allows users to have access to the Web, to download files in seconds, to enjoy Web music and video, and to free up the phone line so users can receive calls while on the Web.

Wireless

Wireless connectivity is possible through either **mobile wireless** or **fixed wireless** (conversion of data to wireless signals that customers receive through a network of transceivers mounted on utility poles, streetlights, and so on). Mobile wireless pipelines have been available for some time and are the pipelines used by cellular phones. With cellular phones, you move in and out of service areas. Mobile wireless service breaks a large service area into smaller areas called cells. For example, when a customer places a call from a mobile unit, the nearest cell, or transmitting station, relays it to a central computer that, in turn, directs the call into the local telephone system. When a customer leaves one cell area and enters another, the computer automatically switches the transmission to the next nearest cell.

Fixed wireless does not utilize client devices moving in and out of coverage areas. Fixed wireless differs from cellular/mobile telephony in that its end-user terminals have a fixed location (for example, affixed to a building); it does not support mobility because the terminals require a power connection. Each fixed wireless subscriber has a small receiver and directional antenna oriented toward the nearest microcell. In the last few years, the number of fixed wireless users grew significantly in the United States—from approximately 200,000 subscribers in 1992 to millions of users today. Fixed wireless networks dropped in price and became more reliable. They are now affordable for homes, home offices, and small businesses. For example, wireless networks, using a wireless access point and a cable/DSL router can support a broadband connection for a small office network. The future is bright for the use of this technology in homes and small businesses.

Future Directions— Unlimited

The rapid growth of telecommunication capabilities from 1995 to 2000 suggests that the capabilities and speed of information transmission by 2020 will have increased **exponentially** (relating to an expression in terms of a designated power of the base). For example, the projection is that Internet users will grow to 2 billion by 2005 and the amount and speed of information transmitted by telecommunications will increase significantly. Presently a **terabyte** (a trillion bytes per second), when sent down a conventional fiber, transmits the equivalent of the entire Library of Congress in a second. To put this in context, rough estimates are that the world's production of information is at around 2 **exabytes** (1,000 **petabytes**, with petabytes being equal to 1,024 terabytes) per year. Fiber-optic communication capacity presently doubles every nine months.

Projections for the future include the following:

- By 2010 the planet will be embedded in a largely unbroken system of data exchange.
- Costs of telecommunication services will continue to fall.
- Numerous new products and services will become available to the general public and to business users. The sophistication of these products and the changes they will bring to people's personal and business lives will be tremendous. Here are only two of the many home products presently under development.

(1) A house with a mind—With a house's heating and cooling, electrical, and security systems plugged into a computer and the Internet, the house has a mind of its own. If you are at your off-site workplace and are worried you left your lights on, you can call your house to tell it to turn the lights off.

(2) Researchers are at work on closets and refrigerators that match information from the Web with your personal data to advise you on daily dilemmas such as what to wear and what to cook.

Telecommunication Messaging Services and Etiquette

Telecommunication messaging systems presented in this textbook include email (presented in Chapter 6), fax (presented in Chapter 12), and instant messaging, cell phones, and standard telephones. Each of these messaging systems has a prominent place in businesses and home offices. Additionally, individuals use these systems extensively for their own personal use.

As you use these messaging services, you must use proper etiquette. Clearly, the growth of telecommunications changes the way you communicate. In the past individuals spent more time talking to people face-to-face or over a standard telephone. Today individuals are involved in telework, working from home offices or occasionally going into the office but frequently communicating with people through email, instant messaging, and cell phones—often leaving a voice message.

When talking face-to-face, you can generally correct any errors you make since you are able to observe the person's reaction to your statements. It is much easier to be

Internet users are expected to grow to 2 billion by 2005.

discourteous to someone when you cannot see him or her. You may quickly lose your patience and find yourself shouting at the person on the other end of the cell phone or using harsh, inflammatory language with the person receiving your email. Since telecommunication messages are more impersonal, you must consider the individuals receiving the messages. Take time to read the numerous suggestions given in this chapter for using proper etiquette.

IM Systems

IM (instant messaging) is changing the way individuals communicate. With IM, immediately after you connect to the Internet and log on to your IM account, you see a **contact list** or **Buddy List** (IM users with whom you communicate frequently). This list lets you know who is online and lets your buddies know

You may find it easier to be rude while talking to a person over a cell phone than when talking with him or her in person.

you are online. Figure 8-1 illustrates how IM works. Most IM services are free on the Internet. For example, Yahoo!®Messenger is available for free at **http://messenger.yahoo.com**.

Benefits of IM

Service and sales businesses are finding IM extremely beneficial for their businesses. IM allows these benefits for clients and businesses:

- Quicker and more complete answers to employee questions. For example, if service representatives do not have complete answers for customers' questions, they may check their online Buddy List to see who is online and then IM the appropriate person for a quick answer. With such an approach, a representative can quickly answer a question for a client while on the telephone with him or her. The service representative does not have to tell the customer he or she will call back later with an answer. The representative obtains an answer and communicates it to the customer quickly and efficiently.

- Increase sales. Ecommerce companies can expect to see their sales improve because of IM. Studies have reported that ecommerce businesses that adopt IM for communicating with customers can expect sales to rise immediately as much as 20 percent.

Research suggests that IM users will continue to grow and that IM will reduce the usage of standard email and telephones. In a study done by InsightExpress℠, 35 percent of respondents stated that they preferred IM to email and 49 percent said they preferred IM to the telephone.[4]

IM Etiquette

Communication is often difficult. When you are communicating face-to-face, you have the added advantage of being able to observe body language in addition to hearing the

[4]"Say Hello to Instant Messaging, The Technology That's Changing How We Communicate," *Smart Computing*, September 2002, 51-53.

**INSTANT MESSAGING
THE PROCESS**

STEP 1   Install software client and open the **IM** client.

STEP 2   The **IM** client sends your computer address, the port assigned to the **IM** client, and the names of everyone on your **Buddy List** to your computer.

STEP 3   The computer creates a file of your contacts and checks to see if any of your buddies are currently logged on. If so, it tells your buddies that you are also logged on.

STEP 4   You then click on the name of the person on your **Buddy List** who is online and begin communication with the person. If several of your buddies are online, you can have a conversation with the group.

STEP 5   When the conversation is complete, you close the message window and go offline. The server then sends a message to the client of each person on your contact list that is currently online, indicating that you have logged off.

FIGURE 8~1 Instant Messaging—The Process

words spoken. You can observe the person's facial expressions and the way he or she is sitting or standing and you can hear the person's tone of voice. With the telephone, you have the advantage of hearing a voice. With IM, you have none of these advantages. You must rely only on the keyed message sent to you. Thus, it is extremely important that you observe certain rules of etiquette. Here are several suggestions that will help make your IM communications more successful.

- Communicate with the buddy or acquaintance, informing the person that you are adding his or her name to your list. Do not merely add the name to your list. This approach lets the person know that you value his or her knowledge and will be asking for assistance or sending information occasionally.

- When you ask a buddy for assistance, be sensitive to the person's time demands. A person may become irritated to see a message appear on the computer screen while he or she is engrossed in something else. Ask whether the person has a few minutes to respond to you. Such politeness and sensitivity pays off in IM just as it does in person.

- Be concise with your IM message. State your request or point as succinctly as possible. Remember that the basic purpose of an IM message is to garner a quick response. A longer message is reserved for email, a memorandum, or a letter, depending on the length and subject.

- When you are not available for IM messages, let your buddies know through status settings offered on the system.

- If your buddy does not respond to a request, do not get angry and fire back an offensive or accusatory message. Try communicating with the buddy later. If the person continues to fail to respond to your requests, drop his or her name from your list of buddies.

- Put into action the effective correspondence techniques you learned in Chapter 6—completeness, clarity, accurateness, promptness, conciseness, courteousness, and positivism.

Telephones

The evolution of telephones from the time that Alexander Graham Bell spoke his famous words, "Mr. Watson, come here. I need you!" in 1876 to today is remarkable. Telephones

THOMSON LEARNING/SOUTH-WESTERN

Good communication techniques are important when communicating by IM.

are one example of the many changes in the telecommunications field. A few of the many features available on business and personal phones are these:

- Caller lists—allowing display of caller names, telephone numbers, and dates of calls
- Storage of names and telephone numbers
- Caller identification
- Voice mail
- Conference calls

Additionally, broadband technology, with its numerous pipelines for sending and receiving video, sound, text, and graphics, is providing options not available in the past. For example, **Internet telephony** (a category of hardware and software that enables people to use the Internet as a transmission medium for telephone calls) provides several applications. These products may be called **IP** (Internet protocol) **telephony**, **VOI** (voice over Internet), or **VOIP** (voice over Internet protocol). With IP, Internet service providers become

telephone providers. Here are some of the services offered with Internet telephony.

- Call waiting allows a subscriber surfing the Web to see a small window pop up identifying the caller and relaying a message from the caller.
- Cisco's™ IP phone includes a virtual assistant that can screen calls and send them to you or to voice mail.
- Software such as NetMeeting™ and CUseeMe™ and digital video cameras allow users to conduct meetings and see each other over their PC monitors while talking.

For individuals who want to use Internet telephony without being tethered to a computer, vendors sell phone cards that allow phone-to-phone traffic to be routed over the Internet.

Cell Phones

Cell phones, which use a wireless pipeline, are standard equipment for many people. They carry their cell phones with them constantly. Individuals enjoy being able to send and receive calls from any location at any time.

In 2002 it became possible for customers of any of the major U.S. cellular carriers to send short text messages via their cell phones. The service, known as **SMS** (short message service), is widely used in Europe and Asia. More than 19 billion communications by short message service were sent worldwide in 2002. Multimedia messaging, a new service recently developed for cell phones, allows cell phone users to send small images. Another cell phone service is the ability to handle financial transactions from point-of-sale terminals and vending machines.

Individuals also enjoy combination cell phones and **PDAs** (personal digital assistants), with the units having some of these capabilities:

- Phone, fax, and email messages delivered into a single mailbox reachable from the phone.
- Digital assistants to forward messages and manage how and when you can be reached.

Digital video cameras allow users to conduct meetings and see each other over their PC monitors.

- Web browsing.
- Speakerphone for hands-free calls.
- IM email.
- Multitasking by talking on the telephone using an earpiece and working on PDA applications simultaneously.

To use your cell phone or your combination cell phone and PDA effectively, become informed on what capabilities the system has by doing the following:

- Reading the manual carefully.
- Checking the information available on the cell phone manufacturer's Website.
- Obtaining the number of your cell phone service provider, which is usually toll-free.

Cell Phone Etiquette

Have you ever been in a crowded airport where the person seated next to you was talking on a cell phone while you were attempting to hear boarding instructions for your flight? Have you ever been out for a quiet dinner with friends and had to contend with a constantly ringing cell phone at the table next to you? If so, you understand that as a society, people are often less than courteous when using their cell phones. Individuals seem to forget that others around them have needs also. You can improve your cell phone etiquette by following these simple but important suggestions.

- In public places, make calls only when necessary, and ask your friends to follow the same rule.
- Keep your telephone voice as low as possible. If, due to the noise around you, you find yourself speaking loudly while using your cell phone, seek a quiet place if possible.
- Keep your calls short.
- Turn off your cell phone when not in use; the constant ringing of a cell phone can become an irritant to others in public

IMAGE BANK/STEVE NIEDORF PHOTOGRAPHY

places. If you are expecting an important call, check your messages frequently.

- Avoid talking on a cell phone while driving, and do not call friends or acquaintances who are in their cars. Cell phone conversations can be distracting, which may cause an accident. If you must make a call while driving, keep the call as short as possible.

Voice Messaging

Today many individuals in the workplace use voice messaging to route calls efficiently. When voice messaging is set up with an effective routing system and a pleasant voice giving directions, the system can be very efficient. However, some voice systems today are not well constructed. You may find yourself in a loop that never allows you to connect with the office or person you want to talk with and unable to speak with an operator.

Additionally, some systems attempt to give too much information, resulting in confusion for the caller.

If you find yourself in such a situation, you may get angry. The call is an important one; yet you are not able to complete it due to an inefficient voice messaging system. When you finally do get to the department or person you need, you may (due to your frustration) find yourself being rude to the person who answers the phone. That person may become angry also, with a verbal fight ensuing between the two of you. Frustrating? Yes—for both individuals. Common? Yes—altogether too common. In fact, according to a January 2002 survey by Public Agenda, 61 percent of Americans believe that rudeness is on the rise in the United States.[5]

---

[5]Leslie Farnsworth, "Why Courtesy Counts," *Parade Magazine*, August 25, 2002, 10.

© GETTY IMAGES/PHOTODISC

When using a cell phone in a public place, be courteous to the people around you by keeping your voice as low as possible.

Voice Messaging Advantages

Organizations do not need to eliminate voice messaging. It is an effective technology when used appropriately. There can be numerous advantages of voice messaging, including the following:

- Greater productivity of workers by eliminating repeated telephone calls when the individual being called is not available
- Greater productivity due to calls being routed to the appropriate individuals and the elimination of calls being transferred
- Less extraneous conversation, with voice messages averaging 30 seconds as compared to regular phone conversations averaging 4 to 5 minutes
- Faster delivery of communications by messages getting through even with time zone changes

Voice Messaging Etiquette

If voice messaging is to be effective, system designers must pay attention to the message content, length, and branching system. If you, as an administrative professional, are involved in helping to design a voice messaging system, you must be certain it is both effective and efficient. Carefully consider the ability of the system to respond to the needs of clients and customers. Here are some disadvantages of a poorly designed system and of employees using a system inappropriately, along with suggestions for making the system more effective.

- A voice message may be too long and complex. The voice message should be succinct and clearly stated. Do not give the caller superfluous information.
- A voice message may have a poorly designed routing system. With each step of the routing system, give callers no more than four options. Instructions should be short, under 15 seconds if possible. Give the most important information or answer the most frequently asked questions first. Tell the callers what they need to do first; then tell them the key to press. For example, a message might be as follows: *To*

transfer to the operator, press zero. If you give the number first, the caller may forget what number to press.

- A voice message may not allow the caller to talk with a person. No one likes to be lost in a voice messaging system that does not allow the caller to talk to a human being. Be certain your system allows for exits to a person at appropriate intervals.
- The voice on a voice message may not sound pleasant. You must create a favorable impression with a voice message not only with what you say, but also with the tone of your voice. Do not talk in a monotone; vary your vocal tone. Also be careful not to record any unpleasant or inappropriate background noise with your message.

In addition to a voice messaging system that routes outside calls to the appropriate department or person, organizations may use voice

Do not use a voice messaging system as an excuse for not answering your phone.

messaging systems on individual phones. Such systems allow employees to receive messages while they are away from their desks and return calls later. Unfortunately, sometimes these systems are misused by employees who put their phones on voice mail regularly, even when they are available at their workstations. At times, you may need to use voice messaging while in the workplace, particularly if you are working on a project where interruptions cause problems. However, make certain that these situations are rare. Do not use a voice messaging system as an excuse for not answering your phone. You can save yourself and the caller time by answering the phone when you are at your workstation. Courteousness to callers demands that you consider their needs and time constraints.

Answer the telephone with a smile in your voice.

Telephone Etiquette

As an administrative professional, you will spend countless hours on the telephone. If you are to be effective in your telephone communications, you must use proper etiquette. Study the suggestions given in the following sections, and apply these suggestions as you use the telephone.

Develop a Pleasant Voice

Regardless of how busy you are, you should answer the telephone with a smile. Have you ever noticed how happiness shows through in the tone of your voice? A smile has the same effect; the caller becomes the beneficiary of your pleasant tone of voice. Treat the voice on the telephone as you would a person sitting across from you requesting information or assistance. Let all callers know you want to help with whatever needs they have.

When you are curt and rude in answering the telephone, you set the stage for a negative conversation. You may be busy, but that does not give you an excuse to be rude. Chances are the person you are talking with is just as busy. Instead, answer the telephone with a smile in your voice that says, *I am happy you called. How may I help you?*

Answer Promptly

When your telephone rings, answer promptly—between the first and second ring if possible and certainly before the third ring. You may lose a potential customer if you are slow in answering the telephone. Even if you do not lose a customer, you may not make a good impression on the person calling. Have you ever been on the receiving end of a telephone that rings five or six times before someone answers? If so, you understand how irritating it can be when the person does not answer the phone promptly.

Speak Distinctly

Your voice carries clearly when you speak directly into the mouthpiece with your lips about an inch away from the transmitter. You cannot speak distinctly with something in your mouth. Do not have gum, food, or a pencil in your mouth when you answer the telephone. Speak in a normal tone of voice; do not shout or mumble. Callers may become irritated if they must ask you continually to repeat what you said or if they need to hold the telephone one or two inches away from their ear.

Identify Yourself and/or the Organization

Your employer will usually instruct you in how to answer the telephone. Many large organizations have voice messaging systems that identify the organization and give callers the options available. Other large companies have individuals who personally answer the phone with the name of the organization and route the person calling. When your telephone rings, identify your office and yourself. For example, you might say, "Human Resources, Carla MacIntosh." If you are using a voice messaging system when you are away from your desk, the message should include the appropriate information. For example, *This is Carla MacIntosh. I am away from my desk now. Please leave your name, number, time of your call, and any necessary information. I will return your call as soon as possible. Thank you.*

Record Messages Carefully

Your employer will not be pleased if you provide him or her with an incomplete or incorrect message. When answering the telephone, you are responsible for getting all necessary information from the caller and recording it accurately. You need to get the following information:

- Person's name (spelled correctly). (If you do not know how to spell the name, ask the caller to spell it and then repeat the spelling to the caller to be certain you recorded it correctly.)
- Organization of the person calling.
- Telephone number, with area code if long distance. (Repeat the telephone number to be certain you heard it correctly.)
- Any message. (If the person leaves a message, get the necessary details. For example, if the caller says he will call your employer tomorrow, you may respond, "May I tell him when to expect the call?" This approach helps avoid delays if your employer is going to be out of the workplace. Your task is to get the two individuals connected as expeditiously as possible and to eliminate numerous repeat calls when your employer is not in.)

Organizations usually provide message pads for recording telephone calls. Another possibility is to send an email to your employer (if the person checks email frequently) containing his or her telephone messages.

Place Calls on Hold Effectively

A caller sometimes requests information that you do not have at your fingertips. You may need to check with someone else or go to your computer file to get the information. When this happens, do not place the caller on hold without his or her permission. You may say, "I need to pull the information from my files. Would you like to hold for a moment while I get it, or shall I call you back?" If the caller agrees to hold, get back to the person as soon as possible. If you are taking longer than you anticipated to find the material, check with the caller within no more than a minute to ask whether he or she would like to continue to hold. When you return to the line, let the caller know you are back by saying "Thank you for waiting."

Do Not Discriminate

If you are presently employed or have been in the past, have you ever found yourself being nicer over the telephone to the president of the organization than to a client you do not know? If the answer is yes, make a point of being friendly before you know who is on the other end of the line. Tell yourself before answering the phone that a friend is calling.

Avoid Gender Bias

Some people still assume that all assistants are female and all executives are male. If you answer the telephone and the voice on the other end is female, do not assume she is an assistant and ask to speak to her employer. When addressing anyone, use terms that connote respect. Do not refer to a woman as a girl, a young lady, a gal, or any other term that implies gender bias. Do not refer to a man as a boy or a guy.

Be Helpful and Discreet

When someone calls and your employer is not in the workplace, tell the caller approximately how long your employer will be gone or ask if someone else can help. Let the person know you are trying to help. Here are two examples of how to handle such a call— the wrong way and the right way.

Incorrect Handling of Call

Pablo Rodriquez: This is Pablo Rodriquez. May I speak with Shareen Edwards?

Administrative Assistant: Ms. Edwards is out of the office.

Pablo Rodriquez: When will she be back?

Administrative Assistant: I expect her back in about two hours.

Pablo Rodriquez: Ask her to call me when she comes in.

Administrative Assistant: Okay.

What is wrong with the conversation? You may be thinking that you do not see any glaring errors. The assistant answered Pablo Rodriquez's questions, which is precisely the point. Mr. Rodriquez had to ask all the questions; he probably thought the assistant was uncooperative. The closing "okay" by the administrative professional was too informal. Additionally, the administrative professional did not get a phone number. Notice the improvement in this conversation.

Correct Handling

Pablo Rodriquez: This is Pablo Rodriquez. May I speak with Shareen Edwards?

Administrative Assistant: Ms. Edwards is out of the office now; however, I expect her back in about two hours. Please give me your telephone number, and I will have her call you when she returns.

Pablo Rodriquez: That would be helpful. My number is 555-0129.

Administrative Assistant: Thank you, Mr. Rodriquez. I will give her the message.

The administrative professional has saved time for Mr. Rodriquez and Ms. Edwards and has probably left a positive impression with Mr. Rodriquez.

Another important point to remember in such a situation is to be discreet. In other words, do not give unnecessary information to the caller. Consider the same situation.

Pablo Rodriquez: This is Pablo Rodriquez. May I speak with Shareen Edwards?

Administrative Assistant: Ms. Edwards went to see Ralph Ijiri at IPI about an advertising matter. She should be back in two hours. Can someone else help you, or may I have her call you when she returns?

What went wrong? The administrative professional gave out entirely too much information. It was not necessary to tell Mr. Rodriquez where Ms. Edwards went, whom she went to see, and why. The assistant could be revealing confidential information. You want to help the caller, but you also must protect your employer by not revealing too much information.

Ask Questions Tactfully

It is your responsibility to learn the caller's name. Usually, a caller identifies herself or himself. If not, ask for a name tactfully. Do not say, "Who is this?" Say, "May I tell Ms. Edwards who is calling, please?" *May* and *please* completely change the approach. The caller usually understands that you are responsible for finding out who is calling and does not resent your asking. Try to put yourself in the other person's place, and ask questions the way you would want to be asked.

Screen Calls

Many executives have two telephone numbers—one that is published and one that is not. The executive uses the inside number to make outgoing calls; the executive may also give the number to close friends or family members who can then dial the office directly. The administrative professional is to screen calls that come from the published number. For example, when the executive receives a call, the administrative professional must determine who is calling and why. The executive may refuse to take certain calls. If someone else in your company can handle the call, transfer it to that person after requesting permission from the caller. If no one is available to take the call or if no one is interested in taking it, let the person know courteously that your employer is not interested. One response might be this: *I appreciate the information; however, Ms. Edwards is not interested in pursuing the matter.*

Be Attentive

As you are talking with the caller, visualize the person. Speak *with* the person, not *at* the telephone. Listen politely to what the person is saying. Do not interrupt or continue to key a document. If the caller is unhappy about an experience with the company, listen to the person's complaint. You will have an easier time dealing with a disgruntled caller after you hear what the caller has to say. Use good listening skills.

- Listen for facts.
- Search for hidden or subtle meanings.
- Be patient.
- Do not evaluate.
- Try to understand the words the caller is using.
- Act on what the caller is saying.

Take notes during a long or involved conversation so you will remember all the information. Use words such as *thank you* often. Let the caller know you care.

Use Correct English

Pay attention to using correct English and pronunciation. People who have a good grasp of the English language develop a negative impression of your organization when they hear *this is her* or some other grammatically incorrect statement.

Avoid Slang

Using slang is neither businesslike nor in good taste. Figure 8-2 provides several slang expressions that are incorrect, followed by more appropriate expressions.

Use the Caller's Name

Individuals like to be recognized and called by name. Use the person's name frequently. For example, say, "Yes, Mr. Jordon. I will be happy to get the information." End the conversation with "It was nice to talk with you, Mr. Jordon."

Transfer Calls Properly

It is often necessary to transfer a caller to another person. Before you transfer a call, explain to the person why it is necessary to do so. Make certain the caller is willing. You may say, *"Ms. Dyer is out of the office now, but I believe Mr. Radman can help you. May I transfer you to Mr. Radman?"* Additionally, give the caller the extension number in case you are disconnected. Stay on the line until the person

---

AVOID SLANG EXPRESSIONS WHEN TALKING ON THE PHONE

Avoid	Say
Yeah	Certainly
Okay	Yes
Un-huh	Of course
Bye-bye	Good-bye
Huh?	I beg your pardon. I did not understand.

FIGURE 8-2 Avoid slang expressions when talking on the phone

picks up the phone and announce the transfer. If the person to whom you are transferring the call is not in, ask if the caller would like to leave a voice message. If the caller does not want to do so, take a number from the caller and have someone return the call.

Terminate Calls Courteously

Thank the person if appropriate. Say *good-bye* pleasantly. Let the person who called hang up first. Treat the handset gently; do not slam it down in the caller's ear.

Handle Problem Calls

Although most individuals are pleasant over the telephone, sometimes a caller is angry or unhappy. Remember that the individual is not angry with you. The person is angry at a situation or an event. Just as you are pleasant to a difficult visitor to your workplace, you are pleasant to a difficult telephone caller. If the person is angry over an organizational issue, listen. Successful administrative professionals defuse many angry callers by letting the callers talk and not becoming emotionally involved in the situations.

Once you listen to the person, try to assist in getting the problem solved. This approach may mean that you suggest a solution or suggest someone who can solve the problem. Do not put the person on hold for a long period of time or mishandle the call by transferring it to an individual who cannot help. Such approaches merely make the caller angrier.

Although you cannot solve every difficult situation and make every telephone caller happy, you should be able to handle most people and situations well if you remain courteous and considerate.

Keep a List of Frequently Called Numbers

A file of frequently called numbers is an excellent time saver. You can keep these numbers in a computer file or in a card file on your desk.

Remember Time Differences

You need to remember time zone differences when placing long-distance calls. There are

Keep frequently called numbers in a file so you can find them quickly.

four standard time zones in the United States—Eastern, Central, Mountain, and Pacific. There is a one-hour difference between neighboring zones. For example, if it is 10 a.m. in New York City (Eastern Standard Time), it is 9 a.m. in Dallas (Central Standard Time). If you call from New York to Los Angeles, you do not want to call at 9 a.m. Eastern Standard Time; it would be only 6 a.m. in Los Angeles (Pacific Standard Time). You might note on your telephone list time differences for frequent callers. Figure 8-3 is a time zone map of the United States.

There are also international time zones. For example, the person who places a call from New York to London must remember that when it is 11 a.m. in New York, it is 4 p.m. in London. If you are placing many international calls, you need to become familiar with the international time zones.

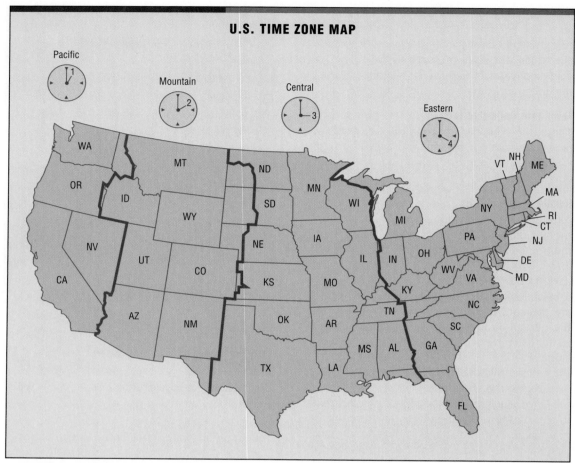

FIGURE 8~3 U.S. Time Zone Map

Your Telecommunications Role

As an administrative professional who understands the importance of keeping abreast of telecommunications technology, your role is twofold. First, you need to keep current on advances in telecommunications. Second, you need to be willing to learn the intricacies of the telecommunications equipment you operate.

If you accept the need to remain current on telecommunications advances, does this mean you must understand the intricacies of each new telecommunications device? Absolutely not! You are not an engineer or a telecommunications expert. However, your job does demand that you pay attention to new developments in telecommunications. You do so by reading publications such as *PCWorld*™ and *Smart Computing*™. You do so by using the Web to learn about new technologies and equipment that are available. In other words, you make it part of your job to have a general knowledge of what is happening in the telecommunications world.

Additionally, you willingly learn the intricacies of new telecommunications devices at your workplace. You eagerly accept training on new equipment. You become proficient in operating the equipment. You become a leader with other administrative professionals in your workplace in using new technology to increase your own productivity and thus the productivity of the organization. ■

SUMMARY

To reinforce what you have learned in this chapter, study this summary.

- Advances in telecommunications affect an individual's workplace and personal life. Telecommunication advances will continue at ever-increasing speeds. Technology will continue to affect how individuals work and live.
- Telecommunication pipelines include analog dial-up, cable, DSL, satellite, and wireless.
- The rapid growth of telecommunication capabilities suggests that the capabilities and speed of information transmission by 2020 will increase exponentially.
- IM benefits include almost instantaneous contact with "buddies" who can assist with information. IM also has the potential to improve sales for ecommerce companies. Research suggests that IM users will continue to grow, with IM having the capacity to reduce the usage of email and telephones.
- Since you cannot observe a person's facial expressions and tone of voice with IM, you must observe appropriate IM etiquette. For example, do not add a buddy to your list without communicating with that person first; be concise with your IM message; let your buddies know when you are not available for IM; and put into action the effective correspondence techniques of completeness, clarity, accurateness, promptness, conciseness, courteousness, and positivism.
- Internet telephony provides hardware and software that enables people to use the Internet as the transmission medium for telephone calls.
- Cell phones are standard equipment for many people. In addition, combination cell phones and PDAs are available that allow phone, fax, and email messages to be delivered into a single mailbox; Web browsing; IM email; and other services.
- With the number of cell phones in use today, appropriate cell phone etiquette becomes important. When in public places, keep your calls to a minimum, your voice as low as possible, and your calls short.
- Since organizations use voice messaging extensively, voice messaging etiquette is essential. Voice messaging systems should route calls quickly and efficiently. The voice on the message must create a favorable impression through the words and the tone of voice.
- Telephone etiquette includes these techniques:
  - Answering promptly
  - Speaking distinctly
  - Identifying yourself and/or the organization
  - Recording messages carefully
  - Placing calls on hold effectively
  - Avoiding discriminatory language and gender bias

- Being helpful and discreet
- Asking questions tactfully
- Screening calls
- Being attentive
- Using correct English
- Avoiding slang
- Using the caller's name
- Transferring calls properly
- Terminating calls courteously
- Handling problem calls
- Keeping a list of frequently called numbers
- Remembering time differences

- As an administrative professional who understands the importance of keeping abreast of telecommunications technology, your role is to remain current on advances in telecommunications and to be willing and eager to learn the intricacies of telecommunications equipment in the workplace.

FIND THE PROBLEM

In your work for People Pharmaceuticals International, you frequently use IM with individuals who report to Sandra Portales, informing them of meetings or asking them for information that Ms. Portales needs immediately. Recently you requested information from three people regarding a new drug under development. You received a reply from two of the individuals; you did not receive a reply from the third person. After one day passed, you sent the following IM to the individual who did not respond.

I sent an IM to you yesterday; I have received no response. I must have the response immediately.

When the individual returned, you received this IM from him:

Sandra knew I was out of town; she gave me an assignment that demanded a trip to Cleveland. Next time check before you send me two IMs and call my assistant.

What is the problem? How should you handle it?

PROFESSIONAL POINTERS

When communicating through email, through IM, or by cell phone, adhere to these rules of etiquette:

- Ask for information rather than demand that you receive it. Use *please* often.
- Use your IM system to let your buddies know when you are not available.
- Before you make a call or write an email or IM covering complicated issues, plan carefully. Be certain you include necessary details.
- When writing email or IMs to internal employees, use proper language, just as you would when writing to a client or customer. Be polite.

- Do not attempt to be clever or cute when writing emails or IMs. Be professional.
- When talking on a cell phone in a public place, remember to follow rules of courtesy: Do not talk too loudly or too long. If you must talk, seek out a place (if possible) where there are a limited number of people.
- Do not handle confidential information via a cell phone in a public place. You never know who might hear and use what you say to the detriment of your organization.

REINFORCEMENT ITEMS

1. Describe three ways that telecommunications affects people's lives.
2. List and describe the major telecommunication pipelines.
3. Describe three messaging services.
4. List three standards of etiquette for cell phone usage.
5. List five standards of etiquette for standard telephone usage.

CRITICAL-THINKING ACTIVITY

Celia Mesa works as an administrative professional for a small law firm, McKay, Carlson & Duffy. Celia started with the firm five years ago when there was only one attorney. Although the firm is still relatively small, there are three attorneys and the number of clients has increased by 300 percent from five years ago. One of Celia's responsibilities is to answer all incoming calls. There is one other administrative assistant in the office (added in the third year of operation), but the person has no phone responsibilities. In addition to answering the telephone, Celia must take care of a myriad of other duties, including keying legal documents and filing correspondence. Mr. McKay was the founder of the firm, and he believes that providing a personal touch is important. He wants his employees to care about the clients. He rejected a voice messaging system in the past because he considered it too impersonal.

Celia is overloaded. She is going to have to ask for additional help—either a third person or a voice messaging system. She knows the voice messaging system would be less costly. What advice would you give to Celia? What should she suggest to Mr. McKay?

VOCABULARY REVIEW

Complete the Vocabulary Review for Chapter 8 given on page 73 of the *Applications Workbook*.

ENGLISH AND WORD USAGE DRILL

Complete the English and Word Usage Drill for Chapter 8 given on page 74 of the *Applications Workbook*.

WORKPLACE APPLICATIONS

A8-1 (Goal 1)

With two classmates, interview three administrative professionals about the impact telecommunications has on the workplace. Write your instructor a short report of your findings using the memorandum form on the Student CD, SCDA8-1. Present an oral report of your findings to the class.

A8-2 (Goals 2 and 3)

Using the Web, conduct a search for the most recent wireless technology; check at least four sources. Write a report to your instructor describing your findings (including costs of services if available) and listing your sources. Use the memorandum form on the Student CD, SCDA8-2 to report your findings to your instructor.

A8-3 (Goal 4)

Refer to the five situations that appear in your *Applications Workbook*, page 75. Respond to each situation. Submit your responses to your instructor.

A8-4 (Goal 4)

Choose a class member to work with. Call each other, recreating the five situations in A8-3. One of you should be the caller; the other, the administrative assistant. Then switch roles and replay each situation. Rate each other on voice quality and the handling of the situations by using the Telephone Rating Form in your *Applications Workbook*, page 76. Individually prepare an action plan on how you can improve your voice quality and/or techniques. Submit your action plan to your instructor.

ASSESSMENT OF CHAPTER GOALS

Did you successfully complete the chapter goals? Evaluate yourself by filling out the form on page 77 of the *Applications Workbook*.

Workplace Mail

chapter 9

LEARNING GOALS

1. Identify mail classifications and mail services.

2. Process outgoing mail.

3. Process incoming mail.

The personal computer as well as the Internet have provided individuals with more ways to communicate. Email communication has greatly increased the amount of information exchanged electronically within the United States and around the world. The computer has also led to the development of prepaid Epostage, which allows people to send traditional mail without having to visit the post office to buy stamps. Even with the widespread use of email, the volume of traditional mail has continued to increase. This increased dependence on traditional mail has spawned the expansion of private companies that handle letters and parcels. FedEx®, UPS®, and others, as well as the United States Postal Service, now provide a variety of services, including express and overnight delivery to compete with instant electronic communication.

An independent entity of the federal government, The United States Postal Service **(USPS)**, is directed by law to provide universal postal communications to all persons residing in the United States. This service, established before the American Revolution, has functioned without interruption for over 226 years. Today, with annual revenues approaching $68 billion, it is the eighth largest organization in the country; and, if included, it would rank as the twenty-sixth largest enterprise on *Fortune's* magazine Global 500. It has a career workforce of nearly 800,000, which makes it one of the largest employers in the nation. Its diverse products and services anchor an $871 billion mailing industry, which, in turn, employs nearly 9 million Americans.[1]

Mail volume per customer has increased over 80 percent since 1970. The delivery network has increased by two-thirds and is currently increasing at about 1.7 million new addresses every year.[2] However, the impact of Internet-related applications on mail volume continues to be uncertain. It is possible that if the economy improves, mail volume will

[1]"Outline for Discussion: Concepts for Postal Transformation," accessed September 2, 2002; available from **www.usps.com/strategicdirection/_pdf/outbody.pdf**.

[2]"FY2002 Annual Performance Plan," accessed September 4, 2002; available from **www.usps.com/strategic direction/_txt/02_app.txt**.

grow accordingly. At the same time, however, electronic mail, **electronic bill presentment and payment** (EBPP) will continue to affect mail volume.[3]

While much of the previous decade marked financial success for the Postal Service, significant marketplace shifts—emerging alternative communication technologies, new competitors both domestic and international, and changing consumer attitudes and behaviors—have altered the landscape. Within the next decade technological innovations such as mobile commerce, broadband Internet access, interactive TV, data mining software, and new printing technologies will change the way businesses and consumers interact. Domestic delivery firms, such as UPS and FedEx, and liberalized foreign posts, such as Deutsche Post World Net™ and TPC™ of the Netherlands, are aggressively competing in postal service markets.

Electronic billing and payment, preauthorized debits to bank accounts and credit cards, and Internet-enabled Electronic Data Interchange will reduce the need for and use of paper bills and payments. Electronic communications will grow at a more rapid pace than traditional hard-copy communications, particularly on the Internet. Using modern technology, advertising will be more targeted, personalized, and interactive.[4]

According to the USPS, the Postal Service delivers hundreds of millions of messages and billions of dollars in financial transactions each day to 8 million businesses and 250 million Americans. In one week, mail volume at the USPS matches the annual volume of United Parcel Service, and in two days, the Postal Service delivers what FedEx delivers in a year.[5]

The Postal Service delivers hundreds of messages and billions of dollars in financial transactions each day to 8 million businesses and 250 million Americans.

The way mail is prepared and processed can have an effect on the operating costs of a business. Company profits may suffer if mail operations are inefficient. For example, assume that you allow a letter that contains an important order to remain on your desk unopened for several days. Several possibilities are likely. The customer will not receive the order on time, will become upset, and will not buy from your company again. The customer may even cancel the order. Regardless, your company may lose a valuable customer due to the improper handling of mail. Additional improper mail-handling procedures that can contribute to increased company costs include failure to:

- Address mail properly.
- Use the proper postage.
- Use the appropriate Zip Code.
- Choose the appropriate mail service.

Efficient handling of workplace mail, both incoming and outgoing, is expected of the administrative professional. This chapter

---

[3]"USPS 5 Year Strategic Plan," accessed September 4, 2002; available from **www.usps.com/strategicdirection/ _txt/fiveyear.txt**.

[4]"USPS 5 Year Strategic Plan," accessed September 4, 2002; available from **www.usps.com/strategicdirection/ _txt/fiveyear.txt**.

[5]"History of the United States Postal Service," accessed September 2, 2002; available from **www.usps.com/history**.

will help you to learn how to process mail efficiently.

Mail Classifications and Services

The USPS, a governmental agency, is the major mail service provider within the United States. The USPS began in 1775 when the Continental Congress appointed Benjamin Franklin as the first Postmaster General.[6] Today the USPS lists its mission as follows:

The vision of the Postal Service for the next five years, therefore, is to become an organization that can improve performance and affordability, implement innovative ways to grow both its revenues and those of the mailing industry, and find flexible, responsive solutions to the challenges raised by technology and the seismic shifts in the global postal business environment.[7]

Since its inception, the USPS has operated by three broad goals. The goal statements developed by the USPS are:

- Earn customers' business in a marketplace where they have choices by providing them with world-class quality at competitive prices.

- Foster an inclusive and welcoming workplace consistent with the values of fairness, opportunity, safety, and security; where everyone is given the knowledge, tools, education, and encouragement to be successful; and where everyone is recognized for and takes pride in his/her participation in customer and Postal Service success.

- Generate financial performance that assures the commercial viability of the Postal Service as a provider in a changing, competitive marketplace and will generate cash flow to finance high-yield investments for

the future while providing competitively priced products and services.[8]

Postal classifications, special mail services, and international mail services available from the USPS are described in the next section.

Postal Service Classifications

If you work in a small organization, you may be responsible for processing the outgoing mail. To do this efficiently, you must know the current postal classifications and rates. To keep advised of current regulations, you can obtain pamphlets from your local post office or visit the USPS Website at **www.usps.com**. The size, weights, and postal rates given in this text became effective on July 1, 2002. The USPS Website and brochures from your local post office will provide you with the most recent information.

Express Mail

The fastest delivery system available from the USPS is **Express Mail**. This service offers next-day delivery by 12 p.m. to most destinations. Express Mail is delivered 365 days a year with no extra charge for Saturday, Sunday, or holiday delivery. All packages must use an Express Mail label; however, Express Mail envelopes and boxes are optional. All supplies are available from local post offices at no additional cost. The maximum weight for this service is 70 pounds, and the maximum length and girth combined is 108 inches. Stamps, postage meters, or Express Mail Corporate Accounts may be used to send express mail. Features of this service include:

- Tracking and tracing on the USPS Website (**www.usps.com**)
- Delivery to post office boxes and rural addresses
- Money-back guarantee
- COD (collect on delivery)
- Return receipt service

---

[6]"History of the United States Postal Service," accessed September 2, 2002; available from **www.usps.com/history**.
[7]"USPS 5 Year Strategic Plan, accessed September 4, 2002; available from **www.usps.com/strategicdirection/ _txt/fiveyear.txt**.

[8]"USPS 5 Year Strategic Plan, accessed September 4, 2002; available from **www.usps.com/strategicdirection/ _txt/fiveyear.txt**.

- Insurance up to $100 at no additional cost
- Additional merchandise insurance up to $5,000

Priority Mail

Priority Mail offers one- to three-day service to most domestic destinations. Items must weigh 70 pounds or less and measure no more than 108 inches in combined distance around the thickest part. The minimum size is $3\frac{1}{2}$ inches high by 5 inches long. Priority Mail envelopes, labels, and boxes are available from the USPS at no additional charge. Materials sent in a USPS Priority Mail flat-rate envelope are charged a standard rate regardless of weight or destination. There is an additional charge for pickup service for all types of Priority Mail.

First-Class Mail

First-Class Mail includes letters, greeting cards, bills, large envelopes, and packages.

There is a set charge for the first ounce of First-Class Mail and an added charge for each additional ounce. The minimum size for First-Class Mail is 5 inches long, $3\frac{1}{2}$ inches high, and .007 inches thick.

Because postal equipment cannot process nonstandardized mail, a nonmachinable surcharge is assessed for First-Class Mail weighing 1 ounce or less with any of the following criteria.

- The height exceeds $6\frac{1}{8}$ inches, length exceeds $11\frac{1}{2}$ inches, or thickness exceeds $\frac{1}{4}$ inch.
- The length divided by height is less than 1.3 or more than 2.5 (length is the dimension parallel to the address).
- It has clasps, strings, buttons, or similar closure devices.
- It is too rigid or contains items such as pens that cause the thickness of the mailpiece to be uneven.

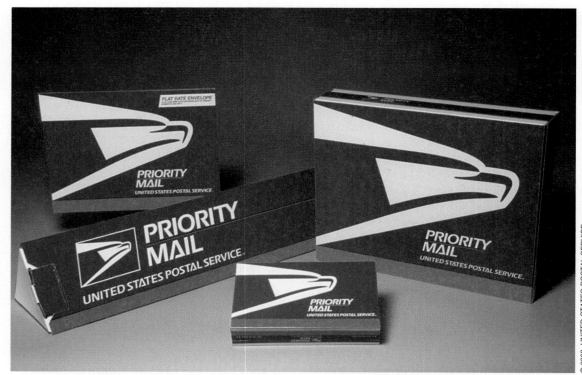

USPS Priority Mail envelopes are charged a standard rate regardless of weight or destination.

- It has an address parallel to the shorter dimension of the mailpiece.

Although postcards are considered First-Class Mail, they are subject to a separate fee structure. Commercially sold postcards cost $.23 to mail; stamped postcards may be purchased from the USPS for $.25. This fee structure assigns a minimum size for postcards of $3\frac{1}{2}$ inches high by 7 inches long by .007 inches thick. The maximum size for a postcard is $4\frac{1}{4}$ inches high by 6 inches long by .016 inches thick. Postcards over the maximum height or length for the card rate receive regular First-Class Mail rates; the nonmachinable surcharge may apply.

Parcel Post

Parcel Post mail consists of pieces 70 pounds or less. The maximum size is 130 inches in combined length and distance around the thickest part. Parcel Post is often used for gifts and general merchandise, but it also may contain books and other matter.

Bound Printed Matter

The maximum weight for **Bound Printed Matter** is 15 pounds, and the maximum size is 108 inches in combined length and distance around the thickest part. Rates are based on weight, shape, and distance. Bound Printed Matter must:

- Consist of advertising, promotional, directory, or editorial material (or any combination of such material).
- Be securely bound by permanent fastenings such as staples, spiral binding, glue, or stitching.
- Consist of sheets of which at least 90 percent are imprinted by any process other than handwriting or typewriting.
- Not have the nature of personal correspondence.
- Not be stationery, such as pads of blank printed forms.

Rates for Bound Printed Matter vary by weight and zone. Check with your local post office or online (**www.usps.com**) for the current fee structure.

Media Mail (Book Rate)

The **Media Mail** category is designed for books, film, manuscripts, printed music, videotapes, and computer-recorded media such as CD-ROMs and diskettes. Media Mail cannot contain advertising. The maximum size is 108 inches in combined length and distance around the thickest part. Rates for Media Mail are determined by weight.

Special Mail Services

In addition to being familiar with USPS mail classifications, you also need to know what special services are available. Being aware of these services allows you to process outgoing mail effectively.

Certificate of Mailing

A **certificate of mailing** provides evidence that an item has been mailed. There is a minimal charge for this service, and you must purchase the certificate at the time of mailing. This service is available for First-Class Mail, Priority Mail, Parcel Post, Bound Printed Matter, and Media Mail.

Registered Mail

Registering mail provides maximum protection and security for valuable items. **Registered Mail** is available only for First-Class or Priority Mail. When you register an item with no declared value, no insurance is necessary. However, if you declare a value on the item, insurance is mandatory. You can combine Registered Mail with COD, restricted delivery, or return receipt (services mentioned in the next section).

Restricted Delivery

With **restricted delivery**, the mailer sends the item by direct delivery only to the addressee or addressee's authorized agent. The addressee must be an individual specified by name. This service is available for First-Class Mail, Priority Mail, Parcel Post, Bound Printed Matter, and Media Mail that is sent Certified Mail, COD, mail insured for more than $50, or Registered Mail. There is an additional fee for restricted delivery.

Registered mail provides protection and security for valuable items.

Return Receipt

Return receipt is a service that provides the mailer with evidence of delivery. This service is available for Express Mail, First-Class Mail, Priority Mail, Parcel Post, Bound Printed Matter, or Media Mail when purchased with one of the following: Certified Mail, COD, Registered Mail, or Mail insured for more than $50.

Generally, you request a return receipt before an item is mailed. However, if you decide that you need a return receipt after mailing the item, you can make the request. You pay more to request a return receipt after the item is mailed than you do at the time of mailing.

Signature Confirmation

You can also purchase **Signature Confirmation** service for an additional fee. This service provides signature proof of delivery as well as the date and time of delivery or attempted delivery. You can purchase this service only at the time of mailing. Mailers can track the delivery information at **www.usps.com** or by calling a toll-free number. The USPS maintains a delivery record, including the recipient's signature. This information is available upon request via fax or mail. There is no acceptance record kept at the office of mailing. The service is available for Priority Mail, First-Class Mail, Parcel Post, Bound Printed Matter, or Media Mail. You can combine Signature Confirmation with the following:

- COD
- Insured Mail
- Registered Mail
- Special handling

Restricted delivery is available if purchased with insurance for over $50, COD, or Registered Mail.

Collect on Delivery (COD)

Collect on delivery (COD) allows the mailer to collect the price of goods and/or postage on the item ordered by the addressee when delivered. You can use COD service for merchandise sent by the following classes of mail:

- First-Class Mail
- Express Mail
- Priority Mail
- Parcel Post
- Bound Printed Matter
- Media Mail
- Standard Mail (B)

With COD service, the amount to be collected cannot exceed $1,000. COD service is not available for international mail or for **APO (air postal office)** and **FPO (fleet postal office)** addresses. Both APO and FPO are military postal addresses.

Certified Mail

For materials that have no monetary value but for which you need a record of delivery, use **Certified Mail**. The mailer is provided with a mailing receipt, and a record is kept at the recipient's post office. Certified Mail is available only for First-Class Mail and Priority Mail. An additional fee is charged.

Insured Mail

You can obtain coverage against loss or damage through **Insured Mail**. Coverage can be obtained for up to $5,000 for Parcel Post, Bound Printed Matter, and Media Mail, as well as merchandise mailed at Priority Mail or First-Class Mail rates. You cannot insure items for more than their value. For items

Use certified mail when your materials have no monetary value but you need a record of delivery.

insured for more than $50, restricted delivery and return receipt service are available.

Money Order

You can obtain **money orders** from the post office. This service provides for the safe transmission of money to individuals or institutions; amounts are available up to $1,000. There is a minimal fee charged for money orders.

Authorization to Hold Mail

The USPS will hold mail at the post office if a mailer requests this service. The mailer must fill out an **Authorization to Hold Mail** form; the service is limited to a 30-day period.

International Mail

The principal categories of International Mail include:

- **Global Express Guaranteed (GXG)**—for mailing high-priority or other urgently needed items, including merchandise, which can be sent to nearly 200 countries and territories around the world. Service is guaranteed to meet destination-specific delivery standards (usually one day) or postage will be refunded.
- **Global Express Mail (EMS)**—for mailing time-sensitive material to more than 175 countries. It provides customers with expeditious handling and delivery on an on-demand basis.
- **Global Priority Mail (GPM)**—for mailing items weighing up to 4 pounds, including merchandise, which can be sent to more than 30 countries around the world. GPM items receive priority service within the USPS and the postal service of the destination country.
- **Letter-Post**—for mailing letters and letter packages, postcards and postal cards, **aerogrammes** (air letter sheets that can be folded and sealed to form an envelope), printed matter, and small packets.
- **International Parcel Post**—for shipping heavier merchandise and printed matter.

All printed matter items, small packets, and parcel post packages can be sent airmail or surface mail. Check with your local post office for specific information about mail service in the country to which you are mailing. The maximum weight limit for Letter-Post rates is 4 pounds.

Special services such as insurance, recorded delivery registered mail, COD, and certified mail are available for international mail customers. Because the regulations regarding these services vary by country, consult your local post office if you wish to use any of these services.

Varieties of international economy services are available as well. To use international economy services, a mailer must have at least 200 pieces or 50 pounds of mailable material. These services require that the sender comply with specific mail preparation requirements. You can obtain additional information regarding international rates and services at **www.usps.com**.

Private Mail Services

Several private companies across the United States offer fast and effective mail services. Four well-known services are FedEx®, United® Parcel Service (UPS), DHL Worldwide Express®, and Airborne Express®. These companies offer service worldwide. You can find information about them on the Internet. Listed here are a few examples of the services provided by FedEx Express®. (Similar services are also provided by other companies.)

Service within the United States includes the following:

- FedEx Same Day®—Delivery within hours in all 50 states, 7 days a week, 365 days a year
- FedEx First Overnight®—Delivery by 8 a.m. or 8:30 a.m. to major markets, depending on destination Zip Codes; available Monday through Friday
- FedEx Priority Overnight®—Delivery by 10:30 a.m. to most U.S. addresses; by noon

Private transportation services, such as FedEx, provide a variety of domestic and international shipping options.

or 4:30 p.m. in remote areas; available Monday through Friday with Saturday service available for an extra charge

- FedEx Standard Overnight®—Delivery by 3 p.m. to most U.S. addresses and by 4:30 p.m. to rural areas; available Monday through Friday

- FedEx 2Day®—Delivery in two business days by 4:30 p.m. and 7 p.m. to residences

- FedEx Express Saver®—Delivery within three business days within the continental United States by 4:30 p.m. and by 7 p.m. to residences

International services include the following:

- FedEx International® Next Flight—Delivery within hours between major cities worldwide, 24 hours a day to more than 210 countries

- FedEx International First®—Delivery by 8 a.m. in two business days to selected international cities

- FedEx International Priority®—Delivery typically in one, two, or three days (depending on destination)

- FedEx International Economy®—Delivery typically in four to five business days to major world markets

- FedEx International MailService℠—Delivery of bulk mailed materials in either 4 to 7 or 7 to 11 international business days

Freight services include the following:

- FedEx 1Day℠ Freight—Delivery by 10:30 a.m. the next business day in most U.S. cities; delivery by noon to most other areas

- Express 2Day℠ Freight—Delivery by noon for most shipments and by 3 p.m. in many other parts of the United States

- FedEx International Priority® Freight—Delivery typically in one, two, or three business days for single pieces, with shipments having at least one piece weighing 151 pounds or more

FedEx offers customers access to a variety of services online at **www.fedex.com**. In fact, more than 2.5 million customers connect with this Internet service daily, and electronic transactions account for almost two-thirds of the shipments FedEx delivers.[9]

A shipper may also use the FedEx Website to prepare a document for shipping. For example, through the Website, you can:

- Prepare and print shipping labels.
- Find the nearest drop-off location.
- Obtain the rate for a shipment.
- Track the status of a shipment.
- Order shipping supplies.
- Find international shipping documents.
- Estimate duties and taxes for international shipments.
- Schedule a pickup.
- Pay invoices.

Electronic Messages

An **electronic message** is the communication of text, data, images, or voice messages between a sender and a recipient by using telecommunications links. As you will learn in other chapters in this text, many communications today are sent through electronic messages. In Chapter 8, you learned about voice mail, which is a type of electronic message. In Chapter 6, you learned about email, another type of electronic mail. Since the coverage of email was extensive in Chapter 6, the information presented here merely serves as a reminder of email's importance in today's workplace.

Email

Workers send millions of messages daily over the Internet, speeding up delivery of important communications and ultimately saving companies millions of dollars. Many of these messages are in the form of emails. In fact, by 2005, it is estimated that nearly a half-million emails will land in inboxes each second.[10] Although many organizations find the use of email to send correspondence beneficial, handling the large number of email messages takes time. A recent survey by the Gartner™ research firm found that the nation's tens of millions of email users spend an average of nearly an hour a day at their workplace and additional time at home managing their email.[11]

Unfortunately, people waste almost half the time spent on email on unimportant messages. To efficiently handle incoming email you should do the following:

- Preview messages. A glance at the subject line should indicate whether reading the entire message is warranted. If not, delete the email.
- Organize your inbox. Keep it clean and well organized so reading your email does not involve sorting through previous messages. Set up folders for messages you want to keep.
- Deal with messages only once. When a message arrives, read it, respond to it, delete it, or file it away in a folder.
- Automate. Create a signature file that you can automatically add to outgoing messages. Create filters so messages are filed as they enter your email inbox. Create standard response emails for frequently asked questions.
- Separate business and personal email accounts (if your company policy allows you to receive personal email using your company account).[12]

Handling large numbers of email will continue to be an important issue for administrative professionals. The time it takes to deal with email messages will continue to increase for workplace employees in the next few years.

9"FedEx Technology," accessed November 8, 2002; available from **www.fedex.com/us/about/overview/technology.html**.

10"When You've Got Too Much Email," USA Today, January 4, 2002.

11"Taking Control of Your Email Inbox", USA Today, February 6, 2002.

12"Taking Control of Your Email Inbox," USA Today, February 6, 2002.

Fax Mail

Another type of electronic message is a fax message. The fax machine is a technology with continued use in the workplace. Even though the growing use of email and more affordable delivery systems have lessened the use of fax, fax is a widely used form of electronic communication.

Fax messages are considered important messages and should be delivered immediately to the addressee, as speed of delivery is one of the reasons for sending a fax. You can assume that all fax messages take top priority unless your employer tells you otherwise.

Outgoing Mail

An administrative professional's responsibilities for handling outgoing mail vary. In a large company, he or she is responsible for preparing the mail for processing by mailroom employees, who, in turn, determine postage requirements, affix postage, seal the correspondence, and sort for the Postal Service. In a small company, the administrative professional usually is responsible for preparing and processing the mail for the Postal Service. Refer to Figure 9-1 to help maximize your postal dollar. Several steps to ensure that you handle outgoing mail properly are described in the next section.

Check Enclosures

An **enclosure** or **attachment notation** at the bottom of a document serves as a flag to the recipient. Use *Attachment* when an item is attached to the document by a staple or paper clip. Use *Enclosure* when the item is merely placed behind the document without being attached. If there is more than one enclosure or attachment, the number should be placed in parentheses after the word *Enclosure* or *Attachment* or itemized as shown below.

> Enclosures (2)
>
> *OR*
>
> Enclosures: Annual Report
> Sales Forecast

When you prepare documents for mailing, be sure to indicate any enclosures or attachments. If the enclosure is the same size as the letter, you can fold the enclosure with the letter. If the enclosure is smaller than the letter (smaller than $8\frac{1}{2}'' \times 11''$), place it in front of the letter. If the enclosure is larger than the

---

BEFORE YOU MAIL THAT LETTER*

To alleviate postal rate increases and maximize your postage dollar, Pitney Bowes Inc.™ recommends several easy strategies.

- Reduce postage expenses up to 20 percent through accurate electronic weighing and rating.
- Eliminate time-consuming trips to the post office with postage resets by phone, online, or via modem.
- Reduce expenses associated with costly address labels and increase mail openability through direct impression printing.
- Ensure the deliverability of mail using address verification software.
- Presort and print postal barcodes to qualify mail for discounts of 30 percent or more.
- Automate folding and inserting (20 times faster than manual processing) for optimum output and accuracy.

*"Before You Mail that Letter," *OfficePro*, January 2001, p. 5.

FIGURE 9~1 Maximize your postal dollar

letter (larger than $8\frac{1}{2}'' \times 11''$), place it behind the letter. Automatic canceling machines are equipped to process only envelopes containing flat contents. If you do enclose bulky items, such as pens, pencils, keys, and so on, key *Hand Cancel* on the outside of the envelope; however, expect to pay an additional fee.

Prepare Envelopes

Your responsibility as an administrative professional is to choose the correct size envelope for the correspondence being mailed. Envelopes that are too large for the items they contain cost the company extra money. Most outgoing correspondence is mailed in No. 10 envelopes. If you need to mail correspondence in a special size envelope, check with the Postal Service to find out about any restrictions. Special sizes of envelopes cost additional money to mail.

Address Envelopes

An incorrectly addressed envelope can cause the delay of an important letter or document and may lead to a loss of money for the company. Always compare the letter and envelope address of outgoing correspondence. Check the address against the letterhead of previous correspondence to be sure the address is accurate. If you keep a mailing list of frequently used addresses, be certain it is up to date.

Adhere to Automation Requirements

The Postal Service uses automated equipment designed to handle the steadily growing volume of mail. As an administrative professional, you are responsible for seeing that outgoing mail is properly prepared for this equipment. Two such machines installed in large post offices are the **multiline optical character reader (MLOCR)** and **remote barcoding systems (RBCS)**. MLOCRs read

Hundreds of envelopes are sorted each minute using USPS automated equipment.

the entire address on an envelope, spray a barcode on the envelope, and then sort the envelopes at the rate of more than nine per second.[13] The RBCS provides barcoding for handwritten mail or mail that cannot be read by OCRs. If the RBCS system is unable to determine the barcode for an address, an image is sent to a reader at a remote location, who then keys in the appropriate barcode information.

Some companies preprint a barcode on their correspondence; you may do so quickly and easily with barcode software. For example, many utility companies print a barcode on the return envelope. If you have not noticed this barcode, you might check the return envelope you receive with your next utility bill.

When addressing domestic envelopes to be read by OCR machines, key the address in all capital letters. Remember to omit punctuation except for the hyphen in the ZIP + 4 designation. Figure 9-2 shows a correctly addressed domestic envelope.

You must meet specific requirements when addressing mail to an international destination. International envelopes can also be generated quickly using computer software.

---

[13]"The Age of Automation," *History of the United States Postal Service*, accessed September 4, 2002; available from **www.usps.com/history**.

Figure 9-3 shows a correctly addressed international envelope.

Seal and Stamp

If you work in a medium to large organization, you usually are not responsible for sealing and stamping the mail. The outgoing mail is sent to a mailroom, where sealing and stamping are done with automated equipment. If your organization is small, you can seal and stamp envelopes using electronic postage or a postage meter.

Electronic Postage

Electronic postage is the name given to postage purchased over the Internet and printed on a company printer. The USPS licenses authorized providers to use the PC Postage brand (and logo) to indicate that their product is compliant with Postal Service criteria. PC Postage products use **Information Based Indicia (IBI)** to produce the postage marks or "stamp." IBI are the postage markings printed on the envelope to indicate that postage has been paid and include a two-dimensional barcode that contains mail-processing and security-related data as well as printed data. Like other forms of postage, such as stamps and meter impressions, IBI are printed on an envelope in the upper right-hand corner or on a label for an envelope or

---

PEOPLE PHARMACEUTICALS INTERNATIONAL
2056 MAIN STREET
DALLAS TX 75201–9898

CONFIDENTIAL

                    ATTENTION MR TROY VANDERLANN
                    BREVARD INCORPORATED
                    5456 HAMMOCK ROAD
                    DETROIT MI 48204–3478

FIGURE 9–2 Domestic addresses must be keyed to meet OCR requirements

PEOPLE PHARAMACEUTICALS INTERNATIONAL
19 RUE SAINT-DIDIER
75116 PARIS
FRANCE

                                        MS JOYCE BROWNING
                                        2045 ROYAL ROAD
                                        LONDON WIP 6HQ
                                        ENGLAND

FIGURE 9~3 International envelopes must be keyed following USPS guidelines

a package. A variety of products exist in addition to PC Postage brand.

Electronic postage is easy to purchase. First, a customer establishes a connection with a PC Postage vendor. A variety of USPS approved vendors are listed at the USPS Website (**www.usps.com**). A customer then purchases postage using an electronic funds transfer or a credit card. Once the postage is purchased, it can be downloaded and stored in a secure device attached to a computer or it can be downloaded and stored on the vendor's server and accessed via the company's Internet site. Electronic stamps can be used for many classifications of USPS mail as well as for selected special services.

Postage Meters

A small organization may also use a postage meter. **Postage meters** are postage-printing machines purchased for use in a home or an office. Envelopes are fed into the meter and are stacked, sealed, weighed, meter-stamped, and counted in one continuous operation. Many of the recent postage meters use IBI technology and print a "stamp" similar to those printed with PC Postage.

The metered-mail imprint serves as postage payment, postmark, and cancellation mark. A postage meter prints directly on envelopes or on adhesive strips affixed to packages. You purchase postage for the postage

meter from the USPS. You can replenish postage meters electronically through telephone line connections. You simply dial-up and download postage anytime, anywhere using a regular phone line connected to your meter.

Another possibility in a small organization is to seal and stamp mail manually. To seal a number of envelopes quickly, place them in a row with the flaps facing up. Run a moist sponge across the flaps, and press them down. You can also save time by purchasing stamps in rolls. Place the envelopes to be stamped face up on the desk. Remove the stamp off the roll, and place it on the envelope. Self-adhesive stamps can be purchased in books or sheets. Sheets are a little more difficult to handle when stamping several envelopes at once. You can order self-adhesive stamps over the Internet and have them delivered to your organization by the postal delivery person.

Establish a Schedule

Determine how often and at what times the local post office dispatches the mail. If you deposit outgoing mail before the established collection times, quicker delivery is possible. If the company has a central mail department, periodic pickups of outgoing mail are usually made from individual departments. In some

PITNEY BOWES

The metered-mail imprint serves as postage payment, postmark, and cancellation mark.

workplaces, outgoing trays are located at a central location. Learn the schedule for these pickups, and have your outgoing mail ready on time.

Maintain Current Mailing Lists

Most companies have correspondence that is sent to a certain group of individuals on a regular basis. As an administrative professional, you are responsible for maintaining a current mailing list. Periodic updating of addresses is essential, as is adding new names to the mailing list. By maintaining your mailing lists on the computer, you can update them quickly and easily. You can print address labels and/or envelopes with barcodes from the mailing lists.

Prepare Mail for Automated Processing

Businesses that prepare mail to meet automated processing requirements can save on postage rates. These automation savings plans are available for letters, flats, or parcels. In order for a business to take advantage of the savings, the mail must conform to specific criteria. Letters and cards that are compatible with the Postal Service's automated processing equipment may qualify for automation rates if they meet the following criteria:

- Must consist of a minimum number of pieces (200 pieces for Standard Mail and 500 pieces for First Class Mail)
- Must have a delivery point barcode on each piece
- Must have an address that has been checked and must be CASS-certified within the last 180 days
- Must have a complete address with ZIP Code or ZIP + 4 code
- Must be a specific shape and size
- Must weigh less than 3.3 ounces

- May not have closure devices such as poly-wrap, polybags, shrinkwrap, clasps, strings, or buttons

These criteria are just a sampling of the requirements for the automation of letters and cards. Check with your local Postal Service to decide whether this process is an effective alternative for your organization. You also may wish to check on requirements for automation of flats or parcels.

In addition to bar coding, it is also important to meter your mail. Mail that has been metered and bar coded reaches its destination sooner because it bypasses several steps within the post office.

Reduce Mailing Costs

Preparing mail for automation is one way of reducing costs, as you have just learned. Several other suggestions also help to control costs:

- Consolidate materials into one envelope; it is less expensive to pay the increased cost per ounce on a heavier package than it is to send an additional envelope.

- Design mail to conform to letter size. Some firms send items such as promotional materials, newsletters, and monthly billing statements in larger envelopes. In order to save money, fold the material to fit into letter envelopes that meet USPS automation requirements (minimum $3'' \times 5''$, maximum $6\frac{1}{2}'' \times 11\frac{1}{2}''$; a maximum thickness of $\frac{1}{4}''$). You can send mailings that fit into letter envelopes at reduced rates over larger envelopes, possibly qualifying for automation discounts.

- Use postcards when possible. Postcards offer these related cost benefits in addition to lower mailing costs:

  - Less staff expense. There are no envelopes, no enclosures to insert, and less staff time needed to prepare the mailing.

  - Immediate impact. If the message is well written, with graphics if appropriate, the reader gets the message without having to open an envelope.[14]

- Eliminate return receipts unless they are necessary. Certified mail may provide all the proof of mailing that you need at a reduced cost.

- If you are mailing a bulky document with copy printed on only one side of the page, reduce the size of the document at the copier and duplex it (copy on both sides of the paper).

- Educate yourself. Know the USPS regulations and private mailer regulations.

- Address mail correctly.

According to USPS surveys, more than 30 percent of all mail pieces have misspelled street or city names, improper state abbreviations, missing or incorrect ZIP Codes, or other inaccurate or incomplete information that slows delivery. Software is available that can scan addressed labels and check them against USPS addresses to make sure the addresses are accurate. Address Element Correction (AEC) focuses on correcting the following address deficiencies:

- Misspellings

- Nonstandard abbreviations

- Improperly joined elements

- Address lines containing data other than the actual address

- Missing elements

Use Software Programs

In addition to the software that can scan addresses and check their accuracy, here is a sample of other software that can help make mailing more efficient.

- Software packages are available that can presort addresses for special rate discounts.

---

[14]"Fight Back: Mail Smarter and Save," *PB Edge*™ *Online*, accessed August 29, 2002; available from **ww3.pb.com/ pbedge/july01_hints.html**.

- Software for coding incoming mail allows an operator to scan the name on any piece of mail, look up the name in a database of employees, and print out a label with the employee's information. It takes two seconds or less to scan an average piece of mail.

- When handling a large number of records, such as checks and credit card statements, software can identify missing documents for reprint and insertion.

Pitney Bowes has a number of software and Web-based products. Some of the capabilities of these products include the following:

- Postage can be downloaded from the Internet and printed onto an envelope.

- Eliminating duplicate addresses and updating address changes with a USPS National Address Database can effectively manage mailing lists.

- Mailing lists can be converted to the standard format required by the USPS for automated handling. First-Class and standard mail can be presorted.

- Rates for FedEx, UPS, USPS, DHL, and Airborne (private mailing and shipping services) are consolidated on one Website.[15]

Use Internet Services

Internet services are available through the USPS and private mailers. For example, the USPS offers a variety of Internet services. One of these services is Mailing Online[SM]. With Mailing Online, users electronically transmit documents and business correspondence with their mailing lists to the USPS. The USPS then sends the documents electronically to commercial printers closest to the delivery point, where the information is printed, put into envelopes, and addressed. The service automatically reviews and standardizes the addresses in the mailing lists according to USPS address standards. If the order is submitted before

2 p.m., it will be in the mail the following business day. This service can be used to mail letters, postcards, flyers, self-mailers, and newsletters.[16]

The USPS Website offers other Internet solutions. Although NetPost[SM] Certified mail allows the customer to submit the documents electronically, the service generates and mails a hard-copy certified document through the USPS. The USPS can also send postcards and greeting cards electronically.

In addition, the USPS offers a variety of payment services with online convenience. For example, the eBillPay[SM] system allows customers to view and pay bills automatically and from multiple bank accounts. The USPS Electronic Postmark is added to all payments. USPS Send Money[SM] allows customers to send or receive money electronically from a checking or money market account. Both parties involved in the transaction must be registered users.

Private mail services such as FedEx and UPS also offer mailers access to Internet services. FedEx allows mailers to address labels, determine rates, and track mailings on the Internet, as mentioned earlier. Internet mailing services will continue to increase for USPS and private mailing services.

Incoming Mail

Responsibilities for handling incoming mail depend largely on the size of the company. One of your responsibilities as an administrative professional in a small firm may be to receive and process the mail. Most large companies, on the other hand, have a centralized mail department that receives and distributes the mail.

As an administrative professional, you need to establish a schedule for handling mail. Know when to expect the mail, whether it is delivered to you by:

---

[15]"Products and Services," Pitney Bowes, accessed September 4, 2002; available from **http://pb.com**.

[16]"USPS NetPost Services," accessed September 4, 2002; available from **www.usps.com/netpost/welcome.htm**.

- The mail carrier (USPS or private carrier).
- The company's mailroom attendant.
- An electronic car, which is a self-powered, unattended, robotlike cart that uses a photoelectric guidance system to follow paths painted on carpeting, tile, or other floor surfaces.

Set aside time each day to handle the incoming mail. Use the following steps when you process mail.

Sort

Once you receive the mail in your organization or department, you must do a preliminary mail sort. If several individuals are in the department, sort the mail according to the addressee. An alphabetic sorter is handy if you are sorting for a number of individuals. After completing the sorting, place the mail for each individual into separate stacks. When this preliminary sort is completed, sort each person's mail in the following order:

- Personal and confidential. The administrative assistant should not open mail that is marked personal and confidential on the outside of the envelope. Place this mail to one side so you do not inadvertently open it.
- Special delivery, registered, certified, or telegrams. This mail is important and should be placed so the individual to whom it is addressed sees it first.
- Fax mail. Most fax mail takes top priority. However, your company may receive "junk fax mail." If so, learn to discard this mail or place it at the bottom of the stack, depending on your supervisor's wishes.
- Regular business mail (First-Class Mail)
- Interoffice communications
- Advertisements and circulars
- Newspapers, magazines, and catalogs

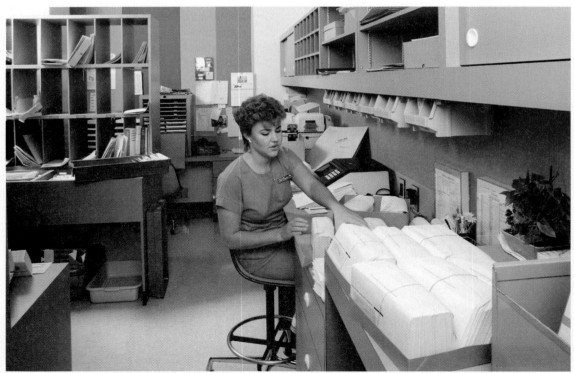

When incoming mail is received, sort it by addressee.

Open

You can open mail in the mailroom (using a machine to slit the envelope) or in the individual's workspace. When opening mail in an individual workspace, you usually use an envelope opener. Even if you have used a machine to open the envelope, you need to follow most of the procedures listed here.

- Have necessary supplies readily available. These supplies include an envelope opener, a date and time stamp, routing and action slips, a stapler, paper clips, and a pen or pencil.
- Before opening an envelope, tap the lower edge of the envelope on the desk so the contents fall to the bottom and will not be cut when the envelope is opened.
- Place envelopes face down with all flaps in the same direction.
- Open the correspondence by using a hand envelope opener or running the envelope through a mail-opening machine.
- Empty each envelope. Carefully check to see that everything has been removed.
- Fasten any enclosures to the letter. Attach small enclosures to the front of the correspondence. Attach enclosures larger than the correspondence to the back.
- Mend any torn paper with tape.
- If you open a personal or confidential letter by mistake, do not remove it from the envelope. Write "opened by mistake" on the front of the envelope, add your initials, and reseal the envelope with tape.
- Stack the envelopes on the desk in the same order as the opened mail in case it is necessary to refer to the envelopes. Save all envelopes for at least one day in case they are needed for reference.

Keep Selected Envelopes

Retain envelopes in the following situations.

- An envelope with an incorrect address—you or your supervisor may want to call attention to this fact when answering the correspondence.

- A letter with no return address—the envelope usually contains the return address.
- A letter written on letterhead with a different return address than that written on the envelope—for example, a person may write a letter on hotel letterhead and write his or her business address on the envelope.
- A letter without a signature—the envelope may contain the writer's name.
- An envelope with a postmark that differs significantly from the date on the document—the document date can be compared with the postmark date to determine how much of a delay there was in receiving the document.
- A letter specifying an enclosure that is not enclosed—write "no enclosure" on the letter and attach the envelope.
- A letter containing a bid, an offer, or an acceptance of a contract—the postmark date may be needed as legal evidence.

Date and Time Stamp

Date and time stamping allows you to verify when a document was received in your workplace. If the postmark date on the envelope and the date on the letter are different from the day you received the letter, you know the letter was held up at some location before getting to you. Stack the opened mail by mail categories when dating and time stamping; for example, make stacks of First-Class Mail, interoffice memorandums, and so on. Then stamp each item in the upper right-hand corner to show the date and time received. You can use a machine that automatically dates and time-stamps or a manual stamp that prints the date and/or time.

Read and Annotate

Busy executives need help with the large amount of mail that crosses their desk each day. As an administrative professional, you can help by scanning the mail and noting important parts of the correspondence. For example, you might underline important elements with a colored pen or pencil, referred to as **annotating**. Annotating also involves making notations about previous actions taken or facts that will assist the reader. You can annotate by writing notes in the margin or by using Post-it® notes or sticky notes. The advantage of Post-it notes is that you can peel off and dispose of them when you and the executive are finished. Here are some examples of possible annotations:

- The enclosure is missing from the letter. Call the person who sent the letter, letting the person know the enclosure is missing and requesting it. Put a note on the letter when making the call as to when the enclosure is expected.
- A discrepancy exists between the amount of a bill and the check received.
- The correspondence refers to a previous piece of correspondence written from your office. Pull the previous correspondence and attach it to the new correspondence, noting the attachment of the previous document.
- A meeting is suggested at a time when the executive is already committed.
- Periodicals can be annotated by:
  - Checking the table of contents for items that might be of interest to your employer. Place a check mark by the title of the article in the table of contents or a sticky note on the page where the article begins.
  - Read articles of interest and highlight the key points in the article.

Figure 9-4 shows an annotated letter that has been dated and time-stamped.

Organize and Present

After you have completed the preliminary mail sort and have opened, date and time-stamped, read, and annotated, you are ready to do a final sort. Here is one method you can use.

- Immediate action. This category consists of mail that must be handled on the day of receipt or shortly thereafter.
- Routine correspondence. Such mail includes interoffice memorandums and other correspondence that are not urgent in nature.

- Informational mail. Periodicals, newspapers, and other types of mail that do not require answering, but are merely for the executive to read, are included here.

Once you have organized the mail into these categories, place the mail in folders. For example, you would use an immediate action folder, a routine correspondence folder, and an informational mail folder. You also might color-code the folders—for example, red for immediate action, blue for routine correspondence, and yellow for informational mail. Place the folders on the executive's desk or in his or her in basket. If the executive prefers not to have the correspondence placed in folders, you should turn over the top piece of correspondence when placing it on the desk or in the in basket so no one who walks in the office can read it. The executive may ask that you present the mail once or twice a day. For example, if outside mail is received in the morning and afternoon, the executive may ask that you organize and present the mail at 10 a.m. and 2 p.m.

Route

More than one person may need to read a piece of correspondence. If so, you can make copies of the correspondence and send a copy to each individual on the list or you can route the correspondence to all individuals by use of a routing slip. The basic question to ask when determining whether to make copies is this: *Is it urgent that all individuals receive the information immediately?* If the answer is "yes," make a photcopy. If the answer is "no," use a routing slip, particularly if the correspondence is lengthy.

A routing slip also provides a reference so you know when and to whom you sent the correspondence in case a question arises about who received the document. When each person on the routing slip receives and reads the copy, he or she initials next to his or her name before sending the copy to the next individual on the list. The last person to receive the correspondence generally returns it to the individual who sent it. You save

AMERICAN FITNESS COUNCIL
4137 Centerville Road, Suite 293
Marquette, MI 49855-3852
Phone: 906 555-0180 ✎ Fax: 906 555-0188

May 6, 2005

May 11, 2005
10:30 a.m.

Ms. Lucia Escamilla
President
Ruther Corporation
2481 Opdyke Road
Bloomfield Hills MI 48304-2355

Dear Ms. Escamilla:

A special dinner meeting of the Board of Directors will be held on Monday, May 23, at the Park West Inn, 18000 Merriman Road, Livonia. The dinner meeting will begin at 6 p.m. Our guest will be Chief Justice Curtis Houser.

We hope your schedule will permit you to join us. Please RSVP by calling Valeria Bracken, 555–0180 with your reply.

Sincerely,

Haifa Karlis

Haifa Karlis
Executive Director

HK/vb

Board of Directors dinner meeting, Monday May 23, Park West Inn

You have a previous commitment—Economic Club

RSVP: Valeria Bracken, 555-0180

FIGURE 9~4 Annotated Letter

copying costs by routing. Figure 9-5 shows a routing slip. Notice the initials placed next to the individuals' names to indicate that they have read the copy, and notice that the sender is requesting that the correspondence be returned to him or her.

Handle Mail When the Executive Is Out

To handle the mail when the executive is away from the workplace, you need to follow these general guidelines:

- Before the executive leaves, discuss how the mail should be handled. Be specific in your questions so you understand your responsibilities. Mistakes in handling mail can be costly to the company.
- When urgent mail comes in, handle it immediately according to the executive's directions; for example, you may give it immediately to the person who is in charge or you may fax it to the executive.
- Answer mail that falls within your area of responsibility in a timely manner.
- Maintain mail that has been answered (with the answer attached) in a separate folder; the executive may want to review it upon his or her return.

- In a separate folder, maintain mail that can wait for the executive's return. Retrieve any previously written correspondence that the executive will need when reviewing the mail; place it in the folder also.

Handle Email

With the number of emails continuing to rise, some executives are asking the administrative assistant to handle email in a similar fashion to regular paper mail. Many of the procedures used to handle incoming mail can be used with email.

- Sort email messages just as you would regular mail. Do not open any email message marked personal and confidential; however, make sure to notify the executive that such a message needs to be reviewed.
- Open email messages and ensure that all attachments have been included.
- Date and time stamping of email is unnecessary since most messages include the time and date the message was sent. However, you might want to confirm that this information is accurate.
- Read and annotate emails as requested by your supervisor. Some software programs

---

Routing and Request

Please...

- ☑ Read
- ☐ Handle
- ☐ Approve

And...

- ☑ Forward
- ☑ Return
- ☐ Keep or Recycle
- ☐ Review with Me

To: B. J. Adams bja
Mark Bilcher mb
Joan Kaufman jk
Brenda Meiyers bm
Robin Todd rt

From: R. Edward
Date: 4-1-2005

FIGURE 9-5 Routing Slip

provide you with computerized sticky notes that you can use for your comments.

- Organize and present the information to the executive.

- Route email messages as appropriate. Sometimes a message requires that you forward it to a group of employees; other times a message should be printed and sent with a routing slip.

- Handle email when the executive is away just as you would regular mail. Handle urgent messages or forward them to the appropriate person, and answer those messages that fall within your area of responsibility. Keep a copy of your responses for your employer's review.

Recycling

You have learned that the workplace continues to generate a great deal of paperwork. This causes serious problems for the environment, with the loss of forests and the use of valuable land to establish more landfills. Review the following facts to learn more about paper use within the workplace.

- Typical businesses generate about 1.5 pounds of waste paper per employee per day.

- Financial businesses generate over 2 pounds per employee per day.

- Nearly half of typical workplace paper waste is comprised of high-grade paper, for which there is strong recycling demand.

- Recycling one ton of paper saves about 6.7 cubic yards of landfill space.

- Every recycled ton of paper saves approximately 17 trees.

- Recycling paper reduces the air and water pollution due to paper manufacturing.[17]

Due to the serious environmental issues involving the use of so much paper, recycling programs are becoming common in businesses. These programs can save millions of

JONATHAN KANNAIR

Recycle office paper.

tons of paper each year. Organizations often provide recycling bins for paper and outsource the collection and shredding of paper to a private vendor. The outsource vendor generally does not charge a fee for this service since he or she is able to collect money for the recycled paper.

In addition to recycling paper, organizations need to use recycled paper products. Recycled paper uses 64 percent less energy and 58 percent less water in the production of the paper than does the production of virgin papers. In addition, manufacturing recycled paper produces 74 percent less air pollution and 35 percent less water pollution than virgin paper production processes.

Organizations also need to research how they can reduce the use of paper in the workplace. Some suggestions include:

- Using both sides of the page (duplex documents).

---

[17]"Fact Sheet: Reducing Office Paper Waste," accessed September 12, 2002; available from **http://es.epa.gov/ techinfo/facts/recypapr.html**.

- Converting scratch paper into memo pads, telephone answering slips, and similar items.
- Printing only the number of copies needed.
- Using electronic mail for sending and receiving messages.

- Reviewing text on-screen to limit mistakes and thus reprinting.
- Installing a central memo board where employees can read interoffice mail.
- Shredding used paper and package materials to use instead of plastic pellets. ■

SUMMARY

To reinforce what you have learned in this chapter, study this summary.

- Mail is classified by the USPS into Express Mail, Priority Mail, First-Class Mail, Parcel Post, Bound Printed Matter, and Media Mail.
- Special mail services include these:
  - Certificate of mailing
  - Registered Mail
  - Restricted delivery
  - Return receipt
  - Signature confirmation
  - Collect on Delivery (COD)
  - Certified Mail
  - Insured Mail
  - Money Order
  - Authorization to Hold Mail
- International mail includes Global Express Guaranteed (GXG), Global Express Mail (EMS), Global Priority Mail (GPM), Letter-Post, and International Parcel Post.
- A number of private mail services across the United States offer fast and effective mail services domestically and internationally.
- Electronic mail includes voice mail, email, and fax mail.
- To ensure proper handling of outgoing mail, these procedures should be followed:
  - Check enclosures.
  - Prepare envelopes.
  - Seal and stamp.
  - Establish a schedule.
  - Maintain current mailing lists.
  - Prepare mail for automated processing.
  - Reduce mailing costs.
  - Use software programs.
  - Use Internet services.
- Responsibilities of the administrative professional in handling incoming mail include the following:
  - Sorting

- Opening
- Keeping selected envelopes
- Dating and time stamping
- Reading and annotating
- Organizing and presenting
- Routing
- Handling mail when the executive is out
- Handling email
- It is important for the environment that businesses recycle paper.

FIND THE PROBLEM

Julie Pagel is the administrative assistant for Marjorie Phillips, the senior vice president of Administration and Planning. Julie has asked Sarah Friendly, a part-time assistant, to stop by Ms. Phillips' office and pick up the outgoing mail on her way to the mailroom each afternoon. Although the company policy clearly states that "personal mail should not be routed through the company mailroom," one or two personal documents are usually included in the items Sarah receives from Julie. Worried that she will get in trouble, Sarah does not pick up the mail on Tuesday. When Julie calls to ask her about it, Sarah says she forgot.

Did Sarah handle the situation effectively? If not, how could she have handled the situation differently?

PROFESSIONAL POINTERS

Here are some tips for processing mail effectively.

- When purchasing mailing equipment, keep in mind that the equipment has a life span of three to five years. You can extend that life span by investing in upgradeable technology.
- Keep current on USPS and private mailing and shipping services by reviewing the Websites of the organizations.
- Compare the costs and services provided, such as time of delivery and convenience of pickup of mailing materials via USPS and private mailing services.
- Use mailing list software to check your mailing addresses. USPS surveys have shown that more than 30 percent of all mail pieces have misspelled street or city names, improper state abbreviations, missing or incorrect ZIP Codes, or other inaccurate or incomplete information.
- Use effective strategies when creating email to save time for the receivers and to handle incoming email messages efficiently.
- To help maintain forests and reduce the land needed for landfills, recycle your paper.
- Reduce the amount of paper you use by printing on both sides of the paper (duplexing), copying only the number of copies you need, single-spacing documents, and using email for in-house communication.
- Purchase recycled paper.

REINFORCEMENT ITEMS

1. Identify and describe six mail services available from the USPS.
2. Identify and describe the principal categories of International Mail offered by the USPS.
3. Describe the suggestions for efficiently handling your incoming email messages.
4. Define the term *electronic postage*, and describe how a business or an individual can obtain electronic postage.

CRITICAL-THINKING ACTIVITY

Protection Plus is a small locally owned insurance agency. Franklin Korey, who has his insurance license and handles some sales, also manages the workplace for the owner and president, Elizabeth Seng. There are three additional sales people and one full-time administrative assistant.

In a recent staff meeting, the topic of email was discussed. Employees are finding it time-consuming to handle the large volume of daily email. In fact, some employees are spending over an hour each day sorting through messages, many of which are unrelated to business matters. At this point in time, the company has no policy regarding personal email. Ms. Seng has asked Franklin to research the issue and provide her with information as to how the employees can better manage their company email.

1. What types of information does Franklin need to find out from other employees?
2. What types of suggestions could Franklin make to help employees better handle their incoming email?
3. What company policies should be in place because of the email problem?

VOCABULARY REVIEW

Complete the Vocabulary Review for Chapter 9 given on page 79 of the *Applications Workbook*.

ENGLISH AND WORD USAGE DRILL

Complete the English and Word Usage Drills for Chapter 9 listed on page 80 of the *Applications Workbook*.

WORKPLACE APPLICATIONS

A9-1 (Goals 1 and 2)

You are given the following items by your supervisor to be send out in the mail. Explain whether you will use USPS service or private mailing or shipping services. If you decide to use USPS service, identify the type of service and mail classification of the item. Use the form provided on the Student CD, SCDA9-1, to record your answers. Submit a completed copy of the form to your instructor.

- A software package stored on two CD-ROMs to a coworker in Raleigh
- A letter addressed to a client in France for delivery the next day
- A contract with a new client in Baton Rouge (proof that the contract is received is necessary)
- A check for $250 for your supervisor's AMA dues
- A report (100-pages, weighing 2 pounds) that must reach the Tokyo office tomorrow morning
- A contract that must reach the Tampa office by 10 a.m. tomorrow
- A letter that must reach California within two days (signature proof is required)
- A congratulatory note to the recently promoted vice president of the Tokyo, Japan, office
- A memo that must reach the Paris office within the next 30 minutes

A9-2 (Goal 2)

Kurt Rupprecht asks you to prepare an email message to Avion LeFevre, (**http://alefever@ppi .com**), an administrative professional, in the Paris office. You need to inform Mr. LeFevre that Susan Portales will be arriving in Paris on American Airlines, Flight 750, on Tuesday, April 23, at 8:15 a.m. Ask that someone be there to pick her up and take her to the Paris office. Request a reply by the afternoon about the arrangements. Submit a copy of the email to your instructor.

A9-3 (Goal 3)

You received the mail items listed on page 59 of the *Applications Workbook*. Sort the mail by completing the form provided on the Student CD, SCDA9-3. In addition, on pages 82 and 83 of your *Applications Workbook* are two letters that were received in the morning mail. Annotate these letters. Submit your sorting plan and the annotated letters to your instructor.

A9-4 (Goal 1)

Work with three classmates. Using the Internet, research the current online services offered by the USPS and FedEx. Prepare a report describing these services. Submit the report to your instructor.

A9-5 (Goals 1 and 2)

A case study is provided on the Student CD, SCDA9-5. Read the case and respond to the questions. Write a summary of your responses to your instructor. Use the memorandum form provided on the Student CD, SCDA9-5a.

ASSESSMENT OF CHAPTER GOALS

Did you successfully complete the chapter goals? Evaluate yourself by filling out the form on page 85 of the *Applications Workbook*.

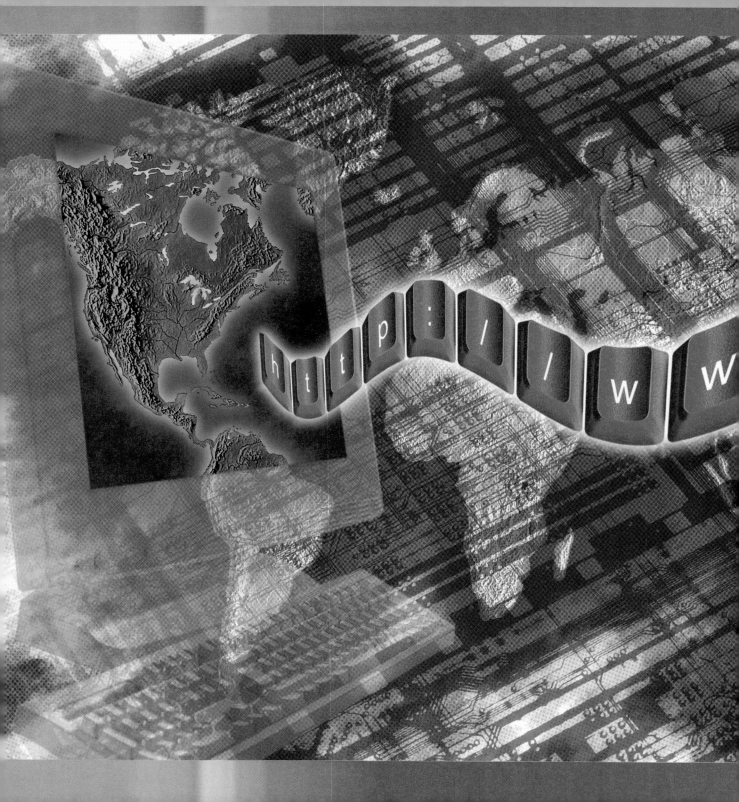

3

Technology

chapter 10

Computer Hardware

1. Identify and explain input devices.

2. Describe computer classifications, computer components, and storage devices.

3. Describe output devices.

4. Identify and describe the types of networks.

5. Identify the future direction of technology.

Computers and the concept of information processing were at one time associated only with those who worked in an office setting. In today's world, computers and the information they gather and disseminate are hardly noticeable, as they have become commonplace.

Consider an evening out with a friend or with family. At dinner, when your server takes your order, he or she typically uses a touch screen to place your order and to send it back to the kitchen. Cooks and preparers can see the orders as well as any special notations (no onions, please!). They can also see the time that you ordered, making an effort to ensure prompt service.

While this initial input of a food order seems simple, a great deal has happened with the inclusion of computer technology in the restaurant business. Managers can follow the service pattern within their establishment, keep track of food supply inventories, and print random customer satisfaction surveys to accompany a customer's bill. They can track food orders by time of day or time of year. All of this information can be used for quality control purposes, to determine staffing levels, or to find out if the latest marketing efforts are successful.

Your next stop, at the movies, brings you to a kiosk where you select a movie and showing time via a touch screen. The machine then prompts you for payment with your credit or debit card. The theater now has access to information it can use to track the number of seats taken during a particular time frame or the number of tickets sold by movie title. With your quick trip to the concession stand for snacks, a data input process similar to the one in the restaurant has begun.

If you bought a new outfit for this occasion, pumped your own gas on the way, or paid a road toll, you created an enormous amount of information that will be processed by computers and then analyzed by someone, somewhere, in the corporate world.

As this example illustrates, the computer (and the data it generates during people's everyday lives) has become commonplace. The computer has also created a need not only for skilled operators of advanced technology, but also for people who understand the concepts of data manipulation and data storage.

Input Devices

Information is created in the workplace in a variety of ways. A supervisor may provide you with a series of reports that need to be keyed and organized by region or cost. An email may be sent to you with an attached draft copy of a report that needs to be **downloaded** (transferred from the Internet or another source to your computer) and corrected, saved, and then resent. You may be required to attend staff meetings where you take minutes on a laptop, edit and format them, and forward them to all attendees. For a supervisor who travels as part of his or her job, lengthy phone messages or random thoughts spoken into a **microrecorder** (a palm-sized voice recorder) may be the preferred way of creating information that, in your hands, will be turned into memorandums, reports, or project summaries.

Once information has been created, it must be entered using an input device. The basic and most recognized computer input device is the keyboard. In the last few years, the mouse, trackballs and track pointers, touch screens and touchpads, as well as infrared information transmission, have become popular. Other input devices include the scanner, voice recognition software, and digital cameras. Each of these technologies continues to evolve in design and performance.

Computer Keyboards

The most frequently used information input device continues to be the computer keyboard. The layout used most frequently is the extended 101-key keyboard, with 12 function keys along the top of the board, a numeric/cursor keypad, and an extra cursor keypad devoted solely to moving the cursor and scrolling within a document.

Portable computers, often referred to as laptop or notebook computers, have keyboards that generally do not replicate the keyboards of the desktop models due to size restrictions. Portables may have smaller-than-usual keys, keys that have dual functions when a special key is activated, keys that are relocated, or some keys that are deleted entirely.

Some keyboards operate on an **infrared** system, a form of wireless information transmission. Infrared systems allow the user to place the keyboard almost anywhere near the computer. The infrared keyboard then beams the information to the processor in a fashion similar to a remote control beaming a signal to a television set.

New hybrid keyboards are also coming onto the market. These small, oftentimes collapsible, keyboards are targeted to handheld computers or to individuals who use a **personal digital assistant (PDA)**. A PDA is a small computer used to track appointments, email, and contacts; it can fit into your hand. Some projected models will have built-in "thumb" keyboards for tapping in short memos, notes, or phone numbers. In addition, several companies have developed foldable keyboards made of aluminum or fabric. These keyboards can electronically sense a finger's touch and recognize the amount of pressure that is applied. These fabric keyboards will allow broader use of handheld computers and PDAs. An added advantage is that they can be folded and used as the protective cover for the device when the input is complete.[1]

Scanners

Scanners allow information to be input directly into a computer without the traditional

---

[1] "Logitech Shows Cloth Keyboard for PDAs," Owen Linderholm, special to *PC World*, March 14, 2002, accessed September 10, 2002; available from **www.pcworld.com**.

Specially designed keyboards are available for PDAs.

key stroking. Scanners can scan text, drawings, graphics, and photos. Scanners come in two basic designs: flatbed scanners and sheet-fed scanners. **Flatbed scanners** are able to handle bound documents since they operate in a similar fashion to copy machines; that is, you lift the top and place the document face down for scanning into your computer system. **Sheet-fed scanners** handle stacks of papers that are loaded into a tray; the paper is then automatically fed through the scanner. Scanner software is available that allows you to modify the copy by:

- Adjusting the image size.
- Retouching, cropping, and manipulating photos.
- Editing the scanned copy.
- Adding notations to the document that will not alter the original scanned image.

In addition, a growing market of **document imaging software** allows users to access scanned documents from virtual filing systems. Users can then view the documents or the document images on their computer screen and return the document to the "file" without leaving their workstation.

A number of specialized scanners are available, including optical and magnetic ink character readers and barcode scanners. These scanners are explained in the next section.

Optical Character Reader (OCR) Scanners

An **optical character reader (OCR)** is a piece of equipment that can read keyboarded and handwritten documents. This technology is widely used by the USPS to scan mail for quicker distribution. Rather than someone having to hand-sort each piece of mail, the OCR scanner reads from the bottom of the address upward, reading the Zip Code, state, and city first and then the street address and finally the company or family name.

Magnetic Ink Character Reader (MICR)

The **magnetic ink character reader (MICR)** is used extensively by financial institutions to read the magnetic ink numbers preprinted on

DIGITAL VISION

Files can be viewed without leaving your desk.

checks and deposit slips. This process provides high-speed reading of financial transaction information and is the key supplier of information to online accounts and ATM machines that provide account balances, withdrawals, or deposit information.

Barcode Scanners

Barcode scanners are the most recognized scanners in use today. From the largest department stores to the smallest mom-and-pop style convenience stores, **barcode scanners** are used to input price information and keep track of inventory. Almost every consumer-purchased product contains a **Universal Product Code (UPC)**, a series of black printed bars of varying thickness read by the barcode scanner. The UPC gives the name of the product and the selling price. Depending on the store, employees may use fixed barcode scanners or handheld scanner units. The

The MICR reads magnetic ink numbers on checks and deposit slips.

store employee and the consumer are alerted to the price of each item as it is scanned. With each high-pitched tone, the price of an item is added to the customer's bill and one unit is subtracted from the store's inventory.

A lottery ticket is an example of a **variable-data barcode**. The code identifies information unique to one particular item. For example, each variety of lottery ticket has its own unique code. Variable barcodes are used on a variety of documents and labels. For example, a packing slip contains barcodes that allow for the tracking, sorting, and expediting of shipments.

Multifunction Devices

Multifunction Devices (MFDs) can print, copy, fax, and scan. These units are designed for the small business or teleworker. Although they are generally sheet-fed, some of the first multifunction units had scanners that could be detached and used as handhelds for scanning bound pages. Hand-held units required a steady hand (and sometimes repeated attempts) until the desired quality of the document image could be achieved. For this reason, the latest in MFDs offer both sheet-fed and flatbed options for scanning and for copying.

The cost of an MFD depends on the features, the number of pages per minute that can be scanned and/or copied, and the image quality. Price ranges for these units start at $129 and can easily reach $599.

Voice Recognition Technology

Undoubtedly, you have an idea of your keyboarding speed and the range of speeds that are attainable. Good keyboardists can key from 100 to 120 words per minute. Excellent keyboardists can be in the 140 word-per-minute range. Today's voice recognition software packages can input data at a rate equal to 160 words a minute, and with options that customize the software to your speaking patterns, these rates can go even higher.

Originally designed to assist visually impaired computer users, voice recognition technology (VRT) has moved into the everyday life of computer users. VRT can be used to lessen repetitive stress injuries caused by continuous keyboarding, to dictate draft or final copy, to access Web pages by voice rather than by clicking on various links, and to dial phone numbers from a computer.

In the early days, VRT was accomplished by **discrete voice recognition** software that required the user to pause between each spoken word. This technology evolved into **continuous speech recognition** programs that allow users to speak normally, using complete sentences and phrases. This type of technology can also be customized to fit individual speech patterns. With advancements in software, computer processing speeds, sound cards, and "quiet microphones," speech recognition technology transforms spoken

MFDs can save valuable space in a small workplace.

words into alphanumeric text and navigational commands that can be recognized by a PC.[2]

Here is how voice recognition technology works. A microphone converts your voice into an analog signal and feeds it to your PC's sound card. An analog-to-digital converter then takes over and converts the voice to a stream of digital data (ones and zeros) that a computer can understand. The software package you are using then takes over to apply specific speech properties to the digital coding.[3]

Voice recognition systems, while advancing rapidly, are far from flawless. Some of the potential drawbacks to these systems and their purported solutions are as follows:

- Extensive training is necessary to learn the software. The software must adjust to a person's voice and speech patterns. On the other hand, when the software misinterprets what was said, the user must make the correction immediately so the error does not appear throughout the final document. As software evolves and storage space is better utilized, common usage dictionaries that come with these programs are expanding. Some programs have up to 250,000 common words in their dictionaries and are capable of using the context of the sentence to select the correct word. (This is especially important in the English language as words such as *there*, *their*, and *they're* were easily misapplied by the earlier systems.)

- Considerable computing power is needed for all continuous speech recognition programs. This is especially true as the power of a

---

[2]Stan Miastkowski, "How It Works: Speech Recognition," *PC World*, April 14, 2000, accessed September 10, 2002; available from **www.pcworld.com**.
[3]Ibid.

software program is increased. Fortunately, storage mediums (discussed later in this chapter) and computer processing speeds have seen phenomenal growth in recent years and, in some cases, are doubling in less than a year's time.

- Outside noise is a problem for voice recognition technology. Even behind a closed door, extraneous noise from the hall, air conditioner, or outside traffic can be picked up and added to the document as nonsense text. A new breed of "quiet" microphones and headset microphones has helped to eliminate these problems. These systems filter out low-level background noises, but they can also filter out information that is not clearly spoken by the operator.

The cost of these systems, much like the cost of computer hardware, has decreased substantially since their inception. Projections are that the technology will continue to improve and that voice recognition technology could become the dominate user interface for information input in the coming years.

Digital Cameras

A **digital camera** is an input device used to take pictures and to store the photographed images digitally, instead of on traditional film. When a digital camera is used in conjunction with a computer, users can insert pictures into a variety of software applications. Photographs may be edited, printed, faxed, or included with email messages. In addition, photographs can be incorporated into electronic presentations; posted on Websites; or included in newsletters, reports, or memos. Electronic images can be stored using a variety of formats, including CDs, DVDs, and Zip drives. These storage methods are discussed later in this chapter.

The quality of a digital camera is often measured by its resolution. **Resolution** describes the sharpness and clearness of an image. Although cameras with higher resolution have better image quality, they are also more expensive. Resolution is measured in **pixels**,

Digital images can be sent with email messages, incorporated into electronic presentations, posted on a Website, or included in newsletters.

or picture elements, which is a single point in an electronic image. The greater the number of pixels the camera uses to capture the image, the better the quality of the image.

Pointing Devices

The mouse was the original pointing device. However, a variety of other pointing devices have been developed. These include the trackball, touch pad, and joystick. A **trackball** is a stationary ball that you roll with the tips of your fingers to move the cursor on the screen. Trackball rollers are typically installed within a keyboard or attached to the side of a keyboard as a removable accessory.

Laptop and notebook computers have a different approach to the traditional mouse or trackball configuration. Some laptops contain a small **touch pad**, or a small window that the user touches to move the cursor on the screen. Cursor movement is a direct reflection of finger movement. To access a drop-down menu, the user must tap the touch pad once or twice, depending on the software application.

Other laptops use a small **joystick**, or a button similar to a trackball, located in the center of a keyboard to manipulate the movement of the cursor. Typically, the joystick works in conjunction with buttons located below the spacebar. The user activates the buttons using his or her thumb.

All of the pointer devices discussed operate via a **graphical user interface (GUI)**, a visual operating system based on buttons, bars, and icons. The devices are not driven by keystrokes. The GUI uses a drop-down menu and various icons for the execution of commands and the choice of program options. The toolbar at the top of a software program is an example of a GUI, with various icons for executing commands.

Touch Screens

With a **touch screen**, the user touches the desired choice on the screen with his or her finger rather than using a mouse or another point-and-click interface. Touch screens are used in a variety of settings, including these:

- Nearly any restaurant where servers can easily input food items ordered.
- Hospitals where doctors can use a touch screen to sign virtual prescriptions for patients.
- Gasoline stations where customers can start the pump by tapping the appropriate type of gasoline and the preferred method of payment.
- Professional buildings where visitors can find the location of a particular business.
- Greeting card stores where customers can create their own personalized greeting card.

Infrared Devices

Many of the input devices discussed so far have been influenced by infrared technology. One common infrared technology is the remote control from the television. Viewers input the desired channel in the remote control; that information then travels across the room to an infrared receiver positioned on the front of the television set. Pointing devices such as mouse devices, trackballs, keyboards, handheld scanners, and printers can be activated or accessed by infrared technology.

To maintain portability, mouse controllers are built in to laptop keyboards.

Pen Tablets and Styluses

Pen tablets allow the user to hold a computer with one hand and use a pen or stylus with the other hand to activate software applications based on a program menu. Pen tablets are typically used for very specific computer needs. Insurance claims adjustors use pen tablets with specific programs that help them total damages and calculate losses. Package delivery personnel use tablets with specialized software that includes time, date, and signature of the receiving party to track deliveries to customers.

The combination of stylus and touch screen technology enables users to write directly onto a screen. This technology is currently in use in a variety of consumer markets. When a person uses a credit card to make a purchase, he or she may be required to submit an electronic signature versus signing a paper copy of the receipt. Advances in technology and software are enabling pen tablets and styluses to create graphics as clear as those drawn directly on paper or painted on a canvas.

Like all new technologies, touch screen and stylus technology will continue to advance. Sweden's mobile phone giant, Ericsson™, has created a Chatpen™. This hardware, in conjunction with Bluetooth™ software, allows someone at a computer screen to witness another person signing a document, locally or at a distance, almost instantly. This product is capable of scanning information or storing information that is written with the pen for input into a PC later.[4]

Hardware Classifications and Components

Once information is created and input, the next step is to process that information electronically. A variety of computer configurations exist that provide users with the ability to process information.

Computer Classifications

Computers are classified by the amount of information they contain and the speed with which they operate. There are five main categories of computers:

- Supercomputers
- Mainframe Computers
- Workstation computers (supermicros)
- Microcomputers (PCs)
- Handheld computers or Personal Digital Assistants (PDAs)

Supercomputers

Supercomputers are the Goliaths of the industry because they are the most powerful and expensive mainframe computers. Until recently, supercomputers were thought to be nearing extinction in the world of business. A decade ago most supercomputers could be found at universities or government agencies, but now nearly half of the world's 500 fastest computers are in corporations.

Supercomputers are multiprocessor systems (imagine linking 2,000 or more personal computers together) using faster processors. The current processing standard for supercomputers is measured in **teraflops** per second; one teraflop equals 1 trillion operations per second. The fastest previous speed on a supercomputer was 368 **gigaflops** per second; 1 gigaflop equals 1 billion operations per second.

The federal government uses supercomputers for tasks that require huge data manipulation. These supercomputers are used in military and government applications, such as worldwide weather forecasting and weapons research. With 1 trillion bytes of memory and more than 160 **terabytes** (1 terabyte equals 1 trillion bytes) of disk storage, a supercomputer can hold six times the information contained in all the books in the Library of Congress. Japan's NEC Corp. released a 35 teraflop supercomputer called Earth Simulator

---

[4]"Ericsson Unveils Bluetooth-Enabled Chatpen," *Newsbytes News Network*, June 18, 2001.

in the spring of 2002. A 100-teraflop super-computer is expected by 2003 or 2004. IBM plans to deliver a supercomputer to the U.S. government in 2004 that will be used to simulate the explosions and decay of the U.S. nuclear weapons stockpile. This computer, dubbed ASCI Purple, is expected to clock in at 100 teraflops, or trillions of calculations per second. In 2005 IBM plans to deliver a second supercomputer to the Department of Energy, dubbed Blue Gene/Lite, running the Linux operating system. This computer will tackle research on global climate change and study interaction between atmospheric chemistry and pollution. It is expected to run 130,000 processors at a theoretical top speed of 360 teraflops—more than triple the speed of ASCI Purple.

Supercomputers will continue to increase in their capabilities. Current projections of processing speeds and hardware capabilities would result in a machine running at 1,000 teraflops, or 1 **petaflop** (1 quadrillion computations per second), by the year 2010. For perspective, operating at 1 quadrillion computations per second, such a computer could do in one second what it would take the entire population of the United States 50 days to do, working nonstop, with hand calculators.[5]

Mainframe Computers

Mainframes are large computers that accommodate hundreds of users completing different tasks. These computers are commonly found in large business and government agencies. Mainframes can support a number of auxiliary devices, such as terminals, printers, disk drives, and other input and output equipment. They are used in companywide applications, such as payroll, accounting, inventory, and purchasing. Mainframe computers and various data backup devices are usually housed in special climate-controlled, dust-free, and highly secure areas due to their cost and the value of the information they contain. Many of these rooms have a floating floor to give technicians access to the multitude of cables required to connect mainframes with terminals and other peripheral devices, but also to protect the equipment from floodwaters and mild earth tremors.

---

[5]Gary H. Anthes, "Supercomputers Make a Comeback," *ComputerWorld*, July 3, 2000, v. 34, no. 27.

Mainframe computers are often housed in special dust-free, climate-controlled rooms.

© GETTY IMAGES/PHOTODISC

Workstation Computers (Supermicros)

Workstation computers (supermicros) are the upper-end machines of the microcomputer (discussed in the next section). They have a large amount of processing power, approaching that of a mainframe. They have a high-speed microprocessor, have significantly increased memory, have increased hard-drive storage capacity over the microcomputer, and are able to serve several users. Yet they are small enough to sit on a desktop. These workstation computers are often **interfaced** (interconnected) with one another or with a company's mainframe computer. Their processing and storage power allow them to retrieve large amounts of file data. Workstation computers can also be used as the mainframe computer, or server, for small business and can be networked with several microcomputers.

Microcomputers (PCs)

Microcomputers (PCs) are the smallest of the desktop computer systems. First introduced in the mid 70s, the personal computer, or PC, began what has become known as the computer revolution. The technology that made this possible was the manufacture of electronic circuits on small silicon chips. A single miniature chip (called a **microprocessor**) contains the circuitry and components for arithmetic, logic, and control operations. Today microcomputers are as powerful as the mainframe computers of several years ago. With the addition of **hard drives** (internal storage capacity), microcomputers can store huge amounts of program data and create data such as reports, databases, and spreadsheets.

Processing speeds of the PC have dramatically increased in recent years with the development of accelerated processing chips. Companies such as Intel®, with their Pentium® Celeron™ and Pentium® 4 processing chips, or Advanced Micro Devices' Athlon™ XP microprocessor, have enabled PCs to run larger applications. This has also resulted in the advancement of educational and entertainment software programs, which will be discussed in Chapter 11.

Personal computing has taken on a portable dimension in recent years. Laptop or notebook computing allows people to take their powerful PCs on the road. Weighing only 3 to 5 pounds, with long-life rechargeable lithium batteries, laptop users can work or play for three or four hours at a time. Newer notebook computers have color displays, hard-drive sizes that rival desktop computers, accelerated processors, and a host of options that used to be available only on desktop models. Today's laptops have built-in modems, sound cards, DVD readers/writers, and infrared technology that will allow information to be beamed into or from the laptop to another computer or handheld.

Handheld Computers

Handheld computers are exactly what the name implies—units that can be easily carried and operated in the hand of a user. The units are often called **PDAs** (personal digital assistants). These systems come in a range of sizes and with a range of applications. The palm-sized units typically allow users to keep

© GETTY IMAGES/PHOTODISC

Information can be exchanged easily between a handheld computer to a desktop computer.

contact information; calendar information; to-do lists; and various levels of word processing, email, and spreadsheet information. Users typically operate these units by writing with a stylus directly on the screen or by tapping on a virtual keyboard. Some of the larger versions of handheld computers open in a similar fashion to the laptop computer. They have small color screens and compact keyboards. These large versions typically have more computing power and enable users to create and edit documents and spreadsheets and to access the Internet.

Due to their smaller size, handheld computers do not have internal disk drives with which to save information. Some handhelds have small chips or sticks where information can be stored and retrieved later. Other units can be interfaced, or synched, into a standard PC, using a special cable. This transfers data so it can then be saved in a variety of storage formats. (Information storage is discussed later in this chapter.)

The basic PDA serves as an appointment book, an address book, a to-do list, and a calculator. In addition, a PDA may allow you to:

- Check your email.
- Retrieve telephone calls.
- Exchange information with a larger computer.
- Read newspaper headlines or books.
- Access the Internet.
- Take digital pictures.

Computer Internal Processing and Storage

Once data has been input into a computer through one of the various input media, processing takes place in the central processing unit of the computer. The unit has two basic parts, the control unit and the arithmetic/logic unit. The central processing unit interacts closely with the primary storage (also called memory), referring to it for instructions and for data. These functions are explained in the next section.

Central Processing Unit

The **central processing unit (CPU)** is the brain of the computer system. This unit accepts and processes information within the parameters of the software program. In other words, if the software program does not tell the computer what to do, it cannot do it on its own. These software instructions are stored in the computer's memory, and as new instructions are sent to the processor, the CPU quickly retrieves the information from the memory and performs the task. This is where the correlation between memory size and processing speed come together. When the processing unit has accomplished what the user has requested (and what the software has allowed it to complete), data is output by the computer to the monitor or printer for the computer user to view.

Arithmetic/Logic Unit

The **arithmetic/logic unit** performs all mathematical calculations. It adds, subtracts, multiplies, and divides. It handles logic operations by comparing alphabetic and numeric data. For example, the unit makes such comparisons as greater than, less than, and equal to an identified number. This unit can also draw logical conclusions based on the arithmetic information it receives. Consider this example: You are working with a personnel program that records leave time for employees. You record five vacation days for an employee, but the employee only has three vacation days available to use. The arithmetic/logic unit will let you know that the employee is not eligible for five vacation days and will give you the number of days that are available.

Control Unit

As its name implies, the **control unit** directs and coordinates most operations of a computer. All instructions to the computer are interpreted in the control unit. For each instruction, the control unit repeats a set of four operations: fetching, decoding, executing, and storing. In other words, the unit retrieves (fetches) information from the computer memory, it translates (decodes) the instructions into commands that the computer processors can understand, it completes the commands (executes), and commits the information to memory (stores).

Memory

Computers use two main types of storage: primary storage and secondary storage. Secondary storage consists mainly of external memory storage such as disks, CDs, and DVDs. (These will be discussed in the next section.) Primary storage is contained within the computer.

Primary storage is a temporary storage place for data, instructions, and information. This memory, like the processing units, is contained in a silicon computer chip on the computer's **motherboard** (the area where the memory and processing chips are placed). Data within computer memory is stored in the form of a code that utilizes a 1 or a 0. These 1s and 0s are called **binary digits (bits)**. Bits are strung together in a series of eight. The string of eight bits are called a **byte** and are the basis of all computer operations. All the letters, numbers, and symbols on a keyboard have a specific eight-digit binary code assigned to them. This is how the computer reads, or interprets, the data that has been input.

Different computers have different amounts of memory. Since the information in a computer is based on bytes, the terms that correspond to memory storage also correlate to bytes. Memory capacities are expressed in thousand-byte units called **kilobytes (KB)**, million-byte units called **megabytes (MB)**, billion-byte units called **gigabytes (GB)**, and trillion-byte units called **terabytes (TB)**. The storage capacity of computers has continued to increase, and there is no reason to believe this trend will end soon.

The two most common categories of memory are random access memory (RAM) and read-only memory (ROM). Both RAM and ROM are present on all computers. **Random access memory (RAM)** is the primary memory at work when you are operating a program. For example, when working in a spreadsheet program, while you are changing or manipulating information, the information is being temporarily stored in the RAM until it is saved on a storage device. **Read-only memory (ROM)** is permanently stored information that cannot be changed; it is vital for the computer's overall operations. When a computer is turned off, the information in the ROM remains; information in the RAM that has not been placed in a storage device will be lost.

Storage Devices

Once information has been processed, it must be saved for future reference or as part of a permanent record of completed projects. Currently there are many ways to store information. As is true with technology, older methods are being improved upon and new methods are being introduced. The most popular storage devices are as follows:

- Floppy disks
- High-capacity disks
- Hard drives
- CDs and DVDs

Floppy Disks

Floppy disks (also referred to as diskettes) were, in one form or another, the dominant storage medium for early computer information processing. Originally introduced as eight-inch-wide disks encased in a flexible plastic envelope, they transformed to 5.25-inch disks and then to 3.5-inch disks in a nonflexible plastic case. Since hard-drive space in early computers was limited, floppy disks were one of the first mediums available that allowed users to store information efficiently. Today a 3.5-inch high-density disk stores 1.44 MB of information. To give you an idea of what this means, a typical single-spaced printed page contains 2,500 to 3,000 characters. One MB stores 400 pages of single-spaced text.

While 3.5-inch disks are still a popular storage medium, they are starting to be

A wide variety of storage devices are available.

replaced by faster and more efficient storage mediums. In fact, current computers are manufactured without 3.5-inch disk drives; in order to use floppy disks, external drives must be purchased.

High-Capacity Disks

This category of storage medium stems from the advancement of disk storage technology. While originally seen as the new horizon in data storage and retrieval, **high-capacity disks** have found themselves as the backup medium of choice for users of personal computers, portable computers, and small businesses. **Back-up storage** is used to make copies of important files or very large files that would be difficult to replicate if the originals were lost, damaged, or destroyed.

High-capacity disks and their drives are often available as options on desktop or laptop computer models, but they can also be purchased as peripherals. **Peripherals** are external self-contained accessories that can be plugged into a computer as needed to make a copy of information or to retrieve stored information. The high-capacity and portability of these systems make them a popular storage medium. Several varieties of high-capacity disks are available:

- **Zip disks** are slightly larger and thicker than a floppy disk and are available in 100- and 250-MB capacities (the equivalent of 75 to 175 floppy disks).
- **SuperDisks** are capable of storing 120 MB or 240 MB of data. Their drives can read SuperDisks as well as floppy disks.
- **Jaz disks** holds 1 GB of data (the equivalent of 850 floppy disks).

Hard Drives

Hard drives, also called **hard disks**, serve as the internal storage device on a computer. They are the large permanent storage centers within a computer and are typically not portable. Originally, hard drives were used to store program information for quicker access. (Rather than having to insert several floppy disks to make a program run, all the required information was installed on a hard disk.) Because technology has greatly increased the capacity of hard disks, they are now an option for information storage. Current personal computer hard drives can store 100 GB or more of data, instructions, and information. Recent developments in technology have boosted hard-drive capacity to the 250-GB range. While hard-drive storage is quickly accessible, it is a good idea to make back-up copies of any information that is not stored on another medium. (Programs can easily be reinstalled; reports and projects cannot be as easily reconstructed.) Hard-disk information can be lost due to extended power failures or failures within the computer hardware itself.

Compact Disks (CDs)

With the advancement of computer processing speeds and memory, software programs have become more complex. As software programs grew, so did the number of floppy disks that were needed to store the programs.

Taking a cue from the music industry, computer programs were soon offered on compact disk, or CD.

Compact disks (CDs) are flat, round, metal disks surrounded by a protective coating of plastic. They are durable but fragile and require special handling. To keep the disks clean and scratch free, they should be stored in their original plastic container, sometimes referred to as a **jewel box**. The discs should be handled by placing your fingers around the edges of the CD.

The storage capabilities of the CD far surpass that of the floppy disk. For this reason, floppy disk drives installed in computers are quickly being replaced by CD drives. CD drives read disks using small lasers. These lasers read patterns on the surface of the disk and convert that information to a series of 1s and 0s, or bits, as mentioned earlier in the chapter. CD drives are also capable of reading music on a CD. With internal or external speakers, you can listen to music while working on your computer.

At this time, CD technology is growing at a phenomenal rate. As new processes for recording and reading information from these disks evolve, the amount of information

Storage devices have increased capacity.

LEFT: © GETTY IMAGES/PHOTODISC. RIGHT: © GETTY IMAGES/EYEWIRE

that can be stored on this medium is steadily increasing. New technology has also led to the creation of various forms of CD storage:

- CD-ROM (compact disk read-only memory)
- CD-R (compact disk-recordable)
- CD-E (compact disk-erasable)
- CD-RW (compact disk-rewritable)

A **CD-ROM** (compact disk read-only memory) is typically used for a commercially purchased software package such as a word processing, spreadsheet, or database programs. The contents cannot be altered by the user, hence the name *read-only*.

A **CD-R** (compact disk-recordable) is a type of CD that allows you to store information. Unlike a floppy disk, once the information has been recorded using a CD-R, it cannot be changed. CD-Rs can be read by any CD drive, however, a specific CD-R drive and software is needed to save information.

Originally called the **CD-E** (compact disk-erasable), a **CD-RW** (compact disk read-writable) is similar to a floppy disk. CD-RWs allow you to store and erase information multiple times. To use this type of disk, you must have a drive capable of using a CD-RW and corresponding software.

Digital Versatile Disks (DVDs)

The **DVD** (digital versatile disk) uses the same format as a CD, but it has much higher disk storage capacities. The DVD is expected eventually to replace the CD-ROM disk. DVDs can hold as much as 17 GB of information, 24.84 times the data of a standard CD. DVDs are available in a variety of formats:

- **DVD-ROM** (digital versatile disk-read-only memory)
- **DVD-RW** (digital versatile disk-rewritable)
- **DVD-RAM** (digital versatile disk-random access memory)

Because of their large storage capacity and high quality, DVDs are the ideal medium for full-screen multimedia presentations. All major personal computer manufacturers now have models that include DVD-ROM drives.

Information Output

Output (data that has been processed into a useful form) is a hardware device that can convey information to the user. Output can be presented in the form of **soft copy** (information that exists electronically and displays for a temporary period of time on a display monitor). Output can also take the form of **hard copy**, or printed information.

Monitors

CRT Monitors

The **cathode ray tube (CRT) monitor** has been the standard since computers became a fixture in the workplace and the home. CRT monitors use the same technology as the screens on a standard television set. Although CRT monitors are available in various sizes, the most common range from 15 to 22 inches. The larger 19- to 22-inch screens are capable of displaying two full pages of text side by side. They are also useful for those whose work require that they have more than one software program open at a time.

The number of pixels that a monitor contains determines the quality of the image on the screen. **Pixels** are the individual dots that make up the image displayed on a CRT. The term **resolution** is used to define sharpness and clearness of an image. The minimum resolution recommended is 800 × 600 for a 15-inch screen; 1024 × 768 pixels or higher is needed if graphics are going to be displayed. High-performance monitors have a maximum resolution of 1600 × 1200 pixels.

In the past, CRT monitor screens had a slight curve in their surface. Current models, like televisions, have gone to a flat screen design. Flat screens reduce glare, reflection, and image distortion. Flat screens are better for the operator in terms of less eyestrain and less eye fatigue.

LCD Monitors

The popularity of laptop computers has led to advances in flat-panel technology. This technology has, in turn, found its way back to desktop computer units as well. **LCDs (liquid crystal displays)** are thin, flat-screen, vibrant monitors that appear to be eroding the market of CRTs. Although LCDs are still more expensive than comparably sized CRTs, analysts project that 40 percent of all monitor sales will be LCD screens by 2003.[6]

An LCD is comprised of two panels that are injected with liquid crystals. As an electric current is passed through the crystals, they let varying amounts of light show through. This, in turn, produces the image seen on the screen. The drawbacks to LCD screens are that rapidly scrolling text or a fast-moving image tends to blur, or leave an image trail. However, the clarity and color accuracy on an LCD is superior to that of a CRT.

---

[6]Tom Spring, "Are you looking at your last CRT?" PCWorld.com, February 13, 2002.

The LCD monitor has a flat-panel screen that allows for the conservation of desk space.

© GETTY IMAGES/PHOTODISC

LCDs also take up less space than CRT monitors. This enables the administrative professional to have more usable desk space at his or her workstation. Some LCD screens have speakers built into their framework, freeing additional space on a workstation. Others LCDs allow the user to alter the appearance of documents on the screen. Increasing the viewable area allows the user to view documents in landscape mode instead of portrait mode.

Image Quality and Size

Better image quality has been proven to reduce symptoms such as headaches, sore eyes, light sensitivity, and neck strain by up to 66 percent. Research also shows that if the quality of the display on the screen is improved, productivity will increase as well. When purchasing a monitor, you should compare the image quality of several models, using the software applications typical to your environment.

In addition to image quality, size is also important. Monitors that are smaller than 17 inches inhibit the user's ability to see more than a few cells on a spreadsheet and to read from multiple applications at one time. Larger monitor screens (19- to 21-inch) provide 50 to 60 percent more visible space than 15-inch monitors.

Printers

The most commonly used output device is the printer. The two most frequently used printer types continue to be the laser and the inkjet.

Inkjet Printers

An inkjet printer is classified as a **nonimpact printer** because it forms characters and graphics on paper without actually striking the paper. **Inkjets** use liquid ink cartridges that spray tiny drops of ink onto a piece of paper to form letters, numbers, and characters. Inkjets are quiet and the print quality is near that of laser printers. Because they are inexpensive, small inkjet printers are used by small organizations and sometimes by large organizations at every workstation. In addition, larger inkjet printers are often networked and used as the main printer for a department.

Inkjet printers are single-sheet feeders. They can be loaded with high-quality letterhead paper for one job and then quickly reloaded with standard weight paper for the next print job. Inkjet printers are also popular options for those who desire colored output. The typical inkjet printer has two cartridge bays: one for black ink and one for colored ink. Color cartridges are filled with the primary colors of ink: red, yellow, and blue. The inkjet blends these colors to match what has been requested in the print job. When purchasing an inkjet printer, make sure to consider the following:

- Speed—Inkjet printers can, on average, print between 10 and 15 pages per minute (PPM). This is an important consideration when determining the volume of printing and the number of users. Printing graphics will significantly decrease the PPM count.
- Cost per page—Ink cartridges usually cost between $20 and $40 per cartridge. However, the number of pages you can print from a single cartridge varies by manufacturer. Some print as few as 20 pages, while others print as many as 300 pages. Typical inkjet printers have operating costs of 5 to 10 cents per page for black and white and 10 to 20 cents per page for color.
- Paper costs—A variety of paper types are available for use with inkjet printers. These include plain paper, photo paper, glossy paper, and banner paper. Some inkjet printers perform better on special inkjet paper or require heavier inkjet paper for color documents.
- Flexibility—Many inkjet printers are capable of printing envelopes, labels, index cards, greeting cards, and transparencies.
- Cost—Inkjets are generally inexpensive, with the price ranging from $50 to $300. However, make sure to include the additional costs, such as special paper and ink cartridges.

Laser Printers

The **laser printer** uses a low-powered beam of light to place charged particles on a drum. As the drum rotates, **toner** (powdered ink) sticks to these charged areas. When paper is rolled underneath the drum, the toner images stick to the paper. A final set of rollers applies heat and pressure to permanently adhere the images to the paper. The result is a quickly produced, sharp-edged image. These high-quality documents can be used directly from the printer for meetings, formal reports, or sales presentations. Laser printers offer an alternative to having documents professionally printed.

Laser printers are also capable of producing high-resolution color graphics. With the appropriate software and special coated paper, laser printers can produce photograph-quality printouts. Laser printers typically allow the user to add memory to the printer. Additional memory may be necessary in the production of detailed graphics. If your printer does not have enough memory, only part of your requested image will be reproduced.

© GETTY IMAGES/PHOTODISC

Inkjet printers are capable of quality black or colored printing.

When purchasing a laser printer, consider the following factors:

- Speed—A laser printer for the home or small business can easily print up to 40 pages per minute (without graphics). Laser printers designed for large workplaces can print more than 1,500 pages per minute.

- Cost per page—Toner cartridge prices range from $50 to $100 for about 5,000 printed pages. This allows laser printers to produce copies at 2 to 3 cents per page.

- Paper costs—A variety of paper types similar to those used with inkjet printers are available for use with laser printers. Remember, expensive paper can increase the price per printed page.

- Flexibility— Many laser printers have more than one paper tray to accommodate different paper sizes or envelopes. Most laser printers are capable of printing envelopes, labels, index cards, greeting cards, and transparencies. In addition, laser printers are often capable of printing on both sides of the page and holding thousands of sheets of paper at a time.

- Cost—As with any computer hardware, the cost for laser printers can vary greatly depending on the speed, resolution, and capacity.

Networked Printers

Many businesses use a **networked printer** (a printer attached to a local area network) so it can serve as the primary printer for several users. The page-per-minute speed of laser printers makes them ideal network printers. In addition, networked printers can provide a cost savings to the business. For example, if specialized functions are required in one department of an organization, the department can use a network printer. This printer can provide additional capabilities (color, stapling, bundling, hole punching, specialized paper size, and so on) for a group of people, rather than purchasing separate printers for each individual.

Multifunction Peripherals

As described earlier in this chapter, multifunction machines print, copy, fax, and scan. If you are considering the purchase of a multifunction peripheral, consider these factors:

- Space—Multifunction devices take up far less space than the machines they replace and can be installed more easily since one hookup takes care of numerous functions.

- Capacity—Multifunction machines are available with varying speeds, print resolution, and capabilities.

- Cost—The cost can range from a low of a few hundred dollars to a high of several thousand dollars, depending on the capabilities and the speed of the machine.

- Downtime—When a multifunction device is broken, you lose all functions—the copier, printer, scanner, and fax. This is an important factor to consider, especially in a small business or home business where there are no backup machines.

Computer Networks

As you just learned, computers and other peripheral equipment can be linked through networks. Networks can be described as many users sharing specific resources such as hardware, software, data, or information. These networks may be LANs, MANs, WANs, or VPNs.

- **Local area networks (LANs)** link various types of technological equipment within a building or several buildings within the same geographical area. Organizations that use LANs may include a college campus, a hospital, or city governmental agencies. Home networks are also considered a LAN. They can be connected through a phone line, cable, or radio frequency (wireless technology).

- **Metropolitan area networks (MANs)** link LANs and technological equipment over a distance equal to the size of a city and its surroundings.

© GETTY IMAGES/EYEWIRE

VPNs allow mobile users to access the company's network server.

- **Wide area networks (WANs)** link technological equipment over an area that can be hundreds of thousands of miles. WANs are often used in state government agencies, organizations with multistate locations, or commercial airlines that operate across the country.
- **Virtual private networks (VPNs)** link mobile users with a secure connection to the company network server. VPNs use the Internet to provide a mobile user with a connection to a main office and help ensure that any data that is transmitted is safe from interception from unauthorized people.

Almost all computers are networked via LANs, MANs, or WANs. These connections allow individuals and computers to talk to each other over distances. Advantages of networks include these:

- Assist in communications. Using a network, individuals can communicate using email,

instant messaging, chat rooms, and videoconferencing. Sometimes these communications occur within an organization's network; other times they occur globally over the Internet.

- Share hardware. Each computer linked by a network can access and use hardware on the network. As described earlier in this chapter, many organizations use a network so departments can share a printer.
- Share information. When using a network, any authorized user can access data and information stored on other computers connected to the network. For example, a university may store student records on a network. This would allow a variety of individuals within the university access to this information.
- Share software. Users can often access software from a network. Most software vendors offer a **site license**, which is a legal

agreement that allows multiple users to run a software package at the same time. Although the fee is based on the number of users or computers connected to a network, the cost is usually less than purchasing individual copies of the software.

The growth of technology and the need for sharing information worldwide have spawned worldwide networks. Businesses and individuals are extensively using the Internet, a worldwide network, and the World Wide Web, one of the features of the Internet.

Internet

The Internet is the world's largest group of connected computers, or network. It connects people from all over the world who wish to exchange information and ideas. The U.S. Department of Defense created the Internet in the 1960s. Today an estimated 459 million people around the world use the Internet. The Internet is used for business, education, and entertainment. In addition, the Internet has become a forum for whatever topic interests the user. Although a plethora of technology makes this worldwide network function, a brief explanation of that technology is presented here.

The Internet is a vehicle for delivering and sharing information among computers around the world. Many computers speak the same electronic language so they can easily exchange information. **Transmission Control Protocol/Internet Protocol (TCP/IP)** is a language that allows computers to communicate over the Internet. This technology manages the transmission of data by breaking it up into packets.

Individuals and businesses interact with the Internet by purchasing a subscription with an **Internet Service Provider (ISP)**. An ISP is a business that sells access to its permanent Internet connection for a fee. Fees are usually based on a standard monthly charge, but may vary by hours of actual connection. Individuals should be aware of their Internet use and pick an ISP accordingly. Services may also be purchased through an **online service**

provider (OSP). An online service provider supplies Internet access as well as additional members-only features, which may include special services such as weather, legal information, games, travel guides, and financial data. A **wireless service provider (WSP)** is a company that provides wireless Internet access to users with wireless modems or Web-enabled handheld computers or devices. Employees and students often connect to the Internet through a business or school network. In this case, the computers are usually part of a LAN that connects to a service provider. Figure 10-1 provides items to consider when selecting an ISP.

World Wide Web

The **World Wide Web** is a large collection of computer files (Web pages) scattered across the Internet. Although the terms *Web* and *Internet* are frequently used interchangeably, the World Wide Web is actually one of the many services available on the Internet. For example, in addition to the Web, the Internet contains news articles, weather information, entertainment (games), email programs, travel information, and encyclopedia information.

SELECTING AN ISP

- How much will you pay for access, and how many hours of connection time does that include?
- What connection speeds and modem types are supported?
- How reliable is the connection? Make sure you won't be bothered by busy signals or slow response.
- What type of technical help is provided?
- What software will you receive?
- If the ISP provider is offering "free" access to the Internet, make sure you fully understand the terms and conditions of the offer.

FIGURE 10-1 Selecting an ISP

The Web was created by Tim Berners-Lee, a consultant at the Swiss research laboratory CERN, as a tool for physicists to share research data. The general public did not use the Web until the creation of Mosaic™, a **Web browser** (an application program that provides a way to look at and interact with all the information on the World Wide Web). From this browser, a number of other browsers have been developed, including Microsoft® Internet Explorer, Netscape®, Neoplanet℠, and Opera®.

In less than 10 years, the Web has changed the way people communicate. In fact, the Web has spawned its own language. A new semi-technical vocabulary that is specific to Web functions has emerged. Some of these terms are listed in Figure 10-2.

To some people, the Internet is business; to others, the Internet is recreation. Information and services available on the Web include:

- *Research.* Individuals can locate endless research information as they search through libraries, publications, government agencies, and news organizations.
- *Travel services.* Individuals and businesses can make travel reservations any time day or night to destinations anywhere in the world.
- *News.* Worldwide news is available almost as it happens.

- *Ecommerce.* The Web allows any business to market itself to a global audience. Anyone with access to the Internet can participate in ecommerce. Although most ecommerce transactions in the past were conducted through desktop computers, today some handheld computers, pagers, and cellular telephones participate in this service.
- *Chat rooms.* People with similar interests meet in chat rooms and speak online with people from around the world.
- *Virtual travel.* Webcams enable users to see places they would not be able to see in real life. Webcams are positioned on famous landmarks (Times Square in New York City and the Eiffel Tower in Paris) and scenic natural areas (Yellowstone National Park). Some are aimed at ordinary individuals at their job or at home so anyone who is interested can take a look.

With the millions of pieces of information available on the Web, one of the biggest challenges is finding the data that meets your needs. Search engines have been developed to help you locate the information you need. These search engines are updated frequently and keep up with new pages that are being created on the Web every minute. Several search engines you may find helpful as you search the Web are listed in Figure 10-3.

WEB TERMINOLOGY

- **Browser**—An information retrieval tool. Some of the Web browsers available are Internet Explorer, Netscape, Neoplanet, and Opera.
- **Downloading**—Receiving information onto a computer from a server on the Internet.
- **Ecommerce**—A financial business transaction that occurs over an electronic network such as the Internet.
- **HTML** (Hypertext Markup Language)—The standard language used for creating and formatting Web pages.
- **HTTP** (Hypertext Transfer Protocol)—The communications standard that enables pages to transfer on the Web.
- **Home page**—The starting page or introductory page of a Website.
- **Hyperlink**—A built-in connection to another related Web page or to part of a Web page.
- **Search engine**—A software program used to find Websites, Web pages, and Internet files.
- **URL** (Uniform Resource Locator)—The addressing system for a Web address.
- **Web server**—A host computer that delivers the Web pages you request.

FIGURE 10-2 Web Terminology

SEARCH ENGINES

The following search engines can help you locate information quickly on the Web:

- AltaVista® (www.altavista.com)
- Ask Jeeves℠ (www.ask.com)
- Canadopedia℠ (www.canadopedia.com) This search engine lists English and French Canadian Websites.
- Google™ (www.google.com)
- Hotbot® (www.hotbot.com)
- Metacrawler™ (www.metacrawler.com)
- SearchEurope℠ (www.searcheurope.com). This is a search engine for Europe.
- Yahoo!® (www.yahoo.com)

FIGURE 10~3 Search Engines

When using the Internet and the World Wide Web, you should remember the following:

- The Internet is public. Even though you may be sitting at a computer at work or at home, other people on the Net can electronically observe your online movements. They can also "listen" to your online chats or read information you post on discussion boards.

- Email is not private. Others can read your email communication unless you are using **encryption software** to encode your messages so others cannot gain access to them.

- Avoid giving out private information such as name, address, phone number, credit card number, Social Security number, or bank account information. Someone can use this information to steal your identity and make purchases with your money.

- The validity of information posted needs to be checked. For example, if you are doing research, you need to check the validity of the source. As you know, anyone can get on the Internet and publish information. You do not want to believe or pass on incorrect information. Ultimately you are re-

sponsible for checking the validity of information you researched on the Internet.

- Files downloaded from the Internet may contain viruses, which you must protect against. You will learn more about viruses and how to protect against them in Chapter 11, Computer Software.

- Harassment can be common in chat rooms, particularly for women. The harassment can range from rudeness, to verbal abuse, to serious sexual harassment. If you are not comfortable with what is happening in a chat room, use the Escape key to get out.[7]

Intranet and Extranet

An **intranet** is a private network that belongs to an organization and is accessible only by the organization's employees. It uses the same technology as the Internet, but is for the private use of the employees. Intranets generally make company information available to employees. Examples of simple intranet applications include electronic publishing of telephone directories, calendars, procedures manuals, benefits information, and job postings. It may also house the company email system. Although an intranet may have a link to the Internet, a **firewall** prevents unauthorized outside individuals from using an intranet.

An **extranet** also operates behind a firewall, but this firewall allows access to selected parts of the in-house network by individuals, companies, and organizations outside the company. This access for non-company personnel is the difference between an intranet and an extranet. A business, for example, may grant extranet access to current customers. The customers need a user name supplied by the company and a password they create to gain access to the site. This access is partial, meaning the customers can access information that pertains to the

---

[7]"Just Like the Real World. . . Use Common Sense to Stay Safe On-Line." *Convince: Guide to Internet Basics* (Volume 6, Issue 10), 96–98.

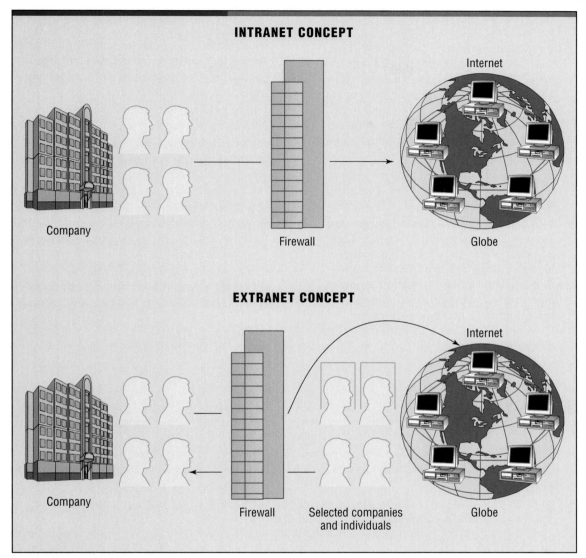

INTRANET CONCEPT

Company

Firewall

Internet

Globe

EXTRANET CONCEPT

Company

Firewall

Selected companies and individuals

Internet

Globe

FIGURE 10~4 Intranet and Extranet Concepts

business relationship now. An extranet, for example, may be used by:

- Banks to provide clients with account information.
- Health institutions to access medical records.
- Businesses to allow stockholders to view their finances.

Future Direction of Computer Technology

Because the computer industry is an ever-changing and dynamic entity, identifying trends is difficult. However, the interest that consumers have shown in specific areas seems to be driving the current wave of technology and research, as follows.

- Laptop computers with DVD-R/RW. Computers are just now being offered with DVD drives. These drives enable users to view DVD content in a free-flowing format similar to home DVD players, but now in a portable device. The technology to be able to record and re-record on DVD is the next logical step.

- Virtual reality systems that allow you to see, hear, and touch computer-generated 3-D images.

- Wi-Fi technology. Wi-Fi is a way for computers to link to a network, such as Ethernet, or the Web via wireless connection. This technology can transfer data up to 11 MB per second using the same 2.4-ghz range that standard cordless phones use. Currently this technology enables the user to be only 300 feet or less from the access point server.

- The widespread distribution of video (DVD) and audio (music CDs) over the Internet. Entertainment companies, claiming for years they have lost revenue because of pirating, that capitalize on the increasing video and audio quality of computer systems.

- Household appliances that operate from verbal instructions.

- Nanotechnological devices (tiny medical robots tinkering with molecules) that patrol the blood stream, killing cancer and viruses and scraping arterial blockages.

- Through MEMS (micro-electro-mechanical systems) materials such as concrete that become smart, able to adapt to shaking in an earthquake.

- Chips implanted in people's bodies that serve as a combination credit card, passport, driver's license, and personal diary. ∎

SUMMARY

To reinforce what you have learned in this chapter, study this summary.

- Information can be input into computers through keyboards, scanners, voice recognition technology, digital cameras, pointing devices, touch screens, infrared devices, and pen tablets and styluses.

- Computer classifications include supercomputers, mainframes, workstation computers, microcomputers, handheld computers, and personal digital assistants.

- The central processing unit is the brain of the computer system. It accepts the data, processes it, and delivers the results to the output device. The other parts of the computer are the arithmetic/ logic unit, the control unit, and memory.

- Computers have two main types of storage: primary and secondary. Primary storage is a temporary storage place for data, instructions, and information. Secondary storage devices consist of floppy disks, high-capacity disks (such as Zip disks, SuperDisks, and Jaz disks), hard drives, CDs, and DVDs.

- Output devices include monitors, printers, and multifunction peripherals.

- Computers within a company may be linked through networks. These networks may be LANs, MANs, or WANs. VPNs link mobile users to a corporate network.

- The Internet and the Web are computer networks that are used worldwide by organizations and individuals.

- An intranet is a network that lets businesses provide employee access to specific business information as well as to the Internet without allowing people from the outside to have access.

- An extranet allows the inclusion of selected individuals, companies, and organizations outside the company to have access to selected company information.
- Technology will continue to influence every area of people's lives in the future, changing the way they work and live.

FIND THE PROBLEM

Rhea Zayas serves as the informal hardware "expert" in the department. She has been working all day on a report that needs to be completed within the hour. While everyone in the department knows she is busy, Francine Miljour has interrupted Rhea three times in the last hour to get her assistance with paper jams in the printer. Once again Francine needs help. Since Rhea is almost done with her project, she agrees to help Francine. When Rhea returns to her desk, her supervisor is waiting for her and asks for the completed project. Upon learning that the report is not ready, Rhea's supervisor is quite upset. How could this problem have been avoided?

PROFESSIONAL POINTERS

Technology, especially in the computer field, is drastically affecting the work of the administrative professional. Opportunities made available by technology are allowing administrative professionals to redefine their roles. Keep these tips in mind as you prepare to enter or re-enter the job market:

- The competitive pressures of business requires that new and more efficient methods continually be sought.
- As an administrative professional, you may be part of restructuring and redesigning your organization. Be a lifelong learner. Keep an open mind about how your work may be reorganized and redesigned.
- Administrative professionals are critical links in accessing, manipulating, and sending information. You need to remain current on workplace technology.
- The administrative professional must possess not only word processing skills, but also a command of graphic arts, interactive video techniques, telecommunications, and computer software installation. Remain current on new developments in these areas through short courses or seminars.

REINFORCEMENT ITEMS

1. Describe and explain three types of pointing devices.
2. Explain the difference between supercomputers and workstation computers.
3. Describe four storage devices.
4. List and explain what considerations should be made when purchasing a printer.
5. Explain the differences between the Internet, intranet, and extranet.

CRITICAL-THINKING ACTIVITY

A computer network connects all of the departments at People Pharmaceuticals. The computer department staff maintains and services software that resides on the system, troubleshoots hardware and technical problems, and monitors the agency's communications. Every employee with a computer logs onto the system with a network name assigned by the computer department and a secret password, which is chosen by the employee. Employees are required to change their password on the first working day of each month.

Ella Leroy, an administrative assistant in the Houston division, spends a great deal of time on the computer and has access to all confidential human resource information. All of her coworkers know Ella has two children, Kevin and Bethany. In the lunchroom last week, Ella was overhead telling a new employee about the system she uses to set her password. In fact, Ella bragged that she uses her children's names as her password so her passwords are easy to remember.

Al Yee, one of Ella's coworkers has repeatedly asked Ella to find out the new department head's salary. Although Ella has refused, over the last week she learned that Al found the information he was seeking. Angry about the new department head's salary, Al has been complaining to anyone in the department who will listen. Ella confronts Al and accuses him of using her password. Al adamantly denies using Ella's information to access the system.

1. Did Ella handle the situation appropriately? If not, what could she have done differently?

2. Can Ella learn whether Al accessed the system using her computer password? Should she file a complaint if she learns someone has been using her password?

3. What other problems could this situation have created?

4. What company policies should be put in place as a result of this situation?

VOCABULARY REVIEW

Complete the Vocabulary Review for Chapter 10 given on page 87 of the *Applications Workbook*.

ENGLISH AND WORD USAGE DRILL

Complete the English and Word Usage Drills for Chapter 10 listed on page 88 of the *Applications Workbook*.

WORKPLACE APPLICATIONS

A10-1 (Goal 1)

For two or three days from your regular daily routine, observe different ways data is created, input, and output. For example, a cash register receipt is the result (or output) from data that was created by a sale. The sale was input into the cash register, with the receipt as the output. Make a list of the methods you observe and the equipment used to record the information. Try to determine how the data is handled or processed by the computer system. In other words, what happens to the data that is input? You may find examples at your local post office, bank, movie theater, and department and grocery stores. If the type of equipment used is not readily apparent to you, ask an employee or manager of the business. Present an oral report of your findings to the class.

 ### A10-2 (Goals 1, 2, 3, and 4)

Using the Internet, locate at least two vendors who offer comparable products in each of the following categories. Use the form provided on the Student CD, SCDA10-3, to record your information. Submit a completed copy of the form to your instructor.

- Computer keyboard
- Computer monitor
- Printer

 ### A10-3 (Goal 5)

Using the Internet, research three examples of the use of virtual reality. Write a short report of your findings, identifying your sources, and submit it to your instructor.

A10-4 (Goal 1)

A case study is provided on the Student CD, SCDA10-5a. Read the case and respond to the questions. Write a summary of your responses to your instructor, using the memorandum form on the Student CD, SCDA10-5b.

ASSESSMENT OF CHAPTER GOALS

Did you successfully complete the chapter goals? Evaluate yourself by filling out the form on page 89 of the *Applications Workbook*.

Computer Software

1. Describe systems software.
2. Describe applications software.
3. Explain software security and ethics.
4. Troubleshoot software problems.

Computers, their processing speed, storage capacity, expandability, and affordability have long been the focus for businesses looking to provide their employees with the latest technology. As hardware technology has continued to develop, so have software programs. In addition to selecting appropriate hardware, being able to select the most efficient software program is equally important. The ability to understand software and its ability to accomplish desired results has become a key responsibility of the administrative professional. Although your role as an administrative professional does not require that you have an in-depth understanding of the inner workings of a computer, it does require that you know the particular software packages you use in the workplace. You may also be expected to select or help to select appropriate software packages for use in your organization.

The intent of this chapter is not to provide detailed information on a specific brand of software; the intent is to give you an overview of the various types of software packages available. (You should also take course work to become proficient in the use of software programs.) This chapter will help you learn how to compare and select software programs. Additionally, you will learn how to care for and maintain software and ways to use software to maintain the efficient operation of computer hardware.

Systems Software

When people speak of software, they are generally referring to the variety of programs that people use for work, communication, or entertainment. However, software programs are running on your computer that you never even see. This type of software is sometimes referred to as systems software. **Systems software** is a program through which the computer manages its own resources, such as the central processing unit, memory, secondary storage devices, and input/output devices.

Systems software controls the many components of a computer system and its devices. In fact, systems software serves as the interface between the user, the applications software, and the computer's hardware. This chapter will discuss the following types of systems software: operating systems and utility programs.

Operating Systems

An **operating system** is a program that contains the instructions that coordinate the computer's outer components (keyboard, printer, mouse, and monitor) and internal components (sound cards, drives, and processing chips). Without operating system software, the computer cannot function. The operating system also contains the instructions that allow you to run applications software. In fact, these programs enable your computer to read and write data to a storage device, send pictures to your monitor, and accept keyboard commands.

A general knowledge about operating systems software will help you to understand how your computer functions. Consider this analogy. When you want to watch a movie at home, you rent or buy a video or a DVD. You turn on the television and the video or DVD player and then insert the movie. Once you press play, you are ready to sit back and enjoy your movie. However, you can perform other functions with the DVD player. You can increase or decrease the volume, pause the movie, or fast-forward or rewind the movie. In other words, once you start the movie, you can control different aspects of playing the movie by entering commands into the video player.

As soon as you turn on your computer, the operating system is copied into memory from the computer's hard disk. This operation prepares the computer to receive your commands. As long as the computer is running, the operating system remains in memory, allowing the computer to communicate with other software programs. The operating

DEANNA ETTINGER

The operating system coordinates the functions of the computer.

system allows you to open a word processing or spreadsheet program, to create a new document so you can key a report, or save a document on the hard drive or another storage device. Just like you have never seen the operating system of a video player at work, you probably have never seen the operating system of your computer at work. Keep in mind, however, that without the operating system, you cannot give the computer any orders or commands.

Currently a number of types of computer operating systems are available. Examples include these:

- Windows®
- Windows for Networks
- Mac® OS
- UNIX®
- LINUX®
- OS/2® Warp Client

Windows

At the time this textbook was written, Windows® XP was the current version of Windows.

This system is Microsoft's fastest and most reliable operating system. In 1992, Microsoft developed **Windows**. Since that time, a number of versions of Windows have been developed. (Each version has upgraded features and expanded capabilities.) Windows XP provides users with a faster start-up; better overall performance; and a cleaner, more simplified appearance. Windows XP is currently available in two versions: Windows XP Home Edition and Windows® XP Professional Edition. Both versions allow you to perform the following tasks:

- Acquire, organize, and share digital pictures
- Download, store, and play high-quality music
- Create, edit, and share videos
- Connect easily and share multiple home computers

Current Windows programs have a **graphical user interface (GUI)** that works in conjunction with the operating system to simplify its use. A GUI uses visual images such as icons, buttons, menus, or other graphical objects to issue commands. These visual images make it easier for the user to give commands to the computer. For example, to print, the user clicks on an icon depicting a printer and to save, the user clicks on an icon depicting a disk.

Developed before the Windows® XP Home Edition, Windows® Millennium is also an upgraded version of the Windows operating system. Windows® ME (pronounced em-ee) has features that were designed primarily for the home user. Internet-browsing software; email software; and programming that allows for digitizing, editing, and storing home movies is included. Windows ME also allows for easy transfer of photos from a digital camera or scanner into the computer.

Windows for Networks

Windows XP Professional and Windows® 2000 Server were developed as an upgrade to Windows NT® Workstation and Windows NT® for Servers (computers that are networked to other computers and peripheral devices). Designed specifically for use in a networking situation, Windows XP Professional Edition offers the following features:

- All capabilities of Windows XP Home Edition
- Greater data security through encryption of files and folders
- Capability to remotely access a computer, data, and its files from another computer system
- Simpler administration of groups of users or computers
- Multiple language user interface
- Support for secured wireless network access

Although the newer versions of Windows are more powerful than earlier versions, they have the same look and feel. This enables prior Windows users to adapt easily to the upgraded system. Each upgraded operating system requires more disk space, more memory (RAM), and a faster processor than previous versions of Windows because the system's features are more complex.

Operating systems can be designed for network use or for stand-alone systems.

© GETTY IMAGES/PHOTODISC

Mac OS

Apple® Computer, Inc., developed the **Mac OS** for use on the Macintosh computer system. Macintosh systems are used primarily in schools and homes and in business operations focused on the manipulation of graphics (art and design, newspaper and magazine layout, and conceptual design). The Mac OS continues to be refined and improved by Apple, with the latest installment being the OS X® system. This system incorporates enhanced multimedia capabilities and has the capability of opening, editing, and saving files created on the Windows platform.

UNIX

The **UNIX** operating system was developed in 1969 at AT&T for use in Bell Labs'[SM] minicomputers. UNIX is now used extensively in the programming and operating of supercomputers and mainframe computers. It is a very powerful operating system, but because it is primarily a command line platform (users must key in "command lines" in order for the computer to complete the desired task) and not a GUI, it is not widely used in the home computing market.

Solaris™ is a version of UNIX that was developed by Sun® Microsystems. This operating system was designed specifically for ecommerce applications because it can manage high-traffic accounts and incorporate the security that is necessary for Web transactions.

LINUX

LINUX is a version of UNIX. Although LINUX was created by Linus Torvalds of Finland, it is now one of the fastest-growing operating systems in the world. LINUX is a free operating system that works with IBM® hardware and software and is fully supported by IBM services. LINUX encourages its users to experiment with and expand the program's capabilities, as long as users share their suggested improvements with other users. LINUX is available in command line and GUI formats and can be downloaded directly from the World Wide Web. Several companies have made commercial versions of LINUX, incorporating more user-friendly features in an effort to increase its popularity in the marketplace.

OS/2 Warp Client

Developed by IBM, OS/2 is also a GUI format operating system. There are two versions of OS/2 operating systems: one for personal and small network use and one for larger corporate network use. This system is capable of running most windows programs, as well as many email and Internet browser programs. OS/2 is often used by businesses because of its strong networking support.

Operating System Functions

The operating system of a computer can be downloaded from the Web or loaded onto a computer system from a CD or from disks. Once the operating system is loaded, unless the computer hardware begins to fail, it does not have to be reloaded. Occasionally, however, updates to the operating system are necessary. These updates optimize the software and the hardware performance.

An operating system is stored on the computer's hard drive. Once the computer is turned on, the operating system software loads into the computer's memory. The three main functions of operating system software are:

- To control computer system resourcess
- To execute computer programs
- To manage data

When purchasing an operating system, consumers must pay careful attention to the **system resources** that the operating system requires. System resources are the amount of hard drive space the software uses when installed and the amount of RAM required for the operating system to function. For example, an operating system may require a minimum of 64–128 megabytes (MB) of RAM and 1.5 GB of free hard drive space. If these resources are unavailable on a computer, the operating system will not perform as it was designed.

Utility Programs

A **utility program** is a type of system software that performs a specific task, usually related to managing a computer, its devices, or its programs. Most operating systems include a variety of utility programs for managing disk drives, printers, and other devices. The most common utility programs offer the following functions:

- Removing computer viruses
- Compressing files
- Viewing files
- Diagnosing hardware problems
- Uninstalling software
- Scanning disks
- Defragmenting disks
- Backing up files and disks
- Displaying screen savers

In addition to single utility programs, **utility suites** can be purchased as well. Utility suites combine several utility programs into a single package. Purchasing additional utilities may offer improvements or additions to those programs that are included with the operating system. In addition, utility program vendors offer Web-based utility services. To use a Web-based service, you pay an annual fee, which allows you to access and use the vendor's programs on the Web. A variety of utility programs are discussed in the next section.

Antivirus Software

The news media is full of reports about computer viruses that infect computers and networks around the world. These viruses are often spread from computer to computer through email or email attachments. Because email is used extensively as a worldwide communication tool, viruses continue to cause damage to computer files. One of the most common types of utility program is antivirus software. **Antivirus software** is a utility program that protects, detects, and removes viruses from a computer's memory or storage devices. When you purchase a computer, it often contains one of the following antivirus

software programs: Norton AntiVirus™, Command™ AntiVirus, or McAfee™ ThreatScan. Be aware of the signs of virus infection listed in Figure 11-1.

Antivirus software is available that can be upgraded as new viruses are created. Computer programmers spend countless hours researching how a virus moves and how it attacks the components of a computer. Once these puzzle pieces are put together, a new antivirus upgrade is made available to those users who have purchased the antivirus software utility. Many software vendors offer Web-based utility services so users can update their software monthly, weekly, or even daily. Once the antivirus software is upgraded, the user can scan the computer for the current virus. In addition, the software program blocks that particular virus from infecting the computer again.

To protect yourself from viruses, adhere to the following guidelines:

- Install an antivirus program on all of your computers, and obtain software updates regularly.
- Do not open email attachments unless they are from trusted sources. Scan all attachments you intend to open.
- Check downloaded programs for viruses.
- Back up your files regularly. Scan the backup program before archiving disks and files.

SIGNS OF VIRUS INFECTION

- An unusual message or graphic appears on the computer screen.
- An unusual sound or music plays randomly.
- Available memory is less than it should be.
- A program or file is suddenly missing.
- An unknown program or file mysteriously appears.
- A file becomes corrupted.
- A program does not work correctly.

FIGURE 11~1 Signs of Virus Infections

- Have a rescue disk made from your anti-virus software. Your software vendor can provide directions on how to create a rescue disk. Following this procedure can prevent downtime due to virus damage.

File Compression

A **file compression utility** shrinks the size of a file. Compressed files take up less storage space than the original file, freeing up room on the storage media and improving system performance. Compressed files are often attached to email to reduce transmission time. Compressed files usually have a .zip extension. When you receive or download a compressed file, you must uncompress it before you can open it. To **uncompress** a file, you restore it to its original form. Some operating systems, such as Windows XP, include file compression capabilities. Two popular stand-alone file compression utilities are PKZIP™ and WinZip®.

Uninstaller

An **uninstaller** is a utility that removes an application and any associated entries in the system files. When you install an application, the operating system records the information it uses to run the software in the system files. The system file entries remain if you delete the files and folders associated with the program without running the uninstaller. Operating systems usually include an uninstaller, although stand-alone programs are also available.

Applications Software

Applications software consists of programs that perform specific tasks for users. This type of software is sometimes called productivity software because it allows people to become more efficient while performing daily activities. In fact, administrative professionals use applications software daily to perform a variety of tasks. Some of these tasks may include:

- Producing letters, memorandums, tables, and reports.
- Maintaining calendar information and appointment scheduling.
- Creating business forms.
- Creating presentations.
- Creating Web pages.
- Creating publications.
- Producing graphics, charts, and diagrams.
- Querying databases.
- Accessing the Internet.
- Sending and receiving email.
- Handling project management.

Applications software allows you to tell the computer how to perform a desired function. For example, you can produce a report through the use of word processing software or a brochure through the use of a desktop publishing program. You can take photos with a digital camera and, using photo-editing and image-editing software, add photographs to the report or brochure. Ask yourself the questions in Figure 11-2 when making a software purchase.

Numerous application software programs are available. The major categories are covered in the next section, and examples of specific programs are discussed. Keep in mind, however, that software programs are frequently revised and new programs are created. Therefore, the software listed is just a sampling of the programs available at the time this textbook was written.

Office Suites

Office suites are software programs that offer the user a variety of software applications in one package. These multiple programs typically include word processing, database, spreadsheet, presentation, and information management applications. Examples of office suites include the following:

- Microsoft® Office
- WordPerfect® Office
- Microsoft® Works Suite
- StarOffice™
- Lotus SmartSuite™

SOFTWARE CONSIDERATIONS

- Do you have the hardware, memory, and storage requirements needed for the software? Will the program run on your existing operating system? Do you have the memory capacity to support the software?
- Does the program offer the software features you need?
- What documentation is available? The program should have an instruction manual that is well organized and easy to read. An index, a glossary of terms, a quick reference guide, illustrations, and examples are helpful.
- What software support is available? Support may be in the form of tutorials and/or hotline assistance.
- Is the program **user-friendly** and **ergonomically sound**. *User-friendly* means the software is almost as easy for the beginner to follow as it is for the experienced user. *Ergonomically sound* means the software is designed to reduce human fatigue.
- Does the vendor have a reputation for providing good service? Is the vendor reliable? How long has the vendor been in business? Will the vendor assist you during package implementation? Does the vendor have a hotline you can call with questions?
- What is the reputation of the software? You can check with individuals who have used the software. You can also read reviews in computer periodicals such as *PC World* and *PC Computing™*.
- Will there be conversion costs? When investing in software, you may have more to consider than the initial purchase. Do you have old files that must be converted to the new software? If so, how long will the conversion take?
- Is the software compatible with other programs you use?
- How much does the software cost? Will there be productivity improvements as a result of using the software?
- Are others in the company going to be using the software? If so, talk with those individuals and agree on a package that will serve all of your needs.

FIGURE 11-2 Software Considerations

One advantage of office suite software is that many of the software functions are activated in similar ways among all programs contained in the suite. The format and look of each application is as similar as possible to add to the ease of use. Menu bars and toolbars are organized in the same way. For example, the process to save a file is the same whether you are using the database component or the presentation software and whether you use the toolbar, the menu bar, or keystroke commands. A second advantage is that information can easily be exchanged among the suite components. For example, a spreadsheet can be easily imported or linked into a word processing document within the suite. For administrative professionals using a variety of applications software, an office suite puts an end to searching for compatible programs.

Bundled Software Programs

Bundled software programs are often sold with a computer as part of a combined hardware/software package. Computer manufacturers provide bundled software, in part, to attract buyers. A common software bundle includes word processing, spreadsheet, presentation, finance, Internet service, and reference works. If you are purchasing a computer with bundled software, ask yourself the following questions.

- What programs do I need? Try to find a bundle that fits your needs.
- What support is offered? Most vendors provide free support during installation. Others support the software that is preinstalled on the computer through subscription plans, Web access, and telephone access.
- Do I need Internet access? Some vendors offer up to 200 hours of free Internet access

through America Online (AOL), MSN®, or another online service.

Bundled software may also include office suites. If you consider the programs you need, bundled software may be what you want—and save you a great deal of money. Generally, the retail value of bundles and services is several hundred dollars.

Word Processing Software

Word processing continues to be the most commonly used type of application software. Word processing software allows users to manipulate documents that contain text and graphics. Elementary school children as well as corporate managers use word processing software to produce a variety of documents, including short stories, research papers, and quarterly earnings reports. The administrative professional uses word processing software every day to create documents such as letters, memos, reports, labels and envelopes, newsletters, and Web pages. Word processing software has greatly improved the productivity of administrative professionals and has become a standard component of the computer workstation.

Typically, a word processing program contains several standard features, including these:

- Wordwrap allows the user to continue to key while the software automatically positions text at the beginning of a line if the text extends beyond the right margin.
- Spell checker checks the text in a document against an electronic dictionary. The dictionary can be customized to include personal, company, or street names that are not included in the original dictionary. The spell checker may also be combined with a thesaurus program, which provides synonyms for words.
- Grammar checker checks to determine whether the text follows basic grammatical rules. Some programs allow you to set the level of the grammar check by varying the

document library you wish the software to search.

- Language programs allow you to change the text to another language supported by the program. Most programs feature several languages.

Additional word processing features are included in Figure 11-3.

Today several word processing programs are available, including Microsoft Word, Corel WordPerfect, and Lotus® Word Pro. Typically, the price of the software corresponds directly to the number of advanced options or features the program contains. These programs have been developed over several years, and each new version contains options that make document production quicker and easier.

Spreadsheet Software

Spreadsheet programs are also widely used in business. A spreadsheet program allows the user to enter data into rows and columns and then to perform mathematical calculations on that data. Although the definition seems simplistic, spreadsheets are powerful programs that take advantage of the mathematical processing speed of a computer to organize data and information into a variety of formats. One of the most important features of a spreadsheet is its ability to perform calculations. Mathematical functions such as addition, subtraction, multiplication, and division are easily accomplished using formulas in a spreadsheet. In addition, when data in a spreadsheet changes, the software automatically recalculates the rest of the worksheet. Some of the functions available in a typical spreadsheet program are shown in Figure 11-4.

For example, assume your employer asks you to total the expenses in your department for the last six months and then to project the expenses for the next five years using a 3 percent increase in the first year, a 5 percent increase in the second year, and a 7 percent increase in the third through fifth year. This type of complex calculation can be handled

---

SAMPLE WORD PROCESSING FEATURES

AutoCorrect	As you key, the AutoCorrect feature corrects common spelling errors, typographical errors, and incorrect capitalization.
AutoFormat	As you key, the AutoFormat feature applies formatting to text. For example, AutoFormat automatically formats a heading, numbers a list, or formats Internet and email addresses as hyperlinks.
Columns	Most word processing packages can arrange text in columns similar to newspapers or magazines.
Grammar Checker	The grammar checker helps check a document for use of capitalization, sentence fragments, punctuation, misused words and subject-verb agreement.
Tables	You can easily organize information into evenly spaced rows and columns using the table feature.
Templates	A template determines the basic structure for a document and contains document settings such as fonts, page layout, special formatting, and styles. Templates exist for letters, memos, Web pages, faxes, and reports.
Thesaurus	A thesaurus supplies synonyms.
Speech Recognition	This feature allows you to dictate text into a word processing program. This function can also be used to activate editing and formatting commands.

FIGURE 11~3 Sample Word Processing Features

SPREADSHEET FUNCTIONS

Future Value	Calculates the future value of an investment
Payment	Calculates the periodic payment for a loan
Present Value	Calculates the present value of an investment
Date	Inserts the current date
Time	Returns the current time
Now	Returns the current date and time
Sum	Calculates the total of a range of numbers
Average	Calculates the average value of a range of numbers
Count	Calculates the number of cells that have entries
Max	Determines the maximum value in a range
Min	Determines the minimum value in a range

FIGURE 11~4 Spreadsheet Functions

---

quickly and easily by a spreadsheet. Changes are also easily accomplished and updated. If your employer asks you to change the percents to 5, 7, and 9, respectively, the worksheet is easily recalculated to reflect these changes.

In addition to performing calculations and automatic recalculations, spreadsheets also have other capabilities. For example, most spreadsheets include the following standard features:

- What-if analysis. This process allows the user to change specific values in a spreadsheet to review the effects of those changes.

- Charting. This feature allows the user to display data in a line, column, or pie chart format. Users also have the ability to customize the charts in a variety of ways, such as adding titles, changing colors, or adding data labels.

- Word processing. Most spreadsheet software incorporate many of the features included in word processing software, such as changing fonts and margins, checking spelling, adding colors, recognizing voice input, and publishing information to the Web.

Spreadsheet programs can be found in office suites or as stand-alone products. Examples of spreadsheet programs include Microsoft Excel, Lotus® 1-2-3 Millennium, and Corel Quattro Pro™.

Presentation Software

Presentation software allows you to present your ideas, messages, or reports to a group of individuals. You can supplement the information with the addition of photographs, drawings, animation, and sound. The presentation can be printed and reproduced as slides, or it can be displayed directly from the computer to a projection screen. Studies have shown that visuals in a presentation assist the audience in understanding the material and increase their retention of the information. Therefore, presentation software has become a widespread tool in the workplace. Although you learned about making presentations in Chapter 7, this section will make you aware of the software features available.

Presentation software programs contain a wide variety of preexisting **layouts** (arrangements of common slide elements such as titles, bulleted lists, and graphics) that can be used to create customized slides. In addition, **templates** (predesigned documents that contain formatting) are available to provide the design framework for a presentation—the colors, text styles, and background elements. Presentation software packages typically include a **clip gallery**, which offers users a variety of clip art images, photographs, video clips, and audio clips. You can also design your own clip art, insert photographs, or include graphics or sound clips downloaded from the Web or from another source on the computer. Although a variety of presentation software packages are available, three common packages include Microsoft PowerPoint, Corel Presentations®, and Lotus Freelance Graphics™.

Presentation software also incorporates some of the features found in word processing software, such as spell checking, text formatting, voice recognition, and publishing to the Web. In addition, once a presentation has been created, it can be viewed or printed as slides, an outline, an audience handout, or a Web presentation. Most presentation software allows the creator to make notes pages, printing the slide frame on a separate page and leaving room for the presenter to write a script or make notes. Presentation software can be purchased as a stand-alone software program; however, it is typically included in most office suite packages.

Database Software

A **database** is a collection of data organized in such a way that it allows access, retrieval, and use of the data. Database programs are used a variety of ways in the workplace. For example, imagine you are asked to find the date of hire for each employee so you can prepare a report that shows the number of years of employment for each individual as well as the average number of years of service by department. If the personnel information is stored in a database management program, the data can easily be organized and presented in the form of a report. Examples of database management programs include Oracle®, Microsoft® Access, Lotus® Approach, and Corel Paradox™.

Most database software programs consist of a collection of tables. Each table contains information specific to one idea. Tables are organized in rows and columns. A **record** is a row in a table, and it contains information about a given person, product, or event. A **field** is the intersection of a column and row in a table, and it contains a specific piece of information within a record.

Data can be manipulated in a variety of ways once it has been entered into a database table. For example, a database program allows you to:

- Sort data alphabetically, geographically, numerically, by date, or by any field you have created.
- Add, delete, or update data.

- Locate data that meets specific criteria (all customers in the state of Michigan, all employees hired in the 1990s, all employees born in March).
- Perform calculations on numeric or currency fields.
- Design reports to present information from one or more tables in a variety of formats.
- Create forms to make data input easier.
- Create validation rules that preclude users from entering invalid data.

Database software programs also incorporate some of the features found in other application software programs, such as spell checking, text formatting, voice recognition, and publishing to the Web. Although many office suites contain a database program, the software can also be purchased as a stand-alone product.

Paint/Image-Editing Software

With graphics being incorporated in word processing documents, in spreadsheets, in presentations, and on Web pages, many paint/image-editing software programs have become available. Administrative professionals use this software to create and modify graphics used in newsletters, presentations, and Web pages. Paint software allows users to draw pictures, shapes, and other graphical images with various on-screen tools such as a pen, brush, and paint bucket. Many of the word processing, spreadsheet, and presentation software programs previously discussed have a paint component built in as part of the program. For example, you can create a graphic image, enhance a clip art image, or change the color of a graphic image in the current versions of Microsoft Word and PowerPoint.

Image-editing software provides all the capabilities of a paint program as well as the ability to modify existing images and photographs. For example, with image-editing software, you can adjust or change image colors, as well as add special effects such as shadows and outlines. Most professional paint software programs include image-editing and photo-editing software.

Personal Information/Contact Manager Software

Personal Digital Assistants (PDAs) are handheld computers that run specifically designed software to help people organize personal and professional information. The software that accomplishes this is referred to as Personal Information/Contact Manager (PIM) software. With a PDA, these software packages allow the user to maintain important contact and calendar information in a remote setting and then share that information with a computer that has PIM software installed.

PIM software allows a user to organize information in the following ways:

- Maintain a calendar of events
- Schedule appointments
- Manage a to-do list
- Establish tickler, or reminder, files
- Maintain listings of phone numbers
- Maintain an address book
- Track business expenses
- Keep notes using a notepad that stores text and graphics
- Maintain email
- Manage calendar sharing

PIM software also has integrated voice recognition and Internet-based applications. The ability to access Web pages, view digital photos, read ebooks, share calendar information, and create address book information via Website links are common functions of personal digital assistants. Examples of PIM software packages include Embedix® Plus PDA, Palm OS® 5, and Microsoft Pocket PC®.

Voice Recognition Software

In Chapter 10, you were introduced to voice recognition as an input device. Voice recognition software enables the user to enter data by speaking into a microphone that is connected to the sound card in a computer. The software instructs the computer to convert the spoken word to computer language. The software then converts the computer code into the written word that appears on a computer monitor.

Today these programs are affordable and easy to use. Examples of stand-alone voice recognition software include Dragon NaturallySpeaking® by ScanSoft™, ViaVoice™ by IBM, and Voice Xpress™ by Lernout & Hauspie. Other examples include Web-TalkIt 2002™ that allows you to interact with your Web browser with simple voice commands and to visit your favorite Websites through simple voice commands. VoiceSecureIt 2002 will allow you to secure your computer system via voice.

In addition, voice recognition technology has been included as a component of many office suites. For example, Microsoft Office XP comes with voice recognition capabilities that are available in all of its components. This technology allows the user to dictate letters and memos, issue commands in all software applications, search the Web, and send and receive messages—all by speaking into a microphone. All voice recognition programs have different capabilities; however, common features include these:

- A vocabulary of over 1 million words
- Input speeds now reaching upward of 160 words per minute
- Voice-activated editing capabilities of previously keyed documents
- Automation of repetitive tasks
- Natural language commands; for example, instructing the program to "put this sentence in italics" and the software interpreting the command

Voice recognition technology has improved dramatically in the past few years; the best systems are 90 to 95 percent accurate. Although this is far better than systems of a few years ago, a 90 percent accuracy rate still means that 1 out of 10 words are incorrect. In addition, when the system is used with unusual dialogue, the accuracy rates decrease to as low as 60 percent (4 words out of 10 will be incorrect). The continuous speech recognition technology used in these software packages makes voice recognition programs more effective than ever before, and these programs are expected to continue to improve. Voice recognition is sure to become a major input device in the workplace in the future.

Communications Software

One of the most common uses of the computer is to communicate and share information. Workers as well as home users have a variety of communications software available to them. These include email, Web browsers, newsgroups, and instant messaging. Online services such as AOL, CompuServe℠, and Prodigy® use built-in browsers. Although Netscape and Internet Explorer combine browsers, email readers, and newsgroup readers into one package, other software packages separate the functions.

IBM PERVASIVE COMPUTING

Voice recognition software is currently available as a component of office suites.

Web Browsers

Internet use will continue to increase as people keep up with the latest news, check the weather, shop for goods, research information, use chat rooms, and so on. A number of software packages are available to improve the Internet experience. The two most common Web browser software programs are Netscape Navigator and Microsoft Internet Explorer. Web browsers provide for effective and efficient online searches; many browsers also allow for the use of other Internet services, such as email and chat rooms.

Email

Email is quickly becoming the primary communication method for personal and internal business correspondence. Email messages can be very simple or can include a word processing, spreadsheet, or database document as an attachment. Administrative professionals use email to create, send, receive, forward, store, print, and delete messages. Many email software programs are available, including Visual Communicator™, Microsoft® Outlook®, Novell GroupWise®, Pegasus™, and Eudora™. In addition, a variety of free email programs, such as Yahoo!® Mail and MSN® Hotmail, exist on the Internet.

Newsgroups

To participate in a newsgroup, you use a software program called a newsreader. A newsgroup is an area on the Web where users can conduct written discussions about a particular subject. To participate in a newsgroup, a user sends a message; other users read and reply to the message. Some newsgroups are private and require that you enter a password to participate. Most Web browsers include a newsreader.

Instant Messaging

Instant messaging (IM) is a real-time communications service offered on the Internet. IM software allows you to track when other people log on and log off of the Internet. Although IM started as a personal communication tool, businesses have found that it is a cost-effective and convenient way to stay in touch with teleworkers and traveling employees. In addition, employees often prefer IM software to email because it provides users with synchronous communications, rather than the store-and-forward method used by email.

Depending on the software you choose, you must enter a screen name or an email address when you activate the software. Several IM software packages are available, including AOL® Instant Messenger™, ICQ™, Yahoo!® Messenger, and MSN® Messenger. Additional IM programs can be downloaded from the Internet. Most of the popular instant messaging programs allow the user to:

- Send notes back and forth with a friend who is online.
- Create a custom chat room with coworkers and friends.
- Share links to favorite Web sites.
- Look at images stored on a colleague's computer.
- Use the Internet instead of a phone to speak with colleagues.

One of the biggest problems with current IM software is the fact that one type of software does not work with another type. To complete an instant message, both users must have the same software. As IM technology continues to progress, standards will be established so different software programs can interact with one another; instant messaging will become as universal as email.

Software Security and Ethics

More individuals and organizations rely on computers to create, store, and manage critical information. Therefore, information must be accessible when it is needed. Users also need to take the necessary steps to protect information from loss or misuse. A variety of software products have been developed to help ensure the security of computer systems.

Privacy Software

With increased use of the Internet, email, instant messaging, and electronic commerce, a new category of software has evolved. Privacy software helps control the information that enters and exits computers linked to public networks. Privacy software can also protect the messages that are being sent. Information on the Web is available to anyone with a computer. How this information is used by companies and individuals is an ethical question that everyone needs to be concerned about.

Large companies that are data aggregators maintain information on millions of people. Their databases store information about where people were born, what they buy, what drugs they use, who they call, how much money they make, what jobs they hold, what bank accounts they have, and what their medical history is.

Although you cannot control the ethics of other individuals, you can behave ethically with whatever information is available to you. You can also protect yourself and your company by using certain security measures that prevent unethical individuals from obtaining the information.

Encryption Software

Similar to the secret codes used by the military, **encryption software** takes a message; scrambles it with various letters, numbers, and symbols; and then sends the message on its way. Once the message has been received, software converts the code back to the original format for reading.

Companies and individuals often send personal and private information over public networks. Email is a prime example of this type of communication. Email may seem like a private communication between the sender and the receiver, but that email message makes many stops along the way to the recipient. At each of those stops, someone can read and/or make a copy of the message. For this reason, encryption software has become popular.

Firewalls

Firewalls are software programs that monitor information as it enters and leaves a computer that is connected to the Web. A firewall can be programmed to block specific types of information and to block hackers who are trying to gain unauthorized access into a system. Firewalls are especially important for businesses that maintain personal and private information, such as physicians, police agencies, and universities. Keep in mind that firewalls are not a cure-all for what can affect a computer. Computer viruses that arrive via email cannot be stopped by a firewall. Also, firewall software cannot prevent the theft of data by individuals within an organization who have access to the information.

Filters

Filtering programs work in a manner similar to firewalls, but they are typically more selective in the kind of information they allow to enter a computer system. A filter can be set to monitor incoming Web pages or email that contains specific content, whether that content is advertisements or adult material.

Security Procedures

Software enables you to manipulate data in a variety of ways. Often this data is highly personal or confidential. To maintain the confidentiality of information, the administrative professional should follow specific guidelines, as follows.

- Back up and carefully store important information so it is not available to other staff members.
- Change your password or access codes frequently. Figure 11-5 offers some dos and don'ts for selecting passwords.
- Password-protect your screen saver to keep your computer secure when you are away from your desk. By doing this, a password prompt will appear when anyone touches the mouse or keyboard on your computer.
- Log off email programs when you are going to be away from your desk. This prevents

---

PASSWORD DOS AND DON'TS

- Do not use real words. A combination of eight or more alphanumeric characters is more difficult to guess or break than a dictionary word or a proper name. Use uppercase and lowercase characters, and avoid simple sequences of letters and numbers, such as ABC123.
- Do not use birth dates, social security numbers, names of pets, or other bits of personal data as a log-in name or password.
- Be original. Do not use the same log-in ID and password on every system or Website you visit.
- Find a mnemonic that works. It's practically impossible to keep track of dozens of unique alphanumeric passwords that aren't words. Your PC, your Internet, and your LAN server accounts require strong passwords. Other sites do not. For those less important sites, you may want to employ a collection of medium-strength user IDs and passwords that are easy for you to remember but hard for others to guess—foreign-language terms or license plate-like phrases. Here's a trick: To create a unique password from one you already use, simply move your fingers to the right or left one key.
- Stay fresh. Immediately change the default password your system gives you; then continue to change your password every two or three months.
- Do not be lazy. Windows and many email programs let you store your password; then they automatically enter it for you the next time you log in to the server. Anyone with access to your computer can log in to the servers you use.
- Keep quiet. Remember, your password is supposed to be a secret. Make sure you keep it that way.
- Store a written copy of your password in a safe place, such as a locked file cabinet. Do not store your password on your computer.

Source: Carol Lane, "Going Private," *PC World* (September 1998), 123.

FIGURE 11~5 Password Dos and Don'ts

others from reading your mail and sending mail with your name and terminal recorded as the sender.

Implementing and performing these workplace practices ensure the safety and integrity of personal and confidential company records.

Software Copying

The development of software programs involves thousands of hours by computer programmers who write code and try to develop functions that will be user-friendly and effective. Software development is an expensive process, but the result is better software for the consumer.

When software is copied illegally, the software companies are not reimbursed for the time and money they spent developing the product. Your responsibility as an administrative professional is to make sure that all copyright laws are followed. Software programs

should be registered; site license information should be submitted, if required; and software should be used only as directed by the issuing company.

Individuals and organizations that illegally copy software can be tried under civil and criminal law. Title 17 of the United States Code specifies that it is illegal to make or distribute copies of copyrighted material, including software, without authorization. Title 18, passed in 1991, instituted criminal penalties for copyright infringements of software. Penalties include imprisonment for up to five years and fines of up to $250,000 for the unauthorized reproduction or distribution of 10 or more copies of software with a total retail value exceeding $2,500. There is one exception to copying: One backup copy of a software program may be made.

Besides the fact that copying software is unethical and illegal, copying software can introduce viruses into a computer system, which may cause enormous problems for the business. Also, companies and individuals who copy software deprive themselves of the benefits of technical support and training provided by many software companies.

Troubleshooting

As you work with computer hardware and software, problems will occur. As an administrative professional, you need to become adept at **troubleshooting**, or determining the problem and finding a solution. As problems occur, you want to be able to handle them quickly and correctly. To be an effective troubleshooter, you need to possess general information about your system. You should be able to answer the following questions:

- What operating system does the computer use?
- How much RAM and ROM does the system have?
- How does the software package function?
- Who within the organization can assist when problems arise? Is there a computer technician within the company? Is there a help desk or help center? Is there an in-house "expert" who can provide assistance?
- Does the computer vendor offer assistance?
- What services does the software vendor offer? How can I contact the vendor?

If you are working within a specific software program and you encounter problems, there are certain troubleshooting steps you can take. The following assistance is available for most software packages.

- Help functions are available for all software packages. Some help functions allow you to

ask questions, scroll through a table of contents, or find assistance through an index.

- Telephone assistance is often available from the manufacturer. Sometimes the assistance is immediate; other times you must wait for the software technician to research the problem and find a solution. Know the manufacturer's phone number for your particular software package.
- Online assistance may also be available. This assistance takes a variety of forms. For example, you send an email asking a question and receive the answer through email, you find an answer to your problem by posting your question on a discussion board and waiting for another user to post a reply, or you find your answer in a list of answers to frequently asked questions that is part of the manufacturer's Website design.
- Manuals or reference books are also available for purchase. These books help with troubleshooting problems, but they may also be a valuable tool when you are learning a new software program. Manuals can provide other information, including step-by-step instructions for more complex software functions, special software shortcuts, and software functions you never used.

As you have learned in this chapter, software is a valuable asset for the administrative professional. It not only increases the productivity of the employee, but also improves his or her quality of work. Using the most effective software product for the task heightens productivity. ■

SUMMARY

To reinforce what you have learned in this chapter, study this summary.

- There are two major categories of software programs—systems software and applications software.
- The purpose of systems software is to regulate how a computer manages its resources.

- Operating systems are sets of programs that contain instructions that coordinate the computer's components.
- Operating systems include Windows, Windows for Networks, Mac OS, UNIX, LINUX, and OS/2 Warp Client.
- The three main functions of operating system software are to control computer system resources, to execute computer programs, and to manage data.
- Utility programs are types of system software that perform specific tasks, including managing disk drives, printers, and other devices.
- The most common utility programs remove computer viruses, compress files, view files, diagnose hardware problems, uninstall software, scan disks, defragment disks, back up files and disks, and display screen savers.
- Antivirus software is a utility program that protects, detects, and removes viruses from a computer's memory or storage devices.
- A file compression utility shrinks the size of a file to free up storage space, to improve system performance, or to reduce transmission time in the sending of email.
- Applications software programs perform specific tasks for users. These programs include office suites, bundled software programs, word processing software, spreadsheet software, presentation software, database software, paint/image-editing software, Personal Information/Contact Manager software, voice recognition software, and communications software.
- When selecting software, a person should ask a number of questions; for example: Does the program offer the software features needed? What documentation is available? What software support is available? Is the program user-friendly?
- Communications software includes Web browsers, email, newsgroups, and instant messaging.
- Privacy software helps control the information that enters and exits computers linked to public networks.
- Encryption software takes a message, scrambles it, and then sends the message on its way. Once the message has been received, it is converted back to its original format.
- Firewalls are software programs that monitor information as it enters and leaves a computer that is connected to the Web.
- Appropriate security procedures must be followed to maintain the integrity of confidential information.
- Unauthorized copying of software is not only unethical, it is also illegal.
- A task of the administrative professional is to solve as many of his or her computer hardware and software problems as possible. In order to do so, the administrative professional must become adept at troubleshooting.

FIND THE PROBLEM

It is a busy time of year at People Pharmaceuticals. End-of-year reports are due from all divisions, including sales, marketing, research and development, payroll, and human resources. All staff members have been asked to compile brief summaries from their specific area of responsibility regarding project updates and new initiatives. Each staff member is to submit his or her report to the division coordinator for review before the final divisional report is prepared. This project has a tight schedule.

Amy Kimball has been working on her summary at every spare moment. She has noticed, however, that Stu Berger spends much of his time playing games and surfing the Web. Amy knows that Stu's procrastination will affect the schedule. In an attempt to apply indirect pressure on Stu, Amy begins to talk about his work ethic with anyone who will listen.

How would you suggest that Amy deal with this situation?

PROFESSIONAL POINTERS

New software programs and upgrades on existing software come on the market frequently. As an administrative professional, you should be committed to staying current with software. Several ways to keep current include:

- Asking to be placed on software vendors' mailing lists for updated literature and announcements of new products.
- Reading computer journals and magazines.
- Enrolling in continuing education courses or workshops on new software.
- Learning from others about the software programs they use.
- Visiting computer retail stores to observe demonstrations of available software.

REINFORCEMENT ITEMS

1. Explain the purpose of systems software. Describe the two types of systems software discussed in this chapter.
2. Identify and describe five types of applications software.
3. Give three examples of ways to keep your passwords secure.
4. Explain what troubleshooting means. List three kinds of troubleshooting assistance that are available for software packages.

CRITICAL-THINKING ACTIVITY

Recent advancements in technology have forced your company to review its daily processes and its use of technology. In order to stay competitive, management has announced that a team of Information Technology (IT) consultants will be spending several weeks evaluating the workflow within your organization and making suggestions about new computer hardware and software that will make operations more streamlined.

By the second day, the administrative professionals are not pleased with the group of specialists. Although the specialists know a great deal about hardware and systems software, they have a limited knowledge of appropriate workplace procedures and the kinds of tasks the administrative professional must complete. Several meetings have been scheduled where the IT professionals talk about current software trends and the latest software releases. Although the specialists have provided examples, the examples deal with management issues of software rather than practical applications. Preliminary recommendations include the following:

- All administrative professionals must change to new word processing and spreadsheet programs. Although the organization is currently using a software suite, the IT specialists believe that changing to a more powerful stand-alone system is the best option. Division heads and vice presidents will continue to use the current software.

- All employees will change to a common calendaring and email program.

What advantages and/or disadvantages do you see with the preliminary recommendations? How can the administrative professionals be sure that the final recommendations best fit their workplace needs?

VOCABULARY REVIEW

Complete the Vocabulary Review for Chapter 11 given on page 91 of the *Applications Workbook*.

ENGLISH AND WORD USAGE DRILL

Complete the English and Word Usage Drill for Chapter 11 listed on page 92 of the *Applications Workbook*.

WORKPLACE APPLICATIONS

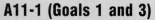

A11-1 (Goals 1 and 3)

Use the Internet to research three current utility software packages or privacy software packages. Find the following information: purpose, price, vendor, and at least two product reviews. Prepare a memo report for your instructor that includes the information described. In addition, indicate whether you would purchase this product, explaining your reasons. A memorandum form is provided on the Student CD, SCDA11-1. Use the following headings in your memorandum:

- Product Information
- Product Purpose
- Product Reviews
- Recommendations

A11-2 (Goal 2)

Work in teams of three. To become familiar with the newest applications software programs on the market, visit a computer store. Choose two similar software packages (for example, office suites, email, or spreadsheets). Compare and contrast these two packages, and make a recommendation as to which of the two packages you would buy and why. Be prepared to present your findings to the class.

A11-3 (Goals 2 and 3)

As part of your assignment at People Pharmaceuticals International, Kurt Rupprecht has asked that you use a word processing program to create a flyer to distribute to all employees that describes at least four strategies employees should consider when choosing passwords. Include a variety of font enhancements, at least one graphic, and a page border. Print one copy of the flyer, and submit it to your instructor.

A11-4 (Goal 4)

Research the following problems and determine how you would solve them. Use any available resources discussed in this chapter. Use the memorandum form provided on the Student CD, SCDA11-4, to prepare a memo to your instructor. Provide your instructor with the solutions and the resources you used to find your answers.

- I have so many windows open that I can't see my desktop. How do I quickly get rid of the clutter?
- I have 300 records in my mail merge. How can I preview just one of the completed letters?
- I have a report that can be no longer than 2,000 words and have a reading level of no more than 10.5. How can I make sure I do not exceed those limits?
- I applied a border to my copy, but it just underlined the text. What did I do wrong?

A11-5 (Goal 3)

In your *Applications Workbook* on page 93 is a handwritten memo from the director in the Information Systems Department. Key the memorandum, making the necessary corrections. Use the memorandum form provided on the Student CD, SCDA11-5. Print a copy of the memo and submit it to your instructor.

A11-6 (Goal 2)

A case study is provided on page 94 in your *Applications Workbook*. Read the case and respond to the questions. Discuss this case with three of your classmates. As a group, write a summary of your responses to your instructor.

ASSESSMENT OF CHAPTER GOALS

Did you successfully complete the chapter goals? Evaluate yourself by completing the form on page 95 of the *Applications Workbook*.

chapter 12

Reprographics

1. Identify the types of copiers that are available.
2. Explain basic and optional copier features and copy quality issues.
3. Describe copier maintenance, copier selection, and copy centers.
4. Demonstrate an understanding of ethical and legal considerations when copying and shredding materials.
5. Describe fax machines, identifying features and selection.

The Information Age, rather than spawning the paperless workplace as was predicted a number of years ago, has actually created a large increase in the volume of paper that is generated in the workplace each day. Administrative professionals make copies of faxes, copies of emails, copies of articles, and copies of reports. Managers print information from the Internet for future reference. Sometimes employees make extra copies of items "just in case" they are needed.

These copies are made with relative ease and speed, merely by the push of a button. Piles of paper are stacked in workplaces, with the size of these piles growing exponentially. The Information Age has produced "information junkies," people who cannot exist without their reports and their reams of printed and copied information.

This chapter, in addition to helping you learn about the various categories of copiers and their functions, will show you how copying can be abused, as well as ways to control this abuse. You will also learn how to select and maintain copier equipment. By studying and practicing the information provided within this chapter, you can become a more knowledgeable and ethical administrative professional.

Reprographics

Reprographics is the process of making copies of documents. It refers to any piece of equipment that produces multiple copies of an original document. This process is not confined to one type of copier or to copiers in general, as copies can be made on fax machines, printers, scanners, and multifunction units.

Copier Classifications

Copiers are categorized by the speed with which a particular unit produces copies and by the estimated average monthly copy count. Four categories of copiers are available today. These categories include low-volume, mid-volume, and high-volume copiers, as well as copier/duplicators.

Low-Volume Copiers

Low-volume copiers typically produce copies in the range of 20-30 **cpm** (copies per minute) and are best suited for environments that require only 100 to 5,000 copies per month. These copiers are one of the fastest-growing segments of the copier market due to their small size, low cost, and advanced feature options. Low-volume copiers are used by teleworkers and small businesses. They are available as basic copier-only models or can be purchased with a variety of features. These features include the following:

- Automatic document feeders
- Sorting (collating)
- Folding
- Duplexing
- Stapling

Low-volume copiers are available in fixed-platen or moving-platen designs. The **platen** is the glass surface upon which the original object is placed and copied. Less expensive machines often use a **moving platen**, which literally moves the item being copied over the copier lens. With a **fixed platen**, the lens and exposure light move inside the copier to scan the image. Fixed-platen copiers are typically more expensive, but they often come with the added features of automatic document feed and additional paper trays.

Mid-Volume Copiers

Mid-volume copiers generate between 25 and 60 cpm and are capable of producing 6,000 to 85,000 copies per month. These copy machines are available with analog and digital technology (discussed later in this chapter) and with advanced features such as sort, fold, staple, and hole punch. Mid-volume copiers are ideal "walk-up environments" due to their copying capabilities and because of their ease of use. Mid-volume copiers are typically the general workplace copiers that employees use to make the copies they need in performing their daily duties.

High-Volume Copiers

High-volume copiers are those machines that can typically be found in a centralized copy center within a mid- to large-size business. These single function or multifunction copiers are capable of producing 50 to 135 cpm and have a monthly production range of 50,000 to 400,000 copies. High-volume copiers are usually equipped with very efficient copy-producing capabilities, including these:

- Microprocessor-controlled job recovery
- Large paper capacities (5,000 sheets or more)
- Advanced editing and copy control displays
- Speed (including copy speed and overall job production speed averaging three-second copies)
- Remote diagnostic technology

© GETTY IMAGES/PHOTODISC

Reprographics is the process of making copies of documents.

Copy/Duplicators

Copy/duplicators are high-performance machines that are generally found in specialized
copy/duplication centers or in print shops.
The machines are capable of producing up to
150 cpm. They are fast and cost-effective alternatives to the large-volume copy machines,
especially when a large number of copies
(5,000 to 10,000) must be completed. Their
monthly capability easily surpasses the
150,000 copy range. Common applications
for these machines are flyers, programs,
forms, and brochures. Copy/duplicators also
have the ability to reproduce copies on a
variety of paper stocks and sizes. Because
their paper path is short and straight, fewer
paper jams occur, even when using nonstandard types of paper. Some models can feed
envelopes without the use of a specialized
envelope feeder tray.

Digital and Analog Technology

Copiers are available in two types: analog
and digital. The traditional copier was created
using **analog** technology, where the image is
translated into fluctuating electronic signals.
Digital copiers look very much like traditional
analog copiers and are just as easy to use.
However, the technology these machines incorporate has made a great deal of difference
in the speed and quality of reprographics.
Although a number of analog copiers are still
used in the workplace today, they are becoming obsolete with the advancements in digital
technology.

Digital technology allows data to be
transferred as a series of bits, rather than as
a fluctuating (analog) signal. Digital copiers
work by scanning the original to be copied,
thus creating a digital image. This image is
then used to create the resulting copies.

BILL ARON/PHOTOEDIT

Copy/duplicators are large machines that are generally found in print shops.

There is less wear and tear on digital copiers because of this scan-once, print-many approach. The technology also means that digital copiers are better at reproducing graphics and photos. Digital copiers have better range and clarity than analog copiers when reducing and enlarging because the original is an electronic image and is easier to manipulate; the original is not a fixed image that is being altered.

While digital copier technology is more expensive than analog technology, the price gap is closing fast. Savings may be realized in other ways, such as:

- Fewer service calls because of fewer moving parts.
- Less down time due to paper jams because of a more direct paper path.
- Faster print runs because of the scan-once, print-many capability.
- Fewer reprints as copy quality is the same from the first copy to the last.

Digital copiers can create an original document from data downloaded directly from a computer, a network, or the Internet. The ability to include these copiers on a network enables editing, formatting, and correcting to be completed quickly. You can also use the copier as a high-speed printer that produces sorted and stapled sets of copies without your having to leave your desk. With added features, these copiers can perform as a fax machine or a scanner.

The benefits of digital technology in copiers include:

- Greater reliability.
- Enhanced image quality.
- Scan-once, print-many reproduction.
- Increased clarity in the reproduction of advanced graphics.

Digital copiers do not sacrifice speed for quality, as most are capable of producing 100 or more copies per minute. One drawback to digital copier technology is that first-copy speed is typically slower than that of analog copiers; extra time is necessary for scanning the original. Digital copiers are usually purchased for use in an environment that requires extended runs or multiple copies.

Multifunction Units (Mopiers)

You learned in the computer hardware chapter about multifunction devices that print, scan, copy, and fax. In addition, you have just been introduced to digital copiers that have the ability to serve as multifunction units when connected to a network. Multifunction units, also called **mopiers**, combine printing, scanning, copying, and faxing into one unit. Mopiers, however, often include additional copier features such as collating, stapling, and hole punching. Mopier units can save time, processing steps, and floor or desk space. (They can even save user frustration by consolidating time-consuming tasks and tedious supply ordering and restocking of a variety of equipment-specific products.) Mopiers are available in the same classifications as the standard copier. They can be low-volume, mid-volume, or high-volume machines and are available with black-and-white or color capabilities. The use of mopiers, or multifunction peripherals, is expected to continue to increase as the prices for these units become more affordable.

Copier Features

Copier features vary depending on the size and price of the unit. You learned earlier about some of the features on various categories of copiers. Basic features are the same on most copiers. Basic as well as special features are presented in this section.

Basic Features

Copiers usually handle two standard sizes of paper—$8\frac{1}{2}'' \times 11''$ and $8\frac{1}{2}'' \times 14''$. Most copiers (with the exception of small low-volume copiers) handle paper sizes of up to a maximum of $11'' \times 17''$. The paper tray, which feeds the paper through the machine,

Multifunction units (mopiers) combine printing, scanning, faxing, and copying into one unit.

needs to be replaced (so clear, dark copies can be produced), the machine will inform the operator.

Special Features

Due to advances in technology, many special features, or options, are available on copy machines. A number of these features are explained here.

Reduction and Enlargement

This feature allows you to reduce the size of the original document by degrees, usually expressed in percentages. For example, you can reduce an original by as much as 200 to 500 percent. Reduced copies can be made of large documents so all filed copies are

can be adjusted for different paper sizes, or there may be separate trays. If a copier has separate trays, one size holds the $8\frac{1}{2}'' \times 11''$ paper, one tray holds the $8\frac{1}{2}'' \times 14''$ paper, and another tray holds the $11'' \times 17''$ paper. The trays snap in and out of the copier for reloading the paper. With a single tray, the appropriate paper for the task being performed must be placed in the tray.

Another basic feature of copiers is the copy counter. Before starting to copy material, the operator sets the counter for the number of copies required. When the appropriate number has been reached, the copier automatically stops. In addition, copiers are equipped with an exposure control that regulates the lightness or darkness of the copies. For example, if a copy is too light, the operator can push a button instructing the machine to make the copies darker.

Copiers are equipped with a feature that shows the cause of a machine malfunction, generally with a code number displayed. If the paper path is jammed, the copier will indicate the problem. If the toner in the machine

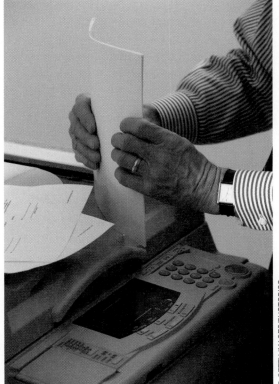

The copy counter and display are basic features of a copier.

uniform in size. Computer printouts that measure 11″ × 17″, for example, can be reduced to fit $8\frac{1}{2}″$ × 11″ paper for easy handling and filing.

An enlargement feature allows an original document to be enlarged by as much as 500 percent. Reductions and enlargements can be made in 1 percent increments. Fine details on an original can be made more legible by using the enlargement feature. Also, reducing or enlarging a copy more or less than the maximum percent allowed by the copy can be done. The copy originally reduced or enlarged (rather than the original) can be copied and reduced or enlarged again.

Automatic Document Feeding

The **automatic document feeder (ADF)** allows you to copy multipage documents without having to lift and lower the platen cover for every sheet. The multipage original document (anywhere from 2 to nearly 50 sheets) can be placed in the feeder. The document will be transported one sheet at a time through a series of drive belts or wheels to the platen, where it will be exposed to the copy lens. The original document is then returned in the same order to a catch bin for retrieval by the user. Document feeders can also be used for quick single copy making.

A variation of the ADF is the **recirculating automatic document feeder (RADF)**. The RADF makes it possible to copy originals that are printed in back-to-back format. The RADF takes the original and delivers it to the platen for copying; then the RADF takes the original through another series of wheels and belts that turn the document over so the other side can be copied. The original is then turned over again and returned to the catch tray. This type of feeder can be an immense time saver; it not only eliminates the need to lift and lower the platen cover, it also eliminates the need to flip, close the platen cover, copy, retrieve, and flip the original again so it is in the correct order from where it started. RADF, however, can add significantly to the price of a copier.

Duplexing

Copying on both sides of a sheet of paper is known as **duplexing**. It is sometimes called back-to-back copying. This feature saves paper and reduces the number of sheets of paper that must be stored in files. Copies are made on both sides of the paper by the push of a few buttons. The duplexing feature, when used with an RADF, enables the user to make two-sided copies from two-sided originals.

Editing

Many copiers have built-in editing features. These standard features include border erasing, centering, and color adjusting. Some advanced features include **marker editing**, which lets you change the color of specific sections of a document to highlight these areas, and **masking**, which allows you to block out areas of sensitive or confidential information. If advanced editing features need to be used on a regular basis, a networked copier is a wise choice. With a networked copier, the document is scanned into a computer, the editing takes place on the screen, and the final image is sent to the copier for production.

Diagnostics

Some copiers are equipped with microprocessors that monitor and identify copy status and copier problems and then display these findings on a readout panel. These machines can automatically call a remote service center via a modem and relay the problem, which can then be repaired remotely through the modem. Other problems can be corrected by the service center dispatching a local service person.

This feature eliminates the need for some service calls by recognizing such problems as paper jams and pulled plugs. In addition, it helps eliminate more serious problems by recognizing when a machine needs service by a trained professional. This feature minimizes copier down time and allows dealers to be proactive rather than reactive when dealing with problems.

Collate and Staple

Copiers can collate only or collate and staple sets of materials.

Interrupt key

This key permits the operator to stop the copier at any point in the copying process. The key is useful in emergencies when the operator wishes to discontinue the copy cycle. For example, if the operator is running a long job, the employer may need three copies of another document immediately. The operator can interrupt the long job, make the three copies, and then resume the copy process without starting over.

Help Button

This user-friendly feature allows the inexperienced operator to get help. The help button flashes instructions in systematic order so the operator can produce copies correctly.

Job Recovery

The job recovery mode stops the copier and remembers how many copies have been made. When you are ready to complete the project, the machine automatically picks up where it left off and makes the required number of

Copiers are available with a variety of special features.

copies. For example, assume the paper path becomes jammed during a job. Without job recovery, you must reprogram the machine and start the job over, losing time and effort. With job recovery, once the problem area is cleared, the job is finished without reprogramming and without wasting a lot of copies.

Automatic Folding

Some copiers will fold 11″ × 17″ copies to get an $8\frac{1}{2}″ \times 11″$ size. With this feature, drawings and schematics are in a convenient format for handling and distribution. The fold can also be **offset** (not folded to the edge of the paper) so folded materials can be placed in three-ring binders.

Touch Control Screen

Many copiers have a color CRT that lets you program a job by touching icons on the screen. The kinds of jobs you can do are illustrated on the screen.

Programmable Memory

If you perform certain complex copy jobs frequently, you can program them into the copier one time and then recall the instructions when you need them again; for example, long reports in which you begin each section of the report on the right-hand page and insert copy onto divider sheets. Other programmable examples include inserting preprinted tabs or colored paper; copying onto special paper stocks, such as cardstock; and controlling copy quality for a page of graphics. Programmable memory allows you to save time and effort.

Book Copy

With book copy, you can place an opened book on the copier without having to turn the book around to copy facing pages. This feature saves considerable time if you copy from books frequently.

Online Binding

Books can be bound with thermal adhesive tape. The tape is available in various colors to coordinate the binding with cover stocks, tabs, and dividers. With this feature, turnaround time on bound work can be quite fast.

Image Shift

When binding books, the image shift allows you to automatically add one-half inch (or whatever space is necessary) to the left margin for binding. In addition, if you are going to place the material in a prepurchased binder, image shift allows you to make the left margin wider so the pages can be hole-punched.

Environmentally Friendly Features

Many copiers incorporate organic photoconductors, recyclable materials, toner-save modes, and energy-save modes. Some vendors offer their own brands of recycled paper and other media transparencies, as well as programs that make it easy for customers to recycle their toner cartridges.

Copy Quality

Millions of copies are made each day in workplaces around the world. These copies are expensive and should be of high quality. Copied documents may have pages missing, may be incorrectly collated, or may be unreadable. Although these errors may be caused by machine malfunctions, they are more often caused by operator errors. To ensure you are producing clear, high-quality copies, follow these procedures.

- Fill copier trays correctly. Before filling a paper tray, check the label on one end of the ream of paper. Look for an arrow pointing up and the words *copy this side first*; put the paper in the copier so this side is facing up. This will reduce paper jams. If packaging instructions are not available, a simple test can help. Hold a manageable stack of paper at each end, and notice how it bends. Then turn the paper over and repeat this process. The side with the greatest bend, or curve, should be the side that faces upward in the paper tray.
- Check the platen before starting to copy. Make sure it is free of debris that would

cause spots or lines on your copies. Remove all staples or paper clips that could scratch the platen or disrupt the copier operation.
- Run one copy and check it before continuing. Ask yourself these questions about the copy:
  - Is the copy free of spots?
  - Is the copy easy to read?
  - Is the copy straight on the page?
  - Did any color reproduce properly?
- If using a collator or sorter, ask the following questions:
  - Have all pages been copied?
  - Are the pages in correct order?
  - Has the correct number of sets been completed?

When you finish a copying job, leave the room or copy area clean for the next person. Be sure you have returned all extra paper or supplies to the appropriate cabinet or storage area. Tear or shred any copies that are inappropriate for use. Follow the guidelines presented in Figure 12-1 regarding copier etiquette.

Other Copier Considerations

The copy machine, as you have read, has become an integral component in today's business world. Workers have become dependent on the many specialized functions that these machines offer. To maximize a copier's usefulness in the workplace, careful consideration must be given to the maintenance of the copier unit, selection of the correct type of unit for the needs of the business, and correct placement of the machine for single or multiple users.

Copier Maintenance

Broken workplace copiers can have a major impact on productivity. The downtime from nonworking copiers can be extremely costly, as is the cost of service, whether it is in the

---

COPIER ETIQUETTE

When sharing a copier with others, be considerate. Observe the following courtesies:

- Try to complete an extensive copying job during nonpeak copying hours. Let colleagues interrupt when they have only a few pages to copy.
- If a problem with the machine occurs while you are copying, try to fix the problem. If you cannot do so, call the key operator in your organization or call a service person. **Do not** leave the problem for the next person to handle.
- When toner runs out, refill it or notify the key operator.
- Replenish the paper supply as necessary.
- When paper jams, remove it.
- If you are using additional supplies such as paper clips, scissors, and so on, return them to their location before leaving the copier.
- If you have made copies that are unusable, destroy them. Shred them or put them in the recycle bin.
- Return the copier to its standard settings.

FIGURE 12~1 Copier Etiquette

form of a maintenance contract (purchased from the vendor when the copier is leased or purchased) or direct service charges when a maintenance contract is not used. To keep maintenance to a minimum, the administrative professional and management have certain responsibilities. Some of these responsibilities are listed in this section.

Responsibilities of the Administrative Professional

As an administrative professional, you are responsible for making a variety of copies. In addition, you are responsible for certain areas of copier maintenance. Keep the following suggestions in mind to keep maintenance to a minimum.

- Store paper properly. As mentioned previously, correct paper handling can increase the productivity of a copier. Paper should be stored in a dry area, away from extreme hot or cold temperatures. Keep the paper flat and, if possible, on a shelf or a pallet above the floor. Since paper is affected by humidity, keep it wrapped and boxed until it is needed. Reseal or box partially used reams of paper.
- Check the paper before you load it into the machine. Some copiers accept varying

weights of paper; others do not. Paper that is wrinkled, curled, or damp can cause repeated paper jams and will eventually harm the internal components of the copier. Paper that has been packaged has very little air in it. It is wise to fan the paper prior to loading it to increase the amount of air between the sheets, which, in turn, allows the paper to feed through the copier one sheet at a time. Fanning the paper also helps get rid of static in the paper and lessens the possibility of a paper jam.

- Be cautious! Copiers have moving parts and parts that become very hot during operation. Touching certain areas inside the copier can result in minor to severe burns. If you attempt to make a minor repair or adjustment, such as removing a paper jam or changing a toner cartridge, be very careful. Jewelry, scarves or ties, or loose-fitting clothes can become caught in the equipment.
- Trust the control panel warning. When the control panel instructs you to add toner, you should do so. The quality of the copy is affected.
- Look for consistency. When a particular problem appears consistently, you should inform the technician of the malfunction. If

you make a list of the types of problems or how the machine reacts in certain situations, you can save repair time and cost.

- Designate a **key operator**, a person who is responsible for making simple repairs. One person who is located near the copier should be responsible for removing paper jams, fixing malfunctions, replenishing supplies, and determining when a repair call is justified. Consistent care adds to the operating life of the equipment.

- Determine how the key operator will be trained. Management may need to be involved in this decision. The vendor usually has personnel who can provide initial training. Check to see if this training is available. If it is not, check the information provided in the copier manual. Proper training of all personnel using the copier will enhance copier productivity and the productivity of the workplace.

- Establish a schedule for the key operator to train all workplace individuals in the use of the copier.

Responsibilities of Management

Although management will most likely make the decisions about maintenance contracts and where the copier is located, you may be asked for input. This section will help you understand the types of issues you may be asked to consider.

- Choose an appropriate location. A copier needs proper ventilation and adequate temperature control. The user also needs sufficient space to place paper and other supplies so the top of a copier is not abused. Paper clips and staples that fall into a machine can cause major repair bills.

- Determine how often preventative maintenance is needed. Preventative maintenance increases the productivity of a copier in the long run by decreasing the number of copier breakdowns. Preventative maintenance typically should occur every three months. Maintenance can be scheduled by independent contractors, through a mainte-

nance agreement purchased from a dealer, or by the manufacturer.

- Related closely to the maintenance issue is the "lease versus buy" option. Leased copiers may include preventative maintenance checks by the leasing company's technicians. However, leases may also have restrictive copy count plateaus that result in the copier being underutilized so extra use charges are not accrued.

- Investigate remote diagnostic systems availability. These systems can detect copier problems before they occur and fix them remotely using an off-site computer.

Copier Selection

Since a copier is used so extensively, consideration must be given to the type of copier that will best serve the needs of the business. Management has the primary responsibility for making the decision. However, as an administrative professional, you may be asked for your input or to serve on a committee that will make a recommendation to management about what copier to purchase. Figure 12-2 lists some questions that should be answered before selecting a copier.

Centralized and Decentralized Copy Centers

Centralized and decentralized copy centers serve different functions and exist for different reasons. Small organizations may have only decentralized copiers, while large organizations often have centralized and decentralized copy centers.

Centralized Copy Centers

What exactly is a centralized copy center? **Centralized copy centers** are located in one central location. These centers exist within large businesses (or within small businesses with large copying needs) to provide in-house copying services for the organization. Employees are typically responsible for producing "large-run copies" the company needs for

---

COPIER SELECTION

Questions the Organization Needs to Answer

- How many copies will be made per month?
- Is there a projected increase or decrease in copy volume during the next three years?
- Will your copy requirements fluctuate during certain times of the year? If so, what are the lowest and highest volumes you can anticipate?
- What materials will be copied? What percentage of copying will be done on letter-size paper? What percentage of copying will be done on legal-size paper? What percentage of copies will be made on other paper sizes?
- What features are necessary? Ask the potential users of the copier what their needs are. A survey may be conducted to determine the needs of the employees.
- Is color necessary?
- What space limitations exist for the copier? If there are space limitations, the size of the copier becomes an issue.
- Will you run card and cover stock, recycled paper, or transparencies? Will forms, directories, reports, and manuscripts be produced?

Questions to Ask During a Demonstration

- What is the quality of the copy?
- Are the copies clean and crisp?
- What is the cost per copy?
- Is there a clear definition between black and white? If it is a color copier, are the colors clear and true?
- Is the machine easy to operate?
- Is the interior easily accessible for removing jammed paper and for replacing toner?
- Will the copier handle special materials, including card stock, cover stock, recycled paper, and/or transparencies?

Questions to Ask Potential Vendors

- What is the purchase price of the machine?
- What is the cost of supplies, especially toner?
- Is key operator training available?
- Does the vendor carry parts for the machine?
- What is the cost of service?
- Are maintenance contracts available? If so, what is the cost?
- Are lease programs available? If so, what is the cost?

FIGURE 12~2 Copier Selection

internal reasons or for presentations to outside groups. Although the main responsibility of employees in centralized copy centers is the reproduction of documents, companies may also employ graphic artists to create graphics or artwork for the documents being produced. Other duties of a centralized copy center employee may include:

- Scheduling projects within the center so the deadlines established by the individuals needing the work can be met.
- Ordering and maintaining supplies.
- Supervising other personnel within the center.
- Maintaining center equipment.

Some companies combine the printing function of the copy center with the mailroom function. In that case, in addition to knowing how to operate copiers, employees need to have knowledge of mailing equipment and procedures. Employees in a centralized copy center may prepare mail for internal as well as external distribution and for this reason may help to design materials that are easier or more economical for the company to mail. For example, the company may want to send all off-site managers a procedures manual. The center would more than likely help to design this manual in such a way that the printing and reproduction are cost-effective and the manual is more visually appealing than it would be in report form. Figure 12-3 lists advantages and disadvantages of centralized copy centers.

Similarly, when the administrative professional takes materials to the centralized copy center, complete and accurate information must be given to ensure that the job is completed correctly. A preprinted form is usually provided by center personnel so the individual submitting the request can check off the type,

size, and color of the paper needed; the number of copies to be run; special instructions, such as enlargement, graphics, or pictures that should be included; and so on. Completing this form accurately ensures the saving of time and money since, more than likely, the job order will not need to be rerun.

In addition, the administrative professional is responsible for delivering the correct originals to the centralized copy center. If errors (factual, typographical, grammatical) are made in the document to be copied, hundreds of reproductions may need to be discarded. The cost in time and in money to the company can be considerable.

Decentralized Copy Centers

Large and small companies use **decentralized copy centers**, in which copying machines are located in close proximity to the employees. This type of copier and copier area is typically referred to as a **walk-up station**. Walk-up stations can include low-volume, mid-volume, or high-volume copiers, depending on the number of employees designated to use the particular machine. In this setting, employees have immediate access to a copy machine instead of having to submit a print job for someone else to complete. However, if a walk-up station is busy, employees may need to wait for others to finish before they can proceed with their own work. Figure 12-4 describes advantages and disadvantages of decentralized copy centers.

Copying Laws, Abuse, and Shredders

As you learned in previous chapters, the technology exists to reduce the number of copies produced in the workplace. The use of computers, email, voice mail, scanning technology, and the Internet should reduce the need for paper copies. Unfortunately, the reverse has proven to be true. Businesses produce more copies than ever before. Billions of

---

ADVANTAGES AND DISADVANTAGES OF CENTRALIZED COPY CENTERS

Advantages:
- Tighter cost controls over equipment and supplies
- Reduction of outside printing costs
- Less unauthorized copying

Disadvantages:
- Dependence on one unit; no backups
- Higher personnel costs; dedicated operator; more walking time
- Longer total job turnaround time
- Underutilization of the equipment with some jobs

Source: "How to Buy Photocopiers," *Library Technology Reports* (March–April 1998), p. 58.

FIGURE 12~3 Advantages and Disadvantages of Centralized Copy Centers

ADVANTAGES AND DISADVANTAGES OF DECENTRALIZED COPY CENTERS

Advantages:
- Backup copiers always available
- Greater user convenience
- Lower personnel costs; no key operator; less walking time
- Faster job turnaround

Disadvantages:
- Higher total equipment, supplies, service costs
- More unauthorized copying

Source: "How to Buy Photocopiers," *Library Technology Reports* (March–April 1998), p. 58.

FIGURE 12~4 Advantages and Disadvantages of Decentralized Copy Centers

copies are made in businesses each year, and many of them are unnecessary. For example, an employee may make 20 copies of a document when he or she knows that only 15 copies are necessary. The additional copies are made "just in case" they are needed. Unfortunately, the employee often ends up throwing the extra copies in the trash. Additionally, employees sometimes make personal copies on workplace copiers. Such behavior calls into question the employee's personal and workplace ethics.

Think back about what you learned in Chapter 3 about ethical behavior. The ethical administrative professional is honest. He or she does not spend company time or resources in copying personal documents. In addition, ethical and legal considerations are inherent in copying due to copyright law. As an administrative professional, you need to be aware of what you can and cannot copy legally. The next sections provide an overview of the copyright law and legal and ethical issues that should be considered before making copies.

Copyright Law

Since you are responsible for a great deal of copying, you need to be informed about the law, highlights of which are given in Figure 12-5. Pay particular attention to the fair-use clause described in Figure 12-6. This clause means that individuals do have the right to reproduce copyrighted materials without

THE COPYRIGHT LAW

Highlights of the copyright law include the following:

- Money, postage stamps, United States bonds, Federal Reserve notes, or other securities of the United States may not be reproduced.
- Birth certificates, passports, draft cards, and naturalization and immigration papers may not be reproduced.
- Driver's licenses, automobile registrations, and certificates of title may not be reproduced.
- Documents that contain the personal information of an individual are protected by the Right of Privacy Act. They may not be reproduced without the individual's permission.
- Material that retains a copyright may not be reproduced without the owner's permission. The fair-use provision allows some exceptions to this provision.

Source: "Circular 21," United States Copyright Office, accessed on October 16, 2002; available at **www.copyright.gov/circs/ circ21.pdf**.

FIGURE 12~5 The Copyright Law

FIGURE 12~6 Fair-Use Clause

permission under certain fair and reasonable circumstances. Deciding whether the copying to be done falls within the fair-use provision must be done on an individual basis.

Further technological advances have affected the copyright process even more. Almost all software is copyrighted. Statements included on software specify the copyright restrictions. For example, under the copyright laws, neither the documentation nor the software may be copied, reproduced, translated, or reduced to any electronic medium or machine-readable form without prior written consent from the company. You learned in the computer software chapter that abuses in copying software take place. These abuses are legally and ethically wrong.

In 1994, the National Information Infrastructure Working Group in Intellectual Property Rights asked the U.S. Patent and Trademark Office to address the shortcomings of the 1976 Copyright Act. The task was to determine whether copyright holders and "fair users" of copyright material could agree to a new set of guidelines that address technological trends in education. The result was the establishment of the Conference on Fair Use (CONFU). This group addressed multimedia, distance learning, visual archives, and digital libraries. The guidelines established by the CONFU address the recent technological trends.

Ethical and Legal Considerations

Each employee in a company should be ethical in the use of copying machines. Each employee should also be aware of the legal restrictions that pertain to the copying of certain documents, such as pages from a textbook. Behaving ethically and legally in document copying means:

- You do not copy documents for personal use.
- You do not copy cartoons, jokes, and similar types of information to distribute to colleagues.
- You do not make copies of documents that you need for an outside professional group or a service organization unless you have approval from your company to do so.
- You do not copy restricted materials, as explained in the previous copyright section.
- You are prudent in making the appropriate number of copies needed.

Control Systems

To reduce the amount of copying abuse by employees, some businesses employ the use of a copy control device. Each copy control device or copy control system works somewhat differently; however, the same basic features exist in each system. For example, if a keypad system is used, the user enters an account number into the keypad; the copier is then activated, or unlocked, and is ready to operate. There are also two types of card systems. With a card system, the card may be preprogrammed for a specific amount of money or number of copies. When the card is inserted into the machine, copying costs are automatically deducted from the total amount of money on the card or from the total allowable number of purchased copies. A card system may also serve as a counting mechanism. In this instance, copy charges can be automatically charged to the issuing department or division. With either card system, a department or division of the company can check copy costs against a specific account number. If abuses are occurring, appropriate action can be taken. With a control system, you can easily see how important it is that each employee be responsible for his or her own copy card or access number.

Public entities such as libraries and schools control copying costs by using coin-operated or card system copiers. The user of the copier pays for the copies directly by inserting money. A twist on this system enables the user to use a card that functions like a debit card. Money is placed into a copy account, and the card is electronically debited with each copy that is made. Most card systems allow the user to add additional monetary value to the card as necessary.

Shredders

Document or records security is a high priority in business today. For that reason, document shredders are found in workplaces of every size. A shredder is a machine that cuts paper into strips or confettilike pieces. Today shredded paper is recycled by many businesses as packing material. Since mailrooms process large amounts of paper and often pack materials for shipping, shredders are used there, among other locations.

Because the Information Age has increased the amount of paper that people handle, shredders have become an integral security measure in business. You should be aware of several features of shredders.

- Auto-reverse. The shredder automatically reverses the rotation of the cutters when it senses that a paper jam is about to occur. This prevents the cutter blades from bending or breaking.

- Crosscut shredding. First-generation shredders cut paper into thin strips and were referred to as **strip-cut shredders**. **Crosscut shredders** cut the paper vertically and horizontally, producing confettilike pieces of paper. While it would be challenging to reassemble a strip-shredded document, it is possible. However crosscut pieces are very difficult to reassemble, even by the most patient person.

- Sheets per pass. **Sheets per pass** refer to the number of sheets of paper that can be fed into a machine at one time. Sheets per pass typically range from 2 to 80, depending on the size of the shredder.

- Throat width. This is the measurement of the width of a sheet of paper that can be fed into a shredder.

- Shredding speed. This is the speed with which a shredder completes it task. Speeds can range from 10 feet per minute up to 120 feet per second.

- Multiple media capabilities. **Multiple media shredders** have been developed that destroy computer tapes, floppy disks, computer disks, and plastic ID cards.

© GETTY IMAGES/PHOTODISC

Do not shred material that needs to be kept for financial, legal, or government documentation.

Identity theft crimes are becoming increasingly widespread, which is a driving force in personal shredder sales. The Supreme Court of the United States has ruled that any unwanted material set at curbside or placed in a dumpster is public domain. This ruling has increased the occurrence of dumpster diving by people seeking to use personal or private records for their own purposes. Anyone who disposes of information without shredding it first is at risk for that information falling into the hands of an inappropriate person.

As an administrative professional, consider the following when shredding information.

- Know the company policy on shredding.
- Do not shred material that needs to be kept for financial, legal, or government documentation.
- Know when a document is confidential or sensitive.
- Shred all appropriate and unnecessary copies.
- Do not toss unnecessary copies in the trash without first determining whether they contain sensitive or confidential information.

Fax Machines

A **fax (facsimile) machine** is a type of copy machine that electronically sends an original document from one location to another via communication networks. With a fax, you can send a document to someone within the same building, in the same city, across the nation, or across the world. A quality fax machine receives and prints a faxed document that is as crisp and clear as the original. The fax process combines copying technology and telephone or satellite communications. There are two basic steps in the fax transmission process:

- The original document is placed in a fax machine, where it is scanned and the "image" of the document is converted into electronic symbols that are transmitted over communication network lines to a receiving fax machine.

- The receiving unit converts the electronic messages back to their original form and prints a copy of the original document.

The fax has become a standard piece of workplace equipment, with sales increasing on a yearly basis. In fact, the fax machine ranks second only to the computer as the most widely used technology in the workplace. Some experts believe that email and the Web will make the fax machine redundant, but as fax machine performance improves and the move to multifunction devices increases, the fax machine appears to have a steady future.

Fax machines can be purchased in either plain paper or thermal paper units. Early fax machines were of the thermal paper variety, but the majority of machines on the market and in use today are plain paper units. Thermal paper is slick, curls quickly, and cannot be written on easily. Thermal paper is also continuous feed paper on a roll. Lengthy faxed documents on thermal paper had to be unrolled and cut apart at the page breaks.

Plain paper faxes offer the flexibility to receive documents on different sizes of paper. If your business occasionally receives faxes on legal size paper, you can buy a fax machine with a legal size paper tray option. Plain paper faxes also allow for different printing options; some use inkjet technology, and some print with laser-jet (photocopier) quality.

In an effort to speed fax transmittal time (and reduce the number of fax-related phone bills), fax machines are now manufactured with built-in expandable memory. Memory in a fax machine allows the original document to be scanned into the machine quickly with the information being stored electronically within the memory. When a connection is made to the receiving machine, the sending machine quickly dumps the information out of its memory and onto the communication lines. On the other end of this communication, the receiving fax quickly takes the information and loads it into its own memory. Once the call is completed and the connection is broken, the receiving fax machine then dumps the information out of its memory and prints the faxed documents.

Keep in mind that fax speed is only as efficient as the slower of the two machines. Your workplace may have a memory-enhanced fax machine, but if the receiving machine does not have storage memory, the call (fax) will still take as much time as the receiving machine needs to process the information.

Fax Features

Numerous features are available on fax machines. Several of these features are discussed in the following section.

Fax Broadcasting

Fax broadcasting is the ability to personalize and transmit to multiple locations simultaneously. You fax a single document, and then a computer individualizes and faxes it to hundreds or thousands of recipients in minutes. Broadcasting is often accomplished at a fraction of the cost of direct mail or overnight services. Transmissions can be scheduled 24 hours a day. However, most documents are sent after business hours when telecommunication rates are lower and fax machines are not busy. The message sits in the recipients' machines, ready to be read first thing the next morning.

Dual Access

Dual access is the term used to describe a fax machine that performs a number of tasks at one time. For example, you can scan a document into memory while transmitting or receiving another document from memory. You cannot, however, receive and send a fax at the same time. If you wish to do that, you must add a second phone line to your unit. Because of features such as dual access and the desire for speedier fax communication, fax machines are commonly being manufactured with 2MB of memory, but are capable of being upgraded to 16-18 MB.

Fax-on-Demand

Fax-on-demand is the service of storing information for instant retrieval via telephone and fax. It allows you to automate your organization's repetitive actions. For example, customers may call asking for product literature, specification sheets, or price lists. Callers follow a voice-prompted menu to choose documents and then enter their choices and fax numbers on their telephone keypads. The documents are automatically sent to the designated fax machine.

Color fax

Color fax makes it possible to scan any high-resolution color image and transmit it anywhere in the world in a few minutes via standard telephone lines. Images can be edited and output to a full-color printer, color display monitor, or another output device. Color faxes, while available as stand-alone devices, are increasingly part of multifunction devices.

Auto dialers

Auto dialers automatically redial a busy number after a minute or two and store from 20 to 200 numbers into memory for one-button code dialing. Some devices can dial numbers when line charges are the lowest so you can transmit information at the cheapest rate. This feature is called **delayed send**.

Portable fax

A **portable fax** (a telephone handset and a small fax machine) fits in a briefcase. If an executive is traveling and does not have a portable fax machine, he or she will find machines available in hotels across the country. Many office supply and copying stores also offer fax machine services.

Elimination of Junk Fax

Businesses have had problems with junk mail clogging their fax machines. With a special device attached to a fax machine, you can eliminate the receipt of junk faxes. The device requires that the sender know your security code as well as your fax number. If the

Portable fax machines are convenient when traveling.

STEWART COHEN

sender does not know the security code, the machine blocks the message. Another way of controlling junk fax is to purchase a fax machine that allows communication with only user-selected numbers stored in the machine's memory.

Internet Fax

The growth of the Internet has spawned Internet-capable fax, which has the ability to bypass the PSTN (Public Switched Telephone Network) by diverting fax traffic to the Internet and thus reducing fax costs. There are no telephone charges. Fax transmission over the Internet operates like email messaging. The message from the fax is forwarded to an email address, and the user picks up the message the same way he or she would pick up an email message. The major disadvantage of

Internet fax through a service provider, such as AOL, is that the immediacy of receipt can be sacrificed. Internet fax may arrive within seconds, minutes, or hours after the initial transmission. In addition, if a person is not connected to the Internet when a fax is being sent, he or she may not receive the message in a timely fashion.

Multifunction Units

As you learned earlier in this chapter, multi-function machines allow the combination of two, three, or four functions. A fax may be a part of a multifunction machine, combining printing, faxing, copying, and scanning (or two or three of these functions) into one machine. In fact, copying ability is a common feature of most fax machines.

Fax Selection

You should ask some questions before purchasing a fax machine.

- How will the fax be used? What are the applications? Will more than one document be sent or received?
- What features are needed? How much memory is needed?
- What type of image quality is needed? Is faxing photographs or graphics a priority?
- Is security necessary? **Confidential mailboxes** (mailboxes to which no other person has access) are available if document security is an issue. Security devices are also available that enable the user to send **scrambled signals** (signals in code).
- What is the vendor's reputation? How long has the company been in business? Is the service quick and efficient? If the company's home office is not local, is a service center located nearby? Does the vendor have a minimum time guarantee for repairing the fax?
- Does the fax machine have a sleep mode, or power-saving mode, for those times when it is waiting for an incoming fax?

- If your workplace receives multiple-page faxes, does the fax machine print the last page first or the first page first? Does the fax print face up or face down? The sorting and resorting of documents on a regular basis can become a nuisance.

- What is the cost of toner or ink the fax machine will use? How many pages per unit will the fax typically print? What about the paper? Does the fax machine require specific paper, or will standard copy paper work? ■

SUMMARY

To reinforce what you have learned in this chapter, study this summary.

- Reprographics is the process of making copies of documents. It refers to any piece of equipment that produces multiple copies of an original document.
- There are three categories of copiers—low-volume, mid-volume, and high-volume copiers.
- Copy/duplicators are high-performance machines typically found in duplication centers or print shops.
- Copier technology is moving to digital. Digital technology provides fast, clear, and high-quality output.
- Multifunction units (sometimes called mopiers) can print, scan, copy, and fax.
- Basic features of copy machines include handling two or three sizes of paper, automatically counting copies, adjusting lightness and darkness, and displaying features that show the cause of a machine malfunction.
- Special features on copiers may include reduction and enlargement, automatic document feeding, duplexing, editing, diagnostics, collate and staple, interrupt key, help button, job recovery, automatic folding, touch control screen, programmable memory, book copy, online binding, image shift, and environmentally friendly features such as toner-save mode and energy-save mode.
- Copy quality must be maintained.
- Because nonworking copiers can have a major impact on workplace productivity, administrative professionals need to know and use proper maintenance procedures.
- When selecting a copier, a number of questions should be asked. Questions include: How many copies per month will be run? What materials will be copied? What copier features are needed? What is the cost of supplies? How reliable is the vendor?
- Centralized copy centers serve the large-volume copying needs of an organization.
- Decentralized centers, providing copiers at various locations throughout an organization, serve low-volume copying needs and ensure quick access by the user.
- Copying abuses are prevalent. Some of these abuses include making too many copies of documents, copying personal information, and copying material that is protected by copyright laws.
- Behaving ethically and legally when copying documents means that one does not copy documents for personal use; one does not copy cartoons, jokes, and similar types of information to distribute to colleagues; one does not make copies of documents that you need for an outside professional group; one does not copy restricted materials; and one is prudent in making the appropriate number of copies needed.
- Copy control devices are installed on copiers to control copy abuses.
- Unnecessary copies of sensitive and confidential information should be shredded.

- Shredders have several features, including auto-reverse, crosscut shredding, sheets per pass, throat width, shredding speed, and multiple media capabilities.
- One should consider the company policy and legal ramifications when shredding a confidential or sensitive document.
- A fax machine is a type of copier that electronically sends an original document from one location to another via communications networks.
- Special features available on fax machines include broadcasting, dual access, fax-on-demand, color fax, auto dialers, portable fax, and elimination of junk fax.
- The growth of the Internet has created Internet-capable fax, which has the ability to bypass telephone lines by diverting fax traffic to the Internet and thus reducing fax costs.
- When selecting a fax machine, one should ask these questions: How will I be using the fax machine? What features do I need? What is the vendor's reputation?

FIND THE PROBLEM

Kurt Rupprecht is the key operator for the department copier. Although he has provided all employees with training on the equipment, every time he goes to make a copy, he encounters a problem. This morning the top of the copier was littered with paper clips and several discarded reports were left on the table. After cleaning up the mess, Kurt copied the financial reports he needed for the board meeting, only to find that someone had left green paper in the paper tray. Kurt quickly redid his copies and went to his meeting. When he went to make a copy after lunch, a large note was taped to the copier, saying the machine was out of order. Upon further inspection, Kurt found a paper jam in the copier. He removed the jam and threw the sign in the trash. Kurt decides to solve the problem. He removes the paper tray and tapes a note to the top of the copier that reads: "If you need to copy, see Kurt!"

PROFESSIONAL POINTERS

It is illegal to quote or copy the work of another individual or organization without giving proper credit for the material. Apply the following procedures when you are keying or reproducing copyrighted material.

- A direct quotation of four or more lines should be single-spaced and indented five spaces from the left margin. Quotation marks are not required when using this format.
- A direct quotation of less than four keyed lines should follow the established line length. Quotation marks should be used at the beginning and end of the quoted material.
- If you must photocopy a published report, a table, material from the Internet, or other material for distribution to others, be sure to credit the original source of the material. You should review the copyright law so you know what constitutes fair use of someone else's work.
- **Plagiarism** is the act of representing another person's work or ideas as your own. Ideas expressed in copyrighted material of another author must be properly credited when used. Quotation marks are not necessary if you paraphrase someone's writing; however, a footnote reference should appear with any expression of ideas not your own.

- Sometimes giving credit for another person's work is not enough. You may need to obtain permission from the individual or organization to use the materials.

REINFORCEMENT ITEMS

1. Describe how a digital copier can save an organization money.
2. Explain the basic features available on most copiers.
3. Describe the advantages and disadvantages of a centralized copy center.
4. Describe what it means to behave ethically and legally with regard to document copying.
5. Describe four special features available on fax machines.

CRITICAL-THINKING ACTIVITY

Burt Keppler is one of the most likable people in the office. He works well with his coworkers, believes in what the company stands for, and tries to put a positive spin on issues that concern his colleagues. Burt is also well known within the local community for his work with disadvantaged children. In a continuing effort to raise funds for these children, Burt uses the workplace copier to print flyers about pancake breakfasts, car washes, bake sales, and other fund-raisers. Burt does not want to spend any of the profits from these events for printing. Is Burt acting ethically? What could Burt do differently? What suggestions could you make to Burt to get his copies made for free?

VOCABULARY REVIEW

Complete the Vocabulary Review for Chapter 12 given on page 97 of the *Applications Workbook*.

ENGLISH AND WORD USAGE DRILL

Complete the English and Word Usage Drill for Chapter 12 listed on page 98 of the *Applications Workbook*.

WORKPLACE APPLICATIONS

A12-1 (Goals 1, 2, and 5)

As a team of three, visit an office equipment/supply store and investigate the types of multifunction units that are available. Select three different units and compare and contrast their capabilities. You should also investigate the following:

- In which copier classification is each unit placed (low-volume, mid-volume, or high-volume)?
- What copy features do the multifunction units have?
- What fax features are available?
- Do the units have network capability?
- Are the units capable of printing on a variety of paper types and sizes?

As a team, prepare a written report of your findings and submit it to your instructor, identifying the store you visited. Use the memorandum form on the Student CD, SCDA12-1. In addition, prepare a 10- to 15-minute presentation on your findings.

A12-2 (Goals 2 and 3)

A case study is provided on page 99 in your *Applications Workbook*. Read the case and respond to the question. Discuss this case with three of your classmates. As a group, write a summary of your responses to your instructor.

A12-3 (Goal 3)

Kurt Rupprecht has been designated as the key operator for his department's copier. When Kurt is on vacation, one of his coworkers must take over this responsibility. Using a word processing program, create a document with clear explanations for Kurt's replacement. Include all of the tasks a key operator must complete to keep copier maintenance to a minimum.

A12-4 (Goal 4)

You have been with your company for six months; you are an assistant to one of the vice presidents. Before joining the company, you worked as an administrative professional for five years. You like your supervisor. She has supported you and has told you that you are doing a good job. However, you have growing concerns about what is happening in the company and in your workplace. In your previous job, you encountered none of these requests; nor did you encounter management's behavior. Here are some of your concerns.

- After only a few weeks on the job, you were asked by your employer to make three copies of a new software package for the other office professionals in your area. You made the copies.
- Your supervisor has repeatedly given you articles from magazines and books and asked you to make several copies. She has then told you to send the articles out to her colleagues across the nation. You have done so.
- Today the president of the company came into your office after a meeting with your supervisor. He handed you a book and asked that you copy and send 15 copies of Chapter 6 to a list of administrators. You made the copies and mailed them.

Remembering what you learned in the chapter on ethical behavior and in this chapter, answer these questions:

- Did you behave ethically? Why or why not?
- Did your supervisor behave ethically? Why or why not?
- Did the president of the company behave ethically? Why or why not?
- What should you do about your growing concerns?

Write a note to your instructor, using the memorandum form on the Student CD, SCDA12-4, answering these questions.

A12-5 (Goal 5)

You have been assigned a research project by your supervisor. Your department needs to replace its aging fax machine with a newer model that uses plain paper and can receive faxes at night when the workplace is closed. Any other features you think are necessary should also be included. Use the Internet to find information about three fax machines that would fit your department's needs. Compare and contrast the machines and make a final recommendation for purchase. Create a short report and submit it to your instructor.

ASSESSMENT OF CHAPTER GOALS

Did you successfully complete the chapter goals? Evaluate yourself by filling out the form on page 100 of the *Applications Workbook*.

Telework

chapter 13

1. Define telework and its advantages and disadvantages.
2. Describe successful teleworkers.
3. Discuss workspace and other considerations.

The growth of telecommunications, including computers, fax machines, cellular phones, and email and instant messaging, has created opportunities for individuals to work in a variety of locations at a variety of times. In fact, an estimated 28.8 million Americans—one-fifth of the adult working population—worked from home, on the road at a telework center, or at a satellite office at least one day a week in 2001.[1] As more and more individuals become "wired," the trend for working anytime and anyplace will continue. An internal telework survey conducted by AT&T found the following:

- Over the last four years, about half of AT&T managers have worked from home at least once a month, about one-quarter at least once a week, and about 10 percent in a full-time "virtual office."
- About 70 percent of those surveyed cited increased productivity due to teleworking.
- This increased productivity is valued at $65 million annually.
- When real estate and job retention savings are included, AT&T saves more than $100 million every year due to telework.[2]

These survey findings are not unique. A similar survey conducted by the Winston Group for the Information Technology Association of America[SM] reported the following findings:

- Telework is widely recognized by most adults as a fast track to a better life.
- Fifty-four percent think telecommuting would improve the quality of their lives. For those with a 1+ hour-per-day commute, this view jumps to 66 percent.
- Thirty-six percent would choose telecommuting over a pay raise.
- Forty-three percent of respondents said they would be a better spouse or parent if they were able to telecommute.

---

[1]John Fetto, "You Can Take it With You," *American Demographics*, February 2002, pp. 10-11.
[2]"AT&T Telework Survey," accessed October 4, 2002; available from **www.att.com/telework**.

- Forty-six percent think the quality of work would improve if they were able to telecommute.[3]

This interest in working anytime, anywhere is not limited to the United States. More and more individuals in other countries are turning to telework. In fact, telework has been embraced in Canada, Switzerland, Finland, Sweden, Germany, and a variety of other European nations. A survey conducted of the European Union showed that the number of teleworkers in Europe doubled in the last three years to 20 million.[4] Telework is on the increase not only in the United States, but also across the globe.

Telework Described

Traditionally, going to work meant leaving home and going to a specific location. However, advances in technology now allow individuals to work in a variety of locations. With the increases in computing and telecommunications technology and the cost for these services falling, more and more individuals are gaining access to these services. Figure 13-1 describes the future of telecommunications technology.

The Internet has opened up a variety of possibilities for individuals who wish to take advantage of current technology. High-speed telecommunications connections, portable computers, email, and instant messaging technologies continue to expand and provide more opportunities for workers. These changes will continue to have a major impact on the workplace of the future, especially on teleworkers. In addition to technology, other factors are leading to the increased numbers of teleworkers:

TELECOMMUNICATIONS STATISTICS

- By the end of 2000, 124 million Americans had access to the Internet (45 percent of the adult population).
- By the end of 2001, over 45 percent of U.S. businesses had access to the Internet.
- By the end of 2001, 30 percent of U.S. businesses had their own Website.
- From 2005 to 2008, over 20 million households will have high-speed data capacity.
- By 2020, all households and businesses will be connected online at very high speeds.

Source: "Work at Home Jobs and the Future," accessed October 4, 2002; available from **http://intlhomeworkers.com/future_of_work.htm**.

FIGURE 13~1 Telecommunication Statistics

- Global competition
- Demand for 24-hour customer support
- Workers' desire for increased flexibility
- Need for companies to reduce overhead[5]

Today, a single assigned workplace for many workers no longer exists. In fact, one in five individuals participates in some form of telework. In addition, about 14.5 million Americans who do not currently participate in telework would like to try it.[6] Interest and participation in telework has continued to increase for a variety of reasons:

- Organizations are investing in more technology.
- Telecommunications costs have dropped.
- Computer use is widespread.
- Lawmakers are promoting alternate worksites to control transportation and pollution problems and to provide employment

---

[3]"U.S. Telework Scene—Stats and Facts," accessed October 12, 2002; available from **www.ivc.ca/studies/us.html**.
[4]"Teleworking Booms in Europe," *ZDNet UK News*, October 9, 2002, accessed October 12, 2002; available from **http://news.zdnet.co.uk/story/0,,t269-s2123557,00.html**.

[5]"Telecommuting," accessed October 4, 2002; available from **www.eworkingwomen.com/experts/telecommute.html**.
[6]John Fetto, "You Can Take It With You," *American Demographics*, February 2002, pp. 10-11.

opportunities for those who are unable to commute from isolated or remote areas.[7]

- Ebusiness has flourished. Many teleworkers own their own Internet business.

Telework Definitions

To understand the concepts in this chapter, you should be familiar with some general terminology. Although the terms *telework* and *telecommuting* are used interchangeably, there are differences between the two. For this textbook, **telecommuting** is periodically working out of a principal office one or more days per week.[8] The emphasis in telecommuting is on the reduction or elimination of the daily commute to and from the office.[9] **Telework** is a broad term used to describe a variety of situations where individuals use telecommunications technology to work from somewhere other than the traditional workplace. These alternative work sites can take a variety of forms.

- **Virtual/mobile telework**—using communications tools and technology to perform job duties from a customer location, an airport, a hotel, or another off-site location.
- **Hoteling**—sharing space with other employees in a specific company location as necessary. Employees can reserve space equipped with phones, PCs, faxes, printers, copiers, email, and Internet access as needed.
- **Satellite center**—a fully equipped workplace in a suburban location. Satellite centers are owned and established by a company and are specifically designed to reduce the commute times of employees.
- **Telework center**—similar to a satellite office, but the space is shared by employees

from a variety of employers. These centers are operated by an independent organization, and employers are charged for the space and services used by their employees. The centers are located closer to employees' homes than their regular company locations.[10]

A self-employed teleworker often works full-time in a home workplace. Many self-employed teleworkers participate in ecommerce. They may own and operate their own Web-based business. The number of Web-based businesses has grown substantially over the last few years, and continued growth in this area is expected. Other individuals telework part-time. A company that allows employees to work one or more days a week in a remote setting, such as those described above, often employs part-time teleworkers.

Interest in Telework

More and more organizations are offering their employees the opportunity to participate in some form of telework. This increased interest has come about for a variety of reasons. The increased accessibility of technology and global economy has influenced the workplace in a variety of ways. In addition, a variety of factors have increased individual interest in telework. Individuals and organizations interested in participating in telework can find research and suggestions through a variety of Web resources. Figure 13-2 provides a list of Web resources that may be helpful to organizations and individuals considering telework opportunities.

Workplace Interest

Dramatic changes have occurred in the workplace. Organizations are downsizing, **outsourcing**, and **off-loading**. Both outsourcing

---

[7]"Time to Take Another Look at Telecommuting," "*HR Focus*, May 2002, pp. 6-7.
[8]"Teleworking, Telecommuting, What's the Difference?" accessed October 4, 2002; available from **www.jala.com/definitions.htm**.
[9]Ibid.

[10]"Introduction: What is Telework?" accessed September 16, 2002; available from **www.att.com/telework/get_started/gs_definitions.html**.

WEB TELEWORK RESOURCES

- **www.abcdependentcare.com**—American Business Collaboration for Quality Dependent Care
- **www.att.com/telework**—AT&T
- **www.gilgordon.com**—provides a variety of teleworking resources
- **www.ivc.ca**—provides a variety of teleworking resources in the United States and Canada
- **www.langhoff.com**—provides tips and advice for teleworkers
- **www.telework.gov**—provides links to sample telecommuting agreements and policies
- **www.telework.com**—provides links to a variety of teleworking resources
- **www.workforce.com**—provides a variety of teleworking articles

---

FIGURE 13~2 Web Telework Resources

and off-loading occur when an organization contracts with individuals outside the organization to complete part of the work of the organization. In today's global economy, organizations must be as flexible as possible, and telework provides organizations with this flexibility. Much of an organization's work can be completed by individual contractors or by individuals employed part-time by the organization. In either case, these individuals are often teleworkers.

Worker Interest

Increased interest in telework from an employee's perspective has occurred due to a variety of factors. Some of these factors include:

- The continued growth of women in the workforce.
- The continued growth in the number of two-career families, with both husband and wife working.
- The need for childcare for young children.
- The increasing longevity of the population, bringing with it the care of the elderly,

which is often the responsibility of two-career families.

- The growth of cities, which often causes transportation problems in getting to and from work.
- The relocation of companies to other cities, with the resulting possibility that some workers do not relocate, but become teleworkers for the company.

All of these factors make the flexibility of teleworking attractive to many people in the workforce. In fact, an increasing number of employees are requesting telework as part of their employment contract. A study conducted by *Office Team*[SM] found that nearly one-third of the workers polled (32 percent) indicated that the ability to balance business and personal demands was the No. 1 career concern of employees.[11] In addition to flexibility, telework provides several other advantages to individuals and organizations.

Advantages to the Individual

Teleworkers describe the following advantages to the concept of working anyplace at anytime.

- Fewer interruptions, which allow for greater focus and improved personal productivity
- Improved job satisfaction
- Increased quality of work/life because of decreased stress associated with balancing work and family obligations
- Increased flexibility in determining work times and daily schedule
- Reduced stress from workspace limitations or interruptions from coworkers, with improved morale, work satisfaction, and motivation
- Reduced commuting time, commuting stress, traffic accidents, and transportation costs
- Less need to relocate
- Fewer absences and personal leave

---

[11]"The Power of Balance," accessed October 4, 2002, available from **www.officeteam.com/PressRoom**.

Results from an annual telework research survey conducted by AT&T suggest that employees who choose to participate in teleworking experience increased productivity. These teleworkers report that they work at least one hour more per day, which is equivalent to about 250 hours (or six additional weeks) each year.[12] Four out of five teleworkers say that the ability to balance the competing demands and responsibilities of work is an important advantage. Additional advantages reported by teleworkers in this survey are included in Figure 13-3.

A number of surveys and studies have demonstrated that telework improves employees' lifestyles, organizational bottom lines, recruitment, and retention capabilities. As was mentioned previously, teleworkers are very happy with their increased productivity, with their ability to balance work and family, and with the feeling that their employers care about their well-being.

[12]"Getting Started. Introduction: Savings and Benefits," accessed September 16, 2002; available from **www.att .com/telework/get_started**.

Disadvantages to the Individual

Disadvantages to the teleworker may include:

* Isolation from other workplace employees.
* Limited or lack of a support group.
* Potential conflict between home and work responsibilities.
* Reduced support for equipment and telecommunication problems.
* Loss of fringe benefits such as paid vacations and insurance coverage if the person is a self-employed teleworker (an individual not employed by an organization).
* Interruptions and distractions from working in a home environment.

Teleworking is not the perfect situation for all employees. It takes the right kind of job/tasks, people, organization, and home workplace settings to be successful. Review Figure 13-4 to determine if you could be a successful teleworker.

Advantages to the Organization

In addition to being advantageous to the individual, telework also has advantages specific

MAJOR ADVANTAGES OF TELEWORK (ACCORDING TO EMPLOYEES)	
Advantage	**Percent of Employees Selecting as an Advantage**
Balances work and family	82
Improves productivity	71
Shows that the firm cares	70
More personal time	66
Employee feels trusted	64
Employee saves money	64
Keep/attract best people	63
Helps environment	61
Company saves money	61
Reduces work stress	55

Source: AT&T 2001–2002 annual employee telework survey.

FIGURE 13~3 Major Advantages of Telework

COULD YOU BE A SUCCESSFUL TELEWORKER?

- Do you have a good understanding of telecommuting? Do you have an appreciation of telecommuting, its pros and cons, and the demands it can make on you?
- Do you have the right job? How much of your work is portable? How much face-to-face contact do you need with people at the workplace? Does your job require ongoing access to equipment, materials, and files that are found only at the workplace?
- How good are you at your job? How familiar are you with your work? Do you know your job well? Do you have a history of reliable and responsible job performance?
- Do you have the right home office environment? Do you have a separate room that is quiet, safe, and insulated from domestic activities and other distractions? Do you have the work tools necessary to do your job? Would members of the household allow you to work without interruption?
- Are you comfortable with IT? Are you comfortable with your computer, its software, email, and remote access capabilities? Do you rely on your tech support to resolve all problems, or are you able to fix some of them on your own?
- Do you have the right supervisor and organizational culture? Is your supervisor supportive of employee needs to balance work with personal life? Does your supervisor evaluate performance by results rather than by the clock? Is your organization supportive of flexible work arrangements?
- Are you an effective communicator? Are you adept at communicating effectively with your colleagues and clients?
- Are you self-disciplined, motivated, and organized? Do you have a proven track record of personal motivation and being able to stay on course without direct supervision? How easily would you be distracted by things around the house?
- Do you have social independence skills?
- Are you susceptible to overwork? Do you have a tendency to overwork?
- Do you see teleworking as a way to balance work and other roles? If allowed to telework, would you be prepared to dedicate 100 percent of your attention to work during your working hours?

Source: "Could You Telecommute?" accessed October 16, 2002; available from **www.telecommutect.com/infoTelecommuters**.

FIGURE 13~4 Could You Be a Successful Teleworker?

---

to the organization. Some of these advantages include:

- Increased productivity and job performance of employees (by 20 percent on average).
- Financial savings from reduced investment in real estate and office space and parking requirements (some $2,000 per employee).
- Reduced absenteeism and health-care related costs (one to two days per year on average).
- Lower long-term disability costs.
- Fewer business disruptions due to emergencies (snow and other storms, power outages, floods, strikes, viral and other illness, and so on).
- Less need to downsize.

- Lower travel costs.
- Improved morale and job satisfaction.
- Improved recruitment and retention of key employees; reduced hiring and training costs.
- Access to labor markets from geographically remote areas.
- Potential for tax credits and other incentives.
- An option to relocating employees.[13]

Because most organizations can benefit from some form of telework, the numbers of organizations participating in a telework program

---

[13]"Advantages and Disadvantages of Telework for Employers," accessed October 16, 2002; available from **www.ivc.ca/proemployer.html**.

are increasing. In fact, according to a survey by an international outplacement firm, telework is the biggest workplace trend in the United States. The high cost of real estate is another major growth factor. Since real estate represents about 20 percent of a corporation's total assets, reducing the amount of money invested in real estate has a major impact on the bottom line. Companies with telework programs report saving as much as 30 percent in reduced overhead expenses.[14]

Disadvantages to the Organization

Disadvantages to the organization may include:

- Difficulty in managing teleworkers.
- Increased costs for employee selection and training.
- Difficulty in evaluating employee performance.
- Expense and difficulty of providing technological equipment and/or support.
- Security of information and files.
- Disruption of organizational culture.

These disadvantages are often found in companies that are starting a telework program. If an organization is going to have a successful program, it must plan carefully when implementing the program. Organizations can decrease the potential for disadvantages if they commit the time needed to identify the jobs best suited to distance work, determine which employees are most suited to telework, and evaluate teleworkers appropriately. A variety of publications and Internet resources are available to organizations that wish to implement a telework program. To initiate or improve a telework program, an organization should follow these suggestions:

- Set specific guidelines. A telework contract can ensure that both sides agree about such areas as hours of availability, what equipment the employer will provide, performance expectations, and training.

- Have a formal training program. Teleworkers and their managers need training on the technical aspects (how to use equipment) and relationship factors (how and when to contact the workplace).
- Provide frequent and constructive feedback. This is important for all employees, especially teleworkers. Make sure teleworkers understand how their work will be reviewed and that their evaluation is tied directly to established job standards and goals.
- Communicate. This is very important for employees who work off-site. Incorporate weekly progress reports, email updates, and virtual meetings. Be flexible and willing to adopt new ways to communicate.
- Help teleworkers stay involved. Be honest about the changes in relationships that occur when people are teleworking. To overcome feelings of isolation, incorporate regular contact with supervisors and other staff, include teleworkers on project team and in promotions, and schedule regular trips for teleworkers to visit the workplace.
- Do not ignore teleworkers' growth and development. See that they get training in their field, the opportunity to participate in professional organizations, and assistance in advancing in the company.
- Recognize when the arrangement is not working. Telework is not for everyone. Document teleworkers' progress and take action to change problem situations.[15]

Advantages to Society

Advantages to society include:

- Enhanced economic development.
- Reduced traffic congestion, consumption of fuels, and pollution.
- Reduced stress and healthcare costs.
- Increased community stability.

Telework encourages individuals to set up and maintain offices in their homes, which

---

[14]June Langhoff, "Telecommuting," accessed October 6, 2002; available from **www.eworkingwomen.com/experts/ telecommute.html**.

[15]"What is the Future of Telework?" *HR Focus*, March 2001, pp. 5-6.

can be accomplished at a relatively low cost. Technology and the Internet provide new business opportunities not available in the past. In addition, more opportunities are available for women since telework allows them to maintain a successful business operation while juggling family and home responsibilities.

Telework decreases transportation issues such as traffic congestion, accidents, and the demand for public transportation. A decrease in the number of individuals who commute to work saves precious natural resources and decreases the amount of toxic emissions into the atmosphere. For example, members of the Metropolitan Washington Council of Governments (COG) recently introduced a program designed to get 20 percent of the DC area's workers teleworking one or more days a week by 2005. If this goal is reached, 70,000

fewer vehicles will be clogging highways at rush hour, 118,000 gallons of gas will be saved, and harmful auto emissions will be reduced by 1.2 tons.[16] In fact, if 10 percent of the nation's workforce participated in teleworking one day a week, people would avoid the frustration of driving 24.4 million miles, they would breathe air with 12,963 tons less air pollution, and they would conserve more than 1.2 million gallons of fuel each week.[17]

When you combine the individual, company, and society benefits of telework, multiplied by thousands of companies and millions of people, you begin to see just how significant the benefits of teleworking can become.

---

[16]"Phone It In," *PC Magazine*, December 4, 2001.
[17]"What Are the Benefits of Telecommuting?" accessed October 1, 2002; available at **www.langhoff.com/faqs .html#how%20many**.

Telework reduces commuting stress and time.

© GETTY IMAGES/PHOTODISC

Successful Teleworkers

Before you consider working as a teleworker for an organization or as a self-employed teleworker, you must think about some issues. To be successful in this type of environment, you need to determine your goals. You need to spend time thinking objectively about what you hope to accomplish. You also must be sure you have the traits necessary to be a successful teleworker.

Based on experiences of a variety of organizations, successful teleworkers typically possess the following characteristics, traits, and skills:

- Goal-oriented
- Self-disciplined
- Independent (works successfully without close supervision)
- Planning and organizing abilities
- Time management skills
- Strong communication skills (written and verbal)
- Strong work ethic
- Self-confident
- Low affiliation needs
- Supportive family/home environment
- Strong performance record
- Technical ability/high job knowledge
- Computer proficiency (hardware, software, peripherals)[18]

This section will help you consider your work options and determine whether you have the characteristics to be a successful teleworker.

Goal Identification

What are your goals? Do the goals listed here match your own? If so, you may be interested in pursuing the possibility of teleworking.

- Independence
- Flexibility
- Control
- Ability to set and maintain a work schedule
- Family time—time with children, spouse, and parents

If you had trouble identifying these goals as your own, perhaps you need to spend some time thinking about your goals. Stephen Covey, a well-known authority in the area of establishing goals, suggests asking these questions as you begin to think about what you want to do.

- What do I think are my greatest strengths?
- What strengths have others who know me well noticed in me?
- What have been my happiest moments in life? Why were they happy?
- When I daydream, what do I see myself doing?
- When I look at my work life, what activities do I consider of greatest worth?
- What quality-of-life results do I desire that are different from what I now have?[19]

Once you ask and answer these questions, Covey suggests that you write a **mission statement** to clarify your goals. A mission statement helps you determine your individual values and your future direction. A thoughtful mission statement:

- Fulfills your own unique capacity to contribute.
- Includes fulfillment in physical, social, mental, and spiritual dimensions.
- Is based on quality-of-life results.
- Deals with both vision and values.
- Deals with all the significant roles in your life—personal, family, work, community.
- Inspires you to achieve.[20]

---

[18]"Telecommuter Profile," accessed October 16, 2002; **www.tipsfortelecommuters.com/telecommuting/profile.asp**.

[19]Stephen R. Covey, Roger Merrill, and Rebecca R. Merrill, *First Things First* (New York: Simon & Schuster, 1994).
[20]Ibid.

To understand more about how a mission statement is written, review Figure 13-5, which shows an example of someone's mission statement. If you would like to practice writing a mission statement, visit the Franklin Covey® Website at **www.franklincovey.com/ missionbuilder/**.

If you are self-employed, you should write a mission statement for your company. Such a statement helps you to stay focused on the direction you have determined the company should take. An example of an organizational mission statement is shown in Figure 13-6.

Personality Traits

In addition to understanding your goals and being clear about them by writing a mission statement that guides you in the pursuit of those goals, you need to be realistic about who you are. What personality traits do you have? How do you like to work? What traits do you have that contribute to your success?

If you are interested in pursuing telework, the following traits are important to your success.

Discipline

Working as a teleworker requires discipline. Working at a home-based workplace means you will encounter a number of distractions. The telephone rings. The doorbell rings. The dog barks. FedEx® delivers a package. One of your customers or clients calls. Being disciplined means you know how to work with these distractions—because you generally cannot eliminate them.

When working from home, discipline involves these activities:

- Set a routine, just as you would in a traditional workplace. Make a to-do list each afternoon, and check it each morning. Check your email and voice mail two or three times a day.
- Establish times to communicate with your company if you are telecommuting.
- Create a visual sign that lets your family know you are working and cannot be disturbed.
- Shut your office door at night. The teleworker can overdo the work hours just as the traditional employee can. Determine the

---

PERSONAL MISSION STATEMENT

My mission is to:

✓ Discover and use all of my talents and abilities.
✓ Treasure my family.
✓ Live true to the principles I hold dear (self-sufficiency, honesty, integrity, and giving).
✓ Be an outstanding worker—one who contributes to my employers and clients.
✓ Provide adequate income for my family.

FIGURE 13~5 Personal Mission Statement

ORGANIZATIONAL MISSION STATEMENT

Pioneer-Standard℠ Electronics, Inc.

We will be the preferred strategic link between our suppliers and customers. We will serve today's needs for electronic components, computer products and services—and tomorrow's needs for technology. We will be among the leading industrial distributors in the world. We will provide our investors with attractive financial growth and our employees with an equal opportunity for personal and professional growth. We take pride in our culture, dedicated to integrity, flexibility, growth, quality, success in all regards. We are committed to doing what we say we will do.

www.pios.com/corporate/corporate.htm

FIGURE 13~6 Organizational Mission Statement

number of hours you will spend working, and then stick to that number. Remember that the most productive worker is a balanced worker—one who knows how to balance work, family, and play.

Self-Starter

A self-starter knows what needs to be done and is eager to get it done. A self-starter is the opposite of a procrastinator. A procrastinator always has an excuse as to why a project cannot be started or cannot be completed. A procrastinator is not successful in a telework environment. Procrastinators are the people:

- Who always have filing to be done.
- Whose desk is stacked with papers they cannot find.
- Who never accomplish what is on their to-do list. (In fact, they probably do not even have a to-do list.)

Let your family know when you are working and cannot be disturbed.

DIGITAL VISION

The self-starter generally has a number of items on his or her to-do list and not only gets them accomplished, but feels a sense of satisfaction at marking the items off the list. The self-starter is eager to begin the next to-do list, enjoying a sense of pride and accomplishment from being able to do a number of tasks well.

Organization

Organization is important on any job, but particularly so in a telework environment. An individual must be organized in order to juggle numerous tasks and successfully confront interruptions. A person working in a virtual environment must be able to plan and organize time well and to implement the time management techniques described earlier in this textbook:

- Setting priorities
- Organizing the workstation
- Simplifying repetitive work
- Handling paperwork as few times as possible
- Using time management systems, such as electronic calendaring and scheduling software

Independence

In the traditional workplace, you generally have someone you can go to for help in solving a problem. Not so in a telework environment. You must be a creative problem solver. If you are working on a report that includes graphics and you cannot get the graphics software to work properly, you cannot go to the computer expert in the next office for help. You must figure out the problem or find someone who can assist you. If your child develops a fever while you are working on a project under a tight deadline, you must solve the problem. Whatever occurs, you must be creative enough to find a solution.

Good Communication

You have already learned the importance of being a good communicator and continuing to grow in your communication skills. These skills are crucial to the teleworker, who must communicate with a variety of people (executives, coworkers, clients, employees at the local print shop, and so on). As a teleworker, you generally do not have the luxury of communicating with these people often enough to learn their communication styles. In addition, contact with these people usually happens through email, videoconferences, voice mail, the telephone, or fax; you may never see them in person. These situations demand that you be a good communicator who strives to improve your skills, as well as a person who cares about others. When communication goes poorly, you must step back and analyze what happened and why it happened. Realize that you can learn from your mistakes. It is a good idea to remember the Golden Rule: Treat others as you would have them treat you.

Self-Confidence

As a teleworker, you need to know what you do well. When you do something well, you need to take the time to congratulate yourself on your success. You may even set up your own reward system—however small. Maybe the reward is as simple as taking a 30-minute walk in the park when you successfully finish a particularly difficult project. You do not have coworkers or a supervisor to tell you when you have done a good job. You must have the self-confidence to be your own support system. Additionally, you must have the self-confidence to admit when you cannot do something well. If this is the case, find someone who can help you, decline the job, or develop the necessary skills.

Strong Work Ethic

The teleworker must have a strong work ethic. No one is around to set the time clock or to determine the length of breaks or lunch. It is important that you set and maintain a schedule that allows you to get your work done. In addition, a project may take longer than you had planned. You must be willing to work long hours if necessary. But you need to be a balanced worker. You do not work late because you were undisciplined or disorga-nized; you work late only occasionally so you can meet a deadline.

Technology Skills

Technology skills are essential for all administrative professionals. As a teleworker, however, technology skills are even more vital. Because teleworkers depend on a variety of computer and telecommunications technology, they must understand the equipment. In addition, a teleworker needs to be self-reliant in troubleshooting problems. Successful teleworkers follow the six tips for system maintenance provided in Figure 13-7.

As a teleworker, you must also be willing to upgrade your knowledge and skills. Read current computer magazines, talk to other teleworkers, and remain up to date on equipment so you can continue to perform your job responsibilities in a satisfactory manner. You may also consider enrolling in course work on the Web or through a community college or university in your area. If you are self-employed, these courses may be tax-deductible and considered continuing education for employment benefits. An accountant can further advise you in this area.

Teleworking Challenges

Disadvantages to teleworking were discussed earlier in this chapter. To overcome these challenges, full- and part-time teleworkers must learn to deal with feelings of isolation, to address family issues, and to be aware of avenues available to troubleshoot technology problems.

Isolation

The biggest challenge for many teleworkers is the isolation. If you have been accustomed to a traditional workplace setting, you will recognize several differences as a teleworker. You cannot chat with a coworker on break. You do not run into colleagues in the hallways or on the elevator. You do not have access to coworkers to discuss new ideas or problem situations. As a full-time teleworker,

---

GOOD HABITS FOR SYSTEM MAINTENANCE

Teleworkers should follow these six habits for system maintenance.

- When in doubt, reboot. From software glitches to frozen screens or applications, a reboot often does the trick.
- Do not install unauthorized software. The IT help desk knows how to handle the applications on your system. Loading new applications can stump them and leave you hanging without answers.
- Know your back-up tools. If your data is stored locally on the PC, back up regularly. Install and use a battery backup.
- Learn the drill. Schedule and perform routine maintenance and upgrades (operating system updates and patches, system defragmentation, virus scans, and system cleanup) to keep the system running smoothly.
- Keep your defenses up. Update your antivirus software and keep the firewall up.
- Log on and learn. Whether it's built-in help features, read-me files, help wizards, or online help, seek out assistance for individual software applications. Visit newsgroups for free advice from others who know the products.

Source: Jeff Zbar, "Controlling the Cost of Remote Support," *Network World*, February 25, 2002, p. 23.

FIGURE 13~7 Good Habits for System Maintenance

you must find ways to lessen your isolation. Suggestions include the following:

- Join a health club; exercise with people; sign up for an aerobics class.
- Arrange to have lunch occasionally with someone in a similar business.
- If you are a telecommuter, take advantage of company-sponsored professional development activities.
- Turn on a news program during your lunch to get in touch with what is happening in the outside world.
- Go to an occasional movie in the afternoon.

As a part-time teleworker, you must also develop strategies to deal with feelings of isolation. The following tips will help you stay in touch with your supervisor and coworkers.

- Contact your manager and/or peers at least once a day. Make it a part of your daily routine.
- Make sure you are accessible by telephone.
- Engage the services of a "workplace buddy" to keep you informed on an informal but regular basis.
- Get more from your visits to the workplace. Use these trips for formal meetings as well as informal lunches.

- Take advantage of email and voice mail technology to supplement telephone conversations. This technology can help maintain communication regardless of time zones.
- Use email and voice mail technology to broadcast personal and project updates. These emails can later serve as proof of work submissions and evidence that you are on target with your project deadlines.
- Continue face-to-face meetings. Encourage planning and/or progress meetings; attend all staff meetings.[21]

Family Issues

Dealing with conflicting job and home demands is often difficult for the teleworker. If you are a teleworker and are married, have a family, or live with other individuals, you must discuss your work arrangements with them. Many people will have misconceptions about you as a home-based teleworker. Some people may assume you are not really working or that you are available to take on additional responsibilities. Obviously, this is not true. Unless you can help these people understand

---

[21]"Tips for Staying In Touch," accessed September 16, 2002; available from **www.att.com/telework/get_started/gs_tips_b.html**.

what you are doing, you cannot be successful as a teleworker. To help deal with family issues, consider the following suggestions.

- Hold a meeting to explain how you will be working and what your work entails.

- Determine a clear division of household tasks. What are your spouse's responsibilities? What are the children's responsibilities? Who does the cooking? Who buys the groceries?

- Find a house-cleaning service or an individual who can come in if needed. Hire someone full-time if the workload becomes overwhelming.

- Determine whether you need someone to help with the children either full-time or after school. If you do, call a childcare referral service and/or ask friends for recommendations. You need to feel confident that you have a competent, caring individual looking after your children.

- Keep the lines of communication open. If you think someone is not doing his or her share, communicate your feelings.

- Do not expect perfection from your family as they perform tasks. Although they may not do it as well as you would, they are doing their part.

- Try to keep your home a low-maintenance one. Do not buy furniture or carpet that requires constant care and cleaning.

With family and friends, make sure they understand that your home is your workplace. Make sure they know your working hours, and help them to understand when you cannot be disturbed. To assist in this effort, close your office door when you are working and post a sign on a bulletin board, indicating your work hours for the day or week. Refer to your home office as your workplace. Do not let family or friends think you can take on extra community and household projects

© GETTY IMAGES/PHOTODISC

A weekly family meeting can be held to assign household tasks.

because your workplace is in the home. Let them know you have business responsibilities that you must complete.

Technological Challenges
As discussed previously, technology is vital if you choose to become a teleworker. You may be working from your home, a client's office, a satellite office, or some other location. You will be using telecommunications technology to accomplish your job. The following suggestions can help you when dealing with technological challenges.

- Learn the telephone numbers of the technical support centers for your software programs, as well as hours of availability. Keep these in a file or on a contact list and handy at all times.
- Use Internet sources. A variety of Internet sites are available that allow you to post questions and/or problems.
- Make a listing of the telephone numbers of the manufacturer of your computer, fax, printer, and so on, and keep the warranty information in a safe and practical place.
- Know how to get assistance with Internet problems; for example, know the telephone number of your ISP provider.
- Take a short course from your local college on a new software program you are going to use.
- Call a temporary agency for part-time support if the job becomes too much for you to handle productively.

If you are a part-time teleworker and remote support is available, follow these tips to optimize your remote support experience.

- Know what you have. Tech support will need to know the type of PC on which you work, the operating system, application versions, the amount of RAM you have, the peripherals you have running, and so on. Get a spiral notebook, write this information down, and keep the notebook handy.
- Reproduce the error. Reboot the PC and try to re-create the problem. If it happens

again, write down the error message—and the steps you took that caused the problem. If the error does not freeze the computer, hit the "Print Screen" button; open a blank document in Word, and Paste (Edit, Paste) the picture of the screen into the document. This will help you explain the problem to tech support.

- Take notes. Before calling, put on your headset. In your spiral notebook, write down the date, start time, and duration of your call. Get the tech support staffer's name and the location, and write down what he or she tells you to do—and the result. Also write down the time the call ended (as this may be the time entered in the computer as the time you called).
- Get help. If someone in the office can help solve the problem faster, conference them into the call. If the help desk staffer is a rookie, politely ask that the call be escalated to a more experienced support representative or engineer.[22]

Workspace and Other Considerations

You need to consider a number of elements when setting up your workspace. What type of work are you going to be doing? How much space do you need? Where should you locate your workspace? What equipment is needed? What types of services will you need?

Type of Work
Before you think about location and size of your workplace, you need to think through your needs. Ask yourself these questions:
- What will my work be?
- Will I be working on highly technical material that requires a distraction-free environment?

---
[22]Jeff Zbar, "Controlling the Cost of Remote Support," *Network World*, February 25, 2002, p. 23.

- Will I be meeting with coworkers and customers or clients in my workspace?
- Do I need a space that will not be invaded by any member of my family?
- Can I share my space with my spouse? For example, if you have a spouse who is a teleworker, is it possible to have a two-person office?
- What environmental factors are important? For example, are you a person who works more productively when close to a window? Can you work in a small space? Do you need a relatively open environment?

Once you answer these questions, you are ready to consider location and size.

Location and Size

Whether you are a part-time or full-time teleworker, a dedicated workspace is essential. A spare bedroom, a basement room, or an unused formal dining area may be the answer. If clients, customers, and/or coworkers will be meeting with you, the space needs to be as close to an entrance as possible. You do not want these individuals walking through your entire house before reaching your office. Regardless of the size of your workspace, keep these ideas in mind when choosing your location.

- Choose a quiet location. If a dedicated space with a door that closes is unavailable, choose an area away from the commotion of your home.
- Separate your work area from the rest of the house. If you do not have a room with a door, find a way to put something between your office and the rest of the house. Remember, when the door is closed, the office is closed.
- Make sure the location you choose has sufficient electrical outlets and telephone jacks to accommodate your equipment needs. Make sure the outlets and jacks are in close proximity to your equipment. Stringing cords across a room can be dangerous.

- Check the lighting. Make sure you have adequate lighting for your equipment. Do not locate your computer so close to a window that the outside light causes a glare on the screen.
- Control the temperature. Working in an environment that is too hot or too cold lessens your productivity. In addition, having your computer against an exterior wall may cause problems due to temperature variations.
- Make the space your own. Create a space that nurtures and improves your state of mind. Choose a functional layout, but add personal touches such as pictures, artwork, plants, or even a fishbowl to make it a place you enjoy.

You must also consider the size of your workspace. Your space needs will be different if you are working full time from a location versus one day a week or month. For example, if you are an occasional teleworker, you may need only a portion of a room. If you are working at home full time, you need a larger desk and additional space for a computer, copier, printer, and other workplace equipment. You may also need filing cabinets and bookshelves. Overall, keep in mind that a productive teleworker has a functional work space.

Furniture

When selecting furniture, look for ergonomically designed furniture. For example, an ergonomic chair promotes healthy posture and more comfortable seating. Select a chair with adjustable armrests, seat, and back and a wheeled base with five coaster arms to prevent tipping. Select a desk that suits your needs and size constraints. If your job is paperwork-intensive, select a desk with a large work surface. Make sure your desk is deep enough so you can place the computer monitor at a comfortable viewing distance and you have ample space for proper ventilation of the monitor.

Create a workspace that nurtures and improves your state of mind.

Adequate storage is also important. You can purchase a desk unit that has built-in storage space. Additionally, you probably need at least one file cabinet and a bookshelf or storage cabinet. Be sure you have enough storage space for your supplies, files, customer information, materials, and business records. Keeping frequently used supplies close at hand increases your productivity. Be sure you are able to keep supplies handy and still have an organized work area.

Equipment and Software

Your equipment purchases should include the basics—a computer, printer, fax, copier, and scanner. You may want to consider multifunction machines, which include a fax, printer, copier, and scanner all in one machine. The following suggestions will help you determine your equipment needs.

- Read computer periodicals such as *Home Office Computing*™, *PC World*, and *PC Computing*.
- Conduct online research; many equipment and software manufacturers advertise their products on the Internet.
- Shop your local computer stores.
- Talk with people who use the technology. For example, discuss the best buys with other teleworkers, computer technicians, or friends who are computer literate.

Once you have purchased your equipment, arrange it in an efficient manner. For example, your computer, printer, fax, scanner, and copier need to be in proximity to each other.

Software is also an important consideration. In addition to telecommunications software, you need access to an email program as well as application software suited to your particular job. You may choose an office suite

DIGITAL VISION

Arrange your equipment in an efficient manner.

that includes word processing, spreadsheet, database, and presentation software; or you may choose stand-alone software. You need to secure a reliable Internet provider and may choose to download a free IM program. Software specific to your organization is often provided to you. Be sure to have the proper licensing for this software. If you are to use this software for more than one client, you may need to purchase the software in the name of your company in order to comply with licensing requirements.

Supplies and Services

If you are telecommuting, your company furnishes you with supplies such as letterhead, memorandum forms, envelopes, business cards, and so on. If you are a self-employed teleworker, you can design your own stationery and business cards. Most word pro-

cessing and desktop publishing programs have the capability to create professional-looking documents. You can also use a local office supply store or printing business to assist in the design and to print the items relatively inexpensively and quickly.

As a teleworker, you may need access to mailing and/or printing services. Although you can purchase software to affix postage to correspondence, you may wish to use a local mailing service if you are sending out large mailings or need special services (certified, return receipt, and so on) for your mail. A printing or copying service can handle special projects you are not equipped to perform at home. Copying, collating, and binding manuals or specialized printing jobs may be completed more efficiently by a printing service.

Health and Life Insurance and Retirement Benefits

If you are a self-employed teleworker, you need to purchase health and life insurance and set up a program for retirement. Talk with several health and life insurance companies, and research the benefits available. You must also consider how you will provide for yourself during your retirement years. Options include **IRAs** (individual retirement accounts) and investments in **mutual funds** (funds that include a combination of stocks and bonds purchased through a mutual fund company) or individual **stocks** (ownership in a company) and **bonds** (debts owed by organizations). You should carefully research the options available to you. You may find it helpful to consult with a financial planner or an investment counselor. Some cities have special organizations dedicated to securing benefits for small businesses. You may want to investigate whether such a service is available in your area.

Lifelong Learning

As a teleworker, you must continue your professional growth. Because you are isolated from the busy workplace and from your coworkers, you may find you are no longer up to date about technological advances. In addition, the emphasis on technology for teleworkers will continue. A variety of options are available to help you stay current in your area of expertise.

- Network with other teleworkers. Attend seminars in your field. Make an effort to meet people at these seminars, get their business cards, and keep in touch with them. As you attend such training, update your resume as appropriate.
- Join professional organizations. Seek organizations of interest to you, perhaps the IAAP, Business and Professional Women^{SM}, or a local service club, such as Rotary^{SM} or the Chamber of Commerce. Stay involved in your community.
- Take classes. Many opportunities are available to expand your knowledge online. Although online courses do not satisfy a need to see people face-to-face, many of the courses have discussion capabilities that allow you to interact with other students. A number of courses are available, ranging from computer courses to liberal arts studies.
- Read. Computer periodicals were suggested earlier in this chapter. Read periodicals relevant to your field. Visit your local bookstore or library for the latest books available.

Technology and the ability to work from any location have spawned the term *virtual assistant*. A **virtual assistant** is an individual who provides administrative support or specialized business services from a distance through the Internet, by fax, by telephone, or by another method of communication. A variety of organizations exist to support and promote virtual assistants. Two of these organizations include:

- IVAA (International Virtual Assistants Association^{SM}); **www.ivaa.org**.
- IAVOA (International Association of Virtual Office Assistants^{SM}); **www.iavoa.com**.

In addition, teleworkers can now obtain specialized certification through specialized programs. One program, called VA Certification, offers two levels of certification: PVA (Professional Virtual Assistant) and MVA (Master Virtual Assistant). The PVA program certifies that individuals have a specific set of skills as well as experience as a teleworker. The skill set is shown in Figure 13-8. The MVA certification is available for teleworkers who have expanded their education with additional course work and more depth of experience. Specific information regarding this certification can be accessed online at **www.va certification.com**. An additional certification program called the CVA (Certified Virtual Assistant) is available from the IVAA. Specific information regarding this program can be accessed at **www.ivaa.org/certified_vas.html**.

Managing the Teleworker

With the increasing number of teleworkers, the experienced administrative professional may be responsible for supervising a teleworker. You learned earlier in this chapter

---

VIRTUAL ASSISTANT SKILL SET

- Experience in supporting executives with administrative needs
- Keen business decision-making skills
- Outstanding customer service techniques
- Crisis management
- Multitasking ability and prioritization skills
- Project management skills
- Self-discipline
- Knowledge of corporate protocol
- Awareness of need for sensitivity and confidentiality
- Proficiency in business English, business law, ethics, and intellectual property
- Proficiency in office practices regarding letters, manuscripts, and other documentation
- Experience and proficiency in core services offered in practice

www.vacertification.com/skillset.html

FIGURE 13~8 Virtual Assistant Skill Set

that disadvantages of telework from an organization's perspective include difficulty in managing, selecting, training, and evaluating employees. Figure 13-9 can help you decide whether telework would be beneficial for your organization.

If your organization is in the beginning stages of implementing a telework program, make sure you follow the suggestions discussed earlier in this chapter. In addition, utilize the Web resources listed in Figure 13-2 to research how other organizations have overcome some of the challenges. Once the program has been implemented, the following suggestions can help you effectively manage teleworkers.

- Provide the necessary tools. If you want individuals to function properly in the workplace, provide the appropriate technology, furniture, and equipment. When confidential information is involved, consider security issues.

- Focus on output. Teleworkers do not need to adhere to the standard 8 to 5 schedule of the traditional workplace. Instead, focus on the work bring produced, and clarify expectations regarding quality and deadlines.

- Make expectations clear. Teleworkers should have an accurate job description. In addition, they should understand what is expected of them with regard to specific deadlines.

- Provide motivation. Out of sight does not mean out of mind. You do not bump into teleworkers by the copy machine, so you must find other ways to keep them motivated. A daily telephone call, a weekly audio- or videoconference, and scheduled face-to-face meetings help keep team spirit alive.

- Set up partners. Partner each teleworker with a buddy or coach in the workplace.

- Keep a few desks available. Retain space for your teleworkers so that when they need to come to the office, they have a work area. If your teleworkers are required to spend one day each week in the office, rotate those days so that not all teleworkers are present on the same day.[23] ■

---

[23]Alexander Garrett, "Managing Home Workers," *Management Today*, May 2002, p. 74.

CAN YOUR ORGANIZATION BENEFIT FROM TELEWORK?

Telework can benefit your organization if:

- Office space represents a large portion of your expenditures.
- Recruitment and retention of specialized individuals is a key concern for your organization.
- The organization is serious about reducing costs and improving efficiency.
- You want to maximize employee performance and productivity.
- You are becoming more and more reliant on information technology.
- You operate across several time zones or want to expand to global markets.
- You want to increase hours of service to customers.
- You spend a lot of money on overtime for staff.
- You want to improve morale and reduce stress.
- You are serious about introducing lifestyle options for employees to help them balance their work with their personal/family lives.

Source: "About Telework," accessed October 16, 2002; available from **www.ivc.ca/part2.html**.

FIGURE 13~9 Can Your Organization Benefit from Telework?

SUMMARY

To reinforce what you have learned in this chapter, study this summary.

- The growth of telecommunications technology has created opportunities for individuals to work in a variety of locations at a variety of times. As more and more individuals become "wired," the trend for working anytime and anyplace will increase.

- Interest and participation in telework has continued to increase as organizations continue to invest in technology, telecommunications costs have decreased, computer use has spread, and lawmakers seek ways to control transportation and pollution problems.

- Alternative work sites can take a variety of forms, including virtual/mobile telework, hoteling, satellite centers, and telework centers.

- Advantages of telework for the individual include greater productivity, greater quality of work/life, increased flexibility, reduced stress, reduced commuting time, less need to relocate, and fewer absences and personal leaves.

- Disadvantages of telework for the individual include isolation, lack of a support group, potential conflict between home and work responsibilities; reduced equipment and telecommunications support, loss of fringe benefits, and interruptions and distractions.

- Advantages of telework for the organization include increased productivity, financial savings, reduced absenteeism, lower long-term disability costs, fewer business disruptions due to emergencies, less need to downsize, lower travel costs, improved morale and job satisfaction, and improved recruitment and retention of employees.

- Disadvantages of telework for the organization include difficulty in managing teleworkers, increased costs for employee selection and training, difficulty in evaluating employee performance, expense of providing technological equipment, security of information, and disruption of organizational culture.

- Advantages of telework for society include enhanced economic development, reduced transportation issues, reduced stress and health-care costs, and increased community stability.

- To be a successful teleworker, an individual must be able to set goals and must be a self-starter. In addition, he or she must be disciplined, organized, independent, and self-confident. The person must be a good communicator and possess a strong work ethic. In addition, technology skills are essential for a successful teleworker.

- Teleworker challenges include isolation, family issues, and technological challenges.

- When setting up a home workspace, one must consider the type of work, location and size, furnishings, equipment, and supplies and services.

- A teleworker must also consider health and life insurance and retirement benefits and be interested in participating in lifelong learning.

- To manage teleworkers effectively, the organization needs to provide the necessary tools, focus on output, make expectations clear, keep employees motivated, set up peer partners, and keep desks available for the teleworker.

FIND THE PROBLEM

Christine teleworks two days a week. Her job requires that she be connected to the Internet. In addition, Christine's supervisor requires that an IM system be activated on her computer when

Christine is working at home in case the office needs to contact her. While she is online during the day, friends and relatives send her messages, preventing her from getting any meaningful work done. Every time a message is sent, a small box appears on her computer screen and Christine is distracted from her work. She looks to see who sent the message in case it is from her supervisor. Christine spends considerable time online at night, chatting with friends and family. What suggestions do you have for Christine to make her teleworking days more efficient?

PROFESSIONAL POINTERS

Ask yourself the following questions if you are considering telework.

- Am I a good problem solver?
- Am I independent?
- Do I communicate well?
- Do I set regular break times for myself?
- Am I flexible?
- Do I control my stress?
- Do I exercise frequently?
- Do I set clear limits on my work?
- Do family members understand my job and my expectations of them?
- Do I hold regular meetings with my family to discuss issues?
- Do I allocate appropriate time for my job and my family?

REINFORCEMENT ITEMS

1. Describe the types of alternative work sites a teleworker may encounter.
2. List five advantages and disadvantages of teleworking for the individual.
3. Describe five personality traits necessary to be a successful teleworker.
4. Describe the kinds of things you need to keep in mind when choosing a location for a home work space.

CRITICAL-THINKING ACTIVITY

Alita has worked as an administrative assistant in a traditional workplace setting for several years. She has become accustomed to a daily routine that includes talking with coworkers and speaking informally with her supervisor. Due to advances in technology, space constraints, and a desire to save money on real estate, the company has decided to offer employees the opportunity to work from home. Alita is comfortable with the daily routine and her contact with coworkers. Although she is hesitant, Alita believes the extra time at home will enable her to be more productive in her workplace responsibilities and her home responsibilities. One month into her teleworking career, Alita has begun staying up late and sleeping in the next morning. She moves from project to project and is beginning to accumulate several piles of paper on her desk. In her prior workplace setting, Alita easily moved completed projects on to the next person, but she has not yet delivered any projects to her supervisor. Alita has three major projects due next week. Although she has begun all of the projects, none of them are complete. Alita is overwhelmed and does not know where to begin. What suggestions could you give Alita to help her complete her projects on time? What suggestions could you give to help Alita become more organized and productive in the future?

VOCABULARY REVIEW

Complete the Vocabulary Review for Chapter 13 given on page 101 of the *Applications Workbook*.

ENGLISH AND WORD USAGE DRILL

Complete the English and Word Usage Drill for Chapter 13 listed on page 102 of the *Applications Workbook*.

WORKPLACE APPLICATIONS

 ### A13-1 (Goals 1 and 2)

Recently several individuals assigned to Sandra Portales, executive vice president and chief operating officer, have indicated an interest in telework. Kurt Rupprecht, her administrative assistant, has asked that you use the Internet to research three telework information sites. Write a short report on the advantages and disadvantages of working from home as well as the personality traits necessary to be a successful teleworker. Cite at least three specific examples or stories from successful teleworkers.

 ### A13-2 (Goal 3)

Work with two classmates. You have decided to quit your job and become a full-time self-employed administrative professional. You have a 10′ × 10′ room in your home that has adequate electrical and telephone jacks. You bought a laptop last month, which includes an office suite and a Web browser. You have no other home office equipment or supplies. Prepare a prioritized list of the items you need to get your business up and running.

To start your business, you have obtained a small business loan of $5,000. Use the Internet office supply catalogs, or visit a local retailer to identify specific items you will purchase with this money. Create a proposal to submit to your bank, indicating what items you will purchase and their cost. Remember, you are working with a limited budget and may not be able to purchase all the items on your prioritized list.

A13-3 (Goals 1, 2, and 3)

Interview two individuals who are employed as teleworkers. You may locate people to interview through Internet resources and interview them online. Ask them to respond to the following items.

• Describe your teleworking situation.

• What personal qualities are necessary in order to be successful?

- If you are employed by an organization, what does your employer provide for you?
- Where is your workspace located? What equipment do you have? What software do you use?
- How do you continue your professional growth?
- What tips would you give a potential teleworker?

Write a report describing your findings, and present it orally to the class. Submit your written report to your instructor.

A13-4 (Goals 2 and 3)

A case study is provided on page 103 in your *Applications Workbook*. Read the case and respond to the questions. Discuss the case with three of your classmates. As a group, write a memo to your instructor that summarizes your responses. Use the memorandum form provided on the Student CD, SCDA13-4.

ASSESSMENT OF CHAPTER GOALS

Did you successfully complete the chapter goals? Evaluate yourself by completing the form on page 104 of the *Applications Workbook*.

4

Records and Financial Management

chapter 14

Filing Rules and Procedures

LEARNING GOALS

1. Explain the importance of records management.

2. Describe and apply alphabetic indexing rules.

3. Describe records storage systems.

4. Explain storage considerations and procedures.

The administrative professional in today's work environment is responsible for taking care of an organization's records. The responsibility for managing and maintaining records continues to increase in complexity. Although there has been a tremendous shift to electronic records and the electronic management of records, organizations continue to generate paper and to rely on paper management techniques. In fact, in 2001, 90 percent of the information shared among organizations was still printed, thereby creating trillions of paper documents annually.[1] Technologies will continue to change. The use of paper records may decrease in some organizations, while in other organizations, the emphasis on paper documents will stay the same or even increase.[2] It is apparent that paper records will not disappear in the next few years. A sound understanding of the function of manual records management and the indexing rules associated with records storage will continue to be an essential skill of the administrative professional. Management of paper documents is presented in this chapter; technological aspects of records management are presented in Chapter 15.

The Importance of Records Management

A **record** is any type of recorded information. For example, information may be:

- Written and recorded on paper.
- Written and recorded on some type of electronic form or **microform** (any medium containing miniaturized or microimages).
- An oral record that captures the human voice and is stored on a CD or a tape.

---

[1]"Spinning Paper Into Gold at Iron Mountain," *Business Week*, September 2001; accessed October 28, 2002; available from **www.businessweek.com/bwdaily/dnflash/sep2001/nf2001094_700.htm**.

[2]Mark Whitehead, "The Myth of the Paperless Office," *Supply Management*, February 28, 2002.

- Email or computerized files stored in an electronic folder.
- Movies stored on DVDs.
- Digital photographs stored on disks.

Whatever the form, these records contain information about an organization's functions, policies, procedures, decisions, and operations. **Records management** is the systematic control of records or the **record life cycle**, which is from creation of a record to its final disposition. This life cycle has five distinct phases:

1. Creation of the record
2. Distribution of the record to internal or external users
3. Use of the record (information gleaned from the record for making decisions, determining directions, and so on)
4. Maintenance of the record (filing and retrieving)
5. Disposition (retaining or destroying after a period of time)

Records are assets to a business just as products, services, management expertise, and a good reputation are assets. Records provide a history of the business. Successful organizations appreciate the need for records. They use the information contained in records to make decisions and plans. The additional value of records to business includes these:

- Legal value by providing evidence of business transactions, such as articles of incorporation, real estate transactions, and contracts
- Financial value through records needed in audits and for tax purposes
- Personnel value through items such as employment applications, dates of hire, employee evaluations, payroll records, and employment termination records
- Day-to-day operational value through such records as policy and procedure manuals, organizational charts, minutes of meetings, information sent to clients and customers, and sales reports

Well-managed records are essential for all organizations and provide the following benefits:

- Reduction of staff time spent searching files for misplaced records
- Quick and easy retrieval of information needed in making management decisions
- Financial savings through systems that provide the most efficient and effective methods of storage
- Protection and storage of archival information needed in perpetuity by the business
- Planned records management systems that allow for growth, evaluation, and updating of methods and equipment
- Trained personnel who understand the importance of records and the need for effective systems and procedures
- Efficient use of space by maintaining records in the most appropriate form and determining the proper equipment for storage

Alphabetic Indexing Rules

The rules for filing may vary slightly from business to business based on specific needs of the organization. Find out what filing rules are used in your organization and use them. ARMA International, the Association for Information Management Professionals℠, has developed rules that are designed to help the administrative professional perform the job of filing more effectively. The rules in this chapter are compatible with ARMA's Simplified Filing Standard Rules and Specific Filing Guidelines.

Rule 1: Indexing Order of Units

A. *Personal Names*
A personal name is indexed in this order: (1) surname, (2) first name or initial, (3) middle name or initial. If it is difficult to determine

the surname, the name is indexed as written. All punctuation is omitted and a unit consisting of just an initial precedes a unit that consists of a complete name beginning with the same letter. The general rule to follow in all indexing is *nothing comes before something*.

Filing Segment	Index Order of Units		
Name	Key Unit	Unit 2	Unit 3
Franklin J. Severson	Severson	Franklin	J
Frederick L. Severson	Severson	Frederick	L
Frederick Lionel Severson	Severson	Frederick	Lionel

B. *Business Names*

Business names are indexed as written, using letterheads or trademarks as guides. Each word in a business name is a separate unit.

Business names containing personal names are indexed as written.

Filing Segment	Index Order of Units			
Name	Key Unit	Unit 2	Unit 3	Unit 4
Howard Ogea Excavating	Howard	Ogea	Excavating	
Howard Oil Company	Howard	Oil	Company	
Huron Mountain Bread Co.	Huron	Mountain	Bread	Co

Rule 2: Minor Words and Symbols in Business Names

Articles, prepositions, conjunctions, and symbols are considered separate indexing units. Symbols are spelled in full. When the word

The appears as the first word of a business name, it is considered the last indexing unit.

Filing Segment	Index Order of Units			
Name	Key Unit	Unit 2	Unit 3	Unit 4
The Gingerbread House	Gingerbread	House	The	
In Nature's Image Taxidermy	In	Natures	Image	Taxidermy
Lawton Interiors by Design	Lawton	Interiors	By	Design

Rule 3: Punctuation and Possessives

Disregard all punctuation when indexing personal and business names.

Filing Segment	Index Order of Units		
Name	Key Unit	Unit 2	Unit 3
Alger-Marquette Community Foundation	AlgerMarquette	Community	Foundation
Bob's Septic Service	Bobs	Septic	Service
E-Z Storage	EZ	Storage	
North/South Collection Agency	NorthSouth	Collection	Agency

Rule 4: Single Letters and Abbreviations

A. *Personal Names*

Initials in personal names are considered separate indexing units. Abbreviations of personal names (Wm., Jos., Thos.) and brief personal names or nicknames (Dick, Liz) are indexed as written.

Filing Segment	Index Order of Units		
Name	**Key Unit**	**Unit 2**	**Unit 3**
J. T. Hinkley	Hinkley	J	T
Jas T. Hinkley	Hinkley	Jas	T
L. Pauline Hinkley	Hinkley	L	Pauline
Liz P. Hinkley	Hinkley	Liz	P

B. *Business Names*

Single letters in business names are indexed as written. If single letters are separated by spaces, index each letter as a separate unit. Index **acronyms** (words formed from the first or first few letters of several words, such as ARMA) and radio and television station call letters as one word. Abbreviated words (Corp., Co.) and names (AT&T) are indexed as one unit regardless of punctuation or spacing.

Filing Segment	Index Order of Units			
Name	**Key Unit**	**Unit 2**	**Unit 3**	**Unit 4**
E C I Inc.	E	C	I	Inc
EG Environmental	EG	Environmental		
KBER Radio	KBER	Radio		
K L Enterprises	K	L	Enterprises	

Rule 5: Titles and Suffixes

A. *Personal Names*

A title before a personal name (Dr., Mr., Ms.), a **seniority suffix** (II, III, Jr.), or a **professional suffix** (D.D.S., M.D., Ph.D.) after a name is the last indexing unit. **Numeric suffixes** (II, III) are filed before **alphabetic suffixes** (Jr., Sr.). If a name contains a title and a suffix, the title is the last unit. Royal and religious titles followed by a given name or by a surname only (Sister Mary) are indexed and filed as written. If a person's professional title comes after the name, it is referred to as a suffix; for example, CPA, CPS.

Filing Segment	Index Order of Units			
Name	**Key Unit**	**Unit 2**	**Unit 3**	**Unit 4**
Gary J. Estevant, II	Estevant	Gary	J	II
Gary J. Estevant, III	Estevant	Gary	J	III
Gary J. Estevant, Jr.	Estevant	Gary	J	Jr
Gaynelle D. Estevant, CPA	Estevant	Gaynelle	D	CPA
Gaynelle J. Estevant, M.D.	Estevant	Gaynelle	J	MD
Sister Gaynelle	Sister	Gaynelle		

B. Business Names

Titles in business names are indexed as written.

Filing Segment	Index Order of Units		
Name	**Key Unit**	**Unit 2**	**Unit 3**
Aunt Joan's Fudge	Aunt	Joans	Fudge
Doctor Frank's Greenhouse	Doctor	Franks	Greenhouse
Dr. Phil's Counseling	Dr	Phils	Counseling

Rule 6: Prefixes—Articles and Particles

An article or a particle in a personal or business name is combined with the part of the name following it to form a single indexing unit. The indexing order is not affected by a space or punctuation between a prefix and the rest of the name; the space and punctuation are disregarded when indexing. Examples of articles and particles are D', Da, De, Del, De la, Des, El, Fitz, L', La, Las, Le, Lo, Los, Mac, Mc, Saint, San, Santa, St., Ste., Ten, Van, Van der, Von, and Von der.

Filing Segment	Index Order of Units		
Name	**Key Unit**	**Unit 2**	**Unit 3**
Mrs. Francis De Gabriele	DeGabriele	Francis	Mrs
Le May's Fine Foods	LeMays	Fine	Foods
St. Germain and McDougal	StGermain	and	McDougal
Alexis Von der Grieff	VonderGrieff	Alexis	

Rule 7: Numbers in Business Names

Numbers spelled out in a business name are considered as written and filed alphabetically. Numbers written in digit form are considered as one unit. Names with numbers as the first unit written in digit form are filed in ascending order before alphabetic names.

Arabic numbers (2, 3) are filed before Roman numerals (II, III). Names with inclusive numbers (33-37) are arranged with the lowest number only (33). Names with numbers appearing in other than the first position (Pier 36 Café) are filed alphabetically within the appropriate section and immediately before a similar name without a number. When indexing numbers written in digit form that contain *nd*, *rd*, *st*, and *th*, ignore the letter endings and consider only the digits.

Filing Segment	Index Order of Units		
Name	**Key Unit**	**Unit 2**	**Unit 3**
5 Step Cleaners	5	Step	Cleaners
5th Street Bakery	5	Street	Bakery
500-700 Rustic Way	500	Rustic	Way
Fifth News Shoppe	Fifth	News	Shoppe
Finally 21 Club	Finally	21	Club
Finally Fantastic Franks	Finally	Fantastic	Franks

Rule 8: Organizations and Institutions

Banks and other financial institutions, clubs, colleges, hospitals, hotels, lodges, motels, museums, religious institutions, schools, universities, and other organizations and institutions are indexed and filed according to the names written on their letterheads. *The* used as the first word in these names is considered the last filing unit.

Filing Segment	Index Order of Units			
Name	Key Unit	Unit 2	Unit 3	Unit 4
Bay de Noc High School	BaydeNoc	High	School	
First Bank of Negaunee	First	Bank	of	Negaunee
Grace United Christian Church	Grace	United	Christian	Church
The Marquette Exchange Club	Marquette	Exchange	Club	The
Northern Michigan University	Northern	Michigan	University	
University of Michigan	University	of	Michigan	

Rule 9: Identical Names

When personal names and names of businesses, institutions, and organizations are identical, filing order is determined by the addresses. Addresses are considered in the following order.

1. City names

2. State or province names (if city names are identical)

3. Street names; include *Avenue, Boulevard, Drive, Street* if city and state names are identical

   a. When the first units of street names are written in figures (18th Street), the names are filed in ascending numeric order (1, 2, 3) and placed together before alphabetic street names (16th Street, 20th Avenue, 25th Drive).

   b. Street names with compass directions (North, South, East, and West) are considered as written (North LaSalle Street). Numbers after compass directions are considered before alphabetic names (North 6th, North Main, SE Main, Southeast Main).

   c. If city, state, and street names are identical, house and building numbers are used. House and building numbers written as figures are filed in ascending numeric order (10 Opdyke Terrace, 2480 Opdyke Terrace) and placed together before alphabetic building names (Opdyke Terrace). If a street address and a building name are included in an address, disregard the building name.

   d. ZIP Codes are not considered in determining filing order.

Filing Segment	Index Order of Units							
Name	Key Unit	Unit 2	Unit 3	Unit 4	Unit 5	Unit 6	Unit 7	Unit 8
Cheryl R. Jackson Chicago, IL	Jackson	Cheryl	R	Chicago	Illinois			
Cheryl R. Jackson Hartford, CT	Jackson	Cheryl	R	Hartford	Connecticut			

(continued)

Filing Segment	Index Order of Units							
Name	Key Unit	Unit 2	Unit 3	Unit 4	Unit 5	Unit 6	Unit 7	Unit 8
Integrated Designs Inc. 1616 5th Avenue Minneapolis, MN	Integrated	Designs	Inc	Minneapolis	Minnesota	1616	5	Avenue
Integrated Designs Inc. One Valley Drive Minneapolis, MN	Integrated	Designs	Inc	Minneapolis	Minnesota	One	Valley	Drive
Iron Bay Books 832 Franklin Building Phoenix, AZ	Iron	Bay	Books	Phoenix	Arizona	832	Franklin	Building
Iron Bay Books 1515 Franklin Building Phoenix, AZ	Iron	Bay	Books	Phoenix	Arizona	1515	Franklin	Building

Rule 10: Government Names

Government names are indexed first by the name of the governmental unit—country, state, county, or city. Next, they are indexed by the distinctive name of the department, bureau, office, or board. The words *Office of*, *Department of*, *Bureau of*, and so on, are separate indexing units when they are a part of the official name. If *of* is not a part of the official name as written, it is not added.

A. Federal

The first three indexing units of a United States (federal) government agency are *United States Government*.

Filing Segment	Index Order of Units (Units 1, 2, and 3 are United States Government for each example)					
Name	Unit 4	Unit 5	Unit 6	Unit 7	Unit 8	Unit 9
Department of Labor Employment Standards	Labor	Department	of	Employment	Standards	
Internal Revenue Service Department of the Treasury	Treasury	Department	of	Internal	Revenue	Service

B. State and Local

The first indexing units are the names of the state, province, county, parish, city, town, township, or village. Next come the most distinctive name of the department, board, bureau, office, or government/political division. The words *State of*, *County of*, *City of*, *Department of*, and so on, are added only if needed for clarity and if in the office name. Each word is considered a separate indexing unit.

Filing Segment	Index Order of Units				
Name	Key Unit	Unit 2	Unit 3	Unit 4	Unit 5
Alabama Highway Patrol	Alabama	Highway	Patrol		
Michigan Department of Education	Michigan	Education	Department	of	
Marquette County Sheriff's Department	Marquette	County	of	Sheriffs	Department
Public Works Department, Branson County	Branson	County	Public	Works	Department

C. Foreign

The distinctive English name is the first indexing unit for foreign government names. Index the remainder of the formal name of the government, if necessary. Branches, departments, and divisions follow in order by their distinctive names. States, colonies, provinces, cities, and other divisions of foreign governments are filed by their distinctive or official names as spelled in English.

Filing Segment		Index Order of Units			
Name	**Key Unit**	**Unit 2**	**Unit 3**	**Unit 4**	**Unit 5**
Principat d'Andora	Principality	of	Andora		
Polska Rzecapospolita Ludowa	Polish	Peoples	Republic	of	
Estados Unidos Mexicanos	United	Mexican	States		

Cross-Referencing

Cross-referencing must be completed when a record is likely to be called for under more than one name. Cross-referencing will save time when there may be confusion about where the record is stored.

Personal Names

When indexing personal names, cross-referencing should be used in the following situations.

- Unusual Names. When it is difficult to determine the last name, index the last name first on the original record. Prepare a cross-reference with the first name indexed first.

Original	Cross-Reference
Thomas Joseph	Joseph Thomas
	SEE Thomas Joseph

- Hyphenated Surnames.

Original	Cross-Reference
HaslittHiggins Francise	Higgins Haslitt Francise
	Francise Haslitt Higgins
	SEE HaslittHiggins Francise

- Change in Name. When an individual changes a name, prepare a cross-reference that refers to the original name.

Original	Cross-Reference
Tacie M (Phelps) Swanson	Phelps, Tacie M
SEE Swanson Tacie M.	

- Similar Names. When names could be spelled in a variety of ways, cross-references are prepared for all possible spellings.

Erickson	Ericsen	Ericsson
SEE Ericsen, Ericsson	SEE Erickson, Ericsson	SEE Erickson, Ericsen

Business Names

When indexing business names, cross-references should be used in the following situations.

Original	Cross-Reference
Kendricks, Bordeau, and Adamini	Bordeau Adamini and Kendricks SEE Kendricks Bordeau and Adamini
	Adamini Kendricks and Bordeau SEE Kendricks Bordeau and Adamini

- Compound Names. When a business name includes two or more individual surnames, prepare a cross-reference for each surname other than the first.

- Abbreviations and Acronyms.

Original	Cross-Reference
IBM	International Business Machines

- Change in Name. When a business changes its name, a cross-reference is prepared for the former name and all records are filed under the new name.

Original	Cross-Reference
Fast Prints	Franklin Print Shop SEE Fast Prints

- Foreign Business Names. The name of a foreign business is often spelled in a foreign language. The English translation is written on the document, and the document is stored under the English spelling. A cross-reference should be placed under the foreign spelling.

Original	Cross-Reference
Federal Republic of Germany	Bundersrepublik Deutschland SEE Federal Republic of Germany

Records Storage Systems

Records can be stored in paper, electronic, or image form. **Records storage systems**, sometimes called filing systems, are the manner in which records are classified for storage. The four basic storage methods are alphabetic, subject, numeric, and geographic. Records in a manual or electronic system may be stored any of these ways.

Alphabetic Storage System

The **alphabetic storage system** uses letters of the alphabet to determine the order in which the names of people and companies are filed. This method is one of the most commonly used storage methods and is found in one form or another in almost every organization. With the alphabetic storage system, the name of the company, the person, or the organization addressed determines the filing order of an outgoing record. The name of the originator (company, individual, or organization) determines the filing order of incoming records. Figure 14-1 illustrates an alphabetic file. This method is based on the filing rules presented earlier in this chapter.

Advantages to the alphabetic storage system include the following:

- It is a **direct access** system. There is no need to refer to anything except the file to find the name.
- The dictionary arrangement is simple to understand.
- Misfiling is easily checked by alphabetic sequence.
- It may be less time-consuming to operate than other filing methods because of direct access.
- Only one **sorting** (arranging records in a predetermined sequence) is required.

There are also several disadvantages to an alphabetic system, including these:

- Misfiling may result when rules are not followed.
- Related records may be filed in more than one place.
- Excessive cross-referencing can congest the files.
- Confidentiality of files is difficult to maintain because the file folders bearing names are seen by anyone who happens to glance at a folder.

Subject Storage System

Subject filing is used to some extent in all organizations. **Subject storage** is used when a file may be looked for more by a topic than by a name. A subject file is actually an alphabetic file. Captions are key words used in locating filed material. The use of clear and concise subject captions is essential to successful subject files. For example, assume a department is working on cancer research. A file labeled CANCER RESEARCH would place all material on the same subject in one folder. In a typical alphabetic file, this information would be spread across a variety of files. See Figure 14-2.

Although subject filing is useful and necessary in certain situations, it is the most difficult and costly method of records storage. Each record must be read completely to determine the subject. It is a difficult method to control since two people reading the same record may have two different ideas as to the subject of the document.

A necessary component of a subject file is an index. The index is a list of all subjects under which a record may be filed. Without an index, it is almost impossible for the subject filing method to function satisfactorily. The list should be kept up to date as new subjects are added and old ones are eliminated. When new subjects are added, the index provides guidance so as to avoid the duplication of subjects. The index may be kept on standard sheets of paper and filed in a notebook or on index cards and filed in a card file box.

Advantages to a subject filing system include these:

- Records about one subject are grouped together.
- The system can be expanded easily by adding subdivisions.
- Most subjects are easy to remember.

Disadvantages to this method include the following:

- It is often difficult and time-consuming to classify records by subject.
- Liberal cross-referencing is necessary since one record may contain several subjects.
- It is necessary to create and maintain an index of subject headings contained in the file.
- It is the most expensive method to maintain since it takes more time to read and file.

Numeric Storage System

Under the **numeric storage system**, file cards and folders are given numbers and arranged

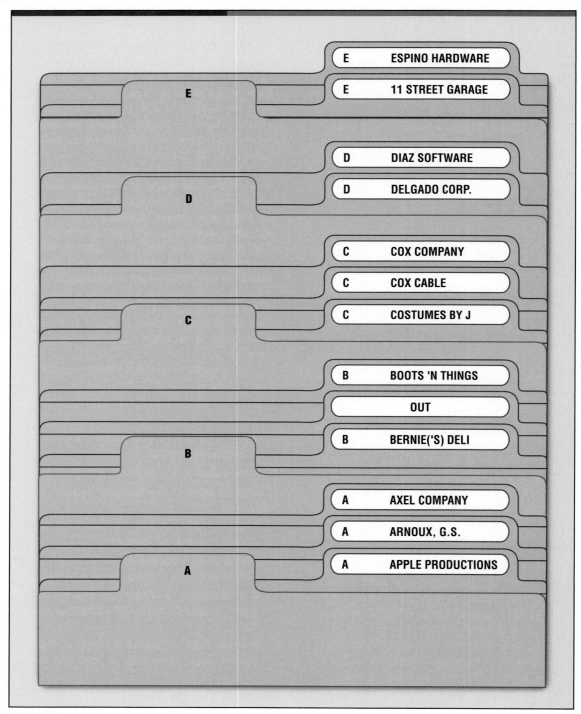

FIGURE 14~1 Alphabetic File

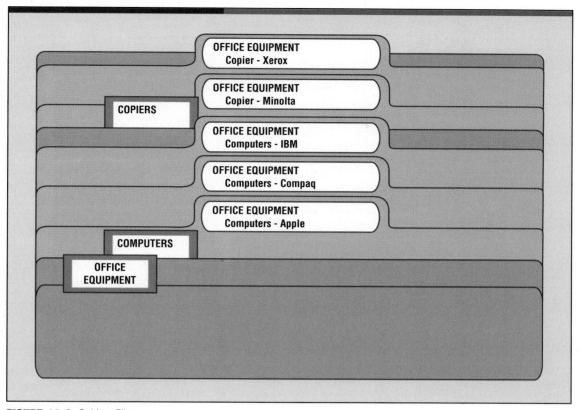

FIGURE 14~2 Subject File

in numeric sequence. Figure 14-3 illustrates a numeric file.

The numeric method of filing is particularly useful in the following situations:

- Insurance companies that keep records according to policy numbers
- Social welfare agencies that maintain records according to case numbers
- Law firms that assign a case number to each client
- Warehouses that stock by part numbers and real estate agencies that list properties by code numbers

The numeric filing system has four parts, including:

1. A card file that includes index cards showing the name and the assigned number.

The card is placed alphabetically in the card file. Figure 14-4 illustrates a numeric card file.

2. A numeric file, which houses the records.

3. An alphabetic general file (for miscellaneous records).

4. An **accession book**, which is a record of the numbers that have been assigned.

The basic procedures used in a numeric filing system are as follows:

- When a document is received for storage, the card file is consulted to see if the correspondent or subject has been assigned a number.

- If a number has already been assigned, the number is placed on the document; the document is placed in the numeric file.

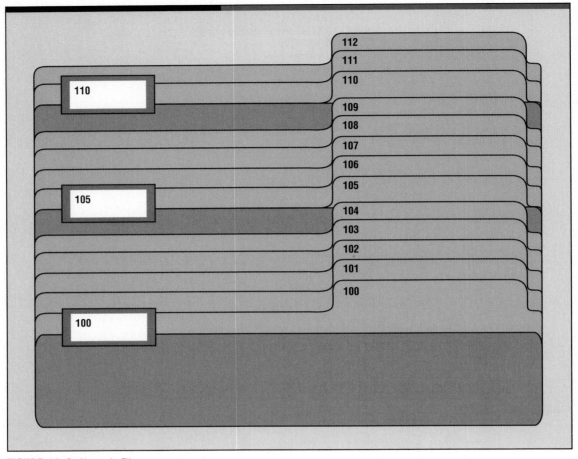

FIGURE 14~3 Numeric File

- If the client is new and no number has been assigned, the record is placed in the general alphabetic file. No number is assigned when there is only one record for a company or subject.
- When several records from the same source have been accumulated in the general alphabetic file, the accession book is consulted. The records are assigned the next available number and then placed in the numeric file.

Advantages of the numeric storage method include these:

- Expansion is unlimited.

- It is confidential. A card file must be consulted before files on important papers can be located.
- Once an index card is prepared and a number is assigned to a record, filing by number is quicker than filing alphabetically.
- Misfiled folders are easily located because numbers out of place are easier to locate than misfiled alphabetic records.

Disadvantages of the numeric storage system include these:

- It is an indirect method: the card file must be consulted before a paper can be filed.

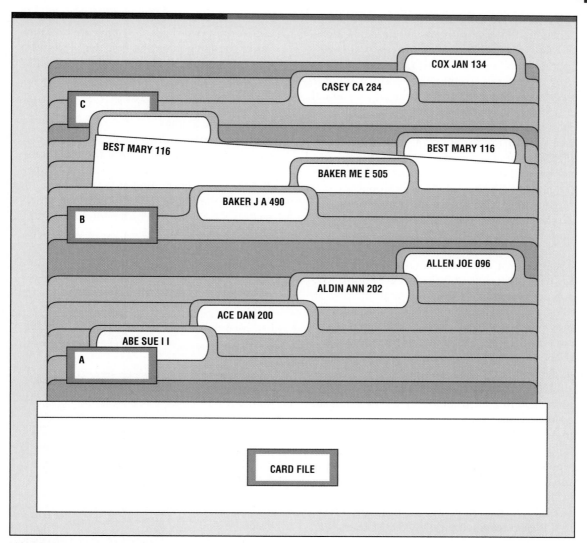

FIGURE 14-4 Numeric Card File

- More equipment is necessary, so the cost is higher.

There are several variations of the basic numeric storage method. Three of these variations include chronologic storage, terminal digit storage, and alphanumeric storage.

Chronologic Storage

A **chronologic storage system** is an arrangement in which records are stored in date order, with the most recent date first. Chronologic storage may be used for filing such items as freight bills, daily reports, and tickler files. The term **tickler file** gets its name from the fact that the file is used to "tickle" your memory and remind you to take certain actions. For example, when something must be taken care of on a certain date, a card is prepared with the necessary information and placed in date, or chronologic, order.

Many software programs include calendaring functions that can serve as an electronic tickler file. To use this type of system, you need to input the information into the computer program so it can remind you to take action. Regardless of whether you are using a manual or electronic system, you must check each morning to see what is to be done that day. The basic arrangement of a manual tickler file consists of a series of 12 guides with the names of the months printed on the tabs and 31 guides with the numbers 1 through 31 representing each day of the month printed on the tabs. The tickler file is generally kept on the administrative professional's desk.

Chronologic storage may also be used as a supplement to a subject system as help in locating records filed by subject. Because the subject system is the most difficult method of filing, you may decide to keep a chronologic index with a subject system. The index would contain the date of the document, the name of the individual or company, and the subject under which the document is filed.

The chronologic system allows you to find records with limited information. For example, assume your employer says, "I need the letter to Armando Bentances that was written in January." With a subject system alone, it would be difficult to locate a record with only the name and date of the letter. A chronologic system allows you to find the letter with the limited information given. A chronologic system is also used within individual folders. For example, the most recent record is always on top so anyone who opens a folder can immediately see the latest record.

Terminal Digit Storage

In the basic numeric method, as the number of files increases, the numbers assigned become higher. When the numbers become several digits long, it becomes difficult to file items correctly. **Terminal digit filing** organizes files by the final digits of the number. The digits are usually separated into groups of two or three. For example, assume you have a file with the number 013746. The last, or terminal,

digits (46) identify the file drawer number. The second two digits (37) indicate the number of the file guide. The first two digits (01) give the number of the file folder behind the file guide. Figure 14-5 illustrates terminal digit filing.

Alphanumeric Storage

Alphanumeric coding combines alphabetic and numeric characters, with the main subjects arranged alphabetically and their subdivision assigned a number. For example, the file guide may have RM-01 RECORDS MANAGEMENT, with the files having RM-01-01 FILING METHODS, RM-01-02 ELECTRONIC FILING SYSTEMS, and so on.

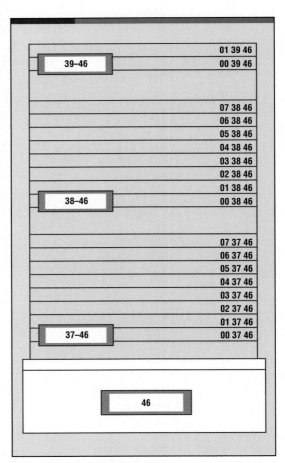

FIGURE 14-5 Terminal Digit File

Geographic System

An additional variation on the alphabetic system is the geographic system. **Geographic storage** is advantageous when the files are requested by location rather than by name. The geographic method is based first on the location of the originators and second on their names. It is particularly useful for:

- Utility companies where street names and numbers are of primary importance in troubleshooting.
- Real estate firms that have listings according to land areas.
- Sales organizations that are concerned with the geographic location of their customers.
- Government agencies that file records by state, county, or other geographic divisions.

In geographic filing, the main divisions may be states, counties, cities, or sales territories. The breakdown into geographic divisions and subdivisions must fit the type of business, its organization, and its need for specific kinds of information. In a geographic file by state and city, for example, file guides are used to indicate the state and city. The file folders are arranged alphabetically behind the guides by company or individual name. Figure 14-6 shows a geographic filing arrangement.

An alphabetic card file is an essential element of a geographic filing system. Records may be requested by the name of the originator rather than by the address. A file consisting of cards with the names of originators in alphabetic order and their complete addresses gives all the necessary information when an individual must locate records without knowing the geographic location.

Advantages to the geographic method include the following:

- It provides for grouping of records by location.
- By glancing at the files, one can see the volume of records within any given geographic area.
- It allows for direct filing if the location is known.

- All the advantages of alphabetic filing are inherent in this method since it is an alphabetic arrangement.

The arrangement of guides and folders makes filing more difficult in the geographic method. In addition, reference to the card file is necessary if the location is not known.

Manual Storage Considerations and Procedures

Records, whether handled electronically or manually, are the memory of a business. Depending on the size of the organization, records may be **centralized** (stored in one central location) or **decentralized** (stored in various departments or branches). Many administrative professionals maintain decentralized files as well as send materials to and retrieve materials from large central files.

Designing Storage Systems

The administrative assistant's filing responsibilities usually go beyond maintaining existing files to include designing and installing various types of files that will best serve the supervisor's need for information. In planning a filing system, three factors must always be considered: findability, confidentiality, and safety.

Findability

The main criterion for judging any system is findability. The administrative professional should think of files as places to find materials, not just places to put materials. Before determining where to file an item, consider these questions.

- How will this information be requested?
- How can I most efficiently locate the information?

Materials must be located quickly, and necessary materials should be removed from a file. It is not always necessary to remove an entire file. Although safely filing materials is

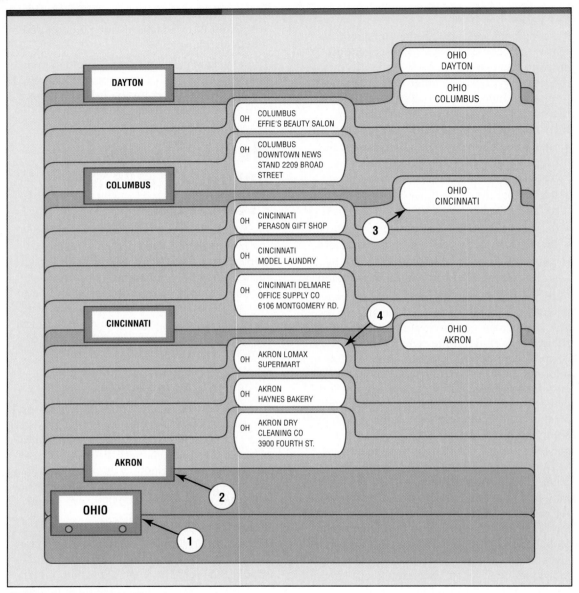

FIGURE 14~6 Geographic File

important, being able to find records in a timely manner is just as important.

Confidentiality

The administrative professional is also responsible for the confidentiality of the supervisor's files. Great care must be exercised to maintain security of highly confidential information. Reasonable protection must also be exercised over less sensitive materials. When working in a highly sensitive area or industry, you often follow a company policy that has been designed specifically for the handling of confidential information.

Safety

The administrative professional is often responsible for the safety of records in the supervisor's workplace. Because many records are irreplaceable, administrative professionals should pay careful attention to security. Many new systems automatically lock when not in use. Safety from fire and water damage must also be considered.

Storage Procedures

When using a manual filing system, certain procedures should be followed before placing a record in the file. These steps include inspecting, indexing, coding, cross-referencing, sorting, and storing.

Inspecting

Incoming records must not be stored until the record has been reviewed and acted upon. Before storing any incoming record, be sure to inspect the record for a release mark. This may be in the form of initials, a stamp, a check mark, the word *file* written on the record, or some other agreed-upon mark. Sometimes records will be placed in the out basket by mistake. If there is no release mark, be sure to check to see if the record is ready to be stored. Copies of outgoing records do not need a release mark since the record has been generated within your organization. Once the original has been signed, the copy can be indexed.

Indexing

Indexing refers to the process of determining the name to be used in storing. This may be the name, the subject, the number, or the geographic location. When indexing incoming letters for alphabetic storage, the letterhead is the most likely name to be used for storage purposes. If the letterhead has no relation to the writer (for example, the letter has been written on hotel stationery or plain paper), use the name or company in the closing lines. When indexing outgoing letters, the company name from the inside address is used as the indexing unit.

In subject storage, indexing means determining the most important subject discussed in the record. If there are two subjects, the record should be filed under one subject and cross-referenced under the other. In geographic storage, the location to be used must be determined. In numeric storage, the name and number to be used must be determined.

Coding

Coding is the process of marking the units of the filing segment (or name) by which the record is to be stored. Coding is important since it saves time in the filing and refiling process. When a document has been removed from the files and must be refiled, the administrative assistant does not need to reread the document if it has been coded. On incoming records, coding is completed before the document is filed. On outgoing records, coding may be done on the record as it is being prepared. The filename assigned to a document is essential in retrieving the record, and it may be used in filing the record as well.

Cross-Referencing

As discussed previously, cross-referencing should be completed when a document may be called for under more than one name. Cross-reference cards or sheets can be purchased from a commercial company, or you can make your own. An example of a cross-reference form is provided in Figure 14-7. Regardless of the storage system used, cross-referencing will help to ensure that records can be found when needed.

Sorting

Sorting is arranging records in the order in which they are to be filed. The records should be sorted first into a few groups and then into the final arrangement. The records may be sorted more than once. For example, items may be arranged into groups of A to C, D to H, I to M, N to S, and T to Z. The last sorting consists of arranging the items in exact alphabetic order. When the last sort is complete, the materials are ready to be filed.

```
┌─────────────────────────────────────────┐
│          CROSS-REFERENCE SHEET           │
│                                          │
│  Name or Subject              File No.   │
│  CUFFEE ROSE                  C–3        │
│                                          │
│  Regarding                    Date       │
│  Bid for pocket calculators   5/4/2005   │
│                                          │
│                                          │
│  SEE                                     │
│  Name or Subject              File No.   │
│  AWB CORPORATION              A–2        │
└─────────────────────────────────────────┘
```

FIGURE 14~7 Cross-Reference Form

Storing

Storing is the process of placing the record in the file folder and then in the file drawer. Rather than filing one record at a time, which is time-consuming, accumulate several records before going to the file drawer. As you are accumulating enough documents to file, you should keep the documents in order at your desk in case someone needs to refer to a record. When filing records, the most recent paper is placed on top. That means that the oldest piece of correspondence is at the back of the folder. The final step in this cycle of the life of a record is disposing of the record when it is no longer needed. You will learn more about disposal in the next section.

Records Retrieval

In all records management systems, whether they are manual, electronic, or image, it is important to be able to retrieve records, retain them for their useful life, and transfer them to other locations to reduce the size of the active files. Manual systems retrieval, retention, and transfer is explained in the following sections. Electronic and image system retrieval, retention, and transfer is discussed in Chapter 15, Records Technology.

If a record is taken from a file, it is necessary to indicate what was taken, who has possession of the record, and when it was removed. It may also be helpful to indicate when the record will be returned. Charge-out procedures using requisition forms and out guides and out folders provide a system for retrieval of records when they are taken from the files.

Requisition Form

A **requisition form** includes a space for identifying the record borrowed, the name and location of the borrower, data about the borrowed record, and the date the record is to be returned to the files. This form may be prepared in duplicate, with one copy kept in a tickler file and the other copy inserted in an out guide or an out folder.

Out Guide and Out Folder

The **out guide** is usually a pressboard or plastic guide with the word *OUT* printed on the tab; it is used to replace a record that has been removed from the files. When an entire folder is taken from the files, papers for a particular originator cannot be filed until the folder has been returned. For continuity in filing, you may choose to use an out folder to take the place of the file that has been borrowed. The out guide or out folder remains in the file until the borrowed record or folder is returned and refiled. Figure 14-8 shows an out guide and an out folder.

Records Retention

As the cost of real estate continues to rise, the need for retention control becomes increasingly important. Filling valuable workplace space with unnecessary documents and file cabinets is not a viable option.

As an administrative professional, you probably will not make decisions about how long important documents should be kept. The legal counsel for a company is generally consulted regarding retention of these types of documents. If the company is large, it may have developed a retention schedule. Figure

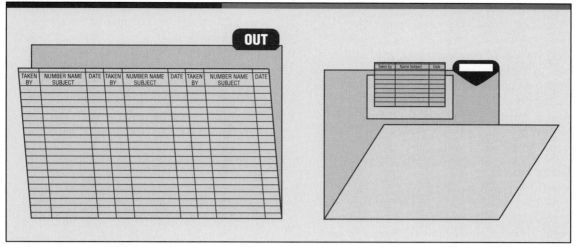

FIGURE 14~8 Out Guide and Out Folder

14-9 shows a portion of a retention schedule. If the company does not have a records retention schedule, the administrative professional should check with his or her supervisor before making any decisions about how documents should be transferred or destroyed.

One useful reference on the retention and legality of records is the *Guide to Record Retention Requirements* published by the National Archives and Records Service. It is available from the Superintendent of Documents, U.S. Government Printing Office, Washington, DC 20402.

Retention and destruction of files have taken on additional importance with the approval in December 1993 of the Revised Rule 26 of the Federal Rules of Civil Procedure. Revised Rule 26 requires organizations to make available all relevant records that must be kept in order to be in compliance with prevailing statutes and regulations. Delay or failure to find information makes an organization vulnerable to financial loss and adverse legal judgments. Disposal becomes important because records kept past legal retention and disposal periods can be a liability.

To understand more about retention control, consider the following categories of records.

RETENTION SCHEDULE

Document	Retention in Years
Accounting	
Payroll (time cards)	3
Expense reports	6
Payroll	8
Corporate Records	
Capital stock and bond records	Indefinitely
Contracts and agreements	Indefinitely
Patents	Indefinitely
Personnel	
Disability and sick benefit records	6
Personnel files (terminated)	6
Withholding tax statements	6

FIGURE 14~9 Retention Schedule

Vital Records

Records that cannot be replaced and should never be destroyed are called **vital records**. These records are essential to the effective, continued operation of an organization and should not be transferred from the active section of the storage area. Some examples of vital records are corporate charters, certain contracts, deeds, and tax returns.

Important Records

Records that are necessary to an orderly continuation of a business and are replaceable only with considerable expenditure of time and money are known as **important records**. Such records should be transferred to inactive storage but should not be destroyed. Examples of important records are financial statements, operating and statistical records, and board minutes.

Useful Records

Useful records are useful for the smooth, effective operation of an organization. Such records are replaceable, but their loss involves delay or inconvenience to the organization. These records should be transferred to inactive files or destroyed after a certain period. Examples include letters, reports, and bank records.

Nonessential Records

Records that have no future value to an organization are considered **nonessential**. Once the purpose for which they were created has been fulfilled, they should be destroyed.

Records Transfer

At some point in the life of a record, you decide to destroy the record, retain it permanently, or transfer it to inactive storage. Two common methods of records transfer are perpetual transfer and periodic transfer.

Perpetual Transfer

With **perpetual transfer**, materials are continuously transferred from the active to the inactive files. The advantage of this method is that all files are kept current, since any inactive material is immediately transferred to storage. The perpetual transfer method works well in organizations where jobs are completed by units. For example, when a lawyer finishes a case, the file is complete and probably will not need to be referred to often. Therefore, it can be transferred to inactive files.

When distinguishing between active and inactive records, the following categories should be used:

- **Active records** are used three or more times a month and should be kept in an accessible area.
- **Inactive records** are used less than 15 times a year and should be stored in less accessible areas than active records.
- **Archive records** have historical value to an organization and should be preserved permanently.

Periodic Transfer

With **periodic transfer**, active records are transferred to inactive status at the end of a stated period. For example, you may transfer records that are over six months old to the inactive file and maintain records that are less than six months old in the active file. Every six months you follow this procedure. This method of transfer works well and is used by most businesses.

Records Disposal

Records that are no longer of any use should be destroyed. If the material is not confidential, the document can be disposed of by simply dropping it in a basket, with the paper being recycled. However, when the information is confidential, the document should be destroyed by shredding. Shredders that cut the paper into confettilike strips are common in the workplace. The shredded paper can then be recycled.

Misplaced and Lost Records

Although you may be very careful in your filing, papers occasionally do get misplaced and lost. When they do, here are some suggestions about how to handle a lost document.

- Look in the folder immediately in front of and immediately behind the correct folder.
- Look between folders.
- Look in the GENERAL folder.
- Check to see if the paper slipped to the bottom of the file drawer.
- Look through the entire correct folder, since a record may be placed out of chronological sequence.

- Look for the second, third, or succeeding unit rather than for the key unit.
- Check for misfiling due to misread letters; for example, C for G, K for H, and so on.
- Check for alternative spellings of words; for example, McDonald or MacDonald.
- Check for the transposition of numbers.
- Look in a related subject file.
- Look in the sorter.
- Look on your desk and on your employer's desk.

If you are unable to find the record, try to reconstruct as much of it as you can by asking your employer about the contents and rekeying the information. Key the words *Replacing Lost Record* at the top of the record, and store it in its correct place within the file.

Basic Supplies and Equipment

Basic manual filing supplies and equipment include file folders, suspension folders, file guides, labels, and file cabinets.

File Folders

A file folder is generally a manila folder that holds $8\frac{1}{2}'' \times 11''$ or $8\frac{1}{2}'' \times 14''$ paper. Other colors besides manila are available, including blue, red, yellow, and brown. The filing designation for the correspondence placed in the folder is keyed on a label that is then affixed to the tab of the folder. Folders are made with tabs of various widths, called cuts. The cuts are straight cut, one-half cut, one-third cut, and one-fifth cut.

Suspension Folders

In addition to standard file folders, you may purchase suspension folders (hanging folders), which have attached metal rods that allow them to hang on the sides of the file drawer. Plastic tabs and insertable labels are used with the folders. These tabs and labels can be

© GETTY IMAGES/PHOTODISC

File folders are available in a variety of colors and cuts.

placed in any position, using the precut on the folder.

File Guides

A file guide is usually made of heavy pressboard and is used to separate the file drawer into various sections. Hollow tabs on the top of the guide provide for a name, number, or letter to identify the section of the file drawer.

File Folder Labels

File folder labels can be purchased in various configurations, including continuous folded strips, separate strips, rolls in boxes, and pressure-sensitive adhesive labels. Different colored labels can speed up the process of filing and finding records and can eliminate much misfiling. It is very easy to spot a colored label that has been misfiled, since that color stands out from the other colors that surround it.

Colored labels can be used to:

- Designate a particular subject (for example, green labels designate budget items and blue labels designate personnel items)
- Indicate geographic divisions of the country
- Designate particular sections of the file

When keying labels for files, consistency should be observed. Suggestions for preparing labels are as follows:

- Key label captions in all capital letters with no punctuation.
- Begin the caption close to the left edge of the label.
- Key the name on the label in correct indexing order.
- Use the same style of labels on all folders. For example, if you decide to use labels with colored strips, be consistent; if you decide to use colored labels, be consistent.
- For lateral file cabinets, key wraparound side tab labels above and below the color bar separator so the information is readable from both sides.

Equipment

Vertical files are the conventional storage cabinet. These files are available in one- to five-drawer sizes. They are also available in sizes to accommodate cards and letter-size records.

Lateral files are similar to vertical files except the drawer rolls out sideways, exposing the entire contents of the file drawer at once. In addition, less aisle space is needed for a lateral file than a vertical file because the drawers extend sideways.

Movable-aisle systems consist of modular units of open-shelf files mounted on tracks on the floor. Files are placed directly against each other. Wheels or rails permit the individual units to be moved apart for access. Movable systems can be manual, mechanical, or electrical. Manual systems are small, with two to four carriages. They require no power; the user merely pushes the files apart. Mechanical systems operate by turning a crank. Electrical systems move carriages with motors.

Lateral file drawers roll out sideways.

THE HON COMPANY

Because movable systems take up less space than standard files, they are used more frequently. Features that provide safety for the file contents as well as the people who work with the files are of top priority for companies using the system. The most basic protection device is a key-operated carriage lock that prevents the system from rolling on the rails. Another safety device is a strip that runs the length of the file cabinet at floor level. Pressure of more than a few ounces stops cabinet movement. Still another safety device is an infrared photoelectric beam. If a person or an object breaks the beam, the system stops movement. When the person or object is no longer breaking the beam, the system resets itself. To ensure safety of materials, users swipe a badge through a card reader, allowing entrance to the system, or users enter a password code. Some systems can be fitted with locking doors. ■

SUMMARY

To reinforce what you have learned in this chapter, study this summary.

- Records management is the systematic control of records from creation to final disposition.
- The Association for Information Management Professionals International (ARMA) has developed alphabetic indexing rules designed to help the administrative professional index records for filing.
- The types of storage systems are alphabetic, subject, numeric, and geographic. The alphabetic system is the most commonly used method of storing materials.
- Variations on the numeric storage system include chronologic, terminal digit, and alphanumeric storage.
- When designing storage systems, it is important to consider findability, confidentiality, and safety.
- Storage procedures include inspecting, indexing, coding, cross-referencing, sorting, and storing.
- Out guides and out folders allow for the retrieval of records taken from the files.
- Records retention involves deciding how long records should be kept. In the retaining and storing of records, consideration should be given to the classification of records. These classifications include vital records, important records, useful records, and nonessential records.
- Records are transferred to storage using perpetual or periodic transfer methods.
- Confidential records should be disposed of through shredding.
- When records are lost or misplaced, a consistent process should be used to find them. This process includes looking in the folder immediately in front of and immediately behind the correct folder, checking for misfiling due to misread letters, and checking for alternative spellings of words.
- Basic manual filing supplies and equipment include file folders, suspension folders, file guides, labels, and file cabinets.

FIND THE PROBLEM

Veronica Forrest is a clerk in the medical records department at a large hospital. Solomon Keyes, a patient services advocate, routinely requests patient files so he can update billing information for patients and insurance companies as new tests and procedures are completed. Since Veronica and Solomon have been working together for several years, they have become somewhat informal in their handling of patient records. Recently some patient files have come up missing. Veronica and Solomon have come under scrutiny because of a lack of a paper trail involving files that have been requested, checked out, and returned. While each of them knows he or she is not responsible for the missing files, they are facing serious questions from their department managers. What could they have done differently?

PROFESSIONAL POINTERS

As an administrative professional, you may have the opportunity to be involved in recommending, implementing, or expanding a records management system. If so, keep these pointers in mind.

- Define the needs of the organization—department, division, or entire company. Know the types of records used, how long they are to be retained, who can have access, and the capacity needed for storage.
- Conduct research and seek information. Based on your identified needs, collect recommendations from representatives of records supplies and systems firms. Solicit input on systems used in other organizations similar to yours.
- Ensure that everyone has adequate training on the system that is chosen.
- Provide a list of the filing procedures/rules as a reference source for all individuals who have access to the files.
- Implement a method for ongoing evaluation of the records management system. Efficiency and cost effectiveness are vital to the success of the system and the business.

REINFORCEMENT ITEMS

1. Describe the record life cycle.
2. Explain how Indexing Rule 4 (Single Letters and Abbreviations) affects the indexing of personal and business names.
3. List the advantages and disadvantages of the alphabetic and numeric storage systems.
4. Explain the factors that must be considered when designing storage systems.

CRITICAL-THINKING ACTIVITY

Dawon Abrego's work space is filled with stacks of papers. He has three neatly piled stacks on his desk and at least eight stacks on the floor. Although he has two vertical filing cabinets, it appears most of the documents do not make it from the stacks to the cabinet. Although many of Dawon's coworkers tease him about his unique filing system, they are impressed that he can locate information in a short period of time. In fact, Dawon's system seems to work quite well for him. He has never had a problem locating information in a timely manner.

Two weeks ago Dawon requested an extended leave from work to take care of personal matters. In his absence, several projects were reassigned to other employees. The majority of these projects could not progress because the employees were unable to locate the necessary information in Dawon's stacks. One employee contacted Dawon, but Dawon could not guide him in locating the information. Although Dawon's supervisor did not approve of his filing methods, it was never an issue because Dawon was able to locate information in a timely manner. Now, however, the supervisor can see how Dawon's method has an impact on the workplace. Dawon will not be back in the office for at least three months. How can the supervisor handle this situation so the work gets done? What suggestions could you make to the supervisor to prevent this type of problem from happening again?

VOCABULARY REVIEW

Complete the Vocabulary Review for Chapter 14 given on page 105 of the *Applications Workbook*.

ENGLISH AND WORD USAGE DRILL

Complete the English and Word Usage Drill for Chapter 14 listed on page 106 of the *Applications Workbook*.

WORKPLACE APPLICATIONS

A14-1 (Goal 1)

Using the Internet, locate two sites that discuss professional records management procedures. Pay careful attention to information and procedures relating to records retention policies, records transfer policies, and records disposal issues. Write a short report on your findings. Submit the completed report to your instructor.

A14-2 (Goals 2 and 3)

In your *Applications Workbook* on page 107 is a list of client names. Correspondence from these clients is to be placed in an alphabetic file. Prepare 3″ × 5″ cards for the card file by listing the clients' names in indexing order. Arrange the cards in alphabetic order. Submit the cards to your instructor.

A14-3 (Goals 2 and 3)

In your *Applications Workbook* on page 108 is a list of client names. Correspondence from these clients is to be placed in a numeric file. Assign numbers to the clients, beginning with 100 for the first name on the list. After assigning the numbers, prepare 3″ × 5″ cards for the card file by listing the clients' names in indexing order and placing the appropriate number on each card. Arrange the cards in alphabetic order. Submit the cards to your instructor.

A14-4 (Goal 2)

The Student CD contains several letters and memorandums that you are to place in a subject file. The files are SCDA14-4a, SCDA14-4b, SCDA14-4c, SCDA14-4d, SCDA14-4e, and SCDA14-4f. Print a copy of each document. Index, code, and sort the correspondence in preparation for filing.

Cross-reference the letter to M. Holms, using the cross-reference form provided on page 109 of your *Applications Workbook*. Turn in the coded documents and cross-reference sheet to your instructor.

A14-5 (Goal 4)

Kurt Rupprecht has decided that your department needs to expand its filing system. Kurt has asked that you use the Internet to research two office supply companies for information on filing supplies and equipment. Kurt anticipates the following needs:

- An additional file cabinet. Research vertical and lateral file cabinets. The cabinets will hold confidential records and need to be secure.
- Suspension (hanging) folders. You need at least 500 hanging folders, tabs, and insertable labels. The current folders use third-cut tabs.
- File folders. You need at least 1,500 colored file folders. The current system includes an assortment of primary colors with third-cut tabs.

Kurt has also asked that you include other new, innovative supplies that are necessary for this system. Prepare a proposal to purchase these items from each of the two supply companies you researched. Make a recommendation as to which company you would choose and why. Submit the completed proposal to your instructor.

A14-6 (Goals 1, 3, and 4)

Work with two or three classmates. Select a local hospital, clinic, law office, insurance company, or other organization in your area. Contact the organization and make an appointment with the individual responsible for records management. Use the information presented in this chapter to develop questions about types of filing systems, equipment, policies, and so on, that you can ask during the interview. Informally interview the individual about the records management practices and procedures he or she follows. Submit your list of questions to your instructor. In addition, prepare an outline of this information to use when making a short oral presentation to the class.

ASSESSMENT OF CHAPTER GOALS

Did you successfully complete the chapter goals? Evaluate yourself by filling out the form on page 110 of the *Applications Workbook*.

chapter 15

Records Technology

LEARNING GOALS

1. Describe the information management systems available.

2. Explain microimage system elements and storage methods.

3. Describe the integration of electronic and microimage systems.

The paperless workplace, touted by early computer manufacturers and business consultants, has proven to be a myth. In truth, computing technology has increased the ability to manipulate so much data, that organizations are actually using more paper than at any other time in history. Businesses are producing reports like never before; email and IM enable employees to run an idea by several coworkers with the push of a button; the Internet allows people to conduct research quickly and efficiently and to share their findings with anyone who is interested. Since computer applications allow an individual to print a document easily, thousands of reams of printed materials are produced daily in business operations.

What is a company to do with all this documentation? As you learned in the previous chapter, several processes and procedures are available to file documents manually. Some companies pay thousands of dollars a month to independent document storage companies. These storage companies promise to provide safe storage of an organization's information. While this can be an effective option, these records may not be as safe as they would be if the organization itself were watching over them. Also, a lengthy turnaround time may be needed to retrieve necessary documents, including submitting a request for a document or file, having the file pulled from storage, and then having it delivered to the workplace (where it may be copied only to be filed away again in a different area).

Companies still produce roughly 25,000 conventional metal file cabinets a week in the United States,[1] and 90 percent of the information shared by organizations today is still printed, creating trillions of paper documents annually.[2] Businesses are producing far more information than can be stuffed into file cabinets or that can be affordably stored in warehouse facilities. Electronic document management has become the immediate future for business document storage. In an increasing number of companies, computers serve

---

[1]Gary Flood, "Flood Warning," *Information World Review*, issue 175, January 2002, p. 32.

[2]Gene Marcial, "Spinning Paper Into Gold at Iron Mountain" *Business Week Online*, September 4, 2001.

as electronic file cabinets that store digitized images of documents that can be retrieved and displayed instantly on a computer screen.

Since you will most likely be using electronic or microimage technology in storing records, you should have some knowledge of the technologies available. Electronic storage systems, microimage systems, and future trends in electronic records management are presented in this chapter.

Information Management Systems

An **information management system** is any records management system where records are input and filed electronically. This type of system includes:

- Inputting data.
- Processing the data through integration with other data, including modifying, editing, deleting, and sorting the data.
- Outputting the data.
- Storing and retrieving the data.

Information in an automated system is entered into the system, processed, stored, and retrieved differently than with a manual system. For example, information in an automated system is entered into the system through a personal computer. This information may be keyed, scanned, or input via voice recognition. Once the information is entered, it is available to be processed. The processing may include performing arithmetic computations, sorting alphabetic lists, sorting numbers, and so on. Output may be stored on computer tape, hard drives, CDs, or DVDs or as microimages on microfilm or microfiche. (Microimage technology is discussed later in this chapter.) A computer terminal can access the information that has been created, manipulated, and stored. See Figure 15-1 for an example.

Electronic Records Management Systems

The first step in understanding electronic records management is to recognize that records management is not the same as document management. A **record** may be any form of information, including a drawing, a sound file, a video clip, or a CD; therefore, records may or may not be a document. Businesses often believe that document management software can handle all their electronic filing and retrieval needs, only to find out that is not the case. The terms electronic records management systems (ERMS) and electronic document management systems (EDMS) are used in this chapter to differentiate the two approaches.

An **electronic records management system (ERMS)** is a mechanism for storing business records through electronic means. This type of system provides the user with the ability to input data; process data by merging with other data; and edit, sort, and delete data. ERMS also provides the user with the ability to output, store, and retrieve this data through simple computer applications.

In today's business climate, ERMS needs to be seriously considered and researched. These systems should conform to legislative requirements regarding the types of information that need to be maintained and easily retrieved. This includes information about employees, business practices, sales, research and development, and taxes. Ideally, anything that can be useful in the event of unforeseen legal action against a company should be saved. Since this can be an inordinate amount of information, electronic records management can be the ideal solution.

An example of an automated ERMS would be the student files at your university. Computer records regarding admissions, financial aid, course schedules, and grades are filed within the electronic records system and are available to many users at one time via student ID number. These records can be manipulated in large groups to prepare course rosters, to provide listings of students who live in a specific state, and to calculate the number of students that come from a specific county within a state or from a specific city within a county.

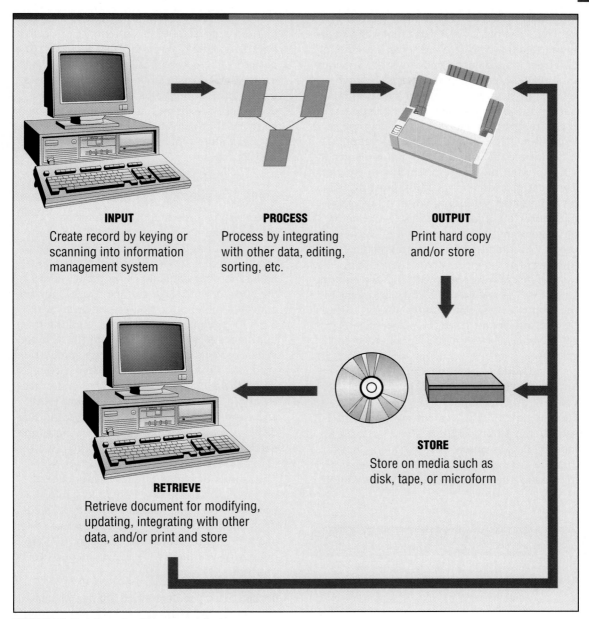

INPUT
Create record by keying or scanning into information management system

PROCESS
Process by integrating with other data, editing, sorting, etc.

OUTPUT
Print hard copy and/or store

STORE
Store on media such as disk, tape, or microform

RETRIEVE
Retrieve document for modifying, updating, integrating with other data, and/or print and store

FIGURE 15~1 Information Management Systems

Electronic Database Systems

An essential task of the administrative professional is to create or follow a plan of active records management. In other words, you must understand the steps of indexing, coding, and storing with an electronic system.

Just as in a paper system, if you do not know where an item is filed, you cannot retrieve it. However, when you use appropriate records management procedures, electronic systems allow you to store and retrieve information almost instantly.

A **database** is a collection of records organized in related files. A **database management system** (also referred to as a relational database management system) is the software that allows a user to perform a variety of records management functions. With a database management system, the user can enter, organize, process, index, sort, select, link related files, store, and retrieve information.

With a database, the information is generally stored in the order in which it is entered. The next record is assigned the next available record number. **Indexing** sorts the records and stores the information based on one or more key fields. The **primary key**, or **keyword**, is a unique record identifier chosen by the user. For example, if you are working in a human resources department and are entering employee information, the keyword might be the employee's social security number. Since no two individuals have the same social security number, it is a unique identifier for each employee.

In addition to entering employee names and social security numbers into a database, you will probably enter other information, such as date of employment, age, address, salary, and so on. With database software, individuals can **query** (ask questions in a format the database understands) to display the information in a variety of ways. For example,

you might query for employees who are making less than $50,000 or for employees who have been employed for at least 15 years. The design of the database allows the user to ask for information efficiently and retrieve it in a useful format. Integrated packages include database, spreadsheet, and word processing software that work together so users can easily move stored information from one application to another.

Electronic Storage Systems

Electronic records management systems and electronic database systems are convenient ways of storing and accessing information in the workplace. However, these systems are limited in their capabilities by the amount of memory, or electronic storage space, they are allocated within a computer system or within a personal computer. At some point, information needs to be withdrawn from the system. When projects are finished, when students graduate, or when employees leave a company, their related records are no longer necessary in an easily accessible system. ERMS and database software can use optical (laser) disks as the storage medium. If you have no need to edit or modify the information, you can store the information on a CD-ROM. Thousands of pages of data can be stored on these types of disks. In addition, information stored on this media cannot be erased or manipulated. A CD is not susceptible to changes in temperature or exposure to computer viruses, and its life expectancy is over 100 years.

Decentralized and Centralized Storage Systems

Decentralized storage refers to information stored by individual computer users on their own disks or tapes. A **centralized storage** system is one in which computers are linked together through a network and the information can be retrieved by multiple users. Typically, the information stored in centralized storage systems cannot be accessed unless the user uses a password or an access code.

Database software allows the user to perform a variety of records management functions.

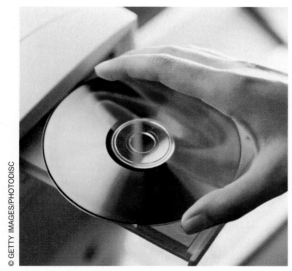

© GETTY IMAGES/PHOTODISC

Individuals often use decentralized systems to store their documents.

Most businesses use a combination of centralized and decentralized systems. For example, as an administrative professional, you generally store the documents you key on a CD or DVD. These documents may be reports, spreadsheets, letters, and so on; other users typically do not need to access this information for use in documents or reports. This is an example of a decentralized storage system.

Personnel information is an example of information stored in a centralized system. This information may need to be accessed by human resources for items such as payroll and benefits and by department managers for information such as vacation time and sick leave.

Storage and Retrieval

When setting up a decentralized electronic filing system, you need to make two decisions. You must determine how you will file the CDs or DVDs, and you must decide on the naming conventions and standards you will use to store these records. Just like a manual filing system, when storing computer-generated information you can create and name folders. Folders can contain subfolders, which allow you to subdivide your information. When

creating folders and naming documents, you can use an alphabetic, subject, numeric, or geographic method. There are a variety of options to consider when naming and storing information. The most important concept is to be consistent. Make sure you organize your computerized folders and documents using the same procedure.

If you are using a centralized electronic system, you must follow the standards within the system. A centralized system allows you to store information for your private use only, as well as to make the information available to everyone on the network. However, some network systems allow only select users to access specific areas within the network. For example, at your university, only certain individuals have access to your grade reports; other employees have access only to financial aid information.

This electronic storage can be compared to file cabinets, drawers, and folders. You create drawers (folders) within the cabinet and smaller sections (additional folders) within the drawers. Accurate indexing is key to the success of an electronic filing system. And as electronic filing incorporates computer-generated documents such as email, word processing files, presentation slides, and electronic spreadsheets, everyone in an organization must learn to identify and tag their documents consistently so the documents can be accurately indexed and retrieved by a variety of users.

Safety and Security

Records must be protected from physical hazards as well as from unauthorized access. Suggestions for safely storing electronic information include the following:

- Store electronic media at room temperature and out of direct sunlight.
- Copy electronic files as a backup system; store the backup copies in a fireproof cabinet or safe.
- Store electronic files at an off-site location. When doing so, you may want to use barcode technology; for example, each tape or

CD case has a barcode label affixed to it so the files stored within can be quickly identified and retrieved.

- Protect against viruses. Several suggestions for protecting against viruses were presented in Chapter 11; you may consider reviewing those recommendations now.

- Keep tapes and CDs stored in their cases when they are not in use. Keep the underside of the CD wiped clean of dust, dirt, and fingerprints.

- If you want to ensure that the files on your disk or tape are not erased, use the write-protect feature. If you are storing information on a CD, use a CD-R instead of a CD-RW.

Security is another important issue when storing electronic documents. Security tips include these:

- Protect the information stored on a tape or CD from unauthorized use by assigning passwords to employees. Only individuals with the appropriate passwords can retrieve information.

- Develop a security policy that ensures safe and reliable operation of the records system.

Electronic files may be stored at an off-site location.

© CORBIS

For example, everyone should log off the system before leaving his or her desk.

- When an employee leaves a company, immediately eliminate his or her password from the system so the person has no access to the data on the system.

Electronic Document Management Systems

An **electronic document management system (EDMS)** is a computer-based system that allows for retrieval of specific documents from an electronic filing system. These systems provide one user or many users with easy computer access to documents that would have been tucked away in a series of file cabinets (or possibly in a long-term storage facility). An electronic document management system typically incorporates one or more key technology components, including document imaging or archiving, workflow software, and computer-output-to-laser-disk (COLD) storage. Therefore, EDMS is the overall process of converting paper documentation into digital information that can be retrieved, displayed, or forwarded to another employee at a computer terminal within a computer network.

As discussed previously in this chapter, one solution for organizing document information was the development of the electronic database. Although the database continues to be an effective business tool, companies realize they need a more flexible system for their records. Companies need to be able to store computer-generated information such as memos, faxes, emails, billings, and sound files. This type of information is sometimes referred to as "unstructured data" since it cannot be reduced to fields and records that are then stored in a traditional relational database. The problem of managing unstructured information led to the development of document management software.

Document Management Software

Document management software can be used to manage electronic, digital, microimage, and paper storage systems. Features of a document management software system include the ability to:

- Code and log in documents.
- Print file labels.
- Track active files, inactive files, vital records, and off-premise storage.
- Provide an inventory of all records within a system or within a specific grouping.
- Follow up on overdue files.
- Track nonpaper documents such as disks, CDs, and microforms.
- Generate activity reports by department and by user.
- Generate and help follow records retention and disposal guidelines.

The escalating cost of maintaining files, mismanaging, and misfiling (with the average cost of retrieving a misfiled document being about $200) has led to increased use of document management software. As these systems become easier to use and the types of storage media continue to change, document management systems will become increasingly important within the business environment. Recent developments in software are allowing records that are stored on a variety of media to work together in the accessing of information.

Digital Archiving

Digital archiving is the practice of converting paper documents to digital format so the data can be stored on a variety of media and then retrieved electronically. This method is commonly referred to as **document imaging**. Using specialized scanning equipment and software, information is transferred to optical media. A LAN-based document system provides all users on the network instant access to documents through their desktop computers. Instead of searching through file cabinets and paper file folders, employees can access an index or a specific filename directly on their personal computer. They no longer need to find a document, copy it, and return it to the filing system. This type of system saves valuable time as employees can view, print,

electronically forward (email), or fax a document to another user without leaving their desk.

The components of a digital archiving system include a computer, a scanner, a storage medium or storage device, a printer, and application software. Optical disks using **WORM** (write once, read many) **technology** prevent any alteration to the original document once it is scanned into the system. With document imaging, electronic sticky notes or highlighted areas can be attached to the imaged document. These notes or highlighted areas do not allow a change to the original document content. This is especially important in today's business environment where record archiving can be instrumental if records are called upon in the event of legal action against a company. The original unaltered documents can be provided when requested and can include a record of when they were scanned, when they were viewed, and what notes were attached regarding action taken with these documents.

Two methods of converting information to digital images exist. The first scans the paper document and replicates the document in digital format. After documents have been scanned, they are annotated with identifying information such as name, date, and account numbers, as mentioned above. Documents can then be referenced and retrieved using computer-based indexing and search criteria. The images can be viewed using a variety of file-viewing software.

A second method of converting documents to digital images uses **optical character recognition** (OCR) to capture data from scanned documents. This method scans documents and converts the content into computer-readable format (text) using specialized software. The text files can then be indexed, similar to indexing imaged files, and located using a contents search. The text approach uses less storage space than the imaging filing system.

Some organizations use a combination approach—filing some documents as images

SOUTH-WESTERN/THOMSON LEARNING

Digital archiving can be used to change paper documents to digital information.

and others as text documents. Regardless of the approach used, document image processing technology is used for capturing document images and storing them for future retrieval and distribution. The image and the text-conversion techniques allow you to distribute documents electronically, annotate them, and otherwise treat them as computer files, without changing the content of the original.

Currently in development are systems that can capture email and instant messages that originated from personal computers or workstations and were sent through company networks or email systems. While there are continuing battles as to the legality of this information gathering, legal outcomes against a business can be determined when this information is preserved in a document management system and can be presented in verified original format.

Storage Methods

Record storage methods were discussed in detail in the chapter on computer hardware. Storage media that were once reserved for large businesses are now available to the public at very reasonable costs. Storage media still consist of computer disks and computer tape, but the more popular options include CDs and DVDs. Both of these laser disc storage media are available in formats that allow information to be recorded once, but read many times. This technology is especially effective for archival preservation of information and for original documentation that should not be altered either in error or on purpose. Other media are available in rewritable format. These media can be used repeatedly for saving changes to a document or to information in a spreadsheet or database.

Advantages of Document Management Systems

Changing from traditional paper filing systems to electronic document management systems provides an organization with many opportunities for cost savings and increased productivity.

- Electronically filed documents decrease the amount of necessary filing space. With this increased space, a company can reallocate traditional filing space for other uses.

- Organizations can increase productivity of employees by eliminating or reducing the amount of time employees spend filing, retrieving, and tracking paper documents and records.

- Increased retrieval speed is also a major benefit. In addition to improved customer relations, increased access speed helps cut costs by reducing the need for additional staffing to handle increased volume for seasonal surges.

- Electronically filed documents do not need to be removed from their filing location, which decreases or eliminates the possibility of missing documents and records.

- With multiple indexes, documents residing anywhere within a system can be easily found by users. Multiple users can also access electronically filed documents concurrently, keeping projects moving and increasing overall company productivity.

Computer-Output-to-Laser-Disc (COLD) Systems

Many organizations are moving toward COLD systems to store information that was historically stored on microfiche, on paper, or on mainframe computers. Although COLD originally stood for *Computer Output to Laser Disc*, today COLD is defined more by the process it represents rather than the actual storage media used.

Storage Process

COLD technology takes report files and rewrites them onto magnetic or optical disks in a special format, which can be retrieved and redisplayed to a variety of system users. As the data are "read" into the system, the associated software builds an index by extracting information from the reports. COLD technology information is copied to a storage media, but it remains accessible to authorized users on a system. This gives users instant access to information. COLD technology brings society closer to the "paperless office" ideal, as the printing, copying, and filing requirements that other systems, including many microimage systems, still require to a certain degree.

Storage Methods

Although original COLD technology stored information on laser discs, updates to the technology allow the user to store information using a variety of formats, including networks, CDs, optical discs, DVDs, or the Internet. The CD or CD-R has become a popular storage solution for COLD data. As mentioned before, CD-R media are an established standard, are inexpensive, and offer rapid retrieval. This is also true of DVD and DVD-R. While DVDs are gaining a following, CD is the current leader in storage media due to the fact that international standards for DVD specifications have not been established.

Advantages of COLD Technology

COLD technology provides users with a variety of advantages over the traditional COM system by:

- Providing instant access to information and eliminating the cumbersome and time-consuming tasks associated with microform retrieval.

- Eliminating all microfilm costs associated with film production, distribution, and retrieval.

- Providing instant access in branch offices or remote sites to current COLD data through network storage instead of duplicating and distributing microfilm reports.

- Providing increased storage capacity. CD and DVD storage capabilities and compression

© CORBIS

COLD technology can be stored on CDs, DVDs, optical discs, or the Internet.

software enable increased storage of documents which allows users to retrieve information efficiently versus searching through several indexes of microimage records.

- Controlling confidentiality of information through normal network system security instead of the physical security necessary for paper and microform records.

Microimage Systems

Electronic records management systems greatly reduce the amount of space required to maintain records and provide for almost instantaneous retrieval of records. However, in some instances, it is more cost-effective to store records in other ways, regardless of the previously mentioned features and benefits.

Consider the following example. Banks need to retain copies of canceled checks. Personnel departments need to retain copies of employment information. Schools need to retain copies of grade reports. Government agencies need to retain birth certificates. Libraries and archives need to retain historical information. Although all of this information could be maintained within document imaging systems, these types of records are not accessed as regularly as most business documentation; therefore, a microimage system provides a more cost-effective approach to these records retention needs.

Microimage Records Storage

Microform is a blanket term used to describe microimage storage media and the related technology. However, two major forms of microimage records storage are in use today: microfilm and microfiche. Both are explained in the following section.

Microfilm

Microfilm is a roll containing a series of frames or images much like a movie film. Each individual record is photographed and reduced to fit the frames of the film. The microfilm reader magnifies these images on a lighted screen as the film is passed through it.

Microfilm is stored on reels or in cartridges, cassettes, or jackets. Reels are desirable for storing and for viewing large volumes of records that do not change. The microfilm itself must be threaded, or fed, into a machine that works in a manner similar to a movie projector. As the reels turn, the film is fed through the reader. Newspapers maintained in a library are ideally suited to storage on reels so a user can roll through the pages quickly, disregarding nonessential materials. Older archived business records might also be stored on microfilm.

Microfilm on cartridges and cassettes requires no threading into a machine and, therefore, is somewhat easier to use. Still another method of storing microfilm is cutting it into strips and placing it into a film "jacket" to protect the individual strips. The jacket storage method allows portions of the file to

EYECOM 9000 READER/PRINTER

Microfilm records are used to store and view large volumes of records that do not change.

be updated easily, since a strip of film can be removed and replaced with a new strip.

Microfiche

Microfiche is a sheet of film containing a series of images arranged in a grid pattern. The word *microfiche* is usually shortened to *fiche* (pronounced "feesh"). Fiche permits direct access to any record without having to advance a roll of film to the desired location within the record. **Ultrafiche** is a variation of microfiche. The standard size microfiche contains 98 frames or images, whereas one ultrafiche can store thousands of images.

Microimage System Elements

In order to produce and use microimage storage media, it is necessary to have a microimage system that encompasses the following phases:

- Converting the records to film
- Processing and duplicating the film
- Displaying and reproducing the film

Converting to Film

Although some companies photograph records in-house, many hire service bureaus or decentralized copy centers to assist in the conversion of documents to microform. Even if your organization outsources this process, as an administrative professional, you may have the responsibility of getting the documents ready for filming. All paper clips and staples must be removed from the records. Attachments to records, such as routing slips and envelopes, should also be removed. Records should then be batched and placed in sequential order. Once this has been done, the records are ready to be "filmed" and are sent on to the processing stage.

Processing

After the material has been filmed, the film must be processed. Again, many organizations use an outside company for this procedure. However, inexpensive processors are available if a company decides to complete the processing in-house.

Duplicating

Sometimes more than one copy of a microimage is required. For example, a bank with several branches may want each branch to have access to the same records. Alternatively, for safety and security reasons, a company may decide to have records stored in two separate places. As an administrative professional, you are not involved in the actual duplication of these records; however, you may be involved in researching, comparing, and contrasting companies that can do this work for you.

Displaying and Reproducing

To read a microimage document, you must first place it in a projector, called a "reader" or a "viewer." A reader displays the microimage in an enlarged form on a screen so it is readable. The typical reader is a desktop unit designed to accept microfiche or microfilm. Additionally, multimedia readers are available, designed to accept two or more different types of microimaged records. Readers

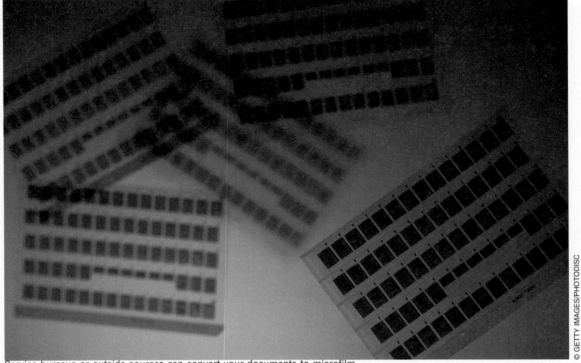

Service bureaus or outside sources can convert your documents to microfilm.

© GETTY IMAGES/PHOTODISC

are also available in a variety of magnifications determined by the reduction ratio of the original microimage and determined by the size of the viewing screen. Some readers have interchangeable lenses to address the different-sized reductions.

Portable readers are lighter in weight and less expensive than desktop readers. An executive on the road can purchase lap readers for use in cars or at outside job locations. If a person often needs a copy of a microimage record, a portable reader may not be the correct choice, but a reader-printer unit would be. With the push of a button, the reader-printer produces a paper copy of the record that is simultaneously being projected on the reader. Electronic repair businesses rely heavily on microimaged schematics and repair manuals. Since these diagrams must be referred to often, being able to print a copy and have it at the repair site can be invaluable.

Storing

Various storage containers are available for each type of microform. These storage containers include trays, cabinets, carousel units, and rotating desktop stands.

Legal Issues

The Uniform Photographic Copies of Business and Public Records as Evidence Act of 1951 allows microforms of certain business documents to be admitted as evidence in courts of law. Federal and state agencies often have their own regulations concerning the substitution of microimaged documents for actual hard copies of documents. If a company plans to duplicate and store records with microimage technology, federal and state regulations must be reviewed to determine whether these microimaged documents can be used as evidence if they are needed during a legal proceeding.

Evaluation

When evaluating whether to implement a microimage records management system, the following points should be considered:

- The cost of the system and the necessary supplies
- The availability of in-house systems, including the added personnel costs
- Costs of having a service bureau film the documents, compared to having the processing done in-house
- Reputation of service bureaus
- Turnaround time on average processing jobs
- Storage costs of filmed documents on-site versus off-site storage and space considerations
- Need for duplicate films
- What records can and cannot be legally filmed

Integration of Electronic and Microimage Systems

Computer and micrographics technologies have come together in the form of computer-output microfilm (COM), computer-input microfilm (CIM), and computer-aided retrieval (CAR). This combination of micrographics and computer technology has made the storage and retrieval of microforms a speedy, inexpensive, and efficient records management option.

Computer-Output Microfilm (COM)

One of the big problems of processing data by computer is the enormous number of paper printouts that are created. When these papers are ready for storage, the space requirements can be excessive and expensive. One result of using the computer in conjunction with microimage records technology is **computer-output microfilm (COM)**. With COM, no paper documents are produced; instead, documents are produced on microforms, which may be microfiche or microfilm.

Here is how the COM process works. Information from the computer is sent directly to microfilm (nothing is printed on paper). Images are created on COM in one of the following ways:

- By displaying the image on a video display screen, which the COM camera photographs
- With a laser, which writes on the film like a laser copier
- With an electron beam, which creates dots that make up the image
- With LEDs (light emitting diodes) and a fiber-optic bundle, which produce the image photographed by the COM camera

Computer-Input Microfilm (CIM)

Computer-input microfilm (CIM) is COM in reverse. Plain language data on microfilm are converted into computer-readable data for use by a computer system. A CIM device converts information into a form the computer can read. Often COM and CIM come together in one system to exchange input and output between the computer and the microimage system.

Computer-Aided Retrieval (CAR)

Computer-aided retrieval (CAR) systems speed up the retrieval of documents on microfilm through use of a computer. They are designed to solve two common problems encountered in manual records management systems—high cost and difficulty of finding documents that have been misfiled. Drawing on a combination of micrographics and computer technology, CAR can result in more effective and economical approaches to document storage and retrieval. With CAR, access to randomly filed documents on microforms is facilitated by the use of the computer.

An example of CAR is as follows. Documents are indexed into a computer by the entry of such data as the date, author, and subject. As data are transmitted to the computer, software establishes and/or updates a series of indexes maintained online with a disk drive. When retrieving documents, the user can request all documents written on a particular date, by a particular person, or about a particular subject. The user has the option of narrowing, broadening, or otherwise changing the search. The outcome is the identification of one or more microfilm addresses containing the desired documents. (This entire process is very similar to an online search using an Internet search engine; however, in this instance, the search is limited to information cataloged on the microforms.) Once the search is complete, the reel, cartridge, or cassette that was identified in the search is used to locate the requested information.

As an added feature in the CAR process, bar coding is now being used. Bar coding consists of placing an identifying unit (such as a name, an identification number, or an invoice number) on a document in barcode format. For example, a barcode is placed on a computer document. As the document is transferred from the computer to the microform, the barcode also appears on the microform. Then during the CAR process, a CAR cartridge reader that has bar coding, scanning, and encoding capabilities retrieves the image.

Integration of Fax and Micrographics

Technology that combines the cost savings and convenience of microfilm and the immediacy of electronic delivery has enabled the administrative professional to send micro-imaged records directly to the computer screen of another user. Say an administrative professional keys an image address and locates the required microimage file. Once the microimage file is inserted into the reader, a computer captures the image and sizes it to the computer monitor. The administrative professional verifies this as the correct file and faxes the image from one computer screen to another computer screen. Automatic cropping and edge detection make it easy to print only selected information and to protect confidential information that may appear on the microimaged record. Optional annotation capabilities give the administrative profes-

sional the ability to add important routing information. With this technology, an administrative professional can take a micrographic image, manipulate it, and send it via fax to anywhere in the world.

Benefits of Integration

The integration of computer technology and microimage records management allows records to be stored in an effective and efficient manner. Listed below are benefits of such systems.

- Space savings. By using microforms instead of paper for document storage, space requirements can be reduced up to 98 percent. This is an important consideration with the escalating cost of floor space. Additional cost savings result from the elimination of file cabinets and filing supplies.
- Cost savings. In a paper-based system, approximately 125 to 175 documents can be filed manually in an hour. The time typically spent filing 2,000 documents is more than 11 hours. However, with integration of microforms and computers, 2,000 documents can be filmed and the coordinating indexing information attached and input in about three hours. Retrieval time is also greatly reduced compared to a manual system.
- Increased productivity. By using an integrated system, the laborious and time-consuming tasks involved in manual sorting, filing, retrieving, refiling, updating, and purging outdated records are eliminated. Employees are able to increase their productivity and to take on other assignments.
- Elimination of lost or misfiled papers. Estimates are that between 4 and 8 percent of all paper documents in a manual filing system are lost or misfiled. With electronic filing systems, problems of lost and misfiled documents are virtually eliminated.
- A secure and easily duplicated storage medium. Microforms and electronic media are difficult for an unauthorized person to access. These forms of storage can also be

reproduced easily and inexpensively so copies of important records can be stored off company premises for protection against fire or other catastrophe.

Records Migration

Whether for legal or financial reasons or to provide historical company data, it is important that records be accessible. As technology changes, many applications and file formats for records that were used just a few years ago are now difficult or impossible to support. As organizations adopt and implement new technology, the challenge of migrating records to new formats becomes very important. Organizations must make sure the technology they use today allows them to access their records 10 years from now. Many organizations that previously disliked microfilm and microfiche now look to them as media that guarantee perpetual access to documents, meaning companies can avoid major migration challenges.

Trends in Records Management

The volume of records will probably continue to increase faster than the rate of disposal. Because of the increase in the amount of information that needs to be stored, as well as continued changes in technological advances that allow for more data to be gathered and processed, you can expect some of the following trends in records management for the future.

- COLD technology will increase in use. Remember, with COLD technology, the information on the system remains accessible to authorized users and is stored for future access.
- The increase in the number and variety of computer-based systems available for

records storage will continue to grow. This growth will result from the increased availability of computerized records management systems. In addition, an increasing number of companies will offer a wide variety of document and records management systems.

- Companies are now realizing the value and the resulting security implications of company email systems and IM programs. New systems are coming online that will be able to capture and commit these messages to long-term storage. These systems capture the information via direct COLD storage or microimage technology or directly into document imaging systems.
- Increased reliance on computerized records management systems in organizations will require that records managers become more involved with technical computer issues and systems. This may require a merger of information systems staff with records management staff. Such a merger will allow a business to perform its work effectively since both departments will have a better understanding of the entire electronic records process.
- Records management standards will continue to be developed throughout the industry. Such standards will assist companies in managing their records. These standards will continue to include a broader legal definition of the types of storage media acceptable in litigation.
- The use of combination systems, which include a wide variety of electronic technologies, will increase. Systems will continue to be produced that provide for the merger and combination of various technologies. An organization must continue to update its stored records so they can be used with innovations. ■

SUMMARY

To reinforce what you have learned in this chapter, study this summary.

- An electronic information management system includes inputting data; processing the data through integration with other data, including modifying, editing, deleting, and sorting the data; outputting the data; and storing and retrieving the data.

- An electronic records management system (ERMS) provides the user with the ability to input data; process data by merging with other data; edit, sort, and delete data; output the data; and store and retrieve data through simple computer applications.

- Database software allows the user to perform the records management functions of entering, organizing, processing, indexing, sorting, selecting, linking, storing, and retrieving within a specific software program.

- Decentralized storage refers to information stored by individuals on their own computer disks or tapes.

- Centralized storage refers to a system in which computers are linked together through a network and the information can be retrieved by multiple users.

- Storage and retrieval in a decentralized electronic filing system require that you determine how you will file the CDs or DVDs and decide on the naming conventions and standards you will use to store the records.

- Records must be protected from physical hazards and unauthorized access.

- An electronic document management system (EDMS) is a computer-based system that allows for retrieval of specific documents that would have been filed in a cabinet or long-term storage facility.

- Document management software can be used to manage electronic, digital, microimage, and paper storage systems.

- Digital archiving is the practice of converting paper documents to digital format so the data can be stored and retrieved electronically.

- Most digital archiving uses CDs or DVDs as their storage media. Both of these formats allow information to be recorded once, but read many times.

- An organization that changes from traditional paper filing systems to document management systems has many opportunities for cost savings and increased productivity.

- Computer-output-to-laser-disc (COLD) technologies will continue to be an important records management tool, offering several advantages.

- Microimage systems provide a suitable storage alternative for many records. These records are placed on microforms—microfilm and microfiche.

- There are laws that determine what types of records can be stored on microforms and still be acceptable in a court of law.

- Computer and micrographics technologies have come together in the form of COM, CIM, and CAR. Many benefits have occurred as the result of the integration of micrographics and computers.

- Fax and micrographics have been integrated, combining the cost savings and convenience of microfilm and the immediacy of electronic delivery.

- Records migration will continue to be an important challenge for organizations. Because technology changes rapidly, organizations must make sure the technology they use to store their records will be supported when the time comes to retrieve those records.

- The expectation for the future is that there will be even greater integration of micrographics with other technologies. Such integration will provide for more effective and efficient storage methods. There will also be widespread use of local area networks and RIM software. More versatile storage equipment will be available. In addition, there will be a merger of computer systems staff with records and information management.

FIND THE PROBLEM

Alex Wargo is a computer technology specialist at People Pharmaceuticals. While the standard operating procedure and the code of ethics for this job forbids accessing the email or Web page history of individual terminal operators, Alex noticed a pattern within the daily access attempts to the company's centralized filing system. Over a period of two weeks, attempts were made through several computers in the marketing division to access the restricted research and development files. The times of the attempted access were all different, as were the passwords entered. If you were Alex, how would you proceed?

PROFESSIONAL POINTERS

The following suggestions will help you manage records more efficiently.

- Determine any problems your organization has in managing records properly. Seek solutions to problems from employees who work closely with the process.
- Prepare a records management manual. This manual should describe the job responsibilities of records personnel and the equipment and systems used for controlling records. Store the manual on a network, allowing all employees access to the most current information.
- Maintain effective operating procedures.
- Measure the efficiency of each process; discard unnecessary procedures and improve necessary ones.
- Develop and adhere to strict records retention policies.
- Seek new technology that will enhance productivity and improve overall efficiency of managing records. Update stored records to accommodate new systems.

REINFORCEMENT ITEMS

1. Describe the difference between centralized and decentralized storage systems, and provide an example of the types of records stored in each system.
2. List and describe the elements of a microimage records management system.
3. Explain three benefits of the integration of electronic and microimage systems.

CRITICAL-THINKING ACTIVITY

Your company purchased a new document imaging system. Although the system won't be up and running for several months and several training seminars must still be conducted, the staff has been instructed to get an early start on this program. All of the paper files from the last fiscal year need to be pulled and prepared for scanning. This process includes batching all work orders by company or client name. (The current manual filing system was organized by date.) The records need to be batched in groups of 20 files, and each batch must include a cover sheet listing the client names that are included in that batch. The file processors are not happy with this conversion; they believe the old system worked fine. They have no idea how the new document imaging system works and do not like the fact that they had no input into the purchase of this system.

1. How could the department managers have made this transition less intimidating?
2. What steps can be taken to give the processors an understanding of how the new system will affect their work and the company's overall operations?

VOCABULARY REVIEW

Complete the Vocabulary Review for Chapter 15 given on page 111 of the *Applications Workbook*.

ENGLISH AND WORD USAGE DRILL

Complete the English and Word Usage Drill for Chapter 15 listed on page 112 of the *Applications Workbook*.

WORKPLACE APPLICATIONS

A15-1 (Goal 1)

Kurt Rupprecht asks you to assist the records manager, Radman Ingells, with two projects. Radman has revised the records retention and disposition schedule to be submitted for review at this week's executive officers' meeting. Using the document on the Student CD, SCDA15-1, make the revisions indicated on pages 113-115 of your *Applications Workbook*. Use the strikethrough feature to show what text should be deleted, and put all new wording in italics. This will aid the reviewers in understanding revisions to the document. Identify the document as Draft 2.

A15-2 (Goal 1)

Radman Ingells asks you to prepare a database that includes information about all employees in the Records and Information System Department. Each employee has completed a form listing a variety of information. The completed forms can be found on pages 116-117 of your *Applications Workbook*. Create a database that includes the information from the forms. Print a copy of the database for your instructor.

A15-3 (Goal 2)

Work in teams of three. Make an appointment to visit two different offices in your area; for example, a school, a hospital, a doctor's office, a lawyer's office, or an insurance office. Request a brief meeting with the individual in charge of records management for the organization. Prepare a list of questions you can ask. (Have your instructor review your questions before you make your visits.) Ask about the types of records and storage mechanisms that are used and how documents created with applications software are organized. You should also ask about safety, security, and retention policies. Write up your findings and be prepared to present them orally to the class. Submit your written report to your instructor.

A15-4 (Goal 3)

A new trend in electronic records management will include capturing and retaining email and instant message communications. Using the Internet, research three journal articles that discuss this new technology, its advantages, and its disadvantages. Using the memorandum form on your Student CD, SCDA15-4, prepare a short memo to your instructor, discussing the information you found.

ASSESSMENT OF CHAPTER GOALS

Did you successfully complete the chapter goals? Evaluate yourself by filling out the form on page 118 of the *Applications Workbook*.

chapter 16

Financial Analyses— Organizational and Personal

LEARNING GOALS

1. Explain payroll deductions, including federal, state, and city taxes.
2. Explain banking changes.
3. Analyze organizational financial statements.
4. Compare and contrast personal investment strategies.

As an educated wage earner and contributing member of a democratic society, your responsibilities include understanding the financial picture of your organization or your self-employment situation, as well as understanding how you as an individual prepare to achieve your financial goals.

Many people take for granted that the organization employing them is financially healthy and stable. Unfortunately, that is not always true. Enron Corporation, a large corporation with home offices in Houston, Texas, is an example of a firm that the public and most of its employees believed was financially stable. However, in 2002, the company declared bankruptcy. Investigations of its financial records revealed corruption. Long-term employees who invested their life savings in Enron stock lost their money; many people were left with few retirement resources. Enron's story of corruption and financial malfeasance became a national concern.

Today's corporate world is a complex one and includes large organizations that are multinational in scope and that constantly change directions and initiatives. These changes occur partly due to ever-expanding technological capabilities. This information comes so fast and frequently that people have a difficult time comprehending all the changes that are occurring. For example, Enron grew quickly to a megacorporation with interests in many parts of the world. The average employee may not have been able to understand the company's entire financial picture.

However, the complexity of corporations does not lessen your need to be knowledgeable about financial issues in the organization for which you work; your need merely increases. If you are to make wise financial decisions related to your present and future financial stability, you must commit to gathering information about your organization's financial picture. Additionally, you must make wise decisions to ensure your financial future.

Wait just a minute, you might be thinking. How can I understand complicated financial statements when it takes a CPA to interpret them? How can I take control of my own

Many large corporations today are multinational in scope.

financial well-being when investing is so complex? The answer is that you take one step at a time and add to your knowledge. As in all other areas, the learning process is ongoing.

This chapter will assist you by providing information on individual payroll deductions, organizational financial statements, and personal investment strategies. An additional focus of this chapter is to help you understand the importance of continual learning in financial areas.

Payroll Taxes

Whether you are working for an organization or are self-employed and earning more than $400 per year, a portion of your salary goes to the federal government in the form of **pay-** roll taxes. These taxes include federal income tax and **FICA** (Federal Insurance Contributions Act) **tax**. Some states and cities also tax personal income. If so, this tax is withheld from your check.

The amount deducted for federal income tax depends on your earnings and the number of dependents you claim. Each employee must fill out form **W-4** (Employee's Withholding Allowance Certificate). Your employer provides this form at the time of employment, or you may download the form from **www.irs.gov**. The amount of income tax withheld by employers is paid quarterly or monthly to a district office of the Internal Revenue Service.

Social Security and Medicare

FICA includes **Social Security** (retirement benefits, survivors benefits, and disability insurance) and **Medicare** (health insurance for senior citizens). Social Security tax rates and the maximum amount of earnings subject to tax are revised frequently by Congress. Figure 16-1 shows the Social Security and Medicare tax rates for 2003.

The amount of your salary deducted for federal income tax depends on your earnings and the number of dependents you claim.

SOCIAL SECURITY AND MEDICARE TAX RATE 2003				
Calendar Years	Maximum Earnings Subject to SS	Social Security Tax Rate	Medicare Tax Rate	Total FICA Tax Rate
2003	$87,000*	6.20%	1.45%	7.65%

*An increase of $2,100 over the 2002 wage base of $84,900

FIGURE 16~1 Social Security and Medicare Taxes

The U.S. government accumulates the money paid for Social Security and Medicare in an account and pays benefits when a person retires or pays benefits to the survivors and/or dependents in the event of the person's death. Under provisions of the Tax Reform Act of 1985, everyone age two or older must have a Social Security number. To obtain a number, you must file an application with your local Social Security office. You will then receive a card with your number on it. The Social Security Administration recommends that every three years you request a statement of your earnings to make certain that they have been reported properly. To get this statement, call your local Social Security office and ask for details.

Federal, State, and City Income Taxes

Forty-one states impose an income tax. New Hampshire and Tennessee apply it only to income from interest and dividends. Seven states (Alaska, Florida, Nevada, South Dakota, Texas, Washington, and Wyoming) do not tax personal income. Selected state income tax rates for 2002 are shown in Figure 16-2.

Some cities also tax personal income. City tax rates are generally less than state tax rates.

Other Deductions

Several other deductions may come from your earnings. Common deductions are these:
- Insurance
- Hospitalization
- Union dues
- Retirement savings plans

Employer Taxes Only

Employers pay several taxes that employees do not. These taxes include both federal and state unemployment taxes. In some states, employees contribute to unemployment taxes, but this contribution is not the norm.

Federal Unemployment Tax

FUTA (Federal Unemployment Tax Act) provides some relief to people who become unemployed as a result of economic forces beyond their control. FUTA pays one-half of the cost of extended unemployment benefits and provides for a fund from which states may borrow, if necessary, to pay benefits. FUTA also covers the costs of administering the Unemployment Insurance and Job Service programs in all states. The FUTA tax rate, as of 2002, is 6.2 percent of taxable wages. It is applied to only the first $7,000 of each employee's earnings per calendar year. Employers who pay the state unemployment tax on a timely basis receive an offset credit of up to 5.4 percent, which means that the net federal tax rate is 0.8 percent.

State Unemployment Tax

SUTA (State Unemployment Tax Act) also provides payments to unemployed workers. State tax rates are based on requirements of state law. Rates vary from state to state, though the maximum tax in most states is 5.4 percent. States often grant reduced rates

SELECTED STATE INCOME TAX RATES 2002

State	Lowest Income Tax Rates	Highest Income Tax Rates
Alabama	2.0	5.0
California	1.0	9.3
Delaware	2.2	5.9
Hawaii	1.4	8.3
Kansas	3.5	6.4
Minnesota	5.3	7.8
New Jersey	1.4	6.3
New York	4.0	6.8
Wisconsin	4.6	6.7

FIGURE 16~2 Selected State Income Tax Rates

to employers who provide stable employment for their employees.

Banking

Banking changes in the last few years have been dramatic. Due to technological innovations, the banks that your parents knew or perhaps even the banks that you knew no longer exist. Today individuals rarely go in the doors of a bank.

- Organizations deposit payroll checks electronically. In fact, most banks encourage businesses, through incentives, to provide this service to their employees.
- Many people use **ATMs** (automated teller machines) to get cash from their accounts. If your payroll check is not deposited automatically, you can deposit the check using an ATM. Most banks also allow you the option of getting your bank balance after each ATM transaction.
- You can access your bank accounts online to check your bank balances, to determine what checks have cleared the bank, and to transfer money from one account to another.

For example, you can transfer money from your regular checking account to your savings account.

- You can pay most of your bills electronically by giving the organizations to whom you pay monthly bills the authority to deduct money from your bank account automatically. Utility companies, credit card companies, mortgage companies, and numerous other companies offer this option. Due to automatic deductions, the number of checks that individuals write each month has dropped considerably. You can also personally authorize bill payment through the online service at your bank. In this way, you control when the deductions occur, instead of payments being made on a set date.
- You can use your banking card as a debit card to pay for purchases such as groceries.
- You can pay for online purchases with debit or credit cards.
- Most businesses also accept checks by telephone, which only requires a check number, the routing number of the financial institution, and the account number. This, too, hastens payments and lessens the use of mail.

Paper checks and other forms of paper banking will still be used in the foreseeable future. However, ATMs, **EFTs** (electronic funds transfers), automatic bill payment, and debit cards will continue to decrease people's use of paper checks.

In addition to automatic bill payments, electronic check deposits, and online banking being convenient for individuals, these options also provide businesses a number of advantages:

- Eliminates the time and expense of writing and distributing paychecks
- Decreases the possible loss or theft of paychecks
- Reduces postage required for mailing checks

Electronic banking will continue to grow in the future and add new services for its customers.

ATMs have become a popular way to withdraw money from checking accounts.

© GETTY IMAGES/PHOTODISC

Organizational Financial Statements

As an administrative professional, you will not be expected to have an extensive knowledge of accounting. However, organizational financial statements, such as the balance sheet and income statement, will help you understand the financial position of your organization. As you begin to acquire personal investments in the form of stocks, bonds, and/or mutual funds, you will be able to analyze in a general way the financial status of your investment companies. Additionally, you will be more knowledgeable about ratios such as P/E ratios—important information when buying stocks.

Income Statement

An **income statement** reflects the financial position of an entity for a particular period. It shows the total amount of money earned and the total amount of expenses involved in earning the money for the period designated. The excess of revenue over expenses is **net income** or **net profit**. If expenses exceed revenue, the results are a **net loss**, or lack of profit.

Balance Sheet

A **balance sheet** shows the financial position of an organization on a certain date—how much the company owns and how much it owes. A balance sheet includes assets, liabilities, and owner's equity. **Assets** are resources owned by the entity. There are two major classifications of assets—current assets and plant and equipment assets. **Current assets** consist of cash and assets expected to be turned into cash, sold, or consumed within a short period (usually one year). **Property, plant, and equipment assets** consist of relatively long-lived assets used in the operation of the entity.

Liabilities are debts of the entity. Examples of liabilities include accounts payable, notes payable, and wages payable. **Current liabilities** are debts that must be paid within one year. **Long-term liabilities** are debts that are not due for a comparatively long period (more than one year). Common long-term liability items are mortgages payable, bonds payable, and notes payable.

Owner's equity is the owner's right to the assets of the entity. Revenues increase in the owner's equity due to selling services or products. If the business is a public corporation (selling stock), this part of the balance sheet is called **stockholders' equity, shareholders' investment**, or **capital**. This section reports the amount of each of the two main sources of stockholders' equity. The first source is capital contributed to the corporation by stockholders and others, which is called **paid-in capital**. The second source is net income retained in the business, which is called **retained earnings**. These two sources equal the total stockholders' equity. Figure 16-4 shows a balance sheet.

Notice the difference in the income statement (Figure 16-3), which reflects the financial position for a particular period of time (a period statement) and the balance sheet (Figure 16-4), which reflects the financial

HOLLOWEL CORPORATION

Income Statement
Year Ended December 31, 2005

(in thousands)

Net Sales	$2,113,843
Cost of sales	1,678,919
Gross Profit	434,924
Operating expenses	
Selling, general and administrative	323,574
Restructuring costs	4,823
Operating income	106,527
Other income (expense)	
Interest income	9,077
Interest expense	(11,328)
Income before taxes	104,276
Taxes on income	52,083
Net income	$ 52,193
Net income per common share	$ 2.02

FIGURE 16~3 Income Statement

position for a particular date (a point statement). In the examples given, the income statement is for a period of one year ending on December 31, 2005. The balance sheet reflects a point in time—December 31, 2005.

Financial Statement Analysis

Before the financial condition of a business can be understood, the financial statements must be analyzed. There are many methods of analysis; several are discussed here.

Comparative Horizontal Analysis

Comparative **horizontal analysis** compares increases and decreases in items for particular periods of time. Figure 16-5, on page 381, shows a portion of a comparative income statement. Notice that the gross profit increase for the period from 2004 to 2005 is 9.8 percent.

Comparative Vertical Analysis

A percentage analysis may also be used to show the relationship of each component to the total within a single statement. This type of analysis is called **vertical analysis**. Figure 16-6, on page 381, illustrates a portion of a balance sheet. Notice that cash and cash equivalents for 2005 are 21.56 percent of the total current assets of $927,700. Each category on the balance sheet is treated as a percent of the total of its section.

Current Ratio

Bankers and other creditors of a business are mainly interested in the current position of an organization. They want to know whether the company has enough money to meet its current operating needs and pay its current debts.

HOLLOWEL CORPORATION

Balance Sheet
December 31, 2005
(in thousands)

ASSETS

Current assets

Cash and cash equivalents	$ 194,367
Accounts receivable	237,401
Inventories	175,300
Deferred income taxes	23,700
Prepaid expenses	45,450
Total current assets	676,218
Property and equipment, net	550,401
Goodwill and other intangibles, net	75,411
Investments	34,821
	$1,336,851

LIABILITIES AND STOCKHOLDERS' EQUITY

Current liabilities

Accounts payable	$ 217,300
Bank credit lines	3,500
Accruals	
Salaries and related expenses	59,400
Restructuring costs	8,900
Other expenses	65,000
Current maturities of long-term debt	6,059
Total current liabilities	360,159
Long-term debt	250,197
Total liabilities	610,356
Commitments and contingencies	8,500

Stockholders' equity

Common stock, $.01 par value, authorized 110,000,000	
Issued 51,955,288	510
Additional paid-in capital	472,413
Retained earnings	244,539
Deferred compensation	533
Total stockholders' equity	717,485
	$1,336,851

FIGURE 16~4 Balance Sheet

MARQUETTE CORPORATION
COMPARATIVE INCOME STATEMENT
For the Years Ended December 31, 2005 and 2004

	2005	2004	Increase (Decrease) Amount	Percent
Sales	$1,830,000	$1,780,000	$50,000	28.1%
Sales returns and allowances	25,000	27,000	(2,000)	(8.0%)
Net sales	$1,805,000	$1,753,000	$52,000	3.0%
Cost of goods sold	1,515,000	1,489,000	26,000	1.7%
Gross profit	$ 290,000	$ 264,000	$26,000	9.8%

Note: Percentages are rounded to the nearest tenth of a percent.

FIGURE 16~5 Portion of Comparative Income Statement

MARQUETTE CORPORATION
COMPARATIVE BALANCE STATEMENT
For the Years Ended December 31, 2005 and 2004

	2005 Amount	Percent	2004 Amount	Percent
Cash and cash equivalents	$200,000	21.56%	$150,000	20.00%
Accounts receivable	363,700	39.20%	320,000	42.67%
Inventories	290,000	31.26%	210,000	28.00%
Deferred income taxes	22,000	2.37%	20,000	2.67%
Prepaid expenses	52,000	5.61%	50,000	6.66%
Total current assets	$927,700	100.00%	$750,000	100.00%

Note: Figures have been rounded to the nearest one hundreth of a percent.

FIGURE 16~6 Portion of Comparative Balance Sheet

One method of determining the current position of a company is to calculate the **current ratio**. This figure is obtained by dividing current assets by current liabilities, as shown here.

$$\text{current ratio} = \frac{\text{current assets (\$173,865)}}{\text{current liabilities (\$56,915)}}$$

$$= 3.05:1$$

An organization's current ratio indicates its debt-paying ability. A current ratio of 3.05 to 1 indicates that $3.05 in cash is being received for every dollar being paid out within the year.

Now compare the current ratios of two different corporations shown in Figure 16-7. Notice that the current ratio of A&E Hardware is greater than the current ratio of Edward's Hardware. A&E Hardware (with its current

CURRENT RATIO COMPARISON OF TWO HARDWARE COMPANIES

	A&E Hardware 2005	Edward's Hardware 2005
Current assets	$350,000	$650,000
Current liabilities	120,000	343,000
Working capital	230,000	307,000
Current ratio	2.9	1.9

FIGURE 16~7 Current Ratio

ratio of 2.9) is in a better position to obtain credit than is its competitor, Edward's Hardware, with a ratio of 1.9. Different business categories have different preferred current ratios, as determined by lending institutions, to decide whether they are currently **solvent** (able to meet their financial obligations without going bankrupt).

Acid-Test Ratio or Quick Ratio

The **acid-test ratio** or **quick ratio** measures the instant debt-paying ability of an organization. It is the ratio of the total quick assets to the total current liabilities. **Quick assets** are cash and other current assets that can be quickly converted to cash. The quick ratio indicates the extent to which total current liabilities can be liquidated on short notice.

Cash, notes receivable, and marketable securities are quick assets because they can be converted to cash quickly. Inventories and prepaid expenses are not considered quick assets because they are further removed from conversion into cash than other current assets. The quick ratio is determined by dividing quick assets by current liabilities. Compare A&E Hardware and Edward's Hardware again—this time using the quick ratio that is illustrated in Figure 16-8. Notice that Edward's Hardware is in a better position to pay its debts, having a quick ratio of 2.45, than A&E Hardware with a quick ratio of 2.04. Edward's Hardware has more cash, marketable equity securities, and accounts receivable that can be quickly converted into cash.

ACID-TEST RATIO COMPARISON OF TWO HARDWARE COMPANIES

	A&E Hardware 2005	Edward's Hardware 2005
Quick assets		
Cash	$ 65,000	$390,500
Marketable securities	60,000	175,000
Accounts receivable	120,000	275,000
Total quick assets	$245,000	$840,500
Current liabilities	$120,000	$343,000
Acid-test ratio	2.04	2.45

FIGURE 16~8 Acid-Test Ratio

Earnings per Share on Common Stock

The **P/E ratio** (price/earnings) is an often-used and often-quoted measure of a stock's value. The P/E ratio is the price of the stock divided by the 12-month earnings per share, with the resulting number being an indicator of a firm's future earnings prospects. *P/E ratios are useful to investors because they allow investors to examine how a company has performed over time and to make intelligent decisions about whether to buy or sell stock.* For example, assume that Fannie Mae's[SM] P/E ratio is 13, which means that a share of stock was selling at 13 times the amount of earnings per share. Also assume that you have tracked Fannie Mae for a period of time and know that its P/E ratio a year ago was at 25 and that its historical low was 10. (Fannie Mae is listed on the New York Stock Exchange and may be tracked in the stock market tables of many newspapers.) What you can conclude from this analysis is that Fannie Mae is selling close to its historical low; thus, Fannie Mae may present a good buying opportunity. The P/E ratio appears in the stock market tables.

$$\frac{\text{price of stock per share}}{\text{annual earnings per share}} = \frac{\text{price-earnings}}{\text{ratio}}$$

Numerous other analytical measures exist that are beyond the scope of this chapter. However, if you are interested in furthering your knowledge of how to measure a company's performance, you may want to consider these profitability measures.

- **Ratio of net sales to assets**—a profitability measure that shows how effectively a firm utilizes its assets
- **Rate earned on total assets**—measures the profitability of total assets
- **Rate earned on stockholders' equity**—shows the rate of income earned on the amount invested by stockholders

Most accounting books explain these measures—their computation and their significance in analyzing a company's profitability.

As an employee and/or an investor, you must be aware of the importance of ethical behavior when preparing financial statements. When fraudulent, financial statements mislead investors and employees, with serious repercussions occurring. The 2002 demise of Arthur Andersen due to its inaccurate auditing procedures of Enron made the public more aware of the consequences of reporting false information on financial statements. As a direct response to the issues raised by the Enron and Arthur Andersen matters, a special bill, H.R. 3763 (Sarbanes-Oxley Act of 2002), was signed by President Bush on July 30, 2002. The bill created a new oversight board for accounting firms that are auditing publicly traded companies. The bill also addressed these issues:

- Auditor independence
- Corporate responsibility at publicly traded companies
- Financial disclosures of publicly traded companies
- Conflicts of interests of financial analysts

Additionally, the law created protections for **whistleblowers** (individuals who bring wrongdoing within an organization to light) at publicly traded companies and imposed new criminal penalties relating to fraud, conspiracy, and interfering with investigations.[1] Corporate management has the responsibility of assuring its stockholders and employees that all financial statements are accurate. Accounting firms hired by management to audit and verify the accuracy of financial statements also have a legal and moral responsibility to ensure that statements are true and accurate.

Investments

Understanding how to invest and beginning to invest early in your professional career are important for your individual long-term financial security. The essence of investing is deciding to forego certain immediate gratification

---

[1]"Summary of Provisions in H.R. 3763, the Sarbanes-Oxley Act of 2002, Relating to Documentation," accessed November 26, 2002; available from **www.arma.org/news**.

coming from the possession of goods in exchange for future income. In an era when individuals cannot expect to be employed by one organization for life and when organizations are continuing to limit the extent of **fringe benefits** (employment benefits given in addition to wages), individuals become responsible for assuring their financial security.

Social Security was, at one point in the history of the United States, considered to be a benefit that provided some measure of security after retirement. However, future Social Security benefits are in question. If you listen to senators and representatives, you hear an ongoing debate about what should happen with Social Security. Although no unanimity exists on how Social Security funds should be handled, there is widespread belief among Congress members that if something is not done to ensure the financial stability of the Social Security system, the funds will be bankrupt in the not-too-distant future. Due to this concern, changes in Social Security may occur. Possibilities include allowing you to invest a portion of your Social Security benefits yourself and/or allowing the government to invest some of the Social Security pool in the stock market. However, even if Social Security remains solvent and provides the benefits that it does today, do not expect to live on it during retirement. The dollars provided by Social Security are not enough to provide you with adequate dollars for retirement—yet another reason why you need to understand investing and do it wisely.

Sound investing is not only important for long-range retirement needs, it is also important for more immediate needs such as a house, college funds for your children, and hospitalization expenses not covered by insurance.

Investing requires that you understand the types of investment opportunities available at your job and that you know how to invest in such securities as stocks, bonds, and mutual funds. Additionally, you need to understand investment vehicles such as stock exchanges and online investing.

Investment Opportunities on the Job

Several types of employer-sponsored retirement plans exist. They all work on the same principle; they are tax-deferred plans, meaning you do not pay taxes on the money you put into the plan. You do pay taxes on the money when you start withdrawing it for retirement. These plans fall into two basic types—defined contribution and defined benefit.

Defined Contribution Plans

With defined contribution plans, the employee decides how much money to invest and where it is to be invested. Two plans often used are **401(k)** plans (for employees of private companies) and **403(b)** plans (for employees of public and nonprofit employers). Employers may contribute to a plan. For example, some employers add 50 cents to every dollar an employee contributes, up to a certain percentage of his or her salary. When you figure this amount into the return on your original investment and add the interest that you earn on all the monies deposited into your account, maximizing your 401(k) or 403(b) investment plan is the first step toward retirement security. This step is generally less risky than direct stock market investments. When you consider the tax savings on original earnings due to tax deferment, 401(k) and 403(b) plans are sound investment vehicles.

Companies may also offer employees the chance to buy stock as part of a 401(k). This option has its down side if you decide to invest your total savings in company stock. A prime example of a situation when it did not work is the Enron fiasco. Many employees invested all of their savings in Enron; when Enron collapsed, their savings were gone.

Defined Benefit Plans

With a defined benefit plan, the employer guarantees the sum received. Defined benefit plans usually require that you work a minimum number of years (usually five) before you are qualified for the money. The value of the dollars in the plan increases as you continue to work for the organization. You

DIGITAL VISION

Several types of employer-sponsored retirement plans exist.

generally receive a larger amount of money in the last five years before retirement, with the goal of the company being to keep you until retirement.

Social Security

All individuals pay into the Social Security system, at a present rate of 7.65 percent of their income. This rate is subject to change by Congress. However, as previously mentioned, the dollars available from this system are not adequate to fund an individual's total retirement needs.

Stocks

Stocks represent shares of ownership in a company. Stockholders invest in a company by buying shares of stock. Stockholders are issued stock certificates that show the number of shares owned. When you buy a share of stock, you become one of the owners of the company. You are entitled to a share of the company's profits that are paid to stockholders as **dividends**. As a stock owner, you are vulnerable to the costs of the company's poor performance, which can mean if the stock goes down, you receive no dividends. If the stock goes down considerably, the company may be forced out of business, meaning you have lost money. History has shown that stocks generally make more money than bonds (explained in the next section) over time, but stocks are also more **volatile** (characterized by unexpected change) than bonds. Most stock is common stock; however, there is a classification of stock called **preferred stock**. The major differences in common and preferred stock are these:

- Preferred stock pays dividends before common stock.
- Dividends are set on preferred stock.

- When dividends are declared, preferred stockholders are paid in full before common stockholders are paid any dividends.
- The market value on common stock may fluctuate more than the market value of preferred stock.

Stocks may be purchased in the following ways:

- Through brokers
- Through financial advisers
- Online

As you consider your investing opportunities, you also need to understand three indices that appear on the stock market pages each day—the Dow Jones℠ Industrial Average, the S. & P. Index™ of 500 Stocks, and the Russell 2000℠ Index.

Dow Jones Industrial Average

The **Dow Jones Industrial Average** (often called *the Dow*) is an average of the stock of 30 well-known companies, such as AT&T and McDonald's®. The editors of *The Wall Street Journal* chose these stocks. This average, due to the well-known and relatively stable companies that make up the Dow, is one indicator used to describe what is happening in the stock market on a daily basis. Even though the Dow Jones represents only 30 stocks, these stocks have been a mainstay in the United States economy for years. If they are down as a group, the possibility of the majority of stocks being down is likely.

S. & P. 500

As the name **S. & P. 500** implies, it represents a group of 500 stocks that Standard & Poor's tracks to get a picture of the stock market. The S. & P. is based on 425 industrials, 25 railroads, and 50 utilities. The index is carefully weighted according to the stocks used. The S. & P., like the Dow Jones, is an indicator of trends in the stock market.

Wise investment in stocks can provide a source of income when you are no longer working.

© GETTY IMAGES/PHOTODISC

Russell 2000

The **Russell 2000** represents 2,000 **small-cap stocks**. Small-cap stocks have a **market capitalization** (how much they are worth by shares that are outstanding to the public multiplied by the price of the stock) of less than 1 billion. In comparison, **mid-cap stocks** have a market capitalization of a few billion and **large-cap stocks** have a market capitalization of 10 billion or more.

By looking at all three indices, you can get a good idea of trends in the marketplace.

Online purchasing is presented in a later section.

Stock Exchanges

The stock market in the United States consists of a number of exchanges, where traders physically stand on the floor of the exchange and buy and sell stocks. The largest stock exchange is the New York Stock Exchange^{SM}, where over 3,000 stocks are listed. You have, no doubt, watched on television the opening and closing bell on the New York Stock Exchange. The organization that became the New York Stock Exchange actually was formed on May 17, 1792, when its traders began trading stocks under a tree in New York City. On March 8, 1817, the traders wrote a constitution, and the name *New York Stock Exchange Board* was adopted. The name was changed to *New York Stock Exchange* in 1863.

Other stock exchanges in the United States include the following:

- Philadelphia Stock Exchange^{SM}
- Pacific Stock Exchange^{SM}
- Boston Stock Exchange^{SM}
- Cincinnati Stock Exchange^{SM}
- Chicago Stock Exchange^{SM}

Additionally, there are numerous global stock exchanges; for example, the Bermuda Stock Exchange^{SM}, the Montreal Stock Exchange^{SM}, the Paris Stock Exchange^{SM}, and the London Stock Exchange^{SM}.

Since people invest globally, information about international markets is provided in *The New York Times* and other newspapers.

© GETTY IMAGES/PHOTODISC

The New York Stock Exchange is a physical place where stocks are bought and sold.

The **NASDAQ**^{SM} (National Association of Securities Dealers Automated Quotation) is an **over-the-counter market**, which means it is not a physical location like the New York Stock Exchange, but an automated information network that provides quotes on stocks for brokers registered with the **NASD** (National Association of Securities Dealers). Trades are done by phone or computer, with traders (members of the NASD) profiting from the spread between a stock's bid and its asking price, rather than a commission. The NASDAQ has the largest number of stocks, approximately 40,000.

Bonds

A **bond** is a certificate that represents a company's promise to pay a definite sum of money at a specified time with interest payable periodically to the holder of the bond. Thus, bonds do not represent a share of ownership in a company like stocks, but are evidence of a debt owed by the firm. A **bondholder** lends money to an organization and, in return, receives a bond, which is a preferred lien against the organization. Several types of bonds may be purchased—corporate, United States treasury, tax-exempt, and municipal. Bonds are relatively safe investments. In times when the stock market is **bearish** (at a low), bonds generally yield a greater return to the investor. However, in a **bullish market** (when stocks prices are increasing), stocks generally yield a greater return to the investor. Figure 16-9 provides information on how the terms *bull* and *bear* in relation to the market came into being. This historical relationship of stocks to bonds in the market is one reason investors like to balance their portfolios between stocks and bonds.

Bonds range in risk from relatively safe Treasury bills to extremely risky high-yield or junk bonds. Listed here are some of the types of bonds.

- U.S. Treasuries. The federal government backs these bonds, which are exempt from state and local taxes. U.S. Treasuries include treasury bills, treasury notes, treasury bonds, and zero-coupon treasuries. **Treasury bills** are a short-term investment. They mature in one year or less, costing at least $10,000. **Treasury notes** mature in two to ten years and pay interest twice a year. The minimum investment is between $1,000 and $5,000. **Treasury bonds** mature in one to thirty years and pay interest semiannually. **Zero-coupon treasuries** pay no interest until they mature, with maturity being from six months to ten years.

- Corporate bonds. Individual companies issue **corporate bonds**, which are fully taxable. Their reliability depends on the issuing company. The safest corporate bonds are **investment-grade bonds**; the riskiest are **high-yield issues** or **junk bonds**.

- **Municipal bonds**. State and local governments issue these bonds. They usually cost $5,000 or more and are free from federal taxes.

- **Mortgage-backed bonds**. These bonds represent ownership of mortgage loans issued or backed by government agencies; they are not tax exempt. They usually cost at least $25,000.

- Foreign bonds. **Foreign bonds** are sensitive to changes in the exchange rate. If the value of the dollar goes up, the bond increases in value. These bonds can help diversify a bond portfolio because interest rates in other countries do not match those of the United States.

Newspapers and financial publications such as *The Wall Street Journal* and *Barron's*™ list bond prices. Websites also provide bond information.

ORIGIN OF STOCK MARKET TERMS *BULL* AND *BEAR*

There are two explanations as to the origin of the terms *bull* and *bear*. One is based on how each animal attacks—the bear by raking *down* with large, sharp claws and the bull by tossing *up* his large, sharp horns.

The second explanation is based on the selling of bearskin by traders. The term *bear* comes from sellers of bearskins who had a penchant for selling bearskins before the bears were caught. In the stock market, the term came to mean speculators who agreed to sell shares of stock they did not yet own because they believed the price would drop. They would quickly buy shares at the dropped price and then sell them for the previously agreed higher price.

Bulls came to mean the opposite of bears. Bulls were individuals who bought heavily, expecting a stock price to go up.

FIGURE 16~9 Origin of Stock Market Terms *Bull* and *Bear*

Mutual Funds

A **mutual fund** is an investment company that pools individuals' money and invests the money in stocks and bonds. Mutual fund companies employ investment advisers who select, buy, and sell investments based on a fund's investment objective. Mutual funds provide one of the simplest ways for the small investor to buy stocks and bonds. Owning several types of stocks and bonds provides some protection for investors against losses. If one investment in the fund does poorly, the other investments can help cushion the blow. However, mutual fund managers do make mistakes, and the investor cannot assume they will not lose money in a mutual fund. History shows a different story—money can be lost. Smart investors take time before investing in funds to look at the history of a mutual fund's performance, just as smart investors look at the history of a particular stock's or bond's performance before investing.

IRAs

An **IRA** (Individual Retirement Account) is a plan that permits individuals to set up a savings plan as opposed to employers setting up the plan, which you learned about earlier in this chapter with 401(k) and 403(b) plans. The IRA is a tax-deferred account that protects the money deposited from taxation until you start to withdraw the money, usually at retirement. The **IRS** (Internal Revenue Service) restricts the types of funds purchased through an IRA. Generally, money can be invested in annuities, stocks, mutual funds, money market funds, trusts, and certificates of deposit. Money cannot be invested in collectibles such as artwork, antiques, gems, and coins. Working spouses can invest $3,000 per year for themselves and $3,000 per year for their nonworking spouses. Types of IRAs are:

- Traditional IRAs that help people who are not covered by an employer-sponsored retirement plan save for retirement.

- Rollover IRAs used to shelter retirement savings that have been taken out of a 401(k) due to a job change.

- Roth IRAs that allow individuals to withdraw money in order to buy a first home or to finance their children's education with no income tax penalty. In order to purchase a Roth IRA, you must have an individual income of less than $100,000 per year or a family income of less than $150,000. In contrast, there is no income limit on the traditional IRA. The Roth IRA has two big advantages—no taxes on earnings growth and an opportunity to pass money on to children tax-free.

- SEP-IRAs (Simplified Employee Pensions) for someone who is self-employed. Contributions are limited to 15 percent or $30,000, whichever is less.

- Simple-IRAs (Saving Incentive Match Plan for Employees) available to the self-employed.

Banks, brokers, or mutual fund companies can set up IRAs for you.

Online Purchasing of Securities

Stocks and bonds may be traded online. You must have basic information about stocks and bonds before attempting to trade online. The following sites can provide a wealth of information about investing.

- **www.marketguide.com**
- **www.briefing.com**
- **www.hoovers.com** (company profiles and financial data)

Once you decide you are ready to invest online, you need to get the help of an online broker. These sites offer names of brokers and other information that can help you understand more about investing.

- **www.schwab.com**
- **www.waterhouse.com**
- **www.fidelity.com**
- **www.harrisdirect.com**

Investment Philosophy

Understanding your own investment philosophy is one of the smartest moves you can make in becoming a sound investor. Presented here are three guidelines in developing a solid investment philosophy.

Guideline 1

Before you begin to invest in stocks, bonds, and/or mutual funds, you need to be clear about your personal investment philosophy. Just as individuals are different in their willingness to take physical risks, they are also different in their willingness to take financial risks. You may be an individual who gets white knuckles whenever you are on a plane that experiences minor turbulence; you also may be willing to take significant financial risks. In other words, tolerance for physical and financial risk taking may be different for the same individual. The important point is for you to understand your financial risk-taking ability. How much risk or how little risk meets your tolerance level? Do you spend sleepless nights when you lose even a small amount of money? On the other hand, if you lose money in investments, do you merely tell yourself you are in for the long haul and not worry?

Guideline 2

Another factor that is important in investing is your time horizon. Are you an individual who needs to see immediate returns on your investments? Are you willing to wait five years to see good returns? Are you willing to wait ten years to see good returns? Your answers

DIGITAL VISION

Stocks may be traded online.

© GETTY IMAGES/EYEWIRE

Do you get white knuckles when there is turbulence in the air?

and what each can mean for you. Do not blindly accept a "tip of the week" from a friend or even a broker. When buying a car or a house, or when making another major investment, you must do your research. For example, when you begin thinking about buying a house, you must pay attention to the following:

- What you can afford
- Where you want to live
- How many bedrooms and bathrooms you need
- What size yard you want

In other words, you become an informed buyer who is clear with the real estate agent about your goals. The same is true of investing. Although you may work with a broker when investing, you must be an educated investor. You must understand the following:

- Your long-term investment goals
- Your level of risk
- Your financial needs in 5, 10, 20, or even 30 years

to these questions can tell you what your time horizon is for experiencing acceptable financial returns.

Guideline 3

Continually educate yourself about the investment world—understand investment vehicles

Then you must be a participant with the broker in determining what stocks, mutual funds, or bonds best meet your needs. Wise investors do not blindly follow anyone's advice. They chart their investment course with qualified assistance from the financial world. ■

SUMMARY

To reinforce what you have learned in this chapter, study this summary.

- Payroll taxes are withheld from your check by your employer. These taxes include federal income tax and FICA tax. The amount of money withheld depends on your earnings and the number of dependents you claim.
- Social Security, deducted by your employer from your check, provides retirement benefits, survivor benefits, and disability insurance. The Medicare portion of the deduction provides health insurance for senior citizens.
- Forty-one states impose an income tax, which is also withheld from your paycheck.
- Employers pay federal and state unemployment taxes. The money from these taxes provides some relief to people unemployed as a result of economic forces beyond their control.
- Today most banking is done electronically using ATMs. People access their accounts online, deposit their paychecks electronically, and pay their bills directly from their bank accounts.

- Knowledge of basic organizational financial statements can help you understand the financial position of your organization.
- An income statement reflects the financial position of an entity for a particular period of time.
- A balance sheet shows the financial position of an organization on a certain date—how much the company owns and how much it owes.
- To understand the financial picture of an organization, you may employ these analyses—comparative horizontal analysis, comparative vertical analysis, current ratio, acid-test ratio, and P/E ratio.
- Understanding how to invest and beginning to invest early in your professional career are important for your long-term financial security.
- Investment opportunities provided by employers may include defined contribution plans and defined benefit plans.
- Personal investment vehicles include stocks, bonds, mutual funds, and IRAs.
- Three indices that can help you understand the direction the stock market is taking include the Dow Jones Industrial Average, the S. & P. 500, and the Russell 2000.
- Before you begin to invest in securities, you need to understand your personal investment philosophy. You need to understand your risk tolerance and your time horizon for investing. Additionally, you need to educate yourself about the investment world. Wise investors chart their investment course with qualified assistance from the financial world.

FIND THE PROBLEM

When you went to work for People Pharmaceuticals, you filled out a W-4 form and listed no dependents. Several months ago you married. Your spouse is going to school full-time and does not have a job. You asked the HR department for a new W-4 and changed your dependent status from zero to one. Your check is automatically deposited by People Pharmaceuticals each month. Four months have passed and you are attempting to reconcile your bank statement. You notice that the amount of money People Pharmaceuticals deposited to your account is considerably more than you had expected. You think an error was made; however, you know you should have reported it earlier. You are embarrassed that you did not notice it sooner. You are tempted to just forget about it. After all, isn't it the responsibility of People Pharmaceuticals or the federal government to find such an error? What is the problem? How should you handle it?

PROFESSIONAL POINTERS

Here are some tips to help you as you work with financial records and investments.
- Double-check figures on all reports that you prepare.
- After keying numerous columns of figures, proofread by having someone else read the figures to you and adding all the columns.
- Keep current on all laws that affect any financial records you are handling.
- Read the financial section of your daily paper.
- Watch TV programs dealing with the economy and investments.
- Commit to reading at least one investment book in the next six months.

REINFORCEMENT ITEMS

1. Explain the payroll deductions that are normally taken from an individual's paycheck.
2. Explain the differences between an income statement and a balance sheet.
3. Define the following terms.
   - Stocks
   - Bonds
   - Mutual funds
4. What is a P/E ratio? How is it computed?
5. Explain what is meant by individual risk tolerance with regard to investing.

CRITICAL-THINKING ACTIVITY

One of the employees of People Pharmaceuticals, Renee Wilson, has decided she needs to begin investing some of her money. Renee grew up in a large family. Her mother and father worked, but there never seemed to be enough money to provide anything but the necessities in life. Renee completed two years of college, but it was a real struggle. She had to work full-time and go to school; her family was not able to help with her financial needs. Renee is now a single parent with a three-year-old son. She wants to be able to give him a college education, and she knows she must start saving for it now. She wants her money to grow as quickly as possible in stable investments. She has come to you for investment advice. What advice would you give Renee?

VOCABULARY REVIEW

Complete the Vocabulary Review for Chapter 16 given on page 119 of the *Applications Workbook*.

ENGLISH AND WORD USAGE DRILL

Complete the English and Word Usage Drill for Chapter 16 given on page 120 of the *Applications Workbook*.

WORKPLACE APPLICATIONS

net A16-1 (Goal 1)
Using the Web, find the latest Social Security and Medicare tax rates. If your state and city tax personal income, find those rates. You should be able to find the information about state income tax on the Web. In order to get the city tax information, you may need to call your city tax office. Write a memorandum to your instructor, detailing the information you learned. Use the memorandum form on the Student CD, SCDA16-1.

A16-2 (Goal 2)

With two or three classmates, interview a bank manager about the technological changes that have occurred in banking in the last few years. Report your findings in an oral report to the class.

A16-3 (Goals 3 and 4)

With two of your classmates, analyze the XYZ Corporation's financial statements in your *Applications Workbook* on pages 121–122. Figure these percentages: comparative horizontal analysis of the income statement (2004 and 2005) and comparative vertical analysis of the balance sheet (2004 and 2005). When figuring the horizontal analysis of the income statement, round the percentages to one decimal place. When figuring the vertical analysis of the balance sheet, round the percentages to two decimal places. On the vertical analysis, compute only *Total current assets*, *Property and equipment*, *Goodwill and other intangibles*, and *Investments and other*. You do not need to compute the individual accounts under *Current assets*. Under *Liabilities and Stockholders' Equity*, compute only *Total current liabilities*, *Long-term debt*, and *Other liabilities*. You do not need to compute the individual accounts under *Current liabilities*. Make notes on both the horizontal and vertical analyses about whether the changes are positive or negative. If the changes are positive, cite the most positive areas. Figure the current ratio and acid-test ratio.

Research the high, low, P/E ratio, and percentage change for a period of one week on the stocks shown below. These companies are listed on the New York Stock Exchange; you can track them in your daily newspaper.

- Alcoa™
- Avon®
- Fannie Mae
- Marathon Oil™
- Mylan Labs™
- Sovereign Bancorp®

Chart the information using a table format. What stock would you purchase (if any) after charting this data?

Write up all information from this project in a report format. Prepare a cover sheet with a project title, the names of the team members, and the date. Submit your report to your instructor.

A16-4 (Goal 4)

Complete the Risk Tolerance and Time Horizon Quizzes on pages 123–126 of your *Applications Workbook*. From your scores on these quizzes, determine what your personal investment strategy should be. Be specific. State whether you would invest in stocks, bonds, mutual funds, and/or IRAs. Answer these questions:

- If you invest in stocks and the market begins to go down drastically, what do you do?
- If you put 50 percent of your money in bonds and the market goes up dramatically, what do you do?
- How do you propose to continue to improve your knowledge of investment strategy?

A16-5 (Goal 4)

Respond to the question at the end of the case presented in your *Applications Workbook*, page 127. Submit your response to your instructor, using the memorandum form on the Student CD, SCDA16-5.

ASSESSMENT OF CHAPTER GOALS

Did you successfully complete the chapter goals? Evaluate yourself by filling out the form on page 128 of the *Applications Workbook*.

5

Meetings and Travel

1 00.01 00
2 00.02 00
 00.03 0
 .05 0
 00.06 00
 00 07 00

chapter 17

Effective Meetings and Conferences

LEARNING GOALS

1. Explain the importance of effective meetings, and describe the wide variety of meeting formats.
2. Describe the roles and responsibilities of individuals associated with a meeting.
3. Describe the responsibilities of the administrative professional in assisting with conventions and conferences.

Meetings are an important component of the workplace; therefore, a great deal of time is spent in meetings. In fact, the average worker spends anywhere from 10 to 50 percent of her or his time at work in meetings. In one year's time, that is 192 to 1,050 hours or 26 to 130 days. While the administrative professional may be at the low end of that range (10 to 15 percent), the average time spent in meetings increases as an individual moves up within an organization. Individuals in upper management positions typically spend 50 to 75 percent of their time in meetings. In addition, as organizations increase their use of teams to solve problems and make decisions, the occurrence of meetings for all employees increases. With such an investment of time (and money) in meetings, they must be effective. This chapter will give you the knowledge and skills you need to assist your supervisor in holding meetings that are productive for all participants—and thus, an efficient use of organizational time. In addition, this chapter will help you develop skills as a meeting planner, leader, and attendee.

Effective Meetings

Why are meetings held? Effective meetings make you and your organization function more efficiently. Many money-wasting activities occur in business because of poor workplace communication. Much of this ineffectiveness could be changed through productive meetings. Voice mail has made phone tag a familiar game. If you are trying to reach someone, you can save time by simply scheduling a quick in-person or audio meeting. Email is another useful technology tool that can be used in place of a meeting at certain times. When you are communicating over long distances or need to send information to more than one person, email is effective. However, do not use email when a face-to-face meeting would be more effective. Do not spend a great deal of time writing an email when you can discuss the issue in person. If you need to discuss an issue in depth, a meeting is the best alternative.[1] The effective meeting is one in which:

- There is a definite need for the meeting.
- The purpose is stated and clearly understood by all participants.
- The appropriate people are in attendance at the meeting.
- An agenda is prepared and followed.
- All members participate.
- There are outcomes achieved because of the meeting.

Although these criteria seem relatively straightforward, few meetings satisfy all of them.

Face-to-face meetings will continue to be a necessary part of the workplace even though electronic meetings are another option. As an administrative professional, you should understand when it is necessary to hold a meeting, the types of meetings that are held, and the types of electronic meeting opportunities available.

Necessary Meetings

Calling a meeting is appropriate when:

- A group needs to be involved in solving a problem or making a decision.
- An issue arises that needs clarification.
- Information needs to be shared with a group.
- Communication needs to occur quickly with a large number of people.

Notice that each situation includes a purpose for the meeting. Once a purpose is identified, considerable planning needs to occur before the meeting takes place. The meeting leader has a role to play if the meeting is to be effective; he or she must understand that role and be well prepared for the meeting. Meeting participants also have a role to play. They must understand the need and purpose of the meeting, prepare before the meeting, and participate actively during the meeting.

Unnecessary Meetings

Unfortunately, many meetings are either unnecessary or ineffective. In fact, millions of dollars are wasted by businesses holding unnecessary meetings, having unclear objectives for meetings, and including people who do not need to be there.[2] Meetings are often called that are not appropriate and should not be held. Meetings are not a good idea when:

- There is no clearly defined purpose for the meeting.
- No consideration has been given to people who need to attend.
- Confidential or sensitive personnel matters must be addressed.
- There are inadequate data for the meeting.
- There is insufficient time to prepare for the meeting.
- There is considerable anger and hostility in the group and people need time to calm down before coming together.
- The same information could be covered in a memo, an email, or a brief report.

One of the ways to ensure that meetings are effective is to differentiate between the need for one-way information dissemination and two-way information sharing. To distribute information, you can use a variety of other avenues, such as sending an email or posting the information on your organization's Website or intranet. Figure 17-1 is a list of meeting behaviors to avoid.

Types of Meetings

The traditional face-to-face meetings where people gather to discuss an issue or a problem continue to be used in organizations.

---

[1]"So Why Do We Still Have Meetings," **www.effective meetings.com**, accessed November 9, 2002; available from **www.effectivemeetings.com/meetingbasics/meetings .asp**.

[2]Paula Gamonal, "Meetings Are Boring and Other Myths," **www.ravenwerks.com**, accessed November 9, 2002; available from **www.ragenwerks.com/practices/meetings.htm**.

MEETING BEHAVIORS TO AVOID

- Hold unnecessary meetings.
- Invite everyone.
- Let people dominate the discussion.
- Allow discussion to wander from the topic.
- Fail to act on decisions made.

Source: Group Meetings, **www.abacon.com/ commstudies/groups/meetings.html**.

FIGURE 17~1 Meeting Behaviors to Avoid

Typical business meetings include staff meetings, committee meetings, project team meetings, customer/client meetings, board of directors meetings, seminars, conferences, and conventions. These meetings may be held face-to-face or through electronic means.

Staff Meetings

Staff meetings are common within organizations. Staff meetings are scheduled on a regular basis where an executive meets with members of his or her staff. For example, an executive may meet with his or her six direct reports as a group every week. The purpose of staff meetings is to review directions, plans, and assignments and to handle routine problems.

Committee Meetings

In most organizations, committees or task forces have been created. A **task force** is formed to deal with a specific issue or problem. Once the problem has been handled or solved, the task force is disbanded. In other words, the task force has a specific beginning and ending. It is organized for a purpose; once the purpose is accomplished, it no longer exists. A **committee** is established for an ongoing purpose. For example, your workplace may have a safety committee that meets regularly (perhaps every month) to identify and address safety concerns. Since safety is an ongoing concern, the committee functions from year to year.

Project Team Meetings

Project teams are frequently used in organizations to accomplish a specific project. For example, a project team may be organized to determine the type of document imaging software that will be used in an organization or to implement quality control policies within a company. Once the project has been completed, the team is disbanded or it takes on another project.

Customer/Client Meetings

Most employers hold meetings with customers and clients. These meetings are generally small, including only one or two people. For example, a lawyer may meet with a client to discuss the evidence in a case. An engineer may meet with a customer to discuss the design of a product.

Board of Directors Meetings

Most large corporations and organizations operate with a board of directors. There are usually **bylaws**, written policies and procedures that clearly define how board meetings are to be conducted. Boards may meet once a month or less. The chairperson of the board conducts the meeting, and strict procedures are usually followed. An agenda is distributed before the meeting, indicating the items to be discussed. If the organization is a public entity in which the open meetings rule applies, notice of the meeting is posted according to legal procedures. Participants generally follow parliamentary procedures as set forth in *Robert's Rules of Order Newly Revised*.

Conventions and Conferences

Conventions are formal annual meetings of the members of a professional group. A convention can involve hundreds or thousands of people. Planning and executing a convention are so complicated that meeting consultants are often hired to assist in carrying out the details.

A **conference** is a meeting where discussion on certain issues or topics takes place. For example, a conference or seminar may be held on topics such as conflict management,

DIGITAL VISION

Board meetings usually follow strict procedures.

written communications, and union negotiations.

Face-to-Face Meetings

While technology can bring people together instantly 24 hours a day, nothing can replace the need for people to meet face-to-face. These types of interactions are not obsolete. More than ever, face-to-face meetings are considered essential to the continued success of organizations. In the age of high-tech communication, face-to-face meetings carry increased importance.[3] The traditional meeting, where people gather for face-to-face discussion of an issue or a problem in one location, has a number of advantages:

- All individuals have a chance to talk informally with other participants before, during, and after the meeting.
- Participants can closely observe others' body language.
- People generally feel more relaxed with the informal setting.
- If the issue to be discussed is a difficult one, the atmosphere allows attendees to deal with the issue effectively.
- A creative, interactive group discussion is more likely.
- Widespread participation among group members is more likely.

Electronic Meetings

The increased emphasis on teamwork and the development of telecommunications technology has contributed to the need and ability

[3]"Today's Technology for Tomorrow's Meetings," *Meetings and Conferences*, July 2002.

to communicate with individuals in remote locations. These electronic options are often referred to as **teleconferencing**. Teleconferencing is a general term applied to a variety of technology-assisted two-way (interactive) communications via telephone, DSL, cable modems, and other high-bandwidth connections. Will electronic meetings eventually replace all traditional meetings? Probably not. If the meeting is collaborative in nature and its purpose is to exchange information, audioconferencing, videoconferencing, and Web conferencing are ideal venues.

The use of teleconferencing continues to increase due to the ongoing globalization and decentralization of corporations. In addition, the wider availability of easy-to-use conferencing and integration tools will keep audio, video and data/Web conferencing growing at a healthy rate.[4]

Audioconferencing

Audioconferencing is a type of conference in which an unlimited number of participants use a voice input unit to participate in a meeting. An audioconference differs from a telephone conversation in that it involves more than two people in at least two locations. This unit may be as simple as a speakerphone or as elaborate as meeting room microphones, speakers, and multipoint "bridge" technology. Bridging services, supplied by telephone and communication services companies, allow multiple locations to dial in to a single phone number which is linked, or "bridged," into one auditory space.[5] Today's speakerphones have superior reception and sound quality, allowing people to participate in the conference from almost any part of the room. Many telephones now allow you to add additional callers to your line by pressing the appropriate conference button. If your phone does not have this capability, a number of communications companies can assist you with audioconferencing. Figure 17-2 provides you with tips for an effective audioconference. Advantages of an audioconference include:

- The ability to assemble individuals on short notice, assuming their schedules allow.
- The ability to connect individuals at any location, nationally or internationally.

[4]Lewis Ward, "The Rise of Rich Media and Real-Time Conferencing," *Business Communications Review*, v. 32, no. 3, March 2002, pp. 53-57.

[5]"Audio and Video Pros and Cons," **www.3m.com**, accessed November 14, 2002; available at **www.3m.com/meeting network/readingroom/meetingguide_audio.html**.

AUDIOCONFERENCE TIPS

- Eliminate or reduce background noise by moving the speakerphone as close as possible to the speaker.
- Mute the phone when your site is not actively participating. Turn the mute function off when someone has a question or comment.
- Save side conversations for after the meeting, even if they are work-related. These conversations compete with the speaker and distract other participants.
- Avoid noises such as tapping pens and shuffling papers; these noises sound louder at remote locations.
- Turn off fans and air conditioning. These sound louder through a speakerphone.
- Shut meeting room doors to keep out workplace background noise.
- Take turns speaking one at a time.

Source: EffectiveMeetings.com, accessed on November 14, 2002; available at **www.effectivemeetings.com**.

FIGURE 17-2 Audioconference Tips

- The use of telephone technology, which is readily available to almost everyone.
- The availability of special technology for supporting large groups and rooms.
- Decreased time and expense associated with travel.

One of the primary disadvantages of audio conferencing is the lack of visual input. However, distributing basic information or confirming the details of previous communication can be handled effectively by email, or a fax can be used to distribute detailed information that includes graphics and text. Other disadvantages to audioconferencing include these:

- Participants cannot see others' body language.
- Without visual cues, it is difficult to manage turn taking when people are speaking.
- Identifying the speaker can also be a problem. Successful audioconferencing requires participants to follow protocols such as announcing who is speaking and asking if anyone else has something to say.
- The potential exists for participants to feel excluded. When many people are in the same room conferencing with individuals in other places, those in the same room have the advantage of being able to see each other. Unless this imbalance is carefully monitored, remote participants may feel left out of the group.

Videoconferencing

Videoconferencing is a system of transmitting audio and video between individuals at distant locations. Videoconferencing is transmitted from a PC-based application (referred to as **desktop videoconferencing**) or by the use of numerous pieces of equipment that have been set up in a specially equipped room.

For two people up to a midsized group, videoconferencing is a valuable alternative to a traditional meeting. It is used when body language is an important element of a meeting. Videoconferencing might not be right for every meeting, but there are times when it is appropriate.[6] Beyond the savings in travel costs that videoconferencing systems generate, there are employee productivity gains because people do not need to travel to and from meetings. A study by WorldCom[SM], Inc., found that an off-site meeting incurs 21 hours in travel, preparation, and meeting time compared with four hours when done through a videoconference.[7]

Although the capabilities for videoconferencing have been around for over 30 years, the recent drop in equipment prices has made it a viable option for the workplace. A basic corporate system costs $5,000 today, compared to $50,000 four years ago. In addition, manufacturers have simplified the videoconferencing process by agreeing on an international standard.[8] Complete desktop videoconferencing systems can be purchased for $500 or less.

Advanced communications and video collaboration have become competitive weapons in business today. The faster and more effectively a corporation makes decisions, the more competitive it can be in the marketplace. Companies today are beginning to realize that videoconferencing is a necessary tool for driving business forward and obtaining a competitive advantage. Figure 17-3 provides tips for setting up effective videoconferences.

Online Conferencing

Online meetings link individual participants through a computer. Other terms used to describe online meetings include computer conferencing, data conferencing, and Web conferencing. **Data conferencing**, which enables two or more people to communicate and collaborate as a group in real time using the computer, is an example of an online

---

[6]Tonya Vinas, "Meetings Makeover," *Industry Week*, v. 251, no. 2, February 2002, pp. 29-30, 32, 35.

[7]James Cope, "Tuning into Travel Savings," *ComputerWorld*, no. 14, April 1, 2002, p. 36.

[8]Roberti Mar, "Meet Me on the Web," *Fortune*, no. 10, Winter 2002, p. 37.

VIDEOCONFERENCE TIPS

- Research several providers of videoconferencing services. Compare prices, accommodations, and technical expertise.
- Scout the location in advance. Visit several videoconferencing facilities so you can judge whether your presenters will feel comfortable in their space.
- Communicate by email with the individuals at the other meeting locations. This communication should take place long before the actual videoconference is scheduled to occur.
- Make a list of the meeting participants, and ensure that everyone needs to attend. Designate a meeting leader.
- Ask for feedback regarding topics and presentations.
- Prepare a detailed written agenda.
- Take time to design the presentation. Make it easy for all the participants to follow.
- Keep each individual's presentation short and simple.
- Rehearse ahead of time. Have the leader arrange the order and flow of the individual presentations. Each presenter needs to be clear, concise, and organized.
- Evaluate the results. After the meeting is concluded, discuss with participants to determine which presentations went well and what can be done to improve the next time.

Source: Len Lipton, "Desire to Videoconference Means Brushing Up Skills," *Los Angeles Business Journal*, November 5, 2001.

FIGURE 17-3 Videoconference Tips

meeting in its simplest form. Data conferencing software allows participants to:

- Share a program running on one computer with other participants in the conference. Participants can review the same information and see the work of the person sharing the application.
- Exchange information between shared applications through a clipboard, transfer files, and collaborate on a shared whiteboard.
- Send files to conference participants.
- Chat with other conference participants by keying text messages or record meeting notes and action items as part of the collaborative process.

The technologies for online conferencing continue to grow and expand. Current technologies allow participants in an online meeting to include data, video, and an audio component, thus embracing all of the technologies described above. IM, document sharing, and streaming video have transformed online meetings. Web conferencing software allows the user to show presentations, field ques-

tions, and poll audiences with the presenter and audience needing only a standard Web browser.[9] The audio portion of a Web conference can be accessed through a telephone line or by using the audio capabilities on the Internet. Online meeting considerations are provided in Figure 17-4.

Advantages and Disadvantages of Electronic Meetings

Just as face-to-face meetings have advantages and disadvantages, so do electronic meetings. Advantages include:

- Savings in travel time, costs, meals, and hotel rooms.
- Presentation of a considerable amount of information concisely through sophisticated audio and video technology.
- Bringing together people with expertise in a number of different areas to discuss problems of mutual concern with a minimum of effort.

---

[9]Bill Roberts, "The Next Best Thing to Being There," *Electronic Business*, v. 28, no. 3, March 2002.

ONLINE MEETING CONSIDERATIONS

- Encourage employees who plan to use these tools to view demonstrations and to be trained to use the tools.
- Ask if online conferencing is appropriate for the planned meeting. Typically, meetings that are relatively passive and that last an hour or less are appropriate.
- Consider breaking half-day or full-day meetings into smaller virtual sessions lasting an hour.
- Resolve any internal network problems.

Source: Bill Roberts, "The Next Best Thing to Being There," *Electronic Business*, v. 28, no. 3, March 2002, p. 42.

FIGURE 17~4 Online Meeting Considerations

- Providing conference information to individuals who are not in attendance.
- Increased availability of software packages and service providers.

Disadvantages to electronic meetings include:

- Less spontaneity between individuals due to a structured environment.
- The tendency to be more formal in nature.
- Inability to see body language of all participants at one time.
- Inability to pick up small nuances of body language over the monitor.
- Little or no socializing time between participants.
- Less chance for effective brainstorming on issues.

International Meetings

In today's global business environment, international business meetings are quite common. These meetings may be face-to-face or electronic. In either situation, you cannot forget that cultural differences exist. If the meeting is to be successful, such differences must be understood and respected. Otherwise, you might have an international incident rather than resolution to a problem. International meetings are more formal in nature. Hierarchi-cal considerations must be considered and dealt with appropriately.

Being prepared for cultural differences is crucial. For example, language has different meanings in different cultures. Consider the following examples.

- Even though the British speak English, they do not speak American English and vice versa. For example, in the United States, *tabling*, means postponing a discussion. In England, to table a subject means to put it on the table for present discussion.
- Values in other countries are different from those values held in the United States. Americans value honesty and directness. However, Asians are more concerned with the quality of an interaction; they do not expect and do not want your complete candor.
- Silence is a form of speech in some cultures. For example, the Swedes value silence, whereas Americans are often uncomfortable with silence.
- In Thailand, it is customary to exchange gifts during the second business meeting. In China, however, gift giving is considered a form of bribery and is actually illegal.

When you are assisting with an international meeting, prior to the meeting, you need to research carefully the culture of participating countries. Your local bookstore or library has resources that can assist you. You can also conduct your research on the Internet. Two Internet resources you should find helpful are **www.executiveplanet.com/index2.jsp** and **www.businessculture.com**. With these sites, you can select your destination country and receive an overview of appropriate etiquette and hints on conducting business in specific areas of the world.[10]

International etiquette is also essential if you are meeting over the Internet. Virtual meetings also need to reflect the customs and

---

[10]"International Etiquette," EffectiveMeetings.com, accessed November 9, 2002; available from **www.effectivemeetings.com/meetingplanning/offsite/rome.asp**.

traditions of the individuals involved. Virtual meetings have the added difficulty of participants not physically being with the people they are meeting. A misinterpreted sentence could lead to a major misunderstanding with no chance for rebuttal.

Meeting Roles and Responsibilities

When organizing a meeting, several individuals play an important part in planning and implementing effective meetings. These individuals include the executive who calls the meeting, the administrative professional who assists in planning and preparing for the meeting, the leader who facilitates the meeting, and the attendees. Each individual or group of individuals has specific roles and responsibilities for the creation of an effective meeting environment.

The Executive's Role and Responsibilities

The executive has a variety of responsibilities when planning a meeting, including determining the purpose of the meeting, setting objectives, determining who should attend, determining the number of attendees, planning the agenda, and establishing the time and place.

Determining the Purpose

Every meeting must have a purpose; without it, there is no need for a meeting. Generally, the executive calls the meeting, so it is his or her role to determine the purpose. When meeting notices are sent out, the purpose should be stated clearly so all participants understand why the meeting is occurring. Although the administrative professional is not responsible for calling the meeting or determining the purpose, he or she must understand the purpose. Understanding the purpose is necessary so that the administrative professional can make appropriate arrangements.

Setting the Objectives

Every meeting should have specific written objectives. Objectives more clearly define the purpose and delineate what is to be accomplished. For example, if the general purpose is to determine the training needs of the organization, the objectives might be to:

- Establish training needs for each department.
- Determine whether the training needs are to be done by internal staff or by an outside consultant.
- Determine the amount of time necessary for training.
- Determine the budget for training.

Meeting objectives should be shared with attendees before the meeting. This will provide them with an understanding of the purpose and objectives and allow them to clarify any questions they may have.

Determining Who Should Attend

The individual who is calling the meeting is generally responsible for determining who should be included. Attendees should be selected based on the type of meeting. If you are planning an information-sharing meeting, you need to invite the people who have the right information. You should also make sure that the people who need to gather the information are planning to attend.[11] The people who should be invited to the meeting are those who:

- Have knowledge that can contribute to meeting the objectives.
- Will be responsible for implementing the decisions.
- Represent a group that will be affected by the decisions.

In addition, you need to consider the backgrounds of the people who are attending. For example, a **heterogeneous group** (a group having dissimilar backgrounds and experiences) can often solve problems more

---

[11] "Is this Meeting Necessary?" *Supervision*, v. 62, no. 11, November 2001.

satisfactorily than a **homogeneous group** (a group with similar backgrounds and experiences). A heterogeneous group can bring varying views to the problem and encourage creative thinking through the diversity that is present. However, a heterogeneous group demands a skilled facilitator to make the meeting productive.

Determining the Number of Attendees

The ideal number of attendees is based on the purpose of the meeting and the number of people who can best achieve the purpose. The best size for a problem-solving and decision-making group is from seven to ten people. This size group allows for creative **synergy** (the ideas and products of a group of people developed through interaction with each other). This size group provides enough people to generate divergent points of view and to challenge what each person is thinking.

Small groups of seven or fewer people are necessary at times. For example, if the purpose of a meeting is to discuss a personnel issue, the employee, supervisor, and human resources director may be the only individuals in attendance. If the purpose of a meeting is to discuss a faulty product design, the product engineer, the manager of the engineering department, and the line technician may be the only people in attendance.

Planning the Agenda

The executive's role is to plan the agenda. The agenda, which should be distributed before the meeting, provides participants with the purpose and objectives of the meeting. Make sure the agenda includes the following information:

- Name of the group, department, or committee
- Date of the meeting
- Start and end times
- Location of the meeting

An agenda is an outline of what will occur at a meeting and helps to ensure that all participants are prepared for the meeting, that each agenda item achieves the desired outcome, and that no time is wasted during the meeting. Figure 17-5 provides the steps to creating an effective agenda. In addition, an agenda should provide:

- The order in which the objectives of the meeting will be presented.
- The individual responsible for presenting the agenda item.
- The action expected on agenda items.
- Background materials (if necessary).

A well-planned agenda saves time and increases productivity in a meeting. By providing attendees with review information before

---

CREATING AN EFFECTIVE AGENDA

- Send an email or memo stating there will be a meeting, including the goal of the meeting and the administrative details such as when and where the meeting will be held.
- Ask participants requesting to have an item placed on the agenda to contact you no fewer than two days before the meeting, indicating the agenda item and the amount of time they will need to present it.
- Summarize the agenda so it includes the agenda item, presenter, and time. Make sure all agenda items are directly related to the goals of the meeting.
- Send the agenda to all meeting participants at least one day in advance. Make sure the agenda includes meeting goals, location, time, and duration.
- Follow the agenda during the meeting.

Source: "How to Create an Agenda, Step by Step," EffectiveMeetings.com; accessed on November 9, 2002; available from **www.effectivemeetings.com/meetingplanning/index.asp#1**.

FIGURE 17-5 Creating an Effective Agenda

a meeting, the leader can use the meeting time effectively.

Establishing the Time and Place

The executive is responsible for establishing the approximate time of the meeting and the general location for the meeting. For example, the executive may tell the administrative professional that the meeting should take place on Tuesday morning. The administrative professional must then check with other attendees (or their administrative professionals) to determine the most appropriate time on Tuesday morning. The administrative professional may have access to an online calendar or scheduling program, which assists in determining an appropriate meeting time. The executive decides whether the meeting should be held onsite at the organization or held at an off-site location such as a hotel conference room.

The Administrative Professional's Role and Responsibilities

As an administrative professional, you have a number of responsibilities when planning face-to-face or electronic meetings. In addition to attending meetings, you must work closely with the supervisor to clarify the meeting's purpose and expectations. Although many of the responsibilities of the administrative professional can be handled independently, you should understand your supervisor's preferences in a variety of areas. When you first join an organization or begin to work with a supervisor, take time before each meeting to understand his or her needs and preferences. Once you have spent some time with a supervisor, you will have less need to discuss details. However, you should continue to discuss the purpose of the meeting, the objectives, and the general expectations. Otherwise, you may make decisions about details that lessen the effectiveness of a meeting.

Confirming the Date and Time

At times, the executive will request to hold a meeting on a specific date and at a specific time. At other times, one or both of these decisions will be left up to the administrative professional. When selecting a date, consider the expected attendees' other commitments. If you know several attendees have a standing monthly meeting on the second Tuesday of the month, try to avoid that day. In addition, you may want to avoid scheduling meetings for Monday mornings and late Friday afternoons. Many employees use Monday mornings to get an overview of the week and to handle pressing items that occurred over the weekend; Friday afternoons are often used to tie up loose ends and to complete projects.

The time of the meeting is also an important consideration. When selecting a time, avoid meetings immediately after lunch and near the end of the day. Keep in mind that meetings should last no longer than two hours; when people must sit longer than two hours, they get restless and lose interest in the topic. If a meeting will go longer than two hours, the leader should schedule short five- to ten-minute breaks for participants, after which the attendees will be better able to focus on the task at hand.

Selecting and Preparing the Meeting Room

When you know the date and time of the meeting and number of attendees, you should select the meeting room. Most businesses have several conference rooms of varying sizes. Be certain to reserve a room that is appropriate for the size of the group. If you choose a room that is too large, participants may feel "lost" in the room. Conversely, if you choose a room that is too small, participants will feel crowded.

Check the temperature controls before the meeting. Remember that bodies give off heat, so the room will be warmer with people in it. A standard rule is to aim for about 68 degrees. Know what to do if the temperature gets too hot or cold during the meeting. A hot stuffy room or a room that is icy cold is a big distraction for people who are trying to make important decisions. Check the ventilation. Is the airflow adequate? Make sure the lighting is adequate and you have enough space and an electrical outlet for whatever equipment is needed.

Determining the Seating Arrangement

The seating arrangement of the room depends on the objectives of the meeting. The five basic seating arrangements are rectangular, circular, oval, u-shaped, and semicircular. Figure 17-6 depicts these seating arrangements.

The **rectangular arrangement** allows the leader to maintain control since she or he sits at the head of the table. This arrangement is also effective when particpants will be talking in groups of two or three. Individuals seated next to or opposite each other have a chance to discuss issues as they arise. However, if discussion is important, the table should not be too long. A long table may make communication difficult because people cannot see the

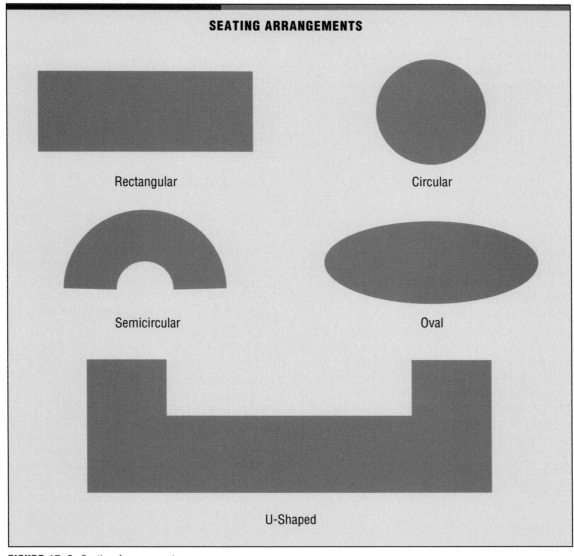

SEATING ARRANGEMENTS

Rectangular

Circular

Semicircular

Oval

U-Shaped

FIGURE 17~6 Seating Arrangements

nonverbal behavior of other participants. A long table may also prevent the leader from taking part in discussions if he or she is seated away from other participants. The rectangular arrangement is most effective in formal meetings.

The **circular** and **oval arrangements** work best when the purpose of the meeting is to generate ideas and discussion and the meeting is relatively informal. These arrangements encourage togetherness, shared communication, and participation. Attendees can make direct eye contact with everyone else in the group. Communication channels are considered equal among all participants since no one person is in a dominant position.

The **u-shaped** and **semicircular arrangements** work well for small groups of six to eight people. The leader retains moderate control since he or she is in a dominant position. The two arrangements are also good for showing visuals because the visual can be positioned at the front of the configuration.

Make certain you have enough chairs for the number of participants who are scheduled to attend. You do not want to have extra chairs; they just get in the way, and it appears as though some people failed to attend. You also do not want to have too few chairs; it appears as though you did not plan properly.

Preparing the Meeting Agenda

All meeting participants should know the purpose and plan of action before coming to a meeting. An **agenda** is an outline of the procedures or the order of business to be followed during a meeting. Participants should receive a detailed agenda at least a day (preferably a week) before the scheduled meeting. It is a good idea to send out the agenda with the meeting notice. The agenda should include the following information:

- Name of the meeting or group
- Date of the meeting
- Start and end times
- Location of the meeting
- Order of agenda items

- Individual responsible for presenting the agenda item
- Expected action on agenda items
- Background materials (if necessary)

You can also allocate a particular time for each item on the agenda. Although doing this is not essential, it does remind people of the importance of time and of adhering to a schedule. The order of the agenda items can vary. Some people believe the most difficult items should be presented first; others think they should be presented last. Check with your supervisor to determine the order that he or she prefers.

The action that is expected on the agenda items should be noted. Notice in Figure 17-7 that the word *ACTION* is listed after specific agenda items. This word denotes that a decision will be made on the item. This approach helps participants know that they should come to the meeting prepared to make a decision.

Preparing Meeting Notices

If the meeting is scheduled within the organization, notify participants by email or through an interoffice memorandum. If you have access to employees' individual online calendars, you can check the schedules of meeting participants to determine whether they are free at the time of the meeting. Be certain the meeting notification includes the following information:

- Purpose and objectives of the meeting
- Meeting agenda
- Location, date, and time
- Background information
- Assigned materials for preparation

You may be responsible for following up on meeting notices. Although you have asked people to let you know if they cannot attend, not everyone will respond. Email or telephone the people who have not responded to determine if they will be present. You also need to let your supervisor know who will be attending the meeting and who will be late. If

MEETING AGENDA

**Planning Meeting
Conference Room C**

April 20, 2005

I. Review of accomplishments on department objectives for
last six months (30 minutes) ....All Managers

II. Proposed budget for next year (20 minutes) ....Juan Menendez

III. Goals for next six months (1 hour) ACTION ....All Managers

IV. Objective planning timelines (15 minutes) ACTION ....Juan Menendez

FIGURE 17~7 Meeting Agenda

a number of people are unable to attend, inform your supervisor. He or she may choose to change the meeting time and/or date.

Preparing Materials for the Leader

Materials for the leader should include:

- The meeting notice with a list of the people who will attend.
- Materials that have been sent out before the meeting.
- Notes that are needed at the meeting.
- Visuals or handouts.

If the leader is a participant in an off-site meeting, you may need to include directions to the meeting location. Using such online sites as **www.mapquest.com**, you can get maps, driving directions, and traffic reports.

Preparing Materials for Attendees

Background materials should be sent to attendees with the meeting notice and agenda. If handouts are to be distributed during the meeting, prepare them well in advance of the meeting. If the handouts are made up of several pages, place them in individual folders. Sometimes attendees are expected to take notes. If so, you might provide a pad of paper in the folder. Extra pencils and pens should be made available for attendees.

Ordering Equipment

Determine what equipment, if any, is needed for the meeting. Follow through to make sure the equipment is available. It is a good idea to make a list of the necessary equipment and note on the list the arrangements that have been made. List the person responsible for obtaining each item. If it is your responsibility, note that. Before the meeting begins, take your list to the room and check it against the equipment there.

Ordering Food and Beverages

For a morning meeting, coffee, tea, and juice can be provided for participants. Water should also be available. If it is an afternoon meeting, you may want to provide coffee and/or soft drinks. It is not necessary to provide beverages. Check with your supervisor to see what he or she prefers.

For a luncheon meeting, you may have the responsibility of selecting the menu, calling the caterer, and arranging for the meal to be delivered. The lunch should be light if you expect the participants to work afterward; a heavy meal often makes people sleepy. If you are aware of participants who have special dietary needs, make special accommodations for them. The caterer can usually recommend a substitute meal.

For a dinner meeting, you may work with an outside caterer or with hotel staff. You are usually responsible for selecting the menu. If you know the attendees, consider their preferences when selecting the food.

Duties during the Meeting

The administrative professional's responsibilities during the meeting are varied. You may be expected to greet guests and introduce them to other participants. Your role is to make them feel comfortable and welcome.

Your main responsibility during the meeting is to take the **minutes** (a written record of a meeting). Sit near the leader so you can clearly hear what is being said. You need to note the names of the people in attendance and those who are absent. A laptop computer can be an efficient way for you to record the proceedings of a meeting. With a laptop, the minutes are almost ready to print (with minor editing) and distribute once you leave the meeting.

If you are taking the minutes of an organizational meeting, such as a board meeting or a professional group, the proceedings are recorded in a formal manner. Minutes contain a record of important matters that are presented in the meeting. Although you do not need to record the entire minutes verbatim, you must record motions verbatim and all other pertinent information. Items that should be included in the minutes are as follows:

- Date, time, and place of the meeting
- Name of the group
- Name of the presiding officer
- Members present and absent
- Approval or correction of the minutes from the previous meeting

You can use a laptop computer to record the minutes of a meeting.

- Reports of committees, officers, or individuals
- Motions made, including the name of the person who made the motion, the name of the person who seconded it, and an indication of whether it passed or failed
- Items on which action needs to be taken and the person responsible for taking the action
- A concise summary of the important points of discussion
- The date and time of the next meeting (if one is scheduled)
- The name and title of the person who will be signing the minutes (the secretary) along with a signature line

Minutes should be prepared in a timely manner, usually 24 to 48 hours after the meeting. Although there is no set format for minutes, some general guidelines should be followed.

- Minutes are generally single-spaced. Margins should be at least 1 inch. If the minutes are to be placed in a bound book, the left margin should be $1\frac{1}{2}$ inches.
- Capitalize and center the heading.
- Subject captions (the agenda's subject captions may be used) should be used for ease in locating various sections of the minutes.
- Use businesslike language. Do not include personal opinions or comments.
- List verbatim any motions made.
- Minutes may or may not be signed. Minutes of board meetings and professional organizations are generally signed. However, routine minutes of meetings within a business may not be signed. If minutes are to be signed, a signature line should be provided.

Routine Follow-up Tasks

Some routine tasks should be followed after a meeting, including these:

- Check the meeting room to see that it is left in good order. Return all equipment. See that additional chairs or tables are removed from the room. Clean up any papers and materials left in the room. If the room needs to be cleaned, notify the cleaning staff.
- Notify individuals who were not present at the meeting but were given duties or assignments.
- Note on your calendar items that require future attention.
- Note on the next meeting agenda any items that need to be considered at that meeting.
- Evaluate the meeting. Consider how you might improve the arrangements for the next meeting. Make notes for your files so you can review them before the next meeting.

The Leader's Responsibilities

To conduct an effective meeting, a leader who is skilled in running a meeting should be put in charge. She or he must understand the purpose of the meeting and be able to engage people in effective conversation around the issues. The leader must also be able to bring closure to the agreed-upon objectives.

Make the Purpose and Objectives Clear

As you have already learned, the purpose of the meeting must be clearly established. The leader of the meeting does not necessarily establish the purpose. For example, assume that an executive of a company calls a meeting. He or she determines what the purpose is before the meeting and makes that purpose clear in writing. Although the executive is the leader of the meeting, he or she may choose to have someone else preside over the meeting. Once the purpose of the meeting is established and sent out in writing to the participants by the executive, the leader's responsibility is to reiterate the purpose at the beginning of the meeting. The leader should also let the participants know the objectives of the meeting—what must be accomplished at the meeting and what must be completed after the meeting.

Adhere to the Agenda

The leader is responsible for keeping the participants focused on the agenda. If the attendees stray from the agenda, the leader must sensitively but firmly bring them back to the agenda. The leader might say, "Thank you for your comments about that issue. We can put that issue on the agenda for a future meeting. Now let's continue with the agenda for today."

Manage Time

The leader must begin the meeting on time, even if several people are not present. Waiting for others to arrive is not fair to the individuals who have made an effort to be on time. Just as important as starting on time is ending on time. The leader must be sensitive to other commitments of participants. Time frames, both beginning and ending, should be established when the notice of the meeting is sent out. The leader is responsible for maintaining these time commitments.

Encourage Participation

Before participants are invited to a meeting, considerable thought must be given to who should attend. The leader should guide, mediate, probe, and stimulate discussion. He or she should allow time for thoughts to emerge. Any group discussion is strengthened by diversity of thinking. The leader should encourage participation from those who may not otherwise

express their views during meetings. The leader can use well-placed questions to draw out less talkative participants. Figure 17-8 provides tips to assist a leader in encouraging participation in a meeting.

The leader is also responsible for making sure that one or two attendees do not dominate the discussion. The leader can guide a balanced and controlled discussion by adhering to the following suggestions.

- Keep the participants focused on the agenda.
- Encourage participation from everyone even if the opinions being expressed are about highly volatile issues.
- Limit the domination of any one person in the meeting.
- Positively reinforce all individuals for their contributions.
- Keep the discussions moving toward the objectives and outcomes that have been determined.

Reach Decisions

The leader is responsible for helping the participants reach a decision about the issue, problem, or direction. Remember that every effective meeting has a purpose and objectives, from which outcomes occur. For example, assume you are setting goals for your department for the next year. One of your goals is to increase the number of customers by 5 percent. How are you going to meet this objective? What steps will you take? Merely saying that a goal is to increase the number of customers does not help the objective get accomplished. Detailed steps as to how, when, and by whom it will be done bring closure to the objective.

Evaluate the Meeting

It is not necessary to complete a formal evaluation for informal meetings within an organization. However, an informal evaluation by the leader (and possibly by the participants) should be completed. The attendees are usually very forthright. They may even tell the leader they found the meeting a waste of time. If an attendee makes such a statement, the

Even if several attendees are not present, the leader should strive to start and end the meeting on time.

© GETTY IMAGES/PHOTODISC

ENCOURAGING PARTICIPATION

- Make it safe. People won't feel comfortable sharing their ideas if they think they may face retribution or ridicule.
- Create a "blame-free zone." Make sure you are looking for ways of improving a process rather than assigning blame to a person or department. The focus should be positive, not negative.
- Act as a "gate keeper." Encourage equal participation by creating openings and asking for input.
- Listen. Listen carefully to the message and the feelings behind it. Explore ideas, rather than debate or defend.
- Contain digression. Limit irrelevant discussion and unnecessarily long examples or stories.
- End the discussion. Make sure all participants have the same impression of what was said, helping to close and decide any necessary issues.
- Test for consensus. Summarize the group's position and state any decisions. Check for agreement of the summary.

Source: "Meeting Skills," *TUFTS University Organizational Development & Training Tip Sheet*, **www.tufts.edu**, accessed November 9, 2002; available from **www.tufts.edu/hr/tips/meeting.html**.

FIGURE 17~8 Encouraging Participation

leader should seek clarification about what the person meant. Regardless of the method of evaluation, after the meeting, the leader should ask himself or herself the following questions.

- Were the attendees participatory?
- Was the nonverbal behavior positive?
- Were the participants creative problem solvers?

- Did the participants exhibit a high energy level?
- Was the purpose of the meeting satisfied?
- Were appropriate decisions made?
- Can I improve on how I handled the issues, the people, or the meeting in general?

If the meeting is relatively formal, the leader may ask participants to fill out an evaluation form, as shown in Figure 17-9.

MEETING EVALUATION FORM

	Yes	No
1. Were the purpose and objectives of the meeting accomplished?	❏	❏
2. Was the agenda received in time to prepare for the meeting?	❏	❏
3. Did the leader adhere to the agenda?	❏	❏
4. Were the appropriate people included in the meeting?	❏	❏
5. Did the leader encourage participation by all members?	❏	❏
6. Did participants listen to one another?	❏	❏
7. Did the meeting start on time?	❏	❏
8. Did the meeting end on time?	❏	❏
9. Did the leader help bring closure to the objectives?	❏	❏
10. Were decisions consistent with the purpose and objectives of the meeting?	❏	❏

FIGURE 17~9 Meeting Evaluation Form

Participants' Responsibilities

As a leader has responsibilities, so do the participants. Their roles are much broader than just attending the meeting. Their responsibilities begin before the meeting and continue after the meeting.

Before the Meeting

Before the meeting, participants are responsible for responding to the meeting notice in a timely manner. In addition, they are responsible for reading any materials that were distributed before the meeting. Participants should make sure they understand the purpose of the meeting and evaluate the meeting materials in relation to the purpose of the meeting. Participants must understand that they have been included in the meeting because the executive or leader believes they have something to contribute. Therefore, they must take their role seriously. If participants have questions before the meeting, they should contact the leader for clarification.

During the Meeting

Participants also have the following responsibilities during the meeting.

- Arrive on time.
- Adhere to the agenda.
- Make contributions.
- Listen to other participants' contributions and respond if they have additional information.
- Respect the leader's role.
- Avoid dominating the discussion.
- Avoid being judgmental of others' comments.
- Be courteous to each individual in the meeting.
- Take notes, if necessary.

After the Meeting

Once the meeting is over, a participant's responsibilities do not end. The participant may be responsible for research, study, or action before the next meeting. The participant may also be asked to work with a small group of people to bring back a recommendation to the next meeting. Whatever follow-up is necessary by the participant, he or she must be committed to carrying out those responsibilities in a timely manner.

Conferences and Conventions

A conference is much larger in scope and has many more participants than a meeting. For example, a company or companies may hold a national sales conference each year to introduce and market the company's new products. Executives may belong to professional organizations in their field of expertise, such as accounting, financial management, or human resources. Many professional organizations hold at least one conference a year, and executives are encouraged to participate as a means of staying current in their field. As an administrative professional, you may belong to a professional organization such as the International Association of Administrative Professionals (IAAP), the American Association for Medical Transcriptionist^{SM} (AAMT), or the National Association of Legal Secretaries^{SM} (NALS). Your role as an administrative professional may be to plan or help plan a national conference.

Before the Event

Preparing for a regional or national conference takes months of work, and the planning is extremely important. Good planning will ensure a smooth, successful conference; poor planning will result in a disorganized, ineffective conference. Two of the most important considerations are to determine the location and to arrange for meeting facilities. Once the location has been determined, you can contact a variety of agencies to obtain information that will assist in your planning.

- Contact the chamber of commerce in the city under consideration. Ask for information about the city and appropriate conference facilities. You can use the Internet to do this.

- Request conference planning guides from hotels and conference centers that will provide you with floor plans of the facilities, dining and catering services, price lists of rooms, and layouts of meeting rooms.

It is important to know how many people are expected to attend overall and approximately how many people will attend each session so rooms large enough to accommodate the attendees can be reserved.

If outside presenters will be speaking at the conference, you may be asked to make their travel arrangements. You should determine the type of accommodations required—room arrangements (single, double, queen- or king-size bed), flight preferences, arrival and departure times, rental car needs, and so on. If an individual is expected to arrive late at a hotel, the hotel should be notified to hold the reservation for late arrival. Find out if someone from the organization will pick up the guests when they arrive in town. If so, the designated person should be given the name(s), times of arrival, flight numbers, hotel accommodations, and other relevant information.

A preregistration period usually takes place during which people can register for the conference (sometimes at a reduced cost). As an administrative professional, you may be responsible for designing the registration form, sending it out, and handling the completed registration forms. You should create a database of registrants if you are responsible for the preparation of name tags, folders, or envelopes containing tickets for special events. You may also be asked to assist with registration at the conference. If the conference is a large one, several individuals may be needed to staff the registration tables.

During the Event

Your responsibilities during the conference may include running errands, delivering messages to participants, and solving problems that arise. Other responsibilities may include checking room arrangements, equipment needs, meal arrangements, and so on. At a conference, you are a representative of the company or organization for which you work. You must present a positive image at all times. Keep a smile on your face, and handle even the most difficult situations with poise and confidence.

After the Event

After the conference, your basic duties involve cleaning up and following up. You may need to assist speakers and guests with transportation to the airport, write letters of appreciation to presenters, and process expense reports.

You may also be responsible for making sure that the proceedings of the conference are published and mailed to the participants. Generally, you are not responsible for the actual writing of the conference proceedings, but you may be asked to work with the conference reporters in producing a comprehensive report based on taped conference sessions. If papers are presented at a conference, each presenter is usually asked to submit his or her paper before the conference. Copies of the papers may then be provided for the participants at the meeting. As a final responsibility, you may be asked to keep a record of problems that occurred and make recommendations for future conferences. ■

SUMMARY

To reinforce what you have learned in this chapter, study this summary.

- The effective meeting is one in which there is a definite need for the meeting, the purpose is stated and understood by all participants, the appropriate people are in attendance, an agenda is prepared and followed, all members participate, and outcomes are achieved as a result of the meeting.

- A meeting should be held when a group needs to be involved in solving a problem or making a decision, an issue arises that needs clarification, information needs to be shared with a group, or communication needs to occur quickly with a large number of people.

- Meetings are not a good idea when there is no clearly defined purpose for the meeting; no consideration has been given to people who need to attend; confidential or sensitive personnel matters must be addressed; there are inadequate data for the meeting; there is insufficient time to prepare for the meeting; there is considerable anger and hostility in the group and people need time to calm down; or the same information could be covered in a memo, an email, or a brief report.

- Typical business meetings include staff meetings, committee meetings, project team meetings, customer/client meetings, board of directors meetings, conventions, and conferences. These meetings may be held in either a face-to-face mode or through electronic means.

- Face-to-face meetings are not obsolete; in fact, in the age of high-tech communication, they carry increased importance. Advantages include informal communication takes place among participants before, during, and after the meeting; participants can closely observe others' body language; individuals feel more relaxed; attendees can deal with difficult issues effectively; interactive group discussion is more likely; and widespread participation among group members is more likely.

- Electronic meetings (teleconferencing) continue to increase because of ongoing globalization of corporations and the wider availability of conferencing and integration tools.

- Audioconferencing tools may be as simple as a speakerphone or as elaborate as a room full of high-tech equipment. Advantages of audioconferencing include the ability to assemble individuals on short notice; ability to connect individuals at a variety of national and international locations; use of telephone technology or special technology to support large groups and rooms; and decreased travel time and expense.

- Disadvantages of audioconferences include the inability for participants to see others' body language, difficulty in managing turn taking when people are speaking, difficulty in identifying the speaker, and the potential for participants to feel excluded.

- Videoconferencing can be accomplished using a PC-based application or by the use of numerous pieces of equipment that have been set up in a specially equipped room. Prices for videoconferencing systems have decreased substantially, and the process has been simplified.

- Online meetings may include computer conferencing, data conferencing, and Web conferencing. Data conferencing software allows users to share a software program, exchange information between shared applications, send files to participants, and chat with other conference participants. Current technologies allow participants to include IM, document sharing, and streaming video.

- Advantages to electronic meetings include savings in travel time, costs, meals, and hotel rooms; presentation of a considerable amount of information; bringing together people with expertise in a number of different areas; providing conference information to individuals who are unable to attend; and availability of software packages and service providers.

- Disadvantages to electronic meetings include decreased spontaneity; a more formal structure; the inability to see and interpret body language; little or no socializing time; and less chance for effective brainstorming on issues.

- International meetings are quite common and may be face-to-face or electronic. In either situation, considerable attention needs to be given to cultural differences that exist.

- The executive's role in meetings is to determine the purpose of the meeting, set the objectives, determine who should attend, determine the number of attendees, plan the agenda, and establish the time and place.

- The administrative professional's role includes confirming the date and time, selecting and preparing the meeting room, determining the seating arrangement, preparing the agenda, preparing meeting notices, preparing materials for the leader, preparing materials for attendees, ordering equipment, and ordering food and beverages. The administrative professional may also be requested to take minutes of the meeting and to perform routine follow-up tasks.

- The leader's responsibilities include making the purpose and objectives clear, adhering to the agenda, managing time, encouraging participation, reaching decisions, and evaluating the meeting.

- Participants' responsibilities include reading materials that were sent out regarding the meeting. During the meeting, participants should arrive on time, adhere to the agenda, contribute, listen to others, respect the leader, be courteous, and take notes. Participants should not dominate the discussion or become judgmental of others' comments.

- The administrative professional's responsibilities for conferences vary. He or she may be asked to plan or assist with the planning of a national conference. Before the conference, he or she may be asked to determine the location and to arrange for meeting facilities, make travel arrangements for outside presenters or speakers, and handle preregistration activities. During the conference, he or she may be asked to run errands, deliver messages, and solve problems as they arise. Cleanup and follow-up duties after the conference include assisting speakers and guests with transportation to the airport, writing letters of appreciation to presenters, and processing expense reports.

FIND THE PROBLEM

Jake Heiden is the mailroom supervisor at People Pharmaceuticals. Jake holds bimonthly staff meetings with his mailroom team to discuss mailroom operations and customer service issues. Jake makes sure his staff is prepared for any problems that arise in the mailroom and within the departments while mailroom personnel are collecting and delivering mail. Over the last two years, problems have been rare since any concerns mentioned to the staff are presented and discussed at the staff meetings. Jake's goal is to address the concern rather than to assign blame.

Dee Snyder, the copy center manager, is frustrated with the negative attitude that seems to exist within the organization about the copy center staff. In fact, there are constant complaints by employees about the staff's inability to meet deadlines, the poor quality of jobs, and the negative attitudes. Copy center staff meetings focus on complaints about work schedules, inadequate time to meet deadlines, and unreasonable staff expectations. In an attempt to build her team, Dee has asked to sit in on Jake's next staff meeting. After the meeting, Dee tells Jake that she is impressed with the positive and productive meeting and asks for advice on how to make her staff meetings more effective. What advice can Jake give Dee?

PROFESSIONAL POINTERS

As an administrative professional, you may be asked to present at meetings within your organization and at meetings of professional organizations. The following pointers can help you present effectively.

- Thoroughly research the topic you are presenting well in advance of the meeting.
- Secure supporting data and documents you can use to clarify the information you are presenting.
- Anticipate the kinds of questions that may be asked about the subject. Write the questions down and outline your answers. This approach will help you remember the issues and be better prepared when you are asked a question.
- Explain your topics in terms the group can understand.
- Be familiar with parliamentary procedure so you do not breach a rule.
- Be concise; do not ramble.
- Exhibit confidence in yourself and your topic.

REINFORCEMENT ITEMS

1. List and describe the typical business meetings discussed in this chapter.
2. List the responsibilities of the meeting leader in conducting an effective meeting.
3. Describe the responsibilities of the administrative professional before a conference.

CRITICAL-THINKING ACTIVITY

Carol has been in charge of the monthly staff meeting for the past six months. Although Carol has been a participant in these meetings for the last three years, her recent promotion has put her in charge. For as long as Carol can remember, the meetings have been held on the first Tuesday of the month from 10 a.m. to noon. All sales representatives assigned to Carol (about 20) are expected to attend.

Carol decides to take a new approach to the traditional monthly meetings. She believes the agendas used in past meetings were too restrictive and decides to allow her staff to use this meeting time to "blow off steam." She eliminates the standard agendas and gives everyone an opportunity to chat informally before the meeting begins.

Carol believed the first meeting went well. All sales representatives were there at 10 a.m., but Carol wanted everyone to have a few minutes to chat. At 10:15, she began the meeting. Several employees had questions about the health insurance policy, and Carol answered them to the best of her ability. Without the policy information in front of her, however, she found a few questions difficult to answer. Carol promised to get the answers and share them at the next meeting. Several individuals were interested in the new telecommuting program that had been adopted by the organization. Although Carol had read the policy, she was not familiar with all the details. Thankfully Albert Greene, who was involved in the pilot program two years ago, was able to provide background information and answer specific questions about the new program. In fact, Albert offered to prepare a PowerPoint presentation for next month's meeting that would explain the company's policies.

Carol thought the second meeting was productive as well. Several employees had questions about the status of recycling within the organization, and Carol was able to answer them all. Staff members were also interested in the upcoming Christmas party, and the details of that event were discussed as well.

By the sixth meeting, there was an obvious change in the tone of the meeting. Most participants did not arrive until 10:20, and Carol could not get the meeting going until after 10:30. Staff members did not participate in the topic discussions, but chatted with coworkers instead. Carol listened to complaint after complaint, becoming frustrated because so little was accomplished. What did Carol do wrong? How can Carol structure future staff meetings so they are more productive? What suggestions can you give to Carol about being a more effective leader?

VOCABULARY REVIEW

Complete the Vocabulary Review for Chapter 17 given on page 129 of the *Applications Workbook*.

ENGLISH AND WORD USAGE DRILL

Complete the English and Word Usage Drill for Chapter 17 listed on page 130 of the *Applications Workbook*.

WORKPLACE APPLICATIONS

A17-1 (Goals 1 and 2)

Using the Internet, find two articles about online meetings. The first article should discuss the future of online meetings; the second article should discuss conducting effective online meetings. The articles should have been published within the last two years. Be prepared to give an oral presentation to the class on the information you found. Summarize the articles using the memorandum form provided on the Student CD, SCDA17-1. Submit the completed summary to your instructor.

A17-2 (Goals 1 and 2)

Work with six or seven of your classmates. Your task is to conduct an effective meeting in front of your class members. Plan the meeting and determine who will be the leader. The meeting topic should be one of the following:

- Audioconferencing
- Videoconferencing
- Online meetings

The group is to prepare a meeting notice (giving the date, time, place, purpose, and objectives of the meeting), an agenda, written materials (if necessary), and an evaluation form. Distribute the meeting notice, agenda, and written materials to the entire class before the meeting. Once the meeting has been held (in front of the class), your group and other class members are to fill out the evaluation form. Submit a copy of the meeting notice, the agenda, written materials, and a compilation of the responses to the evaluation to your instructor.

A17-3 (Goals 1 and 2)

A case study is provided on page 131 in your *Applications Workbook*. Read the case and respond to the questions. Discuss this case with three classmates. As a group, write a memo to your instructor that summarizes your responses. Use the memorandum form provided on the Student CD, SCDA17-3.

A17-4 (Goal 2)

Attend a meeting of a professional organization (this may be a school club or school association). Take notes at the meeting. Prepare minutes from your notes, and submit a copy to your instructor.

A17-5 (Goal 3)

Kurt Rupprecht has just informed you that he is in charge of preparations for his professional organization's convention two years from now. He expects 3,000 attendees at the convention. He estimates one large meeting room will be needed for the entire membership in addition to 10 small conference rooms. Three meals (one dinner and two luncheons) are planned. Kurt does not expect you to plan the entire event but has asked that you use the Internet to research three event organizers he could hire to assist him with the planning. Compare and contrast the three companies or individuals you identify, and make a recommendation to Mr. Rupprecht as to which company or person you would hire and why.

ASSESSMENT OF CHAPTER GOALS

Did you successfully complete the chapter goals? Evaluate yourself by filling out the form on page 132 of the *Applications Workbook*.

Travel Arrangements

chapter 18

LEARNING GOALS

1. Make domestic travel arrangements.
2. Make international travel arrangements.

The fast-paced international business world of today demands that executives travel. Even though the numerous telecommunication systems such as email, IM, audio-conferencing, online conferencing, and videoconferencing allow fast communication internationally, executives need to be able to communicate face-to-face when negotiating business deals and exchanging information. Additionally, with the multinational nature of businesses, executives must visit their organizations' sites in other countries. As an administrative professional, you also may travel for your company or attend national and international conferences with professional organizations such as IAAP. If you are working for a company who has subsidiaries abroad, you may have the opportunity to work in one of the international locations.

Part of your job as an administrative professional is to handle travel arrangements. If you are to handle these arrangements effectively (making appropriate choices with regard to travel arrangements, hotels, land transportation, and so on), you must become familiar with the many travel services available. This chapter will help you understand your options and become proficient at handling travel tasks.

Domestic Travel

In order to save time, executives prefer to travel by air. However, occasionally they must travel by car and rail. This chapter deals mainly with air travel, with brief sections discussing car and rail travel.

Air Travel

Today an air traveler can have breakfast in San Francisco and dinner in New York. The flight takes about five hours, but time zone differences preclude the person from arriving in New York in time for lunch. (New York is in the Eastern standard time zone; San Francisco is in the Pacific standard time zone.) An air traveler can travel from Chicago, Illinois, to Frankfort, Germany, in approximately 8 hours and from Portland, Oregon, to Seoul, Korea, in approximately 11 hours.

During flight time, an executive can read and send email, write letters and reports and send them back to the office for final formatting and mailing, and stay current on news or investments through the Internet. However, computers may not be used during takeoffs or landings due to possible interference with the electronics of the airplane.

During takeoff, flight, and landing, passengers may not use cell phones and PDAs. Passengers may use cell phones before take-off and after landing. A flight attendant announces when they may and may not be used. FCC and FAA rules and regulations specify that no technology that emits a signal is acceptable during a flight. That technology includes cell phones, PDA features built into cell phones, and PDAs with built-in cell phones. Unless you can pull the wireless card out of your PDA or you can turn the cell phone/wireless parts off, you are legally required to keep your cell phone and PDA off during the duration of a flight.

Flight Classifications

The three classes of flight are first-class, business, and coach. Some flights offer all three classes, with business class being offered mainly on international flights. Most airlines offer first class and coach on all flights. However, some airlines, such as Southwest Airlines®, offer coach class only. Additionally, some regional jets (smaller airplanes with the number of seats ranging from approximately 30 to 100) offer only coach, while other regional jets have both first-class and coach.

First-Class Accommodations. The most expensive and luxurious accommodations are **first-class**. Attendants serve generous portions of food, soft drinks, and alcoholic beverages without additional cost. The seats are generally wider and offer more legroom. There are more flight attendants per customer than in coach or business, which means greater attention and service for each flyer. First-class customers board and exit the flight before other passengers. Attendants take passengers' coats

First-class accommodations are the most expensive of the three classes of flight.

and hang them up; they also store passengers' parcels in overhead bins.

Business-Class Accommodations. **Business-class accommodations** are slightly more expensive than coach. The business-class section is located in front of the coach class and directly behind first class or at the front of the plane if first class is not offered. Accommodations may include more spacious seating than coach, complimentary alcoholic beverages, reclining seats, and more food than coach class.

Coach-Class Accommodations. **Coach-class accommodations** provide complimentary snacks and soft drinks, fruit juice, tea, and coffee. Alcoholic beverages are available upon request at a cost. Seats are closer together; however, one airline, American®, has committed to increasing legroom for its passengers by removing some of the seats. Fewer flight attendants are available to serve the needs of passengers.

Privately Chartered Jets

Some small airlines specialize in privately chartered jet service. These planes are generally small, since most private chartering is for small groups of people. The planes may be housed at locations adjacent to regular airports and use the same takeoff and landing runways as the major airlines. Food is available on these jets at an additional cost; flight attendants are generally not available.

Low-Fare Airlines

Several major occurrences in the United States within the last few years have resulted in business management looking at ways to reduce expenses.

- "Enron Effect," with tougher audits of corporations and zero tolerance of **CFOs** (chief financial officers) for sloppy or creative accounting
- Perceived high price of business travel by boards and management
- Downturn of the economy

According to a study done by Unisys Corporation™ and conducted in collaboration with the Association of Corporate Travel Executives™ (ACTE), the use of low-fare airlines is increasing. Of the survey participants, 72.8 percent indicated their organizations increased the number of segments flown on low-fare airlines, with 68.5 percent saying they plan to increase the use of low-fare airlines in the future.[1]

Low-fare airlines fly for less typically due to the following factors:

- Smaller carriers servicing fewer destinations with limited flight schedules
- No meal service—"peanuts only" or some other small snack

Some of the low-fare airlines are as follows:

- America West Airlines™
- Southwest Airlines
- JetBlue Airways

A number of these low-faire airlines fly into secondary airports. According to the Unisys survey, 59 percent of the survey participants reported their companies actively seek to utilize alternative airports, with one of the reasons being that travelers perceive the airports to be less hassle from a security point of view.

Company-Owned Planes

Large organizations may have their own plane or fleet of planes if the amount of travel within the company makes it advantageous to do so. Pilots employed by the organization fly the planes, which are housed adjacent to local airports. Employees of the organization may drive executives to the airport and pick them up at the airport upon their return.

Airline Clubs

For the frequent business traveler, membership in an airline club may be a worthwhile investment. Major airlines provide these clubs in large airports, and membership is available through the individual airlines. Membership fees vary. A variety of travel perks accompany an airline club, including the following:

- Airport lounges
- Computer equipment, fax, and copy machines
- Conference rooms
- Telephones
- Reading material—current periodicals and newspapers
- Complimentary soft drinks, juice, and coffee
- Alcoholic beverages
- Pastries and snacks
- Assistance with airline reservations, seat selection, and boarding passes

Parking Services

Large airports generally provide free shuttle service from airport parking locations; however, you are charged for parking your car. The fee is based on the location of your car

---

[1]"2002 U.S. Business Travel Survey," accessed December 3, 2002; available from **www.btctravelogue.com/**.

Major airlines provide airline clubs in large airports and offer a wide variety of travel perks.

(with lots closer to the airport being more expensive) and the time your car is in the lot.

Since parking at an airport for an extended period can become expensive, private shuttle services in large cities occupy a profitable business niche. Small buses take you to and from the airport. These buses run at frequent times, with generally no more than a ten-minute wait between runs.

Ticketing

Gone are the days of having only one type of airline ticket, the standard paper one that contains tickets for your departure and your return. Although paper tickets are still available (with some airlines charging an additional fee for them), the **e-ticket** is a common form of ticketing. The usual method of delivering e-tickets to customers is by email or fax. E-tickets may be presented at airport ticket counters for boarding passes. Also, some large airports now have self-service technol-

ogy set up in proximity to the airline ticket counters; you insert your flight information from your e-ticket and receive a boarding pass from the machine. This option eliminates standing in line at the airline ticket counter.

Changes or Cancellations

Occasionally you may need to change or cancel flight reservations. Generally, you are charged a penalty for changing a flight. You should ask when booking a flight if you will be charged for changing flight arrangements. If you are making reservations online, the policy is clearly explained. Some airlines will let you bank the ticket for future flights. If you are working for someone who has frequent flight changes, be certain that you know what the airlines' flight change and/or cancellation policies are.

When a change is due to weather, airplane mechanical difficulty, or some other issue that causes the airline to change or cancel the

Private shuttle services in large cities offer transportation to and from the airport at a site located a distance from the airport.

flight, you are not charged. Since you are usually inconvenienced by such a change, the airlines attempt to make the situation as painless as possible. If the change results in your having to stay overnight, the airlines will generally pay for your hotel and give you vouchers that can be exchanged for food.

Ground Transportation

Once executives arrive at their destination, they need some type of ground transportation to their hotel or business site. That transportation may be a taxi or shuttle service to the location. Since taxi service is generally an expensive method of ground transportation, you should compare the cost between taxi service and other methods of ground transportation before making a decision. Some hotels provide free shuttle service to and from the airport. Private concerns also offer shuttle services that are usually less expensive than

taxi service. Limousine service is available at many airports at about the same price as taxi service.

If executives must attend meetings at several locations during their stay, renting a car may be the most economical and convenient method of ground transportation. Toll-free numbers for car rental agencies are listed in the telephone directory. Rental car arrangements can also be made online as you make flight reservations, or they may be made through airlines or travel agents. When renting a car, specify the make and model preferred and the date and time the car will be picked up and returned.

When arriving at the destination airport, executives pick up their cars from the rental location, which may be in the same building as the airport gates or in a separate building. If the car rental is in a separate location, a free shuttle service is available. The cost of a

© GETTY IMAGES/PHOTODISC

Taxi service is one of the more expensive forms of ground transportation.

rental car is generally a daily rate that includes unlimited mileage. However, sometimes a per-mile rate is charged. The size of the car affects the rate; classifications are full-size (the most expensive), midsize (moderately priced), and economy (the least expensive). Insurance is available. However, if executives have their own coverage through a business or personal policy, the insurance is not mandatory. Customers are asked if they wish to purchase extended insurance coverage.

The car will have a full tank of gas when rented. The executive should fill the car with gas before returning it since the rental agency will charge for gas (generally at a higher price than can be obtained at a local gas station) if the tank is not full. Executives can use a company credit card to rent a car and purchase gas. Some organizations prefer to deal with only one car rental agency; you should know your organization's policy before reserving a

car. Most car rental agencies provide maps and assist in planning the best route to a destination. They also will supply information about hotels, restaurants, and tourist attractions if asked. You can also go online to find a map of the area to be visited and information about hotels, restaurants, and tourist attractions. Two Websites for obtaining maps are **www.mapblast.com** and **www.mapquest.com**. By using these online resources, you can obtain detailed directions of an executive's destinations within a city.

Security Tips for Air Travelers

Since 9/11, America's airports are operating under an unprecedented level of security. Being knowledgeable about security measures can help you know how long you need to be at the airport before your plane leaves, understand what not to pack, and feel confident and secure.

Do Not Pack These Items

- Knives of any length
- Any cutting and puncturing instruments, including straight razors, metal nail files, and pocketknives
- Corkscrews
- Weapons—firearms, ammunition, tear gas, and pepper spray
- Aerosol spray cans—hair spray, deodorant, insect repellant, and so on
- Flammable liquids or solids—paints, paint thinners, lighter fluid

Allow Extra Time

- Heightened airport security measures increase the time needed to check in. Arrive approximately one and one-half to two hours before check-in time.
- Consider taking public transportation to the airport. Curbside access is limited and controlled.
- Curbside check-in is available in some airports. Contact your local airport to see whether it is available.
- Cars left unattended in front of terminals are towed.

Observe Airport Security Measures

- Watch your bags and personal belongings at all times.
- Do not accept packages from strangers.
- Report unattended bags or packages to airport security.
- Report suspicious activities and individuals to airport security.
- Be prepared to take your laptop from its case so it can be X-rayed separately.
- Check to be certain you have all your belongings before leaving the security area—wallets, keys, jewelry, cell phones, and so on.

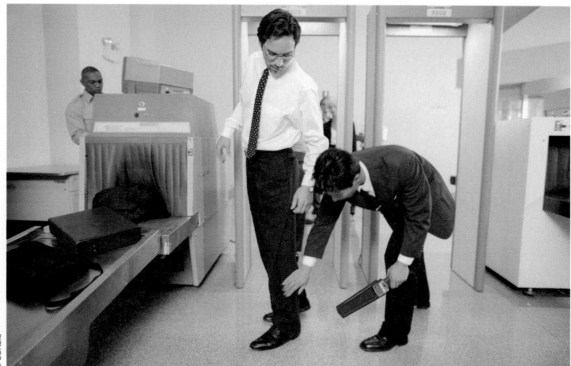

© CORBIS

Heightened airport security measures increase the time needed for check in.

Car Travel

Executives traveling 300 miles or less may prefer to travel by car. Most top-level executives have company-owned or leased cars. Executives can drive their own car and be reimbursed for mileage or rent a car from an agency if they do not have company-owned cars.

Your responsibilities for a car trip may include determining the best route to follow, making hotel reservations, and identifying restaurants along the way. You can use the Internet to find this information. If your employer is a member of **AAA**® (American Automobile Association), you may work with a travel agent employed there to obtain map, hotel, and restaurant information. AAA also provides tour books that give facts about the area being visited, temperatures, hotels and restaurants, and points of interest. AAA's email address is **www.aaa.com**.

Rail Travel

Rail travel is also an option for the executive. Travel by train allows an executive the freedom to work during a trip. Laptops, PDAs, and cell phones may be used. Train stations are generally centrally located within a city, and their fares are usually less expensive than traveling by air. First-class and sleeping accommodations are available on trains, as well as coach accommodations for more economical travel. Dining cars are also available. Travelers can request that meals be delivered to first-class accommodations. You can make train reservations online at **www.amtrak.com**.

Hotel Reservations

You can also make hotel reservations online. Online sites include **www.orbitz.com** and **www.travelocity.com**. These sites allow you to make flight arrangements and car and hotel

Travel arrangements are frequently made online.

reservations at one online location. Additionally, you can telephone a hotel directly or use a travel agent.

When arranging for hotel accommodations, you need the following information from the executive.

- Room rate range
- Accommodations—king- or queen-size bed, smoking or nonsmoking
- Date and approximate arrival time
- Length of stay
- Method of payment

Most hotels ask for a credit card number as confirmation. Many hotels now provide entire no-smoking floors. Find out about the hotel's smoking policy if your employer is concerned about smoke. If the executive will arrive late in the day, you need to inform the hotel staff. Some hotels only hold a room until a specified period—around 6 p.m. If you do not ask for a late arrival time, the hotel may rent the room to someone else. Hotels often confirm reservations by email or fax. Include the confirmation number on the executive's itinerary in case a problem occurs at check-in.

International Travel

Today, with many organizations conducting business around the world, executives often make trips abroad. As an administrative professional, you need to know how to make arrangements for an international trip.

Cultural Differences

When planning a trip to a country for the first time, you should familiarize yourself with the customs and cultures of the people. The expression "ugly American" came about, in part, because Americans are not always sensitive to other cultures when traveling abroad. Consider three situations where Americans made mistakes because they did not understand cultural differences.

Situation 1

A president of an American company meets Hayashi Goro, the president of a Japanese company. The American president makes direct eye contact and extends his hand. With a vigorous handshake and a big smile, he says, "Hello, Mr. Goro." The American president hands the Japanese president his business card, which is printed only in English. As the two presidents begin to walk to their meeting, the American president casually places his arm on the Japanese president's shoulder as an act of friendship. The Japanese president quickly knows the American has done no homework on Japanese culture. Why? Here are the mistakes the American president made.

- In Japan, the last name of the president is given first; his name is Mr. Hayashi. Goro is his first name.
- Although the Japanese generally adopt the Western custom of shaking hands, it is done with a light grip and with the eyes averted. The graceful act of bowing from the waist, however, remains the traditional greeting. Many westerners view the bow as an act of subservience; but the Japanese do not. For the Japanese, a bow signals respect and humility, two qualities coveted throughout Asia.
- The simple act of exchanging business cards is more complex in Japan because the business card represents not only one's identity, but also one's station in life. The American president's card should be printed in both languages—one side in English and the other side in Japanese.
- Prolonged direct eye contact is considered impolite or even intimidating.
- The Japanese are not a touch-oriented society. The American president should avoid any body contact.

Situation 2

At their first meeting, an American visiting Saudi Arabia gives a gift to the president of the company as well as small gifts for his family. What is wrong?

Proper bow etiquette.

It is appropriate to give gifts in Saudi Arabia but not on the first meeting. The interpretation by the Saudi Arabian may be that the gift is a bribe. The spouse of a business acquaintance should not receive a gift; gifts for children are appropriate.

Similar situations can occur when a person is not familiar with the customs of a particular country. It is wise to study the culture before traveling abroad. Help is available through travel agencies, the Web, travel books, international seminars, and **consular offices** in large cities (offices in the United States representing the country abroad and staffed with personnel from the country).

General rules that apply to international travel are provided in Figure 18-1.

Appointments

If you assist the executive in setting up appointments, remember to take into considera-

tion time zone differences. **Jet lag** (a feeling of exhaustion following a flight through several time zones) is a true medical condition that results in prolonged periods of fatigue. Metabolism and medication schedules are upset, in addition to eating and sleeping cycles. As a result, jet lag can greatly restrict an executive's effectiveness. Since it takes the body about a day for each time zone crossed to adapt to the new environment, an executive should take an extra day before meetings begin to recover from the trip. If an executive does not take time for her or his body to adjust to the time differences, fatigue and disorientation can hamper negotiations and cause undue damage to business situations.

However, if an executive does not have the luxury of a full day to recover before appointments, certain techniques generally help with jet lag. For example, when traveling west, two or three days before the flight the executive should postpone bedtime by two or

---

GENERAL RULES FOR INTERNATIONAL TRAVEL

- Learn the appropriate greeting for the country you will be visiting.
- Learn how to say *please* and *thank you* in the language of the country.
- Do not criticize the people or customs of the country you are visiting. Show appreciation for the music, art, and culture of the country.
- Remember that business generally is more formal in other countries than it is in the United States.
- Dress appropriately—generally, business suits for men and conservative dresses or suits for women. Although dress in the United States has become more casual, you cannot assume that is true in other countries.
- Eat the food offered to you. Do not ask what you are being served. Show appreciation to the host.
- Be courteous and respectful at all times.

FIGURE 18–1 General Rules for International Travel

---

three hours. When traveling east, two or three days before the flight the executive should retire two hours earlier than normal. At the same time, the executive can also start shifting mealtimes in the direction of those of the destination city. Although the body clock still must adapt, less jet lag occurs by using these techniques.

Business Cards and Gifts

Executives should have business cards with their name, company affiliation, and address printed in English on one side of the card and the language of the country they are visiting on the other side of the card. The executives from the country visited also have cards and expect to exchange them. In Asia, the exchange of cards is often quite a ceremony. Japanese executives take time to read the card and then store it in a special case. The Japanese consider it rude to simply take the card and put it in their pockets.

Small gifts are usually appropriate for business executives—a nice pen or some similar item. However, before giving a gift, research customs and taboos of the destination country so no embarrassment or hard feelings are involved with the gesture. Additional details concerning gift giving are presented in Figure 18-2.

Flight Classifications

International flight classifications are the same as domestic air travel. Classes of flight are first-class and coach, with business class available on most international flights. Weight and size restrictions for luggage may vary slightly from one airline to another. When traveling abroad, executives must arrive at the airport earlier than normal—generally an hour earlier than for domestic flights. Figure 18-3 lists several international travel tips.

Passports

A **passport** is an official government document certifying the identity and citizenship of an individual and granting the person permission to travel abroad. Most countries outside the United States require a passport. Check the Web or your local travel agent to determine whether the country being visited requires a passport. For example, Canada and Mexico do not require passports. However, even if a country does not require a passport, having one is a good idea because it shows proof of citizenship.

Passport application forms can be obtained from the Web, a travel agency, a passport office, or the post office. One Web address you can access to print passport application forms is **www.travel.state.gov**. However,

GIFT ETIQUETTE

- In English-speaking countries (including Britain, Ireland, Canada, and Australia), gifts are not expected and might even be considered inappropriate. Business gifts are also rarely exchanged in Spain and France.
- Gift giving is important in Hong Kong, Japan, the Philippines, Russia, and Eastern European countries.
- In Filipino business culture, exchanging gifts is an essential step in solidifying business ties.
- In Japan, the best time to present a gift is toward the end of your visit.
- When giving gifts, be certain the gift is made in the United States. For example, do not give a gift to an individual from Japan that was made in Japan.
- Appropriate gifts include pens or pen-and-pencil sets. Items from your home state and books of historical areas of your state are also appropriate.
- Photo albums containing pictures of the people you met on your trip are appropriate gifts.
- Flowers are not a universally acceptable gift for a host. If flowers are acceptable, the color and type of flower are important. For example, in Italy, chrysanthemums are displayed mainly at funerals. In Brazil, purple flowers signify death.

FIGURE 18~2 Gift Etiquette

INTERNATIONAL TRAVEL TIPS

- Investigate duties and U.S. customs limitations. The Custom Service's free brochure *Know Before You Go* can be obtained online at **www.customs.gov/travel/travel.htm**.
- Before you leave home, get a small amount of currency from the country you will be visiting. This way you will have money for a taxi or telephone call before you check into a hotel. The exchange rate at your hotel will not be as good as at a local bank.
- Resist street vendors' foods. It might smell delicious, but you have no idea how long the food has been sitting around at low temperatures.

Excerpted from **www.saf-t-pockets.com/traveltips.htm**

FIGURE 18~3 International Travel Tips

since Websites change, you can use the keywords *passport information* to find other sites. You can also find passport information in the telephone directory by looking under *United States Government, Passport Information* in the Blue Pages or under *Passports* in the Yellow Pages. Figure 18-4 provides information needed to obtain a passport for the first time.

A passport is valid for ten years. After that period of time, you must renew it.

Visas

A **visa** is a document granted by a government abroad that permits a traveler to enter and travel within that particular country. A visa usually appears as a stamped notation on a passport, indicating that the bearer may enter the country for a certain period of time.

Currency

Before leaving the United States, executives can exchange money from certain banks and currency exchange offices for the currency of the country being visited. Newspapers generally report the rate of exchange for various countries. You can also obtain rates of exchange from the Web. For example, **www.xe.com/ucc** allows you to put in the dollars you want to exchange; it then calculates how much those dollars are worth in the country you are visiting. If executives prefer, they can exchange a small amount of money in the United States and then exchange additional money when they arrive at their destination. The executive can exchange any currency left

---

INFORMATION NEEDED FOR OBTAINING A PASSPORT

- A completed application
- Proof of U.S. citizenship through a certified copy of a birth certificate, Consular Report of Birth Abroad or Certification of Birth, Naturalization Certificate, or Certificate of Citizenship. If such proof is not available, the applicant must submit a notice that no birth record exists and provide secondary evidence, such as a baptismal certificate, a hospital birth certificate, a census record, a family bible record, or an early school record
- Proof of identity through such documents as a driver's license, Naturalization Certificate, or Certificate of Citizenship
- Two signed duplicate photographs taken by a photographer within the last six months
- Social Security number
- Applicable fee

FIGURE 18~4 Information Needed for Obtaining a Passport

over at the end of a trip for U.S. currency. Travelers should be aware of the exchange rates in the country they are visiting and pay attention to the exchange rates once in the country. Exchange rates are not always the same; for example, the exchange rate at a bank may be more favorable than the exchange rate at an airport.

The **euro** became the standard currency of Belgium, Germany, Spain, France, Ireland, Italy, Luxembourg, the Netherlands, Austria, Portugal, and Finland on January 1, 1999. The euro will gradually replace national currencies in the form of seven euro notes and eight euro coins. A businessperson traveling to any of these countries no longer needs to worry about currency exchange between the countries.

Health Precautions

Before leaving for a trip abroad, you might check with a physician about vaccines needed or medical precautions to keep in mind for the particular destination. Environmental factors are usually different from the ones experienced in the United States, and it is easy to develop some type of illness as a result of food, water, or even climate of the country you are visiting. A physician may prescribe medications to help you recover from stomach-related illnesses or colds.

In some countries, you should not drink the water unless it is boiled or purified. In these countries, you should rely on bottled water for all activities, including brushing your teeth. Since raw fruit and vegetables are generally washed in water, peel them before eating. In addition to your physician, travel agents can make suggestions about precautions you should take when visiting certain countries.

International Flight Tips

Since international flights are long (unless traveling by the Concorde), an executive should plan carefully and observe certain precautions.

- Investigate duties and U.S. custom limitations. The Custom Service's free brochure *Know Before You Go* is available online at **www.customs.gov/travel/travel.htm**.
- Bring an inflatable neck pillow so you can sleep more comfortably.
- Use earplugs and an eye mask to block distracting noise and light.
- Wear shoes to accommodate feet that may swell during the long flight. Change into a pair of thin socks during the trip.
- Drink at least one glass of water for every two hours of flight time.
- Walk around every so often to stretch your legs.

STEWART COHEN

An inflatable neck pillow, casual shoes, and in-flight movies can make long international flights more comfortable.

- Do in-flight exercises; many airlines publish these exercises in their in-flight magazines.[2]

Transportation Arrangements within the Country Visited

Local arrangements within a country may include hotel, car, and rail accommodations. You should make hotel and rail arrangements before arriving in the country. You can make car arrangements after arriving.

Hotel Arrangements

Hotel reservations can be made through travel agents or airlines at no additional cost. Hotel reservations can also be made online. A section entitled "Online Reservations" presented later in this chapter provides additional information. Some hotels provide breakfast at no additional charge. If administrative assistance or a meeting room is needed at a hotel, a travel agent can arrange for these services; these arrangements can also be made directly with the hotel. However, making arrangements directly may be difficult, particularly if a language difference exists.

Car Rental

Cars are readily available for rent. Executives can arrange for a car after arriving in the city or have the travel agency make arrangements. In most countries, a U.S. driver's license is sufficient. Travelers can obtain an International Driver's License from the AAA. The telephone number of AAA can be found in your local directory. Travelers should obtain appropriate insurance and become familiar with the driving regulations of the country. Conditions are often quite different from those in the United States, including the side of the car on which the steering wheel is mounted, the side of the road on which you drive, and the speed limits on highways.

Rail Transportation

Many countries have excellent rail service (particularly Europe). Service is frequent and relatively inexpensive. A traveler can get from one city in Europe to another in a relatively short period of time with a limited amount of inconvenience. Underground rail transportation in cities such as London is quite good and an inexpensive way to travel. In addition, bus transportation within large cities is dependable and inexpensive.

Organizational Travel Procedures

Since organizational policies about travel arrangements vary, you need to learn the specific procedures followed by your organization. Is an outside travel agency used? Do administrative professionals make travel arrangements for the executives? Is there a set **per diem** (per day) amount for travel? Is a travel advance granted to employees? If administrative professionals make travel arrangements, exactly what are their responsibilities?

Before the executive takes his or her first trip, you should obtain the following information.

- Dates and times for travel
- Cities to be visited; times and locations for appointments or commitments
- Hotel preferences—price range, number of nights, size of bed (full, queen, king), and smoking or nonsmoking room
- Car rental preferences—type of car, size, make, model, number of days of use, and pickup and drop-off locations

Europe offers excellent rail service.

- Company account number to which travel is to be billed or the executive's credit card number
- Arrangements for transportation to the airport or train station
- Appointments to be made—where and when
- Materials and equipment needed—business cards, laptop computer, and so on
- Person in charge while the executive is away
- Correspondence and calls—how they will be handled in the executive's absence

If an executive is traveling by air, you need to know:

- The name of the preferred airline (if the executive has a preference) as well as his or her frequent flyer number. (Most airlines have a **frequent flyer program**, an incentive program that provides a variety of awards after the accumulation of a certain number of mileage points. Awards may include upgrades from coach to first class and free airline tickets.)
- Whether the flight is to be direct (if possible) or whether the executive is willing to change planes. Less expensive flights are often available if the executive is willing to change planes. The downside of changing planes is the hassle of getting from one flight to another and the increase in travel time.
- The class of flight—first-class, business, or coach.
- Seating preference—aisle or window and in what part of the plane.
- Meal preference. Meals are not generally provided now except in first-class sections and on international flights (all classes). However, if meals are provided, travelers generally have a choice of low-calorie meals, low-cholesterol meals, and other special diet needs.

If you are making arrangements for more than one top-level executive to travel to the same location at the same time, company policy may dictate that the executives fly on separate airlines. In case of serious accident when both

When beginning to plan a trip, set up a folder to hold all trip information.

executives are on the same plane, both might be lost to the company.

If executives are traveling by rail, you need to know the type of accommodations needed—coach or first-class.

When you first start planning a trip, set up a folder. Then you can place notes and information relating to the trip in the folder. You have all the information available in one place whenever you need it.

Arrangements by Travel Agency

Travel agencies can make all travel arrangements for the executive. They can schedule the flight, obtain tickets, make hotel reservations, and arrange car rental. They can also see that airline tickets are delivered to your business. Part of their service includes providing an **itinerary** that gives flight numbers, arrival and departure times, hotel reservations, car rental, and other arrangements requested. In addition, travel agencies, through the use of computer software, can give you a list of all airlines leaving at the approximate time the executive wishes to travel and provide an analysis of the lowest fare. Travel agencies will accept major credit cards, or they can bill the company directly.

Travel agencies receive commissions from airlines, hotels, and other service industries when they sell services. However, they may still charge the customer a minimum fee—for example, $50 for all services related to the trip.

Arrangements by Administrative Professional

You may have the responsibility of making travel arrangements. If so, you can choose to telephone airlines, hotels, and car rental agencies directly. However, telephoning can be time-consuming since you often have to hold for an agent. Another method of making reservations is through the Web. Information about online reservations is presented in the next section. Whatever method you use to make travel arrangements, you should com-

pare prices. The travel industry is a competitive one. By taking the time to telephone several airlines and hotels or check several Websites, you generally can save money.

Online Reservations

Advantages of making online travel arrangements include the following:

- Virtual travel agents are available any hour of the day or night and on weekends. You do not have to hold on the Web.
- You can compare fares of different airlines.
- You can find last-minute specials on airfare.
- You can book hotels and cars.
- Some sites offer international travel information, such as passport and visa information, updates on political instability, health scares, and so on.

You can access a number of Websites to make travel plans. In addition to independent sites that allow you to comparison shop for the least expensive airfare, individual airlines have their own Websites. Figure 18-5 lists several Web addresses.

WEBSITE TRAVEL ADDRESSES

- www.travelocity.com
- www.orbitz.com
- www.priceline.com
- www.hotwire.com
- www.aa.com
- www.northwest.com
- www.delta.com
- www.mapblast.com
- www.mapquest.com
- www.flightarrivals.com
- www.roughguides.com
- www.cheaptickets.com
- www.expedia.com

FIGURE 18~5 Website Travel Addresses

Responsibilities before the Trip

In addition to the travel duties of administrative professionals explained in the previous sections, additional responsibilities include the following:

- Preparing an itinerary
- Obtaining travel funds
- Preparing and organizing materials
- Checking the executive's calendar
- Confirming appointments
- Assembling trip items
- Determining how matters will be handled in the executive's absence

Prepare an Itinerary

The itinerary is a must for you and your employer. If you are working with a travel agency, the agency will prepare an itinerary that includes flight numbers, departure and arrival times, car rentals, and hotels. An itinerary is helpful, but it does not include appointments the executive has during the trip, necessary addresses and telephone numbers, and so on. The comprehensive itinerary that you prepare includes all of these items. Figure 18-6 shows a portion of an itinerary. Notice that it includes two different time zones since the traveler is going from Central standard time to Pacific standard time. If your employer is traveling in only one time zone, you need not include the time zones. Your employer may want additional copies of the itinerary for his or her family. Some executives prefer to have the appointment schedule as a separate document. If so, include the date and time of appointments, names of contacts, and location of appointments.

Obtain Travel Funds

Organizations differ in how they handle funds for trips. Most of the time airline tickets are charged directly to the organization. Hotel, meals, and car rental may be charged to a credit card provided by the company. Another practice is for individuals to get cash advances to cover expenses for a trip. To do so, individuals fill out a travel form before leaving, indicating how much money they need. Still another practice is for executives to pay the expenses; they are then reimbursed by the organization upon returning from the trip. Most organizations require employees to turn in a receipt for expenses above a certain amount.

When executives travel abroad, they may take traveler's checks. Traveler's checks can be purchased from most banks and travel agencies. However, since credit cards are accepted in almost all international locations, an executive may find it easier to use a credit card. Executives also have the option of using a combination of traveler's checks and credit cards.

Prepare and Organize Materials

Any number of items may be needed for a trip. If the trip is an international one, items such as passports, medications, business cards, and small gifts may be necessary. Whether the trip is domestic or international, an executive needs certain items, such as reports for meetings and presentation materials. Once the materials are prepared, the administrative professional assembles the appropriate number of copies and places them in the executive's briefcase along with other items necessary for the trip. The traveler generally needs these items:

- E-ticket or plane ticket
- Itinerary
- Hotel confirmation
- Special materials, reports, and so on
- Presentation notes
- Office equipment and supplies—laptop and disks
- Reading materials
- Business cards
- Passport (for international trips)

Check Calendar

Check your employer's electronic calendar and your desk calendar to see if appointments have been scheduled for the period in which your employer will be away. If so, find out

ITINERARY FOR SANDRA PORTALES
April 6–7, 2005

San Francisco Trip

MONDAY, APRIL 6 (DALLAS TO SAN FRANCISCO)

9:30 a.m. CST   Leave DFW International Airport on American
Flight 57 (e-ticket in briefcase)

10:30 a.m. PST   Arrive San Francisco International Airport
[pick up rental car from Hertz (across from
baggage pickup in airport), Confirmation
32786; hotel reservations at Four Seasons, 300
Airport Freeway, telephone 555–3310,
Confirmation 84800]

FIGURE 18–6 Travel Itinerary

whether they are to be canceled or whether someone else in the company will handle them. Then notify the people involved.

Confirm Appointments

Before preparing the itinerary, write, email, or call the people your employer plans to see during his or her trip to confirm the appointments. Obtain correct addresses and directions from the hotel to the location of meetings; make a note of these addresses and directions on the itinerary.

Assemble Trip Items

The administrative professional is responsible for assembling all items the executive needs for a trip. You should take this responsibility seriously. By forgetting to include something, you can cause embarrassment and frustration for the executive. Here is a representative list:

- Plane tickets
- Itinerary
- Travel money and credit cards
- Cell phone
- Business cards
- Hotel confirmation
- Information on organizations to be visited
- Copies of correspondence, presentations, reports, and so on
- Reading materials about the country and culture if visiting an international organization

Determine Office Procedures during the Executive's Absence

Find out who will be in charge during your employer's absence. Check to see if your employer is expecting important papers that should be forwarded. Be sure you understand how to handle all incoming mail, both email and traditional mail. For example, should important correspondence be forwarded to the executive? If so, what items? Are you to answer routine correspondence for the executive? Is mail to be forwarded to another executive for handling? Additionally, check tickler files or pending files for matters that need to be handled before the executive leaves.

Your Responsibilities during the Executive's Absence

You have worked hard and efficiently to facilitate your employer's departure. What happens now? Is it playtime for you? No. Your pace may be somewhat slower while your employer is out of the office, or it may accelerate. Your responsibility is to handle the work flow smoothly and efficiently during your employer's absence. Your employer may want to set up a date and time to check in with you. Touching base gives the two of you a chance to discuss anything that needs to be addressed before the executive returns.

Make Decisions

You must make wise decisions within the scope of your responsibilities during your employer's absence. You should know what matters to refer to someone else in the organization and what matters to refer directly to your employer through a telephone call, an email, or a fax. You should avoid burdening your employer with messages during travel and meeting times. Your responsibility is to make appropriate decisions.

Handle Correspondence

Answer any routine mail within your level of responsibility. If you receive mail that needs immediate attention but you are unable to handle, you can usually refer it to another person designated by your employer. This person should furnish you with a file copy of the reply so your employer will know how the matter was handled. Additionally, your employer may ask that you check and respond to email messages.

Keep Records of Visitors and Telephone Calls

Keep a log of individuals visiting or telephoning your employer. When your employer comes back to the office, you have a log available for him or her to review, which saves time for both of you.

Make Appointments

While your employer is away, you may need to set up appointments. When setting up appointments, remember that your employer will probably have a full day of work to handle on his or her first day back. Keep the calendar appointment free on that day. If you must schedule appointments, set up very few.

Use Time Wisely

Assume that you have handled all routine correspondence and all special matters. Your workday is from 8 a.m. to 5 p.m.; it is now 2 p.m. What should you do? What items need attention? For example, is your filing up-to-date? Do you need to clean out computer files? Does your desk need to be reorganized? Does your employer's desk need to be straightened? Do you know what is happening in the organization? You can read organizational publications, acquaint yourself with new products or newly acquired subsidiaries, and so on. You can also use the time to read business periodicals such as *Fortune* and *Forbes*™. An efficient administrative professional does not waste time; he or she utilizes every minute. You can always do something to increase your personal knowledge and efficiency.

Posttrip Activities

When the executive returns, you should conduct a briefing on the workplace activities

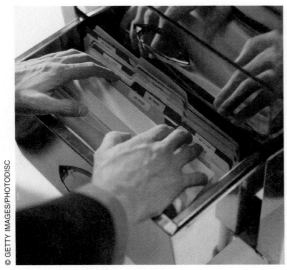

While the executive is away, use free time to clean out files.

- Email messages
- Faxes

Additionally, the executive needs a file of mail that does not require a response, but contains information for the executive, such as informational memorandums, reports, and periodicals. Place this mail in folders by category and date.

The executive may need to write several follow-up letters as a result of the trip. For example, she or he may want to send thank-you letters to the executives contacted on the trip. Customers or potential customers may receive information on products or services. Contracts may be written and mailed. Additionally, the executive may answer correspondence that accumulated or ask you to respond to certain items.

Expense reports need to be filled out. The executive will usually give you a list of receipts from the trip, including flight, hotel, and meal receipts. Your task is to complete the expense report carefully, double-checking all individual figures and totals. Copies of the receipts are usually attached to the expense report. ■

during his or her absence. The executive needs the following information:

- Appointments set up
- Telephone calls and how they were handled
- Correspondence received
- Copies of answers to correspondence

SUMMARY

To reinforce what you have learned in the chapter, study this summary.

- The international business world requires many executives to travel.
- Flight classifications of air travel are first-class, business, and coach.
- First-class accommodations are the most expensive of the three classes and the most luxurious.
- Business-class accommodations are slightly more expensive than coach.
- Coach-class accommodations are the least expensive and offer the fewest amenities.
- Airline tickets may be e-tickets or standard paper tickets.
- After 9/11, America's airports are operating under an unprecedented level of security. Air passengers should be knowledgeable about security measures and how they will impact the time needed to check in at the airport.
- For short trips, an executive may use car or rail travel.
- Hotel reservations are made online, by telephoning the hotel directly, or by working with a travel agency.

- International travel is common in multinational businesses. When traveling internationally, executives need to be knowledgeable about differences in culture. An understanding of how to handle such items as business cards and gifts can be important to the success of a meeting.
- Flight classifications for international travel are the same as for domestic travel.
- When traveling internationally, a passport is needed (with the exception of Mexico and Canada).
- Visas are necessary in some countries. A visa usually appears as a stamped notation on a passport, indicating that the bearer may enter the country for a certain period of time.
- The euro became the standard currency of Belgium, Germany, Spain, France, Ireland, Italy, Luxembourg, the Netherlands, Austria, Portugal, and Finland on January 1, 1999.
- The administrative professional plays a major role in making travel arrangements for executives. Arrangements may be made through a travel agent or via the Web.
- The administrative professional's responsibilities before the trip include preparing an itinerary, obtaining travel funds, preparing and organizing materials, checking the executive's calendar, confirming trip appointments, assembling trip items, and understanding how matters will be handled in the executive's absence.
- The administrative professional's responsibilities during the executive's absence include making certain decisions, handling correspondence, keeping records of visitors and telephone calls, making appointments, and using time wisely.
- Posttrip activities include informing the executive of what occurred during his or her absence from the workplace.

FIND THE PROBLEM

As an administrative professional for People Pharmaceuticals located in the home office in Dallas, you are to hold a seminar on writing effective correspondence for the administrative professionals in the Raleigh, North Carolina, office. You have not been to the North Carolina facility, and you do not know any of the people there. When making your travel arrangements, you call the Raleigh division and ask for directions to the office. The assistant tells you that the office is only 30 minutes from the airport. Your flight is to arrive in Raleigh at noon. Your presentation is to begin at 2 p.m. Your flight leaves Dallas 20 minutes late. Once you arrive in Raleigh, you are held on the plane for 15 minutes, waiting for a gate to open. Then you must wait to collect your luggage. When you finally get to the taxi area, you have only 50 minutes before you are to begin your presentation. The taxi ride from the airport to the office takes 35 minutes because traffic is heavy. You rush into the room ten minutes before the presentation is to begin. You have yet to set up your PowerPoint slides. You begin your presentation ten minutes late, feeling very rushed and nervous from your "ordeal."

What is the problem?

PROFESSIONAL POINTERS

Since many businesses are multinational today, you need to understand the culture and customs of other countries. Listed here is information about greeting customs in Korea, the Philippines, and Taiwan.

Korea

- Western and Korean male friends usually greet each other by bowing slightly and shaking hands. When shaking hands, both hands are sometimes used. Women do not shake hands; they usually nod slightly. When shaking hands, the senior person offers to shake hands first. When bowing, the junior person bows first.
- Prolonged direct eye contact is considered impolite and even intimidating.
- When saying good-bye, the traditional gesture is the bow, but the younger generation has adopted the western custom of waving good-bye by moving their arms from side to side.

Philippines

- Shaking hands is the common custom with men and women.
- Prolonged eye contact is considered impolite.
- Respect is shown to elderly people.

Taiwan

- The western custom of shaking hands is the usual form of greeting, but often a nod of the head is sufficient.
- Business cards are exchanged, but it is considered impolite to scrutinize the card. Business cards are presented using both hands.

REINFORCEMENT ITEMS

1. List five responsibilities of the administrative professional in making travel arrangements.
2. How do tight security procedures in airports affect air travelers?
3. What should be included on an itinerary?
4. Explain five considerations for the international traveler.
5. What duties should the administrative professional perform while the executive is traveling?

CRITICAL-THINKING ACTIVITY

Two months ago Brad Venditti, a friend of yours who works for Clarion Telecommunications, accepted his first full-time position as an administrative assistant. Last week Brad's employer, Judith Malaski, asked him to make arrangements for her to go to Orlando. Brad received the necessary travel information from Ms. Malaski and made the flight reservations. Ms. Malaski requested a rental car for three days while in Florida. She indicated that she had three appointments scheduled. She left the names of the people she would be seeing and the times of the appointments.

Brad handed Ms. Malaski a handwritten list that included numbers, times, and dates of the departure and return flights. Ms. Malaski took one look at the list and asked about the appointment schedule; it was not on the itinerary. She asked if this was his idea of an itinerary. Brad admitted that he did not realize Ms. Malaski would need anything but the flight information and that he really did not know how to prepare an itinerary.

When Ms. Malaski arrived at the airport in Orlando, she called Brad and told him that the rental car agency had no record of the booking. Brad was afraid to tell Ms. Malaski that he forgot to arrange for a car, so he led her to believe the car rental agency made the mistake.

While Ms. Malaski was away from the office, Brad thought he did not have any work to do, so he spent most of his time reading a novel. Several of the employees remarked (with a smile) to Brad that they wished they had it as easy as he did.

When Ms. Malaski returned from Florida, she found the mail in a stack on her desk. It had not been sorted. She told Brad that he must get help in learning how to make travel arrangements. She was clear that she did not want the same snafus to happen again.

Brad called you with a plea for help. What advice would you give him? Answer the following questions:

How should Brad have prepared for Ms. Malaski's trip?

What should Brad have done while Ms. Malaski is away?

How can Brad improve the impression his employer has of him and his work?

VOCABULARY REVIEW

Complete the Vocabulary Review for Chapter 18 given on page 133 of the *Applications Workbook*.

ENGLISH AND WORD USAGE DRILL

Complete the English and Word Usage Drill for Chapter 18 given on page 134 of the *Applications Workbook*.

WORKPLACE APPLICATIONS

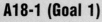 **A18-1 (Goal 1)**

Reread the situation in "Find the Problem." Make travel arrangements, using the Web, for your presentation in Raleigh, North Carolina. Correct the problem that exists in the situation, and make the appropriate travel arrangements. Your presentation is at 2 p.m. on May 5. You will take a taxi to and from the presentation. Since May 5 is on a Friday, you decide to stay over until Sunday. You are staying in the Courtyard by Marriott. Print out a map from the Raleigh airport to the hotel. The hotel's address is 1041 Wake Towne Drive, Raleigh, North Carolina 27609. Since you have never been to Raleigh, you want to do some sightseeing on Saturday. Note on your itinerary the materials you found to help in your sightseeing venture. Prepare an itinerary, noting any materials you need to take with you for the presentation. Submit your itinerary to your instructor.

  A18-2 (Goal 2)

Sandra Portales and Maurice Templeton are traveling to the People Pharmaceuticals location in Guangzhou, China. Kurt Rupprecht asks you to assist him in researching Chinese customs and culture for Ms. Portales and Mr. Templeton, as well as help to make all trip arrangements. With two classmates, conduct the research using the Web and/or the library. Prepare a summary of your findings in a memorandum to Ms. Portales. Using the memorandum form on the Student CD, SCDA18-2a, write a memorandum to Ms. Portales about your findings. List the references you used.

The trip will be from April 5 through April 12. Make flight reservations, using the Web to get the best schedule. Ms. Portales and Mr. Templeton will take a taxi to the airport. A representative from the China office, Chiang Mo, is meeting them at the airport in Guangzhou. Mr. Chiang speaks English; Ms. Portales and Mr. Templeton do not speak Chinese.

You need to make hotel reservations for them in Guangzhou. Book two rooms with king-size beds, no smoking. They will not need ground transportation while in China; the China office will provide transportation.

The meetings scheduled are as follows:

- April 7—Meeting with Niu Lung and Sheng Kuo-fu from 10 a.m. until 2 p.m.
- April 8—Continuation of meeting with Niu Lung and Sheng Kuo-fu from 11 a.m. until 3 p.m.
- April 9—Meeting with Ho Chih-mo and Niu Ta-pei from 9 a.m. until 1 p.m.
- April 10—Continuation of meeting with Ho Chih-mo and Niu Ta-pei from 11 a.m. until 2 p.m.

You are responsible for getting business cards printed for Ms. Portales. Prepare a sample business card for Ms. Portales to review. If Chinese-speaking students are available to assist you, include Ms. Portales's name, address, and telephone number in Chinese on one side of the card.

Prepare a complete itinerary for Ms. Portales and Mr. Templeton. Prepare an appointment schedule. You can find a sample of an itinerary and an appointment schedule in your *Applications Workbook* on pages 135–136.

Using the memorandum form on the Student CD, SCDA18-2b, explain the duties you will be performing during Ms. Portales's absence. Address the memorandum form to your instructor. Submit copies of the two memorandums, the itinerary, and the appointment schedule to your instructor.

A18-3 (Goal 2)

Read Case 18-3 in the *Applications Workbook* on page 137 and respond to the question. Submit your response to your instructor, using the memorandum form on the Student CD, SCDA18-3.

ASSESSMENT OF CHAPTER GOALS

Did you successfully complete the chapter goals? Evaluate yourself by filling out the form on page 140 of the *Applications Workbook*.

6

Career Advancement

chapter 19

Job Search and Advancement

LEARNING GOALS

1. Determine the type of position that matches your skills.
2. Identify sources of job information.
3. Prepare letters of application and resumes.
4. Develop job interview skills.
5. Develop job advancement strategies.

Throughout this course, you improved your skills and prepared to seek a position as an administrative professional. Additionally, during your entire college career, you sought to gain **cognitive** (the mental process of knowing through reasoning) knowledge and to develop skills needed to excel in your chosen profession. Now it is time to think about how you might put your knowledge and skills to work in finding the right job.

Do you have a friend or an acquaintance who constantly complains about his job? Do you have a family member who wishes she never accepted the job she has? If so, you probably understand the importance of spending time finding the right job. *Difficult*, you might be saying to yourself. Perhaps, but well worth all the effort it takes. You want to spend time and energy finding the job that matches your skills and abilities—the one that provides for advancement and growth opportunities. You want a job that you enjoy, one that challenges you, and one with growth potential.

To find the right job demands that you spend time in reflection before beginning the job search process. You must spend part of that reflection time in clarifying your values and reevaluating the skills you have. If you do not engage in these activities, you may find yourself in a job that you like, but in an organization that you believe does not behave ethically. In other words, your values and the organization's values do not match.

Another possibility is that you work in an organization where your skill set does not match the skill set needed for your job. For example, you may have limited experience working in teams and managing teams. You accept a job in which you are responsible for team leadership and management. You are not succeeding. Although you realize the importance of developing the skills, your lack of experience is affecting your performance. Team members do not work together well, and you are constantly addressing difficult issues. You are uncomfortable each time a problem comes up because you do not know how to handle it. You know your skill set does not match the job needs. You are unhappy and frustrated. In fact, you fear and even expect that you will lose your job.

You have a choice in your job search. You can choose to conduct a job search that culminates in a position that allows you to put your unique gifts to work. How do you go about that type of job search? The next section will help you answer that question.

Matching Your Skills, Values, and Interests with Job Possibilities

Chapter 1 introduced you to a number of skills necessary for the administrative professional, including the following:

- Communication (listening, verbal presentation, and writing)
- Human relations
- Time management
- Critical-thinking
- Decision-making
- Creative-thinking
- Teamwork
- Technology
- Leadership
- Anger, stress, and time management

Chapter 1 also introduced you to a number of success qualities:

- Flexibility/Adaptability
- Integrity/Honesty
- Initiative/Motivation

Throughout this course, ethics and values have been stressed. Before you begin your job search, you need to reconsider your own personal values. What are they? Based on your values, what must you consider in your job search? Have you developed different interests due to your educational experiences? If so, what are they? How will these interests affect your job search?

Skill Identification

Before you begin to look for a job, you must take the time to identify the skills you have. Why? For several reasons:

- To help guide your search.
- To help you list your skills on your resume and cover letter.
- To assist you in answering questions well during the interview process.
- To help you succeed on the job.

Value Clarification

In Chapter 2, values were defined as the principles that guide your life, such as honesty, fairness, love, security, and belief in a higher being. You live your values every day even though you may not consciously think about what you are doing. Your values guide you through every task you undertake and through every encounter you have with other people. Thus, you need to be clear about your values as you begin the job search process. If you do not clarify your values, you may end up accepting a job with an organization that operates with values very different from your own. If that happens, you can find yourself unhappy (and possibly not understanding the source of your unhappiness).

Interests

What interests do you have? If you have trouble identifying your interests, try asking yourself this question: If I had the opportunity to talk about something all day long, what would it be? In other words, what are your passions? Are you interested in the medical profession? Do you enjoy working with people who are saving lives? If so, you might want to work in a hospital, a medical doctor's office, or a pharmaceutical organization that researches new drugs. Are you interested in the legal profession and the court systems? If so, you might want to work in an attorney's office or in the local or state judicial system. Do you speak another language proficiently? If so, you might seek a position with a multinational firm, one where you can put your language skills to use. Do you enjoy talking about religious issues? If you do, you might seek work in a church or in a church-related organization, such as a publisher of religious books.

As you consider your interests, also consider the converse. What are your weaknesses? What do you dislike? Do you feel depressed when you are around terminally ill people? If so, you may not want to seek work in the medical profession. Chances are you will not only dislike the work, but you will also feel unhappy much of the time.

Geographical Preference

The job market today is an international one. The Web provides you with an opportunity to identify and apply for jobs internationally. Thus, as you begin your job search, you need to identify your geographical preferences. Do you want to stay in the same city in which you are living now? Do you want to stay in

Before you begin your job search, consider your values and your interests.

© GETTY IMAGES/PHOTODISC

the same state but in a different city? Do you wish to relocate to another state within the United States? If so, where? Are you interested in applying for a job in another country? If so, what country?

Indentifying Sources of Job Information

You need to seek job information from numerous sources. Job sources include the following:

- Networks
- Placement offices
- The Web
- Employment agencies
- Newspapers
- Walk-ins
- Temporary agencies

Networks

Networking is the process of identifying and establishing a group of acquaintances, friends, and relatives who can assist in the job search process. This approach is one of the best strategies for finding a job. In fact, some studies show that as many as 80 percent of jobs are obtained through some form of networking. Employers often fill openings by hiring acquaintances of valued employees. Why? There are various reasons, but the main reason is a financial one. It costs less! A company incurs fewer costs—advertising, finders' fees, and so on. Employing and training a new employee costs an organization a considerable amount of money, so the organization wants to hire the right person. When personnel directors hear about possible applicants from respected employees, they are more confident of the applicants' abilities.

How do you go about networking? First, make a list of 10 people who know you well, who have numerous contacts, and who may be able to assist you in finding a job. Next, contact each person on the list and let the individual know you are looking for an interesting and exciting job. Write down in outline form what you want to say to the person. This approach keeps you focused and does not waste the time of the person you are calling. Tell the person you are seeking a job. If you have not talked with the person for some time, bring her or him up-to-date on your credentials—your education, your experience, and your skills. Be clear about your interests. You might send the person a copy of your resume. Additionally, ask the person you are calling to refer you to anyone else who might be able to help in your job search.

Other tips for networking include these:

- If you have a part-time job, let management know you are ready for a full-time position.
- If you take part in an internship program, let the organization know you are interested in a full-time job.
- Talk with friends in professional, religious, or social organizations about your job needs.

When you get a job, thank the people who assisted you by calling them or writing them a thank-you note.

Placement Offices

Many colleges and universities have placement offices. The counselors in these offices aid students in career planning. Job fairs are a relatively common type of service offered to students. These fairs can be helpful; in attendance are invited representatives from major companies in the area who are seeking employees for their companies. Other services provided by placement offices include these:

- Materials on specific careers
- General occupational information for the city and state
- Writing assistance for application letters and resumes
- Interviewing assistance

Check with your college or university to find out if they have a placement office; if so, ask the counselors what types of services are offered.

The Web

The Web has a variety of resources for job seekers, including tips for resume and cover letter preparation and interviewing. Additionally, you can research companies in which you have an interest and post your resume. You will learn more about writing and posting resumes on the Web under the section entitled "Online Resumes."

Here are a number of Websites that provide job search information and/or allow you to post your resume.

- **www.jobweb.com** provides job search information.
- **www.monster.com** allows you to search for positions and post your resume; it offers career advice and tips on preparing a resume and interviewing.
- **http://careers.yahoo.com** allows resume posting; recruiters can scan resumes without paying a fee.
- **www.flipdog.com** allows resume posting.
- **www.recruitercontacts.com** sends your resume to human resources departments and provides a list of employers who receive it.
- **www.rileyguide.com** provides job search tips.
- **www.careerbuilder.com** allows resume posting.
- **www.ajb.dni.us** lists available jobs.
- **www.hotjobs.yahoo.com** lists available jobs.
- **www.careerjournal.com** is *The Wall Street Journal's* site for job seekers; it offers job-hunting advice and salary tables.
- **www.job.com** allows you to search for jobs and post your resume; it also provides career assessment tests.
- **www.joboptions.com** allows resume posting and provides job-searching capabilities through an extensive job database; it also provides help with resume writing.
- **www.eurojobs.com** offers job opportunities in 42 European countries, manages

applications online, tracks the status of your application, and uses multiple **job robots** (software that compares your resume to employers' ads).

You can also find sites aimed at a particular field by using a search engine such as **www.google.com** and keywords such as *jobs—administrative professional*.

Employment Agencies

There are two types of employment agencies—private and state-operated. Tax dollars support **state-operated employment agencies**. As a taxpaying citizen, you can take advantage of the free services provided by your state-operated agency. **Private employment agencies** charge a fee for their services. Organizations hiring the employee may pay the fee. When private employment agencies advertise jobs in newspapers, they may include the word **fee-paid**, meaning the employer pays the fee. However, if you choose to use a private agency, you need to ask how the fee is paid. If you pay the fee, ask what the amount is. Generally, you must sign a contract with

private employment agencies. Information regarding how the fee is determined should be included in the contract. Read the contract carefully before signing it, and know the laws in your state about paying for an employment service.

When applying for a job listed with an employment agency, be prepared to take tests. The types of tests given to applicants for administrative professional positions include the following:

- Specific software packages, such as Microsoft Word, Excel, and PowerPoint
- Keyboarding speed and accuracy
- Grammar, punctuation, and proofreading skills
- Mathematical aptitude

Newspapers

Employers and employment agencies may list available positions in the Classified Advertisement section of local newspapers, under headings such as *Employment* or *JobCenter*. Employment categories define how jobs are listed. *Administrative, General Office* is one category used for administrative professional positions. These ads describe the positions and the qualifications required. Sometimes specific salary information appears. However, the salary may appear as a range rather than a specific figure. If you are using the newspaper as a source, you should check the Sunday paper. It generally has the largest number of listings.

Walk-Ins

If you are interested in obtaining a position with a certain company or in a particular type of business, going directly to the business or organization may yield successful results. Individuals who are most successful using this approach are those who have a gift for selling themselves. Another essential trait is the ability to handle rejection. You cannot take rejection personally; you may receive more "we

The Web provides a variety of job information, including job postings and hints on preparing resumes.

© GETTY IMAGES/EYEWIRE

have no openings" than "we are hiring for several positions." Before you engage in this approach, find out as much as you can about the organizations you plan to visit. Do not restrict your job search to walk-ins only. It can be a time-consuming process, often with little success. If you do use the walk-in approach, dress professionally and take several copies of your resume. You want to make a good impression, and you may be offered an interview immediately. Be prepared.

Temporary Agencies

A **temporary agency** (one that offers temporary work) is not a source of job information in the usual sense. However, if you are uncertain about where you want to work, a temporary agency can help you learn more about various types of organizations. An agency can place you in a number of different organizations over a short time period. Without a long-term commitment, you can gain a wealth of information to help you decide where you want to work full-time.

Some organizations use temporary agencies as a way to get firsthand knowledge of employees. For example, an organization may hire a temporary worker and be so pleased with the worker's performance, that he or she is offered a full-time job. Temporary agencies also provide an alternative to a full-time job. For example, individuals with young children may decide to work as **temps** (temporary workers) while their children are young.

Preparing Letters of Application and Resumes

You may have excellent job-related skills but little knowledge about applying for a job. Unless you know what is involved, you may become frustrated during the application process. Study this section carefully so you can develop the skills needed to apply for and receive a job offer.

Organization Information

Once you identify organizations of interest to you, spend time learning about each company. How do you get this information? Here are some ways.

- Ask friends, relatives, and acquaintances about the organization.
- Check the organization's Website.
- Obtain the organization's annual report. Most businesses will send you one upon request.
- Consult your local chamber of commerce.
- Ask your college placement office.

Attempt to get answers to these questions:

- What is the organization's service or product?
- What is the organization's stated mission? What are its values and goals?
- How long has the organization been in business?
- Is the organization multinational?
- Does the organization have branches in more than one state within the United States?

© GETTY IMAGES/EYEWIRE

One way to learn about an organization is through reading annual reports and other financial information.

- Is the organization financially secure?
- Is the organization growing?
- Does the organization have a good reputation in the community?
- Is the organization an equal opportunity employer?
- What is the corporate culture?
- How does the organization treat its employees?
- How does the organization compare to its competitors? Is it an industry leader?

Letter of Application

The letter of application is generally the first contact you have with a potential employer and the key, along with your resume, to obtaining an interview. It is a sales letter because its purpose is to sell your abilities. The letter of application makes a favorable or unfavorable impression on the person reading it. If the impression is unfavorable, you have little chance of getting an interview. A poorly written letter suggests that you are disorganized, sloppy, unfocused, and ill suited for employment. Conversely, a well-written letter suggests that you are thorough, conscientious, well organized, focused, and results-oriented.

The basic goals of a letter of application are as follows:

- To state your interest in a position.
- To provide general information about your skills (specific information appears in your resume) and to sell your skills (let the reader know you have something to offer the organization).
- To transmit your resume and request an interview.

State Your Interest in a Position

Consider the following example of an effective beginning.

Your ad in the Sunday paper of The Dallas Morning News™ *stated your interest in employing an administrative assistant who has good*

computer and human relations skills. My associate of arts degree in Business Information Systems and my part-time experiences as an administrative assistant have given me the skills needed.

Provide General Information about Your Skills and Sell Your Skills

Consider this example of a second paragraph beginning.

My courses at Grand Lakes College included six computer courses. I am proficient on several software programs, including Microsoft Word, Excel, and PowerPoint. In my part-time position as an administrative assistant, I had the opportunity to develop and manage a Web page for a small business.

Transmit Your Resume and Request an Interview

The following paragraph provides an example.

My resume, giving further details about my qualifications and experience, is enclosed. I will call you next week to check the status of my application and to explore the possibility of joining your company. You can reach me at 214-555-0171. Thank you for your consideration.

Figure 19-1 provides an example of a letter of application.

Refrain from Using *I* Frequently

The use of the word *I* may cause the reader to think you are self-absorbed, pushy, or boastful. Certainly, you do not want to portray these characteristics in your letter. Here are several examples of the overuse of *I* in a letter.

I am writing to ask for a job.

I will make an excellent administrative assistant.

I think it will be well worth your time to meet with me.

I hope to meet with you soon. I believe such a meeting would be beneficial for both of us.

Use a Return Address

The top of the letter should show your name, address, phone number, fax number (optional), and email address (optional). Figure 19-1 illustrates this format.

Athena S. LeJeune
3412 Abrams Road
Arlington, TX 76003-0743
817-555-0159
email: asle4@web.com

May 26, 2005

Mr. Ian McIntosh
Director, Human Resources
Kline Research Associates
355 Elm Street
Dallas, TX 75201-9834

Dear Mr. McIntosh:

Your advertisement in *The Dallas Morning News* requesting an administrative assistant is most appealing to me. I am eager to talk with you about joining Kline Research Associates in this capacity.

My qualifications include the following:

- An associate degree in Administrative Systems from Edwards College
- One year of work experience in the field
- Excellent human relations and communications skills
- Knowledge of computer software, including Microsoft Word, Excel, and PowerPoint

My resume, giving further details about my experiences and skills, is enclosed. May I have the opportunity to discuss my qualifications with you? I will call you next week to arrange a meeting at your convenience. I look forward to talking with you.

Sincerely,

Athena S. LeJeune

Athena S. LeJeune

Enclosure: Resume

FIGURE 19~1 Letter of Application

Address the Letter Appropriately

When writing a cover letter, you need to know the following information for the inside address and salutation:

- The name of the individual receiving the letter
- The individual's title
- The organization's name
- The mailing address

The salutation should read *Dear Mr./Mrs./ Ms./Dr.* and the person's last name. Do not use a generic salutation such as *Dear Sir* or *Madam*. Do not use *To Whom It May Concern*. A letter addressed to *Dear Sir* or *Madam* suggests to the prospective employer that you do not have much interest in the job since you have not taken the time to find out who should receive the letter. If the recipient of the letter is a woman and you do not know her marital status (and asking is not appropriate), the best approach to use is *Dear Ms.* Figure 19-1 includes an appropriate inside address and salutation in addition to an appropriate return address.

Use Appropriate Layout and Punctuation

If you need a review of letter and punctuation styles, refer to page 508 of the Reference Guide. Standard block style is the most commonly used style; however, modified block style is also appropriate. Mixed punctuation, with a colon after the salutation and a comma after the complimentary close, is the most often used punctuation style.

Figure 19-2 gives some additional tips for writing application letters.

Resume Preparation

A **resume** is a concise statement of your background, education, skills, and experience. Its purpose is to communicate your job skills to prospective employers. It is your personal marketing document. A well-prepared resume markets your education, skills, and experience so effectively that it sets you apart from the

---

TIPS FOR WRITING APPLICATION LETTERS

- Research the organization before writing your letter. One good source of information for most organizations is their Web page.
- Key the letter in proper form using an acceptable letter style.
- Print your letter on high-quality bond paper. Office supply stores sell paper recommended for use in writing letters of application and resumes.
- Use correct spelling, punctuation, capitalization, and grammar. Use the spell and grammar checker on your computer.
- Keep the letter short; put details in the resume.
- Address the letter to a specific person. Do not address an application letter "To Whom It May Concern." If you do not have a name, call the company or check with the placement office, agency, or person who told you about the job.
- Send an original letter for each application. Do not send photocopies. Do not assume one letter is appropriate for all organizations. Personalize each letter by reading and writing to the job notice published by the organization.
- Do not copy a letter of application from a book. Make the letter representative of your personality.
- Use three paragraphs—an opening paragraph in which you provide a brief statement of your interest, a middle paragraph in which you describe your abilities, and a closing paragraph in which you request an interview.
- If you do not own a printer that produces quality work, have your cover letter and resume professionally printed.

FIGURE 19-2 Tips for Writing Application Letters

other candidates for the job. Both the content and the format of the resume are critical to its effectiveness.

There are three general types of resumes—**chronological, functional**, and **targeted/combination style**. In determining the type of resume to prepare, you must consider your purpose and your background.

Chronological Resume

In the chronological resume, your work experience and education appear in reverse chronological order, starting with the most recent experience and education and working backward in time. This style works well for showing progress and growth if the jobs listed reflect increasing responsibility over time. Figure 19-3 illustrates a chronological resume. Figure 19-4 on page 461 provides advantages and disadvantages of this kind of resume.

Functional Resume

The functional resume allows you to concentrate on those skills and abilities that are more applicable to the job you are seeking. It includes the same information as a chronological resume; however, the organization is different. This type of resume clusters your education, experience, and activities so, at a glance, this information supports the job for which you are applying. The functional resume works well for individuals who have recently graduated and for people who have good educational backgrounds and skills but little or no work experience. It also works well if there are periods of time when an individual did not work; for example, a woman took a break from her career to have a child. The functional resume de-emphasizes the gaps and emphasizes your skill sets. Figure 19-5 on page 462 shows a functional resume. Figure 19-6 on page 463 lists several advantages and disadvantages of the functional resume.

Targeted/Combination Style Resume

The targeted (also referred to as combination style) resume, illustrated in Figure 19-7 on page 464, allows you to present your experience in reverse chronological order. This style works best for experienced workers who have held a number of different jobs, know exactly what type of job they want, and can prove they are qualified for the job. It also works well when skills, titles, and organizational names are equally impressive. It does not work well when you do not have several experiences that match a number of skills. It also does not work well when you have multiple skills but a small number of different experiences (job titles or organizations for which you have worked).

Resume Parts

The resume has six basic parts:

- Heading
- Career objective
- Relevant skills
- Education
- Work experience
- Accomplishments

A resume may also include professional affiliations (if they are numerous and relate to the job) and military service.

Heading. The heading includes your name, home address, home telephone number (a cell phone number may be used if you are more accessible through that number), and email address. If you presently hold a job, do not use your work number. It is not ethical to spend time on your present job looking for another job.

Career Objective. This section lets the reader know your present career goals.

Career Objective: A position as an administrative assistant in a challenging job with opportunities to use my technology, communication, and human relations skills.

Notice that this objective did not specify a particular type of organization. If you are interested in a specialized field, you should note that in the objective. You also can list your long-term goal. In that case, your objective might be stated as follows:

Career Objective: A position as an administrative professional in a law firm, with a long-range goal of being a law office manager.

ATHENA S. LEJEUNE
3412 Abrams Road
Arlington, TX 76003-0723

817-555-0159
email: asle4@web.com

CAREER OBJECTIVE

A position as an administrative assistant with the opportunity to use technology and communication skills

COMPUTER SKILLS

Keyboarding at 90 wpm; proficient in Word, Excel, PowerPoint, Access, and Web research

EDUCATION

AAS, Administrative Systems
Edwards College, May 2004
Cum Laude

Relevant Courses: Business communications, organizational behavior, English, computer software, administrative procedures, psychology

EXPERIENCE

Administrative Assistant
Davis & Associates

June 2001 to September 2002
3406 Main Street
Arlington, TX 76842-1899

- Prepared spreadsheets using Excel
- Prepared monthly reports
- Composed letters
- Answered the telephone
- Filed correspondence manually and electronically
- Served on the Quality Improvement Team
- Developed a new records management system

HONORS

- Phi Theta Kappa
- Most Outstanding Student, Business Division

FIGURE 19-3 Chronological Resume

ADVANTAGES AND DISADVANTAGES OF CHRONOLOGICAL RESUMES

Advantages

- Highlights titles and company names; advantageous when the names or titles are relevant or impressive
- Highlights consistent progress from one position to another
- Highlights length of time in each organization

Disadvantages

- Shows gaps in work history
- Shows frequent changes of jobs
- Does not show most impressive or relevant work experience first if it is not the most recent

FIGURE 19–4 Advantages and Disadvantages of Chronological Resumes

If you use a targeted career objective, realize you are limiting yourself to one field.

Relevant Skills. This section gives you a chance to identify your skill strengths. You can list your technology skills, including proficiency in various software packages. You can also list these skills: writing, communication, human relations, critical-thinking, teamwork, decision-making, and other skills that relate to the job.

Education. In this section, list the schools you attended and the degree you obtained (if applicable). You might also list the courses you took that pertain to the position.

Work Experience. List the name of the companies or organizations where you have worked, the dates of employment, and your duties. You may want to reverse the order of education and experience on your resume. For example, if you have a number of years of experience that relate directly to the job, you should list your work experience first. Remember that the resume is a sales piece. You want to call attention to your best selling features first. For a recent graduate who has little work experience, list education after relevant skills. Doing so calls attention to the person's most important qualification—education.

Accomplishments. This section is also titled "Scholastic Honors," "Leadership Accomplishments," or "Professional Interests." If you are a recent graduate, you may have few, if any, professional accomplishments. However, you can list interests you had during your college years or offices you held. For example, listing president of the marketing club or chairperson of the homecoming committee demonstrates leadership ability.

Additional tips for preparing resumes appear in Figure 19-8 on page 465.

References. Do not list references on your resume. The resume is a place to highlight work experiences and skills. However, you may choose to include a section on the resume with the statement "References will be furnished upon request." Take a list of your references with you to all interviews; you may need to list them on an application, or the interviewer may ask you for them. Get in touch with your references before a job search. Let them know you are looking for a job, and ask whether you can use them as a reference. Confirm the addresses and phone numbers of your references, as well as their current employment and job title/duties. A thoroughly completed References section on an application can be a determining factor in the hiring of one applicant over another.

ATHENA S. LEJEUNE   817-555-0159
3412 Abrams Road   email: asle4@web.com
Arlington, TX 76003-0723

CAREER OBJECTIVE
A position as an administrative assistant with the opportunity to use
technology and communication skills

SKILLS
- Computer—Windows, Word, Excel, PowerPoint, Access, Web research
- Keyboarding—90 wpm with high level of accuracy
- Human relations and communications
- Composing letters and reports
- Spreadsheet

Projects
- Prepared monthly reports using Excel
- Researched information for various community presentations using the Web
- Developed a records management system

Writing
- Drafted notes from Web research for employer's review
- Drafted report for Quality Improvement Team
- Composed letters

Teamwork
- Served on Quality Improvement Team to develop a writing workshop for administrative assistants
- Chaired a strategic planning committee

EDUCATION
AAS, Administrative Systems, Edwards College, May 2004
Cum Laude

HONORS
- Phi Theta Kappa
- Most Outstanding Student, Business Division

EMPLOYMENT HISTORY
Davis & Associates, 3406 Main Street, Arlington, TX 76842-1899
Administrative Assistant, June 2001 to September 2002

FIGURE 19~5 Functional Resume

ADVANTAGES AND DISADVANTAGES OF FUNCTIONAL RESUMES

Advantages

- Highlights skills
- De-emphasizes gaps between jobs
- Is more appropriate when changing career fields since skills are highlighted over positions held

Disadvantages

- Does not show advancement from one job to another
- Does not show organizations and titles held
- Is more difficult to review since progression from one position to another is not apparent

FIGURE 19~6 Advantages and Disadvantages of Functional Resumes

The most effective references are previous employers and people who know you well. Personal friends are less effective, although they can provide a character reference for you. Do not select close relatives or religious leaders (unless it is a church-related job). Organizations generally ask for three to five references. Choose your references carefully. Select those individuals who know your qualifications well and will take the time to respond to a reference request. Follow these guidelines when selecting references.

- List people who are employed; they usually are more familiar with what is expected of employees.
- If possible, list at least one person who is in a supervisory or managerial position.
- You may list professors if you performed well in their classes. Do not list a professor for a class in which you earned a C or lower.
- Ask permission to use a person's name before doing so.
- Prepare a reference sheet, listing the references' names, addresses, telephone numbers, and email addresses. Title the sheet "References."
- Common courtesy dictates that you thank your references for allowing you to use their name. You might write a note or send an email to your references, thanking them and telling them of your progress.

Resume Length

If you are an inexperienced job seeker, keep your resume to one page. If you are an experienced job seeker, your resume may require two or perhaps three pages due to your background and experience. Generally, however, your resume should not be longer than two pages. Exceptions exist in certain fields, such as education, where research and publishing are important.

Online Resumes

Many organizations use the Web and online resumes in seeking potential job candidates. Studies show that approximately 85 percent of employers accept online resumes, and many of these employers use online resume services to search for applicants. You can post your resume on any number of search engines:

- www.monster.com
- http://careers.yahoo.com
- www.flipdog.com
- www.recruitercontacts.com
- www.careerbuilder.net

For additional Websites, access a search engine such as Google and key in the words *job search*.

A number of businesses allow you to post your resume directly to their Website. However, if you do post online, know that you

ATHENA S. LEJEUNE   817-555-0159
3412 Abrams Road   email: asle4@web.com
Arlington, TX 76003-0723

CAREER OBJECTIVE

A position as an administrative professional in a law firm, with a long-range goal of being a law office manager

EXPERIENCE

Administrative assistant in the law offices of Davis & Associates, 3406 Main Street, Arlington, TX 76842-1899, June 2001 to September 2002

- Prepared client information using Excel
- Drafted correspondence to clients
- Conducted research on various law-related issues
- Developed an electronic records management system
- Supervised one part-time receptionist
- Implemented voice mail system for office
- Conducted a one-day seminar for high school students interested in working as legal assistants

SKILLS

- Human relations
- Communication
- Composition

EDUCATION

AAS, Administrative Systems
Edwards College, May 2004
Cum Laude

HONORS

- Phi Theta Kappa
- Most Outstanding Student, Business Division

FIGURE 19–7 Targeted/Combination Style Resume

TIPS FOR PREPARING RESUMES

- If you are a recent graduate and have held only part-time jobs, list them.
- If you have not had any paid work experience, list volunteer jobs or leadership positions you have held. Do not insert a category and write "none" under it. If you have nothing to list under the work experience category, omit it from your resume.
- Keep the resume concise—one or two pages preferably (three is the maximum).
- Tailor your resume for the specific job opening, highlighting those areas of your background or work experience that fit the position you want.
- Do not use personal pronouns (I, me, you). They are unnecessary and detract from the impact of the resume.
- Describe your qualifications and skills in specific terms; avoid vague language.
- Check your spelling and grammar usage. Many employers discard a resume if just one spelling, typographical, or grammatical error appears. Do not rely totally on the grammar and spell check feature on your computer. This program does not find all errors, and some errors noted are not errors. You must pay careful attention to the grammar and format. Read and reread the resume several times, and ask someone else who is a good proofreader and grammarian to read it too.
- Take advantage of professional help in writing your resume. Check Web sources, talk with your college placement representatives, and visit a bookstore or library for materials on resume preparation.

FIGURE 19~8 Tips for Preparing Resumes

may be competing with hundreds of job applicants. For example, statistics have shown that a general site such as **www.monster.com** has thousands of resumes posted at any one time, with possibly only a few hundred employers visiting the site for applicants. When posting your resume on a general site, heed these cautions:

- Select a site that allows you to select the type of employer you want to view your resume.
- Find out if there is a charge for updating your resume.
- Date your resume so employers know whether it is recent.
- Remove your resume once you have found a job.

Organizations using online search engines or their home pages to retrieve applications use computer tracking systems to search through resumes and narrow the search to a few individuals. When preparing a resume for scanning by a computer tracking system, follow the guidelines presented here. Remember, you are not creating a different content for the online resume from the one you are sending

by mail. However, you are altering the presentation of the resume so your resume ends up in the top of those selected by the computer.

- Use keywords. The computer may select resumes by special keywords. Many times these keywords are ones listed in the job advertisement. For example, many job notices for administrative professionals ask for specific computer skills—Microsoft Word, Excel, PowerPoint, and so on. Additionally, human relations skills are essential. You should be certain that these keywords appear in your resume.
- Do not use italics, bold, and underlining; scanners do not pick up this format.
- Use a common font, such as Times New Roman or Courier.
- Use capitalization to draw attention to certain information, such as education.
- Avoid abbreviations and jargon; scanners usually do not recognize these words.
- Do not use graphics (even bullets) since the scanner has trouble picking them up.
- Do not use centering, indenting, or other formatting. The best format is for all lines to be left justified.

- Make certain your name is the first item on your resume, followed by your address, telephone number, and email address. Do not use an unprofessional email address. What may have been clever or amusing in college looks immature in business.
- Proofread carefully. Use the spelling and grammar function on your computer. If you are using a name with an unusual spelling or any other anomaly that may cause the spelling and grammar package to highlight the words, click on the "Ignore Once" bar on the spelling and grammar function. You do not want squiggly lines (used to indicate a possible error) to appear on your resume. It will look unprofessional.

Employment Application

You may fill out an **employment application** before or after the interview. In some organizations, all applicants fill out the form. Other firms ask only those people who are seriously being considered for a position to fill out the application. Follow these suggestions when completing an employment application.

- Read the entire application before starting to complete it.
- Print unless your handwriting is extremely neat.
- Answer every question completely. If a question does not apply to you (such as military experience), put NA, meaning "not applicable." Leaving a space blank can give the impression that you overlooked the question.
- Check your spelling. Carry a pocket dictionary so you can look up words you do not know how to spell.
- Have all information with you that you need to fill out the form—dates you attended college, dates of employment, complete addresses of employers, and references. Carry your social security card with you.
- Be honest. State accurately the experience and skills you have. Do not falsify any information. To do so could be grounds for firing. However, do try to state what may

be negative information in a positive manner. For example, most applications include a question asking why you left your last job. If you were fired from your job, you must indicate that fact. However, you can make the statement positively; you can say that your skills did not match those needed by the organization.

Developing Job Interview Skills

Assume you have done well thus far in the application process. Now you have the chance to interview. In order to do well, you must prepare yourself. You may spend several days in preparation; however, consider your time well spent. Your performance during the interview process is critical. If you do not plan well and do not perform well, the job may go to someone else. Conversely, if you do plan and perform well, you may receive a job offer. Remember, the interview gives you the opportunity to market your skills in person.

Portfolio Information

You may want to prepare a **portfolio** of your work to take with you to the interview. Arrange your work attractively in a binder. Here are some possible items to include:

- Letters you have written to demonstrate your writing style
- Research reports you have produced to demonstrate your ability to conduct research and present that research in an attractive format
- Spreadsheets and graphics you have created to demonstrate your knowledge of software

Electronic options also exist for preparing and delivering portfolios. You may choose to prepare an **eportfolio**, one sent on the Web to prospective employers. For example, your eportfolio may be part of a total epackage, including your letter of application and resume. A portfolio can also be prepared and presented on a CD.

Preinterview Nervousness

It is natural to feel nervous before an interview. Most people have such feelings. In fact, nervousness can cause productive behavior; you probably will prepare better because you are concerned that you will not do well. However, you want to control your nervousness. Here are some suggestions for doing so.

- Spend your time and energy before the interview researching the organization, reassessing your skills and abilities, and practicing the interview with a friend. Find someone to ask you possible interview questions. Figures 19-9 and 19-10 list frequent questions asked of job applicants. Review the questions thoroughly; think through your responses carefully. Certain questions are illegal for the interviewer to ask, including questions about the following topics:
  - National origin/citizenship
  - Age
  - Marital status
  - Affiliations
  - Disabilities
  - Arrest record
  - Military record

  Additionally, review Figure 19-11, which lists questions you might ask, and Figure 19-12, which lists frequent interviewing mistakes.

- Research carefully the typical salaries for administrative professionals. You can get some information from the Web. IAAP gives average salaries for various job titles at their Website, **www.iaap-hq.org**. Know what realistic salary expectations are, and be prepared to discuss salary if asked to do so. However, you should not lead a salary discussion. Let the interviewer do that.

- Use stress reduction techniques, such as exercising, getting the proper amount of sleep, practicing visualization, and engaging in positive self-talk. These techniques appear in Chapter 2; you may want to review them now.

- Plan something to do the night before the interview so you do not spend your time worrying about the interview. Go to a movie; go to dinner with a friend.

- Do not place all of your hopes on one interview. As you conduct your job search, select several organizations of interest to you. The more interview experiences you have, the more you will learn. View each interview as a learning experience. After the interview, write down what went right and what went wrong. Learn from the mistakes you made.

Interview Location

Know the exact time and location of the interview. Do not rely on your memory. Write down the time, the address, and the person's name you are to see, and take this information with you to the interview. When traveling to the interview location, allow time for unexpected delays. Make a practice run to the location the day before the interview (at the same time the interview is scheduled) so you can allow appropriate time for traveling and parking.

You must be on time for the interview. Excuses you give for being late do not erase the poor impression you make due to your lateness. When you arrive at the interview location, be pleasant with everyone you see—receptionists, administrative assistants, and so on. Keep a smile on your face, and say "thank you" often. Do not underestimate the impression you make on the receptionists, administrative assistants, or others waiting in the reception area. Sometimes people in the area are employees sent there to evaluate how job applicants react to the stress of waiting for an interview. Additionally, if you drive to the interview, your car should be neat and clean. Do not miss the chance to make a good impression; likewise, do not run the risk of making a bad impression.

Number of Interviews

You may have more than one interview for a particular position. For example, a human resources professional may interview you first.

FREQUENTLY ASKED INTERVIEW QUESTIONS

Questions Relating to Your Interest in the Company and the Job

- How did you learn about this position?
- Are you familiar with our company?
- Why are you interested in our company?
- Why do you think you are qualified for the position?
- Why do you want this job?
- What is the ideal job for you?

Questions Regarding Your Ability to Do the Job

- What are your greatest strengths?
- What is your major weakness?
- Why should I hire you?
- If I talked to your former employer, what would the person say about you?
- What in your past job did you enjoy the most? Why?
- What in your last job did you enjoy the least? Why?
- If I talked with your former colleagues, what would they say about you?
- What can you tell me about yourself?

Questions Regarding Your Education

- Why did you choose your major area of study?
- What was your academic average in school?
- What honors did you earn?
- In what extracurricular activities were you involved?
- What courses did you like best? Least? Why?
- How have the classes you completed as part of your major helped you prepare for your career?

Questions Regarding Your Ability to Fit into the Organization

- If your supervisor asked you to engage in an activity that did not fit your values, what would you do?
- What type of work atmosphere do you prefer?
- Is a sense of humor important at work? Why or why not?
- Tell me about a conflict you have had with someone. How did you handle it?
- What is your definition of diversity?
- How do you handle pressure?
- How would your previous employers and coworkers describe you?

Questions Regarding Experience

- Have you ever been fired or asked to resign from a position?
- Why did you leave your previous job?
- Have you had any problems with previous supervisors?
- What are your greatest strengths?
- What do you not do well?
- What salary do you expect?

FIGURE 19~9 Frequently Asked Interview Questions

FREQUENTLY ASKED INTERVIEW QUESTIONS OF THE RECENT GRADUATE

- How did you choose your college?
- How has your college experience prepared you for a career?
- Describe your most rewarding extracurricular experience?
- Are your grades representative of your abilities?
- Who was your favorite professor? Why?
- How did you pay for school?
- How would your classmates describe you?

FIGURE 19~10 Frequently Asked Interview Questions of the Recent Graduate

QUESTIONS YOU MIGHT ASK

- What are the specific duties of the job?
- Could you tell me something about the people with whom I will be working if I am accepted for the position?
- I read on your Web page that your organization has grown over the last few years. To what do you attribute this growth? Do you expect it to continue?
- When will you make a decision about hiring?

FIGURE 19~11 Questions You Might Ask

FREQUENT INTERVIEWING MISTAKES

- Being late
- Not making eye contact
- Criticizing past employers
- Asking questions about salary and benefits immediately
- Not answering questions concisely
- Being too self-assured (having a cocky attitude)
- Failing to demonstrate interest in the position by asking few questions
- Providing a resume with grammar and typographical errors
- Failing to bring a list of references
- Not articulating interest in the position

FIGURE 19~12 Frequent Interviewing Mistakes

Next, you may interview with your prospective supervisor. Finally, you may have a group interview with your prospective team members.

Team Interviews

A team interview may be with five or six people. Although this type of interview sounds intimidating, it need not be. Tips for a successful team interview are as follows:

- When introductions are made, pay careful attention to the individuals' names.
- Focus on each individual as the person asks questions.
- Listen carefully to the questions asked and answer them succinctly.
- When you ask a question, ask it of the group. If one group member asks you a question you did not understand, address that person and ask him or her to clarify the question.
- Make eye contact with all individuals when answering a question.
- If you find yourself getting nervous, glance occasionally at individuals who have given you positive feedback—ones who have a friendly face, open body language, and positive reactions to your responses. Say to yourself, *This person likes me; I am doing well.*
- Thank the group when the interview is completed. Use their names if possible; it shows you were paying attention.

Virtual Interviews

Occasionally organizations conduct **virtual interviews** (interviews held via technology by an interviewer at a distant location). The virtual interview works in this manner.

Assume you are applying for a job in New York. You live in Texas. The company arranges for you to go to a facility in Texas that has teleconferencing capabilities.

Just as in a traditional interview, you need to be well prepared. When a camera is involved, you may get a little nervous. However, your goal is to relax and treat the situation as though the person interviewing you were in the same room. Suggestions for making a good impression during a virtual interview include the following:

- Dress appropriately, which means dressing conservatively, even if you are applying for a position in a creative line of work, such as art and design. For men and women, a suit is appropriate attire. Women may also wear a conservative dress. Wear a color that looks good on you. Keep your jewelry to a minimum.

- Greet the interviewer warmly and with a smile, just as you would in person. Repeat the interviewer's name. For example, say, *I am happy to meet you, Ms. VanAndel.*

- Sit back in the chair provided; do not sit on the edge of your chair. Sitting on the edge of the chair can connote nervousness to the interviewer.

- Concentrate on the interviewer or interviewers, not on the camera. Try to forget a camera is in the room.

- Pay attention to the body language of the interviewer. Do not spend an inordinate amount of time answering any one question. Be warm and informative, but also concise.

- Enunciate carefully. Poor enunciation is more noticeable on camera than in person.

- Once the interview is over, thank the person and leave the teleconferencing room.

- Keep in mind the hints for traditional interviews (given in the next section). Many of these apply to the virtual interview.

Helpful Interview Hints

- Get a good night's rest before the interview so you will be alert.

In a virtual interview, concentrate on the interviewer or interviewers, not on the camera.

DIGITAL VISION

- Be prepared. Review the material you have gathered about the organization. Think through questions the interviewer might ask and questions you want to ask. Refer again to Figures 19-9 and 19-10 for help in preparing.

- Dress appropriately. As mentioned in the virtual interview section, a suit is appropriate for men and women. Clothing should fit well. If you need to tug on any part of your outfit, you may distract the interviewer and compromise the quality of the interview. Women should never wear a dress that is too short or too revealing. Wear a color that looks good on you. Since bold patterns can be distracting, wear solid colors.

- If you wear an overcoat, hang it in the reception area. Do not take it into the interviewer's office. You do not want to be juggling numerous belongings.

- Keep the amount of jewelry you wear to a minimum. Women should avoid wearing too many bracelets, which may cause noise that is distracting to the interviewer. Women should not wear earrings that make noise or that dangle and may get caught in their hair.

- Have your hair styled and make sure your nails are neat and clean. Good grooming is critical.

- Carry a briefcase. Women should try to do without a handbag so they have one less item to juggle.

- Have several copies of your resume in your briefcase, as well as a list of your references. The interviewer may request your references, or you may need reference names for the application.

- Stand and walk with your head erect and your shoulders back.

- Greet the receptionist with a friendly smile, stating your name and the purpose of your visit.

- Say "thank you." For example, thank the receptionist if she or he offers you a magazine while you are waiting.

- Shake the interviewer's hand with a firm (but not tight) grip.

- Wait to sit down until invited to do so by the interviewer.

- Keep your hand gestures to a minimum. Some movement of your hands while speaking is natural, but do not flail your hands and arms around excessively.

- Display good humor and a ready smile.

- Show genuine interest in what the interviewer says, and be alert to all questions.

- Answer questions truthfully and carefully.

- Be enthusiastic; demonstrate pride in your skills and abilities.

- Be positive.

- Be prepared to tell the interviewer about yourself, but be careful to keep the conversation on a professional level.

- Express yourself clearly using a well-modulated voice.

- Be prepared to ask questions. Acceptable questions you might ask are listed in Figure 19-11.

- Be prepared to take tests. Tests pertaining to basic skills such as keyboarding, spelling, math, proofreading, vocabulary, and reasoning ability are what you can expect. The law demands that any test given must relate to the job for which you are applying.

- At the close of the interview, ask what the next steps will be. Will there be another interview? When can you expect to hear the results of the interview?

- Reiterate your interest in the job (that is, if you remain interested).

- Smile pleasantly and thank the interviewer for his or her time.

- Smile and thank the receptionist as you leave.

What Not to Do in an Interview

In addition to the positive steps you should take, there are certain things you should not do during an interview. These behaviors include the following:

- Avoid nervous gestures and movements, such as tugging at your clothes, fidgeting, and playing with your hair and jewelry.

- Do not invade the personal space of others. Maintain a space distance of three to five feet from the person with whom you are talking.

- Do not furrow your brow or tense your jaw.

- Do not nod your head excessively; such movement can indicate nervousness.

- Do not talk too much. When you talk, take your time.

- Do not smoke or chew gum.

- Do not wear excessive makeup, perfume, or cologne. You may not want to wear any perfume or cologne; some people are allergic to it. Smell can be a strong reminder of situations, so you run the risk of wearing a scent that reminds the interviewer of a past unpleasant event. Your best bet is simply to smell shower fresh.

- Do not interrupt. Let the interviewer complete all questions or statements before you speak.

- Do not ask too many questions. Ask important questions only. Do not ask—When will I get a raise? When may I receive a promotion? When will I receive a vacation? These questions make the interviewer wonder about your commitment to the job. Perhaps you are only interested in the money and the fringe benefits.

- Do not place personal belongings or your hands on the interviewer's desk.

- Do not argue.

- Do not tell jokes.

- Do not comment on the furnishings of the office.

- Do not brag.

- Do not lie. If the organization hires you, you must produce on the skills you listed on your resume and/or mentioned in the interview.

- Do not criticize—your previous employer, the college you attended, and so on. Criticism denotes negativity.

Interview Follow-Up

After the interview, promptly write a **follow-up letter** that includes the following:

- A thank-you for the opportunity to interview.

- A recap of your skills and abilities.

- A statement of your continued interest in the job.

- A reminder of the next steps you agreed on in the interview, such as when the decision is going to be made.

A sample of a letter you might write appears in Figure 19-13.

If no action is taken concerning your application within a reasonable time (one to two weeks), a second follow-up letter or a call may be advisable. The second letter should merely remind the employer of your continued interest in the job. Depending on the situation, you may want to make a third contact with the organization. Being persistent shows your interest in the job, and the organization views it as a plus. However, you do not want to annoy the employer unnecessarily. Use good judgment in determining how many follow-ups are appropriate in each job situation.

Of course, after the interview, you may decide you are not interested in the position. In that case, you should promptly send a courteous letter expressing your appreciation for the interview and explaining that you do not wish to remain a candidate for the position. Although you are not interested in the present position, you may be interested in another position with the organization at a later time. If so, the courteous way in which you decline the first position may ensure you are considered a second time.

If you are turned down for a job, write a thank-you note to the employer expressing appreciation for the chance to interview and asking that your resume be kept on file for future jobs. Even though you did not receive

Athena S. LeJeune
3412 Abrams Road
Arlington, TX 76003-0723
817-555-0159
email: asle4@web.com

May 30, 2005

Mr. Allan Wade
Human Resources Manager
Wright & Associates
2001 Market Street
Dallas, TX 75211-2044

Dear Mr. Wade:

Thank you for the opportunity to interview with you this morning. It was a pleasure to meet you and to learn more about Wright & Associates.

Because of my education and experience, I am confident I can be an asset to your company. My written and oral communication skills are strong, and my technical skills are excellent. The interview today reinforced my interest in joining your team. I was impressed with what I heard from you about Wright & Associates' philosophy of management and the directions the company is taking. I welcome the chance to be a part of your team.

Please give me the opportunity to prove that I can be a valuable employee. You can reach me by calling 817-555-0159 or emailing me at www.asle4@web.com. I look forward to hearing from you soon.

Sincerely,

Athena S. LeJeune

Athena S. LeJeune

FIGURE 19~13 Sample Interview Thank-You Letter

the current job, you want to keep the door open for future possibilities.

Interview Evaluation

If you are interested in a job but do not get it, you may receive a generic reason from the organization. To avoid potential legal problems, most organizations do not give you an exact reason. In addition, you generally do not receive information concerning your interview errors.

You may do very well in an interview and still not get the job. In that case, go over the experience in your mind. Play back what happened. Jot down your thoughts about how you did. Note the questions you had trouble answering. Note any questionable reactions from the interviewer. Think about how you can correct errors before the next interview. Review your thoughts and notes with a trusted adviser. Ask her or him how you might improve. A job rejection is no reason to become depressed. Do not lose confidence in your skills and abilities. Learn from each interview situation. Keep trying and maintain a positive attitude.

If you are offered a job but do not accept it, you still should evaluate the interview situation. You may not have handled some of the questions as well as you could have. Review how you can do it better the next time. Each interview situation provides a chance for you to learn and grow. If you accept the job, let your network of people who have been helping you in your job search know you have accepted a position. Thank the individuals for their help. Such thoughtfulness lets your network know you are appreciative of their help.

Job Offer Evaluation

You have another responsibility after the interview in addition to evaluating yourself on the interviewing process. You need to ask yourself if the organization lived up to your expectations. Even though you did your homework before going to the interview, you may have encountered a few surprises during the interview. When evaluating whether you really want to work for the organization, ask yourself these questions:

- Is the work environment one in which I will be happy and will prosper?
- Will I have a chance to work with people I believe I can respect and admire?
- Will the work be interesting? Will I be able to learn from the job?
- Are the benefits and compensation packages acceptable?

Again, analyze your skills and your values. Will the position match your skills? Are the values of the organization consistent with your own? Remember, your goal is to find the right position for you.

Developing Job Advancement Strategies

Your reward for completing the job search process successfully is getting the position you want. Once you have the position, maintain the same enthusiasm you had when you applied for the position. The organization selected you because you fit its needs. If you fulfill your employer's expectations and demonstrate that you are capable of accepting more responsibility, raises and promotions can be your reward. Several tips to help you succeed are presented in the next sections.

Perform Successfully

Once you have the position, maintain the same enthusiasm you had when you applied for the position. You now have the opportunity to demonstrate the skills you listed on your resume. Additionally, pay attention to what is happening in the organization and learn daily from the people with whom you work and from your experiences.

Listen, Observe, and Learn

Listen to what your supervisor and coworkers tell you. Observe workplace expectations and acceptable behaviors. Pay attention to coworkers who have the respect of their colleagues. Discuss with them how they perform various jobs. Ask questions when you do not understand a task you are given. Asking is much better than doing a task incorrectly. If coworkers volunteer too much information regarding the job, such as unsolicited comments about management or coworkers, refrain from joining in the conversation. Comments you make could come back to haunt you later. Do not take part in gossip on the job.

Ask about the directions of your department. If a strategic plan for the organization exists, read it. If you have not seen a written description for your job, ask your supervisor for one. Study the description. Establish a plan of action for what you intend to accomplish for the next three to six months. Review your plan with your supervisor. Modify the plan as needed.

Grow from the Performance Appraisal

Good supervisors not only provide you with ongoing feedback about your work, they also conduct formal evaluations of your job performance after you have been on the job for three to six months. These evaluations are known as **performance appraisals**. The appraisal consists of a variety of factors—short-range goals that you establish with your supervisor, items that appear on your job description, or a standard evaluation form used for all administrative professionals. Several categories commonly used in evaluations appear in Figure 19-14. Some organizations provide employees with evaluation procedures during the new employee orientation process. If you do not receive information concerning evaluation procedures, ask your supervisor. If a form is used, ask for a copy.

Listen, observe, and learn.

DIGITAL VISION

JOB ASSESSMENT CATEGORIES FOR ADMINISTRATIVE ASSISTANTS

- Organizational skills
- Attendance
- Quality
- Job knowledge
- Cooperation
- Communication
- Problem-solving skills
- Initiative
- Teamwork
- Supervision needed

FIGURE 19–14 Job Assessment Categories for Administrative Assistants

Rather than being afraid of evaluation, accept the evaluation as a chance for you to learn and grow. Listen openly to what your supervisor tells you. Other suggestions to help you learn from a performance appraisal include the following:

- Offer important information relating to your performance that your supervisor may not know. Be prepared to give specifics of what you have accomplished. Prepare a plan for future growth. Although you will not give the plan to your supervisor (unless it is asked for), be prepared to talk about your growth plans.

- Maintain a professional attitude throughout the evaluation.

- If your supervisor makes suggestions for improvement, listen carefully. Do not be upset by criticism. Do not take the statements personally. Realize that you can learn from them. Realize that the criticism is not of you as an individual, but of skills you can improve to perform more effectively.

- Discuss with your supervisor the job expectations for the next evaluation period. Offer to put in writing the goals you will accomplish.

- Accept praise with a smile and a thank-you. Let your supervisor know you will continue to work hard for the organization.

Live Your Values

Throughout this course, the importance of values has been emphasized—values for the organization and values for the individual worker. After several months on the job, you need to ask yourself these questions:

- Am I living my values? If not, why not?
- Are the organization's values clear?
- Do my values mesh with those of the organization?
- Is management living the values espoused by the organization?
- Is this an organization where I can continue to live my values, learn, and grow in my job?

Advance in the Workplace

If this is your first job, learn your job well, work well with others, and learn new ways of doing your job more efficiently before you begin to think of advancement. Remember that you must do your present job well before thinking of advancing to another position. You must prove to your current supervisor that you are an exceptional employee.

Once you have been with an organization for a time and have proven that you have excellent skills, you can begin thinking about advancement opportunities. Find out if there are established career paths in the company. Be aware of the various positions in the company for which you have the requisite skills and abilities.

Excelling in the following attitudes and skills will help you take advantage of advancement opportunities.

- Commitment—Commitment demands understanding the direction of the organization and working hard to produce short- and long-term success for your organization.

- Communication—Improving communication skills is an ongoing process. For example, you must continue to accept and respect people of different cultures, races, ethnicities, and backgrounds; pay attention to verbal and nonverbal behavior; question and paraphrase; listen without evaluating; and use language well.

- Positive attitude—Employers, as well as coworkers, are attracted to positive people. No one likes to work with a person who is negative and who constantly finds fault with everyone and everything. Be positive about your own abilities. Believe in yourself; believe that you can learn to do almost anything you want.

- Networking—Identifying and establishing a group of acquaintances and friends who reach out and help each other is important. As you work within an organization, you can use your communication skills to network successfully with others. You can offer others encouragement, share information with them, and help them succeed. In turn, others will reciprocate with that same help. You should network with people outside your organization so you can acquire a broader frame of reference for your career area. Additionally, you should network with people who have greater power and influence. By doing so, you not only learn from them, but also gain valuable contacts.

Job Change

You may decide to leave a job voluntarily, or you may have no choice. Whatever your reasons for leaving (whether you are unhappy with your position, you are looking for greater opportunities, or you are forced to leave), you must be professional in how you handle your departure.

The Exit Interview

Many organizations ask employees who are leaving to complete an **exit interview**. Generally, an impartial person, perhaps a staff member in human resources, conducts the exit interview. It is not a time to get even, to make derogatory remarks about your supervisor, or to criticize the organization. Keep in mind the old adage about not burning your bridges. You may need a reference from the organization. Be honest in the interview, and present the facts in a positive light if possible. For example, if you are leaving for a job that has greater opportunities for you, you can say, "I am moving to a position with greater responsibilities."

A Layoff or Termination

You may be laid off or fired. With many companies downsizing, layoffs are common. In such a situation, keep in mind that you did not cause the situation. Even though the situation is difficult, the skills, abilities, and experiences you gained from your job can help you find another one. Remain positive. Consider what you want to do next, and mobilize your resources to help you find a position that fits your needs and abilities.

Assume you are fired. Even though you feel rejection and insecurity, it is not a time to consider yourself a failure. It is a time to analyze why you lost your job. Listen to what your employer tells you about your performance. What can you learn for the future?

- If the firing is due to your lack of skills, what skills do you need to develop for the future?

- If the firing is due to your inability to deal effectively with people, what traits do you need to work on?

- If the firing is because of your poor attendance or lack of punctuality, why were you late consistently or why did you miss so many days?

Strive to get answers to these questions. You may want to review your situation with a trusted friend who can help you look at yourself objectively. Your goal is to analyze your weaknesses and then concentrate on what you can do to improve for the future. By learning from your mistakes, you have the opportunity to perform more effectively on your next job. ∎

SUMMARY

To reinforce what you have learned in this chapter, study this summary.

- Before you begin to look for a job, take the time to identify your skills, values, interests, and geographical preferences.

- Sources for jobs include networks, placement offices, the Web, employment agencies, newspapers, and walk-ins.

- Temporary agencies are not job sources in the usual sense; however, they can help someone learn more about various types of organizations.

- When preparing to look for a job, a person should spend time thinking about organizations that are of interest to her or him.

- The basic goals of a letter of application are to state one's interest in a position, to provide general information about one's skills and sell those skills, and to transmit a resume and request an interview.

- When writing a letter applying for a job, one should refrain from using *I* too frequently; use a correct return address, inside address, and salutation; and use appropriate layout and punctuation.

- The three general types of resumes are chronological, functional, and targeted/combination style.

- The six basic parts of a resume are the heading, career objective, relevant skills, education, work experience, and accomplishments.

- References do not appear on a resume; however, an applicant generally needs to provide three to five references when asked by an organization.

- Many organizations accept online resumes.

- When preparing an online resume, one should use keywords; not use italics, bold, and underlining; use a standard font; avoid abbreviations and jargon; not use graphics; and use his or her name as the first item on the resume.

- Job applicants should fill out employment applications completely and honestly.

- These behaviors minimize preinterview nervousness: researching the organization, reassessing one's skills and abilities, practicing interview techniques with a friend, researching salaries for the field, using stress reduction techniques, relaxing the night before the interview, and committing to learning from failed interviews.

- In addition to the traditional face-to-face interview by one person, an applicant may be interviewed by a team or take part in a virtual interview.

- After an interview, promptly write a thank-you letter to the person who interviewed you.

- Once an interview is over, the applicant should evaluate how he or she performed.

- If a position is offered, the applicant should ask himself or herself if the work environment is one in which he or she will enjoy the work and prosper.

- Once the applicant accepts a job, he or she should commit to listening, observing, and learning from the job; growing from performance appraisals; and living his or her values.

- One can advance in the workplace through commitment, communication, a positive attitude, and networking.

- Upon deciding to leave a job, one should do so professionally.

- If experiencing a layoff or termination, one should commit to learning from any mistakes that were made.

FIND THE PROBLEM

Over the last three months, Rory has applied for 12 jobs online. She sent her resume out through **www.monster.com**. She had one response to her online resume, but it did not culminate in an interview. Rory has an associate degree in Office Systems Technology. Her past work experience includes two years of part-time work as a receptionist with a major corporation in the city where she lives. She graduated with a 3.5 grade point average; she held several leadership positions while in college. She was fired from one part-time job, a job she held only three months; and she indicated on her resume that she was fired. She wanted to be honest about the situation. Rory is discouraged and needs help. What is her major problem? What should she change about her strategy for finding a job?

PROFESSIONAL POINTERS

Here are several pointers to help you find the right job in the work world.

- Continue to develop your skills.
- Commit to learning throughout your career.
- Network, network, network.
- Research companies before you apply.
- Stress your accomplishments on your resume and in interviews.
- Do not lie on your resume or in an interview.
- Post your resume online, but do not use it as your only source.
- Stay positive throughout your job search.

REINFORCEMENT ITEMS

1. Why is value clarification important during the job search process?
2. Identify and explain five sources of job information.
3. What are the goals of a letter of application?
4. List the six basic parts of a resume.
5. List and explain three tips for performing successfully on the job.

CRITICAL-THINKING ACTIVITY

Marta Rojo graduated with an AAS degree a year ago. She was an A student; however, she did not take part in outside activities in college. She was a shy, introverted individual; she thought her communication skills were not adequate in social settings. Since Marta was not certain where she wanted to work, she decided to seek various types of jobs through a temporary agency. During the past year, she worked for six companies. Each of her supervisors praised the quality of her work. Two of them offered her full-time employment, but she declined because she did not believe either company fit her long-term goals. Marta believes she has grown tremendously in her communication skills; she now is comfortable in most situations. She decides she wants to work in the health field—a pharmaceutical company, a hospital, or a health research facility. She applied for three jobs in the health field in the last two months. She interviewed for all three jobs; however, none of the three organizations offered her a position. Marta had these experiences during the interviews.

- When asked about her present job, Marta stated that she did not have a full-time job. She did not explain that she had worked for a temporary agency to try different types of positions to help her decide where she wanted to work.

- When asked about her college experience, Marta said she had made good grades but had not done anything outside of her classes.

- When asked about her strengths, Marta responded that she was a capable employee, but she knew she had much to learn.

- When asked by the interviewers if she had any questions, Marta said no.

- Marta was very nervous during the interviews. She did her homework before her interviews, but for some reason, she became anxious before each one.

Marta is discouraged; she wonders whether she will ever find a full-time job. She has not discussed the interview problems and her feelings with anyone. She is embarrassed to admit that she does not have a job offer after three interviews. What advice would you give to Marta?

VOCABULARY REVIEW

Complete the Vocabulary Review for Chapter 19 given on page 141 of the *Applications Workbook*.

ENGLISH AND WORD USAGE DRILL

Complete the English and Word Usage Drill for Chapter 19 listed on page 142 of the *Applications Workbook*.

WORKPLACE APPLICATIONS

A19-1 (Goals 1, 2, and 3)

Using the newspaper and your personal networks, find a position that matches your skills, values, and interests. Prepare a letter of application and a resume. Use an appropriate resume format consistent with your background. Submit copies of your application letter and resume to your instructor. Write your instructor a memorandum, using the form on the Student CD, SCDA19-1, giving the source of the position. If your source was a newspaper, include the date of the publication and the skills requested. If your source was someone from your personal network, include the skills she or he identified as important.

A19-2 (Goals 1, 2, and 3)

Using the Web, find a position that matches your skills, values, and interests. Prepare a letter of application and a resume appropriate for submission on the Web. Review the suggestions for preparing online resumes on pp. 463–466 before you begin. Submit your letter of application and resume to your instructor. Write your instructor a memorandum, using the memorandum form on the Student CD, SCDA19-2, identifying the Website you used and the skills requested.

A19-3 (Goal 4)

Select three classmates to work with on this project. Using the questions listed here, interview your classmates. Alternate with your classmates as the interviewer, the interviewee, and the evaluator. The interviewee is to complete a self-evaluation using the form provided on the Student CD, SCDA19-3a. The two evaluators are to use the evaluation form given on the Student CD, SCDA19-3b to evaluate how the interviewee answers the questions. Once the evaluation for each interviewee is completed, the group should discuss what improvements are needed. Research **www.merck.com** to answer the question *What do you know about the company?*

- What are your goals?
- What are your strengths?
- What are your weaknesses?
- What do you know about the company?
- Why do you think you are qualified for this position?
- Why did you leave your previous job?
- In what type of atmosphere do you work best?
- Do you have any questions?

To help prepare for the interview, review the suggestions given on page 143 of your *Applications Workbook*. Submit the self-evaluation of your interview to your instructor.

A19-4 (Goal 5)

Interview an employed administrative professional. You can conduct the interview by email or in person. Ask the individual these questions:

- What skills and characteristics are necessary for an administrative professional to advance in your organization?
- Are your own values important in advancement? Explain.
- Are communication skills important in advancement? Explain.
- To what do you attribute your success in your position?

Report your findings to the class.

A19-5 (Goal 5)

Review the action plan you prepared in Chapter 2, A2-6. Retake the Stress Audit you completed in Chapter 2, A2-2. Assess whether you have met your objectives in managing your stress, anger, and time, using the Action Plan you prepared in A2-5. Using the Self-Evaluation Chart you prepared in Chapter 1, A1-5, complete Column 2. Review the career plan you prepared in A1-5. Is your career plan still appropriate, or does it need modification due to your growth in this course? If the plan needs modification, make those changes. Submit a memorandum to your instructor, using the form on the Student CD, SCDA19-5. Explain any changes in your strengths and weaknesses from the Self-Evaluation Chart. Explain your progress in managing stress, anger, and time. Identify any changes in your Career Plan.

ASSESSMENT OF CHAPTER GOALS

Did you successfully complete the chapter goals? Evaluate yourself by filling out the form on page 146 of the *Applications Workbook*.

chapter 20

Leadership Theories and Behaviors

LEARNING GOALS

1. Define leadership and describe effective leadership characteristics.

2. Define management and describe its role and responsibilities.

3. Determine your leadership values.

Place and Time

Once you finished your education, you accepted a full-time position as an administrative assistant in the human resources department of People Pharmaceuticals. You enjoy your work; you find it challenging and invigorating. You respect your supervisor and upper management. Management and staff of People Pharmaceuticals live the value statement daily. You find that your values mesh with the values of the workplace. It has now been three years since you began working for People Pharmaceuticals International as a part-time administrative assistant reporting to Kurt Rupprecht.

Situation

Your supervisor surprised you yesterday by suggesting that you apply for a management position in the human resources department. You knew the position was open, but you did not consider applying. You assumed the department would seek someone with a background in management. Your only management experience is in chairing quality teams within the company. Your response to your supervisor was, "I don't have the qualifications; I've never managed anything." His response was, "Don't sell yourself short. You have a number of qualities that will make you an excellent manager—intelligence, creativity, integrity, flexibility, and initiative. Don't forget that you chaired a number of quality teams—and with distinction, I might add. The committees you chaired were extremely pleased with your leadership. Go home and think about it. We'll talk more tomorrow."

You leave his office shocked, but flattered. You decide to give the idea serious consideration. After dinner that evening, you sit down and list the qualities you believe a manager should have. Then you list the qualities you believe you have. You begin to think maybe you can do it. You talk with your family and get their reaction, which is, "Sure, try it. We know you can do anything you want to do."

The next day you tell your supervisor that you will consider the position. The job opening does not close for two weeks, and you want to read at least one management book during that time. You think you need to understand more about the role and responsibilities of managers.

You begin your research by reading the following material.

Leadership—Its Importance

Today's workplace is not the workplace of a generation ago. It is different. You know it is a technological workplace; you live with the technology daily. It is a workplace where constant learning is crucial—and not just learning about the newest technological device you must operate. You must continue to learn about people, about processes, and about communication. The multinational nature of business and the diversity of people in the workplace present new challenges as well as new opportunities. The issues faced by organizations are more complex and more divergent than in the past. The twenty-first-century leader is cognizant of the following facts:

- Strategic thinking is crucial.
- Plans, not problems, drive organizations.
- Actions to situations are proactive rather than reactive.
- Long-term results are more important than short-term results.

What this means is that successful managers are leaders first and managers second.

What is leadership? **Leadership** is the process of influencing others to achieve group and/or organizational goals. Effective leaders operate by a clearly defined set of values. Those values are centered on what is right for an organization, the constituencies it serves, and its employees. When leading, individuals must use wisely the power entrusted by the organization in translating the intentions of individuals or groups into action. **Power** is the ability to act and the strength to accomplish the objectives of the organization. Power is based on one of several factors:

- The leader's position within an organization.
- The leader's knowledge.
- The followers' identification with the leader.
- The ability of the leader to satisfy the followers' needs.

The effective leader uses power well. For example, leaders do not rely on fear or punishment to get something accomplished. Rather, effective leaders are true to the vision, values, and directions of the organization, leading from a principle-centered approach. Employees can then respond to the leader because they believe what the leader does is right. There is no blind faith on the part of employees; there is thoughtful acceptance or open disagreement (with open discussion) concerning the goals of the organization. The leader and the employees move forward because of their faith, respect, and trust in each other.

Leaders versus Managers

A real distinction exists between leadership and management. Leadership means doing the right things, while **management** is defined as "doing things right." Effective leadership relies on leaders bringing the appropriate set of values to the workplace. Leaders' values become apparent only as they guide an organization to accomplish its goals, which benefit not only the organization, but also the external community and the individuals within the organization. The importance of leadership cannot be diminished, and the numerous books written on the subject attest to the fact that true leadership is a skill to be valued and respected.

Management activities, by contrast, are a subset of leadership. The functions of management include planning, managing information, organizing, recruiting, training, controlling, motivating, delegating, and evaluating. These activities are relatively concrete and are quantifiable and measurable. To further help you understand the difference between leadership and management, consider this situation.

A family spends a hot summer afternoon preparing the soil in their front yard and planting beautiful azaleas in the beds. Within two weeks, the azaleas die because the climate is not conducive to growing them. The managers *prepared the soil well and planted the azaleas properly; they even watered the azaleas. They did things right. However, no* leader *emerged to ask the right question, "What plants grow effectively in this climate?"*

Leadership Theories

Over the years, authorities writing in the field have developed and chronicled numerous leadership theories. Although no theory presents every aspect of leadership, each theory helps to add to the body of knowledge concerning leadership and, thus, to a better understanding of the true nature of leadership. Here are three leadership theories.

* Management by Objectives and Self-Control
* Path-Goal Theory
* Visionary Leadership Theory

Management by Objectives and Self-Control

Peter Drucker, an internationally known and well-respected writer in the management field for over 60 years, does not make the distinctions between management and leadership that other writers make. However, he does see the manager as a leader. In one of his recent publications, he tells this story.

A favorite story at management meetings is that of the three stonecutters who were asked what they were doing. The first replied, "I am making a living." The second kept hammering while he

What plants grow effectively in this climate?

said, "I am doing the best job of stonecutting in the entire country." The third one looked up with a visionary gleam in his eyes and said, "I am building a cathedral."[1]

The third person is the true leader—a person with a vision and the ability to make that vision happen.

Using **management by objectives and self-control**, leaders help formulate the objectives for units they supervise, with the objectives defined by the larger goals of the business. Management by objectives makes it possible for managers to control their own performance. Drucker believes the business enterprise needs a principle of management that gives full scope to each individual's strength and responsibility and harmonizes the goals of individuals with the organization. Through management by objectives and self-control, managers can help individuals achieve the larger goals of the organization. Many organizations today adhere to this theory of management and practice it daily. They establish goals, help their units achieve these goals, measure their successes in terms of the goals set, and reward individuals for their achievement.

Path-Goal Theory

The path-goal theory is similar to Drucker's management by objectives and self-control in that it stresses the importance of goals (objectives). The theory states that leaders increase subordinate satisfaction and performance by clarifying and clearing the path to goals established and by increasing the number and kinds of rewards available as individuals meet the goals. The basic assumptions of path-goal theory are that leaders must do the following:

- Clarify paths to goals.
- Clear paths by solving problems and/or removing obstructions.
- Provide appropriate rewards for goal attainment.

---

[1]Peter F. Drucker, *The Essential Drucker* (New York: Harper Business, 2001), 113.

- Offer followers unique experiences beyond what they can provide for themselves.

Visionary Leadership Theory

The two basic types of **visionary leadership** are **charismatic leadership** and **transformational leadership**. Charismatic leaders are just that—charismatic. They are strong, influential, and dynamic. Charismatic leaders are able to articulate a clear vision for the future—one based on values. Their behaviors are consistent with their vision; thus, the employees in their divisions or units learn to trust them. They expect high performance from employees, and they reward employees for their performance. Ethical charismatic leaders have high moral standards that focus on the larger interests of the organization and society.

Transformational leadership is similar to charismatic leadership; however, transformational leaders are successful in getting employees to commit to the larger good of the group and the organization. As the name implies, they are able to help employees see the importance of true transformation—transformation from self-interest to the larger good of the entire organization and community.

As you can see, these leadership theories have certain commonalities and certain distinct differences. As you grow in leadership experience and continue to study leadership theory through observing and reading, you will develop your own leadership style.

Leadership Characteristics

An effective leader has numerous characteristics, including these:

- Lives by a set of values
- Builds a shared vision
- Engenders trust
- Serves others
- Empowers others
- Rewards risk taking
- Moves through chaos
- Is a follower as well as a leader

Charismatic leaders are able to articulate a clear vision for the future—one based on values.

Lives by a Set of Values

Over the course of history, values have been an important point of discussion among leaders and philosophers. Socrates (469-399 B.C.) asserted that virtue and ethical behavior were associated with wisdom; he taught that insight into life would naturally lead to right conduct. Plato (428-348 B.C.) carried Socrates' doctrine of virtue as knowledge further by positing the theory of absolute justice. According to Plato, absolute justice existed independently of individuals and its nature became apparent through intellectual effort. After the rise of Christianity, Catholic theologians St. Augustine and St. Thomas Aquinas dominated ethical thinking. Correct behavior in business dealings and all other activities was necessary to achieve salvation and life after death.

Ethical behavior in business remains the accepted practice today. As you will recall from Chapter 3, ethics is the systematic study of moral conduct, duty, and judgment. The difficult part is how ethical behavior is lived in business organizations. What practices are ethical? What practices are not? Ethical issues form the basis of many debates—not only in business but also in the world today. On the one hand, the public expects ethical behavior from all leaders. Yet individuals are not clear about what ethical behavior is in different situations. Each individual has her or his own definition of what is ethical and what is not. Thus, the debate as to what is right and what is wrong continues. However, few people would disagree that ethics are important and that leaders must live by a sound set of values.

The contention here is that leaders must stand firmly on moral principles. Leaders must work within an organization to define what those principles are and to ensure that the ethical principles become a part of the daily life of the organization. When difficult decisions arise, true leaders stand on their espoused values; in other words, they walk the talk. Although establishing and living a set of values must begin with the top leadership of an organization, values must permeate every level. Ethical leaders insist that employees uphold the values of the organization. In fact, leaders must be clear about the organization's values, embrace those values, and insist that individuals throughout the organization live the values.

In 2002, the United States saw a rash of corporations whose CEOs seemingly lived a set of values that embraced only their own welfare, unconcerned about the welfare of their companies, their employees, and their stockholders. The public and stockholders paid for these CEOs' failings. For example, Enron's Jeff Skilling and Tyco's™ Dennis

DIGITAL VISION

Effective leaders walk the talk; they stand on their espoused values.

Kozlowski cashed in millions of dollars of stock options before their companies collapsed. Skilling made $112 million from his stock options in the three years before the company collapsed; Kozlowski made $240 million before his company failed. According to *Fortune*, "If you're looking for reasons corporate America is in such ill repute, this kind of over-the-top CEO piggishness is a big one. Investors and in some cases employees lost everything, while the architects of their pain laughed all the way to the bank."[2]

Do not forget, however, that most CEOs in corporate America do an excellent job. On a daily basis, they live values that support their corporations, their employees, and their larger communities. They are honest and concerned about the welfare of their corporations and the nation as a whole. Consider two of the companies selected in 2002 by *Fortune* as the *100 Best Companies to Work For*—SAS™ and Whole Foods Market®. SAS, on their Website, makes this statement about employees.

If you treat employees as if they make a difference to the company, they will make a difference to the company. That's been the employee-focused philosophy behind SAS' corporate culture since the company's founding in 1976. At the heart of this unique business model is a simple idea: satisfied employees create satisfied customers. From managers who work on projects alongside their staff members, to the flexible scheduling that allows employees to work hard and play hard on the job, the environment at SAS is designed to enable employees to do great work and to have a life outside of work, as well.[3]

The CEO of Whole Foods Market (another of the *Fortune* 2002 *100 Best Companies to Work For*) believes his salary should stay at an appropriate level. The standard today for all businesses is for CEOs to make about 400 times the average worker; however, the salary

[2]Joseph Nocera, "System Failure," *Fortune*, June 24, 2002, 70.

[3]"Work/Life," accessed December 13, 2002; available from **www.sasinstitute.com/corporate/worklife/index .html**.

for Whole Foods Market's CEO is 14 times the average worker. The philosophy of Whole Foods Market as reported on its homepage is available on the Web at **www.wholefoods market.com/company**.

Builds a Shared Vision

Leaders of organizations can be visionary, but unless they are able to help others within the organization see and share their vision, the vision has little chance of becoming reality. Bill Gates and Paul Allen, as they stood in Harvard Square as college sophomores and pored over the description of a kit computer, had a vision. They were certain that the first personal computer would change the world of computing. They were right. They were able to build an organization (Microsoft) composed of people who shared the same **vision** (a similar picture in people's minds and hearts), and the world was changed.

Leaders with a vision are able to articulate the vision to those with whom they work and to get others within the organization not only to buy into the vision, but also to feel passionate about it. When individuals unite around a vision, they come together to produce a common goal. They understand and articulate their direction. They have the courage to continue to work toward their goal, no matter how difficult the process may be. For individuals who share a vision, work becomes part of a larger purpose, affecting the climate and spirit of the organization. Risk taking and experimentation are common.

Engenders Trust

Effective leaders forge bonds of trust between themselves and the people with whom they work. They create a climate of trust throughout the organization. How do they do this? Here are some of the ways leaders engender trust.

- They live by a stated set of values.
- They are reliable and predictable; they do what they say they will do.
- They are unshakably fair in public and in private.

Serves Others

Effective leaders consider service to others as primary. In other words, effective leaders think first of how they can serve the organization, its goals, its employees, and the larger community outside the organization. For example, effective leaders' values include a commitment to helping people grow, a commitment to diversity, and a commitment to helping the world become a better place. You may view Starbucks'® mission statement, reflecting the company's commitment to the work environment, diversity, and satisfied customers and its contributions to its communities and environment at **www.starbucks.com/aboutus/environment.asp**.

Empowers Others

As you learned earlier, power is the ability to exercise control. The prefix *em* means to "put

Effective leaders engender trust; they are unshakably fair in public and in private.

on to"; thus, **empower** means to pass on authority or responsibility to others. Leaders empower others when they take these actions:

- Provide employees with access to information that will help them increase their productivity and effectiveness.
- Allow employees to take on more responsibility.
- Allow employees a voice in decision making.

Empowered employees feel a sense of ownership and control over their jobs. They understand they are responsible for getting their jobs done. Empowered employees usually are happier individuals; they trust the organization, feel a part of it, and enjoy the rewards the job provides.

Leaders who empower people have a core belief in people, believing they are good, honest, and well intentioned. These leaders believe people do the right thing when they

have the resources available to accomplish a task and understand that leadership is operating from a central core of values, even in difficult situations.

Rewards Risk Taking

Organizations of the twenty-first century, with change as a constant, face risks daily. Ignoring the risks does not make them go away. Organizations cannot take refuge in the status quo, conformity to the norm, or security in the past. None of these stances makes sense if organizations are to be successful. Organizations must be willing to seek new answers to problems, try new approaches, and be flexible. If organizations are to be successful, they must have leaders who take risks and who encourage others to do the same. Wise leaders who take risks demonstrate a number of characteristics, some of which appear in Figure 20-1.

DIGITAL VISION

The effective leader provides employees with information that helps increase productivity and effectiveness.

CHARACTERISTICS OF LEADERS WHO TAKE RISKS

Wise leaders who take risks engage in the following behaviors:

- Gather information wisely
- Work from strengths not weaknesses
- Prepare thoroughly
- Display flexibility
- Envision what can be gained
- Understand what is at stake
- Stay on mission
- Possess the right motives
- Give their followers wins
- March forward with confidence

Source: John C. Maxwell, *The Right to Lead* (Nashville: Thomas Nelson, Inc., 2001), 66.

FIGURE 20-1 Characteristics of Leaders Who Take Risks

Some of the keys to successful risk taking are as follows:

- Trusting in your own abilities
- Being open-minded
- Overcoming fear of mistakes
- Developing support teams

Moves through Chaos

Since chaos is an inevitable part of leadership in the twenty-first century, effective leaders learn from it—from the good and bad experiences that happen. Leaders practice the art of meeting individuals where they are and moving them forward to bring about the desired outcomes. They understand that each situation is different and may be difficult. However, they do not ignore the situation; they move it from the unacceptable to the acceptable.

Is a Follower as well as a Leader

Effective leaders understand that leaders are sometimes followers and followers are sometimes leaders. A **bilateralness** (affecting two sides equally) exists, with leaders not only understanding the importance of following, but also trusting others to know that these people, given the proper opportunities and training, can be leaders too. Men and women who lead at the highest levels are extraordinary. They continue to develop their extraordinary characteristics throughout their lives. Figure 20-2 lists several additional characteristics of uncommon leaders.

Management

You already learned that leadership is often defined as doing the right thing while management is doing things right. Both leadership and management are important. Leadership without management is ineffective, just as management without leadership is ineffective. Astute leaders understand these statements. They understand that values must be lived through the accomplishment of the objectives of an organization. They strive to be effective leaders *and* managers.

CHARACTERISTICS OF UNCOMMON LEADERS

The men and women who lead at the highest level have these traits.

- Futurists—Their dreams are bigger than their memories.
- Catalysts—They initiate movement and momentum for others.
- Optimists—They believe in their cause and their people beyond reason.
- Activists—They are doers and empower others by their actions.
- Strategists—They plan how to use every resource available to be successful.
- Pragmatists—Their legacy is that they solve the practical problems people face.

Source: John C. Maxwell, *The Right to Lead* (Nashville: Thomas Nelson, Inc., 2001), 22.

FIGURE 20-2 Characteristics of Uncommon Leaders

Management's Role

The tasks of organizations must be managed. Without management, goals of organizations are not met, profits are not made (meaning the long-term viability of the business is threatened), and employees often flounder (not knowing what they are to accomplish and when). The role of management is to make things happen; to meet the competition (have a well-thought-out strategy); and to organize people, projects, and processes.

Management's Responsibilities

Management's responsibilities include these:
- Planning
- Managing information
- Organizing (people and projects)
- Recruiting
- Training
- Controlling
- Motivating
- Delegating
- Evaluating

These activities are relatively concrete and are quantifiable, measurable, and accessible. Management's tasks are a subset of leadership. Without the effective management of tasks, leadership fails. Without effective leadership, management fails. Although characteristics of effective leaders and managers appear separately in this text for your ease of understanding, know that the most effective managers are also effective leaders. Conversely, effective leaders are also effective managers.

Planning

Planning involves setting goals and objectives for an organization and developing plans for accomplishing them. Defining these goals and objectives in writing and establishing measurable results is referred to as **MBO** (management by objectives), a theory developed by Peter Drucker, which you learned about earlier in this chapter as a leadership theory. Although MBO has taken on numerous forms and variations, it is present in the planning process.

The planning process in which goals and objectives are set is usually done in two time frames—**long-range planning** (a three- to five-year period) and **tactical planning** (usually a one-year period). Many times top-level leaders (boards of directors, presidents, and executive vice presidents) set the overall goals of organizations. Once these goals are established, managers distribute them to their work units. Then managers, along with their work units, set objectives. Administration holds managers accountable for achieving the objectives defined.

Assume you are a supervisor of three administrative support staff. What is your involvement in the planning process? First, you involve the personnel who report to you. You help them set objectives that support the overall objectives of the organization. Next, you help them state specifically how the objectives will be accomplished—what actions will occur, who is accountable, when the tasks will be completed, what financial resources are necessary, and how the tasks will be evaluated. Figure 20-3 shows a portion of a tactical plan. Once the tactical plan is developed, you hold the employees who report to you responsible for completion of the tasks. You hold periodic sessions with your group to determine what has and what has not been accomplished on the plan. You help your staff get past any roadblocks that occur. In other words, you support them in the accomplishment of their tasks, tasks that support the overall goals of the organization.

Managing Information

A major task of management is managing information. Think for a minute about the amount of information generated by organizations—product information, employee information, financial information, to name only a few. That information is stored on hard drives (where it can be manipulated and revised), distributed to individuals within the company via reports generated in Excel, and distributed to stockholders through annual reports. If this information is to be of value to organizations, their boards, and employees, it must

PORTION OF A TACTICAL PLAN

OBJECTIVE: Train employees on the use of human resources software

Actions	Accountability	Completion	Resources	Evaluation
Provide four training sessions of two hours each for all employees on the software	HR Manager	May 15, 2005	$250 per session for trainer, for a total of $1,000	Employees' ability to use system and written evaluation by employees of training provided

FIGURE 20-3 Portion of a Tactical Plan

be accurate, complete, relevant, and timely. For example, if a drug distributed by a pharmaceutical company is defective and results in harmful reactions by the individuals taking the drug, the pharmaceutical company must receive timely information about its lack of effectiveness (or even danger) so the drug can be recalled. If such information is not obtained, a number of deaths may result. Additionally, the company may be forced out of business due to the problems.

Organizing

Once planning occurs, the work is organized. Organization involves bringing together all resources—people, time, money, and projects—in the most effective way to accomplish organizational goals.

Teams. As you have already learned, teams are a part of most organizations. Some organizations use teams throughout their organizations. For example, assume that all work of the Information Systems Department is done as a team. The team receives an assignment from management, divides the work among its members, and performs the job in a timely manner. If a team member does not perform, the team leader confronts the individual about the problem. Team members evaluate each other, and the evaluations are sent to the supervisor, who discusses them individually with each team member. Team members receive recognition or rewards for a job well done, in addition to salary increases.

Teams are more effective when these conditions are present:
- The job to be accomplished is clear.
- People on the team work well together.
- Individuals share information.
- Individuals have the skills needed to perform the job.
- Rewards are provided for the team.
- Resources are available to reward the team.
- Teams have authority to manage and change how work is accomplished.

Teams are not effective in the following situations:
- When the job to be accomplished is not clear
- When resources are not available for the team to accomplish the task
- When managers are prone to micromanage
- When employees are not empowered to do the work
- When approval is necessary for each decision the team makes
- When team members and management are not willing to take risks

Systems. One system common to all organizations is the human resources system. This system gathers, analyzes, stores, and disseminates information about attracting, developing, and keeping a qualified workforce.

Human resources systems do the following:
- Project the number and types of employees needed.

- Engage in external forecasting to determine factors outside the organization that affect supply and demand for human resources.
- Establish skills needed for various types of jobs.
- Establish salary ranges for job categories.
- Disseminate information to managers.

Recruiting

Using the data provided by Human Resources and in conjunction with Human Resources, supervisors have the responsibility of recruiting new employees. If supervisors are to do so effectively, they must be aware of recruitment sources and laws that impact recruiting and interviewing. For example, when placing advertisements, companies must ensure that the wording of the ad does not conflict with fair employment practice laws. Discrimination statutes prohibit advertisements that show preferences in terms of race, religion, gender,

age, or physical disabilities. An employer cannot advertise for a particular age group. Thus, expressions such as *young person* or *retired person* are illegal in advertisements.

Once recruitment of applicants occurs, companies use three major screening and selection tools:

- Resumes
- Personal interviews
- Testing procedures

Managers or teams of employees sometimes review the resumes of applicants. If you are part of the team, you should be clear about the skills, education, and experience needed for the job. Asking these questions will help you.

- What type of person are we seeking?
- What qualifications does the person need?
- What education and experience does the person need?

DIGITAL VISION

Teams are more effective when members share information.

With that criteria in mind, screen the resumes and select the most qualified individuals to interview. Before the interviewing process begins, make a list of the questions to ask each candidate. Such a list keeps you on target as you begin the interviewing process and helps you treat all interviewees with fairness and consistency. Know what questions are unlawful to ask. For example, these questions cannot be asked.

- Are you married? Single? Divorced?
- What nationality are your parents?
- What is the date of your birth?
- Where were you born?
- Is your spouse a U.S. citizen?
- What does your spouse do?
- To what clubs do you belong?
- What are the ages of your children?
- What church do you attend?

- Have you ever belonged to a union?

Stay current on all laws that affect interviewing. Without the latest information, you may place your organization in jeopardy of a discrimination suit.

The third screening tool is the test. Here, too, legal considerations are important. The test must measure the person's qualifications for the job, not the person as an individual. If you are employing an administrative professional, for example, and a requirement of the job is that the person be able to key at a certain rate with an established degree of accuracy, you can give the person a keyboarding test. You can also give applicants grammar and spelling tests since they must produce documents free of grammar and spelling errors. You cannot ask the applicant to take a math proficiency test unless the use of math is necessary in performing the job.

DIGITAL VISION

Certain questions are unlawful to ask in an interview. The interviewer needs to stay current on what questions are illegal.

Training

After employment, training periods are necessary. No matter how qualified people are for jobs, they must learn the policies and procedures of the organization. Supervisors must assist employees in the job training process. For example, new employees need the following information:

- History of the organization
- Policy and procedures manual
- Evaluation procedures (when evaluation occurs and what criteria and evaluation forms are used)

Other entry-level training includes assistance in the day-to-day procedures of the administrative professional's job—handling mail, using records management systems, writing letters and reports, and answering the phone. Some organizations assign new employees **mentors** (counselors or teachers). The mentor meets with the new employee regularly, introduces the new employee to other people within the organization, answers questions, and trains the employee in order to expedite the process of learning the job and the organizational procedures.

In addition to entry-level training, ongoing training for administrative professionals is necessary due to the rapid changes in technology. For example, employees may need training in a new software program.

Controlling

Organizations exercise a variety of controls in measuring the performance of the organization and individuals within the organization. Some of these measures are as follows:

- Standards
- Budgets
- Benchmarking

As you learned earlier, managers and employees set goals during the planning process. In accomplishing these goals, standards are crucial. For example, an administrative professional may have a performance goal of developing an information management system. Standards are set and questions are developed

around the standards. For example, does the system:

- Provide for quick retrieval of documents?
- Meet the budget requirements established?
- Provide for both electronic and manual storage?

Then the evaluation of the administrative professional's performance includes whether the system is effective.

Benchmarking (the process of determining how well other companies perform functions or tasks) is another method of establishing controls. Organizations may benchmark anything—from the time needed to produce products to the quality of products.

These examples are of **organizational control** (control exercised by the organization). Three other types of control are **group control**, **stakeholder control**, and **individual self-control**.

- Group control involves the norms and values that groups impose on one another through measures such as group acceptance or rejection.
- An example of stakeholder control is evident through boards of directors. Boards, along with CEOs, generally look at the big picture—issues that affect the organization from the outside, such as environmental issues, global issues, and ethical issues.
- Individual self-control is evident through the professionalism of employees. In other words, employees are willing to use their knowledge, skills, values, and ethics to exercise self-control.

Motivating

Effective managers understand the strengths and weaknesses of the people within their unit. Managers also understand what motivates their employees. **Motivation** comes from the Latin word meaning "to move." Motivation may be **extrinsic** (relying on external factors such as salary increases or promotions) or **intrinsic** (from within the person—something is done because it is right and fits the individual's values). Figure 20-4 lists several motivational techniques.

MOTIVATIONAL TECHNIQUES

- Set objectives. Help the employees you supervise establish challenging, measurable objectives. Once the objectives are established, help employees commit themselves to achieving the objectives.
- Give recognition. As a supervisor, you need to become sensitive to the accomplishments of others. You can give recognition in a number of ways: verbal praise for a job well done, a thank-you letter, and recognition in the organization's newsletter.
- Develop a team. Individuals need to be an accepted member of a group. As a supervisor, you can capitalize on this need by building a team of people who work together well. Productivity improves when each person in the group contributes to the overall effectiveness of the team.
- Pay for the job. As a supervisor, know what your employees do and then pay them fairly for their work. Reward employees who consistently perform well with good salary increases.
- Delegate work. Employees enjoy doing meaningful and challenging work. Provide this opportunity by delegating important projects to them.

FIGURE 20~4 Motivational Techniques

Delegating

Delegation is the assigning of tasks to others and then empowering them to get the job done. Delegation can be difficult for a manager, particularly one who has a need to control all aspects of a job. Yet no manager can possibly do everything. One widely accepted definition of management is "getting work done through others." Managers must delegate. Delegation requires that employees receive the proper information and training before a task is assigned. Ineffective managers (unfortunately, they do exist) often have control issues, and they do not delegate well. If forced to delegate by upper management, they may not give employees the proper information or the proper training. As a result, the employees often fail. Such a situation sets up a self-fulfilling prophecy:

- The manager did not want to delegate.
- When forced to delegate, the manager did not give the proper information or training to employees.
- The employees failed due to lack of good information.
- The manager feels vindicated—delegation should not have occurred in the first place. The ineffective manager's view of employees is reinforced: they cannot be

trusted to get the job done. Delegation does not work.

Of course, ineffective managers do not recognize their own failings in such situations.

Effective managers understand the power and necessity of delegation. They also understand that once delegation occurs (and employees are provided the necessary information to get the task done), employees must be trusted to perform.

Evaluating

You learned earlier that once plans for the organization are established, they are evaluated periodically. When evaluating plans, here are some of the questions you need to ask.

- Were plans successfully completed?
- If not, what is the problem?
- Do plans need modification?
- Are certain portions of the plan no longer applicable for the organization?

The evaluation step is an important one. Without it, plans may not be carried out and no one asks why. In other words, plans lose their effectiveness due to lack of follow-up. Additionally, the organization suffers (and may even go out of business) due to the inability to adhere to its plans and deliver a product or service that its customers need.

Another important evaluation piece (and the focus of this section) is evaluation of employees. Is this a difficult job for most managers? Yes, it is. Why? Because the measurement of employee performance is not precise and objective. Human interactions involve subjectivity; they involve factors such as judgment and perception, which are difficult to quantify in objective measurements.

Assume you are managing an administrative assistant. The assistant is responsible for maintaining the records management system and preparing monthly reports. What evaluation measures do you use? Assume you have chosen to use accuracy as a measure. The employee is accurate, but very slow. How long should it take to produce the reports? Is the employee doing a good job if all papers are filed accurately in the system, but there is a three-month backlog of filing? What about other activities the employee must perform? Is the employee required to handle a myriad number of tasks (telephone calls to answer, meetings to attend, a continual flow of new projects to complete) that have not been considered?

You can see the problems. Evaluation of personnel is not easy. As a manager, you should have a carefully defined evaluation system, one that all employees understand and all administrators uphold. Here are several suggestions for maintaining and administering effective systems.

- Maintain a job description for each job, including details of the requirements. Figure 20-5 gives a job description.
- Involve employees in establishing their job descriptions.
- Keep job descriptions current; ask employees to review their job descriptions at least once a year and recommend modifications, if necessary.
- Establish formal evaluation procedures; involve employees in the process.
- Give a copy of the formal evaluation procedure to employees, along with the specific instrument you are using to evaluate their

JOB DESCRIPTION

Job Title: Administrative Assistant
Company: People Pharmaceuticals International
Department: Human Resources

Skills

The position of Administrative Assistant requires these skills:

- Communication
- Time Management
- Critical-Thinking
- Teamwork
- Computer (Microsoft Word, Excel, PowerPoint)
- Keyboarding (accurate at 90 wpm)

Education

Associate degree or equivalent course work

Experience

Two years of workplace experience, with Human Resources experience preferred

Duties

- Input personnel records
- Prepare monthly personnel reports
- Compose correspondence
- Maintain a records management system
- Plan meetings
- Supervise one support staff

FIGURE 20-5 Job Description

performance. Before the formal evaluation procedure, give employees a copy of the instrument again, ask them to do a self-evaluation and justify the ratings they give themselves.

- Evaluate performance on a daily basis. Employees should always know how they are performing. For example, if an employee prepared a report that contained grammatical errors, let the person know immediately. Do not withhold this information and then bring it up six months later during the employee's formal evaluation session.

- As a supervisor, know yourself. Know what your needs and values are. If you come to the workplace tired or upset, do not vent your irritability on others by criticizing the people or their work when your emotions are the problem. Psychologists refer to this phenomenon of transferring problems to others as **projection**.

- Allow adequate time for formal evaluation, which usually occurs every six months or every year. Set aside enough time to do it well. You may need to spend an hour or two with each employee. Also, choose the appropriate place for the evaluation. If you are using your office, ask your assistant not to interrupt you. Do not accept telephone calls during this time. The employee deserves your undivided attention. Close the door to your office to ensure confidentiality. Figure 20-6 provides a number of additional suggestions.

Leadership—Values Communicated and Aligned

Throughout this chapter, the importance of leadership and management were stressed and the differences between the two were identified. To refresh your memory, leadership is the process of influencing others to achieve

---

EMPLOYEE EVALUATION TECHNIQUES

- In the formal evaluation session, establish ground rules at the beginning of the session. For example, you might say, "I will discuss your performance on each objective of your plan and then give you an opportunity to tell me what your assessment is."
- During the formal evaluation session, praise the employee for work well done. Too many managers consider an evaluation period as a time for criticism only. It is not. It is a time to look at the total work of the employee. In what areas is the employee performing in an exemplary manner? In an average manner? Below expectations?
- During the session, stay focused on the topics at hand; keep digressions to a minimum. Present observable behaviors to support your comments.
- Be fair. Analyze the employee's work based on established criteria—not on how much you like or dislike the person. Stay away from personality traits. Stress job performance. Word your comments as positively as possible. Do not say, for example, "Your performance is a problem." Instead, say, "You are doing well in these areas (and list the areas); however, you need to improve in these areas."
- Give the employee an opportunity to talk. Then listen intently, without interrupting, as the employee talks. If the employee makes negative comments, try to understand and accept the employee's feelings. Help the employee know how to handle difficult situations. Do not be offended by negative comments the employee makes.
- Avoid personal areas. Sometimes a supervisor, even with the best of intentions, becomes too involved in the employee's personal life. Do not try to counsel an employee about personal problems. Let a qualified professional handle that area of the employee's life.
- Help the employee establish attainable objectives for improvement, if necessary, and realistic objectives for the next six months or year. If a plan of action for improvement is necessary, help the employee set measurable objectives, with a timeline established for each objective. Evaluate the employee periodically on the improvement plan; do not wait for the next formal evaluation period. Praise the employee for improvement.
- Take notes during the performance evaluation, and urge the employee to do the same. Offer the employee an opportunity to add comments to the final written evaluation, which become a part of his or her file.

FIGURE 20~6 Employee Evaluation Techniques

group and/or organization goals. Leadership is defined as doing the right thing, while management is defined as doing things right. Leaders live by a set of values, build a shared vision, engender trust, use power appropriately, and reward risk taking. Management is a subset of leadership, with management tasks defined as planning, managing information, organizing people and projects, recruiting, training, motivating, delegating, and evaluating. You have learned that a definite link exists between good leaders and good managers. Each manager must have leadership characteristics—characteristics that keep the organization focused on doing what is right. Each leader must have management characteristics—characteristics that keep the organization focused on performing tasks well. Leaders and managers must operate by a set of values that support the organizational goals.

After studying this chapter, ask yourself these important questions:

- Am I interested in developing my leadership skills?
- Do I live by a well-defined set of values?
- Am I willing to help others learn and grow?

Communicating Values and Goals

You learned that effective leaders are clear about their values and goals. However, effective leaders do not stop there. Their next step is to communicate these values and goals in a manner that fits the agendas of the organization and the employees. In other words, successful leaders work in organizations where their values and goals complement and support the values and goals of the organization. They do not join organizations where their values and goals do not match those of the company; they do not stay in organizations where the companys' values and goals are different from their own values and goals. When the organizational goals and the leader's goals are the same, those goals can be successfully communicated to the employees.

Aligning Values and Goals

Once the organizational values and the leader's values are in agreement, the next step for the leader is to align the values with the work of the organization. As planning takes place, the leader articulates the relationship between defined tasks and values and goals. As each task in the planning process is envisioned, the question is this: Does the task support the stated values and goals? If it does not, the task does not become part of the plan. Value-driven leaders understand that success does not come from merely talking about values; leaders understand that success comes from consistently putting values into action. When organizational tasks are aligned around values and when goals are lived by individuals within the organization, ordinary people can and do accomplish extraordinary results.

Earning the Right

Leadership in an organization is an earned right—a person is not born with leadership characteristics. A person must work at developing them. Hard work? Yes! Individuals who

DIGITAL VISION

Leaders effectively communicate their values and goals.

strive to develop the characteristics defined in this chapter, who commit to helping an organization meet its goals, and who commit to helping others within an organization learn and grow earn the right to lead. Whatever position of leadership you find yourself in, whether it is in the workplace, in professional organizations, in volunteer organizations, or in your home, the challenges of leadership demand the very best from you. ■

SUMMARY

To reinforce what you have learned in this chapter, study this summary.

- The twenty-first-century leader understands that strategic thinking is crucial, plans drive organizations, actions to situations are proactive rather than reactive, and long-term results are more important than short-term results. The leader understands that successful managers are leaders first and managers second.
- Effective leaders operate around a clearly defined set of values. Those values are centered on what is right for an organization and its employees.
- Management activities are a subset of leadership.
- Leadership theories add to the body of knowledge concerning leadership and, thus, to a better understanding of the true nature of leadership. The three leadership theories included in this chapter are management by objectives and self-control, path-goal theory, and visionary leadership theory.
- Leadership characteristics include these: lives by a set of values, builds a shared vision, engenders trust, serves others, empowers others, rewards risk taking, moves through chaos, and knows how to follow.
- Management's responsibilities include these: planning, managing information, organizing (people and projects), recruiting, training, controlling, motivating, delegating, and evaluating.
- Leadership is an earned right—not a birthright.

FIND THE PROBLEM

You accepted a management position in your company six months previously. Two months ago you hired an administrative assistant, Mark Erickson. He reports directly to you. His skills are excellent; his keyboard rate is 100 wpm; his grammar and punctuation skills are outstanding; his knowledge of software is commendable. However, for the last month, a few of his coworkers have come to you with complaints. The majority of the complaints concern Mark's poor people skills—he does not help others with projects, he refuses to serve on committees, he rarely speaks to anyone, and he is not interested in being part of any group within the company. In the past, you praised his work; it was and continues to be excellent. You have not talked with him about his people skills because you did not realize there were problems until the complaints started. You did not give him a position description; in fact, you do not think one exists. What is the problem? As his supervisor, what should you do?

PROFESSIONAL POINTERS

Strive to develop these behaviors of effective leaders.

- Effective leaders promote a spirit of cooperation.
- Effective leaders praise employees and work groups for their contributions.
- Effective leaders believe the basic human needs of employees are important. (Employees must believe that an organization cares about them.)
- Effective leaders celebrate the successes of individuals.

REINFORCEMENT ITEMS

1. What is the difference between leadership and management?
2. Define Drucker's concept of management by objectives and self-control.
3. List and explain five characteristics of an effective leader.
4. List and explain five management responsibilities.
5. Explain the meaning of this statement: Leadership is an earned right.

CRITICAL-THINKING ACTIVITY

As a new manager (six months), you instituted a team approach to projects. You believed you were clear in your expectations about how teams should work, but nothing is going as you expected. Two team members are openly hostile, sarcastic, and abusive to each other. They use team meetings to engage in shouting matches. One of the two (Fernando) came to you to complain about the other person (Lorna). He stated that Lorna never liked him and that she uses the team meetings to criticize him. You believe him and tell him you will talk to Lorna about her behavior. However, when you talk with Lorna, she denies that she criticizes Fernando; she believes all the yelling and screaming matches are a result of his actions. You do not know how to handle the situation. You are feeling frustrated and out of control. How can you get control of the situation?

VOCABULARY REVIEW

Complete the Vocabulary Review for Chapter 20 given on page 147 of the *Applications Workbook*.

ENGLISH AND WORD USAGE DRILL

Complete the English and Word Usage Drill for Chapter 20 listed on page 148 of the *Applications Workbook*.

WORKPLACE APPLICATIONS

A20-1 (Goals 1 and 2)

Work with two classmates and interview two supervisors. You can interview them by email or in person. Ask them the questions given here. Report your findings to the class.

- How do you define leadership?
- What characteristics does a leader possess?
- What distinction do you make between leadership and management?
- Does your organization have a published mission and value statement? If so, who developed the statement? May I have a copy of the statement?
- What process do you use to evaluate employees?
- Do you use teams in your organization? If so, do you believe the approach is successful?
- What type of leadership style works best with teams?

A20-2 (Goal 2)

Work with two or three classmates. Here is the situation. You are in the process of employing an administrative assistant for the human resources department. Figure 20-5 lists the skills and experience needed for the job. Review the job description. Make changes to the job description if you think they are necessary. As a group, write 12 to 14 questions you can ask each candidate for the position. Establish a rating scale for each question, using from one to five points as the value of each question. To be certain you are not asking any illegal questions, review the illegal questions given in the textbook. Additionally, research the legality of interview questions online. Present your list of questions, as well as the online resources you used, to your instructor in a memorandum, using the memorandum form on the Student CD, SCDA20-2. List the members of your group on the memorandum after the From heading.

A20-3 (Goal 3)

Using the rating scale on page 149 of your *Applications Workbook*, rate yourself on your leadership potential. Ask one of your classmates to rate you, using the other rating scale provided. Talk with your classmate about how he or she thinks you can improve. Using the memorandum form on the Student CD, SCDA20-3, write a memorandum to your instructor about how you can improve your leadership skills.

A20-4 (Goal 3)

Reread the situation at the beginning of this chapter on page 482. Assume you are offered the management job mentioned in this situation. List the following: (l) your values, (2) your management qualities, and (3) your management experiences, including positions of leadership in school, in the community, or in professional organizations. How will you continue to improve your leadership skills? Submit your responses to your instructor, using the memorandum form on the Student CD, SCDA20-4.

ASSESSMENT OF CHAPTER GOALS

Did you successfully complete the chapter goals? Evaluate yourself by filling out the form on page 152 of the *Applications Workbook*.

Reference Guide

This Reference Guide is a handy and easy-to-use reference to a variety of rules you will use frequently in preparing correspondence. You can use the guide to review grammar and punctuation rules. In addition, the guide includes basic formats for letters and guidelines for business introductions. To assist you in using proper grammar and punctuation as you write and in using correct letter format, read this guide at the beginning of the course and refer to it as needed throughout the course. The parts of the Reference Guide are as follows:

CONTENTS

Abbreviations

1. Use standard abbreviations for titles immediately before proper names.

   <u>Before the Name</u>

   Use periods in abbreviations before the name.

   > Dr. Cindy Bos
   > Mr. Michael Khirallah
   > Rev. Thomas McIntrye

   Spell out titles such as *Reverend* and *Honorable* when preceded by *the*.

   > The Honorable Isabella Martinez
   > The Reverend Elias Enderon

   Abbreviate personal titles such as *Rev., Hon., Prof., Gen., Col., Capt.,* and *Lieut.* when they precede a surname and a given name. When using only the surname, spell out these titles.

   > Prof. James Huddleston
   > Professor Huddleston

   <u>After the Name</u>

   Abbreviate academic degrees with periods or eliminate the periods.

   > Patricia LaFaver, Ph.D.
   > Bryant McAnnelley, J.D.
   > Helene Chen, MS
   > Bryon Nichols, MD

   Abbreviate civil titles in all capital letters with no periods.

   > J. Hansel Zucker, CLU

2. Many companies and professional organizations use abbreviated names. Key these abbreviated names in all capital letters with no periods and no spaces between the letters.

IBM	International Business Machines
YMCA	Young Men's Christian Association

3. Abbreviate certain expressions.

e.g.	exempli gratia (for example)
etc.	et cetera (and so forth)
i.e.	id est (that is)

4. Abbreviate names of countries only in tabulations or enumerations, and key these names in all capital letters. Periods may or may not be used.

   > U.S.A. or USA
   > U.S. or US

   Note: Spell out *United States* as a noun, and abbreviate it as an adjective.

   > The people of the United States are very diverse in race and ethnicity.
   > The median age of the U.S. population is 35.6 years.

5. Write abbreviations for government agencies in all capital letters with no periods and no spaces between the letters.

FTC	Federal Trade Commission
CIA	Central Intelligence Agency

6. Use only one period when an abbreviation containing a period falls at the end of the sentence. In sentences ending with a question mark or an exclamation mark, place the punctuation mark directly after the period.

   > The play began at 8:15 p.m.
   > Does the class start at 9:30 a.m.?

7. Avoid abbreviating the following categories of words unless these words appear in tabulations or enumerations.

   - Names of territories and possessions of the United States, countries, states, and cities
   - Names of months
   - Days of the week
   - Given names, such as *Wm.* for *William*
   - Words such as *avenue, boulevard, court, street, drive, road,* and *building*
   - Parts of company names (such as *Bros., Co., Corp.*) unless the words are abbreviated in the official company name
   - Compass directions when they are part of an address (use *North, South, East, West*) Note: Abbreviate *NW, NE, SE,* and *SW* after a street name.

- The word *number* unless followed by a numeral

8. Use the article *a* before an abbreviation beginning with a consonant sound. Use the article *an* before an abbreviation beginning with a vowel sound.

    an IQ test
    a MBO project

9. When an abbreviation includes an ampersand, generally, do not space before or after the ampersand.

Texas A&M University
P&L statement

10. Form plurals of abbreviations by adding an *s*. If it is confusing to add only an *s*, add an apostrophe *s*.

    Drs.
    A's

Adjectives and Adverbs

1. Adjectives modify nouns and pronouns.

    The *large* dog appeared hungry.
    They were *snobbish*.

- When the word that follows a verb modifies the subject, an adjective is used.

    I feel *bad*. (not *badly*)

- An adverb answers the question when, where, why, in what manner, or to what extent.

    The child ran *quickly*. (not *quick*)
    That tree grows *poorly* in this climate. (not *poor*)

2. Use comparative and superlative forms appropriately. Comparative forms compare two words, while superlative forms compare three words. One-syllable adjectives and adverbs add *er* and *est* to the word to form the comparative and superlative. Adjectives and adverbs with two or more syllables use *more* or *most*, *less* or *least*.

Some two-syllable adjectives are formed either way—*friendlier* or *more friendly*.

    He is *smarter* than she is.
    She is the *most capable* person in the room.

3. Use limiting modifiers carefully. A limiting modifier is a word, phrase, or clause that limits the meaning of a preceding word or a following word. Limiting modifiers include *almost, only, merely, exactly*, and *just*. You must be careful when placing limiting modifiers. Changing the location of the modifier can change the meaning of the sentence. Notice how the placement of *only* in the following sentence changes the meaning of the sentence.

    Only he said he appreciated me.
    He *only* said he appreciated me.
    He said he *only* appreciated me.

Bias-Free Language

In the last few years, people have become more aware of the effect language can have when used to describe characteristics such as gender, race, and physical characteristics. Give careful consideration to the words you use in writing and speaking. This section offers suggestions for avoiding communication biases in three areas—gender, race, and physical characteristics.

Gender Bias

Inclusive usage in language (incorporating both sexes) is extremely important in writing. Avoid exclusive language (words that by their form or meaning discriminate on a gender basis). Examples of exclusive language include words such as *craftsman*, *weatherman*, *fireman*, and *policeman*. Other examples of exclusive language include statements such as these:

> *An engineer relies on his common sense.*
> *The executive answered his phone.*

Eliminate gender-bias statements when writing and speaking. For example, *weatherman* becomes *weatherperson* and *policeman* becomes *police officer*.

Do not write or say *The executive answered his phone.*

Do write or say *The executive answered the phone.*

Strategies for avoiding pronoun gender problems include the following:

- Use the plural of the noun and pronoun.
- Delete the pronoun altogether.
- Replace the masculine pronoun with an article (*the*).
- Use *he* or *she* (but only sparingly).

Ethnic and Racial Bias

Acceptable terms for various races and ethnicities change over time. It is the writer's and speaker's responsibility to be aware of the most acceptable terms. Presently, these terms are the most appropriate ones to use:

- *African American* (some African Americans prefer *black*)
- *Native Americans* or *American Indians*
- *Hispanic* (some individuals prefer *Latinos/ Latinas*, the masculine form ending in *o* and the feminine form ending in *a*)
- When referring to people from the Eastern region of the world, *Asian* is the general term used. People of China are *Chinese*, not *Orientals*.

Biases Based on Physical Characteristics

The most recent term for individuals with disabilities is *physically challenged*. Some groups—but certainly not all—prefer to use *visually impaired* for the blind and *hearing impaired* for the deaf. Since terms do change, you should stay current with the most recent terms.

Business Introductions

Follow these guidelines when making introductions:

- Name the most important person first.
- Say each person's name clearly.
- Add interesting information (if you know something) about each person.

  "Terri Ruiz, please meet Robert Hailey, the vice president for Humber Electronics.

  Mr. Hailey transferred from Cleveland to the Detroit office. Mr. Hailey, Ms. Ruiz is the president of Great Lakes Electric."

When being introduced, follow these guidelines:

- Stand up (both men and women).
- Establish eye contact with the individual.

- Shake hands firmly. However, you do not want to shake hands so firmly that the other person feels as though his or her hand is being crushed. Neither do you want to shake hands so limply that the other person feels no expression of warmth from you.
- Repeat the other person's name.
- Establish conversation with the person. (It does not need to be a lengthy conversation; a brief exchange of words is acceptable.)
- After the conversation is over, let the person know you enjoyed meeting him or her. You might say, "I certainly enjoyed meeting you, and I look forward to seeing you in the future."

Capitalization

1. Capitalize titles of specific courses.

    He took Psychology 121 last semester.

2. Capitalize titles that precede a person's name and abbreviations after a name.

    General Schuman
    Victor Jones, Jr.

    Do not capitalize titles when they follow a personal name or take the place of a personal name. Exceptions include high government titles such as *President, Attorney General, Chief Justice,* and so on when used in formal acknowledgments and lists.

    Louise Fidler, president of Dillon Industries, will speak tonight.
    The President of the United States was in Mexico in March.

3. Capitalize specific trade names of products.

    He bought a Dell computer.

4. Capitalize the first word in each line of a poem.

    Fear corrodes my dreams tonight and
        mist has greyed my hills,
    Mountains seem too tall to climb,
        December winds are chill,
    There's no comfort on the earth, I am
        a child abandoned,
    Till I feel your hand in mine
    And laugh down lonely canyons.
                            James Kavanaugh

5. Capitalize the first word of a direct quotation.

    Kyung-Soon replied, "The sky is the limit."

6. Capitalize compass directions when they refer to specific regions or when the direction is part of a specific name. Do not capitalize directions when they indicate a general location.

    We flew with Northwest Airlines.
    I grew up in the East.
    He lives on the east side of town.

7. Capitalize the first word and all words except articles, prepositions, and conjunctions in titles of books, articles, poems, and plays.

    Effective Business Communication
    The Lion King

8. Capitalize all words referring to the deity, the Bible, the books of the Bible, and other sacred books.

    the Koran
    our Lord

9. Capitalize names of organizations, political parties, religious bodies, and churches.

    Girl Scouts
    the First Presbyterian Church

10. Capitalize names of months, days of the week, holidays, holy days, and periods of history.

    Monday
    Christmas
    the Middle Ages

11. Capitalize names of divisions of a college or university.

    Business Division
    School of Medicine

12. Capitalize names of geographic sections and places: continents, countries, states, cities, rivers, mountains, lakes, and islands.

    Lake Michigan
    New York
    Africa

13. Capitalize names of specific historical events, specific laws, treaties, and departments of government.

    Vietnam War
    Department of Defense

14. Capitalize names of streets, avenues, buildings, hotels, parks, and theaters.

    The Four Seasons Hotel
    Fifth Avenue
    Theater Two

15. Capitalize only the parts of a hyphenated word that you would capitalize if the word were not hyphenated.

> mid-August
> President-elect Aguirre

16. Capitalize names of relatives when they precede a name or when the title is a name. Do not capitalize family titles when they are preceded by possessive pronouns and when they describe a family relationship.

> I telephoned Uncle Ed and Aunt Mary last night.
> Yesterday Mom called me about the tickets.
> My cousin is in town.

17. Capitalize personifications (figures of speech in which inanimate objects or abstractions are represented with human qualities).

> In the autumn, Nature treats us to beautiful colors of gold, orange, and auburn.

18. Do not capitalize business titles when used in magazines, books, and newspapers. The internal practice of many business organizations is to capitalize the titles of company officers and managers.

> Katherine Romero, president of Computer Graphics

Collective Nouns

A collective noun is a word that is singular in form but represents a group of persons or things. For example:

> committee
> company
> department
> public
> class
> board

These rules determine the form of the verb used with a collective noun.

- When the members of a group are one unit, the verb is singular.

> The committee is unanimous in its recommendation.

- When members of the group are separate units, the verb is plural.

> The staff are not in agreement about the decision.

- If the sentence is unclear or awkward, you can address the problem by inserting the words *members of* before the collective noun and using a plural verb.

> The members of the staff are not in agreement about the decision.

Letters and Envelopes

This section provides a review of letter and punctuation styles, placement of letter parts, addressing of envelopes, and folding of letters.

Letter and Punctuation Styles

The main letter styles are block and modified block style with blocked or indented paragraphs. Figure 1 shows the block letter style with blocked paragraphs. (When using block letter style, begin each paragraph at the left margin.) Notice in the block letter style that every line begins at the left margin. Figure 2 shows modified block style with blocked paragraphs. (When using modified block style, the paragraphs may be blocked or indented.) Notice in the modified block style that the date line and the closing lines begin at the center point.

PEOPLE PHARMACEUTICALS INTERNATIONAL

March 3, 2005

Mr. Clint Sabathia
Potomac Insurance Corporation
900 Rogers Park Boulevard
Dallas, TX 75345-3489

Dear Mr. Sabathia

Meredith Nagy would be an outstanding administrative professional for your
company. Meredith was my administrative assistant at Moral Corporation for
two years, from 2000 to 2002. I have not had a more competent administrative
assistant. Her skills are excellent and her work ethic is sound. I would welcome
her back at any time; however, I know she is ready for more responsibility.

If you have any questions about her work with us, please give me a call at
817-555-0133. I would be delighted to talk with you about Meredith's strengths.

Sincerely

Irene Jacobson

Irene Jacobson
Community Relations Director

lc

FIGURE 1 Block Letter Style, Open Punctuation

Marcia Almonte
9346 Centennial Drive
Dallas, TX 76127-9312

March 3, 2005

Dr. Martin Spears
The Mathey Foundation
2895 Grapevine Road
Grapevine, TX 76051-3498

Dear Dr. Spears:

Heart disease affects the lives of many men and women in our nation. Research advances have helped thousands of individuals live longer and more fulfilling lives. Ongoing research is essential in order to reduce the number of deaths from heart disease and to give thousands of individuals a longer life.

Additional monies are necessary to fund research. Enclosed is a brochure detailing the various research projects you have an opportunity to support.

Are you willing to give to this worthwhile cause? Please mail your donation today and know the satisfaction of helping others.

Sincerely,

Marcia Almonte

Marcia Almonte
Heart Volunteer

nak

Enc.

FIGURE 2 Modified Block Letter Style, Mixed Punctuation

There is no punctuation after the salutation and no punctuation after the complimentary close in open punctuation. When using mixed punctuation, there is a colon after the salutation and a comma after the complimentary close. Notice the open punctuation style in Figure 1 and the mixed punctuation style in Figure 2.

Placement of Letter Parts

Date Line	The date (month, day, and year) is positioned approximately one-half inch below the letterhead. If there is no letterhead, position the date line two inches from the top of the page.
Letter Address	The address begins approximately four to six line spaces below the date, depending on the letter's length.
Salutation	Press ENTER twice after the letter address.
Body	Press ENTER twice after the salutation.
Complimentary Closing	Press ENTER twice after the body of the letter.
Name and Title of Writer	Press ENTER four times after the complimentary close.
Reference Initials	Press ENTER twice after the name and title of the writer.
Enclosure Notation	Press ENTER twice after the reference initials.

Second-Page Heading	Create a header for the second page of a letter by using the Header and Footer toolbar. At the left margin of the header box, key the name of the recipient and press ENTER. Key the word *Page* and space; use the automatic numbering feature on the Header and Footer toolbar to insert the page number and press ENTER. Insert the date and press ENTER to leave a blank line between the header and the body of the letter.

Addressing of Envelopes

Your software program automatically copies the letter address from the letter on the screen to the envelope. If the return address is not preprinted on the envelope, you must key it. You can save a return address as a default address; by following this procedure, you need to key the return address only one time. When addressing envelopes, use the tools menu—*Tools, Letters and Mailings, Envelopes and Labels.*

Folding of Letters for Envelopes

Standard Size Envelopes (No. 10—$4\frac{1}{8}'' \times 9\frac{1}{2}''$)

Fold in the manner shown on the next page:

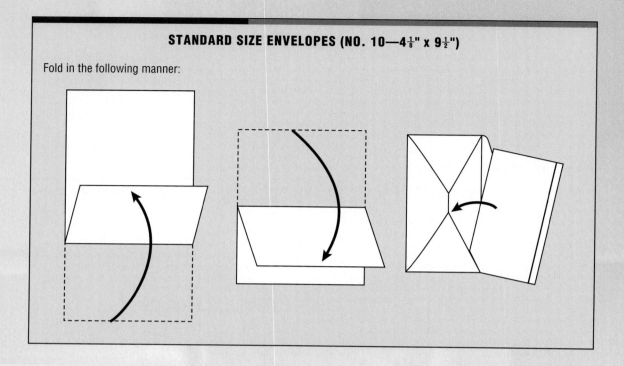

STANDARD SIZE ENVELOPES (NO. 10—4⅛" x 9½")

Fold in the following manner:

Lists

To make information easier to read, you can use lists. Lists may be bulleted, numbered, or lettered. Use bulleted lists when the items presented are of equal importance. Use numbered or lettered lists when the items must be presented in order of importance or occurrence.

You can format lists in the following ways:

When the list items are complete sentences, the following formatting is appropriate.

- The introductory sentence ends with a colon or period.
- Each list items begins with a capital letter.
- Each list item ends with the appropriate mark of punctuation (period, question mark, or exclamation point).

When the list items complete the introductory sentence, this format is appropriate:

- the introductory sentence ends with a comma, semicolon, dash, or no punctuation;
- the list items begin with lowercase letters;
- all items but the last end with a comma or semicolon;
- the second-to-last item ends with *and*; and
- the last item ends with a period.

OR

- The introductory sentence ends with a comma, semicolon, dash, or no punctuation
- All list items begin with capital letters
- There is no punctuation after each list item[1]

Examples

When deciding when and where to place graphics in a report, ask yourself these questions.

- Who is the audience?

---

[1]Andrea J. Sutcliffe, ed., *The New York Public Library Writer's Guide to Style and Usage* (New York: HarperCollins Publishers, 1994), 317–318.

- Will graphics assist the audience in understanding the message?
- Will color help to get the message across?

The software package allows you to determine

- The number of columns needed
- Table style
- Color or black and white

- Number of rows and columns

The package allows you to determine

- the number of columns;
- table style;
- color or black and white and;
- number of rows and columns.

Misused and Easily Confused Words and Phrases

1. *A* or *an* before the letter *h*

   A is used before all consonant sounds, including *h* when sounded.
   An is used before all vowel sounds, except long *u*.

   > a historic event
   > an honor
   > a hotel
   > a useful comment

2. Awhile and a while

   A *while* is a noun meaning a short time.

   > We plan to go home in a while.

   Awhile is an adverb meaning a short time.

   > She wrote the poem awhile ago.

3. About, at

   Use either *about* or *at*—not both.

   > He will leave about noon.
   > He will leave at noon.

4. Accept, except

   > To *accept* an assignment is to agree to undertake it.
   > To *except* someone from an activity is to excuse that person from the activity.

5. Accessible, assessable

   > If something is *accessible*, it can be reached or attained.
   > An object whose value can be estimated is *assessable*.

6. Advice, advise

   Advice is a noun meaning a recommendation.

   > She did not follow my advice.

   Advise is a verb meaning to counsel.

   > The counselor will advise you.

7. All, all of

   Use *all*; *of* is redundant. If a pronoun follows *all*, reword the sentence.

   > Check all the items
   > They are all going.

8. All right, alright

   All right is the only correct usage. *Alright* is incorrect.

9. Among, between

   Use *among* when referring to three or more persons or things.

   > The inheritance was divided among the four relatives.

   Use *between* when referring to two persons or things.

   > The choice is between you and me.

10. Appraise, apprise

    Appraise means to set a value on; *apprise* means to inform.

    > He appraised the house at $300,000.
    > I was apprised of the situation by Jack.

11. Bad, badly

    Bad is an adjective; *badly* is an adverb.

    > He feels bad about losing.
    > The football team played badly tonight.

12. Biannual, biennial

    Biannual means occurring twice a year.
    Biennial means occurring once every two years.

13. Bimonthly, semimonthly

    Bimonthly means every two months; *semimonthly* means twice a month.

14. Can, may

    Can means to be able to; *may* means to have permission.

    > The diskette can be copied.
    > You may leave when you finish your work.

15. Capital, capitol

    Use *capital* unless you are referring to a building that houses a government.

    > The capital of China is Columbus.
    > We toured the United States Capitol in Washington.

16. Cite, sight, site

    Cite means to quote; *sight* means vision; *site* means location.

    > She cited the correct reference.
    > That is a pleasant sight.
    > They sighted a whale.
    > The site for the new building will be determined soon.

17. *Complement, compliment*

    Complement means to complete, fill, or make perfect; *compliment* means to praise.

18. *Council, counsel*

    Council is a noun meaning a governing body.
    Counsel can be a noun or a verb. As a noun, *counsel* can mean a person with whom one consults about a matter. As a verb, *counsel* means to advise.

    > The council meets today.
    > Dr. Baker's counsel helped Kim overcome her fears.
    > Counsel was consulted on the case.
    > He is there to counsel you.

19. *Desert, dessert*

    Desert as a noun means a barren or arid region with low rainfall.
    Desert as a verb means to abandon.
    Dessert is a confection often served at the end of a meal.

    > We traveled through the desert of Arizona.
    > He deserted his family.
    > We had ice cream for dessert.

20. *Farther, further*

    Farther refers to distance; *further* refers to a greater degree or extent.

    > The store is a mile farther down the road.
    > We will discuss the matter further on Saturday.

21. *Good, well*

    Good and *well* are adjectives. *Well* is used to mean in fine health; *good* is used to mean pleasant or attractive.

    > I feel well.
    > She feels good about her job.

22. *Got, gotten*

    Got is preferred to *gotten* as the past participle of get. *Got* is informal when used for *must* or *ought*.

    > I've got to get up at 6 a.m.
    > Improved: I must get up at 6 a.m.

23. *In, into*

    In means located inside an area or limits.
    Into means in the direction of the interior or toward something.

    > She went into the room.
    > She is sitting in the room.

24. *Its, it's*

    Its is the possessive form of *it*.
    It's is the contraction of *it is*.

    > The family had its reunion yesterday.
    > It's probably going to rain.

25. *Percent, per cent, percentage*

    Percent is always written as one word; *per cent* is incorrect.
    Percentage is preferred when a number is not used.

    > He received 56 percent of the vote.
    > The percentage of votes he received is not known.

26. *Principal, principle*

    Principal as an adjective means *main*; as a noun, *principal* means the main person or a capital sum.

Principle is a noun meaning a rule, guide, or truth; *principle* never refers to a person directly.

> The principal character in the play was Geoff.
> The principals in the case are present.
> She held steadfast to her principles.

27. *Respectfully, respectively*

Respectfully means in a courteous manner; *respectively* refers to being considered singly in a particular order.

> She respectfully asked for her grade report.
> The first, second, and third awards will go to Julio, Jody, and Chelsea, respectively.

28. *Stationary, stationery*

Stationary means stable or fixed; *stationery* is writing paper.

> The ladder seems stationary.
> Order three boxes of stationery.

29. *That, which*

Which and *that* are relative pronouns used to refer to places, animals, objects, ideas, and qualities. To improve clarity, many writers make this distinction: The word *which* is used to introduce nonessential information, and a comma is placed before the word. The word *that* is used to introduce a clause containing essential information, and no comma is used.

> In ten minutes, Harry solved the problem that I had been working on for hours.
> The presentation, which would have worked well for managers, had little appeal to the teachers.

30. *Who, whom*

Who is used as the subject of a verb; *whom* is used as an object of a verb or as a preposition.

> Ken is the one who will be at the meeting.
> Lola is the person whom I will hire.
> It does not matter who did what to whom.

Numbers

1. Spell out numbers 1 through 9; use figures for numbers 10 and above.

> We ordered nine coats and four dresses.
> The assistant keyed approximately 60 letters.

2. If a sentence contains numbers above and below nine, be consistent—either spell out all numbers or key all numbers in figures. If most of the numbers are below nine, use words. If most are above nine, use figures.

> Please order 12 memo pads, 2 reams of paper, and 11 boxes of envelopes.

3. Express numbers in the millions or higher in the following manner in order to aid comprehension.

> 3 billion (rather than 3,000,000,000)

4. Always spell out a number that begins a sentence.

> Five hundred books were in his home library.

5. If the numbers are large, rearrange the wording of the sentence so the number is not the first word of the sentence.

> We had a good year in 2003.
> Not: Two thousand and three was a good year.

6. Spell out indefinite numbers and amounts.

> A few hundred voters came to the polls despite the inclement weather.

7. Spell out all ordinals (first, second, third, and so on) that can be expressed in words.

> The store's twenty-fifth anniversary was this week.

8. Use a comma to separate adjacent numbers written in words or figures.

   In 2004, 33 new products came online.

9. Write house or building numbers in figures. However, when the number one appears by itself, spell it out. Spell out numbers one through nine in street names. Write numbers ten and above in figures. When using figures for the house number and the street name, use a hyphen preceded and followed by a space.

   101 Building
   One Main Place
   21301 Fifth Avenue
   122 - 33d Street

10. Spell out ages except when the age is stated exactly in years, months, and days. When presenting ages in tabular form, use figures.

    She is eighteen years old.
    He is 2 years, 10 months, and 18 days old.

Name	*Age*
Bauman, Dan	19
King, Jenna	21

11. Use figures to express dates written in normal month-day-year order. Do not use *th, nd,* or *rd* following the date.

    May 3, 2005
    Not: May 8th, 2005

12. Spell out fractions unless they are part of mixed numbers. Use a hyphen to separate the numerator and denominator of fractions written in words when the fractions stand alone or are used as compound adjectives.

    three-fourths
    one-third cup
    $5\frac{3}{4}$

13. Express amounts of money in figures. Write indefinite money amounts in words.

    $1,000
    $3.27
    several hundred dollars

14. For clarity, numbers in legal documents are sometimes written in both words and figures.

    One hundred thirty-four dollars ($134)

15. Express percentages in figures; spell out the word *percent*.

    10 percent

16. To form the plural of figures, add *s*.

    The 1990s were a challenging time for Raul.

17. In times of day, use figures with a.m. and p.m.; spell out numbers with the word *o'clock*. In formal usage, spell out all times.

    9 a.m.
    10 p.m.
    eight o'clock in the evening

Parallelism

Parts of a sentence that are parallel in meaning must be parallel in structure. Writers should balance a word with a word, a phrase with a phrase, a clause with a clause, and a sentence with a sentence. Notice the examples given below.

NO   The parents tried pleading, threats, and shouting.

YES   The parents tried pleading, threatening, and shouting.

NO   In the past, orders were sent by regular mail, but now overnight delivery is used.

YES   In the past, orders were sent by regular mail; now they are sent by overnight delivery.

Plagiarism

The dictionary definition of plagiarism is "to use and pass off as one's own (the ideas or writings of another)." The derivation of the word comes from the Latin word for kidnapper. It literally means taking someone else's work as your own—not giving credit to someone else for the person's written ideas.

Avoid plagiarism by following these steps:

- When quoting someone else's material exactly as written, use quotation marks and the appropriate documentation.

- When paraphrasing, do not use quotation marks but do document the source. Use your own words but be true to what the source says and means. Do not put your own interpretation on the paraphrase. Be certain that your paraphrasing does not distort what the originator meant.

- Do not document information that is common knowledge; i.e., information that most educated people know.

Plurals and Possessives

1. When a compound word contains a noun and is hyphenated or made up of two or more words, the principal word takes an *s* to form the plural. If there is no principal word, add an *s* to the end of the compound word.

    commanders in chief
    runners-up

2. The plural of letters is formed by adding *s* or *'s*. The apostrophe is unnecessary except where confusion might result.

    CPAs
    the do's on the list

3. Singular nouns form the possessive by adding *'s*. If a singular noun has two or more syllables and if the last syllable is not accented and is preceded by a sibilant sound (*s*, *x*, or *z*), add only the apostrophe for ease of pronunciation.

    the person's computer
    Mrs. Cross's office
    the department's rules
    Ulysses' voyage

4. Plural nouns form the possessive by adding an apostrophe if the plural ends in *s* or by adding *'s* when the plural does not end in *s*.

    ladies' wear
    the children's bicycles

5. When using a verb form ending in *ing* as a noun (gerund), a noun or pronoun before it takes the possessive form.

    Fritz's yelling was excessive.

6. To form the possessive of a compound word, add the possessive ending to the last syllable.

    Her mother-in-law's gift arrived.
    The editor-in-chief's comments were printed in the company newsletter.

7. Joint possession is indicated by adding the possessive ending to the last noun.

    We are near Jan and Keith's store.
    Drs. Edison and Sidhu's article is thought-provoking.

8. In idiomatic construction, possessive form is often used. (An idiom is defined in the dictionary as "a speech form or an expression of a given language that is peculiar to itself grammatically or cannot be understood from the individual meanings of its elements.")

    a day's work
    two weeks' vacation

9. Use the possessive form in cases where the noun modified is not expressed.

>Take it to the plumber's. (shop)

10. Write the possessive form of personal pronouns without an apostrophe.

>This book is hers.
>She will deliver yours tomorrow.

Pronouns

1. A pronoun agrees with its antecedent (the word for which the pronoun stands) in number, gender, and person.

>Carlos wants to know if *his* book is at your house.

2. A plural pronoun is used when the antecedent consists of two nouns joined by *and*.

>*Diana* and *Tomie* are bringing *their* stereo.

3. A singular pronoun is used when the antecedent consists of two singular nouns joined by *or* or *nor*. A plural pronoun is used when the antecedent consists of two plural nouns joined by *or* or *nor*.

>Neither *Lori* nor *Joanne* wants to do *her* part.
>Either the *men* or the *women* will do *their* share.

4. Do not confuse certain possessive pronouns with contractions that sound alike.

its (possessive)	it's (it is)
their (possessive)	they're (they are)
theirs (possessive)	there's (there is)
your (possessive)	you're (you are)
whose (possessive)	who's (who is)

As a test for the use of a possessive pronoun or a contraction, try to substitute *it is, they are, it has, there has, there is,* or *you are.* Use the corresponding possessive form if the substitution does not make sense.

>*Your* wording is correct.
>*You're* wording that sentence incorrectly.
>*Whose* book is it?
>*Who's* the owner of the laptop?

5. Use *who* and *that* when referring to persons. Use *who* when referring to an individual and *that* when referring to a group of people.

>He is the boy *who* does well in history.
>The number of people *that* will be here is more than originally thought.

6. Use *which* and *that* when referring to places, objects, and animals. Use *which* when introducing a clause containing nonessential information. Use *that* when introducing a clause containing essential information.

>The fox, *which* is very sly, caught the skunk.
>The card *that* I sent you was mailed last week.

7. A pronoun in the objective case functions as a direct object, indirect object, or the object of a preposition. Objective pronouns include *me, you, him, her, it, us, them, whom,* and *whomever.*

>The movie was an emotional experience for *her* and *me.* (The pronouns *her* and *me* are in the objective case in this sentence since they function as the object of a preposition.)

8. A linking verb connects a subject to a word that renames it. Linking verbs indicate a state of being (*am, is, are, was, were*), relate to the senses, or indicate a condition. A pronoun coming after a linking verb renames the subject, so the pronoun must be in the subjective case. Subjective pronouns include *I, you, she, he, it, we, they, who,* and *whoever.*

>It is *I* who will attend the play.

9. The pronouns *who* and *whoever* are in the subjective case and are used as the subject of a sentence or clause.

>*Whoever* is in charge will be required to stay late.

10. At the beginning of questions, use *who* if the question is about the subject and *whom* if the question is about the object. To help you know which is appropriate, follow these steps:

- Delete the word *who* or *whom* from the sentence, and fill the gap in thought with *she* or *her*.

- If *she* completes the thought, then *who* is correct.

- If *her* completes the thought, then *whom* is correct.

    Who is going to the party?
    Give the information to *whomever* answers the telephone.

11. Reflexive pronouns reflect back to the antecedent. Reflexive pronouns include *myself, herself, himself, themselves,* and other *self* or *selves* words.

    I intend to do the painting *myself.*

Proofreaders' Marks

SYMBOL	MEANING	MARKED COPY	CORRECTED COPY
^	Insert	two ^ people (*or three*)	two or three people
——ℓ	Delete	the man ~~and~~ ~~woman~~	the man
⊏	Move to left	⊏human relations	human relations
#	Add space	follow/these #	follow these
/	Lowercase letter	in the Fall of 2002 (F struck with /)	in the fall of 2002
⁀‿	Close up space	sum⁀‿mer	summer
∩∪	Transpose	when (is) (it)	when it is
⊐	Move to the right	skills for living ⊐	skills for living
' ∨	Insert apostrophe	Macs book	Mac's book
" ∨	Insert quotation marks	She said, No.	She said, "No."
⊔	Move down	falle ⊔n⊔	fallen
⊓	Move up	straigh ⊓t⊓	straight
¶	Paragraph	¶The first and third page	The first and third page
no ¶	No new paragraph	no ¶The first and third page	The first and third page
◯ sp	Spell out	(Dr.) sp	Doctor
stet or	Let it stand; ignore correction	~~most~~ efficient worker	most efficient worker
____	Underline	<u>Business World</u>	<u>Business World</u>
ital ____	Italics	ital Newsweek (underlined)	*Newsweek*
⊙	Insert period	the last word ⊙	the last word.

Punctuation

Punctuation is important if the reader is to interpret the writer's thoughts correctly. Correct punctuation has its base in accepted rules and principles rather than in the whims of the writer.

The Period

A period indicates a full stop and is used in the following ways:

1. At the end of a complete declarative or imperative sentence.
2. After abbreviations and after a single or double initial that represents a word.

    acct.　etc.　Ph.D.
    U.S.　viz.　p.m.
    Dr.　i.e.　pp.

    However, abbreviations that use several initial letters do not require periods.

    FDIC (Federal Deposit Insurance Corporation)
    FEPC (Fair Employment Practices Committee)
    AAA (American Automobile Association)
    YWCA (Young Women's Christian Association)

3. Between dollars and cents. A period and cipher are not required when an amount in even dollars is expressed in figures.

    $42.65　$1.47　$25

4. To indicate a decimal.

    3.5 bushels　12.65 percent　6.25 feet

The Comma

Use a comma:

1. To separate independent clauses that are connected by coordinating conjunctions such as *and, but, or, for,* and *nor* unless the clauses are short and closely connected.

    We have a supply on hand, but I think we should order an additional quantity.
    She had to work late, for the auditors were examining the books.

2. To set off a subordinate clause that precedes the main clause.

    Assuming no changes are needed, I suggest that you proceed with your instructions.

3. After an introductory phrase containing a verb form. No commas are needed after introductory phrases that immediately precede the verb they modify.

    To finish his work, he remained at the office after hours.
    After planning the program, she proceeded to put it into effect.
    Six miles to the west is the downtown area.
    Between her two daughters sat the matriarch of the family.

4. To set off a nonrestrictive clause. A nonrestrictive clause adds extra or nonessential information to a sentence. In other words, the meaning of the sentence would not change if the information were deleted.

    Our group, which had never lost a debate, won the grand prize.

5. To separate from the rest of the sentence a word or a group of words that breaks the continuity of a sentence.

    The administrative professional, when his work was completed, was willing to help others.

6. To separate parenthetical expressions from the rest of the sentence.

    We have, as you know, two people who can handle the reorganization.

7. To set off names used in direct address or to set off explanatory phrases or clauses.

    I think you, Mr. Bennett, will agree with the statement.
    Ms. Linda Matsuo, our vice president, will be in your city soon.

8. To separate from the rest of the sentence expressions that, without punctuation, might be interpreted incorrectly.

Misleading: Ever since we have filed our reports monthly.
Better: Ever since, we have filed our reports monthly.

9. To separate words or groups of words when they are used in a series of three or more.

   Most executives agree that dependability, trustworthiness, ambition, and judgment are required of workers.

10. To set off introductory words.

    For example, the musical on Saturday was not as lyrical as the last musical I saw.
    Thus, both the man and the boy felt a degree of discrimination.

11. To separate coordinate adjectives. Coordinate adjectives are two or more adjectives that equally modify a noun.

    The large, insensitive audience laughed loudly at the mistake.

12. To set off short quotations from the rest of the sentence.

    He said, "I shall be there."
    "The committees have agreed," he said, "to work together on the project."

13. To separate the name of a city from the name of a state.

    Our southern branch is located in Atlanta, Georgia.

14. To separate abbreviations of titles from the name.

    William R. Warner, Jr.
    Ramona Sanchez, Ph.D.

15. To set off conjunctive adverbs such as *however* and *therefore.*

    I, however, do not agree with the statement.
    According to the rule, therefore, we must not penalize the student for this infraction.

16. To separate a date from a year. Within a sentence, use a comma on both sides of the year in a full date.

    The anniversary party was planned for June 18, 2005.

    He plans to attend the management seminar schedule for April 15, 2006, at the Hill Hotel.

17. Do not use a comma in numbers in an address even when there are four are more digits.

    The house number was 3100 Edmonds Drive.

18. Do not use a comma in a date that contains the month with only a day or a year.

    The accident occurred on June 10.
    The major event for June 2003 was the ethics seminar.

The Semicolon

Use a semicolon in the following instances:

1. Between independent groups of clauses that are long or that contain parts that are separated by commas.

   He was outstanding in his knowledge of technology, including telecommunications and computers; but he was lacking in many desirable personal qualities.

2. Between independent clauses when the conjunction is omitted.

   Everyone in the group enjoyed the meal; many members of the group did not enjoy the movie.

3. To precede expressions such as *namely* or *viz., for example* or *e.g.,* and *that is* or *i.e.,* when used to introduce a clause.

   We selected the machine for two reasons; namely, it is a reasonable price and it has the features we need.

   There are several reasons for changing the routine of handling mail; i.e., to reduce postage, to conserve time, and to place responsibility.

4. Before a coordinating conjunction joining independent clauses containing commas.

   When the task is difficult, the time spent is usually great; and the rewards can be equally great.

The Colon

Use a colon in the following instances:

1. After the salutation in a business letter except when open punctuation is used.

> Ladies and Gentlemen:
> Dear Ms. Carroll:

2. Following introductory expressions such as *the following, thus, as follows,* and other expressions that precede enumerations.

> Please send the following by parcel post: books, magazines, and newspapers.
> The officers elected were as follows: president, Shireen Castroneves; vice president, Malcolm Turnball; treasurer, Ronald Moline.

3. To separate hours and minutes when indicating time.

> 2:10 p.m.   4:45 p.m.   12:15 a.m.

4. To introduce a long quotation.

> This quote from Theodore Roosevelt is a favorite of mine: "It is not the critic who counts. . . ."

The Question Mark

A question mark should be used in the following instances:

1. After a direct question.

> When do you expect to arrive in Philadelphia?

An exception to the foregoing rule is a sentence that is phrased in the form of a question, merely as a matter of courtesy, when it is actually a request.

> Will you please send us an up-to-date statement of our account.

2. After each question in a series of questions within one sentence.

> What is your opinion of the Compaq™ computer? the Hewlett-Packard™? the Dell™?

The Exclamation Point

Use an exclamation point after words or groups of words that express command, strong feeling, emotion, or an exclamation.

> Don't waste supplies!
> It can't be done!
> Stop!

The Dash

Use a dash in the following instances:

1. To indicate an omission of letters or figures.

> Dear Mr.—
> The dollar amounts are—

2. To indicate a definite stop or as emphasis.

> This book is not a revision of an old book—it is a totally new book.

3. To separate parenthetical expressions when unusual emphasis is desired.

> These sales arguments—and every one of them are important—should result in getting the order.

4. To separate appositives (words or phrases that identify the noun or pronoun that immediately precedes it) if the use of commas might cause confusion.

> Concern over terror attacks—biological warfare, attacks on cities, and attacks on government buildings and personnel—is demanding much media attention.

The Apostrophe

An apostrophe is used:

1. To indicate possession.

> The boy's coat; the ladies' dresses; the girl's book

To the possessive singular, add 's to the noun.

> man's work
> bird's wing
> hostess's plans

An exception to this rule occurs when the word following the possessive begins with an *s* sound.

for goodness' sake
for conscience' sake

To form the possessive of a plural noun ending in an *s* or *z* sound, add only the apostrophe (') to the plural noun.

workers' rights
hostesses' duties

If the plural noun does not end in *s* or *z* sounds, add *'s* to the plural noun.

women's clothes
alumni's donations

Proper names that end in an *s* sound form the possessive singular by adding *'s*.

Josh Holtz's house
Andrea Fox's automobile

Proper names ending in *s* form the possessive plural by adding the apostrophe only.

The Walters' property faces the Balderas' swimming pool.

2. To indicate the omission of a letter or letters in a contraction.

it's (it is), you're (you are), we'll (we will)

3. To indicate the plurals of letters, figures, words, and abbreviations.

Don't forget to dot your i's and cross your t's.
I can add easily by 2's and 4's, but I have difficulty with 6's and 8's.
Direct writing is achieved in part by omitting and's and but's.
Two of the speakers were Ph.D.'s.

Quotation Marks

Certain basic rules should be followed in using quotation marks. These rules are as follows:

1. When a quotation mark is used with a comma or a period, the comma or period is placed inside the quotation mark.

She said, "I plan to complete my program in college before seeking a position."

2. When using a quotation mark with a semicolon or a colon, place the semicolon or colon outside the quotation mark.

The treasurer said, "I plan to go by train"; others in the group stated they would go by plane.

3. When more than one paragraph of quoted material is used, quotation marks appear at the beginning of each paragraph and at the end of the last paragraph.

4. Use quotation marks in the following instances:

- Before and after direct quotations.

The author states, "Too frequent use of certain words weakens the appeal."

- To indicate a quotation within a quotation, use single quotation marks.

The author states, "Too frequent use of 'very' and 'most' weakens the appeal."

- To indicate the title of a published article.

Have you read the article, "Anger in the Workplace"?

Omissions Marks or Ellipses

Use ellipses marks (. . .) to denote the omission of letters or words in quoted material. If the material omitted ends in a period, use four omission marks (. . . .). If the material omitted does not end in a period, use three omission marks (. . .).

He quoted the proverb, "A soft answer turneth away wrath, but. . . ."
She quoted Plato, "Nothing is more unworthy of a wise man . . . than to have allowed more time for trifling and useless things than they deserved."

Parentheses

Although parentheses are frequently used as a catchall in writing, they are correctly used in the following instances:

1. When amounts expressed in words are followed by figures.

He agreed to pay twenty-five dollars ($25) as soon as possible.

2. Around words that are used as parenthetical expressions.

> Our personnel costs (including benefits) are much too high.

3. To indicate technical references.

> Sodium chloride (NaCl) is the chemical name for common table salt.

4. When enumerations are included in narrative form.

> The reasons for his resignation were three: (1) starting his own business, (2) relocating to a new area, and (3) wanting to travel.

Spelling

1. Put *i* before *e* except after *c* or when sounded like *a* as in *neighbor* or *weigh*. Exceptions: either, neither, seize, weird, leisure, financier, conscience.

2. When a one-syllable word ends in a single consonant and when that final consonant is preceded by a single vowel, double the final consonant before a suffix that begins with a vowel or the suffix *y*.

run	running
drop	dropped
bag	baggage
skin	skinny

3. When a word of more than one syllable ends in a single consonant, when that final consonant is preceded by a single vowel, and when the word is accented on the last syllable, double the final consonant before a suffix that begins with a vowel.

begin	beginning
concur	concurrent

When the accent does not fall on the last syllable, do not double the final consonant before a suffix that begins with a vowel.

travel	traveler
differ	differing

4. When the final consonant in a word of one or more syllables is preceded by another consonant or by two vowels, do not double the final consonant before any suffix.

look	looked
deceit	deceitful
act	acting
warm	warmly

5. Words ending in a silent *e* generally drop the *e* before a suffix that begins with a vowel.

guide	guidance
use	usable

6. Words ending in a silent *e* generally retain the *e* before a suffix that begins with a consonant unless another vowel precedes the final *e*.

hate	hateful
due	duly
excite	excitement
argue	argument

7. Words ending in *ie* drop the *e* and change the *i* to *y* before adding *ing*.

lie	lying
die	dying

8. Words ending in *ce* or *ge* generally retain the final *e* before the suffixes *able* and *ous* but drop the final *e* before the suffixes *ible* and *ing*.

manage	manageable
force	forcible

9. Words ending in *c* insert a *k* before a suffix beginning with *e, i,* or *y* is added.

picnic	picnicking

10. Words ending in *y* preceded by a consonant generally change the *y* to *i* before a suffix except one beginning with *i*.

modify	modifying	modifier
lonely	lonelier	

11. Words ending in *o* preceded by a vowel form the plural by adding *s*. Words ending

in *o* preceded by a consonant generally form the plural by adding *es.*

> folio   folios
> potato   potatoes

12. Words ending in *y* preceded by a vowel form the plural by adding *s*; words ending

in *y* preceded by a consonant change the *y* to *i* and add *es* to form the plural.

> attorney   attorneys
> lady   ladies

Subject and Verb Agreement

This section presents a review of some of the basic rules concerning subject-verb agreement.

1. When the subject consists of two singular nouns and/or pronouns connected by *or* (*either . . . or, neither . . . nor*) or *not only . . . but also*, a singular verb is required.

   > *Jane* or *Bob has* the letter.
   > Either *Ruth or Marge plans* to attend.
   > Not only a *book* but also *paper is* needed.

2. When the subject consists of two plural nouns and/or pronouns connected by *or* (*either . . . or, neither . . . nor*) or *not only . . . but also*, a plural verb is required.

   > Neither the *managers* nor the *administrative assistants have* access to that information.

3. When the subject is made up of both singular and plural nouns and/or pronouns connected by *or* (*either . . . or, neither . . . nor*) or *not only . . . but also*, the verb agrees with the last noun or pronoun mentioned before the verb.

   > Either *Ms. Salazar* or the *assistants have* access to that information.
   > Neither the *men* nor *Jo* is working.

4. Disregard intervening phrases and clauses when establishing agreement between subject and verb. *One of* is considered singular.

   > *One* of the men *wants* to go to the convention.

5. The words *each, every, either, neither, one,* and *another* are singular. When they are used as subjects or as adjectives modifying subjects, a singular verb is required.

   > *Each* person *is* deserving of the award.
   > *Neither* boy *rides* the bicycle well.

6. The following pronouns are singular and require a singular verb:

   > anybody   everybody   nobody   somebody
   > anyone   everyone   nothing   something
   > anything   everything   no one   someone

   > *Everyone plans* to attend the meeting.
   > *Anyone is* welcome at the concert.

7. *Both, few, many, others,* and *several* are plural. When they are used as subjects or adjectives modifying subjects, a plural verb is required.

   > *Several* members *were* appreciative of the honor.
   > *Both* women *are* going to apply.

8. *All, none, any, some, more,* and *most* may be singular or plural depending on the noun to which they refer.

   > *Some* of the supplies are missing.
   > *Some* of that paper is needed.

9. *The number* has a singular meaning and requires a singular verb; *a number* has a plural meaning and requires a plural verb.

   > *A number* of people *are* planning to attend.
   > *The number* of requests *is* surprising.

10. Geographic locations are considered as singular and are used with a singular verb when referring to one location. When reference is made to separate islands within a geographic location, the plural form is used with a plural verb.

The Hawaiian Islands is their vacation
spot this year.
The Caribbean Islands have distinct
cultures.

Glossary

A

AAA American Automobile Association.

Acceptance favorable reception; approval.

Accession book a record of the numbers that have been assigned in a numeric filing system.

Acid-test ratio or quick ratio measures the instant debt-paying ability of an organization.

Acronyms words formed from the first or first few letters of several words, such as ARMA.

Active records used three or more times a month and should be kept in an accessible area.

Active voice when the subject performs the action.

Acute stress occurs when an individual must respond instantaneously to a crisis situation.

Adapt to make suitable to a specific use or situation.

Aerogrammes air letter sheets that can be folded and sealed to form an envelope.

Agenda an outline of the procedures or the order of business to be followed during a meeting.

Aikido a Japanese soft martial art.

Alphabetic storage system uses letters of the alphabet to determine the order in which the names of people and companies are filed.

Alphabetic suffix Jr., Sr.

Alphanumeric coding combines alphabetic and numeric characters, with the main subjects arranged alphabetically and their subdivision assigned a number.

Amoral lacking moral judgment or sensibility; neither moral nor immoral.

Analog when an image is translated into fluctuating electronic signals.

Analog dial-up connecting devices to a network via a modem and a public telephone network.

Analogies comparisons made of two different things by stressing their similarities.

Annotating underlining important elements within a document or making notations on a document.

Antivirus software a utility program that protects, detects, and removes viruses from a computer's memory or storage devices.

APA American Psychological Association.

APO air postal office.

Applications software programs that perform specific tasks for users.

Archive records have historical value to an organization and should be preserved permanently.

Arithmetic/logic unit performs all mathematical calculations.

Assets resources owned by an entity.

Assumptions something taken for granted or accepted as true without proof.

ATMs automated teller machines.

Attitude position, disposition, or manner with regard to a person or thing.

Audioconferencing a type of conference in which an unlimited number of participants use a voice input unit to participate in a meeting.

Authorization to Hold Mail tells the USPS to hold mail at the post office.

Auto dialers automatically redial a busy number after a minute or two and store from 20 to 200 numbers into memory for one-button code dialing.

Automatic document feeder (ADF) automatically feeds the original document one sheet at a time for copying.

B

Baby boomers individuals born between 1946 and 1964.

Back-up storage used to make copies of important files or very large files that would be difficult to replicate if the originals were lost, damaged, or destroyed.

Balance sheet a financial statement showing the position of an organization on a certain date.

Barcode scanners used to input price information and keep track of inventory.

Bearish expectation of a down market.

Benchmarking the process of determining how well other companies perform functions or tasks.

Biases views based on background or experiences.

Bilateralness affecting two sides equally.

Binary digits (bits) a code utilizing a 1 or a 0 that stores data in computer memory.

Bond a certificate that represents a company's promises to pay a definite sum of money at a specified time with interest payable periodically to the holder of the bond; evidence of a debt owed by a firm.

Bondholder lends money to an organization and, in return, receives a bond.

Bound Printed Matter advertising, promotional, directory, or editorial material that weigh 15 pounds or less.

Brainstorm a sudden clever idea; a group problem-solving technique.

Broadband short for broad bandwidth; a form of digital data transmission that uses a wide range of frequencies to achieve added bandwidth.

Bullish expectation of an up market.

Business ethics the study of just and unjust behavior in business.

Business plan provides the strategic direction for a company's ongoing activities.

Business-class accommodations slightly more expensive than coach, including more spacious seating than coach, complimentary alcoholic beverages, reclining seats, and more food.

Bylaws written policies and procedures that clearly define how board meetings are to be conducted.

Byte eight bits.

C

Cable a pipeline that connects to computers and to a coaxial cable line to provide voice and data transmission.

Cathode ray tube (CRT) monitor uses the same technology as television screens to display images.

cc courtesy copy.

CD-E compact disk-erasable.

CD-R compact disk-recordable.

CD-ROM compact disk read-only memory.

CD-RW compact disk readwritable.

Cell line isolated stem cells from a human embryo that often replicate themselves.

Central processing unit (CPU) accepts and processes information within the parameters of the software program.

Centralized stored in one central location.

Centralized copy centers copiers are located in one central location in an organization.

Centralized storage computers are linked together through a network and multiple users can retrieve the stored information.

CEO chief executive officer.

Certificate of mailing provides evidence that an item has been mailed.

Certified mail the mailer is provided with a mailing receipt, and a record is kept at the recipient's post office.

CFOs chief financial officers.

Change agent individuals who facilitate change and help others accept change.

Charismatic leadership articulates a clear vision for the future (one based on values).

Chronic stress occurs when a distressful situation is prolonged with no rest or recuperation for the body.

Chronologic storage system an arrangement in which records are stored in date order, with the most recent date first.

Chronological resume lists work experience and education in reverse chronological order, starting with the most recent experience, education, and working backward in time.

Circular and oval arrangements seating arrangements that work best when the purpose of the meeting is to generate ideas and discussion and the meeting is relatively informal.

Clip gallery includes clip art images, photographs, video clips, and audio clips that can be inserted into a presentation.

Coach-class accommodations the least expensive of the three classes of flights, including complimentary soft drinks and limited snacks.

Coding marking the units of the filing segment by which the record is to be stored.

Cognitive the mental process of knowing through reasoning.

Collaborative planning working together as a team.

Collect on Delivery (COD) allows the mailer to collect the price of goods and/or postage on the items ordered by the addressee when they are delivered.

Committee a group established for an ongoing purpose.

Communication the ability to make known; to impart; to transmit information, thought, or feeling so that it is adequately received and understood.

Community a group of people with common interests.

Compact disks (CDs) flat, round, metal disks surrounded by a protective coating of plastic.

Compressed workweek, flextime, and job sharing alternatives to the traditional 8 a.m. or 9 a.m. to 5 p.m. workday.

Computer vision syndrome eye complaints related to computer work.

Computer-aided retrieval (CAR) systems speed up the retrieval of documents on microfilm through use of a computer.

Computer-input microfilm (CIM) data on microfilm is converted into computer-readable data for use by a computer system.

Computer-output microfilm (COM) using the computer in conjunction with microimage records technology.

Conciseness expressing the necessary information in a few words as possible.

Conference a meeting where discussion on certain issues or topics takes place.

Confidential mailboxes mailboxes to which no other person has access.

Consular offices offices in the United States representing the country abroad and staffed with personnel from the country.

Contact list or buddy list IM users with whom communication is frequent.

Continuous speech recognition voice recognition technology that allows users to speak normally, using complete sentences and phrases.

Contrived invented or fabricated.

Control unit directs and coordinates most operations of a computer.

Conventions formal annual meetings of the members of a professional group.

Cooperate to work or act together toward a common end or purpose.

Copy/duplicators found in specialized centers or print shops; can produce 150 cpm.

Core hours hours when everyone is in the office.

Corporate bonds issued by individual companies.

Courteousness using good human relations skills in writing.

Cpm copies per minute.

CQI continuous quality improvement.

Creativity having the ability or the power to cause to exist.

Critical thinking a unique kind of purposeful thinking in which the thinker systematically chooses conscious and deliberate inquiry.

Crosscut shredders cut the paper vertically and horizontally, producing confettilike pieces of paper.

CTDs cumulative trauma disorders.

CTS carpal tunnel syndrome.

Current assets cash and assets expected to be turned into cash, sold, or consumed within a short period (usually one year).

Current liabilities debts that must be paid within one year.

Current ratio a method of determining the position of an organization; divide current assets by current liabilities.

D

Data conferencing enables two or more people to communicate and collaborate as a group in real time using the computer.

Database a collection of data organized in such a way that it allows access, retrieval, and use of the data.

Database management system the software that allows a user to perform a variety of records management functions.

Decentralized stored in various departments or branches.

Decentralized copy centers copying machines are located in close proximity to the employees.

Decentralized storage information stored by individual users on their own disks or tapes.

Decision the outcome or product of a problem, a concern, or an issue that must be addressed and solved.

Delayed send dials and sends a fax when line charges are the lowest so the fax is transmitted at the cheapest rate.

Delegation the assigning of tasks to others and then empowering them to get the job done.

Denigrate belittle.

Departmentalization subdividing work and workers into organizational units responsible for a task.

Dependability trustworthiness.

Desktop videoconferencing when a PC-based application is used for videoconferencing.

Digital allows data to be transferred as a series of bits.

Digital archiving the practice of converting paper documents to digital format so the data can be stored on a variety of media and then retrieved electronically.

Digital camera an input device used to take pictures and to store the photographed images digitally, instead of on traditional film.

Digital era a world fueled by numbers.

Direct access a system that does not require referring to anything but the file to find the name.

Direct approach begins with the reason for the correspondence.

Discrete voice recognition voice recognition software that requires the user to pause between each spoken word.

Distress negative stress.

Dividends shares of a company's profits paid to stockholders.

Document imaging see *digital archiving*.

Document imaging software allows users to access scanned documents from virtual filing systems.

Document management software used to manage electronic, digital, microimage, and paper storage systems.

Documentation the process of giving credit to the sources used.

Dow Jones Industrial Average an average of the stock of 30 well-known companies, such as AT&T and McDonald's.

Downloaded transferred from the Internet or another source to your computer.

Downsizing reducing the number of full-time employees in an organization.

Downward communication messages that flow from management to employees of the organization.

DSL digital subscriber line similar to cable; uses wires that run to an organization or a home to provide voice and data transmission.

Dual access describes a fax machine that performs a number of tasks at one time.

Duplex to print on both sides of the page.

Duplexing copying on both sides of a sheet of paper.

DVD digital versatile disk.

DVD-RAM digital versatile disk-random access memory.

DVD-ROM digital versatile disk-read-only memory.

DVD-RW digital versatile disk-recordable.

Dynamic changing rapidly.

E

EBPP electronic bill presentment and payment; the electronic transfer of funds to pay bills.

EEOC Equal Employment Opportunity Commission, a government entity.

EFTs electronic funds transfers.

Electronic document management systems (EDMS) a computer-based system that allows for retrieval of specific documents from an electronic filing system.

Electronic message a communication of text, data, images, or voice messages between a sender and a recipient by utilizing telecommunications links.

Electronic postage postage purchased over the Internet and printed on a company printer.

Electronic records management system (ERMS) a mechanism for storing business records through electronic means.

Ellipses three spaced periods used to indicate a deletion in text.

Emoticons faces produced by the Internet counterculture in answer to email being devoid of body language.

Empathy identification with and understanding of another's situation, feelings, and motives.

Employment application a form indicating an applicant's interest in a position.

Empower to pass on authority or responsibility to others.

Empowerment implies that workers have access to information they need to do the job and the authority and responsibility to do the job without constant checking from the supervisor.

Enclosure or attachment notation indicates that additional printed information is being included with correspondence.

Encryption software encodes messages so others cannot gain access to them; does this by taking a computer message; scrambling it with various letters, numbers, and symbols; and then sending the message on its way.

Eportfolio a method of preparing samples of work and sending them online to prospective employers.

Ergonomics the study of the problems of people in adjusting to their environment; the science that seeks to adapt work or working conditions to fit the worker.

Ergos work.

Ethics the systematic study of moral conduct, duty, and judgment.

Eticket an airline ticket obtained online.

Etymologists specialists in the study of words.

Euro the standard currency of Belgium, Germany, Spain, France, Ireland, Italy, Luxembourg, the Netherlands, Austria, Portugal, and Finland.

Eustress beneficial stress that enables individuals to strive to meet challenges.

Exabyte 1,000 petabytes.

Executive summary a one- or two-page summary of the material contained in a report.

Exit interview an interview conducted by an impartial person when someone is leaving a job.

Exponentially relating to an expression in terms of a designated power of the base.

Express mail the fastest delivery system available from the USPS; next-day delivery.

Extranet a private network that provides for the authorization of selected external individuals to use the network.

Extrinsic in reference to motivation, relying on external factors such as salary increases or promotions.

Extrinsically motivated from outside.

F

Fair having or exhibiting a disposition that is free of favoritism.

Fax (facsimile) machine a type of copy machine that electronically sends an original document from one location to another via communication networks.

Fax broadcasting the ability to personalize and transmit faxes to multiple locations simultaneously.

Fax-on-demand the service of storing information for instant retrieval via telephone and fax.

FDA Food and Drug Administration, a government entity.

Fee-paid the employer pays the fee charged by a private employment agency.

FICA tax Federal Insurance Contributions Act.

Field contains a specific piece of information within a record.

File compression utility shrinks the size of a file.

Firewalls software programs that monitor information as it enters and leaves a computer that is connected to the Web and prevents unauthorized individuals from using an intranet or an extranet.

First-class accommodations the most expensive and luxurious of the three classes of air travel.

First-Class Mail includes letters, greeting cards, bills, large envelopes, and packages sent by the USPS.

Fixed platen the lens and exposure light move inside the copier to scan the image.

Fixed wireless conversion of data to wireless signals that customers receive through a network of transceivers mounted on utility poles, streetlights, and so on.

Flatbed scanners can handle bound documents since they operate in a similar fashion to copy machines.

Flexible capable of being bent or pliable.

Floppy disks a storage medium for computer information.

Focus groups people brought together to talk with an interviewer about their opinions of certain events or issues.

Follow-up letter a letter written after a job interview to thank the interviewer and to recap one's skills and interest in the job.

Foreign bonds issued by corporations outside the United States.

401(k) defined contribution plans for employees of private companies.

403(b) defined contribution plans for employees of public and nonprofit employers.

FPO fleet postal office.

Frequent flyer program an incentive program that provides a variety of awards after the accumulation of a certain number of mileage points.

Fringe benefits employment benefits given in addition to wages.

Functional resume clusters education, experiences, and activities so, at a glance, this information supports the job for which an individual is applying.

FUTA Federal Unemployment Tax Act; provides relief to people who become unemployed due to economic forces beyond their control.

G

Generation Y the group of people born between 1977 and 1995.

Geographic storage records are arranged by geographic location.

Germane having a significant bearing.

Gerunds verbal forms that can be used as nouns.

Gigabytes (GB) one billion bytes.

Gigaflop 1 billion operations per second.

Global Express Guaranteed (GXG) an international mail service used to mail high-priority or other urgently needed items to nearly 200 countries and territories around the world.

Global Express Mail (EMS) an international mail service used for mailing time-sensitive material to more than 175 countries.

Global Priority Mail (GPM) an international mail service that provides priority service for mailing items that weigh up to 4 pounds.

Grapevine messages that may or may not be true and that originate from an unknown source.

Graphical user interface (GUI) uses visual images such as icons, buttons, menus, or other graphical objects to issue commands.

Group control involves the norms and values that groups impose on one another through measures such as group acceptance or rejection.

H

Handheld computers units that can be easily carried and operated in the hand of a user.

Hard copy printed information.

Hard disks see *Hard drives*.

Hard drives the internal storage device on a computer; also called hard disks.

Heterogeneous completely different.

Heterogeneous group a group having dissimilar backgrounds and experiences.

Hierarchical organization organized by rank or authority.

High-capacity disks the backup medium of choice for users of personal computers, portable computers, and small businesses.

High-volume copiers generate 50 to 135 cpm and have a monthly production range of 50,000 to 400,000 copies.

High-yield issues or junk bonds the riskiest of corporate bonds.

Homogeneous like in nature.

Homogeneous group a group with similar backgrounds and experiences.

Honesty genuine; not deceptive or fraudulent.

Horizontal analysis compares increases and decreases in items on a financial statement for particular periods.

Horizontal communication messages that flow from coworker to coworker or from manager to manager.

Hoteling sharing space with other employees in a specific company location as necessary.

I

IM instant messaging.

Important records necessary to an orderly continuation of a business and are replaceable only with considerable expenditure of time and money.

Inactive records used less than 15 times a year and should be stored in less accessible areas.

Income statement reflects the financial position of an entity for a particular period.

Indexing determining the name to be used in storing; sorts the records and stores the information based on one or more key fields.

Indirect approach begins with an opening statement that is pleasant but neutral.

Individual self-control when employees use their knowledge, skill, values, and ethics to exercise control of themselves.

Inferences conclusions derived from premises known or assumed to be true.

Information Age and Knowledge Age describe the current age, with the explosion of information and knowledge made possible by technology.

Information Based Indicia (IBI) the postage markings printed on an envelope to indicate that postage has been paid.

Information management system any records management system where records are input and filed electronically.

Infrared a form of wireless information transmission.

Initiative the ability to begin and follow through on a plan or task.

Inkjets use liquid ink cartridges that spray tiny drops of ink onto a piece of paper to form letters, numbers, and characters.

Insured mail provides coverage against loss or damage.

Integrity and honesty the adherence to a code of behavior.

Interfaced interconnected with other computers or a mainframe.

International Parcel Post an international mail service for shipping heavier merchandise and printed matter.

Internet Service Provider (ISP) a business that sells access to its permanent Internet connection for a fee.

Internet telephony a category of hardware and software that enables people to use the Internet as a transmission medium for telephone calls.

Intranet a private network that belongs to an organization and is accessible only by the organization's employees.

Intrinsically linked being an inevitable part of each other and incapable of being separated.

Intrinsically motivated from within.

Intrinsic from within the person; something is done because it is right and fits the individual's values.

Investment-grade bonds safest corporate bonds.

IP telephony Internet protocol telephony, another term for Internet telephony.

IRA Individual Retirement Account; a plan that permits individuals to set up a savings plan.

IRS Internal Revenue Service.

Itinerary a document giving flight numbers, arrival and departure times, hotel reservations, car rental, and other travel arrangements.

J

Jaz disks high-capacity storage mediums that holds 1 GB of data.

Jet lag a feeling of exhaustion following a flight through several time zones.

Jewel box a plastic case designed to protect CDs.

Job descriptions documents detailing the duties to be performed on the job.

Joystick a button located in the center of a keyboard that is used to manipulate cursor movement.

K

Key operator the individual who is responsible for making simple repairs to the copier.

Kilobytes (KB) one thousand bytes.

Krinein a Greek word meaning "to separate or to choose."

L

Large-cap stocks have a market capitalization of 10 billion or more.

Laser printer uses a lower-powered beam of light to place charged particles on a drum.

Layouts arrangements of common slide elements such as titles and bulleted lists.

LCDs (liquid crystal displays) thin, flat-screen, vibrant monitors.

Leadership the process of influencing others to achieve group and/or organizational goals.

Letter-Post an international mail service for mailing letters and letter packages, postcards and postal cards, aerogrammes, printed matter, and small packets.

Liabilities debts of an organization.

Library of Congress the U.S. national library.

LINUX a version of UNIX that is now one of the fastest-growing operating systems.

Listening actively listening for meaning as well as words.

Local area networks (LANs) link various types of technological equipment within a building or several buildings within the same geographical area.

Long-range planning planning for a three- to five-year period.

Long-term liabilities debts that are not due for a comparatively long period (more than one year).

Low-volume copiers typically produce 20-30 cpm and are best suited for environments that require 100 to 5,000 copies per month.

Loyalty the quality of devoted attachment and affection.

M

Mac OS an operating system developed by Apple Computer for use on the Macintosh computer system.

Magnetic ink character reader (MICR) used extensively by financial institutions to read the magnetic ink numbers preprinted on checks and deposit slips.

Mainframes large computers that accommodate hundreds of users completing different tasks.

Management by objectives and self-control leaders help formulate the objectives for units they supervise, with the objectives defined by the larger goals of the business.

Management doing things right.

Marker editing lets the user change the color of specific sections of a document to highlight these areas.

Market capitalization how much stocks are worth by shares that are outstanding to the public multiplied by the price of the stock.

Masking allows the user to block out areas of sensitive or confidential information.

MBO management by objectives.

Media Mail books, film, manuscripts, printed music, videotapes, and computer-recorded media such as CD-ROMS and diskettes.

Medicare part of FICA designated for health insurance for senior citizens.

Megabytes (MB) one million bytes.

Melting pot the amalgamation of people of different ethnicities and races into one United States of America.

Mentors counselors or teachers.

Metropolitan area networks (MANs) link LANs and technological equipment over a distance equal to the size of a city and its surroundings.

Microcomputers (PCs) the smallest of the desktop computer systems.

Microfiche a sheet of film containing a series of images arranged in a grid pattern.

Microfilm a roll containing a series of photographic frames.

Microform a blanket term used to describe microimage storage media and the related technology.

Microprocessor a single miniature chip that contains the circuitry and components for arithmetic, logic, and control operations.

Microrecorder a palm-sized voice recorder.

Mid-cap stocks have a market capitalization of a few billion.

Mid-volume copiers generate 25 to 60 cpm and can produce 6,000 to 85,000 copies per month.

Minutes a written record of a meeting.

Mission statement helps determine individual values and future direction.

MLA Modern Language Association.

Mobile wireless breaks a large service area into smaller areas called cells.

Modem an acronym that stands for modulate/demodulate; a computer modem modulates data for transmission, and it demodulates incoming signals so the computer's digital processor understands them.

Money orders provide for the safe transmission of money to individuals or institutions.

Monotone a succession of sounds or words uttered in a single tone of voice.

Mopiers the combination of printing, scanning, copying, and faxing into one unit.

Moral conduct a set of ideas of right and wrong.

Moral integrity consistent adherence to a set of ideas of right and wrong.

Morality a set of ideas of right and wrong.

Mortgage-backed bonds represent ownership of mortgage loans issued or backed by government agencies.

Motherboard the area in a computer where the memory and processing chips are placed.

Motivation an incentive to act; a move to action.

Moving platen moves the item to be copied over the copier lens.

MultiFunction Devices (MFDs) can print, copy, fax, and scan.

Multiline optical character reader (MLOCR) a piece of equipment used by the USPS to sort mail.

Multinational referring to businesses that operate from both within and outside the United States.

Multiple media shredders destroy computer tapes, floppy disks, computer disks, and plastic ID cards.

Municipal bonds issued by state and local governments.

Mutual fund an investment company that pools individuals' money and invests the money in stocks and bonds.

N

NASD National Association of Securities Dealers.

NASDAQ National Association of Securities Dealers Automated Quotation.

Negative stress factors that cause emotional and mental upset in people's personal and professional lives; also referred to as distress.

Neophyte a beginner or novice.

Net income or net profit excess of revenue over expenses.

Net loss excess of expenses over revenue; lack of profit.

Networked printer a printer attached to a local area network.

Networking the process of identifying and establishing a group of acquaintances, friends, and relatives who can assist in the job search process.

Nomos natural laws.

Nonessential records have no future value to an organization.

Nonimpact printer forms characters and graphics on paper without actually striking the paper.

Numeric storage system file cards and folders are given numbers and arranged in numeric sequence.

Numeric suffix II, III

O

Office suites software programs that offer a variety of software applications in one package.

Off-loading when an organization contracts with individuals outside the organization to complete part of the work of the organization.

Offset not folded to the edge of the paper.

Online meetings link individual participants through a computer.

Online service provider (OSP) a business that supplies Internet access as well as members-only features.

Operating system a program that contains the instructions that coordinate the computer's outer and internal components.

Optical character reader (OCR) a piece of equipment that can read keyboarded and handwritten documents; widely used by the United States Postal Service.

Optical character recognition scans documents and converts the content into computer-readable format using specialized software.

Organizational control control exercised by the organization.

Organizational culture the ideas, customs, values, and skills of a particular organization.

OSHA Occupational Safety & Health Administration, a government entity.

Out guide used to replace a record that has been removed from the files.

Output data that has been processed into a useful form.

Outsourcing utilizing an outside company or a consultant to take over the performance of a particular part of an organization's business or to complete a project.

Overhead costs salary and benefit costs.

Over-the-counter market not a physical location, but an automated information network that provides quotes on stocks for brokers registered with the NASD.

Owner's equity the owner's right to the assets of the entity.

Oxymoron the combining of incongruous or contradictory terms.

P

P/E ratio the price of the stock divided by the 12-month earnings per share.

Paid-in capital capital contributed to a corporation by stockholders and others.

Parallelism when grammatically equivalent forms are used within a sentence.

Paraphrase to restate the concept in different terms.

Parcel Post mail weighing 70 pounds or less; often used for gifts, general merchandise, or books.

Passport an official government document that certifies the identity and citizenship of an individual and grants the person permission to travel abroad.

Path-goal theory stresses the importance of goals (objectives); states that leaders increase subordinate satisfaction and performance by clarifying and clearing the paths to goals established and by increasing the number and kinds of rewards available when goals are met.

Payroll taxes include federal income tax and Social Security.

pc photocopy.

PDAs personal digital assistants.

Pen tablets allow the user to hold a computer with one hand and use a pen with the other hand to activate software applications based on a program menu.

Per diem means "per day"; the amount of money an employee receives per day for expenses.

Perceive to become aware of directly through any of the senses.

Perfectionism a propensity for setting extremely high standards and being displeased with anything else.

Performance appraisals evaluations of job performance done by a supervisor at periodic intervals of time.

Periodic transfer materials are transferred from active files to inactive files after a stated period.

Peripherals external self-contained accessories that can be plugged into a computer as needed to make a copy of information or to retrieve stored information.

Perpetual transfer materials are continuously transferred from active files to inactive files.

Personal Digital Assistants (PDAs) hand-held computers that run specially designed software to help people organize personal and professional information.

Persuasive approach used to convince someone to do something or to change an indifferent or negative reader's reaction.

Petabyte is equal to 1,024 terabytes.

Petaflop 1 quadrillion computations per second.

Physically challenged describing persons with a physical handicap.

PIM Personal Information Management.

PIN personal identification number.

Pixels individual dots that comprise the image that is displayed on a CRT.

Plagiarism the act of representing another person's work or ideas as your own.

Platen the glass surface upon which the original object is placed and copied.

Portable fax a telephone handset and a fax machine small enough to fit in a briefcase.

Portfolio samples of one's work.

Postage meters postage-printing machines purchased for use in the home or office.

Power the ability to act; the strength to accomplish the objectives of the organization.

Pragmatic relating to an idea or a concept that is understood conceptually and practiced day-to-day.

Preferred stock pays dividends before common stock.

Prejudice a system of negative beliefs and feelings.

Primary key (keyword) a unique identifier of a record.

Primary research original data collected through surveys, observations, or experiments.

Primary storage a temporary storage place within a computer for data, instructions, and information.

Priority Mail one- to three-day service to most domestic destinations.

Private employment agencies charge a fee for assisting in the job search process.

Procrastination trying to avoid a task by putting it aside with the intention of doing it later.

Professional suffix D.D.S., M.D., Ph.D.

Projection the act of transferring one's problems to others.

Property, plant, and equipment assets relatively long-lived assets.

Protestant ethic a work ethic that began as a religious teaching in Europe in the fourteenth century and is still practiced today.

Proxemics the study of personal and cultural use of space.

Public relations the technique of inducing the public to have understanding for and goodwill toward a person, a firm, or an institution.

Q

Query to ask a question in a format a database can understand.

Quick assets cash and other current assets that can be quickly converted to cash.

Quid pro quo Latin meaning "this for that."

Quilt see *salad bowl*.

R

Racial discrimination harassment based on prejudice.

Random access memory (RAM) primary memory necessary for the manipulation of data.

Rate earned on stockholders' equity shows the rate of income earned on the amount invested by stockholders.

Rate earned on total assets measures the profitability of total assts.

Ratio of net sales to assets a profitability measure that shows how effectively a firm utilizes its assets.

Readability the degree of difficulty of the message.

Readability indices formulas such as the Gunning Fog Index that provide the grade level of writing.

Read-only memory (ROM) permanently stored information that cannot be changed.

Recirculating automatic document feeder (RADF) automatically feeds originals that are printed in a back-to-back (duplexed) format.

Record any form of information, including a drawing, a sound file, a video clip, or a CD; a row in a table that contains information about a given person, product, or event.

Records life cycle from creation of a record to its final disposition.

Records management the systematic control of records.

Records storage systems the manner in which records are classified for storage.

Rectangular arrangement a seating arrangement that allows the leader to maintain control since she or he sits at the head of the table.

Registered mail provides maximum protection and security for valuable items.

Remote Barcoding Systems (RBCS) a piece of equipment used by the USPS to determine barcodes for handwritten addresses.

Reprographics any piece of equipment that produces multiple copies of an original document.

Requisition form includes a space for identifying the record borrowed, the name and location of the borrower, data about the borrowed record, and the date the record is to be returned to the files.

Resolution the sharpness and clearness of an image.

Respect showing regard and appreciation for someone.

Response rate the number of people responding to a survey or questionnaire.

Restricted delivery when the mailer sends the item by direct delivery to a specific addressee or addressee's authorized agent.

Resume a concise statement of your background, education, skills, and experience.

Retained earnings net income retained in the business.

Return receipt provides the mailer with evidence of delivery.

Role ambiguity a situation that exists when individuals have inadequate information about their work roles.

RSIs repetitive stress injuries.

Russell 2000 a group of 2,000 small-cap stocks.

S

S&P 500 group of 500 stocks that Standard & Poor's tracks to get a picture of the stock market; includes 425 industrials, 25 railroads, and 50 utilities.

Salad bowl a term used to describe the diversity of the United States; people are no longer melted into one big pot, but retain much of their identity from their homeland and much of their language.

Satellite an orbiting vehicle that relays signals between terrestrial communication stations and the earth.

Satellite center a fully equipped workplace in a suburban location; owned and established by a company.

Scrambled signals signals in code.

Secondary research data or material that other people have discovered and reported.

Self-esteem pride in oneself; self respect.

Seniority suffix II, III, Jr., Sr.

Serendipitous desirable but unsought accidental discovery.

Sexual harassment arising from sexual conduct that is unwelcome by the recipient and that may be either physical or verbal in nature.

Sheet-fed scanners handle stacks of paper that are loaded into a tray and automatically fed through the scanner.

Sheets per pass refers to the number of sheets of paper than can be fed into a shredder at one time.

Signature Confirmation provides signature proof of delivery as well as the date and time of delivery or attempted delivery.

Site license a legal agreement that allows multiple users to run a software package at the same time.

Small-cap stocks have a market capitalization of less than 1 billion.

SMS short message service.

Social Security part of FICA, providing retirement benefits, survivor benefits, and disability insurance.

Soft copy information that exists electronically and displays for a temporary period of time.

Solaris a version of UNIX that was developed by Sun Microsystems and that is used in ecommerce applications.

Sorting arranging records in a predetermined sequence, or the sequence in which the records will be filed.

Spamming sending junk mail or chain letters via email.

Stakeholder control involves groups that exercise certain controls; for example, a board of directors can determine the direction an organization takes through the power granted to the board.

Stakeholders people having an interest in an outcome.

State-operated employment agencies provide job search opportunities free of charge.

Static staying the same.

Stereotyping holding perceptions or images of people or things that are derived from selective perception.

Stockholders' equity, shareholders' investment, or capital public owners' share of a corporation.

Stocks shares of ownership in a company.

Storing placing the record in the file folder and then in the file drawer.

Stress the response of the body to a demand made upon it.

Strip-cut shredders first-generation shredders that cut paper into thin strips.

Subject storage arranging records by their subject.

Supercomputers the most powerful and expensive mainframe computers.

SuperDisks high-capacity storage mediums capable of storing 120 MB or 240 MB of data.

SUTA State Unemployment Tax Act; provides payments to unemployed workers.

Synergy the ideas and products of a group of people developed through interaction with each other.

System resources the amount of hard drive space and RAM required for the operating system to function.

Systems software a program through which the computer manages its own resources.

T

Tact acute sensitivity to what is proper and appropriate in dealing with others, including the ability to speak or act without offending.

Tactical planning planning for a one-year period.

Targeted/combination resume lists experience in reverse chronological order.

Task force a group in an organization formed to deal with a specific issue or problem.

Team a group of people who need each other to accomplish a given task.

Telecommunications the transmission of text, data, voice, video, and images—graphics and pictures—from one location to another.

Telecommuting periodically working out of a principal office one or more days per week.

Teleconferencing a general term applied to a variety of technology-assisted two-way (interactive) communications.

Telework describes a variety of situations where individuals use telecommunications technology to work from somewhere other than the traditional workplace.

Telework center a fully equipped workplace operated by an independent organization and shared by employees from a variety of employers.

Templates predesigned documents that contain formatting.

Temporary agency one offering temporary work.

Temps temporary workers.

Terabyte (TB) a trillion bytes per second.

Teraflop 1 trillion operations per second.

Terminal digit filing organizes files by the final digits of the number.

Territoriality the act of laying claim to and defending a territory.

Tickler file used to remind a person to take certain actions.

Time a resource that cannot be changed, converted, or controlled.

Toner powdered ink.

Topic sentence contains the main idea of a paragraph.

Touch pad a small window the user touches to move the cursor on the screen.

Touch screen a computer screen the user touches with his or her finger to make the desired choice, rather than using a mouse or another point-and-click interface.

TQM total quality management.

Trackball a stationary ball the user rolls with his or her fingertips to move the cursor on the screen.

Transformational leadership similar to charismatic leadership; however, transformational leaders are successful in getting employees to transform from self-interest to the larger good of the entire organization and community.

Transmission Control Protocol/Internet Protocol (TCP/IP) a language that allows computers to communicate over the Internet.

Treasury bills bonds backed by the federal government that mature in one year or less.

Treasury bonds bonds backed by the federal government that mature in one to thirty years.

Treasury notes bonds backed by the federal government that mature in two to ten years.

Troubleshooting determining a hardware or software problem and finding a solution.

U

Ultrafiche a variation of microfiche that can store thousands of images.

Uncompress to restore a file to its original form.

Uninstaller a utility that removes an application and any associated entries in the system files.

Universal Product Code (UPC) a series of black printed bars of varying thickness read by barcode scanners; tells the name of the product and the selling price.

UNIX an operating system used extensively in the programming and operating of supercomputers and mainframe computers.

Upward communication messages that travel from employees to management.

Useful records useful for smooth, effective operation of an organization.

U-Shaped and semicircular arrangements seating arrangements that work well for small groups of six to eight people.

USPS United States Postal Service.

Utility program system software that performs a specific task related to managing a computer, its devices, or its programs.

Utility suites combine several utility programs into a single package.

V

Values principles that guide a person's life, such as honesty, fairness, love, security, and belief in a higher being.

Variable-data barcode identifies information unique to one particular item.

Verbal communication the process of exchanging ideas and feelings through the use of words.

Vertical analysis a percentage analysis used to show the relationship of each component to the total within a single statement.

Videoconferencing a system of transmitting audio and video between individuals at distant locations.

Virtual assistant an individual who provides administrative support or specialized business services from a distance through the Internet, by fax, by telephone, or by another method of communication.

Virtual interviews interviews held via technology by an interviewer at a distant location.

Virtual private networks (VPNs) link mobile users with a secure connection to the company network server.

Virtual/mobile telework using communications tools and technology to perform job duties from a customer location, an airport, a hotel, or another off-site location.

Visa a document granted by a government abroad that permits a traveler to enter and travel within that particular country.

Visionary leadership includes charismatic and transformational leadership.

Visualization using your imagination to help you relax.

Vital records cannot be replaced and should never be destroyed.

VOI voice over Internet.

VOIP voice over Internet protocol.

Volatile characterized by unexpected change.

W

W questions why, what, and who; determine whether the correspondence includes all necessary information.

W-4 Employee's Withholding Allowance Certificate.

Walk-up stations another term used to describe decentralized copy centers.

Web browser an application program that provides a way to look at and interact with all the information on the World Wide Web.

Whistleblowers individuals who bring wrongdoing within an organization to light.

Wide area networks (WANs) link technological equipment over an area that can be hundreds of thousands of miles.

Windows an operating system developed by Microsoft in 1992.

Wireless service provider (WSP) a company that provides wireless Internet access to users with wireless modems or Web-enabled handheld computers or devices.

Workplace politics when the people you know within an organization can be important.

Workstation computers (supermicros) the upper-end machines of the microcomputer.

World Wide Web a large collection of computer files (Web pages) scattered across the Internet.

WORM technology write once, read many technology, which prevents any alteration to a document once it has been scanned into the system.

Y

***You* approach** making every attempt to enter into the feelings of the person who will be reading the letter.

Z

Zero-coupon treasuries bonds backed by the federal government that pay no interest until they mature.

Zip disks high-capacity storage mediums available in 100- and 250-MB capacities.

Index